Theory Construction and Model-Building Skills

Methodology in the Social Sciences
David A. Kenny, Founding Editor
Todd D. Little, Series Editor
www.guilford.com/MSS

This series provides applied researchers and students with analysis and research design books that emphasize the use of methods to answer research questions. Rather than emphasizing statistical theory, each volume in the series illustrates when a technique should (and should not) be used and how the output from available software programs should (and should not) be interpreted. Common pitfalls as well as areas of further development are clearly articulated.

RECENT VOLUMES

PRINCIPLES AND PRACTICE OF STRUCTURAL EQUATION MODELING, FOURTH EDITION
Rex B. Kline

HYPOTHESIS TESTING AND MODEL SELECTION IN THE SOCIAL SCIENCES
David L. Weakliem

REGRESSION ANALYSIS AND LINEAR MODELS: CONCEPTS, APPLICATIONS, AND IMPLEMENTATION
Richard B. Darlington and Andrew F. Hayes

GROWTH MODELING: STRUCTURAL EQUATION AND MULTILEVEL MODELING APPROACHES
Kevin J. Grimm, Nilam Ram, and Ryne Estabrook

PSYCHOMETRIC METHODS: THEORY INTO PRACTICE
Larry R. Price

INTRODUCTION TO MEDIATION, MODERATION, AND CONDITIONAL PROCESS ANALYSIS: A REGRESSION-BASED APPROACH, SECOND EDITION
Andrew F. Hayes

MEASUREMENT THEORY AND APPLICATIONS FOR THE SOCIAL SCIENCES
Deborah L. Bandalos

CONDUCTING PERSONAL NETWORK RESEARCH: A PRACTICAL GUIDE
Christopher McCarty, Miranda J. Lubbers, Raffaele Vacca, and José Luis Molina

QUASI-EXPERIMENTATION: A GUIDE TO DESIGN AND ANALYSIS
Charles S. Reichardt

THEORY CONSTRUCTION AND MODEL-BUILDING SKILLS: A PRACTICAL GUIDE FOR SOCIAL SCIENTISTS, SECOND EDITION
James Jaccard and Jacob Jacoby

Theory Construction and Model-Building Skills

A Practical Guide for Social Scientists

SECOND EDITION

James Jaccard
Jacob Jacoby

Series Editor's Note by Todd D. Little

THE GUILFORD PRESS
New York   London

Library of Congress Cataloging-in-Publication Data

Names: Jaccard, James, author. | Jacoby, Jacob, author.
Title: Theory construction and model-building skills : a practical guide
    for social scientists / James Jaccard, Jacob Jacoby.
Description: Second edition. | New York : The Guilford Press, [2020] |
    Series: Methodology in the social sciences | Includes bibliographical
    references and index.
Identifiers: LCCN 2019030892 | ISBN 9781462542437 (paperback) |
    ISBN 9781462542444 (hardcover)
Subjects: LCSH: Social sciences—Research—Methodology. | Theory
    (Philosophy)
Classification: LCC H62 .J29 2020 | DDC 300.72—dc23
LC record available at *https://lccn.loc.gov/2019030892*

For Marty Fishbein—
a brilliant and inspiring theorist and mentor
—JAMES JACCARD

For Renee and Dana—
in appreciation for the balance and joy they create
—JACOB JACOBY

Series Editor's Note

Theory is an analyst's best friend, while data are the fodder of good theory; but which comes first, the data or the theory? Similarly, some folks never let data get in the way of good theory and some folks never let theory get in the way of good data; but is it this either/or taming-of-the-shrew-like scenario? Constructing a theory is more like crafting an elegant ensemble of logically connected ideas that depict the world and allow knowl edge to leap forward. As Jaccard and Jacoby point out, 90% of our graduate training is on methods for collecting and techniques for analyzing data and only 10% is spent on identifying and crafting the ideas into theories that can be tested.

I have always been a student of good theory and this book is a veritable bible on how to craft testable theories, even before the wonderful enhancements to this second edition. Enhancements include, for example, what constitutes a theoretical contribution and how do you craft one? How do you use a logic model to generate ideas and avoid pitfalls in the theory construction process? How do you use mixed methods and data mining to craft good theory? How do you test a theory and revise it if need be? Jaccard and Jacoby answer these questions with practical wisdom born of extensive experience and uncommon insights.

In addition, the expanded discussion of moderator variables, counterfactual causality, and their *new* 10-step method for generating theory is simply invaluable. Oh, and the new chapters on measurement are absolutely essential because good theory demands good measurement. The operationalization of good theory is way too often neglected in training programs and many seasoned veterans have yet to learn how to do good measurement. Last but not least, they offer insight and wisdom on both interpreting others' theories as well as clearly expressing your own theories.

Their book is transdisciplinary, with many useful examples spanning fields such as anthropology, business, communications, education, economics, health, marketing, organizational studies, political science, psychology, social work, sociology, and so on.

And the companion website is a tremendously useful and helpful resource for students and instructors alike! I will be teaching a course on model building and theory construction. Jaccard and Jacoby is unequivocally the only choice for such a course.

Sadly, Jacob "Jack" Jacoby has departed our worldly sphere. Brilliant thinkers challenge our worldview on humanity and they leave indelible marks that shape us and how we think. Jack was one of our field's finest.

TODD D. LITTLE
Honeymooning at Casa Montana

Preface

Theory construction is at the heart of the scientific process. The strategies that social scientists use to generate and develop ideas are important to understand and foster in young academics and investigators as they prepare for a research-oriented career. Although books have been written about theory construction, there are surprisingly few books on the topic that tackle the problem of teaching students and young professionals, in a practical and concrete way, how to theorize. Students, especially graduate students, take one or more courses on research methods and data analysis, but few experience more than a lecture or two, or read a chapter or two, on theory construction. It is no wonder that students often are intimidated by the prospect of constructing theories.

This book provides young scientists with tools to assist them in the practical aspects of theory construction. It is not an academic discussion of theory construction or the philosophy of science, and we do not delve too deeply into the vast literature on these topics. Rather, we take a more informal journey through the cognitive heuristics, tricks of the trade, and ways of thinking that we have found to be useful in developing theories—essentially, conceptualizations—that can advance knowledge in the social sciences. By taking this journey, we hope to stimulate the thinking and creative processes of readers so that they might think about phenomena in new and different ways, perhaps leading to insights that might not otherwise have resulted. The intent of this book is to provide a practical, hands-on, systematic approach to developing theories and fostering scientific creativity in the conceptual domain. Relative to the majority of books on theory construction, this book is unique in its focus on the nuts and bolts of building a theory rather than on an analysis of broad-based systems of thought.

We have used the book both as a stand-alone text in a course on theory construction and as one of several texts in graduate courses on research and research methodology. In terms of the latter, almost all traditional research methods books include a section or chapter on the nature of theory and/or theory construction. However, the treatment of theory construction usually is brief and of limited practical value. The present book is intended to provide the instructor with a useful source for helping students come up with ideas for research and for fine-tuning the resulting theories that emerge from such thinking. It provides more detail and more practical knowledge than what is typical of chapters in books on research methodology. The social psychologist William McGuire often lamented about how research training with graduate students focuses at least 90% on teaching methods to test ideas but no more than 10% on how to get those ideas in the first place. Despite this difference in emphasis, the process of theory development is fundamental to successful scientific research. Indeed, many would say that there can be no theory testing without theory. An objective of this book is to move toward a needed balance in the emphases given to theory construction and theory testing.

The book can be used in many different disciplines. We draw on examples from the fields of anthropology, business, communications, education, economics, health, marketing, organizational studies, political science, psychology, social work, and sociology, to name a few. Some instructors may prefer more detailed examples in their particular field of study, but we believe that using examples from multiple disciplines helps students appreciate the commonalities and value of multidisciplinary perspectives.

The book has several pedagogical features that enhance its use as a textbook and as a source of learning. First, each chapter includes a section on suggested readings with commentary, where we direct the reader to key references for further study on the topics covered in the chapter. Second, each chapter has a list of key terms that highlights the most important jargon and terminology. Third, each chapter has a set of exercises that encourages the reader to think about the material that was presented in the chapter. We include exercises to reinforce concepts and exercises to apply the concepts to problems of interest. Finally, each chapter has a highlighted box that covers an interesting topic that applies the concepts covered in the chapter or that shows important uses of them. We also created a website that contains supplemental materials to support the book (see the box at the end of the table of contents). The website is intended for use by students, professors, and professionals alike.

CHANGES IN THE SECOND EDITION

In the first edition, we downplayed issues surrounding data collection and data analysis, preferring to keep discussion at a conceptual level. This orientation still dominates the current edition, but we felt it important to more fully recognize that theory often emerges from data collection and data analysis. In the first edition, the emergence of theory from data was front and center in the chapter on grounded and emergent theory because in qualitative research, emergent theory is prominent. However, the emergence of theory from exploratory data analysis was absent for quantitative research. We have added a new chapter, "Emergent Theory: Quantitative Approaches" (Chapter 11), to address this and have retitled our chapter on qualitative approaches (Chapter 10) "Emergent Theory: Qualitative/Mixed-Methods Approaches." The quantitative chapter on this topic prioritizes novel, exploratory methods of quantitative analysis that can help readers generate new theory through data mining. Readers who are less interested in quantitative research may find the core material in this chapter of lesser relevance. However, we have kept this material conceptual as opposed to being steeped in statistical theory and have provided supplemental materials on our website that walk readers through the execution of the methods on popular software at a more practical level.

Another nod to the fact that data often lead to new theory is the addition of a chapter on theory revision (Chapter 15). When we collect data to test a theory, disconfirmatory results can emerge that lead us to revise the theory or abandon it altogether. When faced with disconfirming or only partially supportive data, one can use critical thinking processes to make decisions about whether and how to revise a theory. Chapter 15, "Theory Revision," highlights these processes. Theory revision in light of disconfirming data is as relevant to qualitative researchers as it is to quantitative researchers, so this chapter should be of interest to all.

Measurement and observation are core to science. When we formulate measures, we invoke theory to link measures to the underlying construct the measures are assumed to reflect. When we address measurement error in research, measurement theory also is front and center. As such, measurement theory is a core part of science. Measurement is typically viewed as the province of methodology, but we seek to build a case with two new chapters showing that the practice of measurement is firmly entrenched in theory and that measurement-oriented theory construction is essential for the social sciences. The first chapter on measurement, "General Frameworks" (Chapter 13), emphasizes the concepts of metrics, reliability, validity, and measurement facets. The second chapter, "Types of Measurement Strategies" (Chapter 14), focuses on self-reports, observer reports, and "objective" measures, strategies that form the backbone of social science research. We provide readers with theory construction principles that guide how one thinks about and conceptualizes such measures. Readers who want to contribute to measurement theory will learn useful conceptual tools for doing so. Readers who are not so inclined will still learn about the importance of measurement theory and how to apply that theory to the specific research projects they pursue. This will be true for both qualitative and quantitative researchers because both traditions ultimately use measurement in one form or another.

In the first edition, we wrote each chapter so that it could generally "stand on its own." The idea was that if instructors wanted to change the reading order of chapters, omit certain chapters based on their own or their students' substantive interests, or browse different topics rather than read every chapter, the book would be amenable to these approaches. The new chapters have this same quality.

We also have added new material to most chapters from the first edition. As examples, in Chapter 3, we added a discussion of what constitutes a theoretical contribution and what strategies social scientists can use to make theoretical contributions. This helps orient readers to the remainder of the book. We added a section on conceptual logic models to the chapter on generating ideas (Chapter 4) because such models are key to idea refinement. We expanded Chapter 6, on thought experiments, to give a better appreciation of their role in science and reworked several of the example experiments. We made clearer how thought experiments can be used both by confirmatory-oriented and emergent-oriented theorists. For the chapter on causal thinking (Chapter 7), we expanded our discussion of moderator variables, added a brief discussion on counter-factual causality, and added two ways of generating theory, a 10-step method and a "binder" method. In this chapter, we also added a section on common mistakes made during the theory construction process. We expanded the material on grounded and emergent theory in Chapter 10 to discuss mixed-methods approaches in more depth and to develop the actual thought processes theorists use to construct theories from qualitative data. We also expanded Chapter 16, on reading about and writing theories, and generally updated the book to include practical perspectives that have evolved in theory construction since the first edition.

Our book should be useful (1) in theory construction courses, (2) in proseminars for doctoral students to help them develop their thesis research, and (3) as a supplement to methods courses where instructors can select a subset of chapters for students to read. Young researchers and professors also should find the book of interest independent of courses. We hope that even seasoned researchers will walk away from most chapters with at least one or two new "nuggets of knowledge" they will find useful in their work. In this sense, our intended audience is broad.

As noted, we have created a web page for the book (see the box at the end of the table of contents). This contains useful supplemental information for readers as well as instructional aids for professors.

ACKNOWLEDGMENTS

My dear friend and colleague Jacob Jacoby passed away before writing commenced on the second edition. Despite this, his presence remains even in the new chapters. Jack was an important influence on my life both professionally and personally, and I will always be grateful for the opportunity to have known and learned from him. His legacy will be with us for years. I miss you, Jack.

As with the first edition, a large number of people contributed in diverse ways to the development of the second edition. I again would like to thank students and colleagues who provided feedback on earlier drafts, including David Brinberg, Department of Marketing, Virginia Polytechnic University; Miriam Brinberg, Department of Human Development, Pennsylvania State University; Wendy J. Coster, Department of Occupational Therapy, Boston University; Cynthia G. S. Franklin, Steve Hicks School of Social Work, University of Texas, Austin; Liliana Goldin, Silver School of Social Work, New York University; Guillermo Grenier, Department of Global and Sociocultural Studies, Florida International University; Sean Patrick Kelly, School of Education, University of Pittsburgh; Hailin Qu, Spears School of Business, Oklahoma State University; Rick Sholette, Director, Paraclete Ministries; Michael Slater, School of Communications, Ohio State University; and Weiwu Zhang, Department of Public Relations, Texas Tech University. At The Guilford Press, C. Deborah Laughton, as always, was insightful and supportive in her role as editor. She once again improved the book immensely. It is rare one gets the opportunity for a "do-over" of a project, and I am grateful to C. Deborah for giving me the opportunity. Although all of these individuals contributed significantly to the book, I alone am responsible for any of its shortcomings.

I dedicated the first edition to Marty Fishbein and I do so again here. Marty was an amazing scientist, teacher, and professor who positively impacted my life and those of his many students. It is rare that one has the opportunity to study under and work with a true genius. Jack, I am sure, would once again dedicate the book to his spouse, Renee, and his daughter, Dana, two incredible women. My spouse, Liliana, again contributed to the book in many meaningful ways, and I remain amazed after all these years at her great intellect and breadth, which have been of such immense benefit to me in the form of lively discussions of theory, method, and substance. She is my role model in every way. And a special note of recognition to my daughter, Sarita, who inspires me and serves as my role model every bit as much as her mother.

JAMES JACCARD

Brief Contents

Extended Contents

PART III. FRAMEWORKS FOR THEORY CONSTRUCTION

PART IV. THEORY AT THE LEVEL OF MEASUREMENT

PART V. CONCLUDING ISSUES

15 • Theory Revision

16 • Reading and Writing about Theories

17 • Epilogue

The companion website (*www.theory-construction.com*) includes PowerPoint slides
of all of the book's figures, methodological primers and video demonstrations,
supplemental exercises, and other resources.

Part I

BASIC CONCEPTS

1

Introduction

Few people dispute the central role of theory in the social sciences. Scientists formulate theories, test theories, accept theories, reject theories, modify theories, and use theories as guides to understanding and predicting events in the world about them. A great deal has been written about the nature and role of theory in the social sciences. These writings have spanned numerous disciplines, including anthropology, economics, history, philosophy, political science, psychology, sociology, and social work, to name but a few. This literature has described, among other things, broad frameworks for classifying types of theories, the evolution of theories over time, the lives and scientific strategies of great scientific theorists, and general issues in the philosophy of science. Although this literature is insightful, much less has been written to provide social scientists with practical guidelines for constructing theories as they go about the business of doing their science. Most students are intimidated by the prospect of constructing their own theories about a phenomenon. Theory construction is viewed as a mysterious process that somehow "happens" and is beyond the scope and training of a young scientist trying to find his or her way in the field. Whereas most graduate programs in the social sciences require multiple courses in research methodology so that students will become equipped with the tools to test theories empirically, the same cannot be said for theory construction. In contrast to focusing on methods for testing theory, the current work focuses on methods for generating theory.

The fundamental objective of this book is to provide students and young scientists with tools to assist them in the practical process of constructing theories. It does so via describing in some detail the strategies, heuristics, and approaches to thinking about problems that we have found to be useful over the more than 70 collective years that we have been doing social science research. This book is not an academic discussion of the literature on theory construction or the philosophy of science. We do not delve too deeply into the vast literature on these topics. Rather, we take a more practical journey through the cognitive heuristics, tricks of the trade, and ways of thinking that we have found to be useful in developing theories.

ORGANIZATION OF THE BOOK

The book is organized into five parts. Part I presents the basic concepts that form the backdrop for later chapters. In these early chapters, we consider the nature of science and what it means to understand something. We develop the notion of *concepts* and highlight the central role of concepts in theories. We lay the foundations for communicating to others the concepts in one's theory and then describe what separates science from other ways of knowing.

With this as background, we turn to developing core strategies for constructing a theory, the topic of Part II. In Chapter 4, we focus first on strategies for generating ideas and for stimulating creative thinking. Once you have a set of rough ideas, they need to be refined and focused to meet the criteria of a rigorous scientific theory. Chapter 5 describes strategies for thinking through your constructs and discusses how to develop clear and communicable conceptual definitions of them. We provide numerous strategies for making fuzzy constructs more precise and not overly abstract. Chapter 6 focuses on relationships between variables and develops strategies for making explicit the relationships you posit between variables. We show how to derive theoretical propositions based on a careful analysis of relationships.

Part III considers different frameworks for theory generation. Chapter 7 considers one of the most dominant approaches to theory construction in the social sciences, the framework of causal thinking. This approach elaborates the causes and consequences of different phenomena and views the identification of causal linkages as a central goal of science. Chapter 8 describes strategies for building mathematical models of different phenomena. Our intent here is to make clear the sometimes seemingly mysterious ways in which mathematics and social science theorizing interface. Chapter 9 describes the potential that simulations—in particular, the development of simulations—have for theory construction. Chapters 10 and 11 develop emergent approaches to the construction of theory. Chapter 10 focuses on qualitative methods to identify constructs and relationships on which to focus a theory, whereas Chapter 11 focuses on exploratory quantitative/statistical approaches that allow theory to emerge from data. Some social scientists might argue that these chapters belong in the previous section, where one initially identifies constructs and relationships to include in a theory. As we emphasize throughout this book, theory construction is not a set process, and a case like this could be made for almost every chapter in the current section. This book provides you with key ingredients for constructing a theory. How you choose to mix those ingredients to form your theoretical recipe depends on your predilections and the domains that you are studying. Chapter 12 summarizes 13 broad-based theoretical frameworks that may help in the idea-generation process. These frameworks include materialism, structuralism, functionalism, symbolic interactionism, evolutionary perspectives, postmodernism, neural networks, systems theory, stage theories, reinforcement theories, humanism, multilevel modeling, and person-centered theorizing. The idea is to think about a phenomenon you are interested in from two or more of these perspectives in order to help generate fresh ideas and perspectives.

Part IV focuses on theory construction as applied to measurement. Measurement and observation are, of course, central to science. When we formulate measures, we invoke theory to link measures to the underlying construct the measures are assumed to reflect. As such, measurement theory is a core part of science. Measurement is typically viewed as the province of methodology, but we argue here that key principles of measurement derive from theory and that measurement-oriented theory construction is thus essential. We seek to develop your theory construction skills in this important domain. Chapter 13 emphasizes the concepts of metrics, reliability, validity, and measurement facets. Chapter 14 focuses on self-reports, observer reports, and "objective" measures, strategies that form the backbone of social science research. Both chapters are central to qualitative as well as quantitative research.

In the final section, we first consider theory revision in light of disconfirming data. When we collect data designed to test or evaluate a theory, sometimes results emerge that lead us to revise the theory or abandon it all together. When faced with disconfirming or only partially supportive data, one uses critical thinking processes to make decisions about whether and how to revise a theory. Chapter 15 highlights these processes. Theory revision in light of disconfirming data is as relevant to qualitative researchers as it is to quantitative researchers, so this chapter should be of interest to all. Chapter 16 in this section discusses strategies for reading journal articles and scientific reports so as to make explicit the theories that the authors describe and subject to empirical evaluation. We also discuss strategies for presenting theories in different kinds of reports. We close with an Epilogue that comments on the theory construction process in light of the material covered in previous chapters and that addresses some odds and ends that did not fit well into the other chapters.

We recognize that some chapters will appeal to those with a more quantitative bent to science, whereas other chapters will appeal to those with a more qualitative orientation. We have written the chapters so that each stands on its own, allowing you to skip around as you see fit. Having said that, we strongly urge you to read all the chapters to truly broaden and enrich your toolbox for generating theory. Both qualitative and quantitative approaches are powerful tools for generating ideas and theories. At some point, you will want to master both.

THEORIES AND SETTINGS

This book is written primarily for students and professionals interested in pursuing a career as a researcher in the social sciences. It is intended to provide you with concrete strategies for building upon existing theories and constructing your own theories. Theorizing does not occur in a vacuum. It occurs in the context of individuals pursuing a career in some professional setting, usually an academic setting. At times, we describe how the setting in which you work impacts the way in which you theorize and the kinds of questions you ask. We also discuss strategies for dealing with the constraints you face as a result of these settings.

For us, constructing theory is one of the most rewarding aspects of doing science; it is on a par with the excitement associated with empirically testing and finding support for theory. In all honesty, we probably are more captivated by research that questions the theories we have posited because of the ensuing call to "put on our detective hats" to figure out why we were wrong. This invariably demands that we approach the problem from a new conceptual angle. This book describes some (but not all) of the types of detective hats that we have put on over the years. We hope that we can help to start you down the path of a richer and more productive approach to the construction of theories as you fashion your own strategies and set of detective hats for thinking about phenomena and solving problems.

2

The Nature of Understanding

Reality is merely an illusion, albeit a very persistent one.
—ALBERT EINSTEIN

*The whole of science is nothing more than an extension of
everyday thinking.*
—ALBERT EINSTEIN

Despite the fact that science has been practiced for thousands of years and countless books have been written on the subject, many people still consider it mysterious and forbidding. Perhaps the reason for this reaction is their view of science as something fundamentally different from anything they normally do. Actually, this is not the case. The essence of science is something we all do, which is to try to understand ourselves and the world around us. Scientific research is a process that is designed to extend our understandings and to determine if they are correct or useful. The basic difference between everyday thinking, on the one hand, and science and scientific research, on the other, is that the latter strives to operate according to a more rigorous set of rules. Because science and the process of scientific research can be viewed as extensions of everyday thinking, we find them easiest to explain if we begin by considering how an individual tries to make sense of, and cope with, his or her world.

The present chapter explores the nature of understanding, relying on informal and everyday examples of human thought to draw parallels to scientific conceptions of understanding. In doing so, we build on Albert Einstein's assertion that "the whole of science is nothing more than an extension of everyday thinking." We begin by describing the different ways in which social scientists think about reality, considering the perspectives of realism, social constructionism, critical realism, and hypothetical realism. Next, we address the building blocks of human understanding, namely, concepts and conceptual systems that relate one concept to another. Given that a scientist has evolved a conceptual system to address an issue, he or she then must communicate that system to other scientists. We conclude the chapter by briefly considering the nature of communication so as to set the stage for future chapters on how to derive precise conceptual definitions in theory construction.

THE NATURE OF REALITY

The process of understanding our world and making sense of reality is central to our waking lives. Accordingly, let us be more specific about what we mean by *reality* and *understanding*. Much philosophical thought has been devoted to the question of the nature of reality, and there is controversy among scientists about whether a single objective reality could ever be shown to exist.[1] According to the traditional perspective, termed *realism*, reality exists independent of any human presence. There is an external world composed of objects that follow myriad natural facts and laws. It is up to us to discover these facts and laws. Using this perspective, science has evolved and prospered as an approach for gaining knowledge that mirrors the presumed actualities of the real world.

In contrast to realism, the *social constructionist* perspective holds that reality is a construction of the human mind; that this construction is tied to a particular time and social context; and that what is considered reality changes as the social context changes. In its most extreme form, constructionism maintains that there is no reality and there are no facts until these are conceptualized and shared by some number of people. A more moderate position holds that, though there is an external reality independent of humankind, we can never know its units and true laws—or even if it has units and true laws. All we can know is our interpretation or construction of these experiences. Since the same experiences are open to many interpretations, any or all of which may be correct, the correctness of an interpretation depends on the purposes of those doing the interpreting. Thus, as Scarr (1985) notes:

> We do not discover scientific facts; we *invent* them. Their usefulness to us depends both on shared perceptions of the facts (consensual validation) and whether they work for various purposes, some practical and some theoretical. (p. 499)

As a simple example that drives the point home, we frequently draw a set of parallel lines on a blackboard and ask our students to describe what they see. Some reply "a road," others say "two lines." When we attempt to focus their thinking by saying "Hint: It's a number," three principal interpretations emerge: "Arabic number 11, Roman numeral II, or binary number three." Each of these responses represents a different, but potentially accurate, reconstruction of the same objective reality that reflects that individual's mental perspective. This point is fundamental. Even if the existence of a single objective, external reality could be assumed, the way in which this reality is interpreted can vary within the individual over time and across individuals, and can be heavily influenced by context (e.g., someone immersed in the study of Roman antiquity is more likely to interpret two parallel lines as representing Roman numeral II). Every individual develops his or her own reality, so that a number of different realities may be constructed out of the same set of "objective" facts. As is

---

[1] The discussion that follows is a simplified and not necessarily universally shared perspective on realism, social constructionism, and hypothetical realism. Philosophers and social scientists use these terms in different ways.

increasingly being recognized, it is possible for more than one of these different realities to be correct and useful.

The social constructionist perspective has implications for the way in which science is viewed (see, e.g., Gergen, 1985; Gergen & Gergen, 2003). The principal implications of the social constructionist perspective do not affect so much the way in which scientific empiricism is practiced, but rather the way in which the conceptualizations and outcomes of the assessment process are interpreted. According to the realism perspective, conceptual systems and theories are created so as to mirror an existing reality. The outcomes of the assessment process can be taken as direct representations of that reality, and it is possible to make claims regarding ultimate truths. By contrast, although the social constructionist perspective usually involves the researcher doing virtually the same things as are done in a realism perspective, the recognition that there exist multiple possible realities orients the researcher toward interpretations that reject more absolute perspectives on mapping out a single, existing reality:

> The admission that reality is a construction of the human mind does not deny the . . . value of the construction. Indeed, we get around in the world and invent knowledge that is admirably useful. But the claim that science and reality are human constructions denies that there is any one set of facts that is absolute and real. Instead, it asserts that there are many sets of "facts" that arise from different theory-guided perceptions. (Scarr, 1985, p. 501)

On the one hand, the social constructionist perspective can be discomforting because it makes us less certain of what we do and what we think we know. "How can we know what is right if there is no right?" (Scarr, 1985, pp. 511–512). On the other hand, this perspective enables us to more clearly recognize that any given conceptualization, and the facts that are given meaning by that conceptualization, is a function of the sociocultural time and space in which they occur.

A middle ground relative to these somewhat conflicting perspectives has been articulated by Blumer (1969). According to this view, *reality* is indeed seen through human conceptions of it. But the empirical world also "talks back" to our conceptions in the sense of challenging, resisting, and failing to bend to them. If a knife is plunged into someone's heart, certain ramifications follow (e.g., the heart will cease to function). The ways in which these ramifications are construed and interpreted may vary from one conceptual scheme to another. But the environment has spoken. It is this inflexible character of the world about us that calls for, and justifies, empirical science. Science seeks to develop conceptions that can successfully accommodate the obdurate character of the empirical world. Blumer's view roughly maps onto a philosophy of science known as *critical realism,* though there are many alternative formulations of it (e.g., Manicas, 2006; Sayer, 1992).

Another influential perspective on the debate is that even if it cannot be proven that reality exists, it is useful to assume that it does. This approach has been termed *hypothetical realism.* Here the concept of reality is a heuristic device—something that helps us organize our thoughts and think about matters so as to accomplish certain goals and objectives. Strictly speaking, reality may or may not exist, but we approach the world and our attempts to understand the world as if it does. In doing so, we may be able to accomplish a wide range of goals, but accordingly, we also may be constrained in our thinking. Hypothetical realism derives from a broader approach to epistemology—*pragmatism*. The approach is reflected in the work of philosopher C. I. Lewis (1929), who argued that science does not provide a copy of reality but must work with conceptual systems that are chosen for pragmatic reasons so as to aid scientific inquiry. Assuming a hypothetical reality is one such aid.

In sum, whereas realism embraces a view that external reality exists and the goal of science is to discover the laws that govern that reality, constructionism emphasizes that reality is a construction of the human mind that is tied to a particular time and social context. There are many gradations of these viewpoints, such as the position advocated by Blumer (1969), which emphasizes that reality is seen through human conceptions of it but that there is an empirical world that "talks back" to our conceptions; and hypothetical realism, which recognizes that one may not be able to prove that reality exists, but nevertheless approaches science with a working assumption that it does.

The broader literature on the philosophy of science explores myriad perspectives on how scientists (and laypeople) think about reality. Because this literature presents more nuanced perspectives than what we present here, interested readers are encouraged to pursue it (see Suggested Readings at the end of the chapter).

How Reality Is Experienced

Assuming for the moment that reality exists, how is it experienced by the individual? Most would agree that we experience the world around us as a complex, dynamic flow of unique and unrepeatable phenomena and events. Furthermore, most of these phenomena and events—ranging from those occurring deep in intergalactic space to those occurring in the micromolecular structure of this book—are not directly observable. No wonder, then, that attempting to understand our world can be a difficult process.

   • *Reality appears complex.* Whatever else it is or may be, the world—especially the external world—that we experience is complex. Consider a lecture hall filled with 200 students. Forget about the world beyond our immediate view; to describe, in precise detail, the sizes, shapes, colors (of clothing, objects, etc.), relationships, psychological components, and sociological components of that lecture hall at one instant in time could take months, years, or perhaps even lifetimes.

   • *Reality appears dynamic.* Moreover, things never stay the same. The world at any given instant is different from the world at the very next instant. From the tiniest particles that constitute physical matter to the largest galaxies, things are always in motion. The cells of living organisms are always growing or decaying, and the impulses in the neuronal system are always at work. So even if we were able to describe in infinite detail our hypothetical lecture hall filled with students, once one or more students moved, we would have a set of different relationships and, hence, a different reality.

• *Reality appears unique.* Because of this dynamic quality, the universe at any given instant—and everything in it—is never the same as the universe at any other instant, either previous or subsequent. The water that flows at one particular instant or during any given day down the rivers of New Hampshire, the raindrops that fall on a particular evening in Houston, the expense account dinner that was eaten in Paris—all are unique and can never be repeated precisely. The planet contains more than 7 billion human inhabitants, yet no two people are precisely identical in all respects—from their mundane external features (e.g., fingerprints) to their more complex internal features (how and what they think and feel). Even the inanimate rock lying on the ground is unique. In theory, no two rocks are identical in terms of all their distinguishing characteristics.

• *Reality appears mostly obscured.* Probably the major share of reality remains hidden from direct detection by any of our senses. To be sure, scientific instruments are being developed that enable us to probe more deeply into space, see ever tinier particles of matter and, through functional magnetic resonance imaging, observe how regions of our brains are activated as we think, but the vast majority of nature's secrets still remains mysteriously hidden from direct view. These secrets cannot be seen, heard, tasted, smelled, or touched. With specific respect to human phenomena, whereas many are openly visible (e.g., we can see a person walking, eating a sandwich, purchasing a newspaper), a vast number of others are not. A person's psyche—the inner thoughts and feelings that presumably guide much of our behavior—is one of the most obscure realms of all. We have yet to be able to see what we think is a motive or to point to the resting place of jealousy or pride.

The four characteristics just described—that reality is experienced as complex, dynamic, unique, and mostly obscured—refer to what is often termed the *external environment*. More than a century ago, famed philosopher and social scientist William James (1890) referred to this external environment as "a bloomin', buzzin' world of confusion." These four characteristics apply to individuals' "internal environments" as well.

CONCEPTS: THE BUILDING BLOCKS OF UNDERSTANDING

The Nature of Concepts

Confronted by this array of complex, dynamic, unique, and mostly obscured phenomena, how do individuals manage to make sense out of this world? They do so, almost automatically and often unconsciously, by conceptualizing—that is, by using their mental processes to consider and sort their experiences in terms of the concepts they have acquired and stored in memory. They also develop new concepts to describe things they had never previously experienced. Just as concepts are the fundamental building blocks of everyday thinking, they also are the fundamental building blocks of scientific thinking.

According to *Webster's Dictionary,* the word *concept* refers to something that is conceived of in the mind. It is a generic idea or thought, usually developed from experiencing one or more particular instances. Examples of concepts include *shirt, book, dripping, chair, mother, ice cream, advertising, smashed, home, vacation, memory, love, prejudice, attitude,* and *expectations.* As you can see, concepts refer to things that are tangible and denotable (e.g., shirts) as well as to things that are not as concrete and directly seen (e.g., memory).

Concepts are the building blocks for all thinking, regardless of whether that thinking occurs in the context of everyday living, art, politics, sports, religion, or science. In fact, without concepts, thought as we know it would be impossible. It is our concepts that enable us to achieve some basic understanding of the world.

The most basic level of understanding can be termed *identification.* We understand something, in part, when we can identify it. When experiencing the world about us, we use the concepts we have in mind to identify and classify our experiences: this is an ice cream cone; that is a shirt. Social scientists identify and classify people using concepts such as race, gender, intelligence, and attitudes. Because concepts are so central to all thinking, we examine their nature in somewhat greater detail.

• *Concepts are generalized abstractions.* When an individual has a concept, it means that he or she has a general idea that can be applied across a number of specific instances. Consider the concept *shirt,* for example. Shirts differ in a great number of ways—in terms of their fabric, color or number of colors, sleeve length, number of buttons (or whether they have buttons at all), size and shape of the collar, whether there are pockets and the number of pockets, whether the shirt is squared off at the bottom or has tails, and so on. Yet, having the concept *shirt* in mind is sufficient to enable the individual to sort things into two (or possibly three) categories: shirts, items that have some of the characteristics of shirts but are not shirts, and everything else. When we say that concepts are generalized abstractions, we mean that the general idea subsumes a universe of possible instances. Note, also, that concepts can be "fuzzy" at the margins. Does a woman's blouse qualify as a shirt? What about a woman's halter top? Such fuzziness can lead to disagreements among individuals and scientists alike. For example, a recent controversy in astrophysics involved how to define the concept of a *planet.*

• *Concepts encompass universes of possibilities.* An important feature of concepts—one that has fundamental implications for scientific theory and research—is that each concept consists of a universe of content. As just discussed, the concept *shirt* encompasses a universe of many specific possibilities. The concept *ice cream cone* encompasses a universe of possibilities. The concepts *attitude toward abortion, romantic love,* and so on, all encompass universes of possibilities.

• *Concepts are hypothetical.* Concepts are not reality, just ideas regarding reality. This point is easy to appreciate when concepts or constructs apply to nebulous, amorphous, abstract things, such as *wanderlust, attitude,* or *sustainable development.* But this point also applies to items that are denotable and concrete. For example, although the concept of a *shirt* exists in our minds, we do not walk around with little shirts in our minds. Neither the word *shirt* nor the thought that this word evokes is a shirt. Until and unless neurological science tells us differently, concepts possess no tangible reality, in and of themselves. In this sense, all concepts are necessarily hypothetical, and, although concepts are themselves hypothetical, the things to which they refer include both observable entities (e.g., shirts, tables, dogs), which form part of the external environment, and nontangible phenomena such as love, happiness, and hunger. Although we cannot see a person's hunger directly, we can see the effects of this assumed state and, from these effects, infer its existence. Many of the concepts that populate our minds are of this indirectly observable variety.

- *(Most) concepts are learned.* Most concepts are acquired creations. The infant does not come into the world already possessing the concept *shirt*. Rather, he or she must acquire this concept before being able to use it to understand reality and communicate with others. When individuals experience something completely new and different, they must either acquire or create a concept to be able to identify this experience and distinguish it from all other aspects they perceive. Similarly, the scientist who observes something different under the microscope or in intergalactic space will need to first conceptualize it and then give it a unique label (e.g., *chromosome, quasar*) with which to identify this particular phenomenon and others like it. Although most concepts are learned, there is evidence that certain concepts may be "hardwired," such as the face of a mother as perceived by a newborn (Bednar & Miikkulainen, 2003).

- *Concepts are socially shared.* In order for communication to occur, the set of concepts possessed by one individual generally needs to be similar to the sets possessed by others. Consider trying to discuss the notions of *balks, punts,* and *love–15* with someone who does not understand baseball, football, or tennis, respectively. Or consider a researcher trying to discuss factor analysis with a nonresearcher who has never heard of the subject. Until both parties utilize shared concepts, communication cannot take place. That said, it is important to note that concepts in the social and behavioral sciences often have contested meanings. As examples, after reviewing the scholarly literature, Fishbein and Ajzen (1975) found more than 500 definitions of *attitude,* and Jacoby and Chestnut (1978) found more than 50 definitions of *brand loyalty.*

- *Concepts are reality oriented (or functional).* Although not physical reality themselves, most of our concepts presumably are tied to the external world and used as a guide for interpreting and reacting to this world. Concepts are thus *functional.* If a person's interpretation and labeling of experiences do not mirror the world, then his or her reactions could be dysfunctional, even fatal. Consider the implications of conceptualizing a lethal cobra as a nonlethal garter snake. We develop and share concepts because they seem useful for helping us understand the reality we experience.

- *Concepts are selective constructions.* The world we experience can be conceptualized in almost countless ways. For example, looking at a woman's white blouse, we can think of it as something that provides a socially expected degree of modesty, as something that offers protection from the wind and sun, as something decorative, as something that can be used to wash a car, as a bandage, as a tourniquet, or as a white flag to indicate surrender. The ways in which concepts are applied to describe reality depend on the needs and objectives of the individual doing the conceptualizing.

Concepts, Constructs, and Variables

As might be imagined, the adult individual's mind contains a large number of concepts. Fortunately, most concepts cluster together under broader, more encompassing concepts. For example, *shirts* and *ties* are both examples of *clothing. Cats* and *dogs* are both examples of *mammals,* which, along with *snakes* and *insects,* are examples of *animals.* Such higher-order concepts are called *constructs* because they refer to instances that are constructed from concepts at lower levels of abstraction.

We form and use constructs because they are a powerful means by which we are able to handle greater portions of reality. For example, it is much easier to say "All animals must eat in order to stay alive" than it is to say "All apes, dogs, cats, frogs, snakes, etc., must eat in order to stay alive." Not only do we use constructs because of their greater economy, efficiency, and power, but also because they enable us to achieve a certain degree of order when dealing with the almost infinite number of separate concepts that populate our minds.

One type of construct that is used in many scientific theories is called a *variable.* A variable has, or is composed of, different "levels" or "values." For example, *biological sex* can be conceptualized as a variable that has two levels or values. That is, it can be seen as being composed of two concepts or categories, male and female. *Religion* is a variable consisting of the conceptually distinct categories Protestant, Catholic, Jewish, Muslim, and so on. *Time* is a variable that can be conceptualized as consisting of the categories 1 minute, 2 minutes, 3 minutes, and so on. *Intelligence* is a variable that has different levels ranging from low to high. Many theories in the social sciences focus on variables and the relationships between them, though the way theorists do so often differs considerably. This will become apparent in later chapters.

Variables are important because people and social entities (e.g., families, groups, organizations, nations) are thought to differ depending on the variable category or level that describes them. Males are thought to be different from females. A person with a low IQ score is thought to be different from a person with a high IQ score. Democracies are thought to be different from monarchies.

Although variables are central to many scientific theories, some theoretical approaches eschew variable-oriented approaches to theory construction. These theories tend to rely more on process-oriented characterizations of phenomena and/or on narratives (Mohr, 1982). For example, rather than thinking of gender as a variable that has two levels, male and female, these theoretical frameworks emphasize the many ways in which gender is understood by different individuals, which may include concepts such as *bisexual, transgender,* and *questioning* that are not treated as levels of a variable in a broader theory. (We discuss process-oriented approaches in greater depth in Chapter 10.)

BOX 2.1. Concepts, Cultures, and Values

Concepts are an integral part of science. They form the foundation for the way in which a scientist thinks about a problem. A major tool used by humans in categorizing phenomena is language. Several linguists, such as Benjamin Whorf, have suggested that language is more than a convenient tool for communication. Rather, language shapes the way in which people think about things. Analysis of divergent cultures clearly demonstrates that languages categorize our environment in different ways. Navajo Indians, for example, have color terms that roughly correspond to our *white*, *red*, and *yellow*, but none that is exactly equivalent to our *brown*, *gray*, *black*, *blue*, and *green*. Our *gray* and *brown* are denoted by a single term, as are *blue* and *green*. The Navajo have two different terms to refer to *black*, one focused on objects and the other on darkness. In short, the Navajo language approaches the color spectrum differently from traditional English. Differences in language do not necessarily limit the ability of an individual in one culture to "think" less well than an individual in another culture. Instead, language seems to direct perception and thought into culturally determined channels or categories. This being the case, it is evident that science is influenced by culture, including the way in which we are raised and the way we learn to categorize and relate different concepts. Many concepts are nearly universal, whereas other concepts are culture specific. In this sense, as well as others, science and scientific thought are influenced by the culture and environment in which its practitioners find themselves.

CONCEPTUAL SYSTEMS: THE BASES FOR DEEPER UNDERSTANDING

By enabling us to identify, describe, differentiate, classify, and segregate our experiences, concepts assist us in achieving some rudimentary understanding of our world. Yet, used in isolation, concepts and variables typically provide a limited degree of understanding. It is only when concepts are placed into relationship with each other that they move us toward achieving deeper understanding. Consider the concepts *convict, chair, smashed,* and *hungry*. Although we understand what each of these concepts means separate and apart from each other, as reflected by the statement "The hungry convict smashed a chair," connecting the concepts with each other in this manner leads to seeing a number of relationships, including (1) chairs can be smashed, (2) convicts can smash chairs, (3) convicts can be hungry, and (4) hunger may cause convicts to smash chairs.

Relationships can occur on myriad levels. Examples of relationships include spatial relationships (e.g., the car is *on* the street, parked *next to* the sidewalk); temporal relationships (the blue car reached the traffic light *before* the green car did; adolescence *precedes* adulthood); deterministic relationships (the slip on the ice caused her to fall); kinship relationships (Jon is Robin's brother); and legal relationships (Jon is married to Beth). When two or more concepts are linked together to represent relationships, we have a rudimentary *conceptual system*. It is these conceptual systems that enable us to arrive at deeper levels of understanding.

Over the course of a lifetime, each individual tends to acquire tens of thousands, perhaps even millions, of concepts. When the number of permutations and combinations is considered, it quickly becomes apparent that each person's mind can contain a dizzying array of conceptual systems. The potential exists for all of these systems to get in the way of each other and impede understanding. This is where *selection mechanisms* come into play.

When the mental system is working effectively, concepts useful for understanding and coping with the experiences of the moment come into play. By analogy, it is like the situation involving the college freshman who, while standing on the steps of the administration building during his first day on campus, asks a passerby, "How do I get to the math building?" In answering the question, the passerby might draw a simple map to represent how he or she thinks the freshman should proceed. Clearly, the map would not depict every tree and blade of grass, every section of pavement, every building and parking lot. The only things that the mapmaker includes are those he or she believes will help the freshman get to the desired destination—that is, those items the mapmaker considers to be useful guides to reality. Had the freshman inquired instead "Where is the large oak tree on campus that everyone seems to be talking about?", the map might have contained different elements, even though both maps would be referring to the same physical space.

When coping with the ongoing world, in the previous example, our conceptual systems are analogous to a mental "map," though in real life the systems can take many forms, such as mental narratives, numerical representations, and pictorial representations. The nature of the conceptual system that is invoked depends on the needs of the individual at that moment. It is useful to keep this analogy in mind when we later discuss the topic of scientific theory. At that point, the reader will be able to recognize that, like maps, scientific theories are essentially conceptual systems designed to be useful in identifying, organizing, and, as discussed in the following paragraphs, explaining or predicting some delimited portion of the experienced world.

A core facet of a conceptual system derived to provide insights into a phenomenon is what scientists call *explanation*. Although we may understand that two or more things are related, we may still not understand why this is so. Answering "Why?" involves moving to deeper levels of understanding, with the answers to such questions representing explanation. For example, why do some married couples who have been together for 20 years or more divorce? Why do some schools rely on standardized testing as an indicator of how well they are teaching their students? The answers to such questions are a form of explanation.

Another facet of understanding is being able to predict when something will happen in the future. Although prediction and explanation often go hand in hand, the two are distinct. The person who tells the auto mechanic "Every time I step on the car's accelerator, I hear a rattle in the engine—let me step on it and you can hear what I mean" may be able to predict without being able to explain. Similarly, as a moment's reflection about weather forecasting will reveal, being able to explain how the weather we experienced today came to be does not necessarily mean that we also are able to accurately predict the exact date and time when this precise weather will occur again.

Yet another feature of understanding is that it allows us to differentiate between concepts or events. As Runkel and McGrath (1972) have emphasized, knowledge is "knowledge of differences," namely, how things are similar and how things are different. Understanding a phenomenon implies that we can describe what differentiates it from other phenomena or that we can differentiate instances of it. Knowledge of males and females is knowledge of how males and females differ (or are similar) on different properties, dimensions, or behavior.

Thus, as used here, the term *understanding* encompasses identifying, describing, organizing, differentiating, predicting, and explaining. These basic ingredients of understanding are just as characteristic of the person on the street as they are of the scientist plying his or her profession.

Armed with an understanding of our world, we can begin to achieve important goals. These goals can be numerous and diverse, but two are especially noteworthy: *satisfaction* and *control*. Once we are able to identify, organize, and explain our experiences, the world becomes less of a frightening, unfathomable experience. Thus, if it does nothing else, understanding enables the individual to achieve a measure of peace and satisfaction. Understanding also gives us some ability to control events or relationships. Controlling the environment involves two components: (1) understanding the relevant features of the environment and (2) having the ability to manipulate those features.

COMMUNICATION

Having traversed the terrain from concepts to conceptual systems, we are now ready for a major extension. Up to this point we have focused on what presumably happens in the minds of each of us as we try to come to grips with the world around us. But what happens when we try to communicate this understanding to another person? How do the thoughts in the mind of one person come to be represented in the mind of another? This is a particularly interesting question when we realize that human communication need not involve face-to-face verbal interaction between two people, or even communication occurring at the same time. We are still reading and benefiting from the works of Plato, and much of our communication in this Internet era occurs through written words.

When a person (whom we term the *source*) deliberately engages in communication, he or she does so because there is some thought or feeling that he or she wishes the other party (called the *receiver*) to understand. Communication is typically defined as a process whereby a source transmits a message over a medium to one or more receivers. Unfortunately, the thought that exists in the mind of a source cannot be directly transposed into the mind of a receiver. For the source to communicate a thought (i.e., evoke the intended meaning in the mind of the receiver), the source must convert it into some externally denotable form, such as the spoken word, written words, or some other detectable symbols, and convey these *symbols* to the receiver. In turn, the receiver must then decode—that is, interpret—this overt expression and extract meaning from it—hopefully, the same meaning intended by the source.

The distinction between concepts (as internal mental representations) and symbols (the external observable expressions that are used to represent internal concepts) is important. Using the vocabulary that has evolved, *meaning structure* is the term used to designate the concepts or thoughts that exist in the minds of individuals, and *surface structure* is the term used to designate the symbols that are the externally visible expression of these thoughts. In communicating a particular thought (which we label *Meaning Structure 1* [MS1]), the source uses some surface structure in an attempt to evoke the same thought (Meaning Structure 1) in the mind of the receiver. Should this surface structure evoke some other meaning in the mind of the receiver (say, Meaning Structure 2 or 3 or 4), then we have a miscommunication in which meanings are not common or shared. Should the source succeed in evoking MS1 but also evoke one or more other meaning structures, then we have ambiguous, confusing communication (i.e., a combination of accurate and inaccurate communication).

Suppose the source, trying to communicate that a particular automobile had surreptitiously been taken from its rightful owner, said, "This car is hot." Although the receiver might extract the intended meaning (i.e., MS1—the car is stolen), he or she might also extract some other meaning, such as MS2—the car has just been running hard, and the engine temperature is relatively high; or MS3—the car has been sitting out in the sun and its interior, particularly the seats, would not be a comfortable place to sit; or MS4—the car has excellent high-performance characteristics; and so on. The particular set of surface structure symbols used by the source in this instance does not seem to have accurately conveyed the meaning he or she had in mind.

Just as clearly, the source could have employed any number of different surface structures to convey the intended meaning. He or she could have said, "This car is stolen," or "This is a stolen vehicle." Instead of speaking these words aloud, he or she could have written them out, used Morse code or the gestures employed by American Sign Language, or even tried smoke signals, pantomime, or Braille. Earlier we noted that each concept (e.g., shirt) actually represents a universe of possible meanings. Now we see that each of these meanings can be expressed via a universe of possible symbols. Since symbols tend to possess more than one meaning (i.e., they can be ambiguous), communication—including scientific communication—is enhanced by careful attention to the selection and use of symbols.

Several important points can now be summarized with respect to communication. First, it is necessary to make a distinction between people's understanding of their environment, as represented by the concepts they have in mind, and their description of that environment, as represented by the symbols, usually words, they use to describe their thoughts. Second, a number of different surface symbols could be used to communicate the same underlying meaning structure. Third, communication also requires that the receiver possess a concept comparable to the one in the mind of the source; otherwise, the communication of meaning is difficult. For example, the source could just as well have said, "The frammis is hot." If the receiver had no idea of what a *frammis* was, there would be no transference of meaning. Fourth, for any number of reasons, including "noise" in the channel, though the surface structure may have been precise and accurate, the recipient extracted an incorrect meaning. For example, the receiver may hear only part of what was said and, as a result, believe that the car is not a stolen vehicle. Fifth, even if he or she does extract the meaning intended by the source, the receiver may consider it to be inaccurate or incorrect in its description of reality (e.g., "I don't care what you tell me, that's not a stolen vehicle"). Sixth, just as the concept in our mind (e.g., of a car) is not equivalent to the elements of reality that are so conceptualized, so is the external symbol (e.g., the word *car*) not one and the same with the physical reality it describes. The symbols we use are arbitrary constructions. Finally, meaning must be interpreted in context, and a particular symbol may have different meanings in different contexts. For example, *thin* means something different when it is applied to people than when it is applied to liquids.

Of course, human communication is far more complex and dynamic than this characterization. At this point, it is sufficient to recognize that our discussion regarding concepts and conceptual systems refers to what is happening in the mind of an individual and that to communicate with others regarding these thoughts, the individual must convert thoughts to another system that requires the use of external symbols, usually language. Since much of the scientific enterprise involves the communication of information between individuals, it is important to understand the core elements that underlie that communication. We return to this point in later chapters when we discuss developing conceptual definitions in theory construction.

SUMMARY AND CONCLUDING COMMENTS

The world that we experience is multifaceted, dynamic, unique, and mostly hidden from direct view. At a most basic level, individuals cope with this complexity by forming and using concepts to assign meaning to their experiences. People place concepts into relationships with other concepts and use these conceptual systems as guides to organizing and explaining the world they experience. Scientists disagree about the best way to conceptualize reality, as reflected in the philosophical orientations of realism, social constructionism, critical realism, and hypothetical realism. In order to share and interact with others regarding these conceptualizations, people (scientists) translate their internal concepts into external symbols or language. When both the symbols and the underlying conceptualizations to which they refer are reasonably well shared, the exchange of meaning from one individual to another can take place.

Having described how the individual goes about achieving some measure of understanding of the world, we have provided the foundation for understanding what science is and where it fits into the world at large. In a nutshell, science is just one of a number of approaches (e.g., the arts, religion) for acquiring a deeper understanding of the world we experience. In the next chapter, we examine scientific thought more formally, contrasting it with other ways of knowing things and with some of the core ideas discussed in the present chapter.

SUGGESTED READINGS

Blumer, H. (1969). *Symbolic interactionism: Perspective and method.* Berkeley: University of California Press.

—A cogent discussion of hypothetical realism.

Chomsky, N. (1972). *Language and mind.* New York: Harcourt Brace Jovanovich.

—An in-depth discussion of surface and meaning structures in language as well as how language influences thinking.

Gergen, K. J. (1985). The social constructionist movement in modern psychology. *American Psychologist, 40,* 266–275.

—A brief introduction to social constructionism.

Gergen, M., & Gergen, K. (2003). *Social construction: A reader.* London: SAGE.

—A collection of classic and contemporary articles that encompasses the major viewpoints of social constructionism.

Godfrey-Smith, P. (2003). *Theory and reality: An introduction to the philosophy of science.* Chicago: University of Chicago Press.

—A treatment of major approaches to the philosophy of science, including logical positivism and the perspectives of Popper, Kuhn, Lakatos, Laudan, and Feyerabend, as well as critiques from the sociology of science and feminism. The book also reviews scientific realism, scientific explanation, and Bayesian explanation.

Lakoff, G., & Johnson, M. (1980). *Metaphors we live by.* Chicago: University of Chicago Press.

—A discussion of concepts and constructs and how we use them in our everyday life, from the perspective of anthropology.

Okasha, S. (2002). *Philosophy of science: A very short introduction.* New York: Oxford University Press.

—A brief introduction to major themes in the philosophy of science.

Rosch, E. (1977). Human categorization. In N. Warren (Ed.), *Advances in cross-cultural psychology* (pp. 1–72). New York: Academic Press.

—A discussion of categorization systems from a psychological perspective.

Salmon, W. (2006). *Four decades of scientific explanation.* Pittsburgh, PA: University of Pittsburgh Press.

—A work that traces the major debates about scientific explanation in the philosophy of science from 1845 to 1990.

Scarr, S. (1985). Constructing psychology: Making facts and fables for our times. *American Psychologist, 40,* 499–512.

—Another interesting perspective on social constructionism.

Varela, F., Thompson, E., & Rosch, E. (1991). *The embodied mind: Cognitive science and human experience.* Cambridge, MA: MIT Press.

—A creative account of how laypeople think about concepts and categories in everyday life, integrating research in cognitive science with Buddhist psychology.

KEY TERMS[2]

realism (p. 8)

social constructionism (p. 8)

critical realism (p. 9)

hypothetical realism (p. 9)

pragmatism (p. 10)

concept (p. 11)

identification (p. 12)

constructs (p. 14)

variables (p. 14)

conceptual system (p. 16)

explanation (p. 16)

understanding (p. 17)

meaning structure (p. 18)

surface structure (p. 18)

EXERCISES

Exercises to Reinforce Concepts

1. Explain how everyday thinking is similar to scientific thinking.

2. Describe the nature of *reality* as people typically experience it.

3. What is the difference between realism and social constructionism?

4. What are critical realism, hypothetical realism, and pragmatism?

5. Define the terms *concept, construct,* and *conceptual system.* Explain how each contributes to understanding our environment.

6. What are the major characteristics of concepts?

7. Explain how conceptual systems function as *selection mechanisms.* How does this aid understanding through explanation and organization?

8. Explain how understanding the environment results in prediction and control.

9. Define what is meant by meaning structure and surface structure. Explain how they can result in different forms of communication.

Exercise to Apply Concepts

1. The United States has one of the highest teen pregnancy rates among all developed countries in the world. A social scientist wants to better understand teenage pregnancy in the United States. How would the material in this chapter shape the way in which the scientist might think about this topic?

---

[2]For all key terms, the number in parentheses indicates the page on which the term first appears.

3

Science as an Approach to Understanding

The work of science is to substitute facts for appearances and demonstrations for impressions.
—JOHN RUSKIN (1859)

Chapter 2 described how individuals use concepts and conceptual systems to achieve an understanding of the world, with the premise that scientists draw upon many of these same strategies to construct scientific theories. In this chapter, we delve more deeply into scientific thinking and theorizing. We begin by considering different approaches to understanding, such as theology, philosophy, jurisprudence, the arts, literature, and science. We describe the key characteristics that separate science from these other "ways of knowing." Next, we discuss core concepts in theory construction, including the definition of a theory and the difference between theories, models, and hypotheses. We next consider the different typologies that scientists use to characterize theories and conclude with a discussion of the qualities of a good theory, what constitutes a theoretical contribution, and ways to make a theoretical contribution.

APPROACHES TO UNDERSTANDING

There are many ways of gaining and organizing knowledge about one's world, only one of which is science. All these approaches to understanding involve internal conceptual systems that are communicated among individuals using an externally observable shared symbol system (e.g., words, gestures, mathematics). Being able to use such shared symbol systems opens the door to opportunities for improving and expanding personal understanding. It enables the individual not only to communicate his or her thoughts *to* others, but also to receive communications *from* others. These others may have a more useful way of looking at the world that may lead the individual to revise his or her thinking. In addition, communicating thoughts to others can help individuals clarify their logic through self-reflection during communication.

The existence of shared symbol systems also enables us to tap into the accumulated wisdom of the past. After all, a great number of the things that each of us experiences has been experienced, thought about, and discussed by others at earlier points in time. It is possible that we would find these conceptualizations useful in our own attempt to understand our world. We refer to these bodies of knowledge as *shared meaning systems*. For the present, this term is meant to refer to both the underlying conceptualization as represented in our minds and the externally visible symbols used to communicate regarding this conceptualization.

There are many examples of shared meaning systems. Mythology documents myths that are or were used to explain otherwise inexplicable natural phenomena (e.g., the sun dropping out of view in the evening and mysteriously reappearing the next day), imbuing these phenomena with meanings that made them appear less mysterious. Other perspectives also have evolved over the ages, including those in the diverse fields of theology, philosophy, jurisprudence, the arts, literature, and science, to name a few. Each reflects a different orientation to ordering and understanding the world we experience. The fact that these perspectives have persisted for centuries suggests that each provides a satisfying way of extracting meaning from, and coping with, the world for significant numbers of people. In some key respects, science is like any of the other approaches mentioned here.

Commonalities across All Shared Conceptual Approaches

At least three fundamental characteristics typify all shared approaches to understanding. First, each approach consists of concepts and relationships among these concepts. In this regard, all shared approaches—including science—are like the conceptual systems used by individuals. The basic difference is that the shared systems tend to be more elaborate, more abstract, more stable over time, and more explicit.

Second, all shared belief systems are limited in how much of the world they address. Indeed, if they possessed no such limitation, they would be forced to grasp all of the complexity of the ongoing world as it progressed, and that would be impossible. As a consequence, no single orientation (including science) has an exclusive franchise on arriving at comprehensive understanding. Nobel Prize–winning physicist Victor Weisskopf (1977, p. 411) observed:

> Human experience encompasses much more than any given system of thought can express. . . . There are many ways of thinking and feeling, each of them contains some parcel of what we may consider the truth. . . . Science and technology comprise some of the most powerful tools for deeper insight and for solving the problems we face . . . but science and technology are only one of the avenues toward reality: others are equally needed to comprehend the full significance of our existence.

Recognition of the limits of science has been expressed in many ways. Consider what psychologist Sandra Scarr (1985, p. 500) said:

> Science, construed as procedures of knowing and persuading others, is only one form of knowing by the rules of one game. There are other games in town, some like art more intuitive, some like religion more determined by revelation and faith.

A third feature of shared belief systems is that they generally serve prescriptive and evaluative functions. The *prescriptive function* can be thought of as guidance regarding how we *ought to* approach or respond to some aspect of our world or our experience. The formal systems of religion, for example, provide explicit guidance on such subjects as premarital sex and birth control. In certain instances, the formal system of science indicates what are and are not proper procedures to be followed. For example, scientists should subject theoretical propositions to empirical tests to gain perspective on the viability of the propositions. Prescription provides a basis for evaluation. Given that we have some notion of what should be done, we can evaluate how well what has been done corresponds to what should have been done. The *evaluative function* permits labeling something as being valid or invalid, reliable or unreliable, or proper or not proper relative to what has been prescribed. Shared systems thus provide a template or model against which to evaluate activities that purport to have been taken in accordance with that model.

Special Features of the Scientific Approach

If all shared belief systems consist of the same underlying foundation (concepts and relationships) and each can accommodate only limited portions of our environment, then what distinguishes science from these other approaches? The answer has to do with how the worth of the statements and inferences within the system is assessed. To be taken seriously, any shared system needs to demonstrate that it provides some useful way of describing or coping with the world about us. A variety of avenues is available for assessing this. Perhaps the most common strategy is that known as *consensual validation*. In this approach, the worth of a particular conceptualization is gauged by the degree of acceptance it is granted by others. The fact that other people believe that a particular conceptualization is correct is used as the basis for contending that it necessarily is correct. For example, in the legal context, if a jury agrees that some particular view must be correct (and this view has been sustained on appeal), then its verdict is accepted as being correct within the legal system. Consensual validation also typifies those religions where gaining and retaining adherents are interpreted as bearing on the validity of the underlying tenets. The fact that many believe in the religion is interpreted as an indication of its validity, since "so many people could not be wrong." Consensual validation also surfaces in the arts, where public acceptance might be seen as a form of validation of artistic endeavors.

Expert validation is a related avenue for assessing the value of a particular conceptualization. Here, the decision as to whether a particular conceptualization merits acceptance is determined by selected others who presumably have the knowledge and wisdom to discern what is correct and what is not correct. Examples include relying on professional critics to determine the validity of artistic conceptualizations; on judges to decide the truth of legal matters; and on religious leaders to decide the truth of religious conceptualizations. Another confirmation strategy, *internal validation*, involves the application of formal rules of logic to examine the concepts and relationships within a particular conceptual system. If these concepts and relationships withstand the rigors of intensive logical assessment, then the conceptualization is said to be confirmed. Such a confirmation strategy is often employed in philosophy and mathematics.

Although science also employs consensual, expert, and internal validation (i.e., standards of acceptance), the scientific approach can be differentiated from all others by the fact that it is the only one to place primary reliance on *systematic empirical validation*. Over the long run, scientific conceptualizations tend to be accepted only to the extent that they have been subjected to rigorous and systematic empirical testing and shown to be useful. We consider this important point in greater depth in the next section.

BOX 3.1. The Fringes of Science

Scientific theories are subject to many types of validation. Several critics of science believe that scientists are overly zealous in their application of one type of validation, consensual, and that this can hamper the advancement of knowledge. These critics contend that scientists are too quick to dismiss researchers and theorists "working on the fringes" and that the scientific community only takes seriously that which is acceptable to the prevailing views of that community. Stated another way, science is inherently conservative. As a result of relying on such consensual validation, there are many missed opportunities. A frequently cited example is that of Galileo. Based on his observations with the recently invented telescope, Galileo came to question many widely held beliefs about the universe, such as the Earth being at its center. Ultimately, much of what Galileo posited proved to be true, even though he was subjected to public ridicule and brought before the Inquisition in Rome.

It is, of course, true that strict adherence to prevailing views may blind the scientist to new insights and advances. But this does not mean that the scientific community should approach "fringe" claims without a healthy skepticism. Consider, in retrospect, the case of Galileo. Even though Galileo was ridiculed by the general public, his observations were carefully scrutinized by the scientific community. With the invention of the telescope, scientists had no way of knowing whether what could be seen through the lens was, indeed, accurate. At the time, there was no theory of optics, and what is taken for granted today about the behavior of glass lenses was unknown at that time. Galileo asserted the validity of his telescope by examining objects on Earth with it and demonstrating its accuracy when compared to the case where the objects were directly observable to the human eye. Unfortunately, some distortions occurred at times, such as double images and color fringes. In addition, Galileo observed that while the telescope magnified planets and moons, fixed stars appeared *smaller* in size. Without a theory of optics, Galileo was unable to explain these phenomena, and, as such, the scientific resistance to his ideas may not have been as irrational as commonly portrayed.

Scientists must think carefully about the factors that influence their judgments regarding the validity of a theory, and be explicit about the criteria that they are using when evaluating that theory. Many of the "fringe theories" that occur in the popular press (e.g., biorhythms, the Bermuda Triangle) simply do not hold up under careful empirical evaluation, despite claims by their adherents of being treated like Galileo.

THE ESSENTIALS OF SCIENTIFIC ENDEAVOR

At its core, science can be thought of as consisting of a *conceptual realm,* on the one hand, and an *empirical realm,* on the other. The conceptual realm entails the development of a conceptual system (consisting of concepts, constructs, and their relationships) that can be communicated unambiguously to others. The empirical realm refers to the process whereby the worth of the conceptualization is assessed through the conduct of scientific studies. For example, an organizational scientist might suggest a theoretical proposition (in the conceptual realm) that female applicants who are pregnant will be less likely to be hired for jobs than female applicants who are not pregnant. The scientist then subjects this proposition to an empirical test (in the empirical realm) by designing a study to discern if such bias occurs. For example, managers might be asked to evaluate videotapes of applicants with identical credentials and identical interview behavior, with the only difference between them being that one applicant is obviously pregnant and the other is not (for such a study, see Cunningham & Macan, 2007, who found evidence for such a bias).

Regardless of how detailed, formally explicit, or elegant they may be, by themselves, conceptual systems (such as theories, models, and hypotheses) are not inherently scientific. To be scientific, the systems, or subsets of them, need to be subjected to some form of empirical testing. As Pap (1962) has argued, and Carnap (1936, 1937) and Popper (1963) have concurred, "a scientific statement that claims to say something about the actual world . . . is meaningful if and only if there are possible observations whose outcome is relevant to the truth or falsehood of the statement" (Pap, 1962, p. 24). Science seeks to avoid *metaphysical explanations,* that is, conceptualizations that cannot be subjected to empirical tests. For a conceptual system to be considered scientific, corresponding efforts must be generated toward its empirical evaluation (see Popper, 1968).

As an example, the concept of unconscious influences on behavior had a major impact on psychological theory when the unconscious was first popularized by the theories of Sigmund Freud. However, scientists soon became skeptical of the use of constructs about the unconscious because the constructs could not be validly measured and statements about them could not be subjected to empirical evaluation. It was possible for constructs about the unconscious to be invoked post hoc to explain most any behavior; without the possibility of empirical tests, such explanations could never be falsified. Interestingly, there has been a resurgence in the study of constructs about the unconscious as predictors of behavior as new technologies have become available that purportedly measure facets of the unconscious (e.g., Blanton & Jaccard, 2008; Oswald, Mitchell, Blanton, Jaccard, & Tetlock, 2015).

Just as the testing of theoretical propositions is central to science, it is also the case that empirical systems typically need a corresponding conceptual system to organize them (see Kaplan, 1964, pp. 159–161). Any phenomenon or environment can be thought of as consisting of a great number of empirical relations. "Without some guiding idea, we do not know what facts to gather" (Cohen, 1956, p. 148). It is often said that research should be pursued without preconceived ideas. This is impossible. Not only would it make every research investigation pointless, but even if we wished to do so, it could not be done (Poincaré, 1952, p. 143). When collecting evidence, we must have some hypothesis or guiding ideas as to which evidence is relevant to the investigation at hand, since we can hardly amass all the evidence in the universe. A researcher interested in understanding the bases of poverty in the Maya living in the highlands of Guatemala cannot randomly collect information about the Maya to address this matter. Rather, the investigator thinks about different ways of gaining perspectives on the issue and, in doing so, inescapably imposes a conceptual system, no matter how rudimentary it might be, onto the problem at hand. The basic point is that no observation is free of at least some conceptualization, even a label to name it (Kaplan, 1964, p. 48). We return to this point in greater detail in Chapters 10 and 12.

The necessity for both conceptual and empirical systems cannot be overemphasized. Scientific theories are grounded in empirical tests of theoretical propositions. Without such tests, scientific theories are often said to only represent precursors of science, an argument we consider in more depth below. To be sure, there are notable controversies about the status of theory tests and matters of falsification (see Chapter 15 on theory revision). However, few would argue that a key characteristic of scientific theory is the central role of rigorous empirical protocols underlying the evolution of theory. Correspondingly, even the most applied researcher interested only in answering the question of the moment cannot escape the fact that, regardless of how latent, some form of conceptualization precedes and guides the data he or she collects and the interpretation he or she derives. The emphasis on empirical evaluation and the rigorous protocols by which such evaluation is accomplished are the sine qua non of science and distinguish it from all other approaches to generating understanding.

SCIENCE AND OBJECTIVITY

It is often asserted that scientists are objective in their approach to understanding and that the hallmark of science is its *objectivity*. In some respects, science is anything but objective. Whether consciously or not, the scientist brings to any setting a prior schema (or set of thoughts, beliefs, and assumptions) that is used to filter, interpret, and analyze the world about him or her. This is an inevitable feature of human nature and human thinking. The scientist's schema and values influence the selection and formulation of problems the scientist decides to study, the types of strategies the scientist uses to collect data (since such acts ultimately are determined by how a problem is formulated), and how data are interpreted so as to alter or strengthen the scientist's initial conceptualization.

If, at its very core, science has such subjective characteristics, from where does its reputation for objectivity come? The objectivity of science stems from the fact that the scientist's conceptualization has a corresponding external representation that makes that conceptualization available to others so that they can scrutinize, evaluate, and repeat (or *replicate*) the work of the originating scientist. It is not necessary that other scientists agree on what the implications of these empirically verifiable observations mean. What is critical is that other scientists agree on their empirical existence and could, if they so desired, reproduce them. This characteristic of science has been termed *intersubjectivity* (Babbie, 1973, pp. 18–19; Kaplan, 1964, pp. 127–128). The enterprise of science is predicated upon a foundation of intersubjectivity; in this sense, it is objective.

Although science is heavily influenced by the conceptual schemes of the scientist, there also are aspects of the scientific enterprise that are consistent with the spirit of objectivity. As Blumer (1969) maintains, science attempts to yield perspectives on the obdurate character of our social and physical environment. In doing so, scientists subject their propositions to empirical tests to determine the validity and utility of their statements. They strive to do so in ways that do not bias or prejudge the outcomes of their empirical tests, though they may not always be successful in accomplishing this goal. They consider competing conceptual schemes that lead to opposite predictions and then give preference to the schemes whose predictions follow from the empirical tests. Although pure objectivity is rarely achieved, it still represents a working goal for many scientists, the pursuit of which helps scientists choose between conceptual schemes.

THE PROCESS OF THEORY CONSTRUCTION

What Is a Theory?

As described in Chapter 2, as nonscientists we develop and use conceptual systems to better understand the physical and social world around us. When working as scientists, we do the very same thing. Such conceptualizations may be based on what we observe, imagine, or are stimulated to think about after engaging in mind games of our own, considering what others have said about the issue at hand, or examining empirical observations that have been made. The conceptualization is then given concrete expression via some external symbol system. That is, our ideas are converted into words, numbers, diagrams, and so on. The process of formulating conceptual systems and converting them into symbolic expressions is termed *theorization* or *theory construction*.

Social scientists have defined the term *theory* in many ways. Here are some examples:

> A theory is a symbolic construction. (Kaplan, 1964, p. 296)

> It will be convenient for our purposes to define a theory simply as a set of statements or sentences. (Simon & Newell, 1956, p. 67)

> Basically, a theory consists of one or more functional statements or propositions that treat the relationship of variables so as to account for a phenomenon or set of phenomena. (Hollander, 1967, p. 55)

Although theories differ in many respects, we contend that, at their core, all theories consist of concepts and relationships between those concepts. For this reason, it is sufficient for the purposes of this book to define a theory very simply: A *theory* is a set of statements about the relationship(s) between two or more concepts or constructs.

Scientific theories generally contain three types of propositions or expressions: (1) interesting and/or contributive propositions that have not yet been empirically evaluated but that can be subjected to future empirical tests in accord with rigorous scientific protocols; (2) propositions that have been subjected to prior empirical tests and that have some reasonable degree of acceptance based on that research; and (3) propositions that have not been subjected to empirical tests but that the theorist argues can be taken as givens in their own right (often also referred to as presuppositions or axioms). Our focus in this book is on the thinking strategies and heuristics that scientists use to develop the first type of proposition. As you read future chapters, you will see that scientific theorizing is much more than the simple application of a system of logic to derive theoretical expressions, a subset of which are then subjected to empirical tests. Rather, scientists use their past experiences, in-depth knowledge of a topic, intuition, flashes of insight, creativity, ability to see patterns that others do not see and, yes, even seemingly irrational thought to germinate the seeds of an idea that might ultimately yield a viable and useful conceptual system grounded in empirics.

If empirical evaluation is at the heart of science, are disciplines like theoretical physics reduced to being nothing more than pre-science? Theoretical physics is a branch of physics that uses mathematical models and abstractions of objects to explain and predict natural phenomena. It stands in contrast to experimental physics, which explores phenomena using experiments. Many principles in theoretical physics are, in fact, subject to empirical tests and, in this sense, can be considered scientific; other propositions are subject to acceptance or rejection purely on the basis of their mathematical properties in the system of mathematical logic; and still other propositions are untestable. This has resulted in debates about the scientific status of theoretical physics; see, for example, Smolin, *The Trouble with Physics* (2006), and Hossenfelder, *Lost in Math: How Beauty Leads Physics Astray* (2018), as well as the many reviews of them.

Theories, Models, and Hypotheses

A term often used by scientists when referring to the conceptual realm is *model*. The distinction between theories and models in the social science literature is not always apparent. As examples, various authorities contend that models are a *special type* of theory (e.g., Coombs, Dawes, & Tversky, 1970, p. 4; Kaplan, 1964, p. 263); are *portions* of theories (Sheth, 1967, p. 720; Torgerson, 1958, p. 4); are *derived from* theories (e.g., Pap, 1962, p. 355); are *simplified versions* of theories (e.g., Carnap, 1971, p. 54); represent *correspondence between* two or more theories (Brodbeck, 1968); or represent *specific interpretations* of theories (e.g., Green & Tull, 1975, p. 42). Others consider the terms to be synonymous (cf. Dubin, 1976; Simon & Newell, 1956). At times, the distinctions seem arbitrary and/or eclectic. The fact is that scientists have not reached consensus on the difference between a theory and a model. In our view, expressions of models, like expressions of theories, involve concepts and relationships between concepts. Accordingly, we use the terms *theory* and *model* interchangeably in this book. A *theoretical expression* refers to any external symbolic representation of an internal conceptual system, regardless of whether that symbolic representation is more properly considered a *theory* or a *model* by others and regardless of whether the representation is verbal, mathematical, pictorial/graphic, or physical. The theoretical expressions can be presuppositions/axioms, they can be assertions that have been subject to prior empirical evaluation, or they can be in need of empirical evaluation.

Another term frequently used in scientific theorizing is *hypothesis*. The nature of a hypothesis, relative to theories and models, also is somewhat ambiguous in texts on research methods. Many scientists define hypotheses as empirically testable statements that are derived from theories and that form a basis for rejecting or not rejecting those theories, depending on the results of empirical testing. For example, a researcher might want to the test the theory that people can better recall negative information about a person than positive information. This general proposition is translated into a hypothesis or prediction about what will happen in an experiment where college students are read a list of positive and negative adjectives (prechosen to occur with equal frequency in the English language) and asked to recall the adjectives 2 minutes later. The hypothesis is that the number of negative adjectives recalled by the students will be greater, on average, than the number of positive adjectives recalled. This hypothesis, stated in a form that is part of an empirical evaluation of a theory, was derived from the more general theoretical expression that the theorist seeks to evaluate. Others define a hypothesis as a theoretical statement that has yet to be empirically validated. For example, the proposition that "people can better recall negative information about a person than positive information" would be termed a *hypothesis* until it has been subjected to formal empirical testing.

Like theories and models, hypotheses are statements that involve concepts and relationships between them. For this reason, we often do not distinguish them from theoretical and model-based statements. Given this, we use the terms interchangeably in this book, recognizing that other social scientists may make distinctions between them and that when engaging in theory testing per se, hypotheses can stand distinct from theory (see Chapter 6).

Types of Theories

Philosophers of science have developed typologies of theories so as to better understand the range of theoretical expressions that occur in science. Examples include Albert Einstein's (1934) distinction between constructive and principle theories, Marx's (1951) distinction between reductive and constructive theories, and Kaplan's (1964) distinction between concatenated and hierarchical theories at either molar or molecular levels. More recently, theories have been characterized as humanistic, behavioristic, constructionist, structuralist, functionalist, and so on.

Although all theories focus on concepts and relationships between concepts, theories in the social sciences differ in the fundamental assumptions they make about human behavior. These assumptions lead theorists to think about the same problem in different ways. For example, a humanist may identify and conceptualize an entirely different set of concepts when analyzing school performance in children than the concepts that a behaviorist might consider. The humanist might focus on concepts such as how the child construes the school environment, the child's feelings about school, and the affective quality of the relationship between the teacher and the student. In contrast, the behaviorist might focus on the positive and negative reinforcers that the child is receiving and the nature of contingencies between performance of behaviors and administration of rewards and punishment. Neither conception is more "correct" than the other, although one theoretical approach ultimately might satisfy the criteria of what constitutes a good scientific theory better than the other. We view broad-based typologies of theories, such as those mentioned here, as different launching points for identifying concepts and relationships that we use to organize and understand our world. We discuss such perspectives in Chapter 12 (see also Slife & Williams, 1995).

The Role of Theory in Basic versus Applied Research

An often-heard distinction is that between basic and applied scientific research. The essential difference between these two types of research is difficult to identify. According to one perspective, basic researchers use theories, whereas applied researchers do not. Yet every scientist, even the "strict empiricist," cannot escape the fact that, regardless of how hidden, some form of conceptualization precedes and guides the data that he or she collects and the interpretations he or she derives from it. Hence, reliance on theory would appear to provide an unsatisfactory basis for distinguishing applied from basic research.

Another basis for distinguishing the two approaches emphasizes the intent of the researcher. When the intent is to address and hopefully solve an immediate real-world problem, the research is considered to be *applied*. In contrast, research conducted for the purpose of extending the boundaries of our collective body of understanding, not for the purpose of addressing a pressing problem, is termed *basic*. Theories are seen as being oriented toward basic or applied phenomena, depending on research objectives. According to this view, the applied and basic researcher could design and implement virtually identical studies; yet, because of different research objectives, one would be termed *applied* and the other *basic*.

Another criterion that often is suggested for distinguishing between basic and applied research focuses on the abstractness of the concepts in the conceptual network. According to this perspective, applied research is typically concerned with relatively narrow and circumscribed concepts that are domain specific. For example, the blue jeans manufacturer interested in expanding sales might commission a study to determine whether the buying public contained a sufficient number of people ready for jeans in new colors, styles, and patterns. However, though interested in learning more about such innovators, he or she most likely would not be interested in funding research to learn whether respondents were also innovators in regard to other consumer products (e.g., appliances, pens, foods). Understandably, the objective is to achieve some understanding of a concrete and limited problem. In contrast, basic research is typically interested in broader, less concrete concepts. In the present instance, basic researchers would likely strive to understand and draw inferences regarding innovators in general (i.e., across the range of consumer products) and how these innovative tendencies might be related to a broad spectrum of other concepts and constructs, usually ones that have been suggested and perhaps explored in prior research by others.

There seems to be no single basis sufficient for clearly distinguishing between basic and applied research. Perhaps the best approach is to note a set of attributes that, when employed in combination, seems to provide some basis for making such a distinction. From this perspective, *applied research* can be characterized as research that focuses on an immediate problem; relies on concepts that are relatively narrow in scope; and produces results that are not intended to extend a general body of knowledge. In contrast, *basic research* is characterized as research that is not directly focused on pressing real-world problems; tends to rely on concepts that are relatively broad in scope; and produces findings with the intent of contributing to and extending our basic understanding of the phenomenon in question. In the final analysis, we find the framing of research as either basic or applied to be somewhat of a false dichotomy because much research blends the two orientations to science. For extended discussions of applied versus basic theory and research, see Brinberg and Hirschman (1986) and Brinberg and McGrath (1985).

CHARACTERISTICS OF A GOOD THEORY

How do we know if a theory is a good theory? Several criteria have been proposed for evaluating theoretical expressions. If we assume that the purpose of a theory is to help us better understand our world, then a paramount consideration is whether it does indeed offer such guidance. From this perspective, a primary evaluative criterion is utility. Theoretical expressions are valued to the extent that they serve as useful guides to the world we experience, that is, to the extent that they enable us to achieve some understanding of our world. It is important to recognize that utility is a relative notion. Consider being adrift in the ocean with a leaky life raft. Unless a better life raft is available, we would be foolish to discard the one that leaks—it is the best we have. As another example, though a hand-drawn map may not be 100% accurate, it may be sufficiently accurate to be useful. If a theory is flawed in some respect but still provides unique and useful insights in other respects, it tends to be retained until something better comes along.

Consensual validation is a basis by which scientists often accept or reject theories. This term refers to the degree of consensus among the scientific community about the validity of the theory. If a theory enjoys widespread acceptance, then it is seen as being a "good" theory. The philosopher Karl Popper (1968) believed that adherents of what most scientists judge to be a "bad theory" eventually die off or leave science, rendering the theory obsolete with time.

Shaw and Costanzo (1982) distinguish two broad classes of criteria for determining a good scientific theory: those criteria that are necessary if the theory is to be accepted by the scientific community, and those criteria that are desirable but not essential to acceptance. In the former category, three criteria are crucial. First, internally, the theory must be logically consistent; that is, the theoretical statements within the conceptual system must not be contradictory, nor must the theory lead to incompatible predictions. Second, the theory must be in agreement with known data and facts. Third, the theory must be testable; that is, a theory, or the key components of it, must ultimately be subject to empirical evaluation.

The second class of criteria discussed by Shaw and Costanzo (1982) includes six criteria. First, a theory should be stated in terms that can be understood and communicated to other scientists.

Second, the theory should strive to be parsimonious, adequately explaining a phenomenon, but with a minimum of concepts and principles. Scientists refer to this criterion as Occam's razor, named after 14th-century English philosopher William of Ockham; this principle states that one "cuts away" extraneous concepts and assumptions so as to yield a theory that is parsimonious yet satisfactory in its level of explanation. All other things being equal, preference is given to theories that make fewer assumptions. The fewer the working parts necessary to get the job done, the better the theoretical system.

Third, while recognizing that theories are occasionally so novel that they upset the theoretical applecart (see Box 3.1 on page 25), a theory should be consistent with other accepted theories that have achieved consensus among the scientific community; that is, it should be able to be integrated into existing bodies of accepted theory. Having said that, many notable scientific advancements have occurred when a new theory contradicts accepted theory, so this desideratum should be applied with qualification.

A fourth desideratum is scope. Other things being equal, the greater the range of the theory (i.e., the more of "reality" that it encompasses), the better it may be. Though both Newton's and Einstein's theories of gravity enable us to understand a great many of the same things, the fact that Einstein's theory enables us to understand much more makes it a more powerful and valuable theory. That said, there are times when narrow-range theories tend to hold up better over time than broader-range theories. Also, as discussed in Chapter 4, scientific progress is often achieved by narrowing, not broadening, the focus of theories. Thus, this criterion is somewhat of a two-edged sword.

Creativity or novelty is a fifth criterion that is sometimes suggested for evaluating a theory. A theory that explains the obvious is generally not as highly valued by the scientific community as one that provides a novel insight into an interesting phenomenon.

Finally, many scientists suggest that a good theory is one that generates research activity—which often is a consequence of consensual validation of the theory. A theory that is rich in scope, explicit, interesting, and useful will probably generate a good deal of empirical research. Hence, a yardstick of a good theory is the amount of research it generates. Note, however, that some scientists (e.g., Skinner, 1957) have questioned this criterion, noting that many a theory has led investigators into research enterprises that have been a waste of time.

In sum, good theories, in principle, (1) increase our understanding of the world, (2) are accepted by the broader scientific community (but see Box 3.1), (3) are logically consistent, (4) are in agreement with known data and facts, (5) are testable, (6) are easily understood and communicated to others, (7) are appropriately parsimonious, (8) are consistent with other accepted theories that have achieved consensus (but see Box 3.1), (9) are relatively broad in scope, (10) are novel and original, and (11) stimulate research. When we evaluate the worth of theories as a whole, these criteria are typically invoked in one form or another. Brinberg and McGrath (1985) note that these desiderata sometimes conflict with each other. For example, parsimonious theories tend to be more limited in scope. As such, scientists often must make trade-offs as they construct theories to maximize what the scientific community values.

WHAT IS A THEORETICAL CONTRIBUTION?

One of the most common reasons manuscripts are rejected for publication is that they are judged by editors/reviewers to make an insufficient theoretical contribution. The question then becomes just what constitutes a "theoretical contribution"? Answering this question does not necessarily focus on evaluating a theory as a whole. Rather, the focus is on evaluating a specific product to determine if it is theoretically contributive. Judgments about theoretical contribution are inherently subjective, but most journal editors who have written editorials about the topic emphasize two general qualities, originality and utility (e.g., Corley & Gioia, 2011; Slater & Gleason, 2012). To these we add a third criterion, scope.

Originality

Webster's Dictionary defines *originality* as the quality of being novel or unusual. For journal editors, this quality often translates into the judged *value-added contribution* of a submission relative to extant knowledge. The degree of originality or "value additiveness" varies on a continuum, ranging from low to high. Corley and Gioia (2011) characterize the low end of the continuum as "incremental" and the high end as "revelatory." Huff (1999) makes the analogy of contributing to a current conversation (the low end) versus starting a new conversation (the high end). Conlon (2002) states that contributory theory provides a critical redirection of existing views. Mintzberg (2005, p. 361) argues that strong theoretical contributions "allow us to see profoundly, imaginatively, unconventionally into phenomena we thought we understood." Davis (1971), in his classic article "That's Interesting!", identifies what he believes separates interesting from uninteresting theories, arguing that contributions that are surprising, counterintuitive, and that deny common assumptions represent interesting theory, whereas those that simply affirm audience assumptions are of lesser interest: "The best way to make a name for oneself in an intellectual discipline is to be interesting—denying the assumed, while affirming the unanticipated" (p. 343). Reflecting on paper rejections, Rynes (2002, p. 312) takes Davis's orientation a step further by stating that "reviewers are judging the results not against prior literature, but rather against common sense. . . . " Bergh (2003, p. 136) also emphasizes the surprise element of theoretical contributions: "Is the contribution more of a common sense derivation, or does it represent a novel and unique insight?"

The morphing of originality into surprise value and counterintuition has been the subject of controversy in the social sciences. The criticism is that by emphasizing the clever and nonintuitive, we may miss the important and substantive essence of science that leads to a truly better understanding of the world about us. For example, noted social psychologist John Cacioppo (2004) comments on the field of social psychology as follows:

> We value the prize of a theory that makes non-obvious predictions, that illuminates flaws in social reasoning and interactions, that illustrates not only the inadequacy but the idiocy of common sense. Such work is unquestionably clever, but does the pursuit of the witty at the expense of the comprehensive put personality and social psychologists at risk of becoming the editorial cartoonists of the social sciences? (p. 116)

Cacioppo's concern derives from the growing number of theories and studies in social psychology that focus on cute, fun, clever, or counterintuitive demonstrations rather than on the nuts and bolts of building comprehensive theories of behavior. Novelty and originality are important qualities that editors and reviewers consider when they judge research as making a theoretical contribution, but they also must be careful about equating them with the elements of surprise and counterintuition.

Utility

Another criterion for theoretical contribution that journal editors often emphasize is that of *utility*. Actually, there are two types of utility: (1) utility in the sense of increasing our understanding of the world about us (described above) and (2) utility in terms of practical, real-world implications. Our discussion here focuses on the second type, a criterion that is particularly relevant to audiences/journals that have theoretical *and* applied interests. In such cases, in addition to theory, a premium is placed on tackling problems that affect practitioners/people in real-world settings, or as Hambrick (2005, p. 124) states, problems that derive from "the observation of real-life phenomena, not from scholars struggling to find holes in the literature." In some journals, it is not uncommon for editors to require or encourage reflections in the discussion of a study on "practice implications." Whetten (1989) has elaborated key questions reviewers use to evaluate articles, one of which is "Who cares?" The answer to this question generally focuses on the applied significance of the theoretical product.

Corley and Gioia (2011) lament the too-frequent disconnect between theory and practice. In their commentary, they analyzed differences across almost 20 years of two article types published in the *Academy of Management Review*: (1) the article in the journal formally chosen by the editors as the "best article of the year" and (2) the article in the journal published during that same year that was most cited by other scientists in subsequent years. In only three instances was the same article in both categories. A distinguishing feature Corley and Gioia identified was that the most heavily cited articles tended to focus on practical utility, but this was not necessarily the case for the "best" article. Corley and Gioia concluded that in their discipline (management), it is important for theories to be

> problem driven—that is, in some fashion addressing a problem of direct, indirect, or long-linked relevance to practice, rather than narrowly addressing the (theoretical) "problem" of finding the next mediator or moderator variable or filling theoretical gaps simply because they exist. When we focus mainly on the latter, we end up advancing theory for theory's sake, rather than theory for utility's sake. (p. 22)

When making judgments about practical utility, one might invoke different criteria depending on the substantive domain. What makes a prevention program aimed at neglectful parenting practical and useful might be different from what makes a counseling program for addicts practical and useful, which, in turn, might be different from what makes strategies for reducing racism practical and useful. For prevention programs, for example, criteria surrounding (1) program efficiency (e.g., minimizing cost, discomfort, hassles, and maximizing convenience and sustainability), (2) program effectiveness and the severity of the problem addressed, and (3) program reach (e.g., number of people affected, "defenselessness" of people affected) are central to judgments of program util-ity. Reviewers and editors rarely are explicit about the criteria they use to judge practical utility in a given domain, putting the onus instead on the author to build such a case.

One problem with relying too heavily on practical utility is that sometimes the implications of a scientific discovery may not be readily apparent and, indeed, may take years before the applied value becomes evident. In the early 1500s, mathematician Ger-olomo Cardano developed the concept of imaginary numbers, which focus on the square root of negative numbers. At the time, his work was greeted with suspicion, as was the concept of negative numbers more generally. Little could it be known that imaginary numbers would be key to microchip design and digital compression algorithms respon-sible for today's digital music players. The marine biologist Osamu Shimomura studied the question of why jellyfish glow, a seemingly mundane topic. The work ultimately led to the development of a revolutionary protein tracking tool, the green fluorescent protein, that has transformed modern medical research. Shimomura received a Nobel Prize for his work.

Scope

A third criterion sometimes used by reviewers to judge the degree of theoretical con-tribution is *scope*, although doing so varies by discipline. If a theoretical proposition applies to a wide range of phenomena, then it may be judged as more contributive than if it is narrow in scope. For example, in psychology, the three most highly cited theo-retical articles of all time are by Bandura on the construct of self-efficacy, by Fishbein and Ajzen on their theory of reasoned action (which addresses the impact of attitudes, norms, and perceived control on behavior), and by Barron and Kenny on mediation and moderation (Green, 2018; Ho & Hartley, 2016). Each of these theories can be applied to many different substantive domains and topic areas. In this sense, they have consider-able scope. By contrast, an article that focuses on, say, changes in U.S. conservation atti-tudes over time likely will not be judged as impactful given its narrow scope. Chapter 4 discusses the trade-offs of constructing theories that are broad versus narrow in scope.

Combining Originality, Utility, and Scope

Factors other than originality, utility, and scope obviously come into play when eval-uating the theoretical contribution of research. For example, if the offered theory is logically incoherent or logically questionable, it is not going to be judged favorably. However, assuming such coherence is in place, the originality, utility, and scope of the contribution seem to have high priority in the minds of editors and reviewers. One can think of the originality, utility, and scope of a theoretical contribution in the context of a three-dimensional space, as shown in Figure 3.1. This figure scales each dimension from 0 (low) to 10 (high) and shows four illustrative points in the dimensional space: (1) a contribution that is relatively low on all three dimensions (back lower left), (2) a contribution that is moderate on all three dimensions, (3) a contribution that is high on all three dimensions, and (4) a contribution that is high in originality but low in utility and scope (front lower left). When you seek to create or evaluate a theoretical contribu-

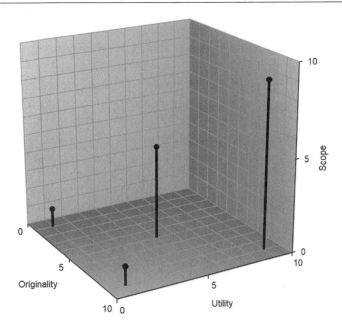

FIGURE 3.1. Originality, utility, and scope.

tion, you might think about where in this three-dimensional space it resides. Contributions that are low in originality, utility, and scope are unlikely to be well received in top-tier journals. This is not to say that research low in these qualities is unimportant. For example, replication studies are not original, but they can be important for scientific progress (see Chapter 15). Contributions that are high in originality, utility, and scope will likely be positively evaluated as contributive. As you construct theory and think about the phenomena you are interested in, how might you maximize the qualities of the originality, utility, and scope of your ideas, essentially moving your work to the upper right space of Figure 3.1? When you communicate your theory to others, how can you frame your presentation so that your project is perceived as being in that section of Figure 3.1? When you read an article and evaluate its theoretical contribution, think about how it fares on originality, utility, and scope. Be specific about where and why you would locate it where you do.

Ways of Making a Theoretical Contribution

As a preview to the remainder of this book, it might be helpful to list selected strategies you can use to make a theoretical contribution, all of which are elaborated in future chapters. We consider 16 such strategies. When you read articles in your discipline, you also can use this list as a guide to articulate the type of strategies the article used to make a theoretical contribution and how original you judge those contributions to be.

1. *Clarify, refine, or challenge the conceptualization of a variable/concept.* Theories work with variables and concepts. One way to make a theoretical contribution is to reframe or reconceptualize a variable/concept in novel ways. You might seek to make a

complex concept simpler or a simple concept more complex. As an example, ethnic identity tends to be viewed as a relatively stable construct that exhibits meaningful across-individual variability in strength; that is, some people identify with their ethnic group more strongly than others do. Instead of a stable ethnic orientation, we might think of the strength of ethnic identity as also having a more fluid, dynamic quality that can shift from one day to the next, depending on situational contexts and the goals of individuals in those contexts. In short, ethnic identity can be viewed as having both stable and transitory components; to explain behavior related to ethnicity, both dynamics need to be taken into account. Extending this idea a bit further, a person of a given ethnic group might be thought of as having multiple cognitive "portfolios" of ethnic identity (e.g., what it means to be Latinx), some of which become salient and actionable depending on the situation (Goldin & Jaccard, 2019; Pabón, 2010). Identifying those cognitive portfolios and the circumstances in which one portfolio becomes salient over another might be useful. Such a reconceptualization of ethnic identity thus might lead to innovative theory. Conceptual definitions are discussed in Chapter 5.

2. *Create a new variable or constellation of variables that are of theoretical interest.* Variables are human inventions and represent ways of categorizing or thinking about people or events. Social scientists sometimes invent or create new variables for the purposes of building new theories, or they create novel variable constellations that might be of interest and import. Chapter 5 describes examples of this strategy as well as heuristics for variable creation. An example of creating a compelling constellation of variables is the *dark triad of personality,* originally proposed by Paulhus and Williams (2002). The dark triad consists of three personality traits: Machiavellianism, narcissism, and subclinical psychopathy. Machiavellianism is the tendency to manipulate people for one's own gains; narcissism is a sense of grandiosity, entitlement, dominance, and superiority; and subclinical psychopathy is characterized by high impulsivity and thrill-seeking coupled with low empathy and low anxiety. The three traits comprising the "dark triad" share common features, namely, a socially malevolent character with tendencies toward self-promotion, emotional coldness, duplicity, and aggressiveness. Grouping these variables together and using a provocative label to characterize the grouping have led to considerable theorizing and research about them as a collective.

3. *Add one or more explanatory variables for an outcome that have not been considered in prior work.* Theoretical contributions can also be made by bringing to bear an explanatory variable that has not been studied in prior research. For example, in sociology, Idler and Benyamini (1997) drew attention to the construct of one's perceived health status as a predictor of mortality, arguing that it is a significant predictor independent of objective indicators of health and other covariates known to be related to mortality (e.g., age, socioeconomic status). Idler and Benyamini considered a range of interpretations that could account for the association and described a research program for "next steps" in building a theory of mortality that included one's perceived health status. Chapter 4 presents heuristics that can help you identify potentially new explanatory variables, and Chapter 7 describes strategies for embedding such variables in a broader theoretical network.

4. *Identify the mechanisms or intervening processes responsible for an effect of one variable on another.* When two variables are linked, theorists often want to know why this is so, that is, what is responsible for the relationship between them. For example, it is well known that there are substantial ethnic and gender differences in the occurrence of HIV infections in the United States. In 2017, Blacks in the United States represented 13% of the population but 43% of the new HIV diagnoses (CDC, 2018). Why? What are the sources of this health disparity? Is it because Blacks, due to poverty, have more limited access to health care? Is it because they make less use of condoms? Is it because of higher needle sharing when they are using illicit injection drugs? Men account for about 75% of individuals living with HIV. Why? What are the sources of this gender-based health disparity? Is it because men are more likely to engage in risky sexual behavior? Is it because men tend to have more sexual partners than women? Another way of making a theoretical contribution is to elaborate new perspectives on the mechanisms responsible for the association between two variables. Chapter 7 discusses this strategy in detail using the concept of causal mediation.

5. *Identify the boundary conditions of an effect of one variable on another.* Theoretical relationships often have *boundary conditions.* Another way of contributing to theory is to identify these conditions (Busse, Kach, & Wagner, 2017). Boundary conditions address the generalizability of a theory, with an eye toward identifying the limits of a theoretical proposition. In economics, for example, lowering the federal interest rate (the interest rate at which banks and credit unions lend reserve balances to other depository institutions overnight) typically leads to an expansion of the economy, but only under certain broader economic conditions. Identifying and elaborating what these conditions are would constitute a theoretical contribution. Ways of theorizing about boundary conditions are described in Chapters 6, 7, and 9.

6. *Identify variables that moderate the effect of one variable on another.* A more subtle variant of identifying boundary conditions is to identify variables that dampen or strengthen the effect of one variable on another variable. These are known more generally as *moderator variables.* As an example, numerous studies find that parents are not as happy as nonparents and that parenthood tends to have a negative effect on subjective well-being (Aassve, Goisis, & Sironi, 2012). Matysiak, Mencarini, and Vignoli (2016) hypothesized that the negative effect of childbearing on subjective well-being would be stronger when parents were experiencing higher levels of work–family conflict. That is, they hypothesized that work–family conflict moderated the adverse effect of having a child on parents' subjective well-being. The strategy of specifying moderator variables is discussed in Chapters 6 and 7.

An interesting form of this strategy is known as *meta-analysis.* Meta-analyses focus on multiple published studies all on the same topic that address the same theoretical relationship between two variables, such as the effect of the number of hours spent watching television programs with sexist content on sexist attitudes. Each study is treated as a separate data point, and specialized statistical methods are used to analyze the statistics reported in each investigation, say, the correlation between exposure and sexist attitudes, across all studies. Moderator variables represented by study characteristics are identified, and the reported correlations are tested to determine if they vary as a function of the hypothesized moderators. For example, a theorist might postulate cohort effects such that the effect of watching sexist television programs on sexist attitudes is stronger for studies conducted in the 1970s versus those conducted in the 1980s versus those conducted in the 1990s, with the effect becoming weaker with each passing decade due to changing societal contexts. This proposition would be tested using meta-analysis. Meta-analyses are often referred to as quantitative literature reviews because they review studies on a given topic but apply quantitative methods to summarize trends across the studies. For an introduction to meta-analysis, see Borenstein, Hedges, Higgins, and Rothstein (2009).

7. *Extend an existing theory or idea to a new context.* Many theories can be applied to new populations, new situations, and/or different problem areas (Pawson & Tilley, 1997). For example, theories have been offered about the causes and consequences of marital dissatisfaction among husbands and wives (Gottman, 1994). Do these theories apply to unmarried couples who live in cohabiting relationships? In 1960, an estimated 439,000 couples were cohabitating in the United States; by 2005, the number had risen to 4.85 million couples (an over-tenfold increase; Jaccard, 2009) and by 2015, it was over 7.5 million couples. Of interest might be how well theories of marital dissatisfaction "import" to dissatisfaction among couple members who are cohabitating.

Applying a well-articulated theory to a new context will not always be seen as innovative unless it is accompanied by new insights relative to the theory or to the substantive domain of interest. Fisher and Aguines (2017) describe seven tactics for elaborating existing theories when they are applied in new contexts: (1) horizontal contrasting, (2) vertical contrasting, (3) new construct specification, (4) construct splitting, (5) structuring specific relations, (6) structuring sequence relations, and (7) structuring recursive relations. *Horizontal contrasting* applies a theory from one context to another but where the level of analysis (e.g., the individual, the organization) remains the same. For example, a theory developed for one type of organization is applied to another type of organization; a theory of couple dissatisfaction for married couples is applied to cohabiting couples. *Vertical contrasting* extends a theory developed to explain constructs and relationships at one level of analysis to another level, such as adapting theories of individual-level decision making to organizational-level decision making, or vice versa. *Construct specification* involves adapting the definition of a theoretical construct in one context to reflect the realities of the new context, thereby advancing theory about the construct. *Construct splitting* splits existing constructs in one context into more nuanced, multidimensional portrayals demanded by the new context. *Structuring specific relations* describes new relationships between the theoretical constructs that are unique to the new context relative to the original context. *Structuring sequence relations* describes how the ordering between variables might change as a function of the new context relative to the prior context. For example, the sequence of steps involved in implementing new policies in hospitals might differ from one medical context to another (e.g., specialty versus general-medicine-focused hospitals). *Structuring recursive relations* involves identifying how reciprocal causal dynamics between theoretical constructs may change as a function of context. When one is seeking to make a theoretical contribution by applying an extant theory to a new context, it usually will be helpful to invoke one or more of these seven processes to strengthen the theoretical contribution.

8. *Identify nuanced functional forms of relationships.* Many theoretical propositions are framed in ways that imply linear relationships between variables. The phrases "as *X* increases, *Y* decreases" and "as *X* increases, *Y* increases" typically imply linear relations. However, variables might be related in nonlinear ways that have nontrivial theoretical and/or practical significance. For example, when mapping how attitudes relate to behavior, one might expect that for some behaviors, only when attitudes toward performing it are quite positive will people be energized enough to put forth the effort to perform the behavior. This suggests that below a certain threshold of attitudinal positivity, attitudes and behavior will be unrelated, but above that threshold, more positive attitudes will lead to higher levels of behavior (see van Doorn, Verhoef, & Bijmolt, 2007). Interventions that change attitudes may have little effect on behavior if that change occurs below the threshold, but they may have appreciative effects if the attitude change occurs above the threshold. Such nonlinear functions may account for inconsistent results in literature reviews of attitude-based interventions. For example, studies that fail to find intervention effects on behavior may have created change below the threshold, whereas studies that observed intervention effects on behavior may have created attitude change above the threshold. Thus, another way to make a theoretical contribution is to specify in more focused ways the function relating two or more variables and elaborating the theoretical and practical implications of that function. This strategy is discussed in Chapters 6, 8, and 11.

9. *Identify unenunciated/unanticipated consequences of an event.* Another way of making a theoretical contribution is to call attention to a new consequence or outcome in a theory, perhaps an "unanticipated consequence." For example, globalization has brought factories to many rural areas of developing countries with the promise of increased economic opportunities, higher income, and steady work. However, the introduction of factories into these communities has produced a host of social and cultural effects, including changes in eating habits, family dynamics, and work patterns that have yielded a mix of community-wide positive and negative outcomes (Goldin, 2009). If a theory does not include all consequences associated with a focal variable, identifying and elaborating new ones can be contributive.

Computer simulations are becoming increasingly popular as a means of generating and refining theory (see Chapter 9). Simulations can take many forms, but they typically deal with complex, large-scale systems that have both elements of randomness as well as dynamic interdependencies. In a strategy known as agent-based modeling, a theorist might create a large population of simulated "units" (e.g., people) on a computer, imbue them with certain attributes or qualities according to a set of computer algorithms/rules, and devise interaction and experiential learning rules for the units, all based on theory. The system is then set in motion on the computer, and the consequences and outcomes that result are noted. Such simulations, for example, are used to model and gain a deeper understanding of phenomena such as traffic congestion, crowd behavior in emergencies, and pollution dynamics, to name but a few. Often, unanticipated emergent outcomes will manifest themselves in the course of the simulation, and documenting these outcomes can make a theoretical contribution. (For an example in the social sciences, see the work on religious diffusion by Whitehouse, Kahn, Hochberg, and Bryson [2012] and the multiple commentaries on their article.) Simulation approaches to theory construction are discussed in Chapter 9.

10. *Enrich and deepen understanding of established quantitative associations.* Theoretical relationships in the social sciences are often tested using quantitative methods. An advantage of quantitative-based approaches is that they allow us to collect data on large numbers of people and to summarize data trends using convenient and revealing statistical methods. Such data also allow one to address complex multivariate questions in ways that the unaided human mind is simply incapable of. However, this efficiency and complexity often comes at a cost, namely, sacrificing levels of detail, richness, and insight that are better achieved through in-depth interviews and/or other qualitative methods. Another strategy for making a theoretical contribution is to identify an interesting theoretical proposition that has been established quantitatively, but then to conduct a qualitative study with respect to it in order to enrich, elaborate, build upon, or even revise it. For example, it is well known that cognitive-behavioral therapy (CBT) is a relatively effective psychosocial treatment for depression, a result that has been shown repeatedly in quantitative-based randomized trials (e.g., Driessen & Hollon, 2010). However, rarely has research conducted in-depth qualitative interviews and/or collected detailed observational data on individuals about their experiences before, during, and after CBT (CBT treatment usually extends over a period of several months). Both theoretical and practical insights are almost certain to emerge in the context of such data collection. For example, quantitative studies tend to find that patients who are married often respond better to CBT; this also is true of patients who are free of comorbid psychiatric disorders. Qualitative research might explore the bases for these documented differential responses to CBT to evolve rich theories surrounding them. Chapter 10 elaborates the concept of qualitative methods.

11. *Develop typologies/taxonomies.* Yet another type of theoretical contribution is to construct a meaningful *typology* or *taxonomy* and then to build theory or practical applications around it.[1] The construction of typologies/taxonomies can be pursued based purely on logic, or it also can use empirics. As examples, Greenberg (1987) categorized theories of organizational justice invoking two dimensions: (a) a reactive versus proactive dimension, that is, a focus on seeking to redress injustice versus a focus on striving to attain justice and (b) a process–content dimension, that is, a focus on the processes used by organizations to ensure outcomes such as pay and recognition are equitably distributed versus a focus on determining the extent to which there are equitable outcomes. Greenberg created a 2×2 typology based on the factorial combination of these two dimensions and then engaged in a theoretical analysis of each cell by and of itself

---

[1]Distinctions are often made between a "typology" and a "taxonomy," but we use the terms interchangeably here; see Chapters 10 and 11 for elaboration.

as well as the four types of theories considered collectively. In this case, the typology served as a means of theoretical synthesis.

In another study, Abraham and Michie (2008; see also Michie et al., 2013) developed a taxonomy of behavior change techniques used in health interventions after acquiring and reviewing the manuals of 195 behavioral interventions. Twenty-six different strategies were identified (e.g., handling time management; providing information about the benefits and costs of action or inaction; providing information about whether others would approve or disapprove of any proposed behavior change; prompting barrier identification and how to deal with barriers; providing general encouragement). The idea was to use this taxonomy to identify which techniques were most effective in different contexts and for different populations.

As a final example, in a qualitative study, Jaccard, Levitz, and colleagues (2018) interviewed contraceptive counselors who help women make decisions related to contraceptives. They explored how counselors felt about expanding the scope of their counseling to include family planning decisions surrounding the timing of a pregnancy relative to the women's current life circumstances and career goals. Based on the interviews, Jaccard and colleagues constructed a taxonomy of challenges and difficulties in implementing such counseling, which was then used to formulate training protocols for counselors and develop theory in this area.

The construction of typologies is discussed further in Chapters 4 and 11.

12. *Import or apply grand theories and frameworks from other disciplines.* Social scientists often distinguish between grand theories and midlevel theories. Grand theories are broad-based, comprehensive frameworks that represent ways of thinking about a wide range of phenomena and that have proven useful across decades of scientific inquiry. Examples include materialism, structuralism, functionalism, symbolic interactionism, postmodernism, and evolutionary perspectives, all of which are discussed in Chapter 12. Midlevel theories are narrower in scope and focus on specific phenomena, usually mapping relationships between variables or concepts in a more limited sense than grand theories. Another form of theoretical contribution is to bring one of the grand theories to bear in a substantive area in ways that provide new theoretical insights into that area. For example, if one is interested in health care delivery systems, what insights might be gained by thinking about such systems from the perspective of materialism, structuralism, and/or functionalism? Examples of this strategy for making a theoretical contribution include Acevedo (2007), Golding and Murdock (1978), Katz (1960), and Timmermans and Almeling (2009).

13. *Synthesize multiple theories into a unified framework.* Yet another form of theoretical contribution is to synthesize multiple theories into a single, more comprehensive theoretical structure that then leads to an even greater understanding of the phenomena of interest. For example, Fishbein and colleagues (2001) sought to integrate the theory of reasoned action, social learning theory, self-regulation theory, the health belief model, and subjective culture theory into a single unified framework for the study of health-related behaviors. Pound and Campbell (2015) characterize the synthesis process as having three steps: (a) *synthesis preparation*, in which parts of relevant theories are extracted and summarized; (b) *synthesis*, in which the theories are compared for points of convergence and divergence and then brought together into a larger whole that resolves points of divergence; and (c) *synthesis refinement*, in which the synthesis is interrogated for further theoretical insights. Pound and Campbell provide examples that use the three steps as applied to sociological theories of health.

14. *Develop a theory of measurement*. Measurement is core to science. Although it is traditionally thought of as a methodological matter, measurement has a theoretical basis around which theory construction can take place (see Chapters 13 and 14). As such, one can develop and evaluate theories about measurement. For example, when people make self-reports of how often they have engaged in a behavior (e.g., voted Democratic, gone to church), they must (a) interpret and comprehend the question asked by the researcher, (b) make a cognitive judgment that constitutes their answer to the question, and then (c) translate the answer in their minds into a response format provided by the investigator. Theorizing about the processes of comprehending, judging, and translating judgments ultimately underlies theories of measurement. As such, contributions can also take the form of theorizing about measurement.

15. *Pit opposing theoretical explanations against one another*. Another strategy for making a theoretical contribution is to pursue a study that pits two competing theories against one another. This is a classic strategy that Platt (1964) called *strong inference*. As an example, Skurka and colleagues (2018) noted that courts in the United States have blocked the use of graphical warnings on cigarette packages based on the premise that they are unnecessarily emotional and scare rather than inform consumers. Skurka and colleagues identified several theories that made opposite predictions about the relationship between negative affect, health risk beliefs, and smoking decisions and competitively tested the theories against one another in multiple experiments. The studies yielded results consistent with theories that asserted informational value for affective information as compared to theories that did not posit such dynamics. Chapters 4 and 15 address the strategy of strong inference in more depth.

16. *Propose alternative explanations to established phenomena*. A related type of theoretical contribution is to posit an alternative explanation to an "established" theoretical proposition and then collect data to evaluate the viability of the alternative explanation. For example, it has been amply documented that adolescent religiosity and drug use are inversely related such that more religious adolescents are less likely to use illicit drugs (e.g., Wallace & Bachman, 1991). This usually has been interpreted in terms of the protective value of religion during adolescence. However, it is possible that this association develops not because religiosity has a causal influence on drug use, but rather, just the opposite. Perhaps youth use or do not use drugs for reasons that have little to do with their religiosity. Instead, as youth become more heavily involved with drugs, they may withdraw from activities that interfere with their drug taking or that go against their preferred predilection to use drugs, such as going to church. In other words, drug use

causes decreases in religiosity rather than religiosity causing lower drug use. Which of these explanations is more likely to be operative is a matter of some interest. Theorizing about such reverse causal dynamics is considered in Chapter 7.

This list of strategies is incomplete, but it provides a sense of the myriad ways one can contribute to theory. Can you generate additions to this list given your substantive interests? Almost all of the strategies are viable for both qualitatively and quantitatively oriented social scientists. The remaining sections of this book provide the tools you will need to pursue one or more of the strategies.

SUMMARY AND CONCLUDING COMMENTS

Individuals are limited as to how much of their environment they can cope with and understand. To acquire deeper levels of understanding, individuals typically rely on shared conceptual systems. A number of different shared conceptual systems exist, including religion, philosophy, law, music, art, and science. Despite their unique variations, all conceptual systems can only provide partial understanding. Each is capable of providing a unique perspective, which may reinforce or expand upon the understanding generated by the others.

Science is generally distinguished from other shared conceptual approaches by the strategy it favors for evaluating its conceptual systems. This strategy, known as systematic empirical confirmation, requires gathering (or, more accurately, generating) relevant information from external observations that can be verified or disproved by observations made by others. In turn, systematic empirical confirmation is predicated upon theorizing. Theorizing involves conceptualizing some phenomena in terms of a set of expressions, encompassing concepts and relationships among them, and then expressing these ideas via a symbol system, typically words and/or numbers. Scientists have described a range of criteria for evaluating theories, some of which are deemed essential whereas others are found to be desirable. Theoretical contributions can take many forms, and as one contemplates devising or evaluating a specific theoretical contribution, one should potentially consider the criteria of originality, utility, and scope. Myriad strategies are available for one to make a theoretical contribution. These include (1) clarifying, refining, or challenging the conceptualization of a variable/concept; (2) creating a new variable or constellation of variables that are of theoretical interest; (3) identifying one or more explanatory variables that have not been considered in prior work; (4) identifying the mechanisms or intervening processes responsible for an effect of one variable on another; (5) identifying the boundary conditions of an effect of one variable on another; (6) identifying variables that moderate the effect of one variable on another; (7) extending an existing theory or idea to a new context; (8) identifying nuanced functional forms of relationships; (9) identifying unenunciated/unanticipated consequences of an event; (10) enriching and deepening the understanding of established quantitative associations; (11) developing typologies/taxonomies; (12) importing or applying grand theories and frameworks from other disciplines; (13) synthesizing multiple theories into a unified framework; (14) developing theories of measurement; (15) pitting opposing theoretical explanations against one another; and (16) proposing alternative explanations to established phenomena. As you focus on one or more of them, you should develop a compelling conceptual logic model for each. The process of theorizing is a complex enterprise that is difficult to teach. The remainder of this book provides the reader with heuristics that may prove useful in such endeavors.

SUGGESTED READINGS

Ben-Ari, M. (2005). *Just a theory: Exploring the nature of science.* Amherst, NY: Prometheus.

—A computer scientist explores the elements that qualify something as science as well as the characteristics of a good theory. Illustrates thinking about theory by a non–social scientist.

Brinberg, D., & McGrath, J. (1985). *Validity and the research process.* Newbury Park, CA: SAGE.

—A classic work on the research process that includes useful discussions of conceptual systems.

Einstein, A. (1934). *Essays in science.* New York: Philosophical Library.

—A discussion of types of theories and the process of theorizing.

Haack, S. (2007). *Defending science—within reason: Between scientism and cynicism.* Amherst, NY: Prometheus.

—A probing account of how science interacts with, and is influenced by, other areas of human endeavor, including literature, jurisprudence, religion, and feminism.

Hempel, C. G. (1966). *Philosophy of natural science.* Englewood Cliffs, NJ: Prentice-Hall.

—A classic book on the general topic of the philosophy of science.

Kaplan, A. (1964). *The conduct of inquiry.* San Francisco: Chandler.

—A thoughtful analysis of the philosophy of science.

Lakatos, I., & Musgrave, A. (Eds.). (1970). *Criticism and the growth of knowledge.* Cambridge, UK: Cambridge University Press.

—A critique of popular conceptions of the philosophy of science.

Loker, A. (2007). *Theory construction and testing in physics and psychology.* Victoria, BC, Canada: Trafford.

—A comparison of theory construction approaches in physics with those in psychology, offering a somewhat jaundiced view of those in psychology.

Parsons, K. (Ed.). (2004). *The science wars: Debating scientific knowledge and technology.* Amherst, NY: Prometheus.

—An edited volume covering a wide range of social and cultural influences on the practice of science.

Popper, K. (1968). *The logic of scientific discovery.* London: Hutchinson.

—A classic on the philosophy of science.

Whetten, D. A. (1989). What constitutes a theoretical contribution? *Academy of Management Review, 14,* 490–495.

—A succinct summary of core questions theorists should be asking themselves as they approach the theory construction process.

KEY TERMS

shared meaning system (p. 23)	applied research (p. 31)
prescriptive function (p. 24)	basic research (p. 32)
evaluative function (p. 24)	originality (p. 34)
consensual validation (p. 24)	utility (p. 35)
expert validation (p. 24)	scope (p. 36)
internal validation (p. 24)	boundary conditions (p. 39)
systematic empirical validation (p. 25)	moderator variable (p. 39)
conceptual realm (p. 26)	meta-analysis (p. 39)
empirical realm (p. 26)	horizontal contrasting (p. 40)
metaphysical explanation (p. 26)	vertical contrasting (p. 40)
intersubjectivity (p. 27)	construct specification (p. 40)
theory construction (p. 28)	construct splitting (p. 40)
theory (p. 28)	structuring specific relations (p. 40)
model (p. 29)	structuring recursive relations (p. 40)
theoretical expression (p. 29)	typology/taxonomy (p. 42)
hypothesis (p. 29)	strong inference (p. 44)

EXERCISES

Exercises to Reinforce Concepts

1. Explain how shared belief systems are useful in our attempt to understand our world.

2. Identify and explain the three fundamental commonalities of shared belief systems.

3. Explain how science is similar to other belief systems. How does it differ?

4. Distinguish between prescriptive and evaluative functions.

5. Identify and define the two basic realms of science. Which is more important and why?

6. Explain what is meant by the intersubjectivity of science.

7. What are the differences between theories, models, and hypotheses?

8. What are the differences between applied and basic research?

9. What are the characteristics of a good theory?

10. What are the elements of a theoretical contribution? Characterize each.

11. Identify strategies that you think are most useful for making a theoretical contribution.

12. What are the seven strategies for elaborating theory when applying it to a new context? Define each.

13. Why is the identification of nonlinear relationships important?

14. How are simulations useful for theory construction?

15. What are the three steps in theory synthesis? Characterize each.

16. In what sense does theory underlie measurement?

Exercises to Apply Concepts

1. From the literature of your choosing, find a theory and describe it. Evaluate that theory using the major criteria discussed in this chapter for evaluating theories. If you have difficulty applying one of the criteria, describe why. Identify other criteria, if any, that you might use other than those discussed in this chapter.

2. Find an article of your choosing and describe the approaches used in that article to make a theoretical contribution relative to the strategies identified in this chapter. Evaluate the quality of the theoretical contribution of the article relative to the criteria of originality, utility, and scope.

3. Pick one of the strategies for making a theoretical contribution and develop and describe a research project that uses it.

Part II

CORE PROCESSES

4

Creativity and the Generation of Ideas

The difficulty lies not in the new ideas,
but in escaping the old ones.
—JOHN MAYNARD KEYNES (1936)

Nobel Prize–winning scientist Murray Gell-Mann was asked by a prospective student at the California Institute of Technology if the school taught the problem-solving methods used by the brilliant Nobel Prize–winning physicist Richard Feynman, also a faculty member at the university. Gell-Mann replied "No," and when the student asked why not, he responded: "Here is Feynman's method. First, you write down the problem." Gell-Mann then squeezed his eyes closed and put his fists against his forehead. "Second, you think really hard." Opening his eyes, he ended by saying: "Third, you write down the answer."

Because Feynman's method probably will not work well for you, this chapter provides more concrete guidance for theory construction. Theory construction involves specifying relationships between concepts in ways that create new insights into the phenomena we are interested in understanding. As we seek to explain something, we do so by invoking concepts and processes that we think influence it or are the basis for it. For example, to explain why some children perform poorly in school, we might think about the characteristics that discriminate good performers from bad performers. When making a list of these characteristics, we will, in essence, identify constructs that are related to school performance. Or, we might want to explain why so many indigent Mayan Indians living in the highlands of western Guatemala are converting from Catholicism to Protestantism. Again, we might try to think about the characteristics that are unique to recent converts, and as we list these attributes, we will be identifying variables or constructs that are related to conversion.

A first step in theory construction often is one of generating ideas about the different strategies discussed in Chapter 3 (e.g., identifying new explanatory constructs and the relationships between them; identifying mechanisms), without initially being too critical about the merits of these ideas. The ideas generated are then subjected to more careful analytic scrutiny, with "bad ideas" being rejected and promising ideas being pursued further. As you choose constructs and relationships to focus upon, you need to refine them so that they meet the rigors of a formal scientific theory. Chapters 5 and 6 discuss strategies for refining and focusing concepts and relationships. The present chapter considers the initial process of idea generation.

There is no simple strategy for generating good ideas or good explanations. It is a creative process that is difficult to articulate, describe, and teach. In this chapter, we briefly review research on creativity to give you perspectives on the mental and social processes involved in the creative process. Next, we describe issues to consider when choosing a topic or problem to study. We then describe 27 heuristics that may help you generate ideas, after which we consider creative strategies used by influential innovators in the social sciences. Finally, we discuss the construction of conceptual logic models to supplement the idea generation process and to help screen out poor ideas. Chapters 7–15 build on the material in the present chapter in more substantive ways. The present chapter is just a start.

ONE SMALL STEP FOR SCIENCE

Name the first great scientist–theorist who comes to your mind. Perhaps it is Albert Einstein. Perhaps it is Isaac Newton. Perhaps it is Sigmund Freud. All of these individuals had a monumental impact on their respective fields of study. Theoretical advances in the social sciences do not, of course, require revolutionizing the field in the way that these individuals did. There is ample room for the more typical yet useful small increments in knowledge that solid theoretical work and research offer (Kuhn, 1962). Indeed, the gradual building of knowledge is an essential aspect of the scientific endeavor. As they attempt to explain variation in behavior, some scientists chip away at answers with the scientific tools equivalent to a small hammer and chisel. Gradually, small bits of knowledge cumulate into larger groupings of knowledge, and eventually we gain a sense of why some people behave one way and others behave another way.

On the other hand, thinking "big" should not be avoided. Instead of approaching explanation with a chisel and small hammer, some theorists prefer to use the scientific equivalent of a sledgehammer, knocking away large chunks of unexplained variation in behavior by focusing on fundamental, pervasive, and important processes. As we discuss below and in Chapter 15, there are forces operating in the scientific environment that reward and punish both approaches.

CREATIVITY

This section briefly reviews research on creativity to provide a sense of the processes that are involved when thinking creatively. After reviewing this research, we extract practical implications for constructing theories.

The Creative Person

Sternberg and Lubart (1996) define *creativity* as the ability to produce work that is both novel (original or unexpected) and appropriate (useful or meets task constraints). Early studies of creativity focused on the concept of genius and the lives and minds of eminent artists, writers, and scientists. For instance, research in the 1950s and 1960s attempted to identify the personality characteristics of highly creative individuals in different fields, including science, mathematics, writing, architecture, and art. As one example, Frank Barron of the Institute for Personality Assessment and Research at the University of California at Berkeley used nomination techniques to identify outstanding creative writers and invited them to participate in extensive testing and interviewing sessions. Some of the writers who participated were world renowned (e.g., Truman Capote, Norman Mailer, W. H. Auden). Barron found that personalities of creative writers were characterized by independence, nonconformity, drive, resiliency, risk taking, ambition, concern with philosophical matters, frankness, social activism, introversion, depression, empathy, intensity, a heightened sense of humor, and trust in intuition (Barron & Harrington, 1981).

Nakamura and Csikszentmihalyi (2001) conducted an intensive case study of Linus Pauling, the eminent scientist whose valence-bond theory has had major implications for the science of chemistry. These authors used the life of Pauling to illustrate that creativity is not just a product of intrapsychic processes but that it fundamentally involves the incorporation of novelty into culture. Creative contributions result from the interaction of three systems: (1) the innovating person, (2) the substantive domain in which the person works, and (3) the field of gatekeepers and practitioners who solicit, discourage, respond to, judge, and reward contributions. At the person level, Pauling possessed characteristics that increased the likelihood of creative contributions, including intense curiosity and a love of science; a quick, playful mind; and an incredible memory that enabled him to draw on vast knowledge bases. He was adept at imaging, which allowed him to analyze complex dimensional structures more efficiently than the typical person can. He also had strong mathematical skills that were needed for analyses in quantum physics. Pauling liked to think about the bigger picture. Importantly, he was gifted at explaining complex ideas in clear and simple terms. It was the latter quality that helped him persuade the field to accept his ideas. As a student, he was receptive to guidance. He was motivated by the skepticism he encountered rather than being paralyzed by it. Nakamura and Csikszentmihalyi go on to describe the social conditions and the state of the field that fostered the acceptance of Pauling's ideas into the "culture" of chemistry.

Research has examined how laypeople and experts view the creative person. For example, Sternberg (1985) found that people's implicit theories of creativity contained such elements as "connects ideas," "sees similarities and differences," "has flexibility," "has aesthetic taste," "is unorthodox," "is motivated," "is inquisitive," and "questions societal norms." He found differences in such characterizations across disciplines. When queried about creativity, professors of art placed heavy emphasis on imagination, originality, and a willingness to try out new ideas. Philosophy professors emphasized playing imaginatively with combinations of ideas and creating classifications and systematizations of knowledge different from the conventional. Physics professors focused on inventiveness, the ability to find order in chaos, and the ability to question basic principles. Business professors emphasized the ability to create and explore new ideas, especially as they related to novel business products or services.

Creative Ideas

Creative ideas provide novel perspectives on phenomena in ways that provide insights not previously recognized. Ideas differ in their degree of creativity, with some ideas being extremely creative and others only marginally so. Sternberg has characterized markedly creative ideas as "crowd defying." He made the following comment on the use of one's intellect to lead as opposed to "defy the crowd":

> Some people use their intelligence to please the crowd, others to defy it. The most tradition-ally intelligent ones hope to lead the crowd not only by accepting the presuppositions of the crowd but also by analyzing next steps in thinking and by reaching those next steps before others do. (2002, p. 376)

By contrast, Sternberg argued, crowd-defying ideas often eschew the presuppositions on which a body of knowledge is based.

Just because an idea is "crowd defying" does not make it useful. Many of Linus Pauling's ideas that were unrelated to his primary contribution were groundbreaking but proved to be wrong, such as the triple helix structure of DNA and the value of vita-min C for fighting colds. Similarly, "crowd-defying" ideas can meet unexpected resis-tance, as was the case with Charles Darwin's theory of evolution and the resistance it engendered not from scientists but from religious groups. Thomas Young's theory of light was so controversial in 1910 that it was viewed as a "negative contribution," only later to be recognized as years ahead of its time. The politics of a creative theorizing are complex, and we delve into this subject in more detail in Chapter 15.

The Creative Process

Research on creativity has also focused on the creative process itself. Amabile (1983) characterized creativity as involving three facets: (1) having high motivation to work on the task at hand, (2) having domain-relevant knowledge and abilities to address the task, and (3) having creativity-relevant skills. Creativity-relevant skills include cogni-tive styles that allow one to cope with complexities and to break one's "mental set" dur-ing problem solving (i.e., to make shifts in one's chain of thought); the use of heuristics for generating novel ideas; and a work style typified by concentrated effort, an ability to set aside problems, and high energy.

Sternberg, Grigorenko, and Singer (2004) developed a theory that conceptualizes creativity as being a function of six resources: (1) intellectual abilities, (2) knowledge, (3) styles of thinking, (4) personality, (5) motivation, and (6) environment. With respect to intellectual abilities, the authors stressed the importance of the ability to see prob-lems in new ways and to escape conventional thinking, the ability to discern which ideas are worth pursuing, and the ability to persuade others about one's ideas. In terms of knowledge, Sternberg and colleagues emphasized the need to know enough about a field to move it forward, but warn that such knowledge also can result in closed and entrenched perspectives. This is one of the major challenges for creative thought—being knowledgeable about a field, but not letting that knowledge channel thinking too much.

With respect to thinking styles, Sternberg and colleagues (2004) argued that creativity requires a preference for thinking in novel ways as well as the ability to think both globally and locally. To invoke an old cliché, one must not only see the trees, but one must also be able to distinguish the forest from the trees. The personality traits that the authors emphasized for creativity included a willingness to overcome obstacles, a willingness to take sensible risks, a willingness to tolerate ambiguity, and self-confidence and assurance. In terms of motivation, Sternberg and colleagues emphasized the importance of task-focused motivation. Numerous studies suggest that people rarely are creative unless they really love what they are doing and focus on the work rather than the rewards that are potentially derived from that work. Finally, the authors stressed the importance of a supportive environment that rewards creative ideas. Without some environmental support, creativity will be suppressed rather than manifested.

Simonton (1988, 2004) has reviewed the literature on scientific genius and studied the lives of great scientists and concludes that creative ideas often happen randomly, spontaneously, and fortuitously. To be sure, for these chance events to have an impact, the individual also must have exceptional logic and intellect to recognize the underlying connections and take advantage of them. But Simonton's thesis is that chance plays a far larger role in scientific creativity than is often recognized. Simonton also notes that creative events are more likely to occur for scientists who have a strong interest in scientific disciplines outside their chosen specialty and for those who tend to be "mavericks" and to think and do the unexpected.

As is the case in many applied arenas, when they have been successful, senior people in advertising tend to write books describing the approach they used to become successful. One such influential book, *Applied Imagination,* was written by Alex Osborn (1963), the "O" in BBD&O, one of the foremost advertising agencies in the United States. In addition to coining the term *brainstorming* to describe a creative process used by small groups, Osborn identified seven stages that he claims characterize the creative process of both groups and individuals: orientation, preparation, analysis, ideation, incubation, synthesis, and evaluation. In the first two stages, Osborn suggested that one should become familiar with the problem or phenomenon of interest, reading, researching, and learning about its essentials and complexity. In the third and fourth stages, Osborn advises that one should consider the problem or phenomenon from as many different perspectives as possible. In the process of doing so, one develops as many different potential solutions or ideas as possible.

Regardless of whether the idea-generation process takes hours, days, or weeks, at some point, the creative well will seem to run dry. At that point, Osborn encourages one to "sleep on it," that is, to let the unconscious mind take over. Get away from the problem or phenomenon for a few hours, days, or (if you can) weeks. Let things incubate and percolate. It is during this period of incubation, often when one least expects it, that the ideas one has generated synthesize into one's most creative insights. For scientists, Osborn's last stage, evaluation, essentially translates into empirically testing one's creative output.

Deciding to Be Creative

Sternberg (2002) emphasizes the importance of "making the decision to be creative." For creativity to occur in science, it typically is preceded by a personal decision to try to think creatively. Sternberg suggests that social scientists should encourage their students to "decide for creativity" and prepare their students for the challenges and obstacles that come from making this decision. "Deciding for creativity" does not guarantee creativity, but without such a decision, there is lessened hope for creativity.

Practical Implications for Theory Construction

While there is a sizeable literature on creativity that we cannot comprehensively review here, our brief consideration of this literature drives home several points you should consider. Creative scientific thinking does not require that you revolutionize a field with every idea you generate. Creative ideas cover the gamut from small and incremental to large and revolutionary, with the small and incremental being much more typical. Creativity, no matter how big or small, means adding something new, and it typically involves "thinking outside the box." Creative people redefine problems, analyze their ideas, and then try to persuade others of the value of their ideas. They take sensible risks and seek connections between ideas that others do not seek; at least at some level, they realize that existing knowledge can be as much a hindrance as it is a help in generating creative ideas. Creative contributions are the result of the interaction of many factors, only one of which is the act of generating the creative idea itself. If you can't communicate those ideas and get people excited about them, the ideas probably will fall flat. Thus, you must consider communication strategies as well as idea-generation strategies.

In our experience, one of the first steps in generating creative ideas is to adopt the proper mindset. Decide to be creative and to think outside the box. Declare to yourself that you are open to mixing the uncommon with the common. Commit to generating ideas without overanalyzing their merits and demerits. You can screen out bad ideas later. Your focus should be on getting a range of ideas, no matter how odd they might seem initially. Adopt a mindset that you are willing to overcome obstacles, to take sensible risks, and to tolerate ambiguity. Most of all, be self-confident and have faith in your intellect. There will be features of your environment (including other people) that discourage creative thinking, and it may be difficult to convince others of the merit of your ideas. But we agree with Sternberg that a crucial first step is making the decision to be creative. Do not expect creativity to be a substitute for hard work. Creativity builds upon hard work.

CHOOSING WHAT TO THEORIZE ABOUT

The first step in building a theory is choosing a phenomenon to explain or a question/problem to address. The reasons scientists choose one particular phenomenon or problem to study rather than another are diverse. Some scientists study a phenomenon because they are genuinely interested in it. For example, a scientist might study the mental processes involved in playing chess because he or she finds such phenomena to be intrinsically interesting. Other scientists study a given phenomenon because of its practical or social significance (e.g., reduction of headaches, poverty, globalization). Graduate students frequently study a phenomenon because their advisors study that phenomenon. Some scientists choose to work in areas for which grant funds are available. Other scientists study a phenomenon because people whom they respect also are studying that phenomenon. In many ways, the selection of a phenomenon to study is a personal matter involving the value system of the theorist. In this sense, science is not "value free." Our values and social milieu impact which phenomena we seek to understand (see Brinberg & McGrath, 1985, for a more extended discussion).

When thinking about a topic or problem to study or a question to answer, it is helpful to ask, "What is interesting about that problem/question?" and/or "Why is that an important topic?" (Alford, 1998). Be careful about selecting areas that are too broad and abstract. For example, choosing to build a theory about "adolescent risk behavior" involves a construct that encompasses such topics as adolescent drug use, tobacco use, sexual risk taking, delinquency, and alcohol use, to name a few. The explanatory mechanisms might be quite different for these various instantiations of "adolescent risk behavior," and it may be too big a task to tackle theorizing about adolescent risk behavior in general. Literally thousands of studies have been conducted to understand each of the separate risk behaviors mentioned here. We do not want to discourage abstract thinking across instantiations of a construct, and indeed, several interesting "grand" theories of adolescent risk behavior in general can be found in the literature (e.g., Jessor, 1994; Jessor & Jessor, 1977). However, when choosing phenomena to study, it is advisable to exercise caution in delimiting the scope of a theory. We offer this advice with reservations because some of the most powerful theories in the social sciences are those that operate at higher levels of abstraction and thus find applicability in multiple content domains. However, when working at the abstract level, the possibility of obscuring important details and lapsing into vagueness poses challenges to confront.

As you think about phenomena to study, you invariably also must think about the population of individuals about whom you will theorize. People differ on many facets, and there are an infinite number of ways in which you can delimit a population. Does the theory you will build apply to infants, toddlers, elementary-age children, preadolescents, adolescents, young adults, adults, and/or older adults? Across what dimensions of the larger population do you want your theory to be applicable? At this point, you may not want to delve into the issue of generalizability (the ability to extend your findings to different populations) too much, but you do want a reasonable sense of who you are going to be theorizing about. The initial decision about who to focus on is not "set in stone" as the theory construction process unfolds. Sometimes in thinking more about your concepts and constructs, you will realize that they apply to a more restricted population of individuals than you initially thought. Or you may realize that they apply to a wider population of individuals than you thought. But at the outset, as you begin your thoughtful endeavors, it usually is best to have a specific population "in mind."

Another strategy for identifying problem areas and questions to focus on is to use the framework of *participatory action research* (McIntyre, 2007; Reason & Bradbury,

2001, 2007). Participatory action research takes many forms, but it generally involves working directly with entities (e.g., social groups, organizations, communities, towns, cities) to identify the problems with which they are faced and the research needed to address those problems, and then implementing that research and the solutions suggested by the research in conjunction with members of the entity in question. Participatory action research is not an exotic variant of consultation; rather, it is designed as active co-research by and for those who are to be helped (Wadsworth, 1998). Although one may decide not to pursue participatory action research in its entirety, certainly the process of interviewing and working with members of the target social entities to identify worthwhile problems on which to work is potentially useful.

Yet another potentially useful heuristic might be that of *question brainstorming*: Based on your knowledge, experience, and/or prior readings in a topic area, generate in a single "brainstorming" session a list of specific questions that easily come to mind and that you would like to know the answers to. Don't critically evaluate the quality of the questions at first—just focus on generating them. For example, if you have a general interest in counseling drug addicts, to generate questions you might ask yourself, "If I was training new counselors on how to counsel drug addicts, what are the 10 questions they would likely want to know the answers to?" Then write out those 10 questions. Or you might ask, "If a drug addict was asking me about treatments for drug addiction, what are the 10 questions he or she would most want answers to?" Then, write out those questions. Once you have generated a list of questions from different vantage points, choose the ones that are most interesting to you and begin to refine them.

It is one thing to try to solve an existing problem or answer an existing question, but creative scientists also identify new problems to solve or new questions to answer. Some of the most influential theorists in the social sciences are individuals who have identified new problem areas to study or who have reframed problems. As examples, in anthropology, John Cole and Eric Wolf (1974) framed issues and questions to define the new field of political ecology, which is the study of how political, economic, and social factors affect environmental issues (see also Enzensberger, 1974). Amos Tversky and Nobel laureate Daniel Kahneman changed the analysis of decision making by bringing to bear the concept of heuristics (i.e., simplified cognitive "rules of thumb") and asking questions about the kinds of heuristics people use when making decisions (Kahneman & Tversky, 1973; Tversky & Kahneman, 1973, 1974). This framework challenged traditional models of decision making that emphasized rational choice and subjective-expected utility frameworks.

LITERATURE REVIEWS

Perhaps the most often recommended strategy for gaining perspectives on a phenomenon or question/problem is to consult the scientific literature already published on the topic. Not only may a comprehensive literature review serve as a useful source of ideas, but it is also an essential prerequisite for scientific research. Having said this, it may surprise you to learn that some scientists do not always seek out the scientific literature when first theorizing about a topic (Glaser, 1978). The idea is that reading the literature may prematurely narrow one's thinking and make it difficult to think "outside the box" in ways that are new and creative. To be sure, if the literature is not consulted initially, it is *always* consulted after the scientist has generated his or her initial ideas. But some scientists prefer to avoid becoming too immersed in a literature when initially thinking about a topic. This is not to say that the topic is approached with a blank slate relative to the existing literature. Usually, the scientist's academic training, past readings, and research over the years provide him or her with perspectives and knowledge that can't help but be brought to bear. But the intent is to rely more on heuristics and cognitive strategies (described below) than on a formal literature review during the initial idea-generation phase.

Having said that, the majority of scientists reject the "hold off reviewing the literature" strategy. Most scientists maintain that reading the literature stimulates ideas that might not otherwise come about. It also provides the scientist with much-needed focus and clarity before embarking on the theory construction process, and it avoids the possibility of spending time inventing the wheel—only to later find out that someone else already invented that very same wheel. These scientists stress the importance of reading the literature thoroughly, critically, and creatively. In the final analysis, there is no one correct way to go about theory generation, and either approach to the extant literature might work well for you. However, the norm is to delve into the extant literature in depth before building your own theory.

HEURISTICS FOR GENERATING IDEAS

We now turn to specific strategies you can use to think about issues in creative and novel ways. These heuristics are ones that we or other scientists have found useful, but they may or may not resonate with you for the particular task on which you are working. We personally do not use every heuristic, and we find that some work better for some problems than for others. The heuristics are only a start to building the tools in your theory construction toolbox. In later chapters, we develop additional ways of thinking that will augment or complement the strategies described here. If you use these heuristics, they may help you think about a phenomenon in ways that are different from how you might otherwise proceed. But if a simple list of heuristics was all it took to generate innovative ideas, then such ideas would abound in science. It is not simple!

Idea Generation and Grounded/Emergent Theorizing

As discussed in Chapter 10, some social scientists argue for the use of emergent methodologies when constructing theories. The essence of these approaches is that theorists should set aside, as much as possible, their preconceptions when studying a phenomenon and let ideas about the concepts and relationships between concepts emerge as they embed themselves in the surroundings and contexts of the groups under study. Theory is thereby "grounded in" and emerges from such data, with the data typically being qualitative in nature.

BOX 4.1. The Nacirema

A strategy for generating ideas used by anthropologists is the careful and systematic observation of others in their cultural contexts. By examining cultures in as objective and systematic a way as possible, insights into behavior become apparent that otherwise would remain hidden. This is illustrated nicely in the following edited account of the Nacirema and their body rituals, as described by the noted anthropologist Horace Miner (1956):

Professor Linton first brought the ritual of the Nacirema to the attention of anthropologists twenty years ago, but the culture of this people is still very poorly understood. They are a North American group living in the territory between the Canadian Cree, the Yaqui and Tarahumare of Mexico, and the Carib and Arawak of the Antilles. Little is known of their origin, although tradition states that they came from the east.

Nacirema culture is characterized by a highly developed market economy that has evolved in a rich natural habitat. While much of the people's time is devoted to economic pursuits, a large part of the fruits of these labors and a considerable portion of the day are spent in ritual activity. The focus of this activity is the human body, the appearance and health of which loom as a dominant concern in the ethos of the people. While such a concern is certainly not unusual, its ceremonial aspects and associated philosophy are unique.

The fundamental belief underlying the whole system appears to be that the human body is ugly and that its natural tendency is to debility and disease. Incarcerated in such a body, a person's only hope is to avert these characteristics through the use of ritual and ceremony. Every household has one or more shrines devoted to this purpose. The more powerful individuals in the society have several shrines in their houses and, in fact, the opulence of a house is often referred to in terms of the number of such ritual centers it possesses. Most houses are of wattle and daub construction, but the shrine rooms of the wealthier people are walled with stone. Poorer families imitate the rich by applying pottery plaques to their shrine walls.

While each family has at least one such shrine, the rituals associated with it are not family ceremonies but are private and secret. The rites are normally only discussed with children, and then only during the period when they are being initiated into these mysteries. I was able, however, to establish sufficient rapport with the natives to examine these shrines and to have the rituals described to me. The focal point of the shrine is a box or chest that is built into the wall. In this chest are kept the many charms and magical potions without which no native believes he or she could live. These preparations are secured from a variety of specialized practitioners. The most powerful of these are the medicine men, whose assistance must be rewarded with substantial gifts. However, the medicine men do not provide the curative potions for their clients; they only decide what the ingredients should be and then write them down in an ancient and secret language. This writing is understood only by the medicine men and by the herbalists who, for another gift, provide the required charm.

The charm is not disposed of after it has served its purpose, but is placed in the charm box of the household shrine. As these magical materials are specific for certain ills and the real or imagined maladies of the people are many, the charm box is usually full to overflowing. The magical packets are so numerous that people

(continued)

forget what their purposes were and fear to use them again. While the natives are very vague on this point, we can only assume that the idea in retaining all the old magical materials is that their presence in the charm box, before which the body rituals are conducted, will in some way protect the worshipper.

Beneath the charm box is a small font. Each day every member of the family, in succession, enters the shrine room, bows his or her head before the charm box, mingles different sorts of holy water in the font, and proceeds with a brief rite of ablution. The holy waters are secured from the water temple of the community, where the priests conduct elaborate ceremonies to make the liquid ritually pure.

In the hierarchy of magical practitioners, and below the medicine men in prestige, are specialists whose designation is best translated as "holy-mouth-men." The Nacirema have an almost pathological horror of, and fascination with, the mouth, the condition of which is believed to have a supernatural influence on all social relationships. Were it not for the rituals of the mouth, they believe that their teeth would fall out, their gums bleed, their jaws shrink, their friends desert them, and their lovers reject them. They also believe that a strong relationship exists between oral and moral characteristics. For example, there is a ritual ablution of the mouth for children that is supposed to improve their moral fiber. The daily body ritual performed by everyone includes a mouth rite. Despite the fact that these people are so punctilious about care of the mouth, this rite involves a practice that strikes the uninitiated stranger as revolting. It was reported to me that the ritual consists of inserting a small bundle of hog hairs into the mouth, along with certain magical powders, and then moving the bundle in a highly formalized series of gestures.

In addition to the private mouth rite, the people seek out a holy-mouth-man once or twice a year. These practitioners have an impressive set of paraphernalia, consisting of a variety of augers, awls, probes, and prods. The use of these items in the exorcism of the evils of the mouth involves almost unbelievable ritual torture of the client. The holy-mouth-man opens the client's mouth and, using the above mentioned tools, enlarges any holes that decay may have created in the teeth. Magical materials are put into these holes. If there are no naturally occurring holes in the teeth, large sections of one or more teeth are gouged out so that the supernatural substance can be applied. In the client's view, the purpose of these ministrations is to arrest decay and to draw friends. The extremely sacred and traditional character of the rite is evident in the fact that the natives return to the holy-mouth-men year after year, despite the fact that their teeth continue to decay.

Miner goes on to describe numerous other features of the Nacirema culture. Now, spell the name "Nacirema" backward and reread Miner's account of the Nacirema. Does it mean something different to you now? This exercise drives home the point that what can seem normal and everyday from one perspective can be seen as unusual, even bizarre, from another perspective. The tendency to see things from our own cultural viewpoint is called an *ethnocentric* perspective. It shapes our thinking in predetermined ways. Creative individuals can often break out of their ethnocentric constraints.

Some grounded theorists reject the idea of doing anything more in theory construction than letting concepts and relationships emerge in the context of careful observation in natural settings. To be sure, creativity and insight are involved in framing the issues to be investigated and in recognizing subtleties in the world that might not be obvious to the casual observer. But the emphasis is on setting aside preconceptions, staying close to the data, and letting theory emerge "from the ground up."

Other grounded and emergent theorists are more open to imposing novel ways of construing and thinking about observed events in their natural settings. These theorists try to think about their observations and their field notes in creative ways, such as by invoking metaphors, making analogies, relating observations to other constructs that form the bases of their own interpretive systems, and so on. For these grounded theorists, one or more of the heuristics discussed in this section may resonate as useful. For an interesting account of creative thinking in anthropology, see Lavie, Narayan, and Rosaldo (1993).

Twenty-Seven Heuristics

This section presents 27 heuristics for thinking about phenomena or questions in a way that might give you new insights and ideas. It assumes you have already identified a phenomenon or problem area to study.

1. *Analyze your own experiences.* This strategy involves thinking about your own experiences and reflecting on what factors have influenced the outcome variable or the phenomenon you are trying to explain based on them. For example, if the outcome variable is social anxiety, you might think about situations in which you have been nervous or anxious and identify the features of those situations relative to other situations that caused you to be nervous. You might think about situations where you overcame your social anxiety and reflect on how you did so. You might think about periods in your life when you tended to be more socially anxious and periods when you tended to be less socially anxious and reflect on what aspects of your life differentiate those periods. The idea is to carefully analyze your own experiences and see if this helps you think about what you are trying to explain in new and creative ways. For grounded theorists, thinking about your field notes and observations relative to your own personal experiences might give you perspectives on how to frame arguments and propositions about the observations you have made.

2. *Use case studies.* This strategy for idea generation involves analyzing a single case (individual, family, group, or organization) in detail and generating ideas based on that case study. It might take the form of formally interviewing a person, family, group, or members of an organization in depth and/or researching archival data and other existing data sources about the person, family, group, or organization. Case studies range from labor-intensive enterprises that take years to complete to simpler gatherings of information about a single person or event. There is a substantial literature on methods for conducting case studies (Cosentino, 2007; Eisenhardt, 1989; Ellet, 2007), and read-

ers are encouraged to consult this literature to gain a better sense of the many forms of case studies. Sigmund Freud used this approach to develop facets of his highly influential psychoanalytic theory. Examples of case studies leading to important theoretical insights in the social sciences abound (see, e.g., Spatig, Parrott, Kusimo, Carter, & Keyes, 2001; Turner, 1970). You should consider the possibility of pursuing case studies as a method for idea generation.

3. *Collect practitioner or expert rules of thumb.* This strategy involves interviewing or researching the ideas of experts in an area who are actively dealing with the phenomenon you want to study (Mayo & LaFrance, 1980). For example, to formulate a theory of the best way to counsel children about grief-related experiences, you might interview professionals who do such counseling to obtain their perspectives on how best to do so. Such practitioners often develop their own implicit or explicit theories about the phenomena (Jarvis, 1998), and eliciting and discussing those theories with them can lead to useful insights. Alternatively, you might interview scientists who study such professionals and/or who conduct research on the matter. Personal interviews (in person, over the phone, through e-mails) with such experts often can yield a richer account of a phenomenon than what you would garner from reviewing the formal scientific literature on the topic. The collected rules of thumb might then serve as the basis for a more formal theory (see Hill, 2006; Kaplan, 1964). In his work on social influence, Cialdini (2003) collected practitioners' rules of thumb for exerting social influence by working in the professions of, and interviewing, insurance and car salespeople, charitable fundraisers, and a host of other professionals who worked in occupations that rely on social influence. Based, in part, on these collected rules of thumb of influence, Cialdini formulated novel theoretical perspectives on persuasion and social influence.

4. *Use role playing.* This heuristic involves putting yourself in the place of another and anticipating how this person might think or behave with respect to the outcome variable. For example, put yourself in the place of another family member, a friend, or someone you know whose experiences might be relevant to the phenomenon you are trying to understand. Think about how they would approach matters. Put yourself in the place of another scientist who has different training from your own and imagine how he or she would conceptualize or think about the problem or explain the phenomenon. Role playing is widely used in organizational training and other applied contexts to foster new levels of understanding and insight (El-Shamy, 2005). Here we are suggesting a technique of "mental role playing," as you intellectually take the role of others and think about their reactions and perspectives. For grounded theorists, thinking about your field notes relative to the perspective you invoke by role-playing relevant others might give you perspectives on how to conceptualize and frame arguments about your observations.

5. *Conduct a thought experiment.* Another tool for generating ideas—one often used by Albert Einstein—is to conduct a *thought experiment* (Ackoff, 1991; Folger & Turillo, 1999; Lave & March, 1975; Watzlawick, 1976). These are hypothetical experiments or

studies that are conducted "in the mind," as if you have collected data and then imagine the results. In this strategy, you think about relevant variables or scenarios and then consider the effects of different variations or manipulations of them, as if you were running an experiment—but instead doing all this in your head. You imagine the results and think about what implications they have for explaining your phenomenon. In other words, to understand fact, think fiction.

A substantial literature exists on thought experiments, primarily in philosophy, political science, economics, and physics. Sorensen (1998) examined thought experiments as used by theorists in a variety of disciplines and concluded that they were central in the theory construction process (see also Nersessian, 2002). Tetlock and Belkin (1996) explored the use of a particular type of thought experiment, namely, the use of *counterfactuals,* to focus on "what-might-have-been" questions. More technically, counterfactuals are subjunctive conditionals in which the antecedents of an event are assumed to be known but for purposes of argument supposed to be false. For example, you might ponder the counterfactual, "If the United States had not dropped atomic bombs on Japan, then the Japanese would have surrendered at about roughly the same time they did." Counterfactual thought experiments can sensitize us to possibilities we might otherwise have ignored, had we not pursued counterfactual thinking.

As an example in the social sciences, an investigator might be interested in the consequences of having an abortion for adolescents in the United States. A counterfactual thought experiment would be to think about the implications of abortion for adolescents if all abortions were illegal. Thinking through this counterfactual circumstance might suggest consequences of having an abortion that the theorist may not have thought of initially. Economist Richard Fogel (1964) used a counterfactual to explore the economic impact of the emerging railroads on American economic growth. He explored the counterfactual of what the American economy would be like had there been no railroads. Interestingly, his detailed exploration of the counterfactual suggested that the railroads did not have a significant impact on the American economy and, more generally, that no single innovation was vital for economic growth in the 19th century.

Try to frame the phenomena you are working with using different thought experiments and counterfactuals. Conjecture by asking the question "what if . . . ?," trying different hypotheticals.

6. *Engage in participant observation. Participant observation* involves observing others in the situations you want to study while you actively participate in those situations. For example, you might live in the community and work with a group of factory workers to get a better idea of factors that influence worker attitudes toward labor unions. Like case studies, participant observation can range from labor-intensive efforts lasting years to more short-lived efforts (Hume & Mulcock, 2004; Reason & Bradbury, 2007). Participant observation, a component of many ethnographic analyses, is a dominant approach for advancing theory in anthropology. It has been used to generate rich theoretical analyses of a wide range of important phenomena. For example, anthropologist Margaret Mead (2001) spent months in Samoa using participant observation to study

the lives of teenagers as she explored cultural influences on adolescence. She dispelled the then-common view that adolescence is a time of "stress and turmoil" as adolescents search for an adult identity. Participant observation is discussed in more detail in Chapter 10. There we see that some social scientists believe that pursuing theory construction without such qualitative data is folly.

7. *Analyze paradoxical incidents.* Sometimes it is useful to isolate and analyze a paradoxical situation. For example, suppose you are interested in the occurrence of unintended pregnancies. As you reflect on this phenomenon, you recognize that some unmarried individuals who are sexually active, do not want to become pregnant, and have positive attitudes toward birth control nonetheless fail to use any form of contraception. This appears to be paradoxical behavior. What could be operating to explain this paradox?

This particular paradox was explored in a qualitative study by Edin and Kefalas (2005), who studied low-income, inner-city young women, mostly Latinas and African Americans, living in the United States. The authors found that about two-thirds of the pregnancies in the women they studied were not planned. Rather, pregnancy occurred by chance, whenever a woman happened to stop using birth control. Contraception often was used at the beginning of a relationship but was discontinued when a relationship "reached another level." Edin and Kefalas report that both men and women in their study interpreted a woman wanting to have a baby by a man as a high form of social praise for that man. Thus, nonuse of birth control was linked to an expression of respect and social praise.

The women in the study tended to see children as giving meaning to a woman's life. Women who placed careers over motherhood were seen as selfish. Childbearing and marriage were not seen as decisions that "go together." This disconnection, however, did not reflect a disinterest in marriage. To the contrary, women held high standards for the men they would be willing to marry. They hoped that the fathers of their children would rise to the occasion and be worthy of being a life-long partner, but they did not count on it. Also, marriage, the women said, was reserved for those men and women who had "made it" economically and were worthy of it. Women thought that both partners should be economically "set" prior to marriage. Indeed, women expressed an aversion to economic dependence on a male. To be worthy of marriage, the women said, couples must demonstrate relational maturity by withstanding hard times together. This can take years to attain. As a result of such dynamics, women were less likely to marry.

The work by Edin and Kefalas provides the beginnings of a theory of why many sexually active, unmarried, inner-city women paradoxically do not seek to become pregnant but fail to use birth control. The women are willing to leave having a baby to chance and see the nonuse of birth control as the sign of a good relationship that can yield the positives associated with childbearing.

As with the other heuristics, analyzing paradoxical incidents can be pursued mentally using the strategies of imagined role playing and examining your own experiences using thought experiments. Or it can take the form of a qualitative study.

8. *Engage in imaging.* Most of the time we think about problems in verbal terms. It is as if we have an internal conversation with ourselves. We subvocally think through our thoughts and ideas. The current heuristic involves setting aside linguistic-based thoughts in favor of visualizing relevant situations and behaviors. For example, in thinking about causes of social anxiety, try to imagine yourself at a party with a few people you know. Try to visualize this situation as graphically as possible and in as much detail as possible. Visualize the setting and the people who are in that setting. Now start playing out the interactions you have with other people. But do not just verbally note these interactions to yourself. Try to imagine them happening, as if you were watching a movie. The general idea is to draw upon imaging and the cues that imaging stimulates as you think about a phenomenon. This strategy tends to engage the right hemisphere of the brain, as opposed to linguistic thoughts, which engage the left hemisphere (Gregory, 1997). Accordingly, new insights may result.

Imagistic thinking and visualization have been found to be common in thought experiments conducted by creative scientists, as they explore in their minds the use of old schema in new situations outside their normal area of application, especially when spatial reasoning is required (Gooding, 1992; Nersessian, 2008). Visual intelligence has been the subject of considerable empirical research (Arnheim, 2004; Barry, 1997; Hoffman, 2000), and its role in the generation of scientific ideas is also being explored (e.g., Clement, 2006, 2008; Nersessian, 2008).

9. *Use analogies and metaphors.* This heuristic involves applying the logic of another problem area to the logic of the area of interest or drawing upon a metaphor. For example, several theories of memory use the metaphor of a "storage bin," where information is placed in long-term memory for later access (Bodenhausen & Lambert, 2003). Long-term memory is seen as consisting of thousands of such bins, which are organized in a complex fashion. Pieces of information relevant to a bin are stacked on top of each other within a bin, with the most recently processed information at the top. Thus, the most recently placed information in a bin is more easily accessed when a person retrieves information from that bin. Of course, the physiology of the brain does not contain physical storage bins, but the metaphor promotes a way of thinking about memory and making predictions about information retrieval processes. Metaphorical thinking thus provides a mechanism for building a theory of memory.

As another example, Randall (2007) used a compost heap as a metaphor for autobiographical memory, arguing that it comes closer than more commonly used computer analogies to capturing the dynamics of memory changes with aging. Randall describes the parallels between composts and such memory-related concepts as encoding, storage, and retrieval and derives an organic model of memory to better understand the psychology of aging.

The process of using analogies can be complex. For example, Clement (2008) gave scientists challenging problems in their areas of study and collected think-aloud protocols as they attempted to solve them. Clement found that scientists tended to struggle with the analogies they generated, often resorting to "bridge analogies" to link the problem with the original analogy. Imagistic simulations and visualization also were often used to think through and explore the application of analogies. The scientists Clement studied engaged in cycles of analogical thought in which they generated, critiqued, and modified series of analogies. They showed great persistence in pursuing analogies. Charles Darwin is known to have worked through a single analogy over a period of years in developing his theory of evolution (Millman & Smith, 1997).

Clement (1988) described four processes scientists use to apply analogies to solve a problem. First, the scientist generates the analogy. Second, the scientist establishes the validity of the analogy in relation to the original problem. Third, the scientist seeks to understand the analogous case. Finally, the scientist applies the findings to the original problem. Clement identified three strategies that scientists use to generate analogies at the first step. First, they might generate an analogy from a well-known principle. This step involves recognizing that the original problem situation is an example of a well-established principle. Second, the scientist might create an analogy by modifying the original problem situation, thereby changing features of it that were assumed to be fixed. Finally, the scientist generates an analogy through association in memory, whereby the scientist is "reminded" of, or recalls, an analogous case.

The use of metaphors in social science theories is common. For example, as noted above, metaphors and analogies are widely used in the analysis of memory and memory processes. In sociology, the classic work of Erving Goffman (1959, 1967) viewed everyday interactions between people using an analogy of actors following scripts, imposing their own interpretations onto the scripts, and employing occasional ad libs. In management, Cornelissen (2004) uses the metaphor of "organizations as theatre" to develop the basic tenets of an organizational theory.

10. *Reframe the problem in terms of the opposite.* This heuristic involves reversing the focus of your thought to a focal opposite. If you are trying to understand the reasons why some people are highly loyal to a brand when purchasing a particular product, it might help instead to think about why people are not brand loyal. The work of William McGuire (1968) is a good example that combines the use of thinking about opposites in conjunction with the metaphorical thinking discussed in the previous section. McGuire, a noted theorist in the field of attitude change, approached persuasion-related phenomena thinking not about how to influence people but instead about how to make people resistant to attitude change. McGuire used biological immunization principles as a metaphor for inducing resistance to persuasive communications. He noted that people are inoculated against many diseases when small amounts of a contaminating virus are introduced into their body. As a result, the body builds up antibodies to resist the virus, thus preventing the full-blown occurrence of the disease should higher levels of viral exposure be experienced later. To make people more resistant to attitude change, McGuire provided them with short, challenging, counterattitudinal messages that would make them think through their attitude in more detail and organize their defenses to counterarguments. These "immunization" challenges, he reasoned, should not be compelling enough to change the attitude, but rather should be just strong enough to mobilize counterarguments and defense mechanisms to combat future persuasive attempts.

McGuire used the immunization analogy to effectively develop a complex theoretical framework for the analysis of persuasion.

11. *Apply deviant case analysis.* Sometimes a certain individual or group of individuals will stand out with respect to a phenomenon as being different from the rest of the crowd. This heuristic focuses on "deviant" cases in the attempt to explain why they are deviant. For example, although most adolescents who have good relationships with their parents do not use drugs, others who have good relationships with their parents do use drugs. Why? What can explain the behavior of these "deviant" cases? In qualitative research, deviant case analysis is a formal method for theory construction in which researchers seek out cases that contradict major patterns in the data with the idea of using those cases to expand theory (see Chapter 10).

In a study of human immunodeficiency virus (HIV) prevention, researchers have identified a small number of individuals whose immune systems almost completely suppress HIV despite the fact the virus annually kills over 2 million people worldwide. Scientists seeking a cure for HIV are conducting extensive analyses of these "deviant cases" (known in the literature as "elite controllers") to determine what sets them apart from those susceptible to HIV, with the hope that doing so will provide insights into the mechanisms through which HIV affects the immune systems of people in general (Gaiha et al., 2019). In developmental science, researchers have identified adults who have achieved success in life despite the fact that they came from challenging backgrounds and were raised in difficult circumstances (Masten, 2014). For example, Werner (2005) summarized the results of the Kauai Longitudinal Study that studied the same youth at ages 1, 2, 10, 18, 32, and 40. Thirty percent of these youth had suffered prenatal complications and were raised in poverty by families typified by discord, divorce, and/or parental psychopathology. Most of the youth exhibited learning or behavior problems by age 10 or they had delinquency records and/or mental health issues by age 18. However, a smaller percentage of the children grew into well-adjusted, confident, and caring adults. Of theoretical interest to Werner was what sets these latter individuals (the "deviant cases") apart from the former individuals and what the implications of these differences are for developmental theory more generally.

12. *Change the scale.* Mills (1959) suggests imagining extreme changes as a method of stimulating thinking: If something is small, imagine it to be enormous and ask "What difference might that make?" If something is pervasive, think about what things would be like if it were not. An example of this heuristic is the research on globalization in the fields of geography, anthropology, political science, and economics. Theorists in these disciplines think about how processes operating at the global level might be mirrored at the local level, as well as how processes operating at the local level might be generalized or altered if they are moved to the global level (Goldin, 2009; Robins, Pattison, & Woodstock, 2005). For example, if we think about the effects and challenges of unionizing workers at the local level, what would happen if we tried to unionize workers at the global level? How might thinking in such terms alter our theories and thinking about unionization at the local level?

13. *Focus on processes or focus on variables.* The dominant tradition in the social sciences is to think in terms of variables. An alternative approach is to think in terms of processes—that is, sets of activities that unfold over time to produce change, to maintain equilibrium in a system, or to get from event A to event B. Abbott and Alexander (2004) describe the implications of thinking about crime and criminals in process terms. Instead of thinking about a criminal as someone who commits a crime, a process analysis views the act of becoming a criminal as consisting of the sequenced actions of getting caught, detained, held, charged, convicted, and sentenced. The often observed inverse relationship between social class and becoming a "criminal" might be due, in part, to the fact that lower-class individuals are more likely to make it through this process-based sequence than middle- or upper-class individuals. Process-oriented models have existed in the social sciences for decades, but they are not as popular as variable-centered approaches (Cederman, 2005; Gilbert & Abbott, 2005). If you tend to think primarily in terms of variables, try thinking in terms of dynamic processes. Conversely, if you tend to think primarily in terms of processes, try thinking in terms of variables.

One strategy for invoking process perspectives is to change nouns into verbs (Weick, 1979). The use of this heuristic is most evident in the field of organizational studies, where process theories change such vocabulary as *order* to *ordering* (Cooper & Law, 1995), *being* to *becoming* (Chia & Tsoukas, 2002), and *knowledge* to *knowing* (Cook & Brown, 1999) so as to invoke process-oriented explanations. The premise of process-based analyses is that organizations are in continual flux and that variable-centered theories are limited because they ignore this flux, capturing only momentary "snapshots" of organizations at a single point in time (De Cock & Sharp, 2007; Sturdy & Grey, 2003).

Process-oriented perspectives are central to the field of processual anthropology, which was articulated by Turner (1967, 1970) in his temporal analyses of rituals. Turner argued that rites of passage are marked by a progression through three stages: (a) separation, when a person becomes detached from a fixed point in the social structure; (b) marginality, when the person is in an ambiguous state, no longer in the old state but not yet having reached the new one; and (c) aggregation, when the person enters a new stable state with its own rights and obligations. Turner characterizes each stage as well as factors that influence movement from one stage to another. This process-oriented view contrasts with structuralist interpretations of rituals.

For those who already think in terms of processes, a way of generating new ideas might be to think instead in terms of variables. Abbott and Alexander (2004) recommend a heuristic of "stopping the clock." The idea is to "freeze" the process at a given point in time and then describe the system in detail at the frozen moment. By "stopping the clock," you broaden the context and apply other heuristics we have discussed to that particular point in the process.

Try analyzing your phenomenon as a dynamic process that fluctuates over time and that entails moving from event A to event B. How do entities get from one point to another? We describe process-oriented frameworks in more detail in Chapter 9 on simulations, Chapter 10 on grounded theory, and Chapter 12 in the context of broader systems of thought.

14. *Consider abstractions or specific instances.* Using instantiation principles discussed in Chapter 5, or the opposite of instantiation, *abstraction*, think about the phenomena at different levels of abstraction. For example, when thinking about what influences people's attitudes toward a political candidate, think about what influences attitudes in general and then apply this to your analysis of attitudes toward political candidates. If you are thinking about what influences people's attitudes in the abstract, then think about what influences a person's attitude toward a political candidate (as well as other specific attitudes) and try to generalize from this position to attitudes in general.

Arie Kruglanski (2004), a noted social psychologist, emphasizes the importance of abstraction in theory construction. Kruglanski states that a key strategy for formulating abstract principles or constructs is to seek commonalities among phenomena and to be skeptical about distinctions. He argues that the surface manifestations of different instances of the same phenomena can be misleading and that different concrete phenomena often are driven by the same underlying principle. The focus should be kept on isolating the gist of the phenomena and identifying what absolutely must be known about it. For example, attitude change, conformity, majority–minority influence, and social power all have a social influence component that may allow you to build a general theory of social influence by looking for commonalities in each of these phenomena. Rather than focusing on domain-specific constructs or processes, strive to isolate underlying principles that generalize across domains. Having said that, Kruglanski also urges caution in the use of abstraction. When abstracting to more general levels, it is possible to obscure important distinctions that should be made. The key is to always ask yourself what is gained and what is lost by moving across different levels of abstraction.

Sociologist Robert Alford (1998), like Kruglanski, views the theory construction process as one of constantly moving back and forth between reflective musings about the implications of abstract concepts to concrete analyses of specific observations. Theory is developed by thinking about concrete instantiations of concepts and then abstracting upward to more general constructs that allow us to make theoretical propositions that generalize across many content domains.

15. *Make the opposite assumption.* Take an explicit assumption and recast it to its opposite. If a phenomenon is assumed to be stable, think of it as unstable. If two variables are assumed to be related, what would happen if they were unrelated? If two phenomena coexist, what would happen if they could not coexist? If X is assumed to cause Y, consider the possibility that Y causes X. This heuristic is similar to the ones discussed earlier, on framing a problem in terms of its opposite and "changing the scale." However, it is distinct in subtle ways.

As an example, it is typically thought that the quality of parent–adolescent relationships influences drug use by adolescents, with better relationships being associated with lower probabilities of drug use. But what if we reverse the causal direction? Is it possible instead that an adolescent's use of drugs negatively impacts the relationship between the adolescent and his or her parents? As another example, it is commonly accepted that adolescents who are religious are less likely to engage in problem behaviors—that is, the religiosity has a protective function. Could it be instead that adolescents who start to engage in risk behaviors (e.g., alcohol or drug use) become less religious? Perhaps lowered religiosity is not a risk factor but instead is just a by-product of the adolescent's engaging in problem behaviors and then rejecting his or her (religious) upbringing in the process. As a final example, it is often assumed that parental childrearing strategies impact child behavior, but it is just as plausible to assert that child behaviors influence parental childrearing strategies.

Abbott and Alexander (2004) provide several additional examples of this heuristic in their book on theory construction. For example, it is commonly assumed that college educates students. But suppose instead we think about all the ways in which college prevents education (e.g., boring classes, emphasizing rote memorization). As we make opposite assumptions and try to marshal support for them, we can gain new insights into the phenomena we study.

16. *Apply the continual why and what.* Given an outcome or dependent variable, ask yourself, "Why do some people do this but other people do not?" or "Why do some people have more of this but other people do not?" For each answer you give, repeat this question again. For example, if the outcome variable is school performance, you might ask, "Why do some people do well in school, whereas others do not?" The answer might be, "because some people are more intelligent and more motivated." Then ask, "Why are some people more intelligent?" and "Why are some people more motivated?" The answer to the former might be "because of the way they were raised." This last answer is vague, so you might ask, "What do you mean by that?" After clarifying this statement, you might ask yourself, "Why were they raised like that?" As you continually probe successive "why" questions for answers and ask, "What do you mean by that?," you might gain new insights into the original question you posed.

Darryl Bem (1970) used this strategy in his analysis of the psychological bases of beliefs. Bem focused his analysis on a belief that people might hold, such as "Smoking cigarettes causes cancer," and he asked people why they believed this to be the case. When given an answer, he would ask them why they believed the answer was true. He would then pose the "Why do you think that is true?" question to the new answer that was given. As he continually pushed beliefs back to their origins, he found that all beliefs rested on one or both of two foundations, namely, (a) the belief that something is true because an authority figure or expert says it is true, and/or (b) the belief that something is true because it was directly experienced (or someone else directly experienced it) and "one's senses do not lie." How do you know, for example, that the sun is the center of the solar system? The answer probably is "because I was taught this in school by my science teacher"—which is invoking an authority figure. The continual "why" heuristic led Bem to derive an interesting theory of the bases of cognitions (see Bem, 1970).

17. *Consult your grandmother—and prove her wrong.* McGuire (1997) coined the term *bubba psychology* to refer to the idea that much of what social scientists "discover" in their research is so banal or obvious that it could have been told to them by their grandmother ("bubba"). Take the obvious and think about how it could be wrong. Try to turn bubba social science on its head. Or, as a variant, extend an obvious "bubba fact" to situations where you might be surprised by their implications. For example, the bubba fact that "being in a good mood increases your life satisfaction" might be extended to a subtler idea that "finding a dollar on the street increases life satisfaction." If you find a dollar, doing so may put you in a good mood. If being in a good mood positively influences your current feelings of life satisfaction, then it follows that finding a dollar on the street should raise your life satisfaction (at least temporarily). People might find the idea that "coming upon a dollar on the street improves life satisfaction" to be more intriguing than the idea that "being in a good mood increases life satisfaction." By extending the obvious to the nonobvious, an interesting theoretical point might be made.

18. *Push an established finding to the extremes.* Take a well-established relationship or finding and consider the extremes of it. For example, it is often held that more eye contact with a person will increase his or her liking of you. But what happens if you make constant eye contact? Too little or too much eye contact may be bad, but an intermediate level of eye contact may be just right. Parents who are affectionate with their children tend to have happier children. But what if a parent is constantly affectionate? Some scientists have suggested that too much of anything eventually backfires or starts to produce opposite effects. What happens at the extremes of your phenomenon?

19. *Read biographies and literature, and be a well-rounded media consumer.* Much of social science focuses on people, and excellent resources for the lives of people are published biographies and autobiographies. These can be a rich source of ideas about many facets of human behavior. Fiction and nonfiction works are filled with insightful analyses, as are movies and other forms of media. The humanities and arts, even though they do not to rely on formal scientific methods, are an invaluable source of ideas and insights. Take advantage of the wealth of knowledge in these different areas.

One of the authors (Jaccard) attended the University of California at Berkeley as an undergraduate and recalls his first meeting in the office of the noted sociologist Erving Goffman. While waiting for Professor Goffman to finish a phone call, Jaccard casually noted the books on his shelves. They included the typical textbooks of a sociological academic, but also among them were popular magazines typically seen at grocery store checkouts, cookbooks, books on fashion, popular self-help books, and other books representing American culture. It was only after taking several courses from Professor Goffman that Jaccard came to appreciate that these resources were a core source of Goffman's ideas about human interaction and American society.

20. *Identify remote and shared/differentiating associates.* Think about the phenomenon of interest to you and try to identify as many causes and consequences of it as you can. Be expansive, listing as many plausible ones as possible. The idea is to create a "free association" scenario in which the list you generate includes "remote associates," that is, things that people are unlikely to think of and that might spark a creative insight. Relatedly, think of people you know or have heard of who perform the behavior or phenomenon you are trying to explain and people you know who do not perform the behavior or phenomenon. Then make a list of the qualities, attributes, and characteristics of each type of person. On what qualities and attributes do they differ, and on

which ones are they the same? What do the similarities and differences tell you about the phenomenon?

21. *Shift the unit of analysis.* When theorizing, we often do so by describing and explaining behavior at the level of individuals. For example, we may want to know why some people are wealthy but other people are poor. Or we may want to know why some people can cope well with a debilitating disease but other people cannot. However, there are also theories that focus on *units of analysis* other than individuals, such as a couple, a family/household, a small group, an organization, or even countries within a world system. In such cases, the outcome variable is not the behavior of the individual but rather the behavior of the "unit." For example, in the context of HIV prevention, we might focus on understanding why *couples* engage in unprotected sex rather than on trying to explain why *individuals* engage in unprotected sex. Or, in the field of organizational studies, we might focus on understanding factors that influence the productivity of *organizations* rather than on the productivity of *individuals* within organizations.

The noted sociologist James Coleman (1994) emphasized the importance of analyzing the functioning of social systems rather than individuals. Note that this is not the same as studying the impact of social systems on individuals, as would be the case, for example, when exploring the impact of work environments on life satisfaction. Instead, the focus is on the behavior of the unit per se—that is, the particular social system in question. According to Coleman, theories of the functioning of social systems can focus either on forces or on explanatory constructs outside the system that impact and shape how the system of interest operates or, alternatively, on forces and processes within the system—that is, the component parts of the system that impact or shape how that system operates. For example, the productivity of an organization may be impacted by the broader economy in which it functions as well as the internalization of an organizational "culture of productivity" on the part of the individuals within the organization.

If you tend to work with phenomena at the individual level, try shifting the "unit of analysis," if plausible, and consider the phenomena from this new "unit" level. As an example, research has explored the effects of alcohol on adolescent tendencies to engage in unprotected sex, and almost all of this research uses individuals as the unit of analysis. However, unprotected sex is a couple behavior, so you could shift the analysis from the individual level to the couple level by focusing on factors that influence whether a given *couple* engages in unprotected sex. One way of analyzing couple behavior is to do so in terms of the different attitudes and characteristics that each couple member brings to the relationship.[1] For example, for condom use in heterosexual couples, the male member has a behavioral orientation toward using condoms, a set of beliefs about using condoms, certain risk-taking orientations, certain alcohol consumption patterns, and so on. This is also true of the female member of the couple; that is, she also brings a behavioral orientation toward using condoms, a set of beliefs about condoms, certain risk orientations, and

---

[1] Throughout this book, we use examples with gender concepts, often using the categories "males" and "females." Current thinking in many areas uses more elaborate categorizations. In some contexts, for example, "males" are referred to as "assigned male at birth" and females as "assigned female at birth." We use simplified labels but recognize the need to sometimes make more fine-grained differentiations. See Box 13.1 on pages 391–392.

certain alcohol consumption patterns. The couple's behavior is a function of the meshing of these two sets of variables, one set from the male and one set from the female.

Four relational models describe possible ways in which the attributes of each couple member combine to impact couple behavior. Consider the case of the effects of alcohol use on couple sexual behavior. The first model, termed the *female influence model,* states that alcohol use impacts the sexual behavior of a couple, but that the primary influence on such behavior is the level of alcohol consumption by the female member of the dyad as opposed to the male member of the dyad. That is, alcohol consumption by the male does not impact the couple behavior, but female alcohol consumption does. The second model, termed the *male influence model,* occurs when male, rather than female, drinking behaviors, influence the couple's sexual activity. The third model, termed the *shared influence model,* conceptualizes the drinking behaviors of both the male and female partners as being independent determinants of couple-based sexual risk behavior. The final model involves more complex couple dynamics and is termed the *interactional influence model.* This model is a variant of the shared influence model in that it accounts for risky sexual couple behavior using the drinking behaviors of both partners, but it allows for configural influence. In addition to the independent effects of the drinking behaviors of both couple members, the interactional influence model posits an interaction effect between couple member drinking behavior, such that as female drinking increases, male drinking behavior becomes more strongly related to risky sexual behavior.

This example frames the analysis around the "components" of the system. However, analyses also could be pursued using unit-level variables as well, such as couple intimacy, relationship length, couple communication, and couple bargaining/negotiation strategies. For interesting perspectives on couple-level analyses, see Kenny, Kashy, and Cook (2006) and the references cited therein. Note that by shifting the unit of analysis from individuals to couples, very different perspectives on the effects of alcohol on unprotected sex have been gained.

Zaheer, Albert, and Zaheer (1999) extend the concept of units of analysis to temporal dimensions. They suggest that thinking about process and change phenomena from the perspective of different units of time can yield new theoretical insights and ideas. For example, if you are building a theory of the dynamics of life satisfaction, what concepts and variables might you focus on if you seek to understand changes in life satisfaction on a daily, monthly, yearly, or decades-long basis? Thinking in terms of these different units of time may produce new ideas and perspectives on life satisfaction.

22. *Shift the level of analysis.* Social scientists focus on explanations at different levels of analysis. One way of characterizing levels of analysis is in terms of proximal versus distal determinants. *Proximal determinants* are the more immediate determinants of behavior, and *distal determinants* are variables that influence behavior but do so through the more immediate determinants. Some theorists explain phenomena using more proximal determinants, whereas others explain phenomena using more distal determinants. We often gain new insights into a phenomenon by shifting the level of analysis we are pursuing, by moving either from proximal to distal analysis or from distal to proximal analysis.

As an example, Jaccard (2009) has presented a framework for thinking about behavior at four different levels. At the first (proximal) level, the explanatory framework asserts a simple proposition: A person's behavior is influenced by his or her intention to perform the behavior. If people intend to do something, they usually will do it, and if they do not intend to do something, they usually will not do it. For example, if a person intends to get tested for HIV, he or she probably will do so; if the person does not intend to get tested for HIV, he or she probably will not do so. In actuality, the relationship between behavioral intentions and behavior is complex—that is, people do not always do what they intend to do. The theory elaborates why this is the case. Factors that affect the intention–behavior relationship include environmental constraints that impede intended behavioral performance; lack of relevant knowledge and skills to perform the intended behavior; the tendency to forget to perform the intended behavior; and the operation of habit and automatic processes.

At the second level of analysis, the near-proximal level, the theory addresses why some people intend to perform a behavior and other people do not. Five classes of variables that impact a person's intention or decision to perform a behavior are the focus of the theory: (a) what the person sees as the advantages and disadvantages of performing the behavior, (b) the normative pressures that the person experiences to perform the behavior, (c) the perceived social image implications of performing the behavior, (d) the person's emotional and affective reactions to performing the behavior, and (e) the person's self-perceived ability to successfully perform the behavior (i.e., perceptions of self-efficacy). For example, what does a person see as the advantages and disadvantages of being tested for HIV; what social pressures are operating for the person to be tested for HIV; how will being tested for HIV affect the person's image he or she conveys to others; what emotional reactions does the person have to being tested for HIV; and what obstacles does the person see to being tested for HIV?

At the next level of explanation are near-distal determinants. These are more general variables that do not reference the target behavior but can shape the proximal and near-proximal determinants of behavior. They include such constructs as (a) personality variables; (b) general values, goals, aspirations, and attitudes; (c) variables related to mental health (e.g., depression, anxiety, stress); and (d) variables related to alcohol and drug use. For example, a person may miss a scheduled HIV test because he or she is depressed or hungover from drinking too much.

The most distal level of analysis focuses on the broader contexts in which behavior occurs: the family context, the peer context, the school context, the work context, the provider context, the religious context, the neighborhood context, the media context, the government/policy context, and the cultural context (for various ethnic groups).

Jaccard (2009) encourages theorists who seek to explain behavior to think about that behavior at the different levels of analysis. Do people intend to perform the behavior in question, and if so, what factors get in the way of their carrying out their intentions? Why do some people intend to perform the behavior, whereas others do not? How do these people differ in their perceived advantages and disadvantages of performing the behavior, the normative pressures that are operating, the perceived image implications of performing the behavior, their emotional reactions to performing the behavior, and their perceived ability to perform the behavior? How are all these variables shaped by their personalities, their broader goals and aspirations, their general attitudes, and other such lifestyle variables? Finally, how is all this influenced by the broader contexts in which they live, including the family context, the peer context, the school context, the work context, the religious context, the neighborhood context, the media context, the government/policy context, and the cultural context?

Most social scientists tend to theorize at only one level of analysis—either at the level of the more proximal determinants of behavior or at the level of more distal determinants of behavior. This focus is perfectly reasonable. However, you might gain insights into the phenomenon you are studying by occasionally shifting your thought process to think about explanatory constructs either at more proximal levels or more distal levels. By thinking about phenomena at these different levels, insights might be gained into the kinds of variables you should focus on at the original level of analysis. For example, even though you might be interested in understanding the political ideologies of voters and how these ideologies influence voting choices, it might be helpful to shift to another level of analysis and ask how different contexts (e.g., the media, work, neighborhood) shape the political ideologies of individuals. Engaging in such an activity might suggest new dimensions of ideology you had not considered or new ways of thinking about ideology that help you better explain the relationship between ideology and voting behavior.

23. *Use both explanations rather than one or the other.* In the area of impression formation, a robust finding is the occurrence of primacy effects: Information about a person that is presented first tends to have a larger impact on impressions than information that is presented later (Anderson, 1965, 1991). One explanation for this difference focuses on "change-in-meaning" processes, whereby the initial information is thought to color or change the meaning of the later information so that it is interpreted to be consistent with the initial information. A second explanation is that the initial information is remembered more easily than later information. More easily recalled information is more influential, hence the primacy effect. A third explanation is that people discount later information that is contrary to the initial information they receive. Research efforts have been made to choose between these explanations (change in meaning vs. accessibility vs. discounting), with somewhat mixed success (Anderson, 1965, 1991; Anderson & Hubert, 1963). Instead of viewing explanations as mutually exclusive, consider the possibility that all of the explanations are operating. Thus, in the impression formation example, perhaps some change in meaning is operating, perhaps there also is some differential recall operating, and perhaps there is some discounting operating, all converging to produce primacy effects. A theory might be devised whereby each of these processes has an "importance weight" reflecting the influence of the process in the formation of impressions. We might then theorize about how the relative magnitude of these importance weights varies across different individuals and across different situations. This approach yields a different theoretical perspective from that of trying to choose the "correct" explanation. (For elaboration, see Poole & Van de Ven, 1989.)

A variant of this heuristic is to invoke the operation of multiple processes rather than a single process when thinking about a phenomenon. Rather than viewing a phenomenon as being influenced by one process or the other, allow both processes to operate. This strategy is well illustrated by the many "dual-process" theories that are popular in psychology. *Dual-process models* take many forms, but the idea is to specify two alternative or complementary processing modes and then build a theory around those processes. For example, Smith, Zarate, and Branscombe (1987) suggest a dual-process model for accessing attitudes: one process that calls a previously formed and previously stored attitude from memory and the other process that accesses a rule from memory to use to form an attitude toward an object to which one is newly exposed. Smith and DeCoster (2000) suggest that people possess two memory systems for storing cognitions: one system that slowly learns general regularities and the other system that forms quick representations of novel events or individual episodes. Petty and Cacioppo (1986) suggest a dual-process model of persuasion based on the systematic processing of a persuasive message (i.e., thinking about the validity of the arguments contained in a message) and the heuristic processing of a persuasive message (i.e., thinking about the source of a message and the characteristics of the source, such as the source's trustworthiness and credibility). Kowalski (2006) offers a dual-process model of thought involving intuitive thinking (which is automatic, effortless, and largely subconscious) and deliberative thinking (which is controlled, effortful, and mostly conscious). Sierra and Hyman (2006) offer a dual-process model of cheating intentions, one based on cognitive thought and the other on anticipated emotions. Although dual-process models are popular in the areas of decision making, memory, and information processing, they also appear in other areas of inquiry. Perhaps the phenomena you are thinking about can be conceptualized in the form of a dual-process framework.

24. *Capitalize on methodological and technological innovations.* Technology is changing rapidly, leading to new methodological tools for social scientists. These advances are opening up new areas for theoretical inquiry and insight. For example, in the past, linking neuroscience findings to human behavior was limited to the exploration of animals removed from their ecological contexts, to observations of patients who suffered trauma, to disorders of localized areas of the brain, and to postmortem examinations. Recent technological advances now permit electrophysiological recording, functional brain imaging, and neurochemical assessments during ongoing human behavior, permitting intriguing interfaces between social science and neuroscience. As an example, Steinberg (2008) suggests that the brain's socioemotional system develops at a much faster rate than the cognitive control system, leading adolescents toward increased reward seeking at a time when control mechanisms are underdeveloped. He hypothesizes that this pattern of brain development accounts for increases in risk-taking behavior during adolescence followed by declines in risk taking during young adulthood, as brain development surrounding control processes "catches up" with those surrounding emotional responses. Steinberg's research has taken advantage of technology-based methodological advances in neuroscience.

As another example, Freud popularized the notion of the unconscious in psychology, but it quickly fell into scientific disrepute when satisfactory measures of unconscious phenomena failed to materialize. Without such measures, unconscious motives could be introduced post hoc to explain anything because there was no way of subjecting unconscious explanations to empirical tests. Recently, psychologists and sociologists have developed methods that purportedly allow for the measurement of unconscious attitudes (Bassili & Brown, 2005; Blanton & Jaccard, 2008). These methods ask individuals to view stimuli on computer screens and to classify them as fast as they can into different categories. Based on how long it takes them to classify stimuli (measured in milliseconds), inferences are made about the attitudes they have toward the stimuli. These methods have opened up new theoretical accounts of human behavior, as both conscious and unconscious phenomena are incorporated into conceptual frameworks.

Keeping abreast of new technologies and methodological innovations is a way of possibly defining new questions and bringing to bear new constructs to understand phenomena you study.

25. *Focus on your emotions.* For many researchers, emotions have no place in theory development, but when studying human behavior, emotions might be tapped for purposes of generating ideas. It is a common practice in anthropology, for example, to record field notes either as an outside observer or in the context of participant observation. Field notes not only involve recording one's observations, but also recording notes about the emotions one is experiencing while making the observations. In traditional anthropology, such notes on emotion were considered to be "warnings" about potential bias in one's observations, such as when one's perceptions of others might be colored by the relationships that had been formed with those others in the context of participant observation. However, more recently, some groups of anthropologists have viewed emotion notes as a source of meaning and interpretation in their own right that may help them formulate theory and gain perspectives on the particular phenomenon being studied (e.g., Cylwik, 2001; Kelinman & Copp, 1993). Anthropologist Renato Rosaldo (1993) used his grief over the death of his wife as a way to understand the intensity of emotions experienced by a group of headhunters, the Ilongot of the Philippines, about headhunting. Rosaldo argues that by attempting to eliminate personal emotions from observations, traditional ethnographies create distortions and misinterpretations of descriptions, thereby undermining explanation.

26. *Find what pushes your intellectual hot button.* Items in the media or discussions with others may evoke in you a sense of disbelief or at least disagreement. Any time you find yourself saying "That can't be right," ask yourself if it is something worth pursuing. As a junior assistant professor discussing the value of advertising with a consumer advocate, one of the authors (Jacoby) found himself disagreeing with the advocate's proposition that "if there is going to be advertising, it should be limited to providing as much concrete information to the prospective consumer as possible." Incredulous, Jacoby contended that, if it were all attended to, too much information likely would discombobulate the consumer, making it more difficult to separate the wheat from the chaff, thereby leading to poorer decision making. The advocate scoffed at the idea. This led Jacoby to conduct research to test his hypothesis. After Jacoby published a series of studies that confirmed the hypothesis, advertisers and public policymakers began thinking differently about how information could best be communicated to consumers. As an example, instead of requiring cigarette manufacturers to list the complete set of 18 health consequences it wanted on cigarette packages, the Federal Trade Commission,

citing this stream of "information overload" research, called for cigarette manufacturers to list only three of these consequences at a time, periodically rotating the consequences to be listed. What have you heard or seen that elicits your disagreement and makes you say "That can't be right"? Is it worth studying?

27. *Engage in prescient theorizing.* When we think about a phenomenon or question, we often adopt a retrospective (what has happened in the past) or concurrent (what is happening now) orientation. As you think of ways to reframe or gain new perspectives on a problem or phenomenon, it might be useful to think about what that problem/phenomenon and the parameters surrounding it might be like 5, 10, or 25 years from now and adjust your theorizing accordingly. How might we need to modify a theory to account for what things will be like in 20 years? What type of trends and clues from today might we take into account to structure our future research and future theories? How might we not only see the coming wave but shape the conceptual conversation about it using theories we frame now? Wayne Gretzky, the famous hockey player, said, "It's not as important to know where the puck is now as to know where it will be." Robert Kennedy, noted American politician, said, "Some men see things as they are, and ask why. I dream of things that never were, and ask why not." As you construct theory, a future focus might lead you to innovative theorizing.

An example that draws on demography is illustrative. Growing populations are typified by age structures that have large numbers of young people and fewer older people. By contrast, populations at replacement-level rates tend to have fairly uniform age structures, which has typified recent growth in the United States. One major exception to this trend was the baby boom that occurred just after World War II, between 1946 and 1964. This period saw a dramatic increase in the number of babies born to U.S. families as soldiers returned from war, peaking at the end of the 1950s when more than 50 million babies were added to the population. This large group of "baby boomers" has been gradually working its way through an otherwise fairly homogenous age structure. Initially, the boomers greatly impacted the demands and dynamics of preschool child care and all other matters associated with infancy and toddlerhood until they aged into the elementary schools. When this happened, they put tremendous burdens on elementary schools to deal with student expansion and the dramatic increase in the demand for teachers to teach them. Once the boomers moved into middle and high school, the elementary schools found themselves overstaffed and overbuilt, posing new challenges to cope with contraction. In the meantime, middle schools and high schools experienced the same expansion–contraction cycle as the elementary schools, followed a few years later by a repeat of the cycle for colleges. As baby boomers have worked their way through the U.S. age structure, they have dramatically upended facets of the U.S. society in ways that touch almost all facets of life. For example, soft drinks tend to be consumed primarily by teenagers and young adults, and the soft drink industry saw tremendous growth and expansion when boomers entered this age range, followed by large contractions thereafter. The response of the industry to the contractions was to put a greater emphasis on global marketing, particularly in countries with large growth rates. Military recruitment went from having access to a large pool of recruits at one point in time to a relatively sudden contraction of that pool. By 2029, when all of the baby boomers will be 65 years of age and over, more than 20% of the total U.S. population will be over age 65 and the stress on the Social Security system and "all things elderly" will be considerable (although this too will dissipate as boomers die and the age structure "normalizes"). A social scientist embarking on his or her career in, say, the 1970s and who was aware of this important demographic trend and its implications for all facets of American society might have forecasted some of the challenges that would arise 20 years hence in the 1990s and embarked upon certain types of research programs in anticipation. The theories forged by this scientist may have included cyclical dynamics of expansion and contraction, facets that otherwise might be ignored.

Other heuristics besides these 27 could be mentioned, and we develop more of them in subsequent chapters. The present list is simply a start. The heuristics can be used effectively in conjunction with the list of "strategies for making a theoretical contribution" described in Chapter 3. For example, one strategy for making a theoretical contribution mentioned in that chapter is to "add one or more explanatory variables that have not been considered in prior work." To identify such variables, you might use one or more of the heuristics described in this chapter. Another strategy from Chapter 3 is to "identify the mechanisms or intervening processes responsible for an effect of one variable on another." To identify such mechanisms, again, you might use one or more of the heuristics described in this chapter.

A compendium of other approaches to stimulating creativity can be found in the volumes by Stein (1974, 1975) and McGuire (e.g., 1997). Nersessian (2008) emphasizes the fact that scientists rarely rely on one heuristic or one cognitive process for generating ideas, but rather notes that an idea might result from the complex interplay of multiple heuristics, such as mixing the use of analogies, thought experiments, and imaging. Try thinking up some heuristics of your own. How can you start to "think differently?" How can you view things from perspectives you are not accustomed to? How can you combine heuristics? Try creating your own list of ways for stimulating creativity.

When the Focus Is on Basic Mental or Biological Processes

Some social scientists focus their theorizing on core processes within the human mind, such as attention, perception, or comprehension, whereas others focus on basic biological processes, such as neural correlates of thought or electrical activity in the brain that is associated with different emotions. Can the heuristics and categories of variables we have described be used by such theorists? Yes. This is not to say that every heuristic will be of use, but if you make a sincere effort to think about phenomena from the perspective of one or more of the heuristics, there is a good chance that new insights will emerge. The use of heuristics—such as interviewing experts, conducting thought experiments, analyzing paradoxical incidents, imaging, using analogies and metaphors, reframing problems in terms of their opposite, using deviant case analysis, focusing on processes, considering abstractions or specific instances, making the opposite assumption, applying the continual why and why not questions, pushing an established finding to the extremes, using remote associates, shifting the level of analysis, and using multiple rather than either/or explanations—all can be applied to the analysis of basic mental, biological, organizational, or sociological processes.

SCIENTISTS ON SCIENTIFIC THEORIZING

Leading social scientists have written many articles on the strategies they use for constructing scientific theories. In this section, we review some of these strategies, focusing on those that complement or augment the heuristics already discussed. One or more of these approaches may resonate with you as you think about your phenomena.

Robert Wyer is an influential social psychologist who studies the phenomenon of information processing. His theory of information processing emphasizes seven processing stages or activities in which individuals engage when processing information: (1) attending to information when it is encountered; (2) interpreting and organizing the information relative to preexisting concepts that are stored in memory; (3) construing the implications of the information for already acquired knowledge about relevant people and events; (4) storing the information in memory; (5) retrieving the information from memory at later times; (6) integrating the retrieved information to make a subjective judgment; and (7) translating this judgment into an overt response. In building a scientific theory about information processing, Wyer (2004) notes that he often compartmentalizes these processes, building a mini-theory for each one separately. He then aggregates these mini-theories to construct his broader theory of information processing. Compartmentalization thus can assist in building theories of complex phenomena. In other words, take it one step at a time.

Wyer (2004) states that he always searches for alternative explanations of a phenomenon. What different assumptions, suppositions, or perspectives might lead to the occurrence of the same phenomenon? When presented with an explanation for a phenomenon, Wyer's immediate reaction is to generate an alternative explanation for it. Then he carefully analyzes the different explanations, deciding either to integrate them or to competitively test them.

Wyer emphasizes the importance of bringing fresh perspectives to theory construction. He expresses reservations about reading the existing literature at the idea-generation phase. The writers of research reports, he notes, can be very effective at conveying their logic and thereby channel the reader's thinking to that of the writers' thinking. He states that he often reads the first few paragraphs of an article and then skips to the Method and Results section so that he can generate his own explanations of the findings. Then he goes back and reads what the authors have to say.

Wyer notes that theories often are metaphorical in character, and he encourages the use of metaphors when theorizing. Wyer was one of the developers of the "bin" theory of memory described in heuristic #9, and his work is typified by the use of rich and creative metaphors.

John Cacioppo (2004) discussed the use of reductionism in his theorizing. *Reductionism* is the attempt by scientists to identify, break apart, or reduce nature into its natural constituents. Identifying the core ingredients of a phenomenon reveals insights into that phenomenon. Although some have criticized reductionism as making the simplistic assumption that "the whole is equal to the sum of its parts," Cacioppo argues that it provides points of entry into complex systems. The idea is not just to describe the smaller parts but to develop a better understanding of the complex system. Reductionism is a strategy for doing so.

William McGuire (2004) argues for the importance of expressing theories using six different modalities: (1) verbal, (2) abstract symbolic, (3) pictorial (or graphic), (4) tabular, (5) descriptive statistical, and (6) inferential statistical. McGuire argues that expressing a theory via multiple modalities can help the theorist grasp the theory better and can increase the likelihood of noticing the implications of a theory and its similarities to and differences from other formulations. As examples, Jacoby (2002) worked with the traditional stimulus–organism–response (S → O → R) model in psychology, which conceptualizes stimuli in the environment as impinging on a person (or, more generally, an organism), who then formulates a response to that stimulus. He asked, "What if the traditional S → O → R model is not depicted linearly but instead is conceptualized as an overlapping Venn diagram?" Representing the framework as a Venn diagram led Jacoby to propose new ways of representing how stimuli, responses, and organismic factors interact, with the result being a richer, seven-sector conceptualization of the traditional S → O → R model. In another realm, Langley (1999) describes several creative visual mapping strategies that can be used for characterizing process-oriented theories, and McGuire provides several additional examples of expressing theoretical propositions in each modality.

Howard Becker, an internationally recognized sociologist, wrote a book called *Tricks of the Trade* (2003) that is filled with heuristics for generating ideas. We describe some of them here, focusing mainly on those that augment the material already presented. One heuristic Becker describes is a *next-step heuristic*. Suppose a person performs a behavior. What are the next steps available to that person? If you graduate from high school, what are the next steps you can take in your life? How does this action (graduating from high school) enhance or constrain the next steps that you can take? If you are late to work, what are your next steps? If you purchase a product (e.g., a car), what are your next steps? Becker argues that theory construction is analogous to a form of storytelling that is constrained by the demands of being logical and consistent with known facts. Stories lead the reader from one step to the next. What events lead up to your "primary event" (i.e., your outcome), and what events follow it? As you think about matters, keep applying a "next step" line of thought: Every time you specify the next step, ask yourself what is the next step that can or should be taken after that.

Another strategy Becker discusses is one of "building a machine to maintain the status quo." Suppose you are interested in academic achievement. What would you need to do to keep the current levels of learning in schools exactly where they are? What steps would you need to take to ensure that neither any improvements nor any decrements were made in student performance? How could you prevent teachers from doing a better job without also making them do a worse job? How could you keep parents from doing a better job without also making them do a worse job with respect to their children and school? If you had to "build a machine" or "design a system" to maintain the status quo exactly as it is, what parts would the machine have, how would they function, and how would they interconnect? As you answer these questions, you may gain insights into how to improve academic achievement.

Social scientists generally try to specify *why* a person performs a particular behavior. As another heuristic, Becker suggests shifting away from this traditional *why* question to focus instead on *where* someone performs the behavior. Think through this strategy in depth. If you interview someone for a case study analysis, probe in detail the question of where the behavior occurs. Such a shift will help you focus on settings and the importance of settings in influencing behavior. For example, someone may buy one brand of beer for personal consumption at home but often select another brand of beer when drinking with his buddies. Another question shift is to ask *how* instead of *why*. Instead of asking why people smoke marijuana, ask how someone came to start smoking marijuana. What were the steps leading up to it? How did the smoker get to the circumstances he or she is in today? A final question shift can be to ask *when* does someone perform the behavior rather than why. By carefully thinking about "where," "how," and "when," in addition to "why" people do what they do, more insights into the phenomena in which you are interested may result.

Yet another strategy that Becker suggests is to doubt everything that anyone in a position of authority or who supposedly is an expert tells you. By accepting nothing as a given, by being a doubter about everything, new ideas suggest themselves.

Abbott and Alexander (2004) have written a useful book describing heuristics to stimulate thinking about social science phenomena, many of which we have already discussed. Additional heuristics they note include (1) questioning scientific propositions that others take as givens (similar to Becker's suggestion, noted earlier); (2) reconceptualizing an action or outcome as not being due to an actor but instead being due to a device or a circumstance, such as when Ralph Nader reconceptualized injuries from car accidents as the result of poorly designed cars that were inherently unsafe rather than the result of speeding drivers; (3) setting conditions, whereby one specifies those conditions under which a relationship holds and does not hold (a topic we take up in detail in Chapter 7), such as stress having a larger negative impact on well-being for people with poor coping skills as opposed to people with good coping skills; (4) adding a dimension, which involves identifying conceptual confounds and controlling for them to see if a relationship still remains (e.g., for the proposition "Women are less likely to pursue mathematics than men": Would this be true if one controlled for or held constant parental encouragement? Would it be true if one held constant mathematical abilities?); (5) splitting, which involves making distinctions that one does not typically make (e.g., as in Epstein's [1983] book *Women in Law,* in which the author argues that traditional studies and characterizations of lawyers apply to male but not female lawyers, or in Joseph Carlin's [1962] book *Lawyers on Their Own,* in which he makes the same argument but for lawyers in small, solo practices); and (6) redefining constructs in novel ways, such as when West and Zimmerman (1987) defined gender not as a variable or as a role but instead as a set of social actions that included making certain gestures and invoking certain symbols in certain contexts, all with the intent of identifying oneself as being gendered.

Finally, Root-Bernstein and Root-Bernstein (1999) identified 13 thinking tools that creative geniuses use as they approach the process of idea generation. They identified these tools based on an analysis of the writings and lives of highly creative individuals in disciplines encompassing the arts, sciences, and humanities. The tools include (1) observing, (2) imaging, (3) recognizing patterns, (4) pattern forming, (5) analogizing, (6) abstracting, (7) body thinking, (8) empathizing, (9) dimensional thinking, (10) thought playing, (11) transforming, (12) synthesizing, and (13) modeling. Many of these strategies map onto the heuristics we have already discussed. Details of each are summarized in Root-Bernstein and Root-Bernstein (1999).

CONCEPTUAL LOGIC MODELS

Chapter 3 identified strategies for making theoretical contributions, and the current chapter describes heuristics you can use to generate ideas for theory development relative to those strategies. A third step in theory construction is to articulate an a priori logic model in support of the theoretical propositions you propose based on the idea-generating heuristics. For example, when trying to explain the occurrence of unintended pregnancies in adolescents, many theorists emphasize the importance of knowledge about sex and birth control as a key determinant: Lack of knowledge about contraception and sex is associated with higher likelihoods of an unintended pregnancy in the ensuing year. Several years ago, after conducting in-depth interviews with adolescents and using some of the heuristics described in this chapter, I (Jaccard) had the insight that many adolescents report they know a great deal about birth control and sex even when they lack such knowledge. I then distinguished the concepts of actual knowledge levels (operationalized using formal knowledge tests) versus perceived knowledge levels (operationalized by asking adolescents to rate how knowledgeable they were about birth control and sex), and I began to formulate a theory about how such self-perceptions may impact unintended pregnancies independent of actual knowledge.

This represents the strategy of "adding a new explanatory variable that has not been considered in prior work" described in Chapter 3 because no one had ever focused on this variable when explaining adolescent unintended pregnancies. Using some of the heuristics described in this chapter, I elaborated theoretical propositions about the relationship between perceived knowledge and actual knowledge, the factors that distort adolescents' self-perceptions of their knowledge levels, and the mechanisms that would account for an independent impact of perceived knowledge over and above actual knowledge. I then developed a conceptual logic model in support of the plausibility of each assertion (e.g., Jaccard, Dodge, & Guilamo-Ramos, 2005; Radecki & Jaccard, 1995).

Logic models take many forms, but when applied to a theory, they are referred to as *conceptual logic models* (Jaccard & Bo, 2018). An a priori conceptual logic model comprises statements/arguments that build a case for the compellingness and justification of one's theoretical assertions. As theorists develop conceptual logic model(s) surrounding their initial ideas, they are forced to think through those ideas in more depth and with greater clarity. Conceptual logic models are thus central to the theory construction process. Stated another way, you can't just specify a set of theoretical propositions without some type of narrative and basis for them. You must convince people (including yourself) that the propositions are viable and make sense. Conceptual logic models accomplish this. Using the language of rhetorical theory, in a conceptual logic model, your theoretical assertion is analogous to a conclusion, and the reasons or a priori arguments that support that conclusion are your premises. If your reasons/premises are weak, then your theoretical assertion is questionable, so strong premises are important. We now discuss three common forms of logic used in conceptual logic models: (1) induction, (2) deductive syllogistic reasoning, and (3) analogical reasoning.

Induction

One type of argument in support of a theoretical proposition is the invocation of prior research that is supportive of it. For example, you might be focused on explaining high rates of suicidal behavior in Asian American youth, and your theory might argue, among other things, that a thwarted sense of belongingness is related to suicide ideation in such youth. In support of this proposition, you might note to your audience (and to yourself) that study A, study B, and study C all found a link between a sense of belongingness and suicidal ideation. For these studies to be supportive of your assertion, they should be methodologically sound, and they also should reasonably map onto the essential elements of your proposition. Specifically, prior studies can differ from your study with regard to the populations they focus on, the time when they were conducted (e.g., 1980 vs. 2018), and the setting to which they apply (e.g., a school setting vs. a clinic setting). The strongest support for your assertion is if studies A, B, and C focused on the key "ingredients" of your theoretical assertion. For example, if your assertion is aimed at Asian American youth, one might question the relevance of study A if it was conducted 20 years ago with elderly white adults in a senior assisted living complex.[2]

Citing past research in this way is a form of inductive reasoning. *Induction* occurs when one provides a limited number of examples and infers a rule or principle from them. In other words, one moves from specifics to the general. For example, John, a top student, was not admitted to college X; Barbara, also a top student, was not admitted to college X; and Joan, a top student, was not admitted to college X. Therefore, it is difficult to gain admission to college X. Applied to the prior example, study A found X to be the case; study B found X to be the case; and study C found X to be the case. Therefore, X is likely to be the case. Again, the important feature of induction is to ensure that the examples used are representative of the general case and are not exceptions. Also, if counterexamples exist, they should be noted and dealt with. When you read a proposed theory in an article, does the logic model(s) for its various assertions use induction? Is the logic sound, or are there weaknesses in it because the exemplars do not really map onto the theoretical expression?

Citing past research that has empirically addressed your proposed theoretical link (or a variant of that link) as a basis for establishing the viability of your theory can be a

---

[2]If the mapping of the facets of prior research is perfect, your study essentially becomes a replication study.

two-edged sword. On the one hand, it does give credence to your assertion and justifies moving forward with further evaluation of it. However, citing such research can also reduce the judged theoretical contribution of your study because you may convince the reader that prior research has already established the theoretical link. You need to build a case that although the prior research is suggestive, there are features of your theory that are distinct and worthy of pursuit.

Deduction

Deduction is another form of reasoning commonly used in conceptual logic models. Deductive reasoning occurs when a conclusion is logically derived from general principles that are assumed to be true. Deduction takes many forms, but one common form used in the social sciences is a *deductive conditional syllogism* that has the form:

> If *A*, then *B*.
>
> If *B*, then *C*.
>
> Therefore, if *A*, then *C*.

Suppose our theoretical proposition is that higher levels of education (*A*) are associated with better health (*C*); that is, "If people have higher levels of education, then they will tend to have better health." To build a case for the viability of this conclusion, we might first seek to establish, perhaps by citing prior research, that higher levels of education (*A*) tend to lead to higher annual incomes (*B*). That is, "If people have higher levels of education, then they will tend to have higher levels of annual income." Next, we seek to establish a case for the idea that higher annual income (*B*) brings about better health (*C*). That is, "If people have higher levels of annual income, they will tend to have better health." Putting these two premises together leads us to the primary theoretical assertion, namely, that people with higher levels of education tend to have better health. By building a strong case for the two premises in the syllogism, the viability of the theoretical assertion becomes compelling. Our research might then empirically test the conclusion and, indeed, might even test the entire syllogism despite prior support for the premises. By testing the entire syllogism, one has increased confidence in the broader conceptual logic model per se.

Journal reports do not use strict "if–then" phrasing nor do they formally express the logic in syllogistic form, but the structure described here often underlies the invoked logic. For example, in a journal report, a theorist might state the following: "Past research has affirmed that higher levels of education tend to lead to higher annual incomes (e.g., Vilorio, 2016) and that higher levels of annual income, by providing greater access to health care, tends to lead to better health (Chetty et al., 2016). It follows from this that higher levels of education should be associated with better health." The strength of the conclusion, as noted, is impacted by the validity of the premises and the extent to which the cited research for each premise maps onto the context of the theoretical assertion, per our discussion for induction. When you read about a theory, does the conceptual logic model for its assertions use deductive conditional syllogisms of this form? Is the logic solid, or are there problems because the premises are weak?

Sometimes an assertion will be justified by using multiple syllogisms, as follows: "Past research has affirmed that higher levels of education tend to lead to higher annual incomes (Vilorio, 2016) and that higher levels of annual income tend to lead to better health (Chetty et al., 2016). As well, higher levels of education tend to lead to higher levels of health literacy (van der Heide et al., 2013), which also are associated with better health (Baker et al., 1997). Taken together, these results suggest that higher levels of education should be associated with better health." This text implies the following syllogistic structure (where A refers to higher levels of education, B refers to higher annual income, C refers to better health, and D refers to higher health literacy):

If A, then B.	If A, then D.
If B, then C.	If D, then C.
Therefore, if A, then C.	Therefore, if A, then C.

This structure leads to a more viable theoretical assertion (if A, then C) because there are two streams of logic for it, not just one (one stream surrounding the effects of higher income on health and another stream surrounding the effects of health literacy on health, both of which are impacted by education). We refer to this structure as the *horizontal structure* of an assertion/conclusion. The more streams of logic underlying an assertion in this context, the more support there is for it, everything else being equal.

Here is an example of a threefold horizontal structure with three reasons supporting the conclusion "if A, then C," where A refers to higher levels of education, B refers to higher annual income, C refers to better health, D refers to higher health literacy, and E refers to lower levels of smoking:

If A, then B.	If A, then D.	If A, then E.
If B, then C.	If D, then C.	If E, then C.
Therefore, if A, then C.	Therefore, if A, then C.	Therefore, if A, then C.

Note that even if one premise is weak (e.g., if A, then E), there are still other logical chains that support the conclusion "if A, then C." As you articulate your logic model in support of a theoretical assertion that takes the form of deductive conditional syllogisms, is it possible to expand the horizontal structure of the assertion with respect to the syllogisms underlying it?

Yet another syllogistic structure extends the chain vertically rather than horizontally, a structure that, in the abstract, might appear as follows:

If A, then B.

If B, then C.

If C, then D.

Therefore, if A, then D.

In this case, there are three premises in the syllogistic chain leading to the final conclusion. For example, the theoretical assertion might be that higher levels of education (*A*) are associated with lower absenteeism at work (*D*). The logic model might be phrased as follows: "Past research has affirmed that higher levels of education tend to lead to higher annual incomes (Vilorio, 2016) and that higher levels of annual income tend to lead to better health (Chetty et al., 2016). In turn, better health is associated with lower absenteeism at work (Darr & Johns, 2008). It follows from this chain of logic that higher levels of education should be associated with lower levels of absenteeism from work." Conclusions with a sizeable underlying *vertical structure* might be more open to criticism because a "break" or weak link anywhere in the chain can undermine the conclusion. As you map out the syllogistic structure underlying a theoretical claim in an article you read, how extensive are the horizontal and vertical structures for it? How valid are the premises?

There are other forms of deductive syllogisms than conditional syllogisms. Types include *categorical syllogisms* (*A:* All societies eventually perish; *B:* the United States is a society; *C:* therefore the United States will eventually perish); *disjunctive syllogisms* (*A:* People either believe in God or they do not believe in God; *B:* most people believe in God; *C:* therefore, only a minority of people do not believe in God); and *enthymemes* (a logical argument that reaches a conclusion but has an implied, unstated premise). For an extended discussion of syllogistic types and their strengths and weaknesses, see Copi and Cohen (2005).

Analogic Reasoning

Yet another form of argumentation in support of an assertion is *analogic reasoning*. This form generalizes from one example to another example, reasoning that the two examples are alike. A theorist might argue that because mice and humans have a similar genetic makeup (mice have about 90% of the same genes as humans), the genetic bases of certain human diseases can be studied with mice, with the resultant theoretical propositions derived from research on mice then being applicable to humans. This is analogical reasoning. In the field of law, analogical reasoning is common, such as when lawyers state that an earlier case serves as a precedent for a current case. The strength of the analogical argument is a function of (1) the actual degree of similarity between the two examples and (2) the relevance of the known similarities to the theoretical assertions being made. The analogy between mice and humans might falter, for example, if the amount of overlap in genes was considerably less than 90% or if the genes that do overlap are irrelevant to the disease being studied.

General Comments on Conceptual Logic Models

Theories can be criticized if the a priori conceptual logic models underlying their assertions are suspect. This is why one of the characteristics of a good theory discussed in Chapter 3 is that the theory be logically coherent. One can question the viability of a theoretical assertion by questioning the premises underlying it. The premises theorists offer in support of theoretical assertions often use inductive logic, deductive conditional syllogistic logic, analogical reasoning, and/or other forms of argumentation (e.g., see our discussion of abduction in Chapter 10). Sometimes premises can be defended by simple appeals to common sense. Other times, we cite research to bolster our premises. In the final analysis, as you build your theory, you will want to elaborate a strong a priori conceptual logic model that supports your assertions and makes them viable.

On a more general level, rhetoricians distinguish three means of argumentation: (1) *logos*, which are strategies that rely on logic, such as induction, deduction, and/or analogical reasoning; (2) *pathos*, which are strategies that rely on emotions and emotional reactions; and (3) *ethos*, which are strategies that rely on expert endorsements of an assertion rather than an underlying logic per se. Science usually is based in conceptual logic models that emphasize logos. As you refine your ideas, the step of constructing a strong conceptual logic model is important. Ideas that initially seemed viable may turn out to be logically deficient. Rhetorical theories have elaborated weak forms of argumentation that one generally will want to avoid when making a case for a theoretical expression. A sampling of them is presented in Appendix 4.1. Also, see Toulmin (2003) for a useful theory of logic and argumentation often used in science.

For examples of conceptual logic models in research articles, see the supplemental materials on our companion website at *www.theory-construction.com*.

SUMMARY AND CONCLUDING COMMENTS

In this chapter, we have provided ways of thinking about phenomena that may help you think of new concepts or constructs or consider relationships between concepts and constructs in novel ways. This chapter is just a beginning; the chapters that follow will augment your theoretical toolbox in more ways. It is not enough for you to passively read about the heuristics we have described and then expect a major, creative idea to hit you over the head (unless you are an incarnation of Richard Feynman). Nor should you give a heuristic a superficial try and then reject it as being simplistic or irrelevant. Force yourself to consider multiple heuristics in depth. Maybe you will ultimately decide a given heuristic is not useful to pursue, but the idea is to stretch your thinking and to try new avenues of thought.

Theoretical advancements in the social sciences can range from the small and incremental to the large and revolutionary. A central process in theory construction is idea generation. When trying to explain something, we want to create new and novel ideas and perspectives that will build on existing knowledge. This is just as true for "small" ideas as it is for large, "revolutionary" ideas. The key to theory construction is to generate numerous ideas from different vantage points and then to screen those ideas in terms of which ones are worthwhile and which ones are not. Once an initial "cut" has been made, the ideas must be subjected to more rigorous explications and analysis, as described in Chapters 5 and 6, and through the use of conceptual logic models.

Creative people tend to be independent nonconformists who have drive and resiliency and are willing to take risks. They typically have a burning curiosity and tend to trust their intuition. The prototype of a creative person differs by profession. Creative ideas provide insights not previously recognized. Ideas differ in their degrees of creativity, with some ideas being extremely creative and others only marginally so. As an emerging scientist, you need to "decide to be creative." As you approach theory construction, you will first identify and frame a problem or question to study and then use heuristics and modes of thinking that help you "think outside the box." We presented numerous heuristics and modes of thinking in this chapter, some of which may resonate better with you than others. In addition to these heuristics, you might develop some of your own. Given the decision to be creative, you now have some of the initial tools for theory construction. The material covered in Chapters 5 and 6 will help you refine your concepts and ideas that much more, and Chapters 7–14 will help you organize and use the above in more systematic ways. The creative process does not follow a set progression. This is just a start.

SUGGESTED READINGS

Abbott, A., & Alexander, J. C. (2004). *Methods of discovery.* New York: Norton.

—A book describing heuristics for thinking about social science phenomena.

Becker, H. (2003). *Tricks of the trade: How to think about your research while you're doing it.* Chicago: University of Chicago Press.

—A book containing some useful tips for generating research ideas.

Jacoby, J. (2002). Stimulus–organism–response reconsidered: An evolutionary step in modeling (consumer) behavior. *Journal of Consumer Psychology, 12*(1), 51–57.

—A description of a revised stimulus–organism–response model that relies on imaging, analogies, and metaphors.

McGuire, W. J. (1997). Creative hypothesis generating in psychology: Some useful heuristics. *Annual Review of Psychology, 48,* 1–30.

—An insightful discussion of 49 strategies for generating research ideas.

Osborn, A. F. (1963). *Applied imagination.* New York: Scribner's.

—A book describing how to encourage the creative process.

Root-Bernstein, R. S., & Root-Bernstein, M. (1999). *Sparks of genius: The thirteen thinking tools of the world's most creative people.* New York: Mariner.

—A discussion of key thought processes used by leading thinkers throughout time.

Simonton, D. K. (1988). *Scientific genius.* New York: Cambridge University Press.

—A study of creativity in science.

Simonton, D. K. (2004). *Creativity in science: Chance, logic, genius, and zeitgeist.* New York: Cambridge University Press.

—A study of creativity in science.

Smith, K., & Hitt, M. (Eds.). (2005). *Great minds in management: The process of theory development.* New York: Oxford University Press.

—An edited book with chapters by 25 great social science theorists about how they developed their theories.

Sternberg, R., Grigorenko, E., & Singer, J. (2004). *Creativity: From potential to realization.* Washington, DC: American Psychological Association.

—A useful book on creativity.

Toulmin, S. (2003). *The uses of argument.* Cambridge, UK: Cambridge University Press.

—A useful theory of rhetoric and logic. This expands on the idea of a conceptual logic model.

Wicker, A. (1985). Getting out of our conceptual ruts: Strategies for expanding conceptual frameworks. *American Psychologist, 40,* 1094–1103.

—More heuristics for generating ideas.

KEY TERMS

creativity (p. 53)

deciding to be creative (p. 56)

participatory action research (p. 57)

question brainstorming (p. 58)

case studies (p. 62)

thought experiments (p. 63)

counterfactuals (p. 64)

participant observation (p. 64)

analogies/metaphors (p. 66)

abstraction (p. 70)

unit of analysis (p. 73)

proximal determinants (p. 74)

distal determinants (p. 74)

dual-process models (p. 76)

reductionism (p. 81)

conceptual logic model (p. 84)

induction (p. 85)

deductive conditional syllogism (p. 86)

horizontal structure (p. 87)

vertical structure (p. 88)

categorical syllogisms (p. 88)

disjunctive syllogisms (p. 88)

enthymemes (p. 88)

analogic reasoning (p. 88)

logos (p. 89)

pathos (p. 89)

ethos (p. 89)

EXERCISES

Exercises to Reinforce Concepts

1. Discuss the role of idea generation and idea screening in theory construction.

2. What are the key characteristics of the creative person?

3. According to Nakamura and Csikszentmihalyi, what are the three system facets that influence the incorporation of novelty into scientific culture?

4. What are the three core factors that Amabile says underlie creativity?

5. What does it mean to "decide to be creative"?

6. What issues and criteria should you consider when choosing a topic area to study? Elaborate on each of them.

7. What are the advantages and disadvantages of doing a literature review before you start thinking about a phenomenon?

8. What are the four processes that Clement describes as characterizing how scientists apply analogies to solve a problem? Describe each.

9. What are the four levels of analysis characterized by Jaccard? Describe each and give examples.

10. Describe the heuristics for idea generation that most resonate with you and discuss why you find them to be the most useful.

11. What is a conceptual logic model? What are the major types of logic used in them? Characterize each.

12. What are the three types of arguments specified by rhetorical theory? Characterize each.

Exercises to Apply Concepts

1. Pick a phenomenon of interest and then generate a set of ideas about factors that influence it, how it functions, or how it influences other factors using one or more of the heuristics discussed in this chapter. Identify the heuristics you used.

2. Create a heuristic for generating ideas that was not discussed in this chapter.

3. Select a journal article of interest to you and critically analyze its conceptual logic model. Indicate the type of logic structures used and comment on the strength of the premises.

Examples of Weak Argumentation

Theories of rhetoric identify weak forms of argumentation or weak appeals that appear relevant to a claim but that may not be relevant. These represent "traps" that scientists should be cautious of as they describe the support for their theoretical propositions, either in presentations or in articles/books. Knowledge of such traps also can help you critically evaluate theories that you read, as sometimes theorists invoke them as a form of weak argumentation. We provide 15 common examples, but there are many morea in practice:

1. *Argumentum ad hominem* (argument toward the man). This strategy praises or criticizes people who make a claim, rather than discussing the claim itself. It occurs when scientists make personal attacks against a critic, which sometimes occurs during debates about a theory.

2. *Argumentum ad populum* (argument to the people). This strategy asserts that because most people believe a claim is true, then the claim must be true. Popular acceptance of a claim does not validate it. Just ask Galileo or Copernicus. In Chapter 3, we stressed the importance of consensus for a theory. The current dictum is a reminder that consensus is not always definitive.

3. *Argumentum ad traditio* (appeal to tradition). This strategy asserts that a claim must be true because it is part of tradition. A variant of this strategy is that because a claim was true in the past, it must be true in the future. Such logic does not always hold.

4. *Argumentum ad verecundium* (appeal to improper authority). This strategy invokes someone with expertise in another area that is not really appropriate for the claim at hand. For example, one might invoke the endorsement of a claim by a Nobel Prize–winning economist about the appropriateness of a reading program for elementary school-aged children.

5. *Argumentum ad misericordiam* (argument from pity). This strategy makes an emotional appeal to try to convince someone to accept a claim based on emotion, independent of the logic underlying it.

6. *Dicto simpliciter* (hasty generalization). This strategy improperly uses inductive reasoning when there are too few samples/examples to prove a point. One is too quick to form a generalization from specific instances.

7. *Non causa pro causa* (not the cause for a cause). This strategy invokes a false cause of an event for the real cause. Consider the claim "Drinking wine in moderation, say a glass a day,

reduces the risk of heart disease." This claim asserts a false cause. More specifically, there are socioeconomic differences in wine drinking behavior, with higher-class individuals being more likely to drink a glass of wine a day than lower-class individuals (who are more likely to drink beer). Better access to health care reduces the risk of heart disease, and upper-class individuals have better access to health care than lower-class individuals. Asserting that drinking a glass of wine a day has beneficial health effects is a position that is *non causa pro causa* because the real source of the effect is social class, not drinking wine. If social class is held constant, there is no association between wine consumption and the risk of heart disease.

8. *Ignorantio elenchi* (irrelevant conclusion). This strategy uses an argument for one claim and redirects it to inappropriately support a different claim. A variant is to change the subject or divert the argument from the real question at issue.

9. *Non sequitur* (it does not follow). This strategy invokes a claim that does not follow from the previous statements or arguments. Logicians often use the term in reference to formal syllogistic errors. For example, arguing that marijuana is a gateway drug to heroin use because almost all heroin users started on marijuana is a *non sequitur*. There are many marijuana users who never use heroin such that the likelihood someone will use heroin, given that they have used marijuana, is extremely low. The logic is flawed.

10. *Argumentum ad ignorantium* (argument from ignorance). This strategy appeals to a lack of information to prove a point or argues that since the claim cannot be disproved, the claim must be true. For example, one cannot prove that ghosts do not exist; therefore they must exist.

11. *Argumentum ad speculum* (hypothesis contrary to fact). This strategy tries to prove something by using hypothetical examples that are not applicable.

12. *Either/or fallacy*. This strategy creates false dichotomies, arguing that there are only two choices when actually there are more.

13. *Equivocation*. This strategy involves using a word or term in a different way than the author used it in the original claim or argument.

14. *Stacking the deck*. This strategy involves ignoring examples that run counter to a claim, focusing only on examples that support it.

15. *Argument from the negative*. This strategy states that because one position is untenable, the opposite position must be true. Both could be in error.

5

Focusing Concepts

People see the world not as it is, but as they are.
—ALBERT LEE

When formulating a theory, researchers usually begin with some phenomenon that they want to understand. Such phenomena can be diverse, ranging from overt, observable behaviors (e.g., smoking cigarettes, purchasing a product) to hypothetical concepts that are not directly observable (e.g., depression, suicidal ideation). The phenomena may focus on entities (schools), groups of individuals (females, Latinxs), processes (automatic processing of stimuli), systems (immune system responses to stress), or time (developmental changes), to name a few. We discussed in Chapter 4 issues surrounding the choice of concepts to include in one's theoretical system. Here, we focus on strategies for specifying and refining conceptual definitions for those concepts that one decides to include in the system.

We begin by describing the process of instantiation—a method for making abstract concepts more concrete—leading us to a formal characterization of the process of specifying conceptual definitions. Next, we consider the problem of surplus meaning, followed by a discussion of practical strategies for formulating clear definitions of constructs. We then discuss multidimensional approaches to constructs and, in turn, selected strategies that social scientists use to literally create variables for use in their theories. Finally, we conclude with a historical note on the concept of operationism as a means of defining constructs.

THE PROCESS OF INSTANTIATION

When formulating a theory, scientists frequently deal with abstract concepts. In fact, one way in which theories differ is in terms of the abstractness of the concepts used in the framework. For example, one theorist might develop a theory of how a person's attitudes are related to his or her behavior. Such a theory contains two concepts, "attitudes" and "behavior," which are quite abstract. A second theorist might develop a theory about how attitudes toward going to college are related to whether or not a high school student attends college. In this case, the same basic concepts are involved ("attitude" and "behavior"), but they are more focused: the concepts now concern a specific type of attitude (the attitude toward going to college) and a specific type of behavior (going to college). In the process of theorizing, scientists usually try to strike a balance between being too specific (and hence, having a theory that is narrow in scope) and being too abstract, to the point where the concepts become "fuzzy" and unmanageable. A process used to refine fuzzy concepts is that of instantiation. *Instantiation* is a deliberate process that involves specifying concrete instances of abstract concepts in order to help clarify their meaning. It is fundamental to science and a crucial process for refining initial theoretical ideas.

Instantiation plays another important role in science. In addition to clarifying concepts at a theoretical level, instantiation is a bridge between the conceptual and the empirical realms where the validity of a theoretical expression is subjected to empirical testing. Instantiation helps ensure that a theory is testable. Given the theoretical expression "Attitudes toward college influence whether a person goes to college," the scientist must devise a strategy for testing whether this statement has any value as a guide to understanding matters. To accomplish this strategy, the scientist might decide to select a group of high school students, measure their attitudes toward attending college, and then later determine whether or not they go to college. Although this strategy may appear straightforward, the scientist pursuing it would quickly be confronted with innumerable questions in the process of implementing it. Should the students be high school seniors only, or should juniors be included? When assessing attitudes, should one make distinctions between attitudes toward community colleges (i.e., 2-year colleges), 4-year colleges, and universities? What about trade schools? How long should the researcher wait to find out if the student has gone to college? 1 year? 2 years? And so on. Each of these questions requires that the scientist focus the concepts, isolate specific instances of them, and then use these instances to test the validity of the more general theoretical expression. Instantiation accomplishes this and is thus an important aspect of designing empirical theory tests.

Most scientists use the term *hypothesis* to refer to the specific empirically based instances that are used to test a more general theoretical expression. For example, based on the theory that "attitudes toward college influence college attendance," a scientist might propose a hypothesis for a study that "the high school seniors in this study will be more likely to attend a 4-year university if they have positive attitudes toward attending college." Although this hypothesis is more concrete, it is still somewhat ambiguous, and, in practice, the scientist would have to be even more specific in the delineation of his or her "hypothesis." Scientists are in disagreement about the exact meaning of the term *hypothesis*. Many scientists refer to the process of specifying a concrete instance of a theoretical expression for purposes of an empirical test as that of stating a hypothesis. Thus, a *hypothesis* is a statement that (1) is derived from a theoretical expression, (2) is more concrete than the originating theoretical expression, and (3) is tied to the empirical realm in such a way as to permit a test of the originating expression. Like theoretical expressions, hypotheses also consist of concepts and relationships. However, hypotheses are usually more limited in scope, more specific, and expressed in testable (or near testable) form. A hypothesis is sometimes called a *focal problem statement* and is a direct result of the process of instantiation.

At some point, almost all theories must be subjected to the instantiation process, either to make the definition of "fuzzy" concepts clearer and more communicable or to derive a direct test of the theory. A theoretical expression usually contains a universe of potential meanings. If the universe of meanings is large, the theoretical expression runs the risk of being vague and ambiguous. Consider the following theoretical expression: "Older people are more knowledgeable than younger people." This expression posits a relationship between two concepts: age and knowledgeability. But what do we mean by each of these concepts? Does "age" refer to chronological age, developmental age (i.e., one's level of maturation), or psychological age ("You're as old as you feel")? To simplify matters, let us assume that we are referring to chronological age. The concept of "knowledgeability" also is ambiguous. A person could be knowledgeable about myriad things, including music, films, television programs, local happenings, world events, geography, aircraft and aviation, his or her family, his or her job, cooking utensils, restaurants, religious events, clothing, consumer products that are generally available, computers, celebrities, photography, and the breeding of tropical fish. It would take an encyclopedia just to list all the possibilities. We need to be more specific about the type of knowledge to which we are referring.

The Nature of Conceptual Definitions

Instantiation involves generating specific conceptual instances so as to make abstract concepts more concrete; it requires posing and answering questions designed to clarify and explicate the meanings of concepts. Nunnally (1967/1978, p. 89) refers to this process as "outlining constructs" or "stating what one means by the use of particular words." The outcomes of this process are termed *conceptual definitions*, which represent clear and concise definitions of one's concepts. Not only do abstract constructs have to be defined as precisely as possible, but even seemingly obvious concepts frequently require explication. Consider a researcher specializing in the design of retail outlets who is responsible for conducting a study to determine where to erect a new shopping center. The researcher may begin by asking people in the target area what they want most in a shopping mall and may learn that "convenience" is highly regarded. The researcher is not, however, quite sure what this means, since, in response to further probing, it is discovered that the same word means many things to many people—including enough places to park one's car, proximity of the shopping center to other places that the individual frequents, and the distance from the individual's home. The researcher decides to explore the issue of distance further. However, the question "How far away is the *XYZ* shopping center?" produces five different replies from five different people: two subway stops; three traffic lights; 10 minutes; 3 miles; and quite far. Faced with such responses, a theorist must think carefully about the essence of a concept and then clearly communicate that essence to other scientists.

SHARED MEANING, SURPLUS MEANING, AND NOMOLOGICAL NETWORKS

Researchers sometimes disagree as to what constitutes the essence of the phenomenon under question. Thus, various conceptual definitions may be provided for the same concept. For example, Jacoby and Chestnut (1977) noted that there were more than 50 definitions of "brand loyalty" in the field of consumer behavior. Given that each investigator makes his or her conceptual definition explicit (by providing clearly articulated and precisely defined propositions), specific points of agreement and disagreement can be identified. The points of agreement may then be assumed to represent the essential (i.e., agreed-upon) core of the concept. Researchers refer to this as *shared meaning,* which can be contrasted with the remainder, which is termed *surplus meaning.* In science, it is better to have concepts that are dominated by shared meaning and that do not have too much surplus meaning.

Some examples will make explicit the relevant issues. Fishbein and Ajzen (1975) reviewed research on attitudes and found more than 500 definitions in the scientific literature. Even a cursory review of this literature made evident that quite different constructs were being invoked to represent "attitudes." Fishbein and Ajzen argued that three distinct constructs were being called "attitude" and that lumping these constructs together under a common rubric was counterproductive to scientific advancement. Although all definitions of attitude recognized that an attitude is directed toward an "object" (e.g., an attitude toward "majoring in psychology," an attitude toward "going to church," an attitude toward "Republicans"), the definitions varied in other respects. One set of constructs used to represent attitudes were people's perceived associations between the attitude object and some other attribute, characteristic, trait, or concept. For example, a person might believe (rightly or wrongly) that Republicans are conservative, that Republicans oppose abortion, that Republicans are from relatively wealthy families, and that Republicans oppose big government. Fishbein and Ajzen referred to such perceived associations as "beliefs." Another set of constructs used to represent attitudes were general feelings of favorableness–unfavorableness, or how positive or negative one felt about the attitude object. Fishbein and Ajzen noted that such affective feelings were an element of most definitions of attitude and, furthermore, that all the standard attitude scaling methods were designed to measure such affective feelings. Because this represented "shared meaning" among the many conceptions of attitude, the authors used the term *attitude* to refer to it. Thus, an attitude toward an "object" is defined as the positive or negative affect that one feels toward that object. The third set of constructs used to represent attitudes in the literature were people's intentions to behave in certain ways with respect to the attitude object. For example, some people intend to vote for Republicans, intend to donate money to Republicans, intend to campaign against Republicans, and so on. Fishbein and Ajzen referred to these constructs as "behavioral intentions." They offered an insightful analysis showing that the kinds of factors that influence beliefs are different from the kinds of factors that influence attitudes, which, in turn, are different from the kinds of factors that influence behavioral intentions.

Hence, Fishbein and Ajzen argued, it makes scientific sense to distinguish between beliefs, attitudes, and behavioral intentions instead of treating them interchangeably as reflecting the same construct.

As another example, there is controversy in sociology and anthropology about ways to define and conceptualize social class. Qualities or characteristics used in the many definitions of social class include occupation, education, income, wealth, land/property ownership, control over means of production, political standing, prestige, reputation, associations with elites, honorary titles, and language, among others. Stratum approaches to social class group people into different classes, including two-class models (powerful and weak), three-class models (lower, middle, and upper class), and multistratum models having as many as nine classifications (Fussell, 1983). The classic work of Karl Marx (1887) defines class in terms of the degree of control over the means of production. Marx also emphasized subjective class (class identity) versus objective class (actual relationship to the means of production). Sociologist Max Weber (1904) defined social class in terms of three components: economic considerations (relative to control over means of production), prestige, and political position. The various characterizations of social class share the assumption that society is stratified in terms of economic-related variables (representing shared meaning), but the many characterizations of social class tend to use additional attributes as a basis for classification, depending on the theory (representing surplus meaning).

Which conceptualization of social class is optimal? The answer to this question is best viewed from the perspective of Meehl's classic work on *nomological networks* (Cronbach & Meehl, 1955; MacCorquodale & Meehl, 1948). According to this framework, the meaning and utility of a concept emerge in the context of the broader theoretical network in which the concept is embedded. Thus, the "most appropriate" definition of social class depends on how the construct is used in the theory being advanced and how it fosters coherence in the overall theory. Of course, it is preferable if conceptual definitions of a construct across different theoretical frameworks have shared as opposed to surplus meaning. But the meaning and worth of a construct ultimately depend on the broader nomological network in which it is embedded. This viewpoint is consistent with recent views of distributed meaning and situated cognition as ways of determining the meaning of constructs (e.g., Hannerz, 1993; Hutchins, 1996).

PRACTICAL STRATEGIES FOR SPECIFYING CONCEPTUAL DEFINITIONS

A reasonable first step in developing a conceptual definition of a construct is to examine the scientific literature to see how other scientists have done so. A comprehensive and careful literature review of previous research that has used the concept will often yield one or more conceptual definitions that other scientists have found to be useful. Often, the difficult task of specifying an unambiguous definition will have already been performed. This is not to say that you should, by fiat, accept the conceptual defini-

BOX 5.1. Etic and Emic Constructs

In anthropology, distinctions have been made between etic- and emic-based approaches to scientific analysis. The terms *emic* and *etic* were coined by the linguist Kenneth Pike and were popularized in anthropology by Marvin Harris. The terms are applied in many different contexts, with somewhat different meanings depending on the subdiscipline. The essence of emic approaches is to understand a culture in the way that members of that culture understand it, to learn the concepts they use, and to try to see the world as they do. By contrast, the essence of etic approaches is to understand a culture in more abstract scientific terms that apply across different cultures and that can be used to make cross-cultural comparisons. The concepts and theories in an etic approach derive from a comparative framework and can be meaningless to the members of the culture under study.

An emic construct is one that reflects the perceptions and understandings of the members of a culture. For example, the concept of "motherhood" would be defined emically by how members of a cultural group view that role. Etic constructs, by contrast, are defined by scientists in more abstract terms and apply across groups (Headland, Pike, & Harris, 1990). The focus is not on how a specific culture defines "motherhood" but rather on a conceptual definition of the concept of "motherhood" as used by the scientific community.

In social science research, a common orientation is to combine etic and emic approaches to theory and measurement. The idea is to build theories of the relationships between variables at an etic level, but to operationalize and measure those constructs at an emic level. For example, a scientist might be interested in the construct of "expectancies" and define them as the perceived advantages and disadvantages of performing a behavior. The actual content of expectancies can vary from one group to another. For example, adolescent males might define "dating" somewhat differently than adolescent females and they might perceive different advantages and disadvantages of dating than females. The idea is to measure the constructs of dating and expectancies in such a way that these different perceptions and conceptions are respected, but to still apply the etic concept of expectancies to try to predict and understand the etic construct of dating behavior.

Examples abound of emic manifestations of etic concepts. For example, in some cultures it is appropriate to mourn individuals who have recently died by wearing black clothes, whereas in other cultures, one wears white clothes while mourning. When greeting one another, it is appropriate for two men to kiss on the cheek in some cultures, whereas such actions would be appalling in other cultures, where a greeting is confined to a simple handshake.

Grounded theorists often work with both etic and emic constructs, and at the etic level, the heuristics and strategies discussed in this chapter can help them refine and articulate their etic-level conceptual definitions.

tions offered in previous work. Perhaps, from your perspective, the definitions miss the essence of the concept or are flawed in one manner or another. However, reflecting on the definitions of others who have thought long and hard about the concept will often be fruitful.

Another useful source is a dictionary. You might be surprised at how often a clear and concise conceptual definition of a term can be found in a dictionary (or might be suggested by looking up the term in a thesaurus). We make it a standard practice to look up any terms for constructs we plan to use in our conceptual system in two or three major dictionaries. To be sure, scientific definitions sometimes deviate from everyday definitions in dictionaries, but consulting a dictionary may help you in the process of specifying a definition with better clarity and insight.

Another strategy for devising a clear conceptual definition is to list the key properties of a concept. *Properties* are the identifiable characteristics of concepts and form the cornerstone for later measurement of the concept and empirical testing. Tables possess such properties as height, width, length, type of composition, and color. When describing a table, we do so in terms of these properties. In practice, most concepts can be described by using scores of different properties. The instantiation process serves both a select-in and a select-out function. It tells us what we must focus on when we are structuring definitions of our concepts, and, at the same time, it puts blinders on us with respect to the remaining aspects of the theoretical expression. Some properties are crucial for conveying the essence of the concept, whereas others may be of less importance. You might try to make a list of the core properties and then assign priorities to them

As an example, behavioral prediction is central to many theories in the social sciences. Many behaviors have four core elements or properties: (1) an action (e.g., talking about drugs); (2) an object or target toward which the action is directed (e.g., to your teenage daughter); (3) a setting (e.g., in your home, while sitting at the kitchen table); and (4) a time (e.g., on Monday night). When researchers measure or conceptualize a behavior, they implicitly, if not explicitly, commit to treating these behavioral elements at some level of specificity or abstraction. For example, the behavior "the number of alcoholic drinks a person has consumed in the past 30 days" ignores or collapses the settings in which the drinking occurs as well as specific times at which drinking occurs. A feature of time is invoked in this example by requiring that the drinking occur in the past 30 days. In addition, the object (alcoholic drinks) represents an abstract category that subsumes multiple instantiations of that category (e.g., drinking beer, wine, hard liquor). Research has affirmed the theoretical importance of being explicit about how each of the four elements of a behavior is treated because the relevant predictors and determinants of that behavior can vary depending on the level of abstraction of the elements (e.g., Ajzen & Fishbein, 1980; Jaccard, 1974). This, in turn, affects the nature of the theory you develop. Thus, providing a clear definition of an outcome behavior of interest involves addressing the four properties of action, target object, setting, and time.

Another heuristic for delimiting the nature of concepts is to successively ask the question "What do you mean by that?" For example, for the concept of "attitude toward African Americans," one might answer the question "What do you mean by that?" as follows: "It is a tendency to act in a consistently favorable or unfavorable manner toward African Americans." One would then focus on key words within the answer, asking the same question: "What do you mean by that?" For example, we might ask, "What do you mean by 'consistently'?" or "What do you mean by 'African Americans'?" If in response to the latter question, the answer is "a person whose ancestry is predominantly African," you might further ask "What do you mean by 'predominantly'?" and "What do you mean by 'African'?" And so on. This process could continue forever, eventually leading to a linguistic nightmare. The idea is to continue with this line of reasoning until you judge that all major ambiguities are clarified and that the meaning of the construct can be clearly communicated.

Another strategy for specifying a concise conceptual definition is to play the role of a journalist who, in the context of an article for a magazine or newspaper, must explain the nature of the variable and its meaning to the public. Write the definition as if you were writing the article. Using this strategy can help you avoid jargon that may carry with it surplus meaning. Even when a conceptual definition is well understood by the scientific community, engaging in this exercise may prove to be useful to ensure that you can articulate all aspects of the definition in a meaningful fashion.

Yet another strategy that can be used to avoid ambiguous jargon is to place yourself in the position of having to define and explain the concept to someone who is just learning the English language, thereby forcing yourself to use more simplified and commonplace terms.

Using a denotive definition strategy is another strategy for articulating a definition (McGuire, 1997). For example, if you want to define "political conservatism," you might assign familiar political figures to different locations on the conservatism dimension and then try to specify which characteristics of each politician made you place him or her where you did.

Creating precise conceptual definitions can also be achieved by articulating or writing out how the concept would be measured in an empirical investigation. Ambiguities in the construct often reveal themselves when the construct must be operationalized at such a concrete level. For example, if you are trying to define a personality trait such as dominance, how would you go about assessing or measuring it in people? Exactly what questions would you ask? As you formulate these questions, the meaning of the concept often will become clearer to you.

A final strategy for specifying a clear conceptual definition is to use principles of grounded theory construction. We defer consideration of this strategy until Chapter 10.

A common trap when offering conceptual definitions is to not provide a definition but, rather, to define the concept by providing examples of it. In general, this tactic should be avoided. Specifying exemplars can be a useful strategy to help you think through the key properties and characteristics of a concept and to convey a sense of the concept to others. However, such exemplars should not substitute for a carefully worded and clear definition.

MULTIDIMENSIONAL CONSTRUCTS

When defining concepts in a theory, it sometimes is useful to think of subdimensions or "subtypes" of the construct. Consider the case of intelligence, a widely used concept in the social sciences. Psychologists became actively interested in the scientific study of intelligence in the early 1900s. At that time, intelligence was conceptualized as a rather broad concept, usually in terms of the capacity to solve complex and abstract problems. Such a conceptualization quickly came under attack as being too abstract and theoretically limiting. Several lines of evidence were used to argue against the global conceptualization. The first was a phenomenon known as the "savant syndrome"—that is, significantly developmentally challenged individuals with one or more highly developed skills. The most intensive study of this phenomenon, conducted by Scheerer, Rothmann, and Goldstein (1945), documented the case of an 11-year-old boy who was healthy and showed no signs of neurological disturbance. He was unable to perform well in school, his general information was quite substandard, he knew the meaning of few words, and he showed virtually no abstract problem-solving skills. His IQ on the Stanford–Binet (a widely used intelligence test) was 50, a very low score. However, there also were some paradoxes. The boy could tell the day of the week for any given date between 1880 and 1950. He could correctly spell many words forward and backward, and he never forgot the spelling of a word once he was told how to spell it. He could play by ear many complex musical compositions and could sing the opera *Othello* from beginning to end. The savant syndrome phenomenon suggested the need to recognize more specialized capacities in the context of the concept of intelligence.

A second perspective on the inadequacy of a general conceptualization of intelligence was provided by a series of factor-analytic studies. These studies postulated different types of intelligence and demonstrated empirically the utility of separating intelligence into different forms. One of the more popular conceptualizations is that of Leon Thurstone (1947), who postulates seven primary mental abilities: number, word fluency, verbal meaning, memory, reasoning, spatial perception, and perceptual speed. The results of factor-analytic studies underscore the idea that general concepts frequently need to be made more specific, and that it is possible to use empirical strategies to help scientists reconceptualize their constructs.

Examples of multidimensional conceptualizations of constructs in the social sciences abound. For instance, theories of risk taking have delineated four types of risk-taking propensities of individuals: (1) physical risk taking (putting oneself in harm's way, physically), (2) social risk taking (taking risks in social relationships), (3) monetary risk taking (taking risks with money), and (4) moral risk taking (taking risks involving the breaking of rules or laws). These "components" of risk taking derive from the proposition that risk taking occurs in different settings and that they can vary as a function of setting. Another example: Theories of social support distinguish four types of support people receive: (1) tangible support (e.g., monetary loans, transportation to and from different places, help with child care); (2) emotional support (providing empathy and understanding for one's feelings and emotions); (3) informational support (providing technical or practical information that a person needs to deal with a problem); and (4) companionship support (providing company for doing fun activities). How people cope with problems and stress is thought to be influenced independently by the four different types of support.

You can often make a theoretical network richer and concepts more precise and clearer by specifying subcomponents or dimensions of a higher-order construct.

CREATING CONSTRUCTS

Social scientists sometimes invent or create variables for the purpose of building new theories. For example, in the 1960s and 1970s, Friedman and Rosenman (1974) created and popularized a personality variable called the Type A and Type B personality syndromes. These syndromes were thought to be risk factors for coronary heart disease. Type A individuals were described as impatient, time conscious, competitive, and as having difficulty relaxing; they are workaholics who are deadline oriented and who internalize stress. Type B individuals were patient, relaxed, and easygoing. There also was a Type AB profile, consisting of people who cannot be clearly categorized into the two types. The Type A versus Type B personality syndromes became the subject of considerable research in the health domain (Friedman, 1996).

Another example is the concept of emotional intelligence (Goleman, 1995; Salovey & Mayer, 1990). As noted earlier, considerable research has been conducted on the concept of intelligence and its ability to predict job and school performance. Intelligence tests are widely used to make placement decisions in schools and to make hiring decisions in organizations. Salovey and Mayer (1990) argued that traditional intelligence tests measure cognitive and problem-solving abilities, but that an equally important ability for success is "emotional intelligence." Emotional intelligence is the ability to monitor one's own and others' feelings and emotions, to discriminate among them, and to use this information to guide one's thinking and actions (Salovey & Grewal, 2005). The core features of emotional intelligence have been subject to hundreds of studies in the social sciences for decades. Salovey and Mayer grouped together some core areas of emotion research, "repackaged" them into a coherent whole, and gave them a provocative label. The result was a noteworthy advance in theoretical and empirical perspectives on emotions (Salovey & Grewal, 2005).

Social scientists use a variety of strategies for "creating" variables. One strategy is to translate an individual-level variable into a contextual-level variable. Using ethnicity as an example, researchers can characterize ethnicity (a characteristic of an individual) at higher contextual levels, such as the ethnic composition of a school that individuals attend, the ethnic composition of the neighborhood in which the schools are located, the ethnic composition of the city in which the neighborhoods are located, and the ethnic composition of the state within which the cities are located. You then can examine how these multiple levels of context, characterized in terms of ethnicity, impact the behavior of individuals or some other outcome. For example, how are the voting preferences of an individual influenced by the political composition of the neighborhood in which the person resides? As another example, you could assess a person's attitude toward smoking cigarettes; the average attitude toward smoking cigarettes of students in the school that a given student attends; the average attitude toward smoking cigarettes of people in the neighborhood where the schools are located; the average attitude toward smoking cigarettes of people in the city where the neighborhoods are located; and the average attitude toward smoking cigarettes of people in the state where the cities are located. You can then examine how these multiple levels of context impact the behavior of individuals. In short, you can describe a context in terms of an aggregation of any individual-level variable.

Another strategy sometimes used for creating variables is to reframe environmental or contextual variables to represent an individual's perceptions. Thus, rather than studying the characteristics of the family environment within which an individual resides, you might study how individuals *perceive* the family environment. Or instead of studying the characteristics of the organizational climate of a business, you might study how an individual *perceives* the organizational climate. Or instead of working with someone's actual social class, you might focus a theory on people's perceived social class. Theories contrasting "perceived" versus "actual" states of affairs are a rich source of scientific theorizing. As an example, Dittus and Jaccard (2000) studied the effects of mothers' disapproval of their child engaging in sexual intercourse on whether the child engaged in sexual intercourse in the next 12 months. Two variables were measured: the mother's actual disapproval of the adolescent engaging in sexual intercourse (as measured on the mother) and the child's perception of the mother's disapproval (as measured on the child). Dittus and Jaccard found only a modest correlation between perceived and actual maternal disapproval, suggesting that mothers were not doing a satisfactory job in conveying their expectations to their children. They also found that both variables were independently predictive of future sexual behavior, though the adolescent perceptions were a somewhat stronger predictor than the actual maternal attitudes.

As you build a theory, you might consider creating new constructs using the strategies described in this section.

AN EXAMPLE OF SPECIFYING CONCEPTUAL DEFINITIONS

It may be useful to consider an example of defining variables that uses some of the principles discussed in this chapter. Suppose we posit a simple theoretical relationship between biological sex (male versus female) and adolescent alcohol use. We might assert that there are sex differences in adolescent alcohol use, with males tending to drink more than females. The first step in our analysis is to consider in more depth the two variables we have specified and to clarify what we mean by each. One construct is biological sex. We might decide that the meaning of this variable is so obvious to the scientific community that we do not need to provide a formal definition of it. The meaning of some variables is consensually accepted by all, and it is not necessary to define every term you use. Note, however, that what is consensual in some research areas will not be consensual in other research areas. For example, the concept of biological sex is a highly controversial one for the Olympic Games. In this context, determining if someone is a male or a female involves complicated issues about genetics and hormone levels. Several years ago, a struggling male professional tennis player underwent a sex-change operation and then played in women's professional tournaments, to the loud objections of many that s/he was not really a female. For the purposes of our theory, however, we might assume that biological sex is a concept whose meaning has social consensus.

The variable of "adolescent alcohol use" is another matter. This is a somewhat abstract and fuzzy concept, and we need to be more explicit about what we mean by it. We first need to be explicit about what we mean by *adolescent* and to which adolescents we are referring. We might decide that we want to restrict our statements to early adolescents (middle-school-age youths) living in the United States. In terms of the behavior, we start by using the four behavioral elements identified earlier (action, target, setting, and time) and analyze the variable in terms of each element. What is the precise action on which we want to focus? Do we want to focus on acquiring alcohol, consuming alcohol, or both? For the adolescent population about whom we are theorizing, it is illegal to purchase alcohol, so gaining access to alcohol is not a trivial matter. We might decide to focus on the act of consumption and ignore issues of acquisition since, in the final analysis, it is consumption that truly interests us. In terms of the target of the behavior, the action is performed with respect to alcoholic beverages. Do we mean a specific type of alcoholic beverage—such as beer, wine, hard liquor, or mixed drinks—or do we want to generalize across all forms of alcoholic beverages? We might decide to theorize about the latter. In terms of the setting, do we care about the particular setting in which alcohol consumption occurs (e.g., drinking alone or drinking with other people), or do we want to generalize or aggregate across settings? We might decide to pursue the latter. In terms of a time frame, over what period of time do we want to examine alcohol consumption? Should it be over the past day, during the past week, during the past month, during the past year, or during one's lifetime? Suppose we decide to focus on "current" behavioral tendencies with respect to alcohol consumption and decide that alcohol use during the past 30 days provides us with a good sense of a person's current drinking habits and orientations. The decision to focus on a 30-day interval is not an arbitrary one, but instead is based on the existing literature on alcohol use, which we do not elaborate upon here.

As we think more about quantifying the alcohol variable, we realize we can actually examine two facets of it. First, people can differ in terms of the number of drinking episodes they have had in the last 30 days. Second, they can differ in how much alcohol they consume during a given episode. This might lead us to distinguish between three dimensions of alcohol use: (1) the frequency of drinking alcohol, (2) the amount of alcohol consumed at each drinking episode, and (3) the total amount of alcohol consumed (obtained by weighting the number of episodes by the quantity consumed at each episode). We do not consider here the methodological challenges that confront researchers in measuring these dimensions. We only note that they are theoretically distinct constructs that represent somewhat different dimensions of alcohol use.

There is yet another dimension of alcohol use we might consider, and that is getting drunk. Some people consume alcohol but never get drunk because they drink in moderation. Others get drunk and, indeed, go out drinking with the explicit intention of getting drunk. The alcohol literature often refers the latter scenario as "binge drinking."

So, instead of simply theorizing about drinking frequency and the quantity of drinks per episode, we might also decide to focus on the number of times an individual became drunk in the past 30 days.

Sometimes, even though they may get drunk, people drink without incident. At other times, people drink too much and get into trouble as a consequence. A person might engage in unprotected sex because he or she is drunk. A person might destroy property or commit vandalism while drunk. A student might skip a class the next day because of a hangover and miss an exam. Yet another possible dimension on which we could focus is that of the experience of negative problems as a result of drinking.

It is possible that sex differences exist with respect to all of these dimensions, or there may be sex differences on just some of them. Do males tend to drink more often than females? Do males tend to drink more on a given drinking episode than females? Across all episodes of drinking, do males drink more alcohol than females? Do males get drunk more often than females? Are males more likely to get into trouble because of their drinking than females? Our fairly simple theory about sex differences in alcohol use has become more elaborated as we refine and critically think about the construct of "alcohol use." Note that we are not obligated to focus our theorizing on all these dimensions. We may choose to focus on all of them or only a subset of them. But it helps in the theory construction process to think through our constructs and then to consciously make choices about where to focus our efforts.

OPERATIONISM

We close this chapter with an important historical note concerning a psychometric controversy that existed in certain areas of the social sciences and that has implications for how we define concepts. Conceptual definitions specify *what* needs to be assessed in empirical science, but the matter of *how* they will be assessed is a distinct issue. This latter function is served by what scientists refer to as *operational definitions*, which are central to the design of empirical tests of a theory. The process of developing an operational definition begins with consideration of the conceptual definition to which it is addressed. The investigator then devotes serious thought to the kinds of operations and procedures that might be employed to provide a satisfactory indication of the concept in question. Consider the notion of "hunger." Conceptually, it can be defined as a craving or need for food or a specific nutrient. In operationalizing "hunger," psychologists have (1) asked people to respond to questionnaire items regarding their degree of perceived hunger; (2) deprived individuals of food for differing amounts of time so as to create more hunger in some than in others (e.g., people deprived for 24 hours must surely be hungrier than those deprived for only 2 hours); (3) measured the amount of food consumed from a standard portion given to each study participant (e.g., 2 pounds of spaghetti), under the assumption that the more a participant consumes (adjusted by body weight and metabolism), the hungrier he or she is; and (4) measured the amount of adversity the person will go through to obtain food. All of these seem to be reasonable procedures for measuring, that is, "operationalizing," hunger.

Unlike conceptual definitions, which often prove difficult to pin down, operational definitions are more concrete and thereby suggest a greater degree of precision and rigor. For this reason, there was a period when many behavioral scientists felt we should abandon conceptual definitions and restrict science to observable operations. This approach was called *operationism*. As examples, some theorists argued that "intelligence tests were what measured intelligence, and intelligence was that which was being measured by intelligence tests" (Bohrnstedt, 1970, p. 84). As another example, instead of considering six purchases of Brand X in a row to be an *indicator* of brand loyalty in consumer psychology, investigators in marketing considered this *to be* brand loyalty itself. In this way, the concept has no identity separate from the instruments or procedures being used to measure it (Jacoby & Chestnut, 1978).

One frequently cited problem with operationism is that if the concept being measured is synonymous with the measurement procedures being used, then even minute changes in method would produce a new concept. The result would be a proliferation of definitions that would lead to confusion and an inability to communicate effectively regarding the concept. "When this occurs, generalizations involving the construct are impossible to make since there is really no single construct under investigation but, instead, a multitude of constructs" (Bohrnstedt, 1970, pp. 94–95). Strict adherence to operationism "means that both the results of an [investigation] and the conclusions the investigators derived from it can never transcend the methodology employed" (Chaplin & Krawiec, 1960, p. 4). Thus, our ability to generalize beyond any investigation is completely abridged. As a consequence of such problems, the physical sciences long ago discarded the approach of defining phenomena strictly in terms of their operations, and the behavioral sciences have since followed suit.

SUMMARY AND CONCLUDING COMMENTS

The process of instantiation involves delimiting and more narrowly defining the concepts developed during theorization. This process of clarifying concepts removes ambiguities and clarifies what is meant by the construct in question. A major weakness occurs in a theory if it relies on concepts that are so abstract that it is hard to know what the theorist truly means by them (e.g., a statement such as "personality influences behavior"). The hallmark of a good theory is one in which the concepts are clearly defined and where the theorist provides clear-cut examples of the constructs as he or she moves toward more precise instantiations of them.

Sometimes the same concept is defined differently in different theories. The extent to which conceptual definitions overlap is referred to as the shared meaning of a construct; those portions of conceptual definitions that do not overlap across theories are referred to as surplus meaning. Although it is desirable for constructs to have shared versus surplus meaning, the worth and meaning of a construct ultimately are judged relative to the broader nomological network in which the construct is embedded.

Many strategies can be used to make abstract concepts more precise and to clarify the meaning of your concepts. These include consulting past literature, using a dictionary, specifying key properties, continually posing and answering the question "What do you mean by that?", placing yourself in the role of a journalist to explain the nature of the variable to the public, placing yourself in the position of having to define and explain the concept to someone who is just learning the English language, and thinking about exactly how the construct in question would be measured in a scientific study. Another strategy is to define subcategories or subdimensions of a construct and then to clearly define and articulate those. It is not enough to simply provide an example of your concepts. Rather, you must clearly define them.

The present chapter has provided perspectives on how to focus and develop conceptual definitions. The next chapter addresses how to focus and develop relationships between constructs using the tool of thought experiments.

SUGGESTED READINGS

Headland, T., Pike, K., & Harris, M. (1990). *Emics and etics: The insider/outsider debate.* Newbury Park, CA: SAGE.

—A debate about, and discussion of, etic–emic approaches.

MacCorquodale, K., & Meehl, P. (1948). On a distinction between hypothetical constructs and intervening variables. *Psychological Review, 55,* 95–107.

—A classic article on types of variables.

Nunnally, J., & Bernstein, I. (1994). *Psychometric theory.* New York: McGraw-Hill.

— A classic study of psychometrics, including a discussion of the importance of conceptual definitions.

Podsakoff, P., MacKenzie, S., & Podsakoff, N. (2016). Recommendations for creating better concept definitions in the organizational, behavioral, and social sciences. *Organizational Research Methods, 19,* 159–203.

—An insightful article on formulating conceptual definitions that elaborates on many of the ideas in the current chapter.

Theory and Psychology, February 2001, Volume 11.

—A special issue containing numerous articles debating operationism.

KEY TERMS

instantiation (p. 96)

hypothesis (p. 96)

focal problem statement (p. 97)

conceptual definition (p. 97)

shared meaning (p. 98)

surplus meaning (p. 98)

nomological network (p. 99)

properties (p. 101)

multidimensional constructs (p. 103)

operational definition (p. 107)

operationism (p. 108)

EXERCISES

Exercises to Reinforce Concepts

1. What are the major functions of instantiation—that is, why do scientists use it?

2. How is instantiation similar to stating a hypothesis or a focal problem statement?

3. What is the difference between shared meaning and surplus meaning?

4. Describe the major strategies for making a fuzzy concept less fuzzy.

5. What is the difference between an operational definition and a conceptual definition?

6. What are the primary objections to operationism?

Exercises to Apply Concepts

1. Choose a concept, provide a conceptual definition of it, and then describe the process you used to create the conceptual definition.

2. Find an example in the research literature of a construct with a fuzzy conceptual definition and provide a clearer definition.

6

Thought Experiments for Variable Relationships

It is sometimes important for science to know how to forget the things she is surest of.
—JEAN ROSTAND (1958)

Albert Einstein (1956) recounted a thought experiment he engaged in as a young man that involved him chasing a beam of light. When he caught up to it, traveling alongside it at the same speed, he envisioned the beam appearing stationary or at rest, though spatially oscillating. How, he wondered, could we know whether we are in a fast uniform motion with another object or truly stationary? Einstein had the insight that nothing in the theory of electromagnetism of the day (the theory of James Maxwell) could account for this phenomenon, so he began to address the paradox formally and mathematically. Einstein's thought experiment became the seed for his revolutionary theory of relativity.

Thought experiments have a rich history in the social, physical, and biological sciences. They have been used in philosophy for decades to clarify philosophical logic and moral dilemmas and by numerous physical scientists, from Galileo to Einstein. *Thought experiments* typically are based on "what if" questions that are framed in order to spark new ways of thinking by combining imagination with analytic thought. Many great inventions undoubtedly have started with a "what if" question (e.g., What if we could get the internet onto a phone? What if we could make cars that drive themselves?).

Counterfactual thinking is a type of thought experiment that we briefly introduced in Chapter 4. Although definitions vary (Starr, 2019), the most common one is that counterfactuals are subjunctive conditionals in which the antecedents of an event are assumed to be known but for purposes of argument are assumed to be false. Counterfactuals usually take the form of a declarative statement or thesis that is to be pondered, such as "If men could become pregnant, then a male birth control pill would be readily available." However, they also are sometimes stated in open-ended ways, such as "What would society be like if men could become pregnant?" Counterfactual thinking is a form of human cognition that all of us engage in, even as children. After experiencing a traumatic event, for example, we might think about what might have happened if we had done something different. Counterfactual thinking involves the ability to think about possible alternatives to events that have occurred, contrary to what actually happened. It is often useful in theory construction to posit counterfactuals for the problem at hand and then conduct an in-depth analysis of it to arrive at new theoretical insights.

Thought experiments, however, are not restricted to counterfactuals. They can be much more elaborate, often taking the form of rich narratives describing sequences of events in more or less elaborated contexts (Nersessian, 2008). The person conducting the thought experiment (the "experimenter") creates the narrative in a way that focuses attention on critical features of the problem. Some realties are suspended (e.g., the fact that a human could never run at the speed of light) but others are maintained. The "experimenter" essentially constructs a mental model of the events in the imagined experiment and then seeks to make inferences about them based on manipulating one or more of the events within that mental model. The thought experiment might provide the "experimenter" access to previously unnoticed consequences or newly apparent details that then result in new insights into the problem. Thought experiments often change over time, with the "experimenter" elaborating upon or streamlining them as his or her thinking evolves, with increased attention being directed toward selected problem facets.

Thought experiments require the ability to imagine, anticipate, visualize, and bring forth detailed memories of prior events into working memory (Nersessian, 2008). The ability to extract principles from the thought experiment also is critical, that is, being able to think abstractly about the specifics of what happens in the experiment.[1] "Experimenters" often must make use of detailed knowledge of the substantive domain to create the thought experiment, but then they rely on their ability to abstract principles from it. Analogies are common in thought experiments, so analogic reasoning skills also are key. Thought experiments do not always lead to problem solutions; instead, they may point to new problems in need of solutions. Box 4.1 on pages 60–61 illustrates an interesting thought experiment, namely, pretending to be a complete outsider but then describing one's own cultural habitat from that perspective.

The thought experiments we consider in this chapter are much narrower in scope, more concrete, and easier to apply than those of Einstein, Galileo, and other famous scientists. Nevertheless, they serve an important function that complements Chapter 5. Chapter 5 provided you with heuristics to help gain clarity about conceptual definitions. Theories often specify relationships between concepts. Just as the concepts in a theory must be clear, so too must theoretical propositions about their presumed relationships. The thought experiments described in this chapter are designed to help you think through relationships you think exist between variables and to develop well-articulated theoretical propositions for those relationships.

We begin by considering the use of thought experiments in emergent theorizing and the variable-centered nature of the thought experiments we present. Next, we make distinctions between different types of variables that are important for conducting the thought experiments. We then describe thought experiments for deriving propositions

---

[1]Concrete thinkers have difficulty moving beyond the facts of the here and now. Abstract thinkers can generalize beyond them. A concrete thinker can think about a particular cat; an abstract thinker can think about cats in general.

about relationships between two variables, considering first the case of the relationship between two nominal variables, next two quantitative variables, and then between a nominal and a quantitative variable. Finally, we introduce the concept of moderated relationships and describe thought experiments for them.

THOUGHT EXPERIMENTS FOR RELATIONSHIPS IN GROUNDED AND EMERGENT THEORY

Grounded theorists typically emphasize the emergent nature of theory, being careful not to impose a priori schemas onto phenomena but instead letting theoretical concepts and relationships between concepts emerge from collected qualitative data. The idea of conducting a thought experiment might seem anathema to this approach, but this is not necessarily the case. Many qualitative theorists believe it is important to read relevant literatures and think in depth about the phenomena they intend to study prior to data collection, even formulating hypotheses about what they might hear and observe. Grounded theorists do not enter a study as tabula rasas. To be sure, they believe it is critical not to let their preconceptions bias their data, but they also believe that prior knowledge and thought can help guide question formulation in ways that ultimately facilitate effective theory construction. When collecting data, it is not uncommon for grounded theorists to explore issues with interviewees in unstructured, open-ended ways at first but then at some point in the same interviews pursue questions in more structured ways in order to probe specific ways the respondents might be thinking about matters. Engaging in thought experiments prior to data collection can assist this latter process and sensitize the theorist to forms of questioning that may be useful during the more structured phases of interviewing.

To provide an example, suppose a qualitative researcher plans to explore the consequences of depression for middle school students by interviewing students, parents, teachers, and school counselors. One such consequence the researcher might anticipate hearing about is the negative effects of depression on performance in school. Applying the thought experiment strategies discussed in this chapter, the researcher may realize that the relationship between depression and negative school performance could be complex and take on one of several different functional forms. For example, one possibility is that relationship is linear: as depression increases, school performance decreases. Another possibility is that lower levels of depression have minimal impact on school performance up to a certain threshold point, after which depression begins to negatively impact performance. Having identified the possibility of this threshold function in thought experiments, the researcher might explore its possibility with interviewees during the structured phases of the interview that will reveal its existence if it is present. In addition, when analyzing the data, the researcher might be sensitive to statements that imply the existence of the threshold dynamics. Again, the researcher is careful to ensure interviewees describe their own construals, perceptions, and feelings, but when analyzing data and structuring follow-up questions, having some awareness of plausible, meaningful relationship functions is useful.

Yet another perspective on the relevance of thought experiments to qualitative research is that many emergent theorists formulate formal hypotheses prior to data collection about relationships they think they will find between variables in their data. The thought experiments described in this chapter can help them think through these hypotheses. To be sure, some grounded theorists eschew the formulation of a priori hypotheses, but others argue that after carefully considering relevant literatures and based on prior experience with a population, it is not unreasonable to formulate expectations about what one might find when addressing a problem or question.

Some grounded theorists prefer process-oriented rather than variable-oriented explanations, such as describing how individuals or entities get from point A to point B. For example, an emergent theorist might articulate the process or steps an organization goes through in moving from a small, fledging start-up company to a large, successful corporation. This is a different mindset than that of describing relationships between variables. Although useful, we believe that even process-focused theorizing often draws on variable-centered frameworks. For example, in a process analysis of government oversight of environmental regulations, a theorist might describe organizational decision processes moving from the initial stage of problem recognition, where an environmental problem created by, say, manufacturing plants is identified, to the final stage of solution implementation, detailing intermediate steps, such as (1) identifying the goals of the oversight agency with respect to the problem, (2) defining possible solutions to the problem, (3) gathering information about the possible solutions, (4) evaluating the different solutions in terms of their advantages and disadvantages, and (5) making a choice as to which solution to implement. A variable-centered orientation might come into play as theorists realize that at a given point in the process, there are variations in how officials behave. For example, some officials who recognize a problem may immediately jump into action to address it, whereas other officials may procrastinate before addressing it. The theorist may wonder why this is the case. What makes some officials procrastinate but other officials not? This question and plausible answers to it fall in the realm of variable-oriented explanations.

Whether theorists identify their approaches as emergent or confirmatory, use methods that are qualitative or quantitative, write their theoretical prose in narrative or mathematical form, or identify their primary orientation to explanation as process- or variable-centered, the fact is that most theories inevitably engage in some degree of variable-oriented analysis of relationships. As such, the thought experiments described in this chapter might be helpful.

DESCRIBING RELATIONSHIPS
WITH DIFFERENT TYPES OF VARIABLES

The way you characterize a presumed relationship between two variables in our thought experiment strategies differs depending on the type of variables involved. An important distinction is whether a variable is nominal or quantitative. A *nominal variable* has different levels, values, or categories, but there is no special ordering to the categories on an underlying dimension. For example, biological sex is a nominal variable that is often treated as having two values or levels, male and female. Religious affiliation is a nominal variable that has the categories Catholic, Protestant, Jewish, Muslim, and so on. The categories are merely labels that differentiate one group from another. Other terms used to refer to a nominal variable are *qualitative variable* and *categorical variable*.

In contrast, a *quantitative variable* is one in which individuals are assigned numerical values to place them into different categories, and the numerical values have meaning in that they imply more or less of an underlying dimension that is of theoretical interest. For example, married couples can be classified into the number of children they have, with some couples having a score of 0, some a score of 1, others a score of 2, and so on. There are different types of quantitative variables (e.g., discrete vs. continuous) and measures of them (e.g., ordinal vs. interval), but the distinctions between them are not critical for our purposes.

It is not necessary to adopt causal thinking to describe relationships, but it is easier to explain the heuristics if we do. More generally, we use a "possible outcomes" approach by Rubin (2005). This approach identifies a presumed cause, X, and a presumed effect, Y, and then asks the "experimenter" (the person doing the thought experiment) to specify what the typical value of Y is when X takes on the value x. For example, if Y is annual income, X is a dichotomous variable about education, and x can be either the values "completed high school" or "did not complete high school," we might seek to specify what the typical (e.g., average) income is when education equals "completed high school" and what it is when education equals "did not complete high school." A theoretical proposition is then derived from this information.

THOUGHT EXPERIMENTS FOR RELATIONSHIPS BETWEEN NOMINAL VARIABLES

Nominal Variables with Two Levels

We begin with a simplistic example to illustrate the general setup of our thought experiments. Later in this chapter, we describe how to derive theoretical propositions from them. Consider gender and political party identification, where gender has the values "male" and "female" and political party identification has the values "Democrat" and "Republican." You believe there may be a relationship between these variables and you decide to use a thought experiment to explore this. You imagine you are able to interview groups of males and females, some of whom are Democrats and some of whom are Republicans. Suppose you intuit that gender impacts political party identification such that females are more likely than males to be Democrats and males are more likely than females to be Republicans. We can translate this belief into the results the thought experiment would yield to articulate it in more depth. First, you construct a two-way table of frequencies, also called a *hypothetical contingency table*. Conceptualize a hypothetical group of 100 females and 100 males and create a hypothetical contingency table for the two variables that looks like this:

	Democrat	Republican	Total
Females			100
Males			100

The "cause" is written as rows, and the "effect" is written as columns. Next, fill in the blank cells of the table with frequencies that reflect your intuition. That is, make up numbers that represent the frequencies you think you would observe in your "experiment" and write them in the table so that they conform to your intuition, knowing the rows must sum to 100. To illustrate, suppose we filled in the table as follows:

	Democrat	Republican	Total
Females	70	30	100
Males	30	70	100

Look at the row for females. It shows that 70 of the 100 females are Democrats and 30 of the females are Republicans. Note that this is the same as saying that 70% of the females are Democrats and 30% of the females are Republican because the total number of females equals 100. Examining the row for the males, we see that 30% of them are Democrats and 70% are Republicans. Shifting our focus to the columns, we see that "females are more likely than males to be Democrats" (because 70% of females are Democrats, but only 30% of the males are) and "males are more likely than females to be Republicans" (because 70% of the males are Republican, but only 30% of the females are). From this data, we create a theoretical proposition: Females are more likely than males to be Democrats and males are more likely than females to be Republicans. The hypothetical contingency table makes the theoretical statement concrete.

Note that, instead of the 70% and 30% figures, we could have captured the same dynamic with a different set of numbers:

	Democrat	Republican	Total
Females	51	49	100
Males	49	51	100

It is still the case in this table that females are more likely than males to be Democrats (51% vs. 49%) and that males are more likely than females to be Republicans (51% vs. 49%). However, the relationship between gender and political party identification is much weaker than before.

Yet another set of numbers that captures the theoretical statement is this one:

	Democrat	Republican	Total
Females	95	5	100
Males	5	95	100

For this table, the effect of gender on political party identification is extremely strong because virtually all females are Democrats and virtually no males are Democrats, and vice versa, for Republicans. In terms of what you theorize, does this seem reasonable to you?

When developing a theory that posits a relationship between two nominal variables, we believe it is instructive to pursue thought experiments with hypothetical contingency tables because it forces you to think through your logic as you try to derive and assign numbers to the cells. It also will give you a sense of how strong you expect the relationship to be. We realize that the numbers that you insert will be somewhat arbitrary and that, at times, you may have little basis for positing a small effect, a medium effect, or a large effect. Nevertheless, we have found it useful at this stage of theory construction to fill out the table and commit to tentative numbers in order to force ourselves to think through the relationship via the numbers we assign. As you generate numbers and try to justify them to yourself, it may have the effect of making you think of things that might not otherwise have occurred to you.

To formalize this exercise, here are the steps you use to clarify the presumed relationship between two nominal variables:

1. Create a contingency table, listing the values of the "cause" as rows and the values of the "effect" as columns.

2. Think of 100 hypothetical people for each row of the table; that is, set the marginal frequency of each row to equal 100.

3. Of these 100 people, specify how many you think will fall into each column category; this represents the percentage of people in each category.

Of course, one would never present the hypothetical table nor describe the thought experiment in a research report. The hypothetical table is merely a heuristic device to help clarify your thinking.

Nominal Variables with More Than Two Levels

Sometimes the nominal variables you work with have more than two levels. You will still approach this situation using the hypothetical contingency table, but now the theory description becomes more complex. As an example, consider the relationship between religious affiliation and political party identification, each of which has three levels. Here is the relevant table:

	Democrat	Republican	Independent	Total
Catholic				100
Protestant				100
Jewish				100

And here are numerical entries we might generate:

	Democrat	Republican	Independent	Total
Catholic	50	25	25	100
Protestant	25	50	25	100
Jewish	50	25	25	100

From this table, we derive the following theoretical propositions:

Proposition 1: Catholics, Protestants, and Jews are equally likely to be Independents

Proposition 2: Protestants are more likely to be Republicans than either Catholics or Jews; Catholics and Jews are equally likely to be Republicans.

Proposition 3: Both Catholics and Jews are more likely than Protestants to be Democrats; Catholics and Jews are equally likely to be Democrats.

The strategy we used for stating the propositions was to focus on each column of the contingency table separately; then we stated what trends were apparent in the numbers we assigned within that column across the different row categories. For example, Proposition 1 focuses on the column for Independents, Proposition 2 focuses on the column for Republicans, and Proposition 3 focuses on the column for Democrats. Reread the propositions more carefully and take note of how we are making statements about row differences within each column. This is a useful strategy for deriving theoretical propositions from contingency tables.

In sum, a heuristic for specifying theoretical propositions about the relationship between two nominal variables is to conduct a thought experiment in which you construct a hypothetical contingency table and then complete cell frequencies. As you do so, articulate the rationale behind the assigned numbers and then derive the propositions using the described principles.

THOUGHT EXPERIMENTS FOR RELATIONSHIPS BETWEEN QUANTITATIVE VARIABLES

Instead of two nominal variables, the theoretical proposition you want to generate and the relationship you want to clarify might involve two quantitative variables. When this is the case, the thought experiment uses a graphical device called a *hypothetical scatterplot*.

Scatterplots

A *scatterplot* is a graph that plots scores or values on one variable, Y, as a function of scores or values on another variable, X. We first provide a sense of what a scatterplot is and then we show how to use it in a thought experiment to help clarify a relationship. Figure 6.1 presents a scatterplot using a simplistic but pedagogically convenient example relating the number of hours individuals work in a week to the amount of money they earn in that week. In this example, there are five individuals, each paid $5 an hour. Here are the data:

Individual	Hours worked	Amount earned
1	20	$100
2	22	$110
3	25	$125
4	23	$115
5	27	$135

The X values (the cause) are always plotted on the horizontal axis, and the Y values (the effect) are plotted on the vertical axis. Consider the first individual. We locate that individual's score on X (20) on the X-axis and then we also locate the individual's score on Y (100) on the Y-axis. We draw an imaginary line up from the located point on the X-axis and across from the located point on the Y-axis (as illustrated in Figure 6.2). We then draw a dot where the two lines intersect. We repeat this procedure for each individual, until the pairs of scores for all individuals have been plotted. The completed scatterplot is presented in Figure 6.1.

Note that there is a systematic relationship between the two variables: The more hours that someone works, the more money the person earns. If we connect the dots that demarcate each individual's pair of scores, we see a straight line, as in Figure 6.3. This is an example of what is called a *linear* relationship. It is rare in the social sciences

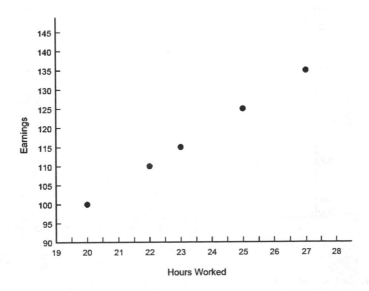

FIGURE 6.1. Scatterplot for earnings as a function of hours worked.

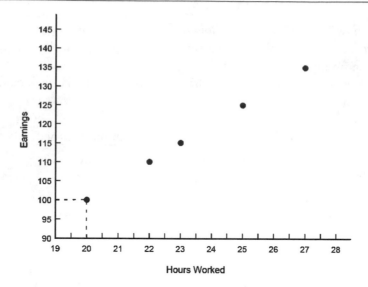

FIGURE 6.2. Scatterplot with dotted lines for earnings as a function of hours worked.

for two variables to have a perfect linear relationship, but sometimes they approximate linear relationships. Figure 6.4 presents a scatterplot showing height and weight for 15 individuals. You can see that the data approximate a linear relationship. We have drawn a line through the data on the scatterplot to emphasize this trend. If there was a perfect linear relationship between the variables, all the points would fall on a straight line. They do not in this case, but there is enough of an approximation that we can reasonably talk about the relationship as if it were linear.

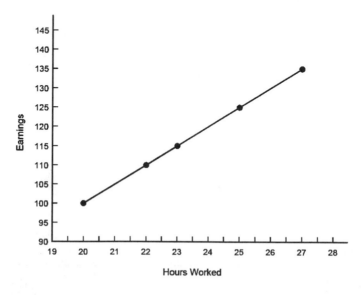

FIGURE 6.3. Scatterplot with dots connected for earnings as a function of hours worked.

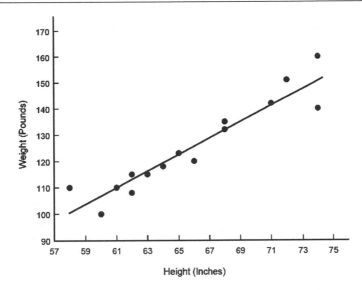

FIGURE 6.4. Scatterplot between height and weight.

Linear Relationships

Linear relationships can be of three types. First, there is a *direct linear relationship* where higher scores on X imply higher scores on Y. This is the case in Figures 6.1 and 6.4. Second, there is an *inverse linear relationship,* where higher scores on X imply lower scores on Y. This case is illustrated in Figure 6.5, which represents the relationship between people's satisfaction with their job and how many days of work they miss (not counting vacations and holidays) over a period of 12 months. The greater the degree of job satisfaction, the fewer the number of days missed. Another example of an inverse relationship is between the amount of exercise people engage in and the probability they will have an early heart attack. The more people exercise, the lower the probability that they will have an early heart attack. A *zero-slope linear relationship* is characterized by a flat line. It means that as X increases, Y is predicted to remain at the same value. Figure 6.6 provides an example of such a relationship. It plots the age of toddlers and how much their mothers say they love them, as rated on a scale from 1 to 5, with higher numbers indicating more love. No matter the age of the toddler, the mother's reported love does not differ.

When describing a relationship between two quantitative variables, theorists often do so with reference to a direct linear relationship, an inverse linear relationship, or a zero-slope relationship. Although we recognize that data seldom are perfectly linear in form, a shorthand heuristic for visualizing the relationship between two variables is to draw a line on a scatterplot that reflects either a direct linear relationship, an inverse linear relationship, or a zero-slope linear relationship, as has been done in Figures 6.7a, b, and c on page 123. The values of X and Y are not written on the axes; instead scores are

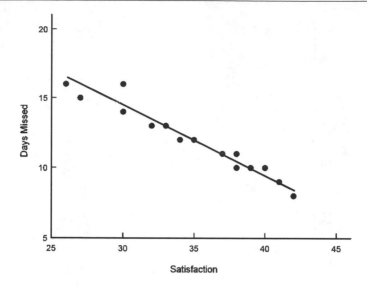

FIGURE 6.5. Example of an inverse linear relationship.

indicated as going from "low" to "high" (again, this is just a shorthand heuristic device). When drawing lines, the steeper you draw the slope of the line, the larger the effect of *X* on *Y*, everything else being equal. Figure 6.8 shows a case of two lines on the same graph that have different slopes, with line *A* reflecting a stronger effect than line *B* (assuming the scales for the two lines are on a common metric). A change in *X* for line *A* produces a greater change in *Y* than a comparable change in *X* for line *B*. These are examples of *shorthand hypothetical scatterplots*.

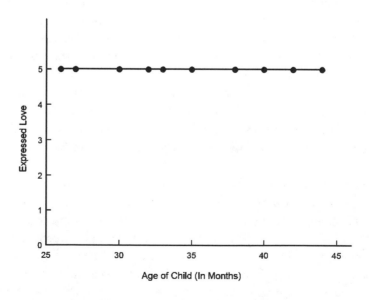

FIGURE 6.6. Example of a zero-slope relationship.

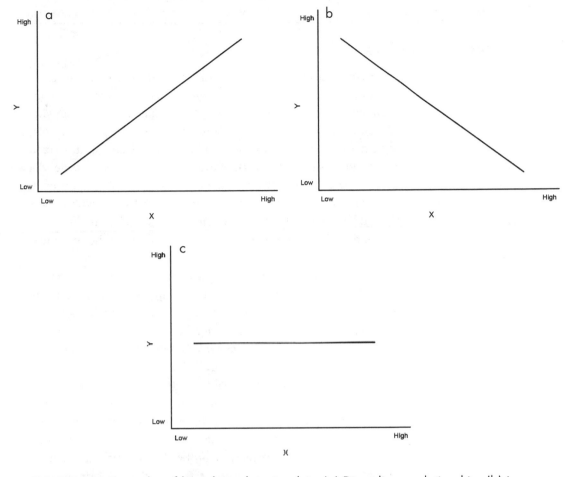

FIGURE 6.7. Examples of hypothetical scatterplots. (a) Direct linear relationship; (b) inverse linear relationship; (c) zero-slope relationship.

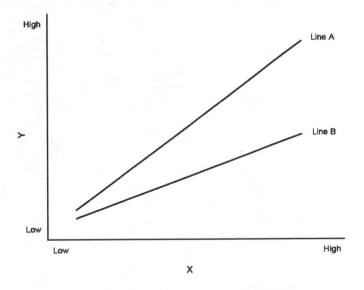

FIGURE 6.8. Example of lines with different slopes.

Nonlinear Relationships

Not all relationships between quantitative variables are linear; some are nonlinear. Consider the shorthand scatterplot in Figure 6.9. This is an example of a nonlinear relationship, called an *inverted-U-shaped relationship* (because it looks like a U drawn upside down). Some quantitative relationships between variables take this form. For example, levels of anxiety about taking a test and performance on that test are often characterized by an inverted-U function. The idea is that increasing anxiety at low levels of anxiety is good and facilitates test performance by increasing the person's attention and arousal. However, at some point, higher levels of anxiety get in the way and start causing the person to worry needlessly and become distracted from the task at hand. This response, in turn, degrades test performance. The result is an inverted-U relationship between test anxiety and test performance.

Figure 6.10 illustrates another common nonlinear relationship, sometimes referred to as an *S-shaped relationship*. At low levels of *X,* there is a *floor effect* such that changes in *X* have no impact on *Y.* Then at some point, increases in *X* begin to lead to increases in *Y.* This continues up to a point, when a *ceiling effect* kicks in, and further changes in *X* have no subsequent effect on *Y.* This type of curve probably better typifies the relationship between job satisfaction and the number of days of work missed rather than the simple linear relationship shown earlier. At very high levels of satisfaction, days of attendance probably "max out" and people simply cannot attend work more, even if they became more satisfied with their jobs. At very low levels of satisfaction, there probably is a point where the dissatisfied worker has missed as many days as he or she can miss without being fired, so yet lower levels of satisfaction probably "bottom out" at this point. Whereas a linear model assumes changes in satisfaction always lead to changes in the number of days missed, the S-shaped relationship posits floor and ceiling effects.

In addition to an S-shaped relationship, variables can reflect an inverse-S-shaped relationship, which is illustrated in Figure 6.11. This might characterize, for example,

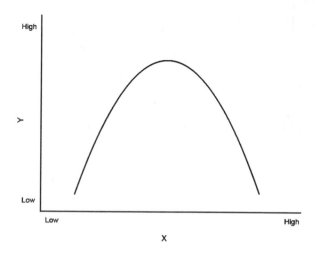

FIGURE 6.9. Example of inverted-U function.

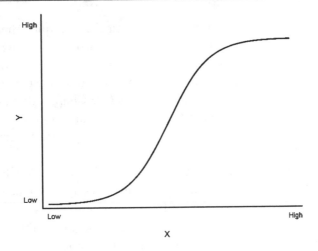

FIGURE 6.10. S-shaped function.

the relationship between age in the elderly and the ability to recall a list of words. Elderly people who are on the younger side are more likely to recall the list perfectly. As people get older, their ability to recall the list may start to decline until they reach an age where none of them can recall much of the list. Just as linear relationships can be direct or inverse, so can many forms of nonlinear relationships.

When Nonlinear Relationships Are Linear Relationships

Social scientists typically think in terms of linear relationships and posit and test their theories in ways that reflect this type of relationship. There are several reasons for this preference, some of which are defensible and others of which are not.

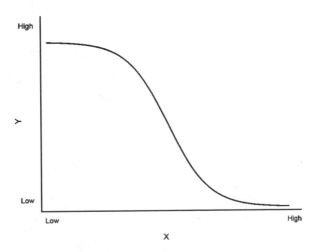

FIGURE 6.11. Inverse-S-shaped function.

One dubious reason is that a family of statistical techniques that assumes linear relationships, known as linear regression and correlation, enjoys widespread use by social scientists. Thus, theorists tend to think in terms of linear relationships because their statistical tools focus on linear relationships. Granted, linear regression methods can be adapted to focus on nonlinear relationships (see Chapter 8), but by far the most common use of regression methods is to test for, and impose, linear relationships on data. Theorists have become too accustomed to thinking in these terms, and perhaps some nonlinear thinking is necessary.

A second reason that theorists tend to ignore nonlinear relationships stems from a general preference for parsimony. The idea is that even though the true function between *X* and *Y* might be nonlinear, the departures from linearity are not sufficient to care about, and it is easier and more parsimonious to describe relationships in linear terms. Examine, for example, the S-shaped relationship in Figure 6.12, onto which a linear relationship has been superimposed. Note that for both relationships, low scores on *X* are associated with low scores on *Y*, moderate scores on *X* are associated with moderate scores on *Y*, and high scores on *X* are associated with high scores on *Y*. Granted there are floor and ceiling effects operating, but, the argument goes, these are of minor consequence in terms of the bigger trends characterizing the relationship. This argument has some validity as long as the departures from linearity truly are inconsequential. If, however, one's theory focuses on the very low or very high values of *X*, then it may be critical to take the nonlinearity into account. For example, suppose there is an S-shaped relationship between self-esteem (*X*) and the depressive symptom of lethargy (*Y*). An intervention might be developed to raise the self-esteem of people with low self-esteem on the assumption that such changes will reduce lethargy. But instead it might be found that changes in self-esteem at the very low end of *X* have no effect on lethargy, given the S-shaped relationship. Because you assumed a linear relationship, you operated under the impression that changes in self-esteem will have a positive effect on the expression of lethargy, even for those with very low self-esteem. The result would be a waste of resources and people receiving an ineffective treatment.

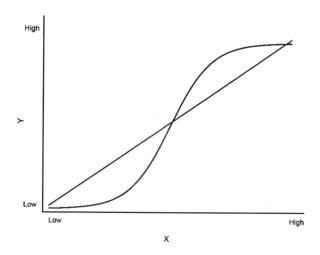

FIGURE 6.12. Linear and S-shaped functions.

A third reason that theorists ignore nonlinear relationships is based on *population partitioning*. Suppose that the true relationship between *X* and *Y* is S-shaped but that the theorist is focused only on a population whose *X* scores occur between the dotted lines in Figure 6.13. For these individuals, the relationship between *X* and *Y* is indeed linear. So it makes sense to theorize accordingly, as long as the theorist does not generalize beyond the *X* values studied.

A Thought Experiment with Hypothetical Scatterplots

If your focus is on a relationship between two quantitative variables, you can develop a theoretical proposition and "clarify the relationship" by drawing a shorthand hypothetical scatterplot for the two variables in the context of a thought experiment. Use linear functions if you think the relationship is linear and nonlinear functions if you think the relationship is nonlinear. Indicate and think through the size of the effect by how steeply you draw your slope. Common nonlinear relationships to consider include the U-shaped, inverted-U-shaped, J-shaped, inverted-J-shaped, S-shaped, and inverted-S-shaped relationships; a threshold function (where scores on *Y* are unchanged as *X* increases at low levels until a threshold point is reached and then a dramatic change in *Y* occurs at that threshold point); and various forms of logarithmic relationships (see Chapter 9). Figure 6.14 illustrates some of these relationships.

As you think about "shapes" of curves that could describe the relationship between your quantitative variables, make sure you can articulate the logic underlying why you think a particular function, and not others, operates. Sometimes you won't be sure about what the most reasonable curve is. You may be able to narrow it to a few possible curves (e.g., direct linear or an S-shaped relationship) but might be unable to choose between them on conceptual grounds. In this case, it is fine to use one of them as a "working assumption" and then develop your theory around it. The default "working assumption" usually is a linear function because of its parsimony and familiarity.

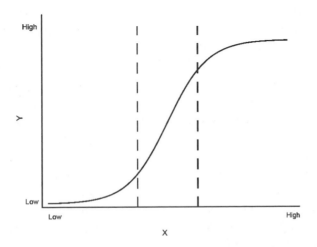

FIGURE 6.13. Focus on part of an S-shaped function.

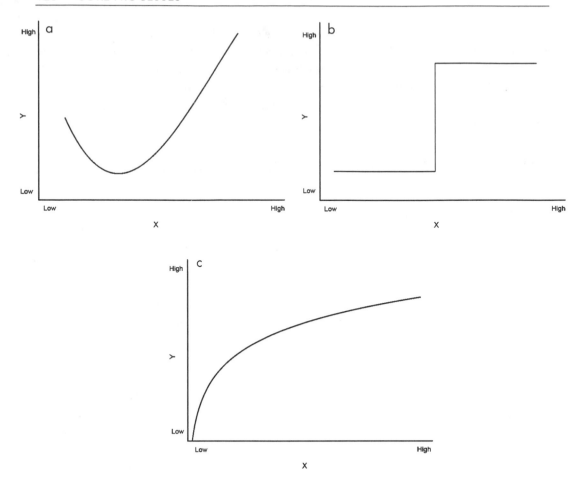

FIGURE 6.14. Additional examples of nonlinear functions. (a) J-shaped function; (b) threshold function; (c) logarithmic function.

When you describe your theory to others, you will need to describe the relationship you are positing. As with the hypothetical contingency table, you will not present the hypothetical scatterplot you used to focus the relationship and derive a proposition. Again, it is a heuristic device used in a thought experiment to help you think through and focus your thoughts. It is rare for social science theories to state a precise mathematical function as we have done here. Rather, they simply state relationships in somewhat loose terms, such as "higher scores on intelligence are associated with higher grade-point averages." To the extent possible, we think it is better to be explicit about the function, such as rephrasing the prior statement to read "higher scores on intelligence have a direct linear relationship with grade-point average." For nonlinear functions, after describing to your audience the logic for the bends or shifts in the curve, you might summarize your logic as follows, using Figure 6.9 as an example: "In sum, we propose that test anxiety has an inverted-U relationship to test performance: Increases in test anxiety at the lower end of the anxiety dimension enhance test performance up to a threshold point, after which increasing test anxiety leads to decreases in test performance."

As an aside, note that the function in Figure 6.9 as applied to test anxiety and performance is symmetrical about the threshold point at the top of the curve. Could there be asymmetry such that the increase in performance as a function of anxiety is less than the rate of decline with comparable increases in anxiety after the threshold point? What could explain such asymmetry? There are many intriguing possibilities in curve shapes, and it should be theoretically fruitful to explore such possibilities in thought experiments and the logic underlying each one. You might be surprised how much this simple exercise can stimulate new, alternative ideas.

In sum, when clarifying the relationship between two quantitative variables, you can do so by conducting a thought experiment for the variables that leads you to a shorthand hypothetical scatterplot. After drawing the scatterplot, state the relationship in narrative terms and articulate your underlying logic. Doing so will help you clearly explicate the form of the relationship.

THOUGHT EXPERIMENTS FOR RELATIONSHIPS BETWEEN NOMINAL AND QUANTITATIVE VARIABLES

When one of the variables is nominal and the other is quantitative, we suggest two different types of thought experiments to help focus the relationship: one using hypothetical means and the other using shorthand hypothetical scatterplots. The first approach is used when the "cause" is nominal and the "effect" is quantitative, and the second when the "cause" is quantitative and the "effect" is nominal. We consider each approach, in turn.

Thought Experiments for a Nominal Cause and a Quantitative Effect: The Use of Hypothetical Means

When a nominal variable is the cause and a quantitative variable is the effect, the thought experiment we recommend uses a *hypothetical table of means*. First, we consider a simple case where the logic is straightforward. Suppose you intuit that high school teachers at private schools have larger annual salaries than high school teachers at public schools. Imagine you have access to the salaries of teachers in schools that are representative of the population you want to make statements about and that you can calculate the average salary of the teachers in the public schools and the average salary of teachers in the private schools. We might generate the following table of hypothetical means to reflect the "results" of our thought experiment:

	Mean Annual Income
Private	$45,000
Public	$40,000

where the "cause" is listed as rows and the hypothetical mean scores appear in the column. The proposed relationship is evident in this table, and although the exercise seems

BOX 6.1. Simpson's Paradox

Scientists have discovered an interesting phenomenon with respect to relationships between variables, called *Simpson's paradox*. This phenomenon refers to the reversal of the direction of an association when data from several groups are combined to form a single group. It is a surprising finding that shows that we must be careful when aggregating results across populations or studies to characterize relationships. Consider the following three scenarios, each of which illustrates the paradox:

Scenario 1

A study examined death rates from tuberculosis in two cities, Richmond, Virginia, and New York City, in 1910. It found the following:

1. The death rate for African Americans was lower in Richmond than in New York City.

2. The death rate for European Americans was lower in Richmond than in New York City.

3. Despite these two findings, the death rate for African Americans and European Americans combined was *higher* in Richmond than in New York City.

Scenario 2

Psychological researchers test two treatments for a mental illness in two separate clinical trials.

1. In trial number 1, treatment A cures 20% of its cases (40 out of 200) and treatment B cures 15% of its cases (30 out of 200). Treatment B has a lower cure rate than treatment A.

2. In trial number 2, treatment A cures 85% of its cases (85 out of 100) and treatment B cures 75% of its cases (300 out of 400). Treatment B again has a lower cure rate than treatment A.

3. Pooling data across the two trials, treatment A cured 45% of its cases (125 out of 300) and treatment B cured 55% of its cases (330 out of 600). So, treatment B has a higher cure rate than treatment A.

Scenario 3

Suppose a university is trying to discriminate in favor of women when hiring faculty to atone for past hiring bias. It advertises positions in Department A and in Department B and only in those departments.

(continued)

1. Five men apply for the positions in Department A and one is hired. Eight women apply and two are hired. The hiring rate for men is 20% and for women it is 25%. Department A thus has favored hiring women over men.

2. For Department B, eight men apply and six are hired, and five women apply and four are hired. The hiring rate for men is 75% and for women it is 80%. Department B also has favored hiring women over men.

3. If we pool the data across the university as a whole, 13 men and 13 women applied for jobs, and 7 men and 6 women were hired. The hiring rate for men is higher than the hiring rate for women.

Why does Simpson's paradox occur? Does it have something to do with the unequal sample sizes in the scenarios? The answer is, not really. For example, in Scenario 3, there were 13 male and 13 female applicants. Also, Department A had 13 applicants, as did Department B. Yet the paradox occurred. How about the fact that the sample sizes were small? This also is not the source of the paradox. If you multiply all the numbers by 1,000 in Scenario 3, the paradox still exists.

Simpson's paradox has a mathematical basis. For eight whole numbers, represented by the letters a, b, c, d, A, B, C, D, it is possible to have the following relationships:

$$a / b < A / B$$
$$c / d < C / D$$

and

$$(a + c) / (b + d) > (A + C) / (B + D)$$

which is what occurs in Simpson's paradox. For example:

$$1/5 < 2/8$$
$$6/8 < 4/5$$
$$\text{yet, } 7/13 > 6/13$$

Simpson's paradox emerges in the three scenarios because a subtle bias is operating, which we explicate using the hiring example in Scenario 3. In this example, more women are applying for jobs that are harder to get and more men are applying for jobs that are easier to get. For example, it is harder to be hired in Department A than in Department B, and more women are applying to Department A than to Department B. Simpson's paradox occurs between either of the two following

(continued)

extremes: (1) when slightly more women are applying for jobs that are much harder to get and/or (2) when many more women are applying for jobs that are slightly harder to get.

When social scientists aggregate across groups of people, they must be careful about the causal inferences they make, as Simpson's paradox illustrates. Simpson's paradox has implications for commonly used methods of research synthesis that aggregate findings across studies, such as the quantitative method of meta-analysis. For other interesting perspectives on Simpson's paradox, see Pearl and Mackenzie (2018).

mundane, it may still be of use because you must commit to an effect size and justify it. As well, just the act of doing the task could generate ideas and clarify your logic as you visualize the more general context. Later in this chapter, we consider hypothetical tables of means that are more complex.

As another example, consider a three-level nominal variable. For this example, the presumed cause is a person's religious affiliation, and the presumed effect is attitudes toward parental notification policies about adolescents seeking an abortion. As background, some states have passed laws stating that if an adolescent under the age of 18 seeks an abortion, then the clinic or hospital that is to perform the abortion must notify a parent or legal guardian. Some people support this policy whereas others oppose it. The attitude is a quantitative variable that ranges from unfavorable to favorable, but it has no natural metric. Whereas "annual salary" in our previous example could naturally be considered in units of dollars, what are the natural units for an attitude? The answer is that there are none. To deal with this problem, we can create arbitrary units ranging from 0 to 10, with 5 being a middle, neutral, or "moderate" attitude, numbers lower than 5 representing increasingly negative attitudes, and numbers greater than 5 representing increasingly positive attitudes. We now imagine an experiment in which we are able to interview large numbers of Catholics, Protestants, and Jews in our target population. We imagine we can determine each person's true attitude (on the 0 to 10 metric) and that we can calculate the average attitude for each groups. Here is the hypothetical table of means we developed:

	Attitude
Catholics	7.0
Protestants	5.0
Jews	4.0

The theoretical proposition that we can derive from this table is as follows:

> **Proposition:** Religious affiliation is associated with the attitude toward parental notification such that Catholics have, on average, more positive attitudes than Protestants who, in turn, have more positive attitudes, on average, than Jews.

As with the hypothetical contingency table method, the theoretical proposition is specified by focusing on the column of hypothetical means and then stating the trends in the assigned numbers across the different row categories.

Thought Experiments for a Quantitative Cause and Nominal Effect: The Use of Hypothetical Probabilities

Consider the theoretical proposition that the degree to which a person is liberal affects his or her political party identification. Political party identification is a nominal variable (e.g., Democrat vs. Republican), whereas liberalness is a quantitative variable that varies from low to high on an underlying continuum. When the cause is quantitative and the effect is categorical, different types of thought experiments can be used. A thought experiment format we have found helpful uses a combination of the hypothetical contingency table and the hypothetical scatterplot. We illustrate the approach using a two-level categorical variable.

For this thought experiment, we turn the nominal variable into a quantitative representation so that we can draw a hypothetical scatterplot between two "quantitative" variables. The X-axis of the scatterplot describes values of the "cause" or, in this case, liberalness. On the Y-axis, we plot the probability that people with a given liberalness score are Democrats. We imagine that we are able to interview a large number of people from the population of interest and to determine their true degree of liberalism. Needing to create a metric for liberalness, we decide to do so using a metric that ranges from 1 to 5, where individuals with a score of 5 are extremely liberal, individuals with a score of 4 are quite liberal, individuals with a score of 3 are moderately liberal, individuals with a score of 2 are slightly liberal, and individuals with a score of 1 are not at all liberal. We then create a hypothetical contingency table using the "cause" as rows and the "effect" as columns, much like our previous case with two categorical variables:

	Democrat	Republican	Total
Liberalness = 5			100
Liberalness = 4			100
Liberalness = 3			100
Liberalness = 2			100
Liberalness = 1			100

Next, we fill in the numbers that we think capture the relationship, just as we did in the contingency table method. For example, we might fill in the following numbers:

	Democrat	Republican	Total
Liberalness = 5	70	30	100
Liberalness = 4	60	40	100
Liberalness = 3	50	50	100
Liberalness = 2	40	60	100
Liberalness = 1	30	70	100

A cell entry reflects the percentage of people with a given liberalness score whom we think will be Democrats or Republicans. For example, we intuit that 70% of people who are extremely liberal will be Democrats and 30% will be Republican; of people who are quite liberal, we expect 60% to be Democrats and 40% to be liberal; and so on. Do you agree with these entries? Most of our colleagues felt that the disparities between being a Democrat versus being a Republican should be more extreme at the upper end of the liberalness metric; for a liberalness score of 5 ("extremely liberal"), our colleagues felt the values in the row should have been closer to 95 and 5 rather than 70 and 30. This ultimately led to rich discussions between us as to why (or why not) this should be the case. By sharing the thought experiment with colleagues, or by having colleagues do the experiment independently and then comparing and discussing entries, richer theories and ideas can evolve.

We next convert these percentages to probabilities by dividing entries by 100:

	Democrat	Republican
Liberalness = 5	.70	.30
Liberalness = 4	.60	.40
Liberalness = 3	.50	.50
Liberalness = 2	.40	.60
Liberalness = 1	.30	.70

We now arbitrarily select one column on which to focus; in this case it will be the Democrats. The choice is arbitrary because the probability for Democrats is the mirror image of the probability for Republicans. We next construct a scatterplot of the relationship (see Figure 6.15) between the liberalness scores and the probability of being a Democrat (using the entries in the Democrat column). Note that the relationship is direct and linear in form. But perhaps instead of direct linear, the relationship is nonlinear. Indeed, any number of the nonlinear relationships we discussed earlier could potentially apply (sometimes a more elaborated liberalness metric in the table might be needed in such cases, such as a 0 to 10 metric). The scatterplot in Figure 6.15 implies the following theoretical proposition:

Proposition: The probability of being a Democrat is a direct linear function of liberalness such that as liberalness increases, the probability of being a Democrat increases.

To use this heuristic device, you need not go through the somewhat laborious process of generating probabilities as we did to construct Figure 6.15. We did this for pedagogical reasons and to illustrate the benefit of sharing such tables with colleagues. Instead, all you need do is create a shorthand scatterplot that draws the function that you think relates the X variable to the "probability of being in category y" for the Y variable. When there are more than two categories for Y, you will need to describe the X and "probability of y" function for each Y category separately because it is only in the two-category case that the one set of probabilities (e.g., for Democrats) is the mirror image of the other set of probabilities (e.g., for Republicans). There are some mathematical nuances in such cases (e.g., outcome probabilities at a given X value must sum to 1.0), but consideration of these is beyond the scope of this book.

In sum, a tool that you can use for clarifying the relationship between a quantitative cause and a nominal effect and deriving theoretical propositions about relationships is a shorthand scatterplot wherein the nominal variable is recast using probability values. As with prior examples, grounded theorists can pursue such thought experiments before or after data have been collected to help them articulate in more precise ways the trends their qualitative data suggest or that are expected to occur in their data.

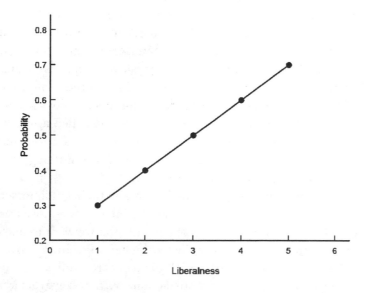

FIGURE 6.15. Liberalness example.

THOUGHT EXPERIMENTS FOR MODERATED RELATIONSHIPS

Thus far, we have considered thought experiments for clarifying, thinking about, and deriving theoretical propositions for bivariate relationships. There is another type of relationship that is important in theory construction, called a *moderated relationship*. Moderated relationships involve three variables and focus on cases where the strength or nature of a relationship between two variables changes depending on the value of a third variable. For example, we might theorize that inflation has a bigger influence on economies in underdeveloped countries as opposed to developed countries. Or we might theorize that higher levels of education are more likely to translate into job opportunities for Whites as opposed to Blacks. This section articulates the nature of moderated relationships and thought experiments you can use to clarify them. Moderated relationships are discussed in detail in Chapter 7.

Thought Experiments Using Hypothetical Factorial Designs

To work with moderated causal relationships, we rely on a thought experiment that uses a *hypothetical factorial design*. Begin the task by identifying the cause, effect, and moderator variable in your theory. Consider, as an example, the case where we examine how satisfied adolescents are with their relationships with their mothers as a function of gender. The outcome variable is the adolescent's relationship satisfaction with his or her mother (Y), and the presumed cause is gender (X). We introduce new terminology by referring to the presumed cause (gender) as the *focal independent variable,* a term often used in the literature on moderated relationships. We might intuit that girls will be more satisfied with their relationships with their mothers than boys will because girls have more in common with their mothers and are more likely to have similar interests to their mothers. However, we might also think this gender difference could vary as a function of the age of the adolescent (Z), namely, that adolescents start to grow apart from their mothers as they become older. This is truer for boys than for girls. For example, as boys and girls go through puberty and experience the physical changes associated with maturation, girls become more like their mothers physically and their interests may remain congruent with those of the mother as a result. By contrast, as boys become physically more mature, they drift away from their mothers. Age is called a *moderator variable* because it is thought to moderate the effect of gender on adolescent maternal relationship satisfaction. How might this dynamic be concretized in a thought experiment to formalize and think through a theoretical proposition?

To simplify, we represent the age of adolescents by their grade in school and use only two grade levels, seventh and eighth grade. We imagine we have access to a large number of youth who are representative of the population we want to make statements about. We imagine we are able to measure the true maternal relationship satisfaction for each adolescent on a metric from 0 to 10, with higher scores indicating higher levels of satisfaction and 5 representing moderate satisfaction. We first construct a factorial table in which we list the levels of the moderator variable as columns and levels of the focal independent variable as rows:

	Grade 7	Grade 8
Female		
Male		

Next, we imagine we are able to calculate mean values for our imagined population, and we fill in hypothetical mean scores for satisfaction with one's mother to reflect our intuition of what the typical score is for each group. We might think that girls in grade 7 are quite satisfied with their maternal relationship, so we assign an 8.0 to that cell. This satisfaction likely persists through eighth grade, so we also assign eighth-grade females an 8.0. Females are likely more satisfied with their maternal relationships than boys, we reason, so we assign a 7.0 for boys in the seventh grade. To account for boys drifting apart from their mothers as they get older, physically mature, and become more "other oriented," we assign a 6.0 to eighth-grade males. Here is the revised table with the numerical entries:

	Grade 7	Grade 8
Female	8.0	8.0
Male	7.0	6.0

Let's examine this table more closely. The gender difference for seventh graders is represented by the mean difference between females and males in the first column. This difference is

$$M_{F7} - M_{M7} = 8.0 - 7.0 = 1.0$$

where M_{F7} is the hypothetical mean for females in grade 7 and M_{M7} is the hypothetical mean for males in grade 7. We can calculate a similar gender difference for eighth graders:

$$M_{F8} - M_{M8} = 8.0 - 6.0 = 2.0$$

If the gender differences are the same at both grade levels, then the value for the first difference should be identical to the value of the second difference. But this is not the case, as seen by differencing the two differences:

$$IC = (M_{F7} - M_{M7}) - (M_{F7} - M_{M7})$$
$$= (8.0 - 7.0) - (8.0 - 6.0)$$
$$= 1.0 - 2.0 = -1.0$$

where IC stands for *interaction contrast*. We use this term because a moderated relationship maps onto an interaction effect in factorial designs. An interaction contrast in a factorial design compares the effect of a focal independent variable at one level of the moderator variable with the effect of the focal independent variable at another level of the moderator variable. The table on the previous page yields a nonzero interaction contrast value, so the numbers we entered imply a moderated relationship. The interaction contrast can be verbalized in the form of a theoretical proposition, as follows:

> **Proposition:** Gender differences in adolescent relationship satisfaction with their mothers during grade 8 are larger than gender differences in grade 7.

We find it useful to work through each cell of the factorial design and assign numerical mean values that we think seem reasonable. We then look to see if an interaction effect is evident in our ratings by formally calculating the interaction contrast value. If it is nonzero and judged to be large enough to be meaningful, we formulate a theoretical proposition accordingly. As in prior examples, we think about the magnitude of the effects we built into the table and discuss our "results" with colleagues to see if they agree or disagree with our entries. Grounded theorists might seek to clarify a moderated relationship using a thought experiment to the extent they hypothesize the possible presence of such a relationship or to the extent they think there is a reasonable chance a moderated relationship will manifest itself in the data. They generally would summarize such a result, however, in narrative form.

A simple way of capturing the numerical computations for an interaction contrast in a factorial table with two rows (the focal independent variable) and two columns (the moderator variable) is as follows:

	Grade 7	Grade 8
Female	a	c
Male	b	d

Then calculate $(a - b) - (c - d)$ to obtain the value of the interaction contrast. If this value is nonzero, then a moderated relationship is present. If the value is zero, there is no moderated relationship. Of interest is whether $(a - b)$ is smaller or larger than $(c - d)$ and by how much.

To formalize this strategy for clarifying moderated relationships:

1. Create a factorial table with the moderator variable as columns and the focal independent variable as rows.

2. Fill in plausible hypothetical mean values on the outcome variable for each cell of the table.

3. Calculate first the effect of the focal independent variable at each level of the moderator variable and then the interaction contrast to determine if there is a moderated relationship.

We now consider more complex moderator analysis.

Hypothetical Factorial Designs with More Than Two Levels

Sometimes your variables will have more than two levels. For example, suppose that instead of grades 7 and 8, we had grades 7, 8, and 9 in our population and performed our thought experiment with these three grade levels. Here is the table we would work with:

	Grade 7	Grade 8	Grade 9
Female			
Male			

We again go through the process of assigning outcome values to each cell of the design, thinking through each one and verbalizing our logic for one cell's number relative to those of the other cells. As we engage in this process, we invariably think thoroughly about the dynamics at play. Suppose we generate the following numbers:

	Grade 7	Grade 8	Grade 9
Female	8.0	8.0	8.0
Male	7.0	6.0	6.0

To concretize the moderated relationship in the table and to derive our theoretical propositions, we need to compare the gender difference in relationship satisfaction at all possible pairs of levels of the moderator variable. The easiest way to do this is to construct all possible 2 × 2 subtables from the larger table, including the assigned values in each table. In the current example, there are three 2 × 2 subtables. Here they are with the value of the 2 × 2 interaction contrast computed beneath each:

	Grade 7	Grade 8
Female	8.0	8.0
Male	7.0	6.0

$(8 - 7) - (8 - 6) = -1$

	Grade 7	Grade 9
Female	8.0	8.0
Male	7.0	6.0

$(8 - 7) - (8 - 6) = -1$

	Grade 8	Grade 9
Female	8.0	8.0
Male	6.0	6.0

$(8 - 6) - (8 - 6) = 0$

From this, we generate our theoretical propositions, one for each subtable:

Proposition 1: Gender differences in adolescent maternal relationship satisfaction during grade 8 are larger than the gender differences in grade 7.

Proposition 2: Gender differences in adolescent maternal relationship satisfaction during grade 9 are larger than the gender differences in grade 7.

Proposition 3: Gender differences in adolescent maternal relationship satisfaction during grades 8 and 9 are the same.

We, of course, would describe the conceptual logic model for each proposition when presenting them, elaborating them as appropriate.

For another example with more than two levels, consider the case where we want to evaluate the effect of dual ethnicity on expressions of depression. We conduct a thought experiment in which we imagine three groups of people living in the United States, people who are Black, people who are Latinx, and people who are both Black and Latinx, half of whom are males and half females. We imagine we can determine each person's true level of depression as reflected on a metric from 0 to 10, where 0 indicates no depressive symptoms, 3 some presence of depressive symptoms, 6 moderate presence of depressive symptoms, and 9 considerable presence of depressive symptoms. We conceptualize levels of depression (Y) as the outcome, the moderator variable as gender (Z), and the focal independent variable as ethnic identity. This yields the following table:

	Male	Female
Black		
Latinx		
Black and Latinx		

Here is the table with the values of hypothetical means that we felt were reasonable inserted into the cells:

	Male	Female
Black	3.0	4.0
Latinx	3.0	4.0
Black and Latinx	4.0	6.0

Here is some of the logic we used. First, we assumed that being Black or Latinx carries with it extra stressors due to discrimination and the challenges of being in a minority ethnic group in U.S. society. We further reasoned that being both Black and Latinx would create a "double stigma," thereby adding to depression. We also reasoned that females would show higher levels of depression than males, a common finding in prior research. Interestingly, when we showed the table to colleagues, some suggested that dual ethnicity might be protective rather than risk-inducing; that being able to draw on the strengths of two ethnic groups rather than one would lead to lower levels of depression. In short, our colleagues would have completed the table differently than we did. This difference, in turn, led to rich discussions of the underlying dynamics.

To develop theoretical propositions from the table, we again form all possible 2 × 2 tables (using the shorthand "Both" to refer to individuals who are Black and Latinx). Here are the tables:

	Male	Female
Black	3.0	4.0
Both	4.0	6.0

(3 − 4) − (4 − 6) = 1

	Male	Female
Latinx	3.0	4.0
Both	4.0	6.0

(3 − 4) − (4 − 6) = 1

	Male	Female
Black	3.0	4.0
Latinx	3.0	4.0

(3 − 3) − (4 − 4) = 0

If all of the interaction contrasts in the 2 × 2 subtables equal zero, then there is no moderated relationship. In this case, two of the three interaction contrasts are nonzero, so a moderated relationship exists. Here are the theoretical propositions that emerge from the tables:

Proposition 1: Being Black and Latinx as compared to just being Black has a larger detrimental effect on depression for females than for males.

Proposition 2: Being Black and Latinx as compared to just being Latinx has a larger detrimental effect on depression for females than for males.

Proposition 3: The effect of being Black versus being Latinx on depression is the same for both males and females.

Note that each proposition focuses on a different 2 × 2 subtable and its corresponding contrast.

Hypothetical Factorial Designs with Quantitative Variables

To focus a moderated relationship in which a quantitative variable is either the focal independent variable or the moderator variable, you still form a factorial table of hypothetical means, but now you might group the values of the quantitative variable into "high," "medium," and "low" categories. Consider the case where the moderator variable is the gender of the adolescent (Z), the focal independent variable is how much time a mother spends with her child (X), and the outcome variable is relationship satisfaction with the mother (Y). You might conjecture that the time spent with boys will not impact relationship satisfaction, but it will do so for girls. The presumed mechanism is that for girls, the more time the mother and daughter spend together, the more the daughter will identify with the mother, leading to a closer relationship. By contrast, boys will not identify with the mother as much, even with increased time together. The table with the hypothetical means (ranging from 0 to 10, with higher scores indicating higher satisfaction) appears as follows:

		Male	Female
	High	5.0	8.0
Time	Medium	5.0	7.0
	Low	5.0	6.0

You calculate all possible 2×2 subtables, as before. They are:

	Male	Female
High	5.0	8.0
Medium	5.0	7.0

$$(5 - 5) - (8 - 7) = -1$$

	Male	Female
High	5.0	8.0
Low	5.0	6.0

$$(5 - 5) - (8 - 6) = -2$$

	Male	Female
Medium	5.0	7.0
Low	5.0	6.0

$$(5 - 5) - (7 - 6) = -1$$

These tables lead to the following theoretical propositions:

Proposition 1: The effect of spending relatively large amounts of time together versus more moderate amounts of time together on relationship satisfaction is stronger for females than for males.

Proposition 2: The effect of spending relatively large amounts of time together versus small amounts of time together on relationship satisfaction is stronger for females than for males.

Proposition 3: The effect of spending relatively moderate amounts of time together versus small amounts of time together on relationship satisfaction is stronger for females than for males.

Each proposition describes in words the "results" of the interaction contrasts for each 2×2 subtable. As before, you elaborate the mechanisms underlying each proposition.

Hypothetical Scatterplots and Quantitative Variables

There is a different way of conceptualizing this example moderated relationship that takes advantage of the fact that both X and Y are quantitative variables. Specifically, we can draw a hypothetical scatterplot between them at selected levels of the moderator variable—in this case, one for our imagined males and one for our imagined females. This has been done in Figure 6.16. Note that although both relationships are linear, the line is steeper for females than it is for males, suggesting that the relationship between X and Y differs for the two groups. This relationship can be characterized in terms of a theoretical proposition as follows:

Proposition: The direct linear effect of time spent together on relationship satisfaction is stronger for females than for males.

In this case, the focus is on describing the differences in the slopes of the two scatterplots.

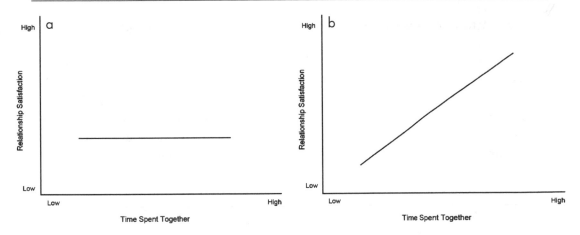

FIGURE 6.16. Hypothetical scatterplots for moderated relationship. (a) Males; (b) females.

Summary for Moderated Relationships

Moderated relationships involve scenarios where the strength or nature of a relationship between two variables varies as a function of a third (moderator) variable. One strategy for clarifying moderated relationships and forming theoretical propositions about them is to conduct a thought experiment that uses a hypothetical factorial design.

BROADER USES OF HYPOTHETICAL FACTORIAL DESIGNS IN THOUGHT EXPERIMENTS

Rosnow and Rosenthal (1989) suggest that certain kinds of questions consistently capture the interest of theorists when they are using factorial designs in their research. They refer to these questions as contrasts that are "conceptually wired in" to factorial designs. We describe these "wired in" contrasts/questions here in case you want to consider them in thought experiments that use hypothetical factorial designs. Perhaps they will lead to additional insights or theoretical angles you had not contemplated.

Suppose we want to evolve a theory about how the ethnicity of a person accused of a crime impacts guilt judgments about the accused by jurors of the same ethnicity versus jurors of a different ethnicity. Upon reflection, we might make up the following thought experiment: We first picture people who are serving as jurors for a robbery trial. The evidence against the defendant is implicative but the case is not "cut and dry." The defendant has an alibi, but the alibi has been provided by an untrustworthy friend. After the trial but before meeting in the jury room to deliberate, we are able to know each juror's initial judgment on the probability that the defendant is guilty. (Probabilities range from 0.00 to 1.00, with a zero meaning that the accused is "definitely not guilty," a 1.00 that the accused is "definitely guilty," and a 0.50 that it is "50–50" that the accused is guilty.) Suppose for the trial that the accused is Black for some of the jurors but European American for other jurors. That is, people participate in different trials that are identical in every respect (including the physical characteristics of the accused) except for the skin color of the defendant (black or white) and except for the fact that the defendant is formally identified as either African American or European American in the court paperwork that jurors see. Suppose further that some of the jurors in each trial are Black and others are European American. This thought experiment yields four different scenarios that constitute a 2 × 2 hypothetical factorial design in which the two factors are the ethnicity of the defendant and the ethnicity of the juror. Here is the operative table:

	Ethnicity of the Juror	
Ethnicity of the Accused	Black	European American
Black		
European American		

As part of the thought experiment, we intuit the average probability of the juror-judged likelihood of guilt for each cell. After much thought, we generate the following entries:

	Ethnicity of the Juror	
Ethnicity of the Accused	Black	European American
Black	0.50	0.75
European American	0.60	0.50

We now specify the "wired-in" contrasts identified by Rosnow and Rosenthal (1989). To illustrate these contrasts, we revise the table by adding marginal means to it, as follows:

	Ethnicity of the Juror		
Ethnicity of the Accused	Black	European American	Marginal
Black	0.50	0.75	0.62
European American	0.60	0.50	0.55
Marginal	0.55	0.62	

A marginal mean is the average of numbers in the respective row or column associated with that marginal mean. The marginal mean for Black jurors is (0.50 + 0.60)/2 = 0.55; the marginal mean for Black defendants is (0.50 + 0.75)/2 = 0.62; and so on.

Relationships Characterized by Main Effects

One set of questions that might be of interest focuses on the *main effects* in the factorial table, which reference the marginal means for each factor. For example, the main effect of juror ethnicity focuses on the marginal means for juror ethnicity. Looking at these means, we can posit that guilt judgments generally are more likely to be made by European American jurors than by Black jurors. From this, we formulate the theoretical proposition:

Proposition 1: In general, European American jurors are more likely to find a defendant guilty than Black jurors.

As we reflect on this proposition and the numbers we entered, we try to articulate the logic that might justify it. We then repeat this process examining the main effect for the second variable, in this case, ethnicity of the defendant. The marginal mean for Black defendants is 0.62 and for European American defendants, 0.55. This leads to our second proposition:

Proposition 2: In general, Black defendants are more likely to be found guilty than European American defendants.

Relationships Characterized by Simple Main Effects

The second class of comparisons described by Rosnow and Rosenthal (1989) is called *simple main effects.* The best way to conceptualize these types of effects is to assign one of the variables the role of the focal independent variable and the other the role of the moderator variable. For this example, we will use ethnicity of the defendant as the focal independent variable and ethnicity of the juror as the moderator variable. A simple main effect refers to the effect of the focal independent variable at a given level of the moderator variable. For example, looking at the factorial table, we see that for Black jurors, there is less of a chance that Black defendants are judged to be guilty (a probability of 0.50) than European American defendants (a probability of 0.60). For European American jurors, there is a greater chance that Black defendants are judged to be guilty (a probability of 0.75) than European American defendants (a probability of 0.50). These two simple main effects lead to the following propositions:

Proposition 3: For Black jurors, Black defendants are less likely to be found guilty than European American defendants.

Proposition 4: For European American jurors, European American defendants are less likely to be found guilty than Black defendants.

The theorist would then articulate the logic underlying each of these propositions separately.

Relationships Characterized by Interaction Contrasts

The final class of relationships described by Rosnow and Rosenthal (1989) is the interaction contrast. As already discussed, these contrasts compare the effects of the focal independent variable at one level of the moderator variable with the effects of the focal independent variable at another level of the moderator variable. The effect of defendant ethnicity on judgments of guilt for Black jurors is $0.50 - 0.60 = -0.10$ versus $0.75 - 0.50 = 0.25$ for European American jurors. The difference between these two effects is $-0.10 - 0.25 = -0.35$. Because this interaction contrast is nonzero, it suggests the presence of a moderated relationship. This leads us to our final theoretical proposition.

> **Proposition 5:** Defendant ethnic differences for Black jurors are smaller and in the opposite direction of defendant ethnic differences for European American jurors.

The logic underlying this proposition would then be developed.

In sum, if you create a thought experiment that represents a hypothetical factorial design, Rosnow and Rosenthal suggest that you consider main effects, simple main effects, and interaction contrasts as possible sources of theory development and specification. You need not consider all of them, but often each will be of substantive interest.

SUMMARY AND CONCLUDING COMMENTS

When constructing a theory, in addition to clearly articulating the constructs in that theory, you will want to articulate the (expected) relationships between constructs. Whereas Chapter 5 presented heuristics for focusing concepts, this chapter presented strategies for clarifying theoretical relationships in the form of thought experiments. These included the use of hypothetical contingency tables, hypothetical mean tables, shorthand hypothetical scatterplots, hypothetical probability scatterplots, and hypothetical factorial designs. The approaches we discussed are not exhaustive, and we illustrate others in later chapters. However, if you carefully scrutinize every relationship in your theory using thought experiments, and try to articulate the logic and reasoning underlying the proposed relationships, you will be that much further along in the process to conceiving a well-thought-out theoretical framework. This is true for both confirmatory and emergent-theory-oriented scientists.

SUGGESTED READINGS

Jaccard, J., & Becker, M. (2001). *Statistics for the behavioral sciences.* Belmont, CA: Wadsworth.
  —An introductory statistics text describing scatterplots, contingency tables, means, and factorial designs.

Nersessian, N. (2008). *Creating scientific concepts.* Cambridge, MA: MIT Press.
  —An interesting book on the nature and construction of thought experiments in the physical sciences.

Pearl, J., & Mackenzie, D. (2018). *The book of why*. New York: Basic Books.

—A discussion of relationships focusing on causality that includes a discussion of Simpson's paradox in Box 6.1 on page 130.

Starr, W. (2019). Counterfactuals. In *Stanford encyclopedia of philosophy*. Retrieved from *https://plato.stanford.edu/archives/spr2019/entries/counterfactuals*.

—A review of the role of counterfactuals in philosophy.

William, T. (2015). *Mind games: 25 thought experiments to ignite your imagination*. Zaze and Drury Publishing.

—A popular press book with examples of thought experiments. Though not science oriented, it will give you a sense of the spirit of "what if" thought experiments.

KEY TERMS

thought experiment (p. 111)

nominal variable (p. 114)

quantitative variable (p. 115)

hypothetical contingency table (p. 115)

scatterplot (p. 118)

direct linear relationship (p. 121)

Inverse linear relationship (p. 121)

zero-slope linear relationship (p. 121)

shorthand hypothetical scatterplot (p. 122)

inverted U-shaped relationship (p. 124)

S-shaped relationship (p. 124)

floor effect (p. 124)

ceiling effect (p. 124)

population partitioning (p. 127)

hypothetical table of means (p. 129)

hypothetical probabilities (p. 133)

moderated relationships (p. 136)

focal independent variable (p. 136)

moderator variable (p. 136)

interaction contrast (p. 137)

main effect (p. 144)

simple main effect (p. 145)

EXERCISES

Exercises to Reinforce Concepts

1. What is the difference between a categorical and a quantitative variable?

2. Describe the hypothetical contingency table approach to focusing the relationship between two categorical variables. Describe how you would derive theoretical propositions from the table.

3. Describe a scatterplot.

4. Describe the hypothetical scatterplot for focusing relationships between quantitative variables.

5. Draw a scatterplot that shows a positive direct linear relationship; draw one that shows an inverse linear relationship.

6. Draw a graph with two linear relationships on it, but one with a stronger effect as reflected by the slopes.

7. Describe how two variables that are nonlinearly related can exhibit a linear relationship.

8. What are some of the reasons why a theorist might prefer working with linear rather than nonlinear relationships?

9. Give an example of a moderated relationship.

Exercises to Apply Concepts

1. Conduct a thought experiment that describes a relationship between two quantitative variables of your choice. Derive relevant theoretical propositions from this experiment.

2. Conduct a thought experiment that describes a relationship between two qualitative variables of your choice. Derive relevant theoretical propositions from this experiment. Have a colleague or classmate do the same after describing the thought experiment to him or her. Compare your "results" and resolve the discrepancies.

3. Conduct a thought experiment that describes a relationship between a qualitative and a quantitative variable of your choice, using the hypothetical mean approach. Derive relevant theoretical propositions from this experiment. Have a colleague or classmate do the same after describing the thought experiment to him or her. Compare your "results" and resolve the discrepancies.

4. Conduct a thought experiment that describes a relationship between a qualitative and a quantitative variable of your choice, using hypothetical probabilities. Derive relevant theoretical propositions from this experiment. Have a colleague or classmate do the same after describing the thought experiment to him or her. Compare your "results" and resolve the discrepancies.

5. Conduct a thought experiment using a factorial table of hypothetical means with variables of your choice. Derive the full set of theoretical propositions corresponding to main effects, simple main effects, and interaction contrasts.

Part III

FRAMEWORKS FOR THEORY CONSTRUCTION

Causal Models

Every why hath a wherefore.
—WILLIAM SHAKESPEARE

Life is a perpetual instruction in cause and effect.
—RALPH WALDO EMERSON

Causal thinking, and the causal modeling that often goes with it, is probably the most prominent approach to theory construction in the social sciences.[1] In this framework, people or units (e.g., families, organizations) are conceptualized as varying on some construct. Theorists are interested in understanding what *causes* this variation. For example, people differ in how smart they are. The question is, "Why is this?" What *causes* variability in intelligence? People differ in how much money they make. Why is this? What *causes* variability in income? People differ in what they buy, how much they eat, for whom they vote, the organizations they join, and how much of themselves they devote to work. Why is this? What causes this variability? Causal thinking tries to explain variability by identifying its causes.

If something causes variability, then that something also varies. People differ in how smart they are, in part, because they are raised differently by their parents. In this case, variability in intelligence is due to variability in childrearing activities. People differ in how much money they make because they differ in how much education they have. Variability in income is due, in part, to variability in achieved education. Causal analysis identifies relationships between variables, with the idea that variation in one variable produces or causes variation in the other variable.

In addition to identifying causes of variables, causal analysis also specifies the "effects" of variables. Thus, a theorist might be interested in the consequences of being rich versus poor or the consequences of being stressed versus relaxed. Causal analysis takes many forms, but the essence of causal modeling is the focus on cause–effect relationships.

---

[1]We use the term *model* instead of *theory* because *model* is typically used in the scientific literature when referring to causal thinking.

In this chapter, we provide strategies for building a causal theory. We begin by identifying two types of relationships: (1) predictive or associational relationships that are unconcerned with causality and (2) causal relationships. We then discuss the nature of causality in general as well as the role of the concept of causality in grounded/emergent theories. Six types of relationships are identified that form the core of causal models in the social sciences: direct causes, indirect causes, moderated relationships, reciprocal causality, spurious effects, and unanalyzed relationships. Each of these relationships is then elaborated in the context of a 10-step approach to constructing a causal theory. After describing this approach, we describe a second strategy for building a causal theory, called the *binder approach*.

TWO TYPES OF RELATIONSHIPS: PREDICTIVE AND CAUSAL

Predictive Relationships

Predictive relationships focus on the question "Is variability in *A* related to variability in *B*?" Note that, at this level, the focus is on mere association; there need be no presumption or implication of causation, only that variations in *A* are related to variations in *B*. If we can identify and verify such a relationship, then we can use our knowledge of variation in *A* to predict variation in *B*, without any need to explain why the association occurs or what causes variability in *B*. For example, one branch of personnel selection is concerned with predicting the potential success of job applicants. The goal of this research is to identify variables that will predict this success. In essence, the scientist does not care whether a causal relationship exists between the variables used to predict success and actual success; he or she is only interested in *predicting* job success. In instances where the focus is on prediction rather than causation, the terminology associated with the two variables are *predictor variable* and *criterion variable*.

An interesting example of a purely predictive orientation is the method used to develop the Minnesota Multiphasic Personality Inventory (MMPI), a widely used test of maladaptive psychological orientations. When the test was constructed, different groups of individuals who had been diagnosed with specific psychological problems were administered a large number of questionnaire items and asked to agree or disagree with each. For example, individuals who had been diagnosed as hypochondriacs indicated their agreement or disagreement with hundreds of items. The same items were completed by a group of "normal" adults, and the responses were then compared for the two groups. Any item that had an agreement pattern that differentiated the two groups became a candidate for inclusion in the final scale, no matter how unusual the item seemed. The result was a subset of 20 or so items to which people with hypochondriasis showed a unique response pattern relative to "normals." If an individual in the general population, when given the MMPI, showed the same response pattern across the items as the hypochondriasis group, then they were declared as likely having hypochondriasis. The MMPI contains some truly bizarre items in terms of content, leading many laypeople who take the test to wonder exactly what is going on. But the test has been carefully developed to have predictive utility, and it often does a reasonable job in correctly diagnosing individuals.

Causal Relationships

Distinct from predictive–associational relationships are causal relationships. These relationships invoke the notion of causality, with the idea that one of the variables in the relationship, X, influences the other variable in the relationship, Y. The nature of causality has been debated extensively by philosophers of science (e.g., Bunge, 1961; Cartwright, 2007; Frank, 1961; Morgan & Winship, 2007; Pearl, 2009; Pearl & Mackenzie, 2018; Rubin, 1974, 1978; Russell, 1931; Shadish, Cook, & Campbell, 2002), most of whom agree that causality can be an elusive concept that is fraught with ambiguities. In fact, the famous philosopher Bertrand Russell (1931) was so flabbergasted by the difficulties with the concept that he suggested the word *causality* be expunged from the English language.

Scientists generally think of causality in terms of *change*. Variable X is said to be a cause of Y if changes made to the crucial properties of X produce changes in Y. Hume (1777/1975) argued that it is impossible to ever demonstrate that changes in one variable *produce* changes in another. At best, we can only observe changes in one variable followed at a later time by changes in another variable. Such coexistent change, he notes, does not necessarily imply causality. For example, an alarm clock going off every morning just before sunrise cannot be said to be the cause of the sun rising, even though the two events are intimately linked.

Russell (1931) argued that causality can be established unambiguously only in a completely isolated system. If one assumes no other variables are present or operating, then changes in X that are followed by changes in Y are indeed indicative of a causal relation. When contaminating variables are present, however, it is possible for a true causal relationship to exist, even though observations show that X and Y are completely unrelated to each other. Similarly, a causal relationship may not exist, even though X and Y are found to be related. Having shown this using formal logic, Russell turned to the problem of how one could ever know that one is operating in a completely isolated system to demonstrate causality, such as in a highly controlled laboratory setting. The only way to be confident that the system is isolated, he argued, is if changes in X unambiguously produce changes in Y in that system. But at the same time that we want to assert the existence of an isolated system because changes in X produce changes in Y, we also want to assert that X produces a change in Y because we are operating in an isolated system. Such reasoning, Russell argued, is tautological.

As you might imagine, the underlying issues for conceptualizing causality and how one establishes causal relationships are complex. They have been debated by extremely bright philosophers of science and scientists for decades, and we certainly are not going to resolve the matter here to everyone's satisfaction. After reading the relevant literature carefully and giving the matter much thought, we agree that, in a strict sense, causality of the type that traditional social scientists seek to infer is difficult to demonstrate unequivocally. Strong adherents to experimental methods take exception to this view, and we respect that. However, we personally find that the arguments of Blalock (1964), Bunge (1961), Hume (1777/1975), Russell (1931), and a host of others, taken as a whole, raise reasonable doubts that causality as pursued in the social sciences can be unambiguously demonstrated.

If causality is so difficult to demonstrate, then why is the concept dominant in social scientific theories? Our answer is that the concept of causality is a type of mental model that social scientists use to help us think about our environment, organize our thoughts, predict future events, and even change future events. By thinking in causal terms, we are able to identify relationships between variables and often manipulate those variables so as to produce changes in phenomena that are socially desirable to change. Causal thinking has been used to invent lasers and transistors, to fly us to the moon, and has resulted in all kinds of rather remarkable human inventions. Pearl (2009) argues that *"deep understanding* means knowing not merely how things behaved yesterday but also how things will behave under new hypothetical circumstances, control being one such circumstance" (p. 415, original emphasis). Causal frameworks can provide such understanding.

Although we may rarely be able to unambiguously demonstrate causality between variables central to the social sciences, we certainly can have differing degrees of confidence that a causal relationship (of the form that "changes in X produce changes in Y") exists between variables. Scientific research, in our view, is conducted to establish strong, moderate, or weak levels of confidence in theoretical statements that propose causality. In particle physics, the classic five-sigma standard defines certainty as a 99.9999% chance of something being true, such as whether humans have caused climate change. While this may rarely be attainable with social science theories, it does underscore the role that the concept of confidence plays in scientific inference.

There are some features of causality on which most social scientists agree. First, as noted, if X causes Y, then changes in X are thought to produce changes in Y (but see Sowa, 2000, and Lewis, 2000, for alternative conceptualizations). Second, a cause always must precede an effect in time. Third, the time that it takes for a change in X to produce a change in Y can vary, ranging from almost instantaneous change to weeks, months, years, decades, or centuries. Fourth, the nature and/or strength of the effect of X on Y can vary depending on context. X may influence Y in one context but not another context. Finally, cause and effect must be in some form of spatial contact or must be connected by a chain of intermediate events. We return to each of these points in later sections of this chapter.

An increasingly popular view of causality in the social sciences uses a counterfactual framework that grew out of the work of Lewis (2000). To illustrate the basic idea, when analyzing the causal effect of a treatment (X) on an outcome (Y), the counterfactual of interest is comparing the potential outcome that would occur if a person receives the treatment versus the potential outcome that would occur if that same person did not receive the treatment under all the same circumstances. If the potential outcomes are different, causality is implied. Based on this fundamental counterfactual premise, scientists and philosophers have posited an elaborate "theory of causality" as well as scientific prescriptions for establishing causality (see Menzies, 2017; Pearl, 2009; Pearl & Mackenzie, 2018).

Not all scientific theories rely on the concept of causality. In fact, certain areas of physics did not progress until the notion of causality was deemphasized (see Sowa, 2000). Nevertheless, causality remains the dominant system of thought in the social sciences.

CAUSALITY AND GROUNDED/EMERGENT THEORY

Causal explanation has been the subject of controversy among grounded/emergent theorists (Maxwell, 2004). There is a vocal group of grounded theorists who have challenged traditional views of causality and who offer perspectives that are more consistent with qualitative methods and process-oriented explanations. Among the alternative frameworks are causal realism (Salmon, 1984, 1989, 1998), constructive empiricism (van Fraassen, 1980, 1989), and ordinary language philosophy (Achinstein, 1983), to name a few. One of the more popular alternatives, causal realism, argues for a real, though not "objectively" knowable, world. Causal realism holds that phenomena within the objective world are so intertwined and so dependent on one another in such complex ways that simple variable-centered notions of causal regularities are inadequate. There are several variants of causal realism, but we do not digress into these here. Our focus in this chapter is on the more dominant variable-centered approaches to causal explanation. We consider the other approaches in Chapter 10. Even if theorists are committed to process-oriented perspectives or other explanatory frameworks, we believe it will be helpful at times to "think outside the box" by contemplating direct relationships, indirect relationships, moderated relations, spurious relationships, reciprocal causes, and feedback loops per traditional causal thinking. Doing so might provide fresh insights for framing one's theory. Chapter 12 elaborates such meta-triangulation strategies in theory construction, namely, the building of theories from the perspective of multiple paradigms (Lewis & Grimes, 1999).

TYPES OF CAUSAL RELATIONSHIPS

When two variables have a causal relationship, the presumed cause is sometimes called the *independent variable* or the *determinant,* and the presumed effect is called the *dependent variable* or the *outcome variable.* Causal models have one or more of six types of "causal" relationships in them. The six relationships capture the universe of relationship types used in causal modeling. In this section, we first briefly characterize these relationships to provide an overview of them, and then we delve into each type in detail. The six relationships—(1) direct causal, (2) indirect causal, (3) spurious, (4) moderated causal, (5) bidirectional causal, and (6) unanalyzed—are shown in Figure 7.1. In this figure, a variable is indicated by a box, and a causal influence is represented by a straight arrow emanating from the cause and pointing to the effect. We discuss the curved arrow later. This type of figure is called a *path diagram* or an *influence diagram.* There are other graphical tools for representing causal theories (such as the directed acyclic graph advocated by Pearl [2009]), but we rely on traditional influence diagrams here.

A *direct causal relationship* is one in which a given cause is assumed to have a direct causal impact on some outcome variable. For example, frustration is assumed to influence aggression. As another example, the quality of the relationship between a mother and her adolescent child is assumed to influence whether the child uses drugs, with poor relationships being associated with higher levels of drug use. Figure 7.2a illustrates this latter relationship.

An *indirect causal relationship* is one in which a variable influences another variable indirectly through its impact on an intermediary variable (see Figure 7.1). For example,

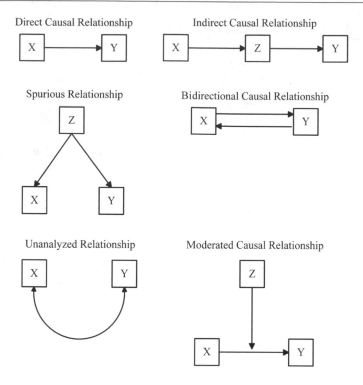

FIGURE 7.1. Relationships in causal models.

failing to accomplish a goal may lead to frustration, which, in turn, causes someone to aggress against another. In this case, failure to obtain a goal is an indirect cause of aggression. It only influences aggression through its impact on frustration. Frustration is formally called a *mediating variable,* or more informally, a *mediator,* because other variables "work through" it to influence the outcome. Indirect relationships are sometimes called mediated relationships. Figure 7.2b illustrates an indirect relationship between the quality of the relationship a child has with his or her mother and adolescent drug use. The quality of the relationship is assumed to impact how much the adolescent orients toward working hard in school, with better relationships leading to working

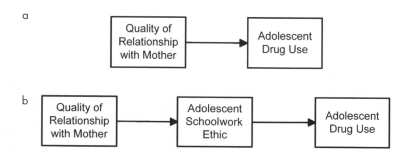

FIGURE 7.2. Examples of direct and indirect relationships. (a) Direct relationship; (b) indirect relationship.

harder. Students who work hard in school, in turn, are assumed to be less likely to use drugs. Figures 7.2a and 7.2b illustrate an important point: What is a direct relationship in one theory can be an indirect relationship in another theory.

A *spurious relationship* is one in which two variables are related because they share a common cause, but not because either causes the other (see Figure 7.1). As an example, if we were to select a random sample of all people in the United States and calculate the correlation between shoe size and verbal ability, we would find a moderate relationship between the two variables: People with bigger feet tend to have more verbal ability. Does this mean that a causal relationship exists between these variables? Of course not. The reason they are correlated is because they share a common cause: age. A random sample of people in the United States will include large numbers of children. When children are young, they have small feet and they can't talk very well. As they get older, their feet grow, as does their verbal ability. The common cause of age produces a correlation between shoe size and verbal ability, but it is spurious.

A *moderated causal relationship,* like spurious and indirect relationships, involves at least three variables (see Figure 7.1). In this case, the causal relationship between two variables, X and Y, differs depending on the value of a third variable, Z. For example, it might be found that a given type of psychotherapy (X) is effective for reducing headaches (Y) for males but not for females. In this case, the causal relationship between exposure to the psychotherapy and headache reduction is moderated by gender. When gender has the value "male," X impacts Y. However, when gender has the value "female," X does not impact Y. Gender is called a *moderator variable* because the relationship between the presence or absence of psychotherapy (X) and headache reduction (Y) changes as a function of (or is "moderated by") gender.

A *bidirectional or reciprocal causal relationship* exists when two variables are conceptualized as influencing each other (see Figure 7.1). For example, in the area of reproductive health, a theorist might posit a bidirectional influence between a woman's belief that the rhythm method is effective in preventing pregnancy (X) and her attitude toward the rhythm method (Y). A woman may have a positive attitude toward the rhythm method because she believes it is effective. Simultaneously, she may believe it is effective, in part, because she has a positive attitude toward it, via a mechanism that involves rationalization of her attitude.

The final type of relationship is an *unanalyzed relationship.* In Figure 7.1, the two variables for this type of relationship are connected by a double-headed curved arrow. This arrow signifies that the two variables are correlated but that the theorist is not going to specify why they are correlated. The correlation may be spurious or it may be due to a causal connection of some kind. The theorist wants to recognize the correlation between the variables, but trying to explain it is beyond the scope of the theoretical effort.

Most causal models have more than one of these six types of relationships in them. We provide an example of a multivariate causal model in Figure 7.3. In this model, there are several direct relationships. How hard an adolescent works in school is assumed to be a direct cause of drug use. The quality of the relationship between the mother and child is assumed to be a direct cause of how hard the adolescent works in school. The quality of the relationship between the mother and child has an indirect causal relationship with drug use that is mediated by how hard the child works in school. The amount

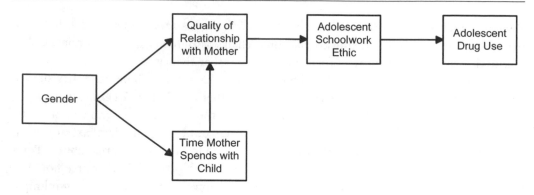

FIGURE 7.3. Multivariate causal model.

of time that a mother spends with her child is assumed to have a direct influence on the quality of the relationship between the mother and child. Gender of the adolescent is assumed to have a direct impact on the amount of time that a mother spends with her child, with mothers spending more time with girls than boys. Gender also has a direct influence on the quality of the relationship between mothers and their children, with mothers having better relationships with girls than boys. Note that because gender influences both the amount of time spent with the child and the quality of the relationship between mother and child, it is a common cause for these variables. Hence, some of the association between time spent together and relationship quality is spurious. However, the straight causal arrow between the time spent together and relationship quality indicates that the theorist believes some of the association is not spurious. Rather, some true causal influence is also operating. In this case, the association between the two variables is thought to have two components: (1) causal and (2) spurious.

Note also in this model that the amount of time a mother spends with her adolescent is an indirect cause of drug use. The indirect effect works through two sequential mediators: (1) the quality of the relationship with the child and, in turn, (2) how hard the child works in school. There are several other more distal indirect relationships in this model; try to identify them. There are no moderated relationships, nor are there any unanalyzed relationships in this model. It is not necessary for a theory to contain all six types of relationships we described earlier.

A common distinction in causal theories is between exogenous and endogenous variables. An *endogenous variable* has at least one causal arrow pointing to it, whereas an *exogenous variable* has no causal arrow pointing to it. In Figure 7.3, for example, gender is an exogenous variable, and all other variables are endogenous variables. We occasionally use this terminology.

CONSTRUCTING THEORIES WITH CAUSAL RELATIONSHIPS

We now discuss a 10-step process for constructing causal models. We draw on the heuristics discussed in Chapter 4, while explicating in more depth the six types of relationships in Figure 7.1. It is not possible to convey this material in a straightforward, linear fashion, so be prepared for digressions. The approach we describe is not the only way to develop a causal theory. We illustrate, for example, an alternative approach after describing the current one, called the binder approach. We have found both approaches useful, but we often deviate from them in our own theory construction efforts.

IDENTIFYING OUTCOME VARIABLES

The 10-step approach we describe involves first identifying an outcome variable and then specifying some causes of that variable. Identify an outcome variable that you want to explain. Perhaps you are interested in understanding why some people are Republicans but other people are Democrats or Independents. Or you might be interested in understanding why some people become alcoholics but others do not. In Chapter 4, we discussed strategies for choosing outcome variables. Apply those strategies to select an outcome to focus on.

Some researchers approach theory construction using a reverse process; that is, they specify a variable of interest and then ask what are the consequences or "effects" of it. For example, a theorist might be interested in self-esteem and in the consequences of having low versus high self-esteem. Or a theorist might be interested in poverty and want to explore the effects of poverty on people's lives. There is more than one way to go about theory construction. If you prefer the latter approach, then the concepts and strategies we discuss below are still applicable, but will have to be adapted somewhat. We specify when such adaptations are required.

Some researchers decide to build a theory of the effects of an intervention on an outcome. For example, an educational researcher might develop a program to improve reading skills and plan to build a theory around its effects on reading. He or she plans to conduct a study in which an experimental group receives the intervention and a control group receives the standard reading curriculum. In this case, you already have a designated "cause" or independent variable (the intervention group vs. the control group), and you also have identified an outcome variable or "effect," reading ability.

IDENTIFYING DIRECT CAUSES

We start the theory construction process by specifying two or three variables that are direct causes of the outcome variable. We do not specify more than two or three direct causes at this initial step because we ultimately will subject each direct cause to considerable elaboration. The theory might become overwhelming at later stages if we work with too many variables initially. Additional direct causes always can be added at a later point.

Use the heuristics and strategies discussed in Chapter 4 to identify your initial set of direct causes, and use the strategies discussed in Chapter 5 to ensure that the concepts with which you are working are clearly defined. You also can apply the thought experiments described in Chapter 6 to clarify the relationships. When specifying a direct cause, remember that your goal is to explain why there is variation in the outcome variable you have chosen. If the outcome variable is popularity, for example, then you want to know what causes people to differ in their popularity. What makes some people more popular than others? What factors influence popularity? If the outcome variable is teacher apathy in schools, then you want to know why some teachers are apathetic and other teachers are not. When specifying your direct causes, keep this focus in mind.

If you adopt the strategy of choosing an initial variable but want to treat it as a cause rather than an effect, then identify two or three variables that the variable is thought to impact. For example, if the primary variable of interest is Latinx acculturation to U.S. culture, you might use drug use as one "effect" (under the supposition that increased acculturation increases drug use) and performance in school as another "effect" (under the supposition that increased acculturation increases performance in school). Whichever approach is used, you should now have a theory with two to three direct effects in it. Be sure that you can articulate the logic underlying each direct effect in your model.

Finally, if you are building a theory of the effects of an intervention, you already specified (from the previous section) a direct effect of the intervention (intervention vs. control) on the outcome (e.g., reading ability). In this case, we will work with this single direct cause.

To make the next tasks manageable, we recommend that you draw your theory using an influence diagram as in Figures 7.1–7.3. By the end of this chapter, your diagram will be complex, but at this stage, it should be simple, consisting of a few direct causes, in the spirit of a direct effect in Figure 7.1. As you complete each step that follows, continually update your path diagram. The steps will add complexity to your theory, and you will need to use the diagram as an aid to avoid being overwhelmed by what is to come.

INDIRECT CAUSAL RELATIONSHIPS

Turning Direct Relationships into Indirect Relationships

Once you have identified a few direct causes, the next step is to try to turn the direct causes into indirect causes. That is, we identify variables that mediate the direct relationships and then insert these variables into the theoretical system. For example, suppose that our outcome variable is drug use in adolescents and one of the direct causes is the quality of the relationship between the child and the mother of the adolescent. We expect that adolescents with better relationships with their mothers will be less likely to use drugs. If we ask ourselves the question "Why do you think that quality of the relationship impacts drug use?," we might answer that adolescents who have a good relationship with their mothers work harder in school in order to please them, and this increased focus on school is why adolescents are less likely to use drugs. Contained in this answer is a mediator variable, namely, the increased focus on school. What was a direct relationship can now be turned into an indirect relationship: Quality of the relationship impacts the adolescent's focus on school, which, in turn, impacts drug use. We refer to this strategy for generating a mediator as the *why heuristic*.

We can take this a step further and attempt to turn the newly established direct relationship between "school focus" and "drug use" into an indirect relationship. We ask ourselves, "Why do you think working hard and focusing on school impacts drug use?" We might answer, "because then adolescents have less time for after-school activities that expose them to drug use." We now have a new mediator, namely, avoidance of risk situations. It can be used to turn the direct relationship between "school focus" and "drug use" into an indirect relationship using "avoidance of risk situations" as a mediator. This new variable is somewhat vague, and we need to apply the focusing strategies discussed in Chapter 5 to clarify it, but that is not the point here. The main idea is that you can expand a theoretical framework that has direct causes by turning direct causal relationships into indirect causal relationships through the specification of mediators. You continue to do this until you reach a point where you just don't want to further explicate mediators for the targeted direct effects. That is, you are at a place where you want to close this aspect of the theoretical system and move on to other features of the theory.

In sum, to turn a direct causal relationship into an indirect causal relationship, ask yourself the question "Why is it that X influences (i.e., reduces or increases) Y?" As you articulate your answer to this question (substituting the actual variables names for X and Y), therein will lie a potential mediator variable. Why is it that higher levels of education lead to higher levels of income? Your answer to this question is a potential mediator. Why is it that males tend to drink more alcohol than females? Your answer to this question is a potential mediator.

Partial versus Complete Mediation

Once you have specified a mediator and added it to your influence diagram, you are confronted with a new issue. Examine Figure 7.4a, which shows an indirect relationship where the impact of X on Y is mediated by Z. According to this model, the *only* way in which X influences Y is through Z. Stated another way, Z completely mediates any impact X has on Y. Therefore, Z is a *complete mediator*.

But another possibility exists. Maybe Z only partially mediates the effects of X on Y. Perhaps in addition to the mediated effects of X on Y through Z, X also has an independent effect on Y that can't be accounted for by Z. This scenario is illustrated in Figure 7.4b. In this case, Z is said to be a *partial mediator* of the effect of X on Y. As an example, the quality of the relationship with the mother impacts the adolescent's work ethic in school, which, in turn, influences the adolescent's drug use. Perhaps in addition to these effects, the quality of the relationship with the mother has an independent effect on drug use, over and above its effect through the adolescent work ethic. If so, this represents partial mediation: The adolescent's schoolwork ethic mediates some of the impact of quality of the maternal relationship on drug use—but not all of it.

In any causal system, once you introduce a mediator, you must next decide if the mediator is a complete or partial mediator. After inserting the mediators into your diagram, you must further adjust the theory either by drawing arrows to represent partial mediation or excluding arrows to reflect complete mediation, per Figures 7.4a and 7.4b.

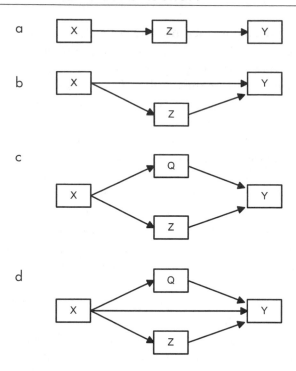

FIGURE 7.4. Complete and partial mediation. (a) Complete mediation; (b) partial mediation; (c) complete mediation with two mediators; (d) partial mediation with two mediators.

What if you are not sure which to specify, complete or partial mediation? Here is the approach we use in such cases. For partial mediation, you are essentially stating that there is some mechanism other than Z by which X influences Y. What is that other mechanism? If you can articulate it, then partial mediation is called for; if you cannot articulate it, then complete mediation is the answer. In essence, we take the direct effect between X and Y in Figure 7.4b and try turning it into an indirect effect by identifying a second mediator, Q. This is illustrated in Figure 7.4c. If we can identify Q, then partial mediation in the model is called for; if we can't think of Q, then complete mediation is the answer. Continuing with our drug use example, we might conjecture that in addition to adolescents' schoolwork ethic, the quality of the mother–adolescent relationship also impacts how much adolescents are willing to allow their mothers to keep track of their activities on weekends: If the relationship between the mother and adolescent is poor, then the adolescent will resist the mother's attempts to monitor him or her. If the relationship is good, then the adolescent may not resist as much. Thus, the quality of the mother–adolescent relationship (X) impacts not only the adolescent's schoolwork ethic (Z) but also parental monitoring (Q), and both of these variables (X and Q) are thought to impact adolescent drug use. In this case, we are justified in hypothesizing partial mediation, as per Figure 7.4b, because we are able to specify a reasonable mechanism for it.

If we specify Q, then why not just incorporate it into the theory? Of course, we could very well do this, but then the issue becomes whether the two mediators, Z and Q, considered together, are complete or partial mediators of the causal effect of X on Y.

That is, perhaps now the model should appear as in Figure 7.4d instead of Figure 7.4c. To add the direct path from X to Y over and above Q and Z, we would need to be able to articulate yet a third mediator. At some point, you decide to close out the system and let a direct path between X and Y stand so as to reflect partial mediation without formally bringing additional mediators into the model. If pressed, you could articulate one, but you simply do not want to complicate the theory further.

Parenthetically, the concept of mediation has recently been reconceptualized using the concept of counterfactuals, leading to more fine-grained distinctions between complete and partial mediation, especially for cases where moderation and mediation are combined. Interested readers should consult Muthén (2011), Valeri and VanderWeele (2013), and VanderWeele (2015).

Alternative Strategies for Turning Direct Effects into Indirect Effects

There are two other ways to bring indirect causal relationships into your theory. Pick one of your direct causes, X, and now treat it as an outcome variable. Then use the heuristics discussed in Chapter 4 to identify causes of this cause. Identify a few such causes and add them to your influence diagram. You will now have indirect relationships between these new causes and the original outcome variable that are mediated by your initial direct cause. The variable that originally took the role of a direct cause now takes on the additional role of mediator. We call this strategy the *cause-of-a-cause heuristic*.

Figure 7.5 illustrates this dynamic for the drug use example. The initial direct cause was the quality of the relationship between the mother and the adolescent (see Figure 7.5a). We then treat the quality of the relationship as an outcome variable and ask what factors influence it. We might conjecture that the gender of the child impacts the quality of the relationship and then add this to the theory (see Figure 7.5b). Now the original direct cause is a mediator. Note that at any point in the process, we can try to turn a direct cause into an indirect cause using our first strategy of answering the question of "why." For example, "Why is it that the gender of the adolescent influences the quality of the relationship between the mother and the adolescent?" Our answer to this question might be "because mothers spend more time with girls than boys," which yields a mediator. This causal dynamic is illustrated in Figure 7.5c, which further augments the theoretical system. Also, any time we create a mediator, we also must make decisions about complete or partial mediation. In Figure 7.5c, we have assumed complete mediation.

Of course, there will be some causes, such as gender or race, where it does not make sense to treat them as an outcome variable and where this strategy is inappropriate. This will also be true when the initial "cause" is an intervention with random assignment to groups.

Another strategy for turning a direct relationship into an indirect one is to treat your outcome variable as a cause of some new variable. In other words, make your effect a cause. What variables might your outcome variable influence? For example, for the theory in Figure 7.5c, we might reason that adolescent drug use impacts performance in school, so we add this outcome to the mediational chain, per Figure 7.5d. Note that in doing so, we have turned our original outcome variable into a mediator variable that

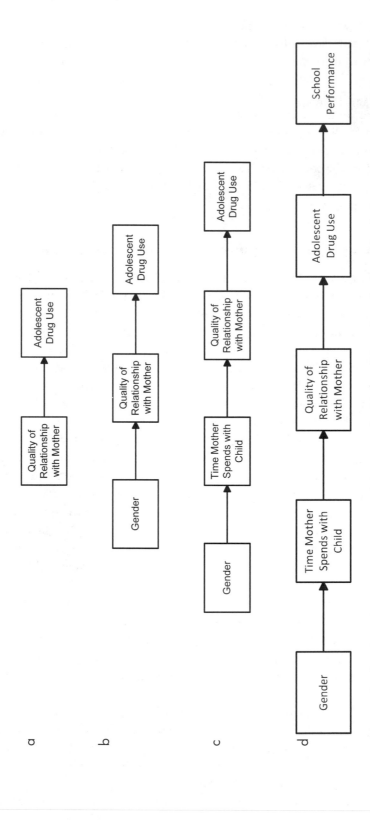

FIGURE 7.5. Example of making the cause an outcome. (a) Direct relationship; (b) quality of relationship becomes an outcome; (c) inserting a mediator; (d) introducing an effect of an outcome.

mediates the effects of our original direct causes on our new outcome variables. We call this strategy the *effect-of-an-effect heuristic*. With the "new" mediator, you must decide on partial mediation or complete mediation.

Summary of Mediation

In sum, there are three heuristics for creating indirect effects in your model. First, the *why* heuristic involves focusing on a direct causal relationship between X and Y and asking "Why does X influence Y?" The answer to this question contains the mediator. Second, the *cause-of-a-cause* heuristic treats one of your direct causes as an outcome and identifies causes of it. Third, the *effect-of-an-effect heuristic* treats your outcome as a cause and identifies consequences of it. Once you add a mediator, you must decide about partial or complete mediation with respect to it. Complete mediation is called for if you are unable to articulate any mechanism other than Z by which X impacts Y; partial mediation is in order if you can specify such a mechanism. Apply these heuristics to one or more of the direct relationships in your model and draw the mediated relationships into your influence diagram. Add partial mediation causal arrows, if appropriate.

MODERATED CAUSAL RELATIONSHIPS

The next step in the theory construction process is to consider the addition of moder ated causal relationships. As noted, a moderated causal relationship involves three variables: a cause (X), an effect (Y), and a moderator variable (Z). The essence of a moderated relationship is that the strength or nature of the effect of X on Y varies as a function of Z. Some examples will be helpful. It is well known that the amount of education people attain tends to impact their annual income, with higher levels of education leading to higher levels of annual income. Suppose in a statistical analysis of a large metropolitan area in the United States, it is found that each year of additional education is worth about $3,000 more in annual income. We might ask if the value of an additional year of education is the same for Blacks and European Americans in the region. A subgroup analysis might find that the worth of an additional year of education is $2,000 for Blacks and $4,000 for European Americans. In this case, the strength of the effect of education on annual income differs as a function of ethnicity; ethnicity is a moderator variable.

As another example, it is well known that stress impacts anxiety; that is, the more stress people are under, the more anxious they become, everything else being equal. Some people have good coping strategies that allow them to deal effectively with stress, while other people have poor coping strategies for dealing with stress. For those with good coping strategies, stress will have less of an impact on anxiety than people with poor coping strategies. The quality of coping strategies thus moderates the effect of stress on anxiety. For additional examples, see Chapter 6.

A heuristic we use to identify possible moderated relationships is called the *stronger-than heuristic*. This heuristic asks if the effect of X on Y will be stronger in some circumstances than in others and/or stronger for some individuals than for others. Whereas mediation asks the question of *why* X impacts Y, moderation asks the question "For *whom, where,* and *when* does X impact Y?" For example, we might ask, "For whom does X influence Y, and for whom does it not?" We then seek to identify the characteristics that distinguish these two groups, and in doing so, we identify a moderator variable(s). Or we might ask, "In what contexts does X influence Y, and in what contexts does it not?" We then identify the characteristics that distinguish these different contexts, and in doing so, we identify a moderator variable(s). Or we might ask, "When (in terms of time or timing) does X influence Y, and when does it not?" We then identify the defining characteristics that distinguish these time periods (e.g., during adolescence but not during adulthood; during the early stages of grieving but not the later stages) to identify a moderator variable(s). In many research programs, plausible moderators include age, gender, social class, and ethnicity. Examine every direct relationship that is in your theory as drawn in your influence diagram. For each relationship, ask yourself, "Are there some circumstances where the impact of this effect will be stronger than in other circumstances?" "Are there some groups of people for whom the effect will be weaker or stronger?" "Are there some points in time when the effect will be stronger or weaker?" As you answer these questions, try to abstract variables that capture or represent the distinguishing characteristics of the moderating dynamics. Use the methods described in Chapter 5 to focus these variables and the methods in Chapter 6 to clarify the relationships.

Of course, you may not want to pursue this strategy for every direct cause in your theory, but the potential for doing so exists. Draw into your influence diagram the moderated relationships you have identified. Your theory now should include direct causal relationships, indirect causal relationships with either partial or complete mediation, and moderation.

Mediated Moderation

Next, you should consider the possibility of adding *mediated moderation* relationships. This type of relationship combines an indirect and moderated relationship (see Figure 7.6a). Note that Z is a traditional moderator variable that impacts the strength of the effect of X on Y. However, we have inserted a mediator of the moderating effect, Q, into the model. For example, suppose we think that gender moderates the impact of a multisession employment enhancement program (designed to make participants more employable) on future employment such that the program will be more effective for females than males. Using the why heuristic, we ask, "*Why* is the program more effective for females than for males?" We might conjecture that females will be more likely than males to attend all of the program sessions because females tend to be more conscientious and better planners than males. We then insert the program attendance variable as a mediator of the moderator effect, per Figure 7.6b.

As before, any time you add a mediator, there is the possibility of complete or partial mediation. The same is true for mediated moderation. It may be that the mediator accounts for only some of the moderating effects of Z on the effect of X on Y. Figure 7.6c illustrates the mediated moderation dynamic for the employment program but with

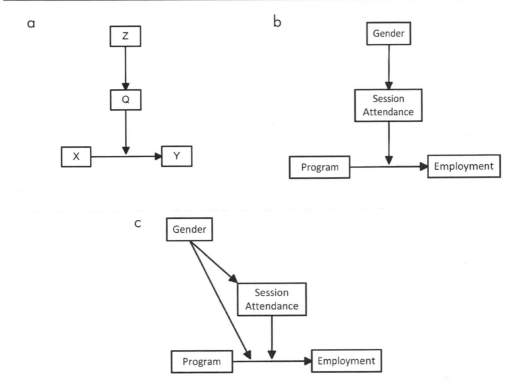

FIGURE 7.6. Mediated moderation. (a) General mediated moderation; (b) treatment–employment example with full mediation; (c) treatment–employment example with partial mediation.

partial mediation. Determine for your theory if you want to assume complete or partial mediated moderation for the mediated moderation effects you add.

Moderated Mediation

Next, consider the possibility of adding a *moderated mediation* relationship. Moderated mediation occurs when the strength of a path signifying mediation varies as a function of some variable, Q (see Figure 7.7a). For example, for females, Z might be a complete mediator of the effect of X on Y, whereas for males, Z may be only a partial mediator of this effect. In this case, the mediational properties of Z depend on the value of the moderator variable, Q. Moderation can occur at any or all of the paths surrounding mediation. In Figure 7.7a, moderation operates at the level of two of the paths involved in mediation but not the third path. An example that maps onto Figure 7.7a would be the case where a program to prevent overly aggressive driving (X) is thought to impact future instances of aggressive driving (Y) by teaching participants anger management skills (Z). Q is gender, the moderator variable—the theorist feels there will be gender differences in the effects of the program on anger management skills such that females will learn them better than males because women are generally more capable of controlling their emotions than men to begin with. In addition, the direct effect of the program

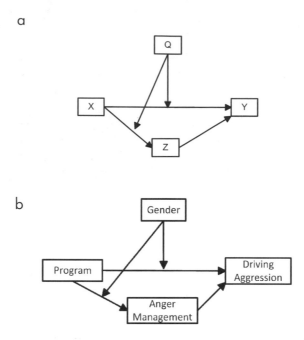

FIGURE 7.7. Moderated mediation. (a) General moderated mediation; (b) treatment–driving aggression example of moderated mediation.

on future driving aggression over and above anger management skills is thought to be stronger for females than for males. Figure 7.7b presents the diagram for this example.

Now use the stronger-than heuristic to identify relevant moderator variables for one or more of the mediated effects in your model. Be sure you can articulate the logic underlying them.

Moderated Moderation

A final possibility to consider is *moderated moderation*. This relationship is diagrammed in Figure 7.8a, where Q moderates the moderating qualities of Z. We give special labels to X, Z, and Q. Y is the outcome variable, X is the focal independent variable, Z is a *first-order moderator variable*, and Q is a *second-order moderator variable*. The first-order moderator is conceptualized as directly moderating the effect of X on Y. The second-order moderator moderates this moderating effect. As an example, people with a sexually transmitted disease (STD) may be reluctant to obtain an STD test because of the felt stigma associated with obtaining the test. Stigma is the focal independent variable (X), and testing behavior is the outcome variable (Y). A theorist may conjecture that stigma will have a larger impact on the decision to obtain a test for females as opposed to males. However, these gender differences, the theorist reasons, should be more pronounced in European Americans than African Americans. Figure 7.8b presents the influence diagram for this example. Consider if you want to include moderated moderation in your theory and add it accordingly. Be sure you can articulate a conceptual logic model for it.

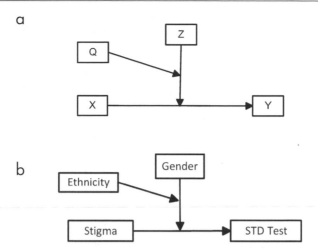

FIGURE 7.8. Moderated moderation. (a) General moderated moderation; (b) stigma–STD example of moderated moderation.

Summary of Moderated Relationships

Moderated relationships can be incorporated into a theory by asking questions about whether the effect of X on Y will be equally strong in all circumstances or equally strong for all individuals and at all times—that is, using the stronger-than heuristic. This heuristic asks if the effect of X on Y will be stronger in some circumstances than in others or stronger for some individuals than for others or at some points in time than at others. The possibility of a moderated relationship can be considered for all direct causes in your theory as well as for mediated relationships in the form of moderated mediation. If you add a moderator variable, then you should consider the possibility of adding mediated moderation, either partial or complete. You also can consider moderated moderation.

RECIPROCAL OR BIDIRECTIONAL CAUSALITY

There Is No Such Thing as Simultaneous Reciprocal Causality

Reciprocal or bidirectional causal relationships occur when a variable, X, influences another variable, Y, and Y also influences X (see Figure 7.1). Strictly speaking, there can never be simultaneous reciprocal causation because there always must be a time interval, no matter how infinitesimally small, between the cause and the effect. If we mapped out the true causal dynamics within a time frame for a reciprocal causal relationship between X and Y to exist, the operative dynamic would appear as follows:

$$X_{t1} \rightarrow Y_{t2} \rightarrow X_{t3} \rightarrow Y_{t4}$$

where X_{t1} is variable X at time 1, Y_{t2} is variable Y at time 2, X_{t3} is variable X at time 3, and Y_{t4} is variable Y at time 4. It is only when we are unable to capture the dynamics at this more microscopic level, and must instead work with coarser time intervals, that the dynamic of the reciprocal causal relationship illustrated in Figure 7.1 applies. Essentially, by working with coarser time units, the more fine-grained temporal causal dynamics already have played themselves out (which is known in the causal modeling literature as the *equilibrium assumption*). Conceptually, we are working with variables that now reflect the past alternating causal dynamics that operated across the more fine-grained time interval. There is nothing wrong with theorizing at the level of coarser time units, as long as we appreciate the underlying logic.

As an example, consider performance in school as measured by grade-point average and drug use by adolescents. It is likely that performing poorly in school puts adolescents at risk for drug use, as their interests drift away from doing well in school. At the same time, school performance is probably adversely affected by drug use, interfering with students' ability to complete their homework and to concentrate on tests. A causal chain that describes this dynamic is

$$SP_{t1} \rightarrow DU_{t2} \rightarrow SP_{t3} \rightarrow DU_{t4}$$

where *SP* represents school performance at time *t*, *DU* represents drug use at time *t*, and the numerical subscript attached to *t* represents later time points as the numbers increase in value. If one is unable to assess these processes at the finer-grained time intervals where the causal dynamics are operating, and if these processes have already played themselves out when the assessments of drug use and school performance are made, then the resulting causal representation that captures what has transpired is this:

This influence diagram essentially reflects a summary of the sequential dynamics.[2]

As a next step in the theory construction process, consider introducing reciprocal causality into the system. This should not be done in too cavalier a fashion in the interest of parsimony and the difficulties that reciprocal causation can create for empirical tests of the theory. But if you believe that a reciprocal relationship is called for and that it is theoretically important, then include it.

Feedback Loops: Adding Mediators to Reciprocal Causation

Theories sometimes include *feedback loops*, an example of which is shown in Figure 7.9a. How satisfied supervisors are with their workers is thought to impact how satisfied workers are with their jobs—that is, workers like their jobs better if their boss is happy with them. Worker job satisfaction, in turn, impacts the productivity of the worker, with more satisfied workers being more productive. The productivity of workers, in turn, feeds back and impacts how satisfied supervisors are with their workers (*X*). Such feed-

---

[2]Exceptions to this logic have been noted, such as when two cars, *A* and *B,* collide frontally; *A* caused *B* to be damaged at the same instance *B* caused *A* to be damaged. Such exceptions are rare in social science theories, with the logic described here being far more common.

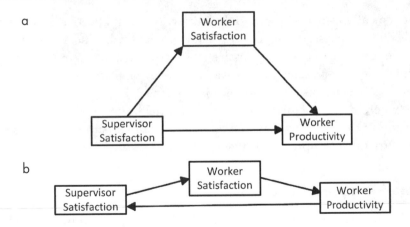

FIGURE 7.9. Feedback loops as reciprocal causation. (a) Traditional feedback path diagram; (b) redrawn feedback loop.

back loops are merely a reciprocal causal relationship with a mediator variable inserted into the causal chain. This is evident if we redraw Figure 7.9a as in Figure 7.9b.

Now, add any mediators to your reciprocal causal relationships using the *why heuristic* discussed earlier (e.g., answer the questions "Why does *X* influence *Y*?"; "Why does *Y* influence *X*?"). You can add mediators to either one or both causal paths in the reciprocal relationship. We illustrate the latter case in Figure 7.10a. In this example, increases in exposure to violent programs on television desensitize viewers to the nega-

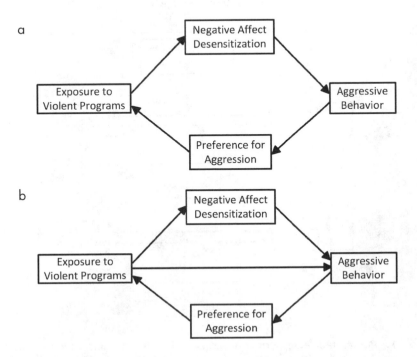

FIGURE 7.10. Feedback loop with two mediators. (a) Complete mediation; (b) partial mediation.

tive affect typically associated with violent behavior. Such affective desensitization, in turn, leads to more physically aggressive behavior in everyday life. Increased aggressive behavior can lead one to prefer aggressive styles more generally, and such preferences, in turn, might lead to a preference for watching television with programs that portray such behaviors (i.e., television programs with violence). Figure 7.10b presents the same model but where partial mediation is assumed for the link between exposure to violent programs and aggressive behavior. One could add a similar path from aggressive behavior to exposure to violent programs, if appropriate.

Moderated Reciprocal Causation

Reciprocal dynamics may operate in some situations but not in others or for some individuals but not for others. This suggests that moderator variables can be added to one or both of the reciprocal causal paths. Such moderators, as before, can be identified using the stronger-than heuristic. Figure 7.11a illustrates the case of a moderator variable associated with one causal path in a reciprocal causal relationship. In this example, the educational aspirations of a high school student (referred to as the "target person") are impacted by the educational aspirations of his or her best friend (referred to as the

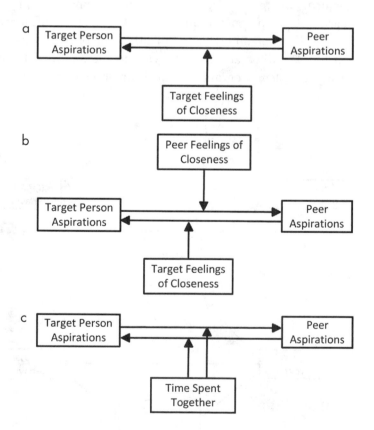

FIGURE 7.11. Moderated reciprocal causation. (a) One-moderator variable model; (b) two-moderator variable model; (c) one moderator variable, two moderated relationships.

"peer"), and the educational aspirations of the best friend are, in turn, impacted by the educational aspirations of the target person. The strength of the former path is moderated by how close the target person feels to his or her best friend; when the target person does not feel that close to his or her best friend, the peer's educational aspirations will have less influence on the target person's aspirations. Figure 7.11b illustrates the case of two moderator variables, one associated with each causal path. This model is the same as that of Figure 7.11a, but it now includes how close the best friend feels to the target person as a moderator of the impact of the target person's educational aspirations on the best friend's educational aspirations. Figure 7.11c illustrates the case of a single moderator variable for both causal paths, namely, the amount of time the two friends spend together: The less time they spend together, the weaker is the presumed impact of both paths.

Of course, you can add multiple moderators, mediated moderators, or moderated moderators when introducing moderator variables into reciprocal relationships. Make additions to your influence diagram accordingly and articulate the underlying logic for the modifications.

SPURIOUS RELATIONSHIPS

In the theory construction process, we usually do not set out to create spurious relationships. Rather, spurious relationships naturally emerge as we work through the other facets of theory construction. The next steps we recommend often create spurious effects within a theory. Before describing these steps, we want to emphasize that spurious effects are not inherently bad, nor are they something to be avoided. In empirical research that tests theories, critics often question a theoretical test by claiming that an observed relationship in the data used to assert a direct causal relationship may, alternatively, represent a spurious relationship. It is one thing to criticize a scientist for conducting a flawed empirical test of a proposed causal link, but this is not the same as recognizing that many phenomena have common causes in the real world. For example, a fear of contracting AIDS might simultaneously influence one's use of condoms, number of sexual partners, and frequency of sexual engagements. These last three variables should exhibit some correlation with each other because they share the common cause of fear of AIDS. These correlations are not artifacts. They reflect the operation of a meaningful common cause, and social scientists should embrace them.

Spurious relationships can have more than one common cause. For example, the sexual risk behaviors noted in the previous paragraph can have ethnicity as a common cause as well as the fear of AIDS. In addition, two variables can have a combination of common causes and direct effects, as was illustrated in our prior discussion of Figure 7.3. In that figure, (1) the mother–adolescent time spent together impacts the quality of the relationship between the adolescent and the mother and (2) both of these variables have gender as a common cause.

We now discuss two additional steps to consider when building your theory, each of which can create spurious relationships. If they do, the spuriousness often is theoretically interesting.

Adding Outcomes

First, consider adding more outcome variables to your theory. Recall that the first step in the theory construction process was to identify a single outcome variable that you were interested in explaining. Now consider other such outcome variables, variables that are conceptually related to your initial outcome variable. For example, if your initial outcome variable was use of condoms, perhaps you might add the number of sexual partners and frequency of sexual intercourse as outcomes. On the one hand, it might be interesting to map the effects of the direct causes you specified for condom use onto these variables as well. On the other hand, you may choose not to add other outcomes, deciding that the system is appropriately focused on the one outcome you initially chose. If you add new outcome variables, then you will indeed have to specify how *all* of the variables currently in your theory are related to them by adding appropriate causal paths. Note that this step is not exactly the same as using the effect-of-an-effect heuristic discussed earlier; the outcomes you add may or may not be impacted by your original outcome.

Specifying Causal Relationships between Existing Variables

Finally, for *all* of the variables in your theory, map out the causal pathways, if any, between them. As an example, Figure 7.12a represents how your theory may have looked after the step of identifying an outcome variable, *Y*, and then adding a few direct causes, *X*, *Z*, and *Q*. At this stage, you had made no statements about the causal relationships between *X*, *Z*, and *Q*. Now is the time to consider them. Could *X* influence *Q* or *Z*? Could *Z* influence *Q* or *X*? Could *Q* influence *X* or *Z*? Figure 7.12b shows one example of causal relationships you might impose on the existing variables. As you create new direct or indirect effects, consider elaborating them using all of the tools we have described thus far (e.g., mediation, partial mediation, moderators, moderated mediation, mediated moderation, and moderated moderation).

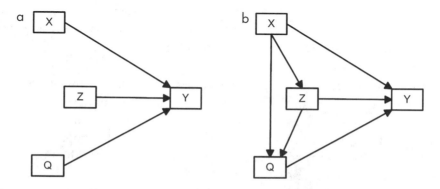

FIGURE 7.12. Mapping causal relationships among all variables. (a) Original specification; (b) mapped specification.

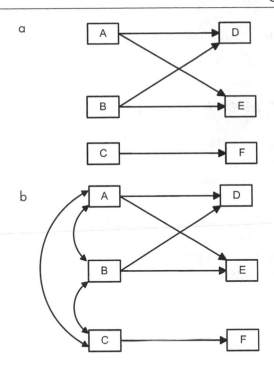

FIGURE 7.13. Examples of exogenous and endogenous variables. (a) Three exogenous and three endogenous variables; (b) unanalyzed relationships between exogenous variables.

UNANALYZED RELATIONSHIPS

In causal models, typically one is uninterested in causal relationships between the exogenous variables. Causal relationships might exist between them, but you must close out the theoretical system at some point, and elaborating those casual relations is of secondary importance. Hence, you choose to ignore these causal dynamics, but you need to recognize that the exogenous variables are correlated. It is traditional to create unanalyzed relationships between all the exogenous variables in a causal model, unless there is a strong theoretical reason for saying there is a zero correlation between them. Figure 7.13a shows a model without the unanalyzed relationships indicated, whereas Figure 7.13b shows the same model with the unanalyzed relationships indicated by the curved, double-headed arrows. Note in these models there are no curved arrows connecting endogenous variables. For example, variables D and E are expected to be correlated because they share common causes (variables A and B), but there is no curved arrow between them. The arrow is omitted because a correlation between D and E is implied by the causal structure, and it would be redundant to draw the curved two-headed arrow between them. Similarly, there is no curved two-headed arrow drawn between variables A and D because a correlation is implied by the fact that A is a cause of D. To reduce the clutter of path diagrams, such redundancies are omitted.

At this point, you should draw the curved two-headed arrows among all of your exogenous variables or, if it makes your influence diagram too cluttered, omit them but put a note at the bottom of the drawing stating that all exogenous variables are assumed to be correlated.

EXPANDING THE THEORY YET FURTHER

We have covered a great deal of ground, and you now have many tools you can use to engage in the theory construction process. Your influence diagram is potentially complex. However, we are not through. Before closing out the theoretical system, there are some remaining details to consider. These include temporal dynamics, disturbance terms, incorporation of a measurement theory, revisiting the existing literature, considering sign reversals, and sharing ideas with colleagues. We discuss each of these topics in turn. Before proceeding, you may want to first step back to synthesize and get comfortable with the prior material.

Temporal Dynamics

Three Types of Temporal Effects

Thus far, we have assumed that the theory you have developed does not involve longitudinal features. But almost any set of variables can be examined at two points in time, three points in time, or multiple points in time. Thus, another facet you can consider adding to your theory is that of longitudinal dynamics. This addition can magnify the complexity of the theory considerably. To illustrate, consider a theory that consists of just one outcome and one direct cause at the same point in time. Let the cause, X, be the number of friends a child has in sixth grade and let the effect, Y, be depression. The proposed theoretical relationship is that children with fewer friends are more likely to be depressed. Suppose we add a second time point, the start of seventh grade, and add the same variables to the theory at this point in time. Figure 7.14 presents a causal structure that illustrates three types of causal paths in the longitudinal model that results.

First, paths a and b reflect the *contemporaneous effects* of the number of friends on depression. These causal paths are the effect of X on Y within a given time period. Second, paths c and d reflect *autoregressive effects*, that is, where a variable at one point in time is assumed to influence a person's standing on that same variable at a later point in time. For example, depression in grade 6 may impact depression in grade 7, and the number of friends children have in grade 6 may influence the number of friends they have in grade 7. Finally, paths e and f reflect *lagged effects*. These are the effects of a variable at time 1 on the other variable at time 2, independent of the aforementioned contemporaneous and autoregressive effects. For example, the number of friends that children have in grade 6 may impact child depression in grade 7. Similarly, a child's depression in grade 6 may impact the number of friends he or she has in grade 7.

When you add a longitudinal component to your theory, consider adding contemporaneous effects, autoregressive effects, and/or lagged effects between the variables. You do not need to add each of these effects; you should add them only if there is conceptual

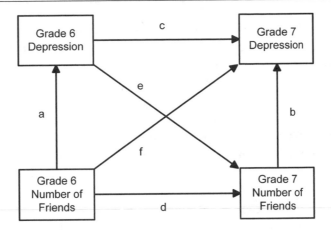

FIGURE 7.14. Models with temporal dynamics: theory with two time points.

justification for doing so. Each of these effects can be elaborated upon using all the heuristics we have described previously (e.g., mediation, moderation, mediated moderation).

Figure 7.15 presents a theory with three time points: grade 6, grade 7, and grade 8. This theory does not include all of the possible contemporaneous, autoregressive, and lagged effects. Nevertheless, we present it to illustrate the additional complexities with multiwave longitudinal models. For example, path *a* reflects lagged effects from a time 1 variable to a time 3 variable. Thus, one must consider not only the possible effects of variables at time $t - 1$ on variables at time t, but also the independent effects of variables at time $t - 2$ on variables at time t.

Choice of Time Intervals

In the preceding example, we theorized about temporal dynamics using a 1-year interval between points. Why 1 year? Why not 6 months or 18 months? In longitudinal models, the choice of a time interval can be important. As an example, suppose a treatment to

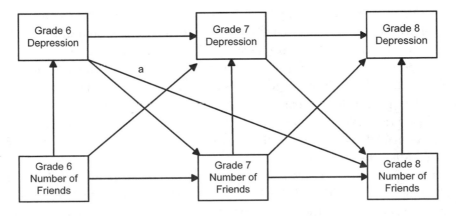

FIGURE 7.15. Three-wave theory.

reduce child depression targets the parents of the child and teaches them more effective parenting skills for dealing with their child. The effect of the newly acquired skills on child depression will not be instantaneous. It will take time for the parents to apply them, for the child to notice a difference, and for the relationship between the parent and child to change to a positive enough state that the child starts to become less depressed. Suppose it takes a minimum of 3 months for the intervention to have its effect. Suppose further that an investigator chooses to evaluate the effects of the intervention 2 months after treatment. There will seem to be no treatment effect, even if the treatment has done what it was intended to do. If the researcher had waited 1 more month, an entirely different conclusion would have resulted.

When working with longitudinal models, the choice of time intervals can influence the kinds of causal paths you include. You must carefully think through the time intervals you select and have a rationale for the intervals on which you ultimately settle. You should think about how long it takes for effects to manifest themselves in every longitudinal link in your theory.

Disturbance Terms

You also can consider pursuing a subtler facet of theory construction, although most theorists leave this to researchers who perform empirical tests of their theories. Our own preference is to be thorough and to provide researchers with a well-developed theoretical roadmap for purposes of theoretical tests, so we generally undertake this next step. But do not expect to see it often at the level of theory description, and you need not do so here.

Consider the simple theory in Figure 7.16a. This theory has two direct causes, wherein variables X and Z are assumed to influence variable Y. A fourth "variable," d, is represented by a circle. This variable represents all unspecified variables that influence Y other than X and Z. This is called a *disturbance term,* and its presence explicitly recognizes that not all causal influences on a variable have been specified. Only endogenous variables have disturbance terms. Traditionally, each endogenous variable in a theory has a disturbance term associated with it.

Consider another example in Figure 7.16b. There are two endogenous variables and they share a common cause. These variables are tobacco use and drug use, and the common cause is gender. The theory posits that males are more likely than females to smoke cigarettes and that males also are more likely than females to use drugs. There is a disturbance term for each of the endogenous variables to acknowledge that many factors other than gender impact tobacco and drug use.

But there is a problem with this theory. According to the theory, smoking cigarettes and drug use in adolescence are correlated *only* because they share the common cause of gender. In reality, these two constructs have many other common causes. For example, social class impacts both tobacco and drug use, with more economically disadvantaged people having an increased tendency to smoke cigarettes and to use drugs. Essentially, social class resides within the disturbance term for smoking cigarettes and for drug use. If the same unspecified cause is in each disturbance term, you would expect the two disturbance terms to be correlated. Figure 7.16c presents a more plausible theory that includes this correlation between disturbances. According to this theory, cigarette smoking and drug use are correlated for two reasons: (1) they share the common cause of gender and (2) they share other common causes that are unspecified by the theory and that reside in both disturbance terms, as reflected by the presence of correlated disturbances.

A well-developed theory provides explicit statements about which disturbance terms in the framework are correlated and which are not. The lazy way out for a theorist is to simply assume that all disturbance terms are correlated. But this is not satisfactory, and it can create difficulties for testing the theory empirically. A better approach is to carefully consider every pair of disturbance terms and try to articulate a common cause that resides in each. If you can articulate such a variable, then it makes sense to posit *correlated disturbances*. If you cannot articulate any such variable, or if its effects are thought to be trivial, then you should not posit correlated disturbances.

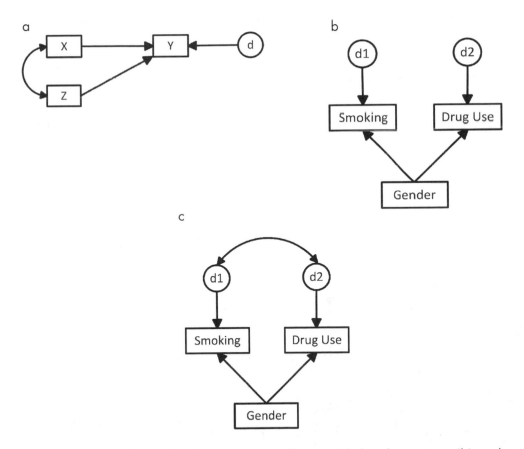

FIGURE 7.16. Examples of disturbance terms. (a) Theory with disturbance term; (b) smoking and drug example with uncorrelated disturbance terms; (c) smoking and drug example with correlated disturbance terms.

For models with a longitudinal component, many theorists have a "knee-jerk" reaction that disturbances at two points in time must be correlated. Figure 7.17 illustrates a direct cause at two points in time with correlated disturbances. We object to such mindless theorizing. Again, if one can articulate a compelling rationale for correlated disturbances, then by all means, correlated disturbances should be incorporated into the theory. Otherwise, correlated disturbances should be viewed with theoretical skepticism.

If you are able to articulate a variable that resides in two disturbance terms to create correlated disturbances, why not just explicitly incorporate the variable into the theoretical system? For example, for the cigarette and drug use example in Figure 7.16, why not explicitly bring social class into the theoretical system? This, of course, is the desirable route. But as in the identification of mediators, at some point we want to close out the theoretical system and work only with the variables we have specified. By including disturbance terms and correlated disturbances, we are explicitly recognizing the operation of other variables, but we choose not to give them a central focus in our theory.

For your influence diagram, add disturbance terms to each of your endogenous variables and then think through if correlated disturbances should be added for each pair of disturbance terms.

Latent Variables, Structural Theory, and Incorporation of a Measurement Theory

Some theorists take matters yet a step further by incorporating a measurement theory into their conceptual frameworks. We mention the general idea here, but develop it in more detail in Chapters 13 and 14. Any empirical test of a theory necessarily requires

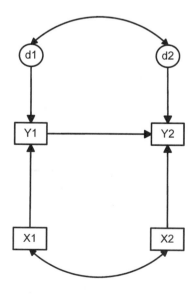

FIGURE 7.17. Example of correlated disturbances in a longitudinal model.

researchers to develop and use measures of the theoretical constructs. Just as one can build a theory linking one concept to another concept, so too can one build a theory linking a construct to a measure of that construct. Some theorists combine both types of theories into a single overarching framework.

Measurement theories make a distinction between a latent variable and an observed measure of that variable. The *latent variable* is, in principle, the true construct that you are interested in making statements about—for example, depression. Although we can see the symptoms and overt manifestations of depression, we can't directly observe the seat of depression in a person's mind. Instead, we rely on some observable response(s) to assess the latent variable, such as a multi-item inventory of depression that a person might complete. Figure 7.18a contains one representation of a measurement model. The latent variable of depression is contained in a circle, and the observed measure thought to reflect depression is contained in a square (the label *AR* stands for *adolescent report* of depression). A causal path is drawn from the latent variable to the observed measure, under the assumption that how depressed a person is influences how he or she responds to the questions on the inventory. There also is an error term, (*e*), that reflects measurement error; that is, factors other than depression may influence a person's responses on the inventory. Ideally, measurement error is minimal, but it is a fact of life for many research endeavors. The relationship between the latent construct and the observed indicator is usually assumed to be linear, but it could also be nonlinear.

Sometimes we obtain multiple indicators of a construct. For example, a researcher might obtain a self-report of depression from an adolescent as well as a report from the adolescent's mother about how depressed the child is (*MR*). A measurement model for this scenario is presented in Figure 7.18b. The latent variable of depression is assumed to influence both of the observed measures, and each measure is assumed to have some

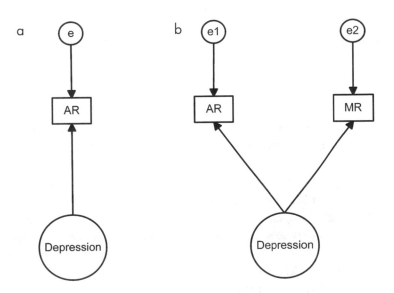

FIGURE 7.18. Measurement models. (a) Single indicator; (b) multiple indicators.

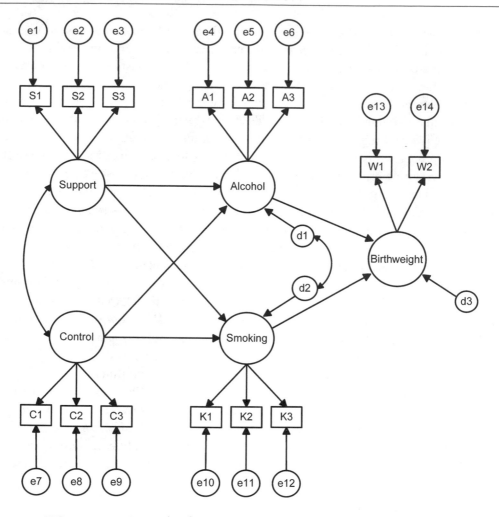

FIGURE 7.19. Example of integrated structural and measurement model.

measurement error as reflected by the presence of error terms. The errors are assumed to be uncorrelated because we cannot articulate any viable reason why we would expect them to be correlated. However, one can introduce correlated measurement error, if appropriate.

Figure 7.19 presents an example of a more elaborate theoretical framework that incorporates a theory about the relationship between constructs as well as a measurement theory. Although it appears somewhat intimidating, it is a straightforward model. There are five latent constructs, and the main substantive theory is focused on them. The portion of the diagram focused on the causal relations among the latent variables is called the *structural model*. The primary outcome variable in this model is the birthweight of a newborn. Birthweight is thought to be influenced by two factors: how much alcohol the mother consumes during her pregnancy and how much she smokes during her pregnancy. Both of these variables are thought to be influenced by two other variables. The first determinant is the extent of support the mother receives from friends and relatives who can help her quit smoking and drinking. The second is the mother's locus of control. *Locus of control* refers to the extent to which the mother believes that what happens to her is beyond her control. The theory is that the more a mother thinks that what happens is not under her control, then the more likely she will be to keep smoking and drinking during pregnancy. These two latent exogenous variables are assumed to be correlated. Each of the three latent endogenous variables has a disturbance term, indicated by a circle with a *d* inside of it. The disturbances are assumed to be correlated for alcohol use and smoking.

The portion of the diagram with arrows from the latent constructs to the observed measures constitutes the *measurement model*. Each of the latent variables has multiple indicators; that is, the researcher obtains three measures of each construct, except birthweight, which is measured using two different indicators. In the interest of space, we do not describe these measures, but note that each is assumed to be fallible, that is, subject to some measurement error (see the circles ranging from e1 to e14). The measurement errors are assumed to be uncorrelated. The theorist assumes that all of the relationships are linear in form. Figure 7.19 provides the researcher with an explicit roadmap to test the combined structural and measurement theories.

We will not ask you to incorporate a theory of measurement into your influence diagram at this point. You need more background in measurement theory, which we provide in Chapters 13 and 14. However, it is useful at this point to recognize that there are two types of theories, structural theories and measurement theories, and that often it is desirable to integrate the two into one comprehensive framework. Our focus in this chapter has been on structural theories.

Revisiting Your Literature Review

Before closing out the theoretical system, you will want to revisit all of the relevant scientific literature on your outcome variable and the other variables included in your theory that you read before embarking on the theory construction enterprise. In relation to this literature, which variables have you included in your theory that the literature has failed to include? These represent innovations on your part. What relationships have you elucidated that the literature has failed to elucidate? These also represent potentially new contributions to scientific knowledge. What variables has the literature suggested that are omitted from your theory? You should consider bringing these into your theory. What relationships has the literature established that you have not included or that contradict you? Make adjustments to your theory accordingly.

Two Final Steps

There are two final steps we recommend. First, take every direct relationship you have specified and try reversing its sign. That is, if the relationship is positive, try making it

BOX 7.1. Finding Sources for a Literature Review

A major strategy for developing ideas about causal models is reading about research that has been conducted in the area in which you are working. There are several methods for locating relevant literature. One procedure involves the use of computer searches of scientific journals and books, which are available in most college libraries (e.g., PsycINFO, Medline). In this procedure, you specify a set of "keywords" to search. For example, if you are studying attitudes toward abortion, you might do separate searches on the keywords *abortion*, *attitudes toward abortion*, or *pregnancy resolution*. The computer then scans the titles and abstracts of a large number of scientific journals, and a list of the titles and abstracts of all relevant articles that contain the keywords is provided. Check with your librarian for details about accessing these databases and conducting an electronic search.

In our experience, a computer search is only as good as one's ability to generate a good list of keywords. The results of such a search may miss important articles because the author of an article did not use one of your keywords in the abstract or title. Also the search can include a good number of irrelevant articles. We often search first on an obvious keyword and then scan the abstracts of the "hits" to get ideas for additional keywords. We then follow up the initial search with more searches based on these new keywords.

A second approach to identifying relevant literature is called the "grandfather method." In this approach, you first identify scientific journals where relevant articles are likely to have been published (this list can frequently be generated with the help of a professor or some other "expert," as well as the above computer search strategy). You then go to the Table of Contents of each issue of each journal for the past 5 years and identify articles that seem relevant based on their titles and abstracts. If an article is deemed relevant, you secure a copy of it, read it, and then examine its reference section for additional relevant articles, based on what you read. Then you locate these cited articles and repeat the process for each of them. The result will be a set of articles that appeared in the major journals and articles that were cited by these articles. The key to this method is to examine the bibliography of every article you locate, to further identify relevant research.

Another approach for identifying relevant literature is to use the Science Citation Index and/or the Social Science Citation Index. These are reference books or databases contained in most college libraries; they list, for a given author of a given paper, all of the articles published by other individuals who have cited the paper (an online version of both indices also exists). If you are aware of the author of a major article in the area in which you are working, then the citation index can be a useful way of identifying other researchers who have cited that article in the context of their published research. The relevant publications of these other researchers can then be identified by information provided in the citation index.

Another strategy that can augment an index search is to use the Internet to locate the websites of scientists who have published in the area in which you are

(continued)

working. Many professors and applied scientists maintain websites, on which they post their most recent research papers for downloading, some of which have not yet been published.

A final strategy is to use Google Scholar, a specialized search tool developed by the website Google for identifying papers and articles that have cited other papers and articles (see the Google website for details at *www.google.com*).

Once you have identified the relevant literature, read it! Don't simply look at summaries of the research.

inverse and see if you can articulate a logic that would justify this sign reversal. As an example, a theorist might assume that people with more knowledge about a topic will be better able to remember the contents of an essay they read about that topic because (1) they likely have more interest in the topic and (2) they have more elaborated cognitive structures in long-term memory that they can use to integrate the essay information. This logic posits a positive association between prior knowledge and recall. Is it possible for this association to be negative instead? Is there a conceptual logic model that would justify a sign reversal? Perhaps people with a great deal of knowledge will think they "know it all" about the topic and therefore read the essay more superficially than people who feel they have something to learn. This lessened processing vigilance may lead those with higher levels of knowledge to have poorer recall of the essay material. If a presumed relationship in your theory is inverse, try making it positive in sign and see if you can articulate a logic that justifies this reversal. If a presumed relationship in your theory is positive in sign, try making it inverse and see if you can articulate a logic that justifies this reversal. If you are able to articulate compelling logic for both a direct and an inverse relationship, then you essentially have specified competing theories that lead to opposite predictions. It is then an empirical question as to which theory is correct. Also, as you consider relationship sign reversals, new mediators or moderators might come to mind.

As a final step, show your theory to friends and colleagues and discuss it with them. Ask them what they think about it. Do they agree or disagree with it? Can they suggest variables you have left out or variables you should drop? Pursue input from diverse sources. When this is done, close out the theoretical system. Pick a portion of the model to conduct your next research project on, either the portion that you are most interested in or the portion that you feel makes the most important contribution and pursue your research accordingly.

Summary of Steps

We conclude this section by listing the sequence of steps you might use to construct your theory based on the preceding discussion:

- Step 1: Identify the outcome variable in which you are interested.
- Step 2: Using heuristics from throughout this book, identify two or three direct causes of the outcome.

  (*Note:* You could instead articulate the first two steps as: (1) specify a variable in which you are interested and (2) identify two or three consequences or outcomes associated with that variable. Or specify a single direct cause consisting of an intervention and an outcome. Whatever the sequence, you want to have at least one direct effect in your theory at this juncture.)

- Step 3: Turn the direct causes into mediated effects using either the *why* heuristic, the *cause-of-a-cause* heuristic, or the *effect-of-an-effect* heuristic.
  - Step 3a: For each mediator, specify complete or partial mediation.
- Step 4: For every direct effect in the model, consider adding a moderator variable. You can focus or elaborate each moderated relationship using the strategies described in Chapter 6.
- Step 5: Expand and refine the mediated and moderated portions of the model.
  - Step 5a: For every mediated effect in the model, consider adding moderated mediation.
  - Step 5b: For every moderated effect in the model, consider adding mediated moderation.
  - Step 5c: For every moderated effect in the model, consider adding moderated moderation.
- Step 6: For every direct effect in the model, consider adding reciprocal causation.
  - Step 6a: Consider turning a reciprocal causal effect into a feedback loop by adding mediators.
  - Step 6b: If feedback loops are added with mediators, consider the issue of partial versus complete mediation.
  - Step 6c: For every reciprocal causal effect in the model, consider adding moderated reciprocal causation.
  - Step 6d: For every moderated reciprocal causation effect, think about adding mediated moderation and/or moderated moderation.
- Step 7: Consider adding new outcome variables to the system.
- Step 8: Consider adding temporal dynamics to the model, including contemporaneous effects, autoregressive effects, and lagged effects.
- Step 9: Fine-tune the relationships and logic of your model.
  - Step 9a: Map causal relationships among all exogenous variables.
  - Step 9b: Add disturbance terms for all endogenous variables and consider the need to add correlated disturbances.
  - Step 9c: Focus all concepts and all relationships using strategies from Chapters 5 and 6.

○ Step 9d: Revisit your initial review of the literature and make changes to the theory, as appropriate. Flag innovations in your theory.

○ Step 9e: Consider sign reversals for all direct relationships in your theory.

- Step 10: Get feedback on the model from your colleagues and select that portion of the theory to conduct your next research project on.

THE BINDER METHOD

There is an alternative approach for constructing an innovative causal model based on a method which I (Jaccard) have used throughout my career, a method I call the *binder method*. With this approach, I first conduct an extensive search of the literature using the methods described in Box 7.1 on pages 184–185 for an outcome variable or topic area I am interested in. For each relevant article I locate, I print a hardcopy of the first page. The first page usually has the full citation information on it, the article abstract, and the first part of the introduction section that sets the stage for the reported research.[3] Accumulating these first pages, I order them from oldest to newest and then read every first page. I begin with the oldest article so that I can gain a sense of how the research has evolved over time. After obtaining an overview of the field in this fashion, I sort the first pages into piles that represent groups of articles that seem to "go together." When approaching this task, I do not rely on a carefully derived set of classification rules; instead, I let the criteria "emerge" as I am sorting, based on my intuition, my social science training, and the "feel" I have recently acquired for the literature as a whole after reading all first pages. If a given article fits into more than one pile, I make a second copy of its first page and place it in both piles. I then ask one or two of my friends or graduate students to perform the same task, after which we compare our respective piles and discuss emergent criteria that seemed to be used to place articles into the different piles. After these discussions, I go through all the articles again and perform a final sort, this time ordering the articles within a pile from most recent to oldest. Each pile essentially represents a "subarea" of research in the topic area, and all the piles taken as a collective represent an organizational scheme I have imposed on the literature. I then place all the first pages in each pile into a binder with a labeled divider between each pile.

At this point, I choose a pile that most interests me and acquire and read all of the articles within it, from most recent to oldest. Invariably, I cannot help "peeking" at articles in some of the other piles, but I usually concentrate on the one target pile. I then select an article in the pile that best maps onto my interests. For this article, I draw an influence diagram that reflects the theory the article tested and affirmed (for how to do this, see Chapter 16 on reading about theories and the supplemental materials online at *www.theory-construction.com*). When I read the second article, I modify this diagram to include new relevant outcomes, new explanatory variables, new direct effects, new mediators, new moderators, and new reciprocal causal relations suggested

---

[3]If a key book is identified in my literature search, I seek to find a thorough review of it to use as my first page or I read the book and write a one-page summary to use.

by the article. I repeat this exercise for the third article, the fourth article, and all the remaining articles in the pile until I have a large influence diagram that reflects "what we know" based on past research. At times, an article in the pile will not be relevant to the emerging, literature-based theory, in which case I skip it. Sometimes, I split the emerging theory into several influence diagrams and work with them separately, to make things manageable. My approach to constructing influence diagrams is fluid rather than rigid.

With the model(s) reflecting the past literature in hand, I begin the task of theory construction. First, using heuristics from Chapter 4, I think about whether there is a key explanatory variable that the literature has ignored. If I identify one, I add it to the diagram and think through how it "fits" in the model relative to other variables. Next, I target an existing path/relationship that particularly interests me and think about how I might expand it in novel ways, say, by elaborating mediators of it or by specifying moderators that qualify it. I might use the why heuristic to generate mediators; or I might think how I can make the outcome a cause using the effect-of-an-effect heuristic; or I might use the cause-of-a-cause heuristic to add a new mediational chain. For each new mediator I consider whether partial or complete mediation is justified. I use the stronger-than heuristic to identify moderators, and then I consider adding mediated moderation, moderated mediation, and/or moderated moderation. All the while, I am thinking carefully about viable conceptual logic models for every theoretical link I add (per Chapter 4) as well as possible sign reversals. I also look for places in the model where potential reciprocal causality has been overlooked in the literature. Once identified, I construct mediation and moderation around those reciprocal relationships. When the process is complete, I usually am able to identify where in the model I can make a reasonable theoretical contribution. However, I do not stop there. I next bring a longitudinal focus to the model (or subportions of it), thinking about causal dynamics over time and potential lagged and autoregressive effects that might be intriguing. Finally, I place my influence diagrams and the extensive notes I made when constructing them at the beginning of the "pile" in the binder, after the divider but before the date-sequenced first pages.

Then, it is onto the next pile, where I repeat the entire process, which continues until I have exhausted all the piles. Sometimes while working on one pile, I get an idea for the model of another pile and bring that idea to it. Once a year, I conduct a new literature search starting where I left off the prior year. I find new relevant "first pages" and integrate them into the binder into the appropriate subsections (piles). I revisit my old influence diagram and update it after reading the new articles in each pile.

My students and colleagues who come by my office see rows of labeled binders on the bookshelves, befuddled by what I possibly could be doing with them. Over the years, I have tried to move to electronic versions of the binders, but it just does not afford the flexibility of viewing multiple first pages simultaneously and experimenting with different sortings. Having said that, with digitized first pages or articles, it is easier to search through first pages or articles for key terms and to copy and paste key phrases or paragraphs. The choice of modality is whatever works best for you. The binder method takes practice as you learn to create workable "piles," efficiently translate what is in an article into an article-specific set of causal essences, and then integrate the article's essence into the overarching influence diagram. If you try the binder method, make modifications to suit your thinking strategies and cognitive habits.

COMMON MISTAKES DURING CAUSAL THEORY CONSTRUCTION

Having overseen doctoral dissertations for over 40 years, we see our students make some common mistakes as they approach causal theory construction for dissertation research. Probably the most frequent mistake is to work with a model that is too complex, containing too many variables, too many relationships, or both. In short, the theory they propose is unwieldy for purposes of empirical research. It may seem ironic for us to mention this mistake because both the 10-step and binder methods of theory construction usually result in large, cumbersome models. It is indeed desirable to have a comprehensive overarching theory of a topic area that elaborates the many variables and operative relationships at work. However, it usually is not feasible to empirically evaluate the overarching theory in a single study. The resources, demands, time, and effort usually are too daunting. Instead, we focus our students on a subportion of the larger theory and encourage them to pursue high-quality research on that subportion in ways that allow one to comprehensively understand it. Once accomplished, students can then focus on another subportion of the model in a different research project and build a corresponding comprehensive understanding of it. As one methodically works through the different subportions of the overarching theory, one is essentially engaging in programmatic research. At some point, the elements of the research program can be pieced together to garner perspectives on the overarching theory. It is for this reason that programmatic research is so important.

A second common mistake is to work with variables that are too abstract and fuzzy and/or relationships that are too abstract or fuzzy. It is important to be clear and precise when describing concepts and relationships. Chapters 5 and 6 should help in this respect.

A third common mistake is to specify a poorly developed conceptual logic model in support of theoretical assertions. This problem can be addressed using the principles developed in Chapter 4. (See also the supplemental materials on our companion website at *www.theory-construction.com*.)

Finally, some students come forth with proposals that make an insufficient theoretical contribution. Chapter 3 can help address such cases.

PERSPECTIVES ON THE CONSTRUCTION OF CAUSAL THEORIES

Path Diagrams as Theoretical Propositions

Using either the 10-step or binder method, what likely started as a fairly simple theory and influence diagram has probably blossomed into an elaborate theoretical product. An invaluable aid to developing the theory in both approaches is the influence diagram that we continually referenced, updated, elaborated, and expanded. Many theories in the social sciences are simple three- or four-variable systems consisting only of direct causal relationships. Such theories are straightforward to describe using narratives, and it is easy to keep in mind the overall framework the theorist is describing. However, as theories grow in complexity, readers may need some type of pedagogical device to help them see the broader framework in a unified way. Influence diagrams are useful in this regard. An influence diagram summarizes many theoretical propositions that, if expressed verbally, would constitute a long list. Every causal path in an influence diagram represents a theoretical proposition, and the absence of causal paths also can reflect theoretical propositions, such as propositions about complete mediation versus partial mediation. To illustrate, consider the structural model in Figure 7.19 on page 182. Here are the major theoretical propositions that derive from this path diagram:

Proposition 1: The birthweight of a newborn is influenced by how much a mother smokes during pregnancy. The more a mother smokes during the pregnancy, the lower the birthweight of the newborn. This relationship is assumed to be linear.

Proposition 2: The birthweight of a newborn is influenced by how much alcohol a mother consumes during pregnancy. The more alcohol a mother consumes during the pregnancy, the lower the birthweight of the newborn. This relationship is assumed to be linear.

Proposition 3: The amount a mother smokes during her pregnancy is influenced by the extent of her support network. The more support the mother has to quit smoking, the less she will smoke during her pregnancy. This relationship is assumed to be linear.

Proposition 4: The amount a mother smokes during her pregnancy is influenced by her locus of control. The higher the locus of control, the less she will smoke during her pregnancy. This relationship is assumed to be linear.

Proposition 5: The amount of alcohol a mother consumes during her pregnancy is influenced by the extent of her support network. The more support the mother has to quit drinking, the less she will drink during her pregnancy. This relationship is assumed to be linear.

Proposition 6: The amount of alcohol a mother consumes during her pregnancy is influenced by her locus of control. The higher the locus of control, the less she will drink during her pregnancy. This relationship is assumed to be linear.

Proposition 7: The effects of locus of control on birthweight are completely mediated by how much a mother drinks and how much a mother smokes.

Proposition 8: The effects of the support network on birthweight are completely mediated by how much a mother drinks and how much a mother smokes.

Proposition 9: The association between how much a mother drinks and how much she smokes during pregnancy is a function of the common causes of locus of control and the extent of support network.

Note that these propositions omit statements about correlated errors and the measurement model.

Years ago, when submitting grant proposals to secure funding to conduct research, it was common practice to list the specific aims and formal hypotheses early in the proposal and then to coordinate discussion of the literature, elaboration of measures, and specification of data collection and data analysis around the three or four theoretical propositions stated in the aims section. This also was a common practice in scientific reports, where the introduction of the report would culminate in the formal statement of three or four hypotheses. However, as theory becomes multivariate and complex, which is more often the case in modern-day social science, these traditions become inefficient and detract from effective communication. Influence diagrams can be a useful tool for summarizing theoretical propositions efficiently. Each path in the diagram can be labeled with a + or a – to indicate if the presumed relationship is assumed to be positive or inverse. Nonlinear relationships can be described in the text, either verbally or mathematically, using principles discussed in Chapter 9.

Unfortunately, some scientists fail to appreciate that influence diagrams represent multiple hypotheses and theoretical propositions. Thus, you may receive criticism in a grant proposal or a research report for not formally stating specific hypotheses, despite the fact that you have presented a clear and explicit influence diagram.

Another potential problem with the use of influence diagrams comes from the opposite end of the spectrum. Some reviewers of proposals and reports do not believe you have a theory unless you have presented a diagram. We have served on numerous review panels and have observed instances where a research project is said to "lack theory," only to see a similar project move forward uncriticized simply because it had a diagram with boxes and arrows. The variables in the influence diagram were poorly defined and fuzzy, the posited relationships were not well thought out or articulated, and crucial variables were omitted. Because there were boxes and arrows, however, the research was deemed as having a viable theoretical base.

We raise these issues so that you will not be discouraged if you are criticized for not specifying hypotheses after having presented a well-articulated influence diagram, and so you will not be lackadaisical and think you can get by with any diagram. If you use the heuristics described in this chapter and previous ones, if you carefully focus your concepts and relationships, and if you articulate the logic underlying every path, you should be on sound theoretical footing.

The Use of Causal Analysis in Grounded/Emergent Theorizing Revisited

The development of theory using the methods described in this chapter has emphasized an a priori approach to theory construction. However, there is no reason why the concepts that we have developed cannot be applied to grounded and emergent theory construction after qualitative data have been collected. Specifically, the grounded/emergent theorist can approach the analysis and interpretation of qualitative data by constructing an influence diagram that captures conceptually the causal relations among variables that emerge from the data. When framing and approaching data, the theorist can think about direct causes, indirect causes, partial and complete mediation, moderated relationships, bidirectional relationships, and spurious relationships; he or she can think about mediated moderation, moderated mediation, and moderated moderation. In short, the causal framework can be used as a blueprint for the types of relationships that grounded/emergent theorists think about as they approach the theory construction process from the qualitative data they have collected. We provide examples of this approach in Chapter 10.

SUMMARY AND CONCLUDING COMMENTS

The building blocks of all causal theories are six types of relationships: (1) direct causal relationships, (2) indirect (mediated) causal relationships, (3) moderated relationships, (4) reciprocal causal relationships, (5) spurious relationships, and (6) unanalyzed relationships. This chapter described two approaches, a 10-step method and a binder method, to developing the skeleton of a causal theory. Each approach works with the generation of an influence diagram in conjunction with careful analysis of each path in that diagram, using concepts like partial and complete mediation, moderated mediation, mediated moderation, moderated moderation, feedback loops, temporal dynamics (including contemporaneous effects, lagged effects, and autoregressive effects), disturbance and error terms, and latent variables. Numerous heuristics for thinking about causal effects were presented and coupled with Chapters 3, 4, 5, and 6 for generating and refining ideas, your toolbox for theory construction should now be that much fuller. Future chapters provide yet further strategies for constructing innovative theories.

SUGGESTED READINGS

Blalock, H. M. (1964). *Causal inferences in non-experimental research*. Chapel Hill: University of North Carolina Press.

—An excellent discussion of the concept of causality and methods of theory construction.

Blalock, H. M. (1983). *Theory construction*. San Francisco: Jossey-Bass.

—A discussion of general methods of theory construction.

Bunge, M. (1961). Causality, chance, and law. *American Scientist, 69*, 432–488.

—A clear discussion of aspects of causality.

Cartwright, N. (2007). *Hunting causes and using them*. New York: Cambridge University Press.

—A more advanced discussion of the concept of causality, particularly as applied in the field of economics.

Howard, G. S. (1984). The role of values in the science of psychology. *American Psychologist, 40*, 255–265.

—A discussion of how values influence the way we theorize.

Manicas, P. (2006). *A realist philosophy of social science: Explanation and understanding.* Cambridge, UK: Cambridge University Press.

—A more advanced discussion of causal realism and a critique of traditional views of causality.

Maxwell, J. (2004). Using qualitative methods for causal explanation. *Field Methods, 16*, 243–264.

— An introduction to alternative views of causality as used in grounded theories.

Morgan, S., & Winship, C. (2007). *Counterfactuals and causal inference.* New York: Cambridge University Press.

—A lucid discussion of the use of counterfactuals in the analysis of causality.

Pearl, J. (2009). *Causality: Models, reasoning, and inference.* New York: Cambridge University Press.

—A comprehensive discussion of causality from many perspectives.

Pearl, J., & Mackenzie, D. (2018). *The book of why.* New York: Basic Books.

—An entertaining read for Pearl's approach to causal analysis using counterfactuals.

Salmon, W. C. (1998) *Causality and explanation.* New York. Oxford University Press.

—A discussion of the approach of causal realism.

Zetterbert, H. (1965). *On theory and verification in sociology.* Totowa, NJ: Bedminster Press.

—A discussion of strategies for theory construction using the concept of causality.

KEY TERMS

predictive relationship (p. 152)

predictor variable (p. 152)

criterion variable (p. 152)

independent variable (p. 155)

determinant (p. 155)

dependent variable (p. 155)

path diagram (p. 155)

direct causal relationship (p. 155)

indirect causal relationship (p. 156)

mediating variable (p. 156)

mediator (p. 156)

spurious relationship (p. 157)

moderated causal relationship (p. 157)

moderator variable (p. 157)

bidirectional causal relationship (p. 157)

reciprocal causal relationship (p. 157)

unanalyzed relationship (p. 157)

endogenous variable (p. 158)

exogenous variable (p. 158)

why heuristic (p. 160)

partial mediator (p. 161)

complete mediator (p. 161)

cause-of-a-cause heuristic (p. 163)   contemporaneous effects (p. 176)

effect-of-an-effect heuristic (p. 165)   autoregressive effects (p. 176)

stronger-than heuristic (p. 165)   lagged effects (p. 176)

mediated moderation (p. 166)   disturbance term (p. 178)

moderated mediation (p. 167)   correlated disturbances (p. 179)

moderated moderation (p. 168)   latent variable (p. 181)

equilibrium assumption (p. 170)   structural model (p. 182)

feedback loops (p. 170)   measurement model (p. 183)

moderated reciprocal causation (p. 172)   binder method (p. 187)

EXERCISES

Exercises to Reinforce Concepts

1. Distinguish between causal and predictive relationships.

2. What are the five common features of the construct of causality on which most social scientists agree?

3. Identify and define the six basic types of relationships in causal models and give an example of each.

4. What is the essence of a causal relationship? Why have some philosophers objected to the notion of causality?

5. If causality in the social sciences can rarely be proven, why is the concept still useful in science?

6. What is a path or influence diagram?

7. What strategies or heuristics can you use to turn a direct relationship into an indirect relationship? Create an example using them.

8. What is the difference between partial and complete mediation?

9. What heuristics do you use to identify moderated relationships?

10. What is the difference between mediated moderation, moderated mediation, and moderated moderation?

11. How are feedback loops indirect effects?

12. Why is there no such thing as an instantaneous reciprocal causal relationship?

13. What heuristics might lead to the addition of spurious effects in a theory?

14. Are spurious effects always bad? Why or why not?

15. What is the difference between an exogenous and an endogenous variable?

16. What are the three types of relationships that incorporate temporal dynamics into them?

17. How is the time frame important for analyzing mediation or causal effects?

18. Under what conditions do you specify correlated error?

19. What is the difference between a structural model and a measurement model?

20. Describe the binder method for theory construction.

Exercises to Apply Concepts

1. Find a study in the literature and describe the theory it tests using a causal framework. Draw an influence diagram of the theory. Provide conceptual definitions of each construct and be explicit about the nature of each relationship in the theory.

2. Using the 10-step method discussed in this chapter, construct a causal theory. Include an influence diagram of it and an accompanying narrative describing it. Give precise and clear conceptual definitions of each variable, using the strategies in Chapter 5. Clarify the relationships and develop a conceptual logic model for key paths, per Chapter 4.

3. Apply the binder method to a topic of your choice, but focus your theorizing on a single "pile." Keep the topic concrete and simple.

Mathematical Modeling

Even if there is only one possible unified theory,
it is just a set of rules and equations.
                —STEPHEN W. HAWKING (1988)

This chapter describes an approach to theory construction called *mathematical modeling*. Like causal modeling, the approach involves describing relationships between variables, but the emphasis is on describing those relationships using mathematical concepts. Mathematical models can be used in conjunction with causal thinking, but social scientists who use mathematical modeling tend not to think in terms of indirect causes, mediated relationships, and moderated relationships in the way we outlined in Chapter 7. Instead, they focus on thinking about functions and describing relationships mathematically based on functions. They more often than not use nonlinear relationships. Our focus here is not on integrating causal and mathematical modeling as approaches to theory construction. Rather, we merely wish to provide you with an additional tool for your theory construction toolbox, mathematical modeling, as you strive to gain insights into the phenomena you want to study.

Constructing mathematical models can involve complex mathematics that go well beyond the background of many of our readers. Entire books have been written on mathematical modeling that assume years of study of calculus and formal mathematics. Our treatment must, accordingly, be limited, and we provide only a general sense of building mathematical models and thinking as a math modeler would. However, the chapter should be a good starting point for delving into this approach in more depth using the suggested readings at the end of the chapter.

Mathematical modeling is common in the physical sciences, but it is used less often in the social sciences. In this chapter, we provide you with a sense of mathematical modeling as it is pursued in the social sciences. We first expose you to basic concepts and terms you will encounter as you read about math models or pursue mathematical modeling. More specifically, we distinguish between categorical, discrete, and continuous variables; differentiate axioms and theorems; introduce the notion of a function;

use linear functions to identify key features of functions; and describe the difference between deterministic and stochastic models. We also provide an intuitive overview of derivatives, differentiation, integrals, and integration in calculus, as well as key notions of model identification and metrics. We next describe five commonly used functions in math models: logarithmic functions, exponential functions, power functions, polynomial functions, and trigonomic functions, as well as functions for categorical variables. We conclude our background section by considering ways of transforming and combining functions and building functions for multiple variable scenarios.

Following the presentation of these concepts, we describe the phases of building a mathematical model and then provide two examples of such models in the social sciences. We then briefly characterize chaos theory and catastrophe theory as influential mathematical models. Our initial discussion may seem a bit fractured as we develop one mathematical concept after another. Be patient. Later sections will pull it all together.

TYPES OF VARIABLES: NOMINAL, DISCRETE, AND CONTINUOUS

In Chapter 6, we distinguished between nominal and quantitative variables. A nominal variable has different levels, values, or categories, and there is no special ordering to the categories along an underlying dimension. The categories are merely labels that differentiate one group from another (e.g., "male" or "female" for the variable of gender). In contrast, a quantitative variable is one in which individuals are assigned numerical values to place them into different categories, and the numerical values have meaning in that they imply more or less of an underlying dimension that is of theoretical interest.

Mathematical modelers make distinctions between discrete quantitative variables and continuous quantitative variables. A *discrete variable* is one in which there are a finite number of values between two values. For example, for the number of children in a family, there is a finite number of values between one child and four children, namely, the values of two children and three children. We do not think of there being 1.5 children in a family. For a *continuous variable,* however, there is an infinite number of values between any two values. Reaction time to a stimulus is an example of a continuous variable. Even between the values of 1 and 2 seconds, an infinite number of values could occur (e.g., 1.001 seconds, 1.873 seconds, 1.874 seconds).

Whether a variable is classified as discrete or continuous depends on the nature of the underlying theoretical dimension and not on the scale used to measure that dimension. Tests that measure intelligence, for example, yield scores that are whole numbers (e.g., 101, 102); hence, the scores are discrete. Nevertheless, intelligence is continuous because it involves a dimension that permits an infinite number of values to occur, even though existing measuring devices are not sensitive enough to make such fine distinctions. In the reaction time example, the measurement of time can be very precise with modern equipment, but there even is a limit to the precision possible with measures of time. Such limits in the precision of measurement do not make the underlying dimension discrete. Reaction time is continuous in character.

Although social scientists often rely on discrete measures of continuous constructs, they build models with those measures as if they were continuous. As long as the measures are composed of many values, this practice usually is not problematic. It is only when the number of values in the measure of a continuous variable is small that problems can arise and special considerations in the modeling effort need to be made (see Chapter 13 for elaboration).

The distinction between discrete and continuous variables is important because the strategies used to construct a mathematical model differ depending on whether the quantitative variables are discrete or continuous. We devote most of our attention to the case of continuous variables, but we occasionally consider nominal and discrete variables as well.

AXIOMS AND THEOREMS

The term *axiom* is used in many ways in the social sciences, but in mathematics, an axiom is a mathematical statement that serves as a starting point from which other mathematical statements are logically derived. Axioms are "given." They are not derived through deduction, nor are they the subject of mathematical proofs. They are starting points. By contrast, a *theorem* is a statement that can be logically derived from, or is proven by, one or more axioms or previous statements. The use of these terms and the many variants of them (e.g., proposition, lemma, corollary, claim, identity, rule, law, postulate, principle) vary somewhat depending on the branch of mathematics, but this characterization captures the essence of axioms and theorems as used in mathematical models in the social sciences.

FUNCTIONS

Functions are central to mathematical modeling. A simple analogy for thinking about functions is to think of a machine that you put something into and get something back, based on what you input. For example, you might press a key that inputs the number 3 into a machine and out comes the number 9. You might press another key that inputs the number 5 into the machine and out comes the number 15. The machine in this case represents the function "take the input value and triple it." Functions in math typically involve numbers as inputs and outputs.

Suppose we decide to name our machine *Jack*. We can write the function that the machine performs as follows:

$$\text{Jack}(X) = 3X$$

This equation states that whatever the value of X, the value of "Jack of X" will be triple it. The traditional notation is to name the machine f (for "function") and write it as follows:

$$f(X) = 3X$$

All functions have what are called a domain and a range. The *domain* is the set of possible input values, and the *range* is the set of possible output values. The domain and range often are stated mathematically rather than listed as individual numbers. For example, for the function

$$f(X) = \sqrt{X - 3}$$

the domain or possible input values is any number greater than or equal to 3 (because you can not calculate the square root of a negative number), and the range or possible output values is any value greater than or equal to 0.[1] The domain is any number that produces a "meaningful output" that will not cause the machine to malfunction (e.g., the number 2, which would require us to calculate the square root of −1). A shorthand way that mathematical modelers use to express the domain is "the domain is $\{X \mid X \geq 3\}$," where the symbol "|" is read as "given that." This expression states that the domain is equal to X, given that X is greater than or equal to 3. This may seem cryptic, but it is an efficient way of stating a domain or a range. For example, I might have a function where the domain is $\{X \mid X > 0\}$ and the range is $\{Y \mid Y > 0\}$.

Functions can apply to more than a single input. For example, the function $f(X,Z) = X - Z$ has two inputs, X and Z, and an output that is the difference between them. For example, if $X = 5$ and $Z = 2$, the function $f(X,Z)$ yields the output 3.

Functions are the foundation of mathematical models. When one "maps" a function between Y and X, one attempts to specify what function applied to values on X will produce the values of Y. A central task in mathematical modeling is that of mapping functions.

LINEAR FUNCTIONS

One of the most commonly used functions in the social sciences is the *linear function*. In this section, we describe the nature of linear functions and then use them to illustrate basic issues in building mathematical models. In later sections, we consider other functions.

The Slope and Intercept

The Slope

Consider the two-variable example we used in Chapter 6 to develop the idea of a linear relationship, namely, the number of hours an employee worked, X, and the amount of money paid to the employee, Y. Assume a scenario where each of four individuals works at a rate of $1 per hour. Their scores are:

---

[1] For pedagogical reasons, we restrict all examples in this chapter to real numbers.

Individual	X (hours worked)	Y (dollars paid)
1	1	1
2	4	4
3	3	3
4	2	2

The relationship between X and Y is illustrated in Figure 8.1, which uses a scatterplot with connected dots. As indicated by the straight line on the scatterplot, there is a linear relationship between X and Y. This relationship can be stated mathematically as

$$Y = X$$

In other words, the number of dollars paid equals the number of hours worked.

Suppose the individuals were not paid $1 per hour, but instead were paid $2 per hour. The scores on X and Y would be as follows:

Individual	X (hours worked)	Y (dollars paid)
1	1	2
2	4	8
3	3	6
4	2	4

In this case, the relationship between X and Y can be stated as

$$Y = 2.00X$$

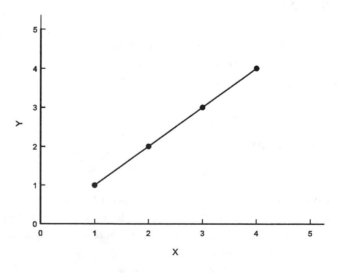

FIGURE 8.1. Linear relationship with slope = 1.

In other words, the number of dollars paid equals 2 times the number of hours worked. Figure 8.2 presents a scatterplot of these data (line B) as well as the data from Figure 8.1 (line A). (Line C is explained on p. 203.) Notice that we still have a straight line (and, hence, a linear relationship), but, in the case of $2 per hour, the line rises faster than with $1 per hour; that is, the slope of the line is now steeper. Technically, the slope of a line indicates the number of units that variable Y changes when variable X increases by 1 unit. It is the rate of change in Y given a 1-unit increase in X. When the wage is $2 per hour, a person who works 1 hour is paid $2, a person who works 2 hours is paid $4, and so on. When X increases by 1 unit (e.g., from 1 to 2 hours), Y increases by 2 units (e.g., from $2 to $4). The slope that describes this linear relationship is therefore 2. In contrast, the slope that describes the linear relationship $Y = X$ is 1.0, meaning that as X increases by 1 unit, so does Y. One way in which linear relationships differ is in terms of the slopes that describe them.

The slope that describes a linear relationship can be determined from a simple algebraic formula. This formula involves first selecting the X and Y values of any two individuals. The slope is computed by dividing the difference between the two Y scores by the difference between the two X scores; in other words, the change in Y scores is divided by the change in X scores. Algebraically,

$$b = (Y_2 - Y_1)/(X_2 - X_1) \tag{8.1}$$

where b represents the slope, X_1 and Y_1 are the X and Y scores for any one individual, and X_2 and Y_2 are the X and Y scores for any other individual. In our example, inserting the scores for individuals 1 ($X = 1$, $Y = 2$) and 2 ($X = 4$, $Y = 8$) into Equation 8.1, we find that the slope for line B is

$$b = (2 - 8)/(1 - 4) = 2.00$$

This is consistent with what was stated previously.

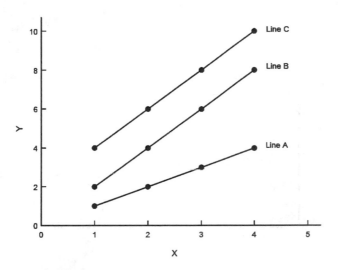

FIGURE 8.2. Example of linear relationships with different slopes or intercepts.

The value of a slope can be positive, negative, or 0. Consider the following scores:

Individual	X	Y
1	2	3
2	1	4
3	4	1
4	3	2

Inserting the scores for individuals 2 and 4 into Equation 8.1, we find that the slope is

$$b = (4 - 2)/(1 - 3) = -1.00$$

Figure 8.3 presents a scatterplot of the data for this relationship. The relationship is still linear, but now the line moves downward as we move from left to right on the X-axis. This downward direction characterizes a negative slope, whereas an upward direction characterizes a positive slope. A slope of 0 is represented by a horizontal line because the value of Y is constant for values of X.

In sum, a positive slope indicates a *positive* or *direct linear relationship* between X and Y, whereas a negative slope indicates a *negative* or *inverse linear relationship* between X and Y. In the case of a positive relationship, as scores on X *increase,* scores on Y also *increase.* In the case of a negative relationship, as scores on X *increase,* scores on Y *decrease.* For instance, the slope in Figure 8.3 is –1.00, meaning that for every unit X increases, Y decreases by one unit.

The Intercept

Let us return to the example where individuals are paid $2 per hour worked. Suppose that in addition to this wage, individuals are given a tip of $1.50. Now the relationship is

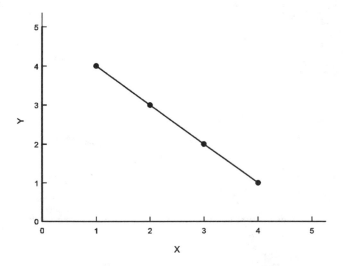

FIGURE 8.3. Example of a negative slope.

$$Y = 1.50 + 2.00X \qquad (8.2)$$

Line C of Figure 8.2 plots this relationship for the four individuals. If we compute the slope of this line, we find it is 2.00, as before. Notice that lines C and B are parallel but that line C is higher up on the Y-axis than line B. The amount of separation between these two lines can be measured at the Y-axis, where $X = 0$. When $X = 0$, the Y value is 1.50 for line C and 0 for line B. Thus, line C is raised 1.50 units above line B. The point at which a line intersects the Y-axis when $X = 0$ is called the *intercept,* and its value is denoted by the letter a. Another way of thinking about the intercept is that it is the value of Y when X is zero.

Linear relationships can differ in the values of their intercepts as well as the values of their slopes. The general form of a linear equation is

$$Y = a + bX \qquad (8.3)$$

Stated more formally, the linear function is

$$f(X) = a + bX$$

where a and b are constants representing an intercept and slope and X is a variable. A variable, Y, is described by this function if $Y = f(X)$, and the function is $Y = a + bX$. Equation 8.3 is called a *linear equation.*

DETERMINISTIC VERSUS STOCHASTIC MODELS

Any linear relationship can be represented by Equation 8.3. Given values of the slope and intercept, we can substitute scores on X into the linear equation to determine the corresponding scores on Y. For example, the linear equation $Y = 1.50 + 2.00X$ tells us that an individual who works for 2 hours is paid \$5.50 because the Y score associated with an X score of 2 is

$$Y = 1.50 + 2.00X = 1.50 + (2.00)(2) = \$5.50$$

An individual who works for 3 hours is paid $Y = 1.50 + (2.00)(3) = \$7.50$, and an individual who works for 4 hours is paid $Y = 1.50 + (2.00)(4) = \$9.50$.

When one variable is a linear function of another, all the data points on a scatterplot will fall on a straight line. However, rarely in the social sciences will we encounter such situations. When two variables only approximate a linear relationship, we need to add a term to the linear equation to accommodate random disparities from linearity. The term is called a *disturbance* or *error term,* yielding the equation

$$Y = a + bX + e$$

where e is the difference between the observed Y score and the predicted score based on the linear function. The errors are assumed to be random rather than systematic because if the errors were systematic, then some meaningful form of nonlinearity would be suggested and would need to be modeled. It is important to keep in mind that e is an unmeasured variable that reflects the disparity between scores predicted by the model and observed scores.

Formal mathematical models do not include an error term when specified at the theoretical level. In this sense, they are deterministic rather than probabilistic. However, when testing mathematical models empirically, it is common for researchers to include an error term because there usually is some random "noise" that creates disparities from model predictions. A common practice is to identify the function that seems appropriate for predicting and understanding a phenomenon and then, in data-based tests of the model, to add an error term to accommodate the hopefully small but random discrepancies that seem inevitable. A model is better if the discrepancies from predictions are trivial and have no practical consequence.

In the world of mathematical models, you will encounter distinctions between deterministic and probabilistic models. A *deterministic model* is one in which there is no random error operating. The model performs the same way for any given set of conditions. In contrast, a *probabilistic model* is one in which some degree of randomness is present. Probabilistic models are also sometimes referred to as *stochastic models*.

MODEL PARAMETERS

Adjustable Parameters and Parameter Estimation

Mathematical models typically include variables that are measured as well as constants whose values can be derived logically or estimated from data. For example, in the linear function

$$f(X) = a + bX$$

there is a variable, X, and two model constants that need to be specified, the intercept, a, and the slope, b. Constants such as the intercept and the slope are called *adjustable parameters* or *adjustable constants* because their values can be set by the theorist to different values so as to affect the output of the function. For example, we might state that annual income is a function of the number of years of education, where the function is defined as $f(X) = 1,000 + 5,000X$. If the number of years of education is 2, then output of the function is $1,000 + (5,000)(2) = 11,000$. By contrast, we might state that the function is $f(X) = 2,000 + 4,000X$. If the number of years of education is 2, then the output of the function is $2,000 + (4,000)(2) = 10,000$. The slope and intercept are adjustable constants that affect the output value of the function as different values of X are submitted into the function.

When one is unsure as to what the value of the adjustable constants should be, then certain strategies can be used to estimate their values empirically based on data. For example, in a linear model where the relationship between Y and X is linear, except for the presence of random noise (i.e., $Y = a + bX + e$), a researcher might obtain data for the values of Y and the values of X for a group of individuals and then use traditional least-squares regression methods to estimate the values of the intercept and slope.

Mathematical models differ in the number of adjustable constants they include and in the number of constants that must be estimated from data. Models with many parameter values that must be estimated are less parsimonious and often present greater challenges for testing than models with fewer estimated parameters. When the value of an adjustable parameter is specified a priori by the theorist and is not estimated, it is said to be *fixed*. When the value of the adjustable parameter is estimated from data, it is said to be *estimated*. Thus, you will hear reference to fixed parameters and estimated parameters in math models.

RATES AND CHANGE: DERIVATIVES AND DIFFERENTIATION

Parameters in a mathematical model often are subject to meaningful interpretation. In the linear model, $Y = a + bX$, the slope reflects the predicted change in Y given a 1-unit change in X. It is calculated using Equation 8.1, which we repeat here:

$$b = (Y_2 - Y_1)/(X_2 - X_1)$$

The slope is meaningful because it provides a sense of how much change in Y we can expect, given a change in X. Note that in the linear model, it does not matter where the change occurs on the X continuum. A 1-unit change on X, at the low end of the X continuum, will produce the same amount of change in Y as a 1-unit change in X at the high end of the X continuum. The value of the slope tells us how much change this is.

The slope is, in essence, a rate of change in Y, given a unit change in X. More generally, if we describe the change in Y between any two points as

$$\Delta Y = Y_2 - Y_1$$

and the change in X between those same two points as

$$\Delta X = X_2 - X_1$$

then the rate of change in Y relative to the change in X is the ratio of these

$$\text{Rate of change} = \frac{\Delta Y}{\Delta X} = \frac{Y_2 - Y_1}{X_2 - X_1}$$

which, in this case, is the value of the slope. If $\Delta Y = 4$ and $\Delta X = 2$, then the rate of change of Y relative to a unit change in X is $4/2 = 2$.

The property of equal amounts of change at all points on the X continuum does not apply to nonlinear relationships. Consider the nonlinear relationship between Y and X shown in Figure 8.4. At low values of X, small changes in X result in no change in Y,

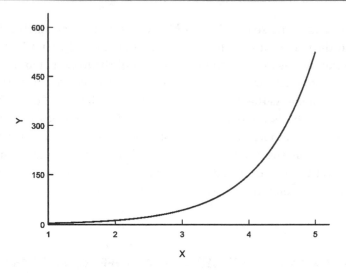

FIGURE 8.4. Nonlinear relationship for derivative example.

whereas at high values of X, small changes in X result in large changes in Y. The impact of a 1-unit change in X differs depending on the part of the X continuum at which the change occurs.

When analyzing change, two fundamental concepts from calculus are helpful: derivatives and differentiation. *Derivatives* refer to the concept of instantaneous change, and *differentiation* refers to algebraic methods for calculating the amount of instantaneous change that occurs. Let us explore these concepts in more depth.

Instantaneous Change

Suppose we want to measure the speed of a car a person is driving between two towns, Town A and Town B, that are 120 miles apart. Let Y be the distance traveled by the car. When the car is in Town A and just about to begin its journey, the car has traveled 0 miles, so we set $Y_1 = 0$. When the car reaches Town B, it has traveled 120 miles, so we set $Y_2 = 120$. Now let X be the amount of time the car spends traveling. Before the car leaves Town A, $X_1 = 0$ hours. Suppose when the car finally reaches Town B, the car has been on the road for 2 hours. This means that $X_2 = 2$ hours. Using the logic from above, the rate of change in Y as a function of X is

$$\text{Rate of change} = \frac{(Y_2 - Y_1)}{(X_2 - X_1)} = \frac{\Delta Y}{\Delta X} = \frac{(120 - 0)}{(2 - 0)} = 60 \qquad (8.4)$$

or 60 miles per hour. A 1-unit change in time (X, as measured in hours) is associated with a 60-unit change in distance (Y, as measures in miles).

The value of 60 miles per hour represents the average speed of the car during the entire trip. But it is probably the case that the car did not travel at a speed of exactly 60 miles per hour during the entire trip. At times, it probably was driven faster and at other times, slower. Suppose we wanted to know how fast the car was going 15 minutes into the trip. One way of determining this number is to define values for X_1 and Y_1 at 14 minutes and 59 seconds into the trip and then to define X_2 and Y_2 values at 15 minutes and 1 second into trip. We could then apply Equation 8.4 to this more narrowly defined time frame. Although the result would give us a sense of how fast the car was being driven 15 minutes into the trip, it would not tell us how fast the car was being driven at *exactly* 15 minutes into the trip. We want to know at the very instant of 15 minutes into the trip how fast the car was going, that is, what its rate of change was at that particular instant. It is this concept of instantaneous change to which a derivative refers. The velocity that the car is traveling at an exact point in time maps onto the notion of a derivative.

For a nonlinear relationship such as that in Figure 8.4, it is possible to use differentiation to calculate the instantaneous rate of change in Y at any given value of X. The derivative is the (instantaneous) slope of Y on X at that given point of X. It is analogous to specifying the speed at which a car is being driven at a specific point in time. For some modeling problems, calculating a derivative by the process of differentiation is straightforward. For other problems, it can be quite complex. Methods of differentiation are taught in calculus and need not concern us here. The main point we want to convey is that in many forms of mathematical modeling, rates of change in Y as a function of changes in X are described using the language of derivatives, and it is important that you have a sense of that language.

For linear models, the instantaneous rate of change in Y at some point on the X continuum is the same as the instantaneous rate of change in Y at any other point on the X continuum. By contrast, for the nonlinear relationship in Figure 8.4, the instantaneous rate of change depends on where on the X continuum the change is occurring. In Figure 8.4, the derivative (i.e., instantaneous rate of change) when X = 1 is 0.04, whereas when X = 4, the derivative is 1.98. We calculated these values using calculus. A common notation for signifying a derivative is dY/dX. A common phrase for describing derivatives is to state "the value of the derivative at X = 4 is 1.98." If the derivative has the same value at all points on X (as is the case for a linear relationship), then one refers simply to "the derivative" without specifying the value of X at which the derivative is calculated.

You also may encounter a derivative expressed as a rate of change (ΔY and ΔX), but invoking what is called a limit, perhaps as follows:

$$\lim_{\Delta X \to 0} \frac{\Delta Y}{\Delta X}$$

The left-hand part of this expression contains the abbreviation *lim* (for the word *limit*), and the entire expression describes symbolically the idea of instantaneous change. Specifically, this expression is read as "the change in Y relative to the change in X as the change in X approaches its lower limit of zero" (analogous to the case where we calculated speed at exactly 15 minutes into the trip). The expression is just a way of referring to a derivative in a more formal way.

In sum, derivatives are useful concepts for describing rates of change in Y as a function of X. For nonlinear functions, the rate of change in Y will differ depending on where on the X continuum the change is occurring. A derivative is an index of instantaneous change at a given X value. It is a slope, but a special one, namely, an "instantaneous" slope.

DESCRIBING ACCUMULATION: INTEGRALS AND INTEGRATION

When describing mathematical models, many theorists emphasize derivatives, that is, rates of change. There is another concept in calculus that is sometimes emphasized: the *integral*. This concept reflects the amount of something. The process of calculating an integral is called *integration*. To gain a sense of what an integral is, consider the well-known function in statistics of the probability density function for a standard normal distribution. This function, often presented in statistics texts, is the basis for calculating the "area under the curve" in a normal distribution. Figure 8.5 presents a graphical representation of this function, as it often appears in statistics books. The various X values on the horizontal axis are standard scores, with a mean of zero and a standard deviation of 1. One can specify any two points in this distribution, say, a value of 0 and a value of 1, and then calculate the area under the curve between these two points. If one scales the total area under the curve to equal a value of 1.00, then the area under the curve between two X scores is the proportion of the total area that falls between the two points. For example, the area under the curve between the X values of 0 and 1 is 0.3413 (see Figure 8.5). Between the X values of 1 and 2, the area under the curve is 0.1359. Between X values of –1 and 1, the area under the curve is 0.6826. Graphically, an integral is the area under the curve between two points. The integral for the values 0 and 1 in Figure 8.5 is 0.3413. The integral for the values 1 and 2 is 0.1359. Because it focuses on

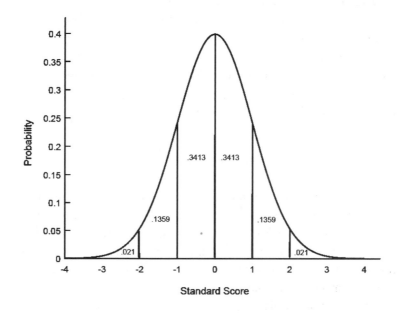

FIGURE 8.5. Area under the curve for a standardized normal distribution.

the area under the curve, one can see that, roughly speaking, an integral refers to "the amount of something."

A common use of integrals in mathematical models is to characterize accumulations, that is, to determine how much of something has accumulated. Many phenomena accumulate. For example, we accumulate money in savings accounts. Also, frustration accumulates with each stressful event experienced within a short time span. Although the mathematical details of integration are well beyond the scope of this book, when one uses the concept of integrals, one often does so in the context of building models of phenomena that accumulate.

JUST-IDENTIFIED, OVERIDENTIFIED, AND UNDERIDENTIFIED MODELS

Mathematical models also vary in their identification status. *Model identification* refers to cases where the values of model parameters must be estimated from data. A *just-identified* model is one for which there is a unique solution (i.e., one and only one solution) for the value of each estimated parameter in the model. Consider an analogy from algebra, where we might be given two equations with two unknowns of the following form:

$$23 = 2X + 3Z$$
$$9 = X + Z$$

For these two equations, there is a unique solution for X and Z: $X = 4$ and $Z = 5$.

An *underidentified* model is one for which there is an infinite number of solutions for one or more of the model parameters. In the equation

$$10 = X + Z$$

there is an infinite number of solutions for X and Z (e.g., $X = 10$ and $Z = 0$ is one solution; $X = 9$ and $Z = 1$ is another solution). Models that have one or more parameters that are underidentified are often problematic.

An *overidentified* model is one for which there is a unique solution for the model parameters, *and* more than one feature of the model can be used to independently estimate the parameter values. Using the algebraic analogy, consider the following equations:

$$10 = X + Z$$
$$18 = 2X + Z$$
$$12 = X + 2Z$$

There are three equations with a total of two unknowns, and any given pair of equations, no matter which pair, can be used independently to solve for the unknowns. In models for which parameter values must be estimated and the function fit is not perfect (i.e., there is an error term such that the model is stochastic), model parameters that have overidentified status are desirable because one can obtain independent estimates of those parameter values.

In sum, when reading math models, you may encounter references to a model as being just-identified, underidentified, or overidentified. Models that are underidentified are unsatisfactory.

METRICS

When developing mathematical models, theorists give careful consideration to the metric on which the variables in the model are measured, especially when nonlinear modeling is involved. This is because the accuracy of a mathematical model and the inferences one makes can be (but are not always) influenced by the metric of the variables. Depending on the variable metric, a theorist might resort to different functions in the mathematical model to describe the relationships between variables. For example, for the variable time, the model form and parameters introduced into the model might vary depending on whether time is measured in milliseconds, seconds, days, weeks, or years. The nature of metrics poses difficulty for some constructs in the social sciences because the metric used to measure them is arbitrary. For example, when a researcher uses a 10-item agree–disagree scale to measure peoples' attitudes toward religion, the metric might be scored from –5 to +5, or from 0 to 9, or from 1 to 10. In some math models, the choice of scoring matters, so an arbitrary metric can create difficulties.

TYPES OF NONLINEARITY

Thus far we have considered a simple mathematical model—the linear model—to introduce several concepts in mathematical modeling. The linear model has two adjustable parameters, a slope and an intercept, that typically are estimated rather than fixed by the theorist. In this section, we introduce other functions that are nonlinear in form and that can be used in mathematical models. There are many classes of functions, and we cannot begin to describe them all. Here we focus on five major classes of functions (the linear function makes six classes). The idea is to give you a sense of some of the nonlinear functions that can be used to build a math model. After presenting the functions, we describe strategies for modifying and combining them to build even more intricate mathematical representations. As we describe the different functions and the modifications to them that can be made, you will see the wide range of tools available to a math modeler when characterizing relationships between variables.[2]

---

[2]Our discussion of functions and the graphic representations of them draws on concepts described by W. Mueller (see *www.wmueller.com/precalculus/index.html*).

BOX 8.1. Reading Mathematical Models

When reading mathematical models, social scientists with more limited mathematical backgrounds sometimes feel intimidated by the presence of equations. Because equations make clear and unambiguous statements about the presumed relationships between variables, you should embrace equations, not avoid them. When confronted with an equation that seems complex, here are some things you can do to help work your way through it. First, make a list of the variables in the equation and a list of the adjustable constants. Make sure that each of the variables in your list is clearly defined and that the metrics of the variables are specified. Second, determine if the equation contains any of the major functions we discuss. For example, is a power function present? Is an exponential function present? Is a logistic function present? Once you recognize a familiar function form and you have a sense of the family of curves associated with it, then the substantive implications of the equation should start to become apparent. Remember, the fundamental form of the function can be altered using transformations, so be sensitive to the presence of a function that has a transformation imposed on it. Sometimes the function is "disguised" by the adjustable constants attached to it. Third, for each adjustable constant, think about what it is accomplishing and why it was included in the equation. Is it just a scaling factor, or does it have substantive interpretation, like a slope in a linear relationship? Finally, you can use your favorite statistical package (e.g., SPSS) or graphics software to apply the equation to hypothetical data you generate and then examine the curve graphically and see what happens to it as you change values of the adjustable constants or change the hypothetical data used to generate it. Also, keep in mind the conditional nature that multiplicative functions imply; that is, when you see the multiplication of two variables in an equation, then the size of the derivative (i.e., the size of the effect) of one of the variables in the product term is dependent on the value of the other variable in the product term.

If you encounter mathematical symbols with which you are not familiar, then you can usually find their meaning on the Internet. Below are some commonly encountered symbols. A useful website for learning about many areas of mathematics at many different levels is called "Ask Dr. Math": *mathforum.org/dr.math*.

Common Symbols That Reflect Important Numbers

π = the ratio of the circumference to the diameter of a circle, the number 3.1415926535 . . .

e = the natural logarithm base, the number 2.718281828459 . . .

γ = the Euler–Mascheroni constant, the number 0.577215664901 . . .

ϕ = the golden ratio, the number 1.618033988749 . . .

∞ = infinity

(continued)

Symbols for Binary Relations

= means "is the same as"
≠ means "is not equal to"
< means "is less than"
≤ means "is less than or equal to"
> means "is greater than"
≥ means "is greater than or equal to"
± means "plus or minus"
≅ means "is congruent to"
≈ means "is approximately equal to"
≃ means "is similar to"
≐ means "is nearly equal to"
∝ means "is proportional to"
≡ means "absolute equality"

Symbols from Mathematical Logic

∴ means "therefore"
∵ means "because"
∋ means "under the condition that"
⇒ means "logically implies that"
⇔ means "if and only if"
∀ means "for all"
∃ means "there exists"

Symbols Used in Set Theory

⊂ means "this set is a subset of"
⊃ means "this set has as a subset"
∪ is the union of two sets and means "take the elements that are in either set"
∩ is the intersection of two sets and means "take the elements that are in either set"
∅ refers to the empty set or null set and means "the set without any elements in it"
∈ means "is an element of"
∉ means "is not an element of"

Symbols for Operations

n! means "the factorial of"
∑ means "the sum of"

(continued)

$\prod$ means "the product of"

$\wedge$ means "to the power of"

$\int$ means "the integral of"

Additional Notations

Greek letters are used to refer to population parameters, Roman, usually italic, letters are used to refer to sample statistics.

A number raised to 0.5 or to ½ is the same as the square root of the number. A number raised to the power of -1 is the same as the inverse of the number.

To describe functions, we often use three concepts: (1) concavity, (2) proportionality, and (3) scaling constants. *Concavity* refers to whether the rate of change on a curve (the first derivative) is increasing or decreasing. A curve that is concave upward has an increasing first derivative, and a curve that is concave downward has a decreasing first derivative. In terms of proportionality, two variables are proportional to one another when one variable is a multiple of the other. More formally, Y is proportional to X if $Y = cX$, where c is a constant. The value c is called the *constant of proportionality*. For proportionality, doubling X doubles Y, tripling X triples Y, and halving X halves Y. Two variables are said to be inversely proportional when there is some constant c for which $Y = c/X$. In this case, doubling X halves Y, tripling X cuts Y by one-third, and halving X doubles Y. *Scaling constants* refer to adjustable parameters in a model that have no substantive meaning but are included to shift a variable from one metric to another. For example, to change meters to centimeters, we multiply the meters by the constant 100, which shifts the metric of length to centimeters. As we describe different functions on the following pages, we occasionally do so in terms of the concepts of concavity, proportionality, or scaling constants.

Logarithmic Functions

The logarithmic function (often referred to as the *log function*) has the general form $f(X) = \log_a(X)$, where a is a constant indicating the base of the logarithm. Logs can be calculated for different bases, such as the base 10, the base 2, or the base 8. The log base 10 of the number 100 is written as $\log_{10}(100)$, where the subscript is the base and the number in parentheses is the number for which you are calculating the log. If n stands for the number for which you are calculating the log, and a is the base of the log, then the log is the solution for b in the equation $n = a^b$. For $\log_{10}(100)$, we solve for b in the equation $100 = 10^b$, so the log base 10 of the number 100 is 2 (because $10^2 = 100$). The value of $\log_5(25)$

is 2 because $5^2 = 25$. Sometimes you will encounter a log expression with no base, such as log(1,000). When this happens, the log is assumed to have a base of 10. So log(1,000) = 3 (because $10^3 = 1,000$).

There is a special logarithm, called the natural log, that uses a constant called e as its base. The number e appears in many mathematical theories. Its value is approximately 2.71828. The number e was studied in depth by Leonhard Euler in the 1720s, although it was first studied by John Napier, the inventor of logarithms, in 1614. It has some remarkable mathematical properties (which we will not elaborate here) and is referred to as *Napier's constant*. The natural log of a number is signified by the expression ln(n). For example, the natural log of 10 is signified by ln(10). It equals approximately $\log_{2.71828}(10) = 2.302585$.

Figure 8.6 presents sample graphs of log functions. When expressing the relationship between two variables, rather than using a linear function, one might use a log function. Log functions are sometimes used to model growth or change when the change is rapid at first and then slows down to a gradual and eventually almost nonexistent pace (see Figures 8.6a and 8.6b).

Log functions share many common features: (1) The logarithm is undefined for negative values of X (where X is the number for which you are calculating the log); (2) the value of the log can be positive or negative; (3) as the value of X approaches zero, the value of the log approaches negative infinity; (4) when $X = 1$, the value of the log is 0; and (5) as X approaches infinity, the log of X also approaches infinity. For the function $\log_a(X)$, the function output increases with increasing X if $a > 1$ and decreases with increasing X if a is between 0 and 1.

Exponential Functions

The *exponential function* has the general form $f(X) = a^X$. The function yields output that increases in value with increasing X if $a > 1$ and decreases in value with increasing X if a is between 0 and 1. Figure 8.7 on page 216 presents examples of common exponential curves. These curves are often used to refer to growth, such as when people say a population is "growing exponentially." With exponential growth or change, the larger a population gets, the faster it grows. For decreasing exponential growth or change, the smaller the population gets, the more slowly it decreases in size. As it turns out, exponential functions are simply the inverse of log functions, so the two functions mirror-image each other's properties. For exponential functions, if a is between -1 and 0, then the output value is a damped oscillation as X increases, and if a is < -1, it is an undamped oscillation as X increases (see the later section on trigonometric functions for a discussion of oscillation).

Social scientists often modify the exponential function to create functions that reflect growth or change with certain properties. For example, using the fact that any number raised to the power of 0 is 1, the following equation can be used to describe exponential growth over time:

$$Y = s_0 e^{(kX)}$$

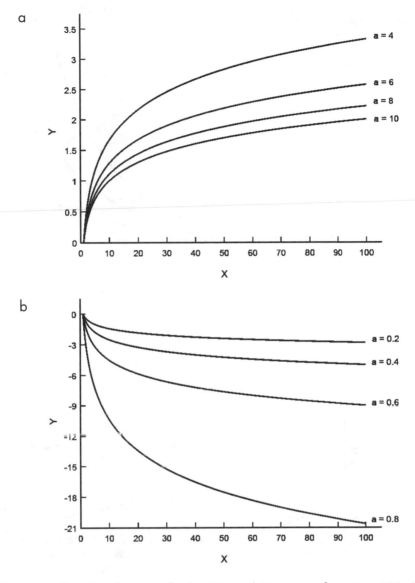

FIGURE 8.6. Graphs of log functions for $\log_a(X)$, with X ranging from 1 to 100. (a) $a > 1$; (b) $0 < a < 1$.

where Y is the population size at a given point in time, X is the duration in time since a predetermined start time, and s_0, e, and k are constants. In this case, e is Napier's constant. The value of s_0 is fixed at a value equal to the population size at the predetermined start time. Note that when $X = 0$, the population size will equal the population size at the start time (because any number raised to the power of zero is 1.0). For this function, Y increases geometrically with a doubling time equal to $0.6932/k$. A graph illustrating this function appears in Figure 8.8 on page 217, where the starting size of a population is $s_0 = 5,000$, where $k = 0.333$ (yielding a doubling time of just over 2 years), and where

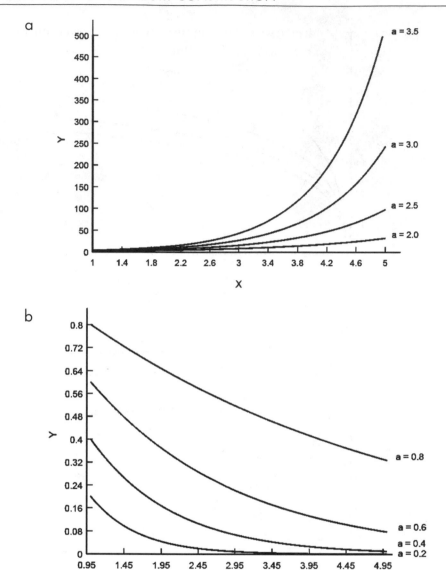

FIGURE 8.7. Graphs of exponential functions for a^X, with X ranging from 1 to 5. (a) $a > 1$; (b) $0 < a < 1$.

X ranges from 0 to 5 years. When expressing the relationship between two variables, rather than using a linear or log function, one might use an exponential function, such as that illustrated in Figure 8.8.

Power Functions

Power functions have the general form $f(X) = X^a$ where a is an adjustable constant. For positive values of X greater than 1, when $a > 1$, the curve will be concave upward, and when *a* is between 0 and 1, the curve will be concave downward. Power functions often have a similar shape to exponential and logarithmic functions, with the differences between the functions sometimes being subtle. When the difference is small, it does not matter which function is used to create the model. But differences can exist. Exponential functions increase by multiples over constant input intervals. Logarithms increase by constant intervals over input multiples. Power functions do not follow either of these patterns. Power curves eventually outgrow a logarithm and undergrow an exponential as *X* increases. A practical example of the function differences is the modeling of the spread of HIV, the virus that causes AIDS. During the early stages of the epidemic, it was thought that the number of HIV cases was growing exponentially, but in later analyses, the function was found to be better mapped by a power function. An exponential model yielded overestimates of the number of cases forecast in future years, which in turn led to overestimates of the required resources to deal with the epidemic (e.g., hospital space, medications; see Mueller, 2006).

Figure 8.9 presents some examples of power functions, and Figure 8.10 on page 219 plots a power function and an exponential function on the same graph to illustrate some of these properties. When expressing the relationship between two variables, rather than using a linear, log, or exponential function, one might use a power function instead.

Polynomial Functions

Polynomial functions are simply the sum of power functions. The general form of a polynomial function is

$$f(X) = a + bX^1 + cX^2 + dX^3 \ldots$$

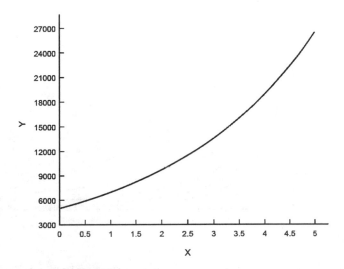

FIGURE 8.8. Exponential growth for $Y = s_0 \, e^{(kX)}$.

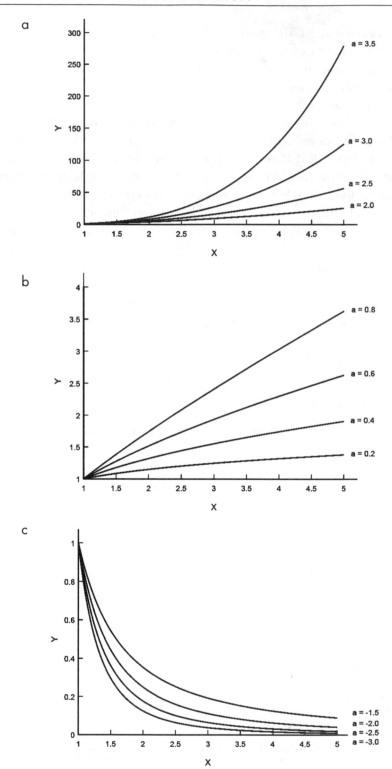

FIGURE 8.9. Graphs of power functions for X^a, with X ranging from 1 to 5. (a) $a > 1$; (b) 0 < a < 1; (c) a < 0.

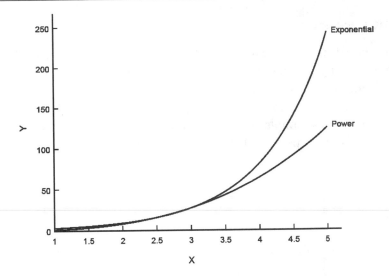

FIGURE 8.10. Example of power and exponential functions.

where X continues to be raised to the next highest integer value, and each term has a potentially unique adjustable constant. Polynomials can model data with many "wiggles and turns," but the more wiggles and turns there are, the greater the number of power terms that are required to model it. Notice that when only a single term for X is used with a power of 1, the polynomial model reduces to a linear model. The adjustable constant a is typically viewed as a scaling constant. Adding one term to the linear model (i.e., adding the term cX^2) allows the model to accommodate a curve with one bend. A polynomial model with three terms ($a + bX^1 + cX^2 + dX^3$) will accommodate a curve with two bends. A polynomial model with four terms will accommodate a curve with three bends. In general, for k bends, you need $k + 1$ terms.

The most popular polynomial functions in the social sciences are the quadratic and cubic functions. They are defined as

$$\text{Quadratic: } f(X) = a + bX + cX^2$$
$$\text{Cubic: } f(X) = a + bX + cX^2 + dX^3$$

Figures 8.11 and 8.12 provide an example of each type of curve, and Figure 8.13 on page 222 illustrates a polynomial function with seven terms. The quadratic model is effective for modeling U-shaped and inverted-U-shaped relationships as well as J-shaped and inverted-J-shaped relationships. The cubic function is effective for modeling S-shaped curves. In Figure 8.12b we manipulated the scaling constant, a, to create separation between curves so that you can better see the trends. Figure 8.13 illustrates how diverse a "curve" that large polynomials can create. When expressing the relationship between two variables, rather than using a linear, log, exponential, or power function, one might use a polynomial function.

Trigonomic Functions

Trigonometric functions are typically used to model cyclical phenomena. The two most common functions are the sine function and the cosine function, which have the form $f(X) = \sin(aX)$ and $f(X) = \cos(aX)$, where a is a constant, *sin* is the sine, and *cos* is the cosine. The sine and the cosine functions repeat the values of their outputs at regular intervals as X increases. Simple transformations of the sine and cosine functions can reproduce many forms of periodic behavior. For example, some people have suggested

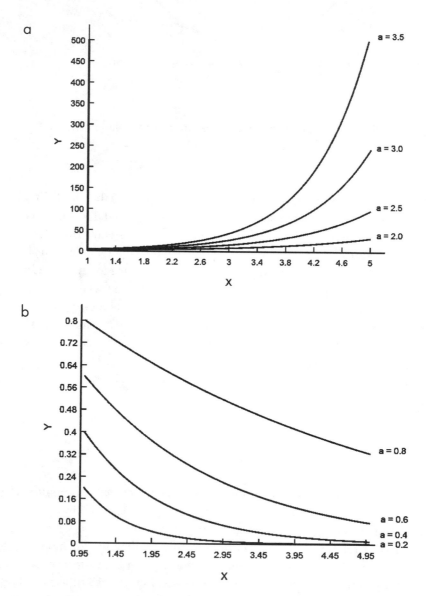

FIGURE 8.11. Quadratic functions. (a) Function $a + bX + cX^2$, with $a = 0$, $b = .5$; (b) function $a + bX + cX^2$, with $a = 0$, $b = -1$.

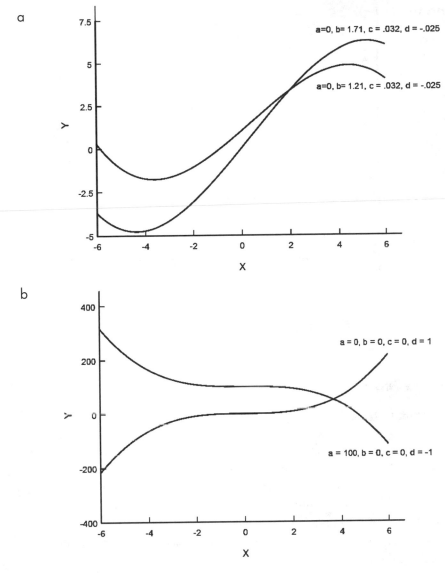

FIGURE 8.12. Cubic functions. (a) Function for $a + bX + cX^2 + dX^3$; (b) additional functions for $a + bX + cX^2 + dX^3$.

that rhythmic cycles, called biorhythms, reflect active and passive phases in the physical aspects of everyday life. The phases of biorhythms are modeled using a sine function of the form $f(X) = \sin(.224*X)$, where X is the number of days since a baseline index is taken. Output values range from 1 to –1, with positive values indicating increasingly high energy and negative values indicating increasingly low energy. Figure 8.14 on page 223 plots the output values for 120 days, starting at day 0. As noted earlier, certain types of cyclical phenomena also can be modeled using exponential functions with negative values of a in the expression $f(X) = a^X$.

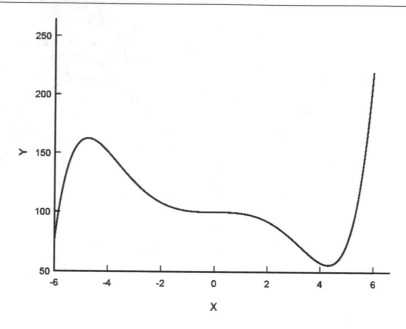

FIGURE 8.13. Polynomial function with seven terms.

Choosing a Function

In sum, a wide range of functions are available to the math modeler for describing the relationship between variables, including linear functions, logarithmic functions, exponential functions, power functions, polynomial functions, and trigonometric functions, to name a few. We have only scratched the surface of the many strategies a mathematical modeler can use. As you become familiar with functions and the curves they imply, you should be able to make informed choices about modeling relationships between variables. Mathematical modelers sometimes select functions for their models a priori, based on logic, and other times they make decisions about appropriate model functions after collecting data and scrutinizing scatterplots or smoothers. In the latter case, the model chosen and the values of the adjustable parameters are still subjected to future empirical tests, even though preliminary data are used to gain perspectives on appropriate functional forms. You can gain perspectives on the curves implied by different functions by creating hypothetical data and applying the different functions to them. We provide information on how to do this using the statistical package SPSS in Appendix 8.1 to this chapter, and also provide information about other graphics software.

FUNCTIONS FOR NOMINAL VARIABLES

Thus far, we have considered only functions involving quantitative variables, but functions also can be specified for nominal variables. Consider as a simple example the

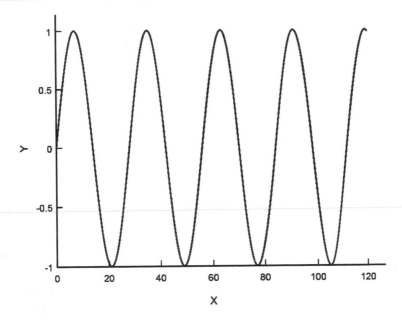

FIGURE 8.14. Sine function.

relationship between whether or not someone uses an umbrella as a function of whether or not it is raining. The relationship between these two nominal variables is expressed as follows

$$f(x) = \begin{cases} \text{umbrella,} & \text{if } x = \text{raining} \\ \text{no umbrella,} & \text{if } x = \text{not raining} \end{cases}$$

where one uses an umbrella if it is raining and one does not use an umbrella if it is not raining.

Sometimes mathematical modelers create quantitative representations of nominal variables and then analyze the quantitative translations using the quantitative functions described earlier. For example, one could specify a mathematical function relating the probability of carrying an umbrella to the probability of it raining, with both variables differing on a probability continuum of 0 to 1.0. The function might then be expressed as an exponential function, as in Figure 8.7a.

In some cases, functions involving nominal and quantitative variables are stated in terms of a table of values rather than symbolically. For example, suppose we specify whether someone is a Democrat or Republican as a function of scores on a 7-point index (e.g., response to a rating scale) of how conservative or liberal he or she is. The scale consists of integers ranging from −3 to +3, with increasingly negative scores signifying more conservativeness, increasingly positive scores signifying more liberalness, and the score of zero representing a neutral point. The function $Y = f(X)$ might be stated as

X	Y
–3	Republican
–2	Republican
–1	Republican
0	Democrat
1	Democrat
2	Democrat
3	Democrat

In this representation, the person is said to be a Republican if he or she has a value of –1, –2, or –3. Otherwise, the person is a Democrat.

Another approach to representing a function with a nominal variable is to use a graph. For example, the liberal–conservative and party identification function might be as shown in Figure 8.15.

ADVANCED TOPICS:
MANIPULATING AND COMBINING FUNCTIONS

One creative aspect of mathematical modeling is deriving new functions from old functions so as to create models that are better suited to describing the relationship between variables. We saw hints of this capability for polynomial functions (which combine power functions). Another class of functions, which we did not discuss, divides one polynomial function by a second polynomial function rather than summing polynomials. These are called *rational functions*. We now describe examples of manipulating and combining functions.

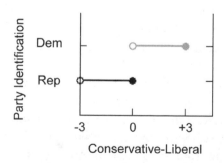

FIGURE 8.15. Graphical representation of a function with a qualitative variable.

Function Transformations

One way of modifying functions is to add adjustable parameters to them. Given a function $f(x)$, one can add or subtract an adjustable parameter, a, after the rule described by $f(X)$ is applied: that is, $f(X) \pm a$. This has the effect of shifting the output values upward (in the case of addition) or downward (in the case of subtraction). These transformations are called *vertical shifts*. The output of a function also can be multiplied by the parameter a after the rule described by $f(X)$ is applied; that is, $a \times f(X)$. This transformation vertically stretches (when $a > 1$) or squeezes (when $a < 1$) the graph of the function. Such transformations are called *vertical stretches* or *vertical crunches*. Another possibility is to add or subtract a from $f(X)$ before the rule described by $f(X)$ is applied; that is, $f(X + a)$ or $f(X - a)$. These transformations typically move the graph of the function left when adding a positive value of a or right when subtracting a positive value of a. Such transformations are called *horizontal shifts*. Finally, one can multiply X before the rule described by $f(X)$ is applied; that is, $f(aX)$. These transformations horizontally stretch (when $a < 1$) or squeeze (when $a > 1$) the graph of the function. Such transformations are called *horizontal stretches* or *horizontal crunches*. Coupled with the possibility of forming inverses for many functions, mathematical modelers have considerable flexibility in manipulating traditional functions with the use of vertical shifts, horizontal shifts, vertical stretches, vertical crunches, horizontal stretches, and horizontal crunches. If you begin your modeling efforts with a traditional function that is approximately correct in form, then transformations such as these allow you to fine-tune the form of the curve to your problem. An example is the classic bounded exponential model, which we now consider.

Recall that the exponential function is $f(X) = a^X$. A simple set of modifications to this function produces what is called a *bounded exponential model*. This has the form

$$Y = a + (b - ce^{-X})$$

where a, b, and c are adjustable constants and e is Napier's constant. The term ce^{-X} is essentially an exponential function where $a = e$ and the exponent is multiplied by an adjustable constant, c. This creates a decaying exponential curve, which is then subtracted from a fixed upper bound or limit reflected by the value of b. As the decaying exponential dies out, the difference from b rises up to the bound. The parameter a is a scaling constant. This kind of function models growth that is limited by some fixed capacity. Figure 8.16 presents an example of this curve, as well as a traditional exponential curve.

Combining Functions

Another strategy that math modelers use is to combine functions. A popular function in the social sciences is the *logistic function*. It has the general form $f(X) = c/(1 + ae^{-bX})$ where a, b, and c are adjustable constants and e is Napier's constant. A logistic function is a combination of the exponential growth and bounded exponential growth functions illustrated in Figure 8.16. In the logistic function, exponential growth occurs when the function outputs for X are small in value. However, this turns into bounded exponential growth as the function outputs approach their upper bound. A logistic function is plotted in Figure 8.17. Note the shapes of the curve to the right and left of the broken line in Figure 8.17 and compare these with the curve shapes in Figure 8.16. The result of combining the exponential growth and the bounded exponential growth functions is an S-shaped curve. The logistic function is a special case of a broader function known as the *sigmoid function*, which generates curves having an S shape.

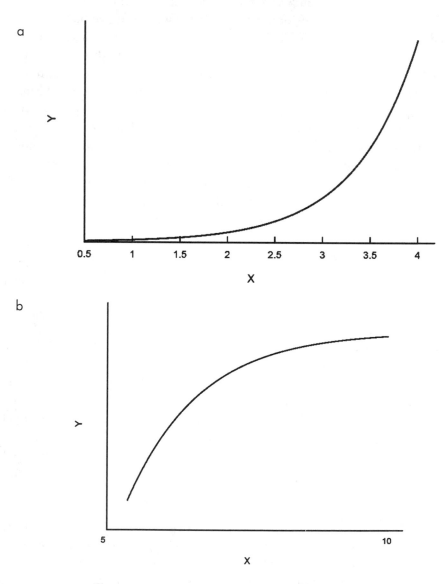

FIGURE 8.16. Exponential and bounded exponential model. (a) Exponential function; (b) bounded exponential function.

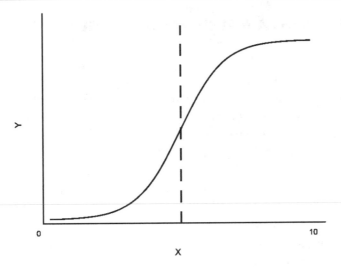

FIGURE 8.17. Logistic function.

Combining multiple functions using processes such as those described for the logistic function is another tool available to math modelers. It is not uncommon for a theorist to break the overall relationship into a series of smaller component segments, specify a function to reflect each segment, and then assemble the component functions into a whole in one way or another.

In sum, functions can be manipulated with adjustable constants and subjected to vertical and horizontal stretching and crunching. Functions also can be combined to form even more complex functions (as in the case of the logistic function). Traditional mathematical modeling opens up a wide range of tools for describing relationships for the theorist to consider.

MULTIPLE VARIABLE FUNCTIONS

All of the functions we have described use a single input variable. However, functions can involve more than one input variable, and the multiple variables can be combined in a wide variety of ways to yield output. For example, the traditional linear function for a single variable can be extended to include multiple variables (e.g., X and Z) using the following functional form

$$f(X, Z) = a + bX + cZ \qquad (8.5)$$

where a, b, and c are adjustable constants. As another example, consider the function

$$f(X, Z) = a + bXZ \qquad (8.6)$$

where a and b are adjustable constants. In this case, the output is a multiplicative function of the two input variables. We make use of this function below.

PHASES IN BUILDING A MATHEMATICAL MODEL

Math modelers typically use four phases to construct a mathematical model. First, the modeler identifies the variables that will be included in the model and identifies the metrics on which the variables are measured. Textbooks on mathematical modeling tend to view the variables and metrics as givens and devote little attention to how the variables and metrics are selected. Of course, this is a nontrivial issue, and how one chooses which variables to include is the subject of much of this book. Second, the modeler thinks carefully about the variables, the metrics, and the relationships between the variables, and proposes a few candidate functions that might capture the underlying dynamics. He or she might think about the implications of the functions and what predictions they make at both moderate and extreme input values. Eventually, a working function is settled on, typically a function that includes several adjustable constants. Sometimes the values of the adjustable constants are logically determined, and the modeler fixes the constants at those values. More often than not, the values of the adjustable constants are estimated from data. Third, the modeler collects empirical data, estimates values of the adjustable constants from the data if necessary, and examines the degree of fit between the output values of the function and the values observed in the real world. At this point, if performance of the model is unsatisfactory, a new function might be tried or the original function might be modified to accommodate the disparities. Fourth, given revisions of the function, the model is applied to a new set of data to determine how well the revised model performs. If the model does a good job of reproducing observations in the real world and if the model makes conceptual sense, it will be selected as the model of choice.

This, of course, is an oversimplification of the process of building math models, and there are many variants of it. Our main point is that building math models is usually a dynamic process that involves much more than simply specifying a function.

AN EXAMPLE USING PERFORMANCE, ABILITY, AND MOTIVATION

Educational researchers have long argued that performance in school is a function of two factors: a student's motivation to perform well and his or her ability to perform well. This relationship is often expressed in the form of a multiplicative model, as follows:

$$\text{Performance} = \text{Ability} \times \text{Motivation} \tag{8.7}$$

The basic idea is that if a student lacks the cognitive skills and capacity to learn, then it does not matter how motivated he or she is; school performance will be poor. Similarly, a student can have very high levels of cognitive skills and the ability to learn, but if the motivation to work and attend to the tasks that school demands is low, then performance will be poor. The multiplicative relationship reflects this dynamic because, for example, if motivation is zero, then it does not matter what a person's score on ability is—his or her performance will always equal zero. Similarly, if ability has a score of zero, it does not matter what a person's motivation score is—his or her performance will always equal zero. Although this makes intuitive sense, the dynamics might be different from those implied by Equation 8.7, as we will now illustrate.

Our first step is to specify the metrics of the variables involved, since they do not have natural metrics. Performance in school might be indexed for individuals using the familiar grade-point average metric that ranges from 1.0 (all F's) to 4.0 (all A's), with decimals rounded to the nearest tenth (e.g., 2.1, 3.5). Ability might be indexed using a standard intelligence test that has a mean of 100 and a standard deviation of 15. Motivation might be indexed using a 10-item scale that asks students to agree or disagree with statements such as "I try hard in school" and "Doing my best in school is very important to me." A 5-point agree–disagree rating scale (1 = strongly disagree, 2 = moderately disagree, 3 = neither agree nor disagree, 4 = moderately agree, and 5 = strongly agree) provides the range of possible responses. The responses to each item are summed to yield an overall score from 10 to 50, with higher scores indicating higher levels of motivation.

Note that neither of these metrics takes on a value of zero. Hence, the dynamic of having "zero" ability or "zero" motivation discussed here cannot occur. Indeed, one might question whether there is such a thing as "zero" intelligence (i.e., a complete absence of intelligence). Is a psychological zero point on this dimension even possible? Suppose we decide that although a complete absence of intelligence is not theoretically plausible, a complete absence of motivation to do well in school is plausible. One way of creating a motivation metric with a zero point is to subtract a score of 10 from the original motivation metric. Before this operation, the motivation metric ranged from 10 to 50. By subtracting 10 from the metric, it now ranges from 0 to 40, which includes a zero point.

However, there is a problem with this strategy. Just because we can mathematically create a zero score on the motivation scale by subtracting 10 from it, we cannot conclude that the score of zero on the transformed scale reflects a complete absence of motivation on the underlying dimension of motivation. What evidence do we have that this is indeed the case? Perhaps a score of zero on the new metric actually reflects a somewhat low level of motivation but not a complete absence of it. The issue of mapping scores on a metric onto their location on the underlying dimension they represent is complex, and consideration of how to accomplish this is beyond the scope of this book. We will work with the original metric of 10–50 and not make explicit assumptions about where on the underlying motivation dimension these scores locate individuals. We suspect that, based on the content of the items, students who score near 50 are very highly motivated to perform well, and students who score near 10 are very low in (but not completely devoid of) motivation to perform well. But a separate research program is required to establish such assertions (Blanton & Jaccard, 2006).

Suppose that a student has a score of 100 on the IQ test and a score of 30 on the motivation test. Using Equation 8.7, multiplying the ability score by the motivation score, we obtain $100 \times 30 = 3,000$, and we would predict a GPA of 3,000! Of course, this is impossible because a student's GPA can range only from 1.0 to 4.0. We need to introduce one or more adjustable constants to Equation 8.7 to accommodate the metric differences and to make it so that a predicted GPA score falls within the 1.0–4.0 range. For example, if we let P stand for performance, A for ability, and M for motivation, we can allow for the subtraction of a constant from the product to make an adjustment in metric differences, modifying Equation 8.7 as follows:

$$P = (A)(M) + a$$

where a is an adjustable constant whose value is estimated from data. Note, for example, that if $a = -2,997$, then this is the same as subtracting 2,997 from the product of A and M. But perhaps subtracting a constant is not enough to account for the metric differences. For example, a score of 120 on the IQ test coupled with a score of 50 on the motivation test would yield a product value of 6,000, and subtracting a value of 2,997 from it would still produce a nonsensical GPA. A second scalar adjustment we might use is to multiply the product term by a fractional adjustable constant, which yields the general equation

$$P = b(A)(M) + a$$

where b is a second adjustable constant (in this case, b would be a fraction) designed to deal further with the metric differences. Its value also is estimated from data. The terms on the right-hand side of this equation can be rearranged to yield

$$P = a + b(A)(M) \tag{8.8}$$

If you compare Equation 8.8 with Equation 8.3, you will note that Equation 8.8 is simply a linear function, so performance is assumed to be a linear function of the product of $(A)(M)$. Not only do the constants a and b take into account the different metrics, but the value of b also provides substantive information as well; namely, it indicates how much change in performance (GPA) one expects given a 1-unit increase in the value of the product term $(A)(M)$.

Figure 8.18 plots the relationship between performance and motivation at three different levels of ability based on Equation 8.8, where values of a and b have been empirically determined from data collected for a sample of 90 students. In this example, $a = -2.0$ and $b = 0.0015$. The slope of P on M for any given value of A is bA. Several features of this plot are worth noting. First, note that the effect of motivation on performance is more pronounced as ability increases. This is evident in the steeper slope ($bA = 0.165$) for the two variables when the ability score is 110 as compared with the slope when the ability score is 100 ($bA = 0.150$) and, in turn, as compared to the slope when the ability score is 90 ($bA = 0.135$). These differences in slope may seem small but they are probably substantial. For example, when the ability score is 110, a 10-unit change in motivation is predicted to yield a $(0.165)(10) = 1.65$-unit change in GPA; when the ability score is 100, a 10-unit change in motivation is predicted to yield a $(0.150)(10) = 1.50$-unit change in GPA; and when the ability score is 90, a 10-unit change in motivation is predicted to yield a $(0.135)(10) = 1.35$-unit change in GPA.

Second, note that at each of the different levels of ability (90, 100, and 110), the relationship between motivation and performance is assumed to be linear. Is this a reasonable assumption? Perhaps not. Perhaps the relationship between performance and

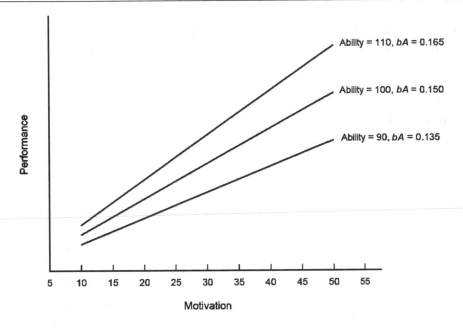

FIGURE 8.18. Example for Performance = Ability × Motivation.

motivation at a given ability level is better captured by an exponential function in the form of one of the curves in Figure 8.7a. For example, when motivation is on the low end of the motivation metric, increasing it somewhat may not have much impact on performance. It will still be too low to make a difference on performance. But at higher levels of the motivation metric, increasing it will have an impact on performance. This dynamic is captured by the exponential functional forms illustrated in Figure 8.7a. Or perhaps a power function in the form of one of the curves in Figure 8.9a is applicable. Power functions have the same dynamic as the exponential function in Figure 8.7a, but they "grow" a bit more slowly. Or perhaps an S-shaped function in the form of the curve in Figure 8.17 applies, with floor and ceiling effects on performance occurring at the low and high ends of motivation, respectively.

The multiplicative model specified by Equation 8.7 assumes what is called a *bilinear interaction* between the predictor variables; that is, it assumes that the relationship between the outcome and one of the predictors (in this case, motivation) is always linear no matter what the value is of the other predictor (in this case, ability). To be sure, the value of the slope for the linear relationship between P and M differs depending on the value of A (as noted earlier), but the function form is assumed to be linear. One can modify the model to allow for a nonlinear relationship between performance and motivation at different levels of ability, say, in accord with a power function, as follows:

$$P = a + b(A)(M^c) \tag{8.9}$$

where c is an adjustable constant whose value is estimated from data. This model allows for the possibility of a function form like those of Figure 8.9a.

Another notable feature of Figure 8.18 is that at the lowest value of motivation, there is a small degree of separation between the three different lines. The amount of separation between the lines reflects the differences in the effect of ability (at values of 90 vs. 100 vs. 110) on performance when motivation is held constant at the same value. But perhaps the amount of separation should be a bit more or a bit less than what is modeled in Figure 8.18. Equation 8.10 can be further modified to allow for a different amount of separation between the lines than what Equation 8.9 implies, as follows:

$$P = a + b(A)(M^c) + dA \tag{8.10}$$

where d is an adjustable constant whose value is estimated by data. The logic of adding this term is developed in Appendix 8.2 and is not central to our discussion here. The main points we want to emphasize are the following: (1) The rather simple theoretical representation in Equation 8.7 has nontrivial conceptual ramifications by specifying that the relationship between performance and the predictor variables is captured by the dynamics of a bilinear interaction when, in fact, the interaction may have a different functional form. (2) When building a mathematical model, the metrics of the variables usually have to be addressed (although our next example illustrates a case where this is not necessary). (3) There may be multiple features of the model (e.g., the separation between curves at different levels of one of the component terms as well as the shape of these curves) that must be specified that are not always apparent in simple representations such as Equation 8.7.

The fact is that the often-presented model of Performance = Ability × Motivation is poorly specified. Applying principles of mathematical modeling helps to produce a better-specified theory that makes implicit assumptions explicit and highlights complexities that should be taken into account (see Appendix 8.2).

AN EXAMPLE USING ATTITUDE CHANGE

As another example of a mathematical model, we consider a model of attitude change from the communication literature that was developed by Fishbein and Ajzen (1975). The model concerns the case where a source is trying to persuade the recipient of a persuasive message to change his or her belief in something. A belief is conceptualized as a subjective probability that ranges from 0 to 1.00, much like a probability in mathematics. For example, people might believe with a probability of 0.20 they will contract lung cancer if they smoke cigarettes. Or people might believe with a probability of 0.30 a particular brand of toothpaste is the best for fighting tooth decay. The model shows three probabilities that are of interest: (1) the subjective probability that the recipient holds prior to receiving the persuasive message, P_0; (2) the position that the recipient perceives the source takes in his or her persuasive message, also reflected by a subjective probability, P_S; and (3) the subjective probability of the recipient *after* hearing the persuasive message, P_1. For example, the recipient might have an initial belief corresponding to a subjective probability of 0.20, perceive the source as arguing that the target belief should have a subjective probability of 0.70, and after hearing the arguments of the source, will revise his or her subjective probability to be 0.60. These three variables, P_0, P_S, and P_1, are measured variables in the theoretical system.

The amount of belief change that occurs is the difference in subjective probabilities before and after the message, or $P_1 - P_0$. It is the central outcome variable. Fishbein and Ajzen were interested in understanding factors that impact how much belief change occurs, so they constructed a mathematical model to reflect the underlying dynamics. Let BC represent belief change and be formally defined as $P_1 - P_0$. Fishbein and Ajzen begin by assuming that the amount of belief change that occurs is a function of the discrepancy between the recipient's initial position and the perceived position of the source; that is, $P_S - P_0$. If a source argues in favor of the exact same position of the recipient, then $P_S - P_0 = 0$, and no belief change will occur. It is only when the source takes a position that is discrepant from the recipient's that belief change can occur. The more discrepant the position taken by the source relative to the recipient's initial position, the greater the potential for belief change. We thus begin with a simple model based on a difference function:

$$BC = (P_S - P_0) \tag{8.11}$$

Not everyone will accept the arguments in a persuasive message. People differ in the likelihood that they will accept a message, with some people having a low probability of message acceptance, others having a moderate probability of message acceptance, and still others having a high probability of message acceptance. Fishbein and Ajzen introduced a parameter into the model to reflect the probability that a recipient would accept the arguments of a message; this parameter is signified by P_A. Equation 8.11 thus becomes

$$BC = P_A(P_S - P_0) \tag{8.12}$$

with the constraint that P_A must range from 0 to 1.0 to reflect a probability metric. If a person completely accepts the message, then $P_A = 1.00$ and the amount of belief change will equal the discrepancy between the recipient's initial position and the position the recipient perceives the source as taking. If a person completely rejects the message, then $P_A = 0.00$ and there is no belief change. If the person is somewhat accepting of the source's message (i.e., P_A is somewhere between 0.00 and 1.00), then the amount of belief change is proportional to P_A, holding $(P_S - P_0)$ constant.

Next, Fishbein and Ajzen address factors that impact the probability of acceptance of a message. One important factor is how discrepant the message is from the recipient's initial position. In general, people are more likely to accept messages that argue in favor of their existing beliefs as opposed to messages that argue against their existing beliefs. If we let D represent the absolute discrepancy between the recipient's initial position and the perceived position of the source (i.e., $D = |P_S - P_0|$), then the probability of acceptance can be modeled as

$$P_A = (1 - D) \tag{8.13}$$

Note that when $D = 0$, the source is arguing the same position that the recipient already believes and the probability of acceptance is 1.00. As the source's message becomes increasingly discrepant from the recipient's initial position, the probability of acceptance decreases to a minimum of 0.00.

Fishbein and Ajzen recognized that there are factors that can facilitate the acceptance of a message independent of message discrepancy. For example, if the source is a trustworthy and credible person, the exact same message may be more likely to be accepted than if the source is untrustworthy or lacks credibility. Fishbein and Ajzen introduced an adjustable constant to reflect these facilitating conditions, which they labeled f. Equation 8.13 was modified to

$$P_A = (1 - D)^{1/f} \tag{8.14}$$

with the constraint that f be greater than 0. Fishbein and Ajzen thus use a power function to capture the underlying dynamics, where $1/f$ is an adjustable constant. Figure 8.19 presents sample curves for the probability of acceptance as a function of D at different values of f. Note that when $f = 1$, the relationship between the probability of acceptance and message discrepancy is linear with an intercept of 0 and a slope of 1. As f exceeds 1, the probability of acceptance increases rapidly at lower levels of discrepancy and remains high even as message discrepancy increases. As f decreases in value from 1, the probability of message acceptance decreases rapidly at lower levels of discrepancy and remains low as message discrepancy increases.

Equations 8.12 and 8.14 can be combined to yield a single equation. Starting with Equation 8.13, we have

$$BC = P_A(P_S - P_0)$$

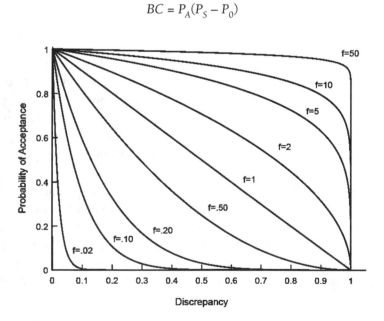

FIGURE 8.19. Fishbein and Ajzen model for probability of acceptance.

Since $P_A = (1 - D)^{1/f}$, we can substitute the right-hand side of Equation 8.14 for P_A, which yields

$$BC = (1 - D)^{1/f}(P_S - P_0)$$

and since $D = |P_S - P_0|$, further substitution yields

$$BC = (1 - (|P_S - P_0|))^{1/f}(P_S - P_0)$$

The belief that a person has after hearing a persuasive message can be further specified by recognizing that $BC = (P_1 - P_0)$, so if we subtract P_0 from both sides of the equation, we obtain

$$P_1 = [(1 - (|P_S - P_0|)^{1/f}(PS - P_0)] - P_0 \tag{8.15}$$

Equation 8.15 is a mathematical model that predicts the belief that someone holds after hearing a persuasive message. Although it may appear a bit intimidating to the mathematically uninitiated, it is based on reasonable communication principles and is reasonably precise in the functional forms it posits. The model makes use of observed measures as well as adjustable constants and incorporates a power function. In empirical applications, P_0, P_1, and P_S are measured variables, and f is an adjustable constant whose value is estimated from data. The value of f is expected to vary across contexts where factors that facilitate message acceptance vary. For further discussion of this model and its implications, see Fishbein and Ajzen (1975).

CHAOS THEORY

An area of mathematical modeling that is receiving increased attention in the social sciences is that of *chaos theory*. In normal parlance, *chaos* refers to disarray. In chaos theory, this also is true, but something systematic is thought to underlie the chaos; what appears chaotic actually has a systematic function generating it. The task of the theorist is to map this function.

Chaos theory is typically applied to changes in systems over time, with the state of a system at time $t + 1$ being impacted by the state of the system at some previous time, t. As an example, consider the simple function

$$X_{t+1} = 1.9 - X_t^2 \tag{8.16}$$

where $t + 1$ refers to the time period following time t. For example, perhaps the time interval in question is a week and suppose that the value of X at time t is 1. Then applying Equation 8.16, the value of X 1 week later (i.e., at time $t + 1$) should be $1.9 - 1^2 = 0.9$. At week 2, this input value is substituted into the right-hand side of Equation 8.16, and the result is the predicted value of X at week number 3. It is $1.9 - 0.9^2 = 1.09$. To predict the value at week 4, the previous value is again substituted into the right-hand side of Equation 8.16 and the result is $1.9 - 1.09^2 = 0.712$. And so on. The pattern of data is plotted in Figure 8.20, which plots the value of X at each week in a series of weeks. The pattern appears to be unsystematic and chaotic with large swings in values. But note that the underlying process is anything but haphazard. The data were the result of a clearly specified and simple function (Equation 8.16). There was no random error in the system. Rather, the "disarray" was systematically generated. The task of the chaos theorist is to identify patterns that appear to be chaotic and to find the function that generates that "chaos."

In math modeling, the term *difference equation* refers to the case where a variable at time t is a function of a variable at time $t - 1$. If the variable at time t is a function of the immediately preceding point in time, it is called a *first-order difference equation*. If it is predicted from time $t - 2$, it is called a *second-order difference equation*. If it is predicted from time $t - 3$, it is a *third-order difference equation*. And so on.

Chaotic modeling tends to require precise measurement, and results can be dramatically influenced by the slightest "noise" or measurement error in the system. Current analytic methods for chaos models tend to require large numbers of observations. Although chaos theory is typically applied to the analysis of systems across time, the properties of space and distance can be used in place of time. Thus, theorists often distinguish between *spatial chaos* and *temporal chaos*. Temporal chaos models that focus on discrete time intervals (e.g., every 10 years; at 3-, 6-, and 12-month intervals) are called *discrete time models,* and those that use time continuously are called *continuous time models.*

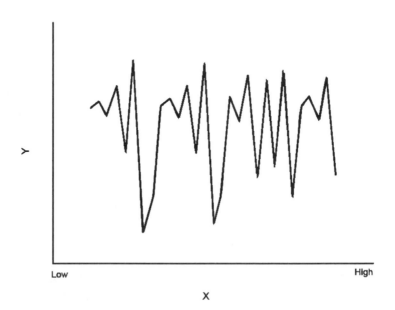

FIGURE 8.20. Chaos theory example.

A wide range of phenomena is potentially chaotic, including epidemics, economic changes, the stock market, and the mental state of depression, to name a few. However, it is controversial as to whether a truly chaotic system can be isolated in the real world, in the sense described in this chapter (i.e., with a stable, generating function underlying the chaos).

Variants of chaos theory include attempts to identify limits of predictable versus unpredictable patterns of data. For example, air flow over the wing of an airplane might be smooth and predictable when the wing is placed at low angles facing the wind. However, the air flow becomes chaotic and unpredictable at larger angles. One could attempt to determine the largest angle that permits smooth air flow, thereby yielding some understanding of this "chaotic system."

CATASTROPHE THEORY

Catastrophe theory is another area of mathematical modeling that is receiving attention in the social sciences. A catastrophic event is one where a large and rapid change in a system output occurs even though the system inputs are smooth and continuous. A simple example that captures the idea of catastrophic events is that of increasing the load on a bridge. One can keep adding weight to a bridge and see how the bridge deforms in response to that weight. The deforming of the bridge proceeds in a relatively uniform manner, showing increasing levels of bending. At some critical point, however, additional weight causes the bridge to collapse completely. Phenomena that might be analyzed using catastrophe theory include the occurrence of a nervous breakdown, drug relapse, divorce, a revolution occurring in a society, a demonstration turning into mob violence, or movement from one developmental stage to another in the context of a stage theory of development.

Catastrophe theory, developed by Rene Thom (1975), postulates seven fundamental mathematical equations to describe discontinuous behavior. Catastrophe theory relates outcome variables to what are called *control variables,* which essentially are explanatory variables. The relationships between the variables are expressed mathematically using nonlinear, dynamic systems that rely on different forms of polynomial functions. The spirit of catastrophe theory can be captured intuitively in a model of aggression in dogs as developed by Zeeman (1976). The behavioral outcome ranges from flight to attack, and the response on this dimension is thought to be a function of two emotions that represent control variables: fear and anger. When fear and anger are at their neutral points, then simple increases in either fear or anger lead to a continuous increase in flight or attack responses, respectively. However, if anger is increased in an already fearful dog, then the potential for a sudden jump from flight to attack can occur. Similarly, if fear is increased in an already angry dog, a sudden jump from attack to flight can occur. The mathematical models developed by Thom and expanded by other mathematicians are designed to model such dynamics. Catastrophe theory represents another area of mathematical modeling that is starting to receive attention from the social sciences.

ADDITIONAL EXAMPLES OF MATHEMATICAL MODELS IN THE SOCIAL SCIENCES

Mathematical models exist in all of the major subdisciplines of the social sciences. Most of the subdisciplines have journals that are devoted exclusively to mathematical modeling (e.g., *Journal of Mathematical Psychology, Journal of Mathematical Sociology, Journal of Quantitative Anthropology, Marketing Science*). Mathematical models also appear in more mainstream journals, but with less frequency. It is impossible to describe the many areas in which mathematical models have been developed, but in this section, we provide a brief sampling to highlight the diversity of applications.

One area where mathematical models have been prominent is in the analysis of human decision making. This endeavor has involved applications of expected-utility theory, linear regression models, Bayesian probability models, and information theory models, to name a few. The models use mathematics to document both the strengths and limitations of humans as information processors when making decisions. Mathematical models also are prominent in theories of memory, learning, language, bargaining, and signal detectability. Mathematical models have been used extensively in the analysis of social networks involving units such as institutions, communities, elites, friendship systems, kinship systems, and trade networks. Mathematical models of political behavior have explored such issues as voting and fairness. Behavior genetics relies heavily on mathematical decompositions of the effects of unique environmental influences, shared environmental influences, and genetic influences on human behavior in the context of twin studies. Spatial models are used to analyze residential and neighborhood patterning and the effects of this patterning on a wide range of phenomena. Geostatistical techniques explore spatial autocorrelation structures and then use mathematical models to estimate values of variables across regions. Our list could go on, but hopefully, these provide you with a sense of the diverse areas to which mathematical models have been applied.

EMERGENT THEORY CONSTRUCTION AND MATHEMATICAL MODELS

It may seem heretical to use the terms *grounded/emergent theory* and *mathematical modeling* in the same sentence, but there is no reason why some of the concepts developed in this chapter could not be used within emergent theory frameworks. For example, as one thinks about the conceptual relationships that emerge from qualitative data, are these relationships linear or nonlinear in form? If nonlinear, might they be described by logarithmic, exponential, power, polynomial, sine, or cosine functions? Although one might not be able to address this question formally and mathematically, perhaps the qualitative data and field notes are at least suggestive of a more precise operative function. Could some systematic combination of variables underlie what seems to be chaos? Is there anything to be gained by thinking about qualitative data in terms of the logic of multiplicative modeling? And so on.

We noted earlier that mathematical modelers usually give short shrift to how the variables they decide to include in their models are chosen. Certainly, an emergent theoretical framework might help them select their variables in informed and creative ways.

SUMMARY AND CONCLUDING COMMENTS

Mathematical modeling is an elegant framework for constructing theories. The emphasis of mathematical modeling is thinking in terms of functions and how to describe relationships between variables in mathematical terms. Functions specify how input variables should be operated upon mathematically to produce outputs. One of the most commonly used functions in the social sciences is the linear function, which has two adjustable constants, a slope and an intercept. The intercept is the output value of the function when the input X equals zero, and the slope is the change in the output given a 1-unit increase in X. Rarely do data conform to a perfect linear function. Model disparities are accommodated through the addition of disturbance or error terms to models. Errors are assumed to be random and inconsequential for the purposes at hand. Models without errors are deterministic, and models with errors are stochastic.

Mathematical models vary in their number of adjustable constants and the meaning of those constants/parameters. Some parameters reflect rates of change in function output per unit change in function input. These rates are best captured using the concepts of derivatives and differentiation from calculus. Derivatives refer to the concept of instantaneous change, and differentiation refers to mathematical methods for calculating the amount of instantaneous change that occurs. Integrals focus on "areas under the curve" or accumulation, and integration refers to the methods used to calculate integrals.

Mathematical models also differ in their identification status, with some models being underidentified, others just-identified, and still others overidentified. A just-identified model is one for which there is a unique solution for each estimated parameter. In an underidentified model, there are an infinite number of solutions for one or more of the model parameters. In an overidentified model, there is a unique solution for the model parameters, and there also is more than one feature that can be used to independently estimate a parameter value. Finally, mathematical models vary in the metrics they rely upon for the input variables. The metrics of variables can affect the type of functions used to describe the relationships between variables and how the parameter variables are interpreted.

Although the assumption of linear relationships is ubiquitous in the social sciences, nonlinear relationships could very well be more common. Five major classes of nonlinear functions are logarithmic functions, exponential functions, power functions, polynomial functions, and trigonometric functions. Logarithms are used to model growth or change, where the change is rapid at first and then slows to a gradual and eventually almost nonexistent pace. Logarithmic models reflect rates of increase that are inversely proportional to the output value of the function. Exponential functions are the inverse of log functions, with the two functions mirroring each other's properties. Power functions have a similar shape to exponential and logarithmic functions, but differ at higher values of the input X. Power curves eventually outgrow a logarithmic function and undergrow an exponential function. Polynomial functions are the sum of power functions and can accommodate phenomena with "wiggles and turns." The more bends there are in a curve, the greater the number of polynomial terms that are needed to reflect those bends. Trigonometric functions are used to model cyclical phenomena, with the most common functions being the sine and cosine functions.

Functions can be manipulated through transformations and can be combined to form new functions. For example, the often-used logistic function is a combination of a bounded exponential function and an increasing exponential function. Combining and manipulating functions is a key ingredient in building effective mathematical models. A typical theory construction process involves breaking up the overall process into a series of smaller component processes, specifying a function to reflect each component, and then assembling the component functions into a larger whole.

When functions involve more than one input variable, additional levels of flexibility and complexity are introduced, as the input variables are combined additively or multiplicatively. With multiple input variables, the theorist often thinks of the function relating each individual input variable to the output variable and then combines the different variables and their functions, while taking into account the synergistic interaction between the input variables. When choosing functions to use in a model, it is advisable not to overparameterize the model or to add parameters that are not subject to meaningful substantive interpretation.

Mathematical modeling represents a sophisticated way of thinking about relationships between variables. The approach is underutilized in the social sciences, and we believe that theory construction efforts can benefit from thinking about phenomena from this perspective.

SUGGESTED READINGS

Abramowitz, M., & Stegun, I. (1974). *Handbook of mathematical functions, with formulas, graphs, and mathematical tables.* New York: Dover.

—A classic on a wide range of functions. A bit dated, but still informative.

Aris, R. (1994). *Mathematical modeling techniques.* New York: Dover.

—A description of mathematical modeling techniques, with a bent toward the physical sciences.

Bender, E. (1978). *An introduction to mathematical modeling.* Mineola, NY: Dover.

—A description of math modeling through hundreds of examples; a book primarily oriented to the physical and engineering sciences.

Moony, D., & Swift, R. (1999). *A course in mathematical modeling.* New York: Mathematical Associates of America.

—A good introduction to mathematical modeling.

Saunders, P. (1980). *An introduction to catastrophe theory.* Cambridge, UK: Cambridge University Press.

—A midlevel book on catastrophe theory.

Williams, G. (1997). *Chaos theory tamed.* Washington, DC: Joseph Henry Press.

—An excellent presentation of chaos theory.

KEY TERMS

discrete variable (p. 197)

continuous variable (p. 197)

axioms (p. 198)

theorems (p. 198)

function (p. 198)

domain (p. 199)

range (p. 199)

linear function (p. 199)

slope (p. 199)

intercept (p. 203)

deterministic model (p. 204)

probabilistic model (p. 204)

stochastic model (p. 204)

adjustable parameter (p. 204)

fixed parameter (p. 205)

estimated parameter (p. 205)

derivative (p. 206)

differentiation (p. 206)

integral (p. 208)

integration (p. 208)

model identification (p. 209)

just-identified model (p. 209)

underidentified model (p. 209)

overidentified model (p. 209)

concavity (p. 213)

constant of proportionality (p. 213)

scaling constant (p. 213)

logarithmic function (p. 213)

Napier's constant (p. 214)

exponential function (p. 214)

power function (p. 216)

polynomial function (p. 217)

trigonometric function (p. 220)

rational function (p. 224)

vertical shift (p. 225)

vertical crunch (p. 225)

horizontal shift (p. 225)

horizontal crunch (p. 225)

bounded exponential function (p. 225)

logistic function (p. 225)

sigmoid function (p. 226)

bilinear interaction (p. 231)

chaos theory (p. 235)

difference equation (p. 236)

first-order difference equation (p. 236)

spatial chaos (p. 236)

temporal chaos (p. 236)

discrete time model (p. 236)

continuous time model (p. 236)

catastrophe theory (p. 237)

EXERCISES

Exercises to Reinforce Concepts

1. What is the difference between an axiom and a theorem?

2. What is a function?

3. How do you interpret the value of a slope and intercept in a linear relationship?

4. How do you calculate a slope in a linear relationship? How do you calculate the intercept?

5. Why would you add an error term to a model? How does this relate to the terms *stochastic* and *deterministic* modeling?

6. What is the difference between a derivative and differentiation?

7. What is integration?

8. Why are metrics important to consider when constructing a mathematical model?

9. Briefly describe the major types of nonlinear functions.

10. What are the major types of transformations affecting functions, and what effects do they have?

11. What criteria are used in choosing a function?

12. Briefly characterize chaos and catastrophe theory.

Exercises to Apply Concepts

1. Find an example of a mathematical model in the literature and write a summary of it. Discuss each of the key parameters in the model and what those parameters represent. Develop the model's conceptual and substantive implications.

2. Develop a mathematical model for a phenomenon of interest to you. Begin by identifying your outcome variable and then variables that you believe are related to it. Specify the functions relating the variables and add relevant constants to the equations, as appropriate. Justify conceptually each function and each constant. Decide if the model should be deterministic or stochastic. Start simple and then build complexity into the model accordingly.

3. Pick a phenomenon of interest to you and try to apply either chaos theory or catastrophe theory to it. Describe the new theory as completely as you can.

SPSS Code for Exploring Distribution Properties

This appendix presents syntax from SPSS that can be used to examine curves produced by different functions.

First, open SPSS with the data field blank. We will use the syntax editor. The first step is to create a variable with a large number of cases, say 100,000. This is accomplished with the following syntax:

```
INPUT PROGRAM.
LOOP #I = 1 TO 100000.
END CASE.
END LOOP.
END FILE.
END INPUT PROGRAM.
COMPUTE X = $CASENUM.
EXECUTE.
```

The last entry in the LOOP command (100000) specifies the number of cases to generate. Numbers are generated in a variable called X, and these numbers range from 1 to the number of cases generated. These can be transformed to take on any metric you wish. For example, to have them range from 0 to 1, multiply X by .00001. To have them range from –5 to +5, multiply by .00001, subtract 0.5, and then multiply the result by 10. And so on.

Next, we compute the function we are interested in graphing. Suppose it is a log to the base 10. SPSS offers numerous built-in functions, and in this case, we use the syntax

```
COMPUTE XX=LG10(X).
GRAPH
/HISTOGRAM=XX.
```

The last two lines construct a histogram of the data, and the shape of the function will be evident from this. You can add adjustable constants and perform various transformations discussed in the chapter, as desired.

The major function commands available in SPSS are arsin, artan, cos, exp, lg10, ln, sin, and sqrt. These are defined in the help menu in SPSS. One also can work with a wide range of statistical functions, including the logistic function. Note that it is possible to calculate a log to any base from the natural log. The logarithm base a of any number is the natural logarithm of the number divided by the natural logarithm of the base. For example, to calculate $\log_2(100)$, evaluate the expression $\ln(100)/\ln(2)$.

There are a host of graphic software programs (for both PC and Mac) designed for scientists that allow them to graph a wide range of functions easily and quickly. These include CoPlot, DPlot, Sigma Plot, and Grapher. We are fond of DPlot. Other statistical software programs that have good graphics packages are S Plus, R, and Statistica.

Appendix 8.2

Additional Modeling Issues for the Performance, Ability, and Motivation Example

This appendix describes details for the example modeling the effects of ability and motivation on performance, where the relationship between performance and motivation is nonlinear instead of linear at a given level of ability. We assume the reader is versed in standard statistical methods and psychometric theory. We illustrate the case first where motivation is assumed to impact performance in accord with a power function, with the shape of the power function changing as a function of ability. Then we mention the case where the relationship between performance and motivation is assumed to be S-shaped, with the form of the S varying as a function of ability.

We build the power function model by first positing that performance is a power function of motivation,

$$P = a + bM^c \tag{A.1}$$

where a and b are adjustable constants to accommodate metrics and c is an adjustable constant to isolate the relevant power curve in light of a and b. According to the broader theory, the effect of motivation on performance varies depending on ability (e.g., when ability is low, increases in motivation will have negligible effects on performance, but when ability is moderate to high, increases in motivation will have a more substantial impact on performance). Stated another way, the shape of the power curve will differ depending on the level of ability of students, such that the value of c is some function of A. In addition, it is likely the case that the adjustable constants a and b vary as a function of A. To simplify matters and to develop the underlying logic, we will assume that c is a linear function of A, that a is a linear function of A, and that b is a linear function of A. This yields the equations

$$c = d + fA$$
$$a = g + hA$$
$$b = i + jA$$

where $c, d, f, g, h, i,$ and j are adjustable constants that conform to the respective linear models.

Using substitution principles, we can substitute the right-hand side of these equations into A.1, which yields

$$P = (g + hA) + (i + jA)(M)^{(d + fA)}$$

Expanding, we obtain

$$P = (g + hA) + iM^{(d + fA)} + jAM^{(d + fA)}$$

We can rewrite this equation using the more familiar symbols of a and b for adjustable constants in regression analysis:

$$P = a + b_1A + b_2M^{(b_3 + b_4A)} + b_5AM^{(b_3 + b_4A)}$$

This model can be fit to data and the values of the adjustable constants estimated using nonlinear regression algorithms in SPSS or some other statistical package. The adjustable constants are amenable to interpretation, but we forgo explication of this here. Additional interpretative complications present themselves if the metrics involved are arbitrary, but we do not pursue such matters here either (see Blanton & Jaccard, 2006).

One intuitive way of seeing the implications of the function once the values of the adjustable constants are estimated is to calculate predicted scores that vary M by 1 unit at select values of A. These can be graphed and then subjected to interpretation.

An alternative approach to modeling the data that uses methods that are more familiar to social scientists is to use polynomial regression. In this approach, performance is assumed to be a quadratic function of motivation. Although the full quadratic curve most certainly is not applicable (because it is U-shaped), the part of the curve that forms the right half of the "U" could apply. The model includes adjustable constants to isolate this portion. We begin by writing a model where performance is a quadratic function of motivation

$$P = a_1 + b_1M + b_2M^2 \tag{A.2}$$

and the adjustable constants in this equation (the intercept and the regression coefficients) are modeled as being a linear function of ability (we could use a nonlinear function, but for the sake of pedagogy, we assume a linear function), yielding

$$a_1 = a_2 + b_3A$$
$$b_1 = a_3 + b_4A$$
$$b_2 = a_4 + b_5A$$

Using the substitution principle, we substitute the right-hand sides of these equations for their respective terms in Equation A.2, which produces

$$P = (a_2 + b_3A) + (a_3 + b_4A)M + (a_4 + b_5A)M^2$$

Expanding this yields

$$P = a_2 + b_3A + a_3M + b_4AM + a_4M^2 + b_5AM^2$$

Rearranging and relabeling the constants to conform to more traditional notation yields the model

$$P = a + b_1A + b_2M + b_3AM + b_4M^2 + b_5AM^2$$

This model can be fit using standard least-squares regression.

To model an S-shaped function, one can stay with polynomial regression but extend the logic to a cubic function. The basic idea is to express performance as a cubic function of motivation

$$P = a_1 + b_1M + b_2M^2 + b_3M^3$$

and then to model the adjustable constants as a function of A. Finally, use the substitution method to derive the more complex generating function.

Alternatively, one can use a logistic function to capture the S shape and then model the adjustable constants within it as a function of A. This approach requires the use of nonlinear algorithms in estimating the adjustable constants.

9

Simulation as
a Theory Development Method

In theory, there is no difference between theory and practice.
But in practice, there is.

—A Computer Scientist

To this point we have examined how causal thinking and mathematical modeling provide frameworks for theory construction. Another approach that can help in the theory construction process is the use of simulations, particularly when the phenomenon being studied is a complex and dynamic process. Simulations can be used to generate theory in their own right, or they can be used as a complement to causal and mathematical modeling.

Most readers likely are aware of the simulations used for training airline pilots and sharpening their ability to handle unanticipated and infrequently occurring contingencies. These devices are gyroscopically controlled rooms constructed so that their interior looks, feels, and operates like the criterion aircraft cockpit to a pilot during the actual in-flight operation of that aircraft. Another familiar form of simulation is business games and management simulations, which are used by industrial organization and business schools to train managers and students. Less well known, however, are the large number of simulations that are being pursued by economists, political scientists, psychologists, and sociologists, among others, to gain perspectives on theories of complex social systems.

For example, in 2008, the economy of the United States dropped precipitously into a recession with the collapse of several large banks, insurance companies, and investment firms. The swings in the stock market and the economic responses of investors confounded traditional economic theory that embraced the notion of equilibrium. Equilibrium theory views markets as the product of a balance of forces that respond primarily to new information about, for example, problems a company is having or changes in the housing supply (Farmer & Geanakoplos, 2002). However, the volatility of the markets made clear that something more was at work. Many economists felt that the volatility reflected, in part, the complex dynamics operating between thousands of traders who compete, interact, and trade with one another on a daily basis. Thus, it is not enough to apply the principle of equilibrium. One also must take into account these thousands of relationships to better appreciate market volatility. Economists developed simulations where thousands of artificially intelligent "agents," represented on a computer, were programmed to have different investing orientations, habits, and social and business networks with other traders. The simulations set the agents about their way to interact and transact their business on a daily basis over an extended period of time, the equivalent of, say, several weeks. Observations were then made about how the simulated market behaved across this more extended time period, especially as the researcher introduced new information into the system. The results of such agent-based simulations provided new perspectives on traditional economic theories of equilibrium as well as the effects of other policy-based innovations on aspects of market volatility (Farmer & Geanakoplos, 2002; Westerhoff, 2008).

The level of complexity of these simulations, with the hundreds of thousands of interactions between agents that are captured over extended time periods, could not possibly be addressed by traditional methods. By using such agent-based simulations, economists were able to evaluate the effects of changes introduced into the system or the effects of changing one or more underlying assumptions about, for example, agent orientations or agent networks, on higher-level system outputs. This evaluation was then used to generate new theories of market volatility.

In this chapter, we consider how simulations can be used to develop theory. We begin by defining simulation strategies and then discuss some of the uses of research-based simulations. After describing different types of simulations, we consider the core activity of analyzing criterion systems for purposes of designing simulations. It is at this stage that new ideas and theory clarification often occur. We then discuss the strategies of virtual experiments and agent-based modeling as theory construction strategies and conclude by identifying resources that will facilitate the conduct of simulations.

DEFINING SIMULATIONS

According to *Webster's Dictionary*, a simulation is defined as "the imitative representation of the functioning of one system or process by means of the functioning of another." The original system that one seeks to simulate is called the *criterion system,* and the imitative representation of that system is called the *simulation*. The criterion system is generally more complex, whereas the simulation is a simpler representation that incorporates only selected characteristics of the criterion system. Different simulations of the same criterion system may thus assume different layers of complexity, depending on how many and just which features are incorporated. The criterion systems may be virtually anything, including physical entities, social entities, corporate or organizational entities, economic systems, mental processes, and military maneuvers. Moreover, the simulation system can attempt to represent the characteristics of the criterion system using a variety of forms, including physical, pictorial, verbal, mathematical, and logical approaches. Our attention is confined to simulations developed for studying some aspect of human systems at either the individual or group level.

A distinction can be made between *pedagogical* and *research simulations*. Pedagogical simulations are developed primarily to be used as training aids. In contrast, the principal function of research simulations is as a strategy for developing, testing, and extending conceptualizations. Because pedagogical simulations often can be used as research tools, the difference between pedagogical and research simulations generally is one of emphasis. Suppose engineers in the process of designing a new aircraft wanted to determine which of several different instrument panel configurations would generate optimal speed and accuracy of a pilot's response. By installing these configurations in a simulator and using an appropriate sample of test pilots, they could conduct research to answer this question.

THE USES OF RESEARCH SIMULATIONS

Research-related simulations serve two basic functions: (1) to build and clarify theories and (2) to test theories. Our emphasis in this chapter is on the first function. Developing simulations generally requires the theorist to think about the criterion system in comprehensive terms. Doing so can force confrontation with the inadequacies of one's original conceptualization, thereby revealing the need for more detailed explication of the conceptualization. This, in turn, often results in the expansion or clarification of the original theory. Thus, apart from the data that may be generated when conducting the simulation at some later point in time, the sheer act of developing a research simulation can be viewed as an aid to theory generation and clarification.

THE DIFFERENCE BETWEEN SIMULATIONS AND LABORATORY EXPERIMENTS

Although simulation and experimentation can be integrated in a single study, when not integrated, the characteristics of the typical simulation contrast sharply with those of experimentation. Whereas fully experimental designs involve "tight" investigator control over both the presentation of the stimuli and the sequence of events, simulation allows for events, their sequence (the "information flow"), and perhaps even the consequences to be determined by the research "participants." Whereas experimentation usually reflects an effort either to eliminate nonfocal factors and/or hold them constant, simulations generally permit these factors to vary freely. Whereas experimentation generally concentrates on a limited number of independent and dependent variables, simulations generally include a greater number of variables, particularly potential causes of the variable of interest. Whereas to achieve their goals, experiments "tie" and "untie" variables (and levels of variables) in ways that may divorce them from everyday reality, simulations strive to keep these factors "tied" in a manner that is consonant with the way in which they are associated in the everyday world criterion system. The presence of more background variables coupled with more complex representations of independent variables produces a "richer" environment out of which sometimes emerge unexpected or "serendipitous" findings that serve to extend the researcher's conceptualization. Whereas experiments are admirably suited for evaluating the input(s) and outcome(s) of a process, simulations tend to place greater emphasis on the process itself.

Many research simulations are developed and used because they are amenable to manipulations that would be impossible, impractical, or too costly to perform with the criterion system itself. In this sense, they are a form of experimentation and are comparable to a laboratory experiment. Simulations are particularly useful when the phenomenon of interest is enmeshed in a complex, dynamic system, and the researcher's intent is to extrapolate from the findings to what is probable under real-world conditions.

BASIC SIMULATION VARIETIES

Simulations can be described in terms of a number of features, and any specific simulation can be identified as possessing some features and not others.

All-Machine versus Person–Machine Simulations

One important distinction is between all-machine and person–machine simulations. *Person–machine simulations* involve one or more human participants as an integral part of the operation of the simulation. In contrast, *all-machine simulations* simulate human behavior and/or mental functioning in the absence of any direct interaction with a human participant. There are two major subvarieties: *physical analog simulations,* which use some sort of physical model to simulate human dynamics, and *mathematical simulations,* which rely entirely on mathematics and computer programs. Artificial intelligence exemplifies a behavioral science domain where the emphasis is on developing computer programs that resemble intelligent thought.

Descriptive versus Analytic Simulations

A distinction is sometimes made between descriptive and analytic simulations. Descriptive simulations emphasize structure, whereas analytic simulations emphasize process. The object of a *descriptive simulation* is to reproduce the physical structure of the criterion system in as much detail as possible, usually on a smaller scale. In contrast, an *analytic simulation* seeks to reproduce the process of the criterion system. Whether the simulation reproduces the physical appearance of the criterion system is of little importance. "The important factor is that the components and variables being investigated respond in a manner comparable to that of the behavior of the real system" (Dawson, 1963, p. 223). Most research simulations are analytic—that is, the criterion system is dynamic, containing characteristics that operate in sequence and over time—and the simulation seeks to represent this process.

Real-Time versus Compressed-Time versus Expanded-Time Simulations

The focus on process raises another distinction. In *real-time simulations,* the process under study takes the same amount of time as it takes in the criterion system. *Compressed-time simulations* focus on phenomena that are extended in time in the criterion system (e.g., interaction patterns between groups over a 2-year period) and enable these patterns to be studied in a much shorter time period, say, 15 minutes. In contrast, *expanded-time simulations* slow down rapid processes so that they can be studied more carefully.

Deterministic versus Nondeterministic Simulations

Another common distinction is between deterministic and nondeterministic simulations. In *deterministic simulations,* the precise outcome is determined by the initial input, whereas in *nondeterministic simulations,* the outcome is determined by some combination of the initial input with "chance" events that occur during operation of the simulation. In other words, deterministic simulations do not build "noise" into the system, whereas nondeterministic simulations do.

Free versus Experimental Simulations

A related distinction is between free and experimental simulations. The defining characteristic of a *free simulation* is that events that occur during the simulation are shaped, in part or entirely, by the behavior of the participants themselves. In contrast, all information that reaches the participant in an *experimental simulation* is preprogrammed by the researcher. Although participants in the experimental simulation believe that they control their own fate (at least to some degree), in point of fact, they do not. This defining characteristic renders the experimental simulation more like the standard laboratory experiment than like the free simulation because the independent variables remain under complete control of the experimenter (Fromkin & Streufert, 1976, p. 425).

Macro- versus Microsimulations

Other ways of describing simulations involve distinguishing them in terms of their scope. *Macrosimulations* involve large-scale criterion systems that include many people and/or variables. An example would be an attempt to simulate the gold-trading system of the free world. *Microsimulations* involve few people and/or variables. At one extreme, a microsimulation would refer to a single type of process (e.g., acquiring information from the outside world as a basis for reaching a decision) going on in the mind of a single individual.

Content-Oriented Simulation

Simulations are often categorized in terms of the specific domain of content they address. Some of the more popular content-oriented simulations in the behavioral sciences include international simulations (Guetzkow, Akger, Brody, Noel, & Snyder, 1963; Silverman & Bryden, 2007), economic system simulations (e.g., Schubert, 1960; Westerhoff, 2008), small group/social process simulations (e.g., McGrath & Altman, 1966; Suleiman, Troitzsch, & Gilbert, 2000), interpersonal bargaining–negotiation simulations (Deutsch & Krauss, 1960; Luce & Raiffa, 1957), organizational simulations (Lomi & Larsen, 2001), and cognitive process simulations (Jacoby, Jaccard, Kuss, Troutman, & Mazursky, 1987; Newell & Simon, 1972; Sun, 2006), to name a few.

THE ANALYSIS OF CRITERION SYSTEMS AS A BASIS FOR THEORY CONSTRUCTION

When developing a research simulation, one begins by developing a conceptualization (essentially, a theory) as to what constitute the essential features of the criterion system that need to be represented in the simulation. Next, one strives to build a simulation that corresponds to the essential features of that conceptualization. Decisions must be made about which features of the criterion system to include and which features to omit. Once designed, the simulation can be used to test a variety of theoretical propositions and to provide feedback on them. In practice, the first two activities go through several iterations, being refined and extended at each iteration. In part, this is because certain features of the criterion system may be so pervasive that, like water to the deep sea dweller, their importance initially goes unrecognized, becoming apparent only after one tries to implement the initial version of the simulation and realizes that something important is missing. This leads to a refined conceptualization of the criterion system, which, in turn, leads to incorporating additional layers of sophistication into the simulation. Throughout the process of simulation development, the goal is to approximate key features of the criterion system as closely as possible and in as much detail as is necessary to answer the question at hand. It is during this phase of simulation design that theory construction and development often occurs. As the theorist carefully analyzes the criterion system, trying to capture and think through the key elements of it that must be captured in the simulation and those elements that can be omitted, important variables and possible relationships between those variables often become evident. We illustrate two case studies of this phenomenon.

Simulation of Information Accessing in Consumer Purchase Decisions

Jacoby developed an informal theory of information accessing during decision making and a program of research based on that theory using simulation technology. The initial simulations were developed in reaction to limitations perceived to be inherent in studies Jacoby had conducted on the subject of information overload in consumer decision making. According to the overload hypothesis, by increasing the amount of information to which a decision maker must attend during a brief period of time, a point will be reached beyond which the decision maker's ability to cope with this information is strained and the quality of his or her decision making deteriorates. Conducted in 1971–

1973 (e.g., Jacoby, Speller, & Berning, 1974; Jacoby, Speller, & Kohn, 1974), the overload studies came about in response to arguments from consumer advocates who maintained that, when it came to communicating with consumers, "more information is better." The overload studies were designed to assess whether this "more is better" assumption, or the competing overload hypothesis, would be empirically confirmed.

The overload studies employed variations of a common methodological protocol. First, questions were used to ascertain each research participant's preferences for various features of a test product. Assume that the test product was ready-to-eat breakfast cereal. Each participant would indicate his or her preferences on such characteristics as type of grain (oat, rice, wheat, etc.), whether or not it was sweetened, whether or not it contained dry fruit, the size (in ounces) of the package, the price, and so on. Next, participants were randomly assigned to the cells of a fully experimental factorial design where one factor was "number of brands" and the second was "number of features described for each brand." Each factor had several levels (e.g., 4, 8, 12, or 16 brands for the first factor, and 4, 8, 12, or 16 features for the second factor). Thus, depending on the cell to which he or she was assigned, the participant would receive as little as 16 items of information (4 brands × 4 features per brand), or as much as 256 items of information (16 brands × 16 features per brand) to consider. Third, the research participants were instructed to examine and evaluate *all* the information provided to them and use this information as the basis for selecting the brand they would most prefer.

The dozen or so studies that Jacoby conducted found that, regardless of the products tested and whether the participants were undergraduates or adult heads of households or lived in the United States, Puerto Rico, or Germany, the pattern of findings generally reflected an overload effect. That is, the ability to select the brand that most closely matched one's ideal brand improved with modest amounts of information, then decreased as the amount of information increased beyond some optimal level. Reports of these findings began surfacing in most consumer behavior textbooks, in marketing and advertising executive deliberations, and in regulatory agency policymaking. For example, the 1981 Federal Trade Commission Staff Report proposing precautionary language in cigarette labeling cited the overload studies as the basis for its recommendation to have no more than three specific health hazards indicated at a time on cigarette packages and to rotate these warnings periodically.

Analysis of the Criterion System

As early as 1974, Jacoby began to express reservations about the applicability of these findings to the everyday world of consumer decision making (see Jacoby, 1975, 1977, 1984). The disparity between the conditions of assessment and key features of *in vivo* consumer decision making convinced Jacoby that demonstrating that overload was *possible* using laboratory experimentation provided little basis for contending that it was *probable* in everyday life (the criterion system). To examine whether overload occurred in the field would require developing an empirical system or simulated environment that more closely paralleled and incorporated many of the key features of the criterion system. The objective was to devise a simulated environment that would enable the researcher to examine how and how much information consumers acquired when left to their own devices, prior to making a purchase decision. This led to an intensive analysis of the criterion system.

Attention initially was limited to consumer choice behavior as it might occur in the context of a typical full-service supermarket, with the combination of consumer plus environment constituting the criterion system. This system was conceptualized as consisting of (1) a decision maker who, at least in part, relies on information acquired from the outside world; (2) a task environment containing a set of choice options (e.g., different brands of breakfast cereal), each of which has associated information (e.g., price, size, ingredients); and (3) an objective that the decision maker brings to the choice context (e.g., "Out of those available, select the breakfast cereal I would most like to buy"). Considering how these three components typically played out *in vivo*, the following features emerged as key characteristics of the criterion system.

First, information exposure in the criterion system was *consumer-determined*, not experimenter-determined. Consumers in the real world are *active*, not passive, information seekers. That is, they do not enter supermarkets and passively wait to be force-fed certain fixed quantities of information (as was characteristic of the overload experiments). Rather, they actively seek and attend to information on their own. Hence, to better understand what was probable in the real world, the simulation had to permit the participant an active stance in acquiring information from an available pool of information.

Second, the task environment is saturated with information that can be used during decision making. Consider the following. The consumer usually has a choice of supermarkets and grocery stores, with each of these outlets containing an overlapping but somewhat different assortment of products. Full-service American supermarkets at that time typically contained more than 25,000–35,000 different items on their shelves, almost all of which appeared in packages that contain considerable amounts of information. For example, the typical American supermarket contains at least 50–80 different brands of breakfast cereal (out of more than 150 such nationally available brands). Even if one disregards all the photographs and drawings, most breakfast cereal boxes contain more than 100 separate items of information. The *information-intensive* nature of this environment is rendered even more complex by the fact that, in many product categories, the available brands (e.g., Crest toothpaste, Coca-Cola) come in different sizes, flavors, colors, and the like.

Third, to avoid being overwhelmed by this complexity, the consumer's prechoice information-seeking behavior reflects great *selectivity*. Consumers generally confine their shopping to one store and, when there, may not go down every aisle. Within any given aisle, they generally do not consider products in every product category. Even within a product category they do consider, as the number of options (i.e., brands, sizes, variations) increases, the consumer is less likely to consider all the available options. And when the consumer does pick up a package for one brand, he or she is not likely to attend to all the information that appears thereon. Thus, consideration of the criterion system suggested that consumers operating *in vivo* are highly selective in regard to how much and just which information they attend to.

Fourth, *memory* plays a critical role in decision making. Consumers need not and likely would not expend time or effort to acquire information from the external environment if they already had that information in mind. When it comes to frequently purchased nondurables, knowing a product's brand name enables one to bring forth from memory a considerable amount of directly relevant information. For example, seeing the brand "Budweiser" might stimulate the consumer to recall such things as the product being a domestic, not foreign, brew, the manufacturer's name (Anheuser Busch), the manufacturer's principal place of business (St. Louis), the packaging (which contains red and white colors and an "A and eagle" logo), the brewing process involving beechwood aging, and around the end of the year, its advertising including Clydesdale horses. Sometimes what is brought forth from memory provides a sufficient basis for arriving at a purchase decision. At other times, we need to update or augment information in memory (e.g., what is the item's current price?) or, when considering something new, acquire information from the external environment as a basis for arriving at our decisions.

Additional reflection suggested a fifth important aspect of the criterion system. All participants in the information overload studies were given information in a set sequence. More than likely, this did not correspond to the sequence in which participants would have acquired the same information had they been left to their own devices. Since the scholarly literature contained a sufficient number of reports to show that the *sequence* in which information is obtained could be important, it was considered necessary that the simulation permit participants to assess information in any sequence they desired.

Thus, as the basis for developing the initial simulation, the criterion system (consisting of both the external information environment and the consumer's internal information processing) was conceptualized as reflecting the following key characteristics: In arriving at his or her purchase decision, the consumer relies on both internal and external sources of information and, especially in regard to the latter, is active and selective in determining just which, how much, and in what order information is acquired. This analysis also led to the recognition that, given the vast amounts of information available in the decision environment (say, a supermarket or drug store), one could not study the entire environment but needed to focus instead on a limited portion of that environment (e.g., a product category such as toothpaste). Attention thus was confined to studying whether the information overload effect would surface—as it had in the laboratory experiments—when individuals were permitted to operate in ways that more closely paralleled their behavior in selecting a brand of toothpaste or shampoo in naturalistic settings.

An Early Simulation

Jacoby developed these simulations before personal computers were available on a widespread basis, so several rather crude versions of the simulated environment were implemented relative to the simulations now in place. One early simulation consisted of a "strip board" device that presented participants with a matrix of information about different brands (e.g., of toothpaste or of cereal). The brands were represented in columns (e.g., the first column was labeled Brand A, the second column Brand B, and so on), and the rows were represented as information dimensions (e.g., price, size). The cells of the matrix contained the specific information about a given brand and a given information dimension where the row and column intersected. Although the row and column labels for the brands and information dimensions were visible, the information in the cells of the matrix was covered by horizontal strips of opaque tape. Each strip ran horizontally, covering the brand-specific information for all brands on a single type of information. For example, one strip covered the prices for each of the available brands; another strip covered the size, and so on. Research participants could remove a strip, one at a time, thereby revealing the information in the cells for all brands on that type of information. For example, pulling off the tape strip over the price information would reveal the prices in the cells for all the brands. The simulation participants were told that they could acquire as much or as little of the information as desired, removing none, one, several, or all of the tape strips before making their choice about the brand they would choose. Furthermore, they were told they could do so in any order they desired. In some simulations, information identifying the brand name (e.g., Crest) was available. Therefore, if acquired, this information would enable the participants to access information about the brand and manufacturer from their memory. In other simulations, this type of information was absent from the information pool.

Though crude, the strip board simulations represented significant improvements relative to prior research strategies. First, although scholars generally agreed that decision making was a *dynamic process* that unfolded over time, almost all of the research on decision making conducted to that point relied on static, cross-sectional, or simple pre–post assessment methodologies. The prior overload research was typical of this genre. In a sense, it was "outcome research," not "process research." Crude as it was, the strip board device enabled information acquisition to be studied dynamically, as it occurred, rather than relying on cross-sectional verbal assessments made before (e.g., "What information do you intend to use?") or after the fact (e.g., "What information did you use?").

Second, comparing poststudy debriefings with the information that the simulation participants acquired during the simulation led to greater appreciation of the fact that not all aspects of decision making operate at consciously retrievable levels. As information processors, we may attend to information of which we had no prior knowledge and therefore could have had no intention to seek out or attend to. Moreover, evidence suggests that we are not capable of recalling all the information that we do acquire, or the sequence in which this information is acquired (see McGuire, 1976; Nisbett & Wilson, 1977). Without having to rely on fallible memory or verbal reports about search behavior, the simulation directly assessed information-accessing *behavior* as it unfolded. It also enabled us to directly examine just which information was ignored instead of having to ask potentially leading questions to make such determinations.

Interestingly, these features of the simulations were viewed as a strength by some methodologists and a weakness by others. On the one hand, the attempt to simulate core features of the criterion system led to a more accurate representation of the role of the information acquisition process in the real world. On the other hand, many facets of information acquisition were out of the experimenter's control (e.g., the amount of information accessed, the sequence in which information was accessed), making it more challenging to arrive at causal inferences from the collected data.

Iterating Simulations and Iterating Theories

As noted earlier, when building a simulation, a researcher must often go through several trial-and-error steps, what we call *iterations,* in order to obtain a reasonably faithful representation of the criterion system. In the process, new variables to include in the system might suggest themselves, and new relationships to focus on also might become salient. As one iterates the system, one also gains theoretical insights, and revisions to the theory often occur as well. In this way, not only does the simulation become an improved representation of the criterion system, but theory becomes "iterated" and improved as well. Although theoretical revisions based on data are a natural part of all methods of science, a unique facet of this dynamic for simulation research is that the scientist is concerned not only with improving theory but also with improving the simulation, so it can be used more effectively in future research.

To illustrate this iterative process, consider the strip board simulation and limitations that were revealed by implementing it. One limitation that became apparent involved the restrictions it placed on information acquisition. Although the strip board enabled us to study the acquisition of types or categories of information (e.g., flavor, price), it did not permit us to analyze the acquisition of single pieces of information associated with a specific brand (e.g., the flavor of Crest toothpaste). Subsequent developments, especially computerized versions of the simulation, circumvented this problem. Research with the strip board device also failed to accommodate the fact that real-world decision makers generally live with the consequences of their decisions. This led to a further change in the simulation to include authentic consequences. For example, simulation participants were told in advance that they would receive several "cents-off" coupons that could be redeemed at local stores, but only for the brand they selected. The simulation thus incorporated an element of *consequentiality,* an important feature of the criterion system.

Spurred partly by conceptual considerations as well as the availability of more powerful computers, the simulation continued to undergo several theory–simulation–theory iterations. For example, unlike purchase decisions made in supermarket settings— which involve consumers attending primarily to two dimensions of the external information environment, namely, "options" (brands) and "properties" (information provided on packaging for brands)—*in vivo* decision making often has decision makers obtaining option and property information from different sources. Hence, the simulation was extended to permit testing of such "properties × options × sources" information environments (e.g., Chestnut & Jacoby, 1980; Hoyer & Jacoby, 1983). Predecision information acquisition rarely occurs in a vacuum. Generally, decision making takes place in the context of important antecedents, such as things the decision maker sees, reads, or hears prior to engaging in decision making. In the consumer context, such antecedents include advertising, pertinent news articles, comments by salespersons, and word-of-mouth communications from family and friends.

The simulation also was extended to examine the impact of such incoming communications on information search (e.g., see Sheluga & Jacoby, 1978). In a modification that may hold the greatest potential for both extending and testing theory, the simulation was further revised to allow scientists to study the *incremental impact of item-*

by-item information acquisition on such phenomena as uncertainty reduction (Jacoby et al., 1994), brand evaluations (Johar, Jedidi, & Jacoby, 1997), and attitude formation (Jacoby, Morrin, Jaccard, Gurhan, & Maheswaran, 2002). Finally, as the simulation was extended to examine information accessing in other types of decision making (e.g., real-world security analysts reaching buy–sell decisions for which there was a hard criterion for evaluating performance; e.g., Jacoby et al., 2002; Morrin et al., 2002), it was found that the theory that had evolved in regard to supermarket decision making had to be revised in several substantial respects, again reflecting the iterative relationship between simulations and theory development.

This discussion demonstrates how, in developing simulations to test theories, the process of simulation development can contribute to theory development. Building a reasonably faithful simulation requires that one undertake a thorough analysis of the criterion system. Since the simulation is essentially a reflection of one's theory of the criterion system, this analysis often will reveal key assumptions and other facets that help refine and extend the seminal conceptualization. This was the case for Jacoby as he developed the simulation for analyzing consumer information accessing. Thus, even when the motivation for designing the simulation may be the development of a research tool for testing theories, doing so can lead to theoretical insights before testing ever takes place. And once the simulation is tested, recognition of its limitations may also suggest ways for extending one's theory.

Virtual Environments, Augmented Environments, and Avatars

Another example of the use of simulations for theory development is recent work with *virtual environments*. In this research, participants either wear a head-mounted display that immerses them in a three-dimensional, computer-generated virtual environment, or they view a computer screen that has an engrossing and realistic virtual environment. In some studies, the participant is hardwired so that his or her body movements are shown on the computer screen. The virtual world typically is viewed from a first-person perspective, so that the screen mimics what one would see from one's own eyes. Virtual humans, called *avatars*, can be introduced into the environment, and the researcher controls in real time how the avatars act and react in interactions with the research participant.

The use of avatars and virtual environments is becoming more common in social science research and applications. This research has explored the use of avatars and virtual environments for the study of such diverse phenomena as online counseling, fear of public speaking, dating and interpersonal behavior, treatment of acrophobia (fear of heights), acquisition of medical knowledge by medical residents, consumer purchase decisions, interpretation of facial expressions, nicotine craving, eating disorders, and friendship formation, to name a few. The studies have led researchers to posit basic questions about the generation of virtual environment simulations, such as the amount of visual fidelity that is required for an avatar to seem human, how the avatar should interact with the environment so as to appear natural, the perceptual and memory skills that an avatar should be programmed to display in order to be perceived as normal, and the amount of unpredictability and emotion that should be shown by the avatar so as to appear normal. In essence, a new set of questions about human behavior and perception has emerged in response to the simulation problem of designing a realistic avatar. As social scientists have addressed these questions, they have embarked on collaborations with artists, computer programmers, and graphic designers to form multidisciplinary teams for analyzing the subtleties of human actions and social perceptions—teams that, prior to simulations with virtual environments, simply did not interact with one another. The result has been promising new perspectives on basic mechanisms of perception and human interaction, independent of research that is formally conducted using avatars.

In addition to virtual environments, another technology is that of *augmented realities* (ARs). This approach enhances rather than replaces a person's environment. AR technologies can manipulate all of the human senses, including smell, touch, and hearing. It can create virtual objects and remove objects from the field of vision. One typically views one's environment through a digital headset, which is configured to alter what the user sees, hears, or smells.

There is no question that with the increasing speed, processing capacity, and power of computers, virtual environments, augmented realities, and avatars will be a useful tool not only in society more generally but in social science research. As simulations become increasingly popular, ways of thinking about the human criterion system will expand accordingly.

SIMULATIONS AND VIRTUAL EXPERIMENTS

Another way in which simulations are used during the initial stages of theory construction is to use all-machine simulations to conduct *virtual experiments* that provide feedback on initial theoretical propositions. Once the theory is revised and refined so that it behaves well in the virtual experiment, it is applied to real-world dynamics (Davis, Bingham, & Eisenhardt, 2007; Sastry, 1997; Sterman, 2000). As an example, Davis, Eisenhardt, and Bingham (2005) unpacked the global construct of "market dynamism" into four subcategories: velocity, complexity, ambiguity, and unpredictability. They then designed a computer simulation of market systems to examine the effect of each component on market behavior and ran the simulation with three of the components held constant and the fourth construct varying. They did this for each component, in turn, and then amended their initial theory based on the results of the simulation. This theory was then applied to real-world market dynamics (see also Repenning, 2002).

AGENT-BASED MODELING

Smith and Conrey (2007) describe a simulation-based approach to theory construction called *agent-based modeling*. This approach uses the spirit of virtual experimentation and was illustrated in the example at the beginning of the chapter on the economic recession in the United States. Agent-based modeling focuses on "agents," who usually are simulated individuals, and variables that describe those agents and their environment. Rather than specifying the causal relationships between agent and environmental variables in the simulation, the emphasis of agent-based modeling is instead on specifying the interactive processes that operate between agents, between environments, and between agents and environments. The simulation then examines the output from the activation of the processes based on different system inputs.

An example of agent-based modeling is the work of Kalick and Hamilton (1986) on dating choices. Correlational studies have suggested that individuals tend to date those who are of equal attractiveness to themselves, often referred to as "attractiveness matching." Very attractive people tend to date very attractive people, moderately attractive people tend to date moderately attractive people, and unattractive people tend to date unattractive people. In traditional research, the correlation between a person's attractiveness and that of his or her partner is usually about 0.50. Some psychologists have hypothesized that people do not try to date potential partners who are more attractive than them because of fear of rejection and because people are more comfortable around people of similar attractiveness. In contrast to this correlational research and such conclusions, experimental studies suggest that people prefer to date very attractive partners, no matter what their own level of attractiveness is. How can this disparity between the correlational and experimental research be resolved?

Kalick and Hamilton (1986) conducted a computer simulation in which they created a population of 1,000 agents (i.e., simulated people), representing 500 males and 500 females. The individuals were randomly assigned a level of attractiveness ranging from 1 to 10. The male and female agents interacted at random, and based on the other's attractiveness, one extended a dating offer to the other. If both agents made a dating offer, they were classified as a couple and were removed from the dating pool. This process continued until all agents had been matched.

In one condition, a dating offer was extended if the partner's attractiveness was roughly similar to the agent's level of attractiveness. Under this algorithm, the simulation produced a correlation between attractiveness levels for the final group of couples of about 0.85, which was too high relative to what correlational studies find. In another simulation trial, the probability that an agent extended an offer to a partner who had an attractiveness rating of 10 was set at 1.0; to a partner who had an attractiveness rating of 9, the probability of extending an offer was set at 0.90; to a partner who had an attractiveness rating of 8, the probability of extending an offer was set at 0.80; to a partner who had an attractiveness rating of 7, the probability of extending an offer was set at 0.70; and so on. Thus, the more attractive the partner, the more likely it was that he or she would be extended a dating offer. Under this algorithm, the correlation between attractiveness levels for the final group of couples was about 0.50, which maps on well to the correlational evidence. In studying the simulation results, Kalick and Hamilton found that the most attractive agents tended to couple up early on, so that the average attractiveness of the dating pool declined over time. This, in turn, resulted in the attractiveness of the couples decreasing over time. It was only through this analysis of the process of interaction dynamics that the correlational and experimental evidence in other studies could be reconciled.

BOX 9.1. Agent-Based Modeling of Segregation

Almost 50 years ago, Thomas Schelling (1971) conducted one of the first agent-based modeling studies in sociology focused on the topic of segregation. By today's standards, the study was crude, but it was highly influential. Schelling wondered what would happen if people wanted to live in a neighborhood where a certain fraction of the people were like themselves. He used a checkerboard and represented one type of people with pennies and the other type with dimes. Note that the pennies and dimes could, in principle, reflect different ethnicities, people of different socioeconomic status, or whatever. He randomly placed 10 dimes and 10 pennies on the checkerboard. For a given "agent" (i.e., coin), Schelling classified the agent as "satisfied" if the agent was surrounded by at least 30% of agents of the same type in adjoining squares (i.e., all squares touching the agent's square). If an agent was "not satisfied," it was moved to a randomly selected open square on the checkerboard. All dissatisfied agents were moved at the same time in the same round. After the round was complete, a new round began, and dissatisfied agents were once again tabulated and moved to new locations. Schelling executed hundreds of rounds (by hand!) and also varied the satisfaction threshold (10% vs. 30% vs. 50%, etc.) to examine the effects of it on segregation. When the threshold percent was set high, the results were what Schelling expected, namely, the checkerboard would quickly segregate into areas of all pennies and all dimes. What was surprising was that even with low thresholds, there were many dense clusters of pennies and dimes. High degrees of segregation in the coin "communities" emerged at a macro level even in the presence of fairly "weak prejudices" on the part of individual community members. Schelling argued that unless one could reduce prejudices to extremely low levels—such that most everyone was comfortable being the sole type of coin in their neighborhood—segregation dynamics would emerge. Schelling's work was controversial at the time because racial segregation in neighborhoods was thought to be due to strong prejudices. Schilling's work suggested otherwise. Critics of Schilling's study pointed out that "people are not ants" and that they have complex, multifaceted reasons for moving. Although Schelling's approach was indeed simplistic, his study energized decades of work on the impact of micro-motives on macro-outcomes. In 2005, Schelling was awarded the Nobel Prize in Economics for his body of work on the topic. With the advent of powerful computers, complex agent-based models (e.g., using more than two ethnicities, using diverse thresholds mixed throughout the population, including subsets of individuals who seek out diversity) have yielded rich theories of residential preference models and the links between micro-motives and macro-outcomes.

Agent-based modeling frameworks are popular in psychology, sociology, and economics (Gilbert & Abbott, 2005). They have been applied to such diverse domains in sociology as the diffusion of norms, innovations to voting, the clumping of local networks into larger social structures, and the evolution of social structures, to name a few (Cederman, 2005). A wide range of agent-based modeling applications in public health have been reviewed by Tracy, Cerdá, and Keyes (2018). Agent-based models of the diffusion of innovations have been described by Zhang and Vorobeychik (2017) and Kiesling, Gunther, Stummer, and Wakolbinger (2012). Jackson, Rand, Lewis, Norton, and Gray (2017) have reviewed agent-based modeling in social psychology. Agent-based modeling strategies also can be used to evaluate counterfactuals, what-if, and virtual policy experiments that might otherwise be infeasible in real-life settings, thereby informing theory development (see Marshall & Galea, 2015).

RESOURCES FOR CONDUCTING SIMULATIONS

The Suggested Readings at the end of this chapter provide useful resources for learning more about simulations. There are a host of computer languages for use in simulations, with a prominent one being NetLogo, which can be found at *ccl.northwestern.edu/netlogo*. NetLogo is a free, reasonably user-friendly modeling environment. More advanced tools include MASON (by Luke, Cioffi-Revilla, Panait, & Sullivan, 2004), and Repast (by North & Macal, 2005).

SUMMARY AND CONCLUDING COMMENTS

A simulation is the imitative representation of the functioning of one system or process by means of the functioning of another. The original system that one seeks to simulate is called the *criterion system,* and the imitative representation of that system is called the *simulation.* Simulations can be an effective tool for theory construction, especially for problems focused on criterion systems that are complex and dynamic. Simulations differ from laboratory experiments in that simulations generally allow participants to control the flow of events (whereas in laboratory studies, the experimenter is often the one controlling), and noise and irrelevant factors are embraced rather than eliminated. Whereas laboratory experimentation generally concentrates on a limited number of independent and dependent variables, simulations generally include a much greater number of variables. That said, we should note that laboratory experiments and research simulations can also be integrated, so that a given simulation has participants randomly assigned to different treatment and comparison groups.

Research simulations serve two basic functions: (1) to build and clarify theories and (2) to test theories. Among the different types of simulations are pedagogical versus research simulations, descriptive versus analytic simulations, real-time versus compressed-time versus expanded-time simulations, deterministic versus nondeterministic simulations, free versus experimental simulations, all-machine versus person–machine simulations, macro- versus microsimulations, and simulations varying in the content domain that is of interest.

One way in which simulations contribute to the theory construction process is by forcing the theorist to engage in a focused analysis of the criterion system in directions that might not otherwise have occurred. A second way is through the conduct of virtual experiments. In this approach, a theory is translated into a computational model, and this computational model is subjected to initial validation by applying the model to hypothetical scenarios. Agent-based modeling is an extension of virtual experiments that also provide perspectives on theory.

The use of simulations for theory development is not without critics. Some scientists believe that simulations are too removed from reality and make too many simplifying assumptions. Simulations (especially those that do not involve human participation), the argument goes, simply cannot capture adequately the dynamic elements of how humans interact with their environment. The result is theories that are either too simple or, by virtue of their underlying mathematics and computer code, too complex. There are at least two counterarguments. First, since tightly controlled experiments and surveys conducted via interviews and self-administered questionnaires are generally unable to capture adequately the dynamic elements of how humans interact with their environment, behavioral simulations provide unique value for developing and testing theories regarding human behavior. Second, simulations may in fact be closer to the real-world phenomena they seek to study than are survey questionnaires and laboratory experiments.

Think about a phenomenon of interest to you. How would you design a simulation to analyze factors that impinge on it? Conduct a careful criterion system analysis from the perspective of trying to create and implement a simulation. What assumptions are you making? What core constructs and processes do you need to capture? What are the dynamic interrelations among them? Can you conduct a virtual experiment to gain insights into your theory and refine or expand it? What starting values would you put in place and vary? What variables would you unpack and how? What assumptions would you make? What new features might you add to the system? As you attempt to answer such questions, the richness of your theory should increase.

SUGGESTED READINGS

Davis, J., Bingham, C., & Eisenhardt, K. (2007). Developing theory through simulation methods. *Academy of Management Review, 32,* 480–499.

—A condensed discussion of a wide range of simulation strategies as applied to theory construction about organizations.

Gilbert, N., & Troitzsch, G. (2005). *Simulation for the social scientist.* New York: Open University Press.

—A description of simulation strategies used in the social sciences.

Smith, E., & Conrey, F. (2007). Agent-based modeling: A new approach for theory building in social psychology. *Personality and Social Psychology Review, 11,* 87–104.

—An introduction to agent-based modeling perspectives in the social sciences.

Sun, R. (2006). *Cognition and multi-agent interaction: From cognitive modeling to social simulation.* New York: Cambridge University Press.

—A solid introduction to agent-based modeling.

Wilensky, U., & Rand, W. (2015). *An introduction to agent-based modeling: Modeling natural, social, and engineered complex systems with NetLogo.* Cambridge, MA: MIT Press.

—An excellent introduction to agent-based modeling and programming using Net-Logo.

KEY TERMS

criterion system (p. 249)

simulation (p. 249)

pedagogical simulation (p. 250)

research simulation (p. 250)

person–machine simulations (p. 251)

all-machine simulations (p. 251)

physical analog simulations (p. 251)

mathematical simulations (p. 251)

descriptive simulations (p. 251)

analytic simulations (p. 251)

real-time simulations (p. 252)

compressed-time simulations (p. 252)

expanded-time simulations (p. 252)

deterministic simulations (p. 252)

nondeterministic simulations (p. 252)

free simulations (p. 252)

experimental simulations (p. 252)

macrosimulations (p. 252)

microsimulations (p. 252)

content-oriented simulations (p. 252)

virtual environments (p. 259)

avatars (p. 259)

augmented realities (p. 260)

virtual experiments (p. 260)

agent-based modeling (p. 260)

E X E R C I S E S

Exercises to Reinforce Concepts

1. What major functions do simulations serve?

2. There are a variety of different types of simulations. Identify and describe six of these.

3. For what principal reasons do scientists use simulations?

4. What is a criterion system? Provide three examples. Select one of the examples and identify the key features of this system that you think would need to be represented in any simulation designed to study that criterion system.

Exercises to Apply Concepts

1. Find an example of a simulation in the research literature. Describe it in detail. Propose a future simulation based on this one that will advance the theory underlying the simulation.

2. How would you go about developing a simulation of friendship formation? Of communication in your work environment? Of selecting a college or college major? Choose one of these topics, or another one of your choice, and describe the basic structure of a simulation that you would set up to help you derive a theory about the chosen phenomenon.

10

Emergent Theory
Qualitative/Mixed-Methods Approaches

People will occasionally stumble over the truth, but most of the time
they will pick themselves up and continue on.
                              —WINSTON CHURCHILL (1940)

The most popular methods of scientific analysis in the social sciences are based on confirmatory frameworks whereby a scientist begins with a well-articulated theory and then subjects that theory to empirical testing. The theory typically is derived from common sense, knowledge of previous research, and the type of logical and creative processes described in Chapter 4. An alternative approach to theory construction is called *grounded theory*. This approach emphasizes letting theory emerge from data rather than using data to test theory. Typically, the data are collected by qualitative methods that may include observation, analysis of archival records, structured and unstructured interviews, and focus groups, to name but a few.

There are areas in the social sciences that tend to rely on *emergent theory* orientations but that do not fall into the formal camp of grounded theory. The grounded theory approach has its roots in sociology, and a specialized jargon and methodology has built up around it. Although we will refer to many aspects of grounded theory in this chapter, we consider theorizing more from the perspective of anthropology, where emergent theorizing has been a cornerstone of the discipline for over 100 years. Readers with formal anthropological training will at times be surprised by some of the grounded theory jargon we use, and readers with more formal training in grounded theory will sometimes see us deviate from prescribed practice. But the spirit of both approaches should come through, and the suggested readings at the end of the chapter can serve as the basis for further study and elaboration.

We begin this chapter by providing an overview of grounded and emergent theorizing. We then discuss stereotypes in the field that associate quantitatively oriented approaches to science with positivism and grounded/emergent approaches with constructivism. We argue that, in practice, use of qualitative or quantitative data collection

267

strategies is not inherently tied to specific epistemologies, at least not in the extreme way that is sometimes suggested. We next discuss how grounded/emergent theorists typically frame problems and questions, and we examine the role of literature reviews in this process. We then describe six different types of data that grounded/emergent theorists often rely on. This overview conveys a sense of the richness of the data sources used when constructing a theory. They include archival records, direct observation, structured and unstructured interviews, focus groups, virtual ethnographies, and directive qualitative methods. Next, we discuss the concepts of memo writing, theoretical sampling, and the analysis and coding of data, drawing out their implications for theory construction. We finish with a discussion of cognitive strategies theorists use for abstracting theoretical assertions from qualitative data; mixed-methods research strategies; and, finally, the range of potential products that qualitative research can produce.

GROUNDED AND EMERGENT THEORY: AN OVERVIEW

Grounded theory is associated with the classic work of Glaser and Strauss. The first application of grounded theory was published in the book *Awareness of Dying* (Glaser & Strauss, 1965). Their book *The Discovery of Grounded Theory* (1967) was written 2 years later to make explicit the methods that had been used in this research. The book became the basis for grounded theory approaches. Glaser and Strauss were heavily influenced by *symbolic interactionism,* a general theory of human behavior proposed by George Herbert Mead (1932) and later articulated by the noted sociologist Herbert Blumer (1969; see Chapter 12). Symbolic interactionism is based on three premises: (1) that people act toward things based on the meanings of those things to them, (2) that meaning is derived from social interactions (i.e., the meaning of objects emerges socially through our interactions with others), and (3) that meaning is the result of an interpretive process used by people to deal with the stimuli they encounter. According to Glaser and Strauss, an important part of theory construction is discovering the meanings that different objects have to people and how their interactions are impacted by and define these meanings. These goals are best accomplished through intensive qualitative work based on direct contact with, and immersion in, the social world of those being studied.

Early writings on grounded theory emphasized that researchers were to set aside, as much as possible, any of their preconceived ideas about the phenomenon of interest and instead let relevant concepts and relationships emerge from rich qualitative data. In later years, some grounded theorists have maintained this orientation, whereas others have encouraged the use of prior knowledge to help explore the nature of meanings (Glaser, 1992).

Grounded theory construction typically begins by framing the research problem and initial research questions in general terms. Data collection then commences in which the researcher pursues data that are rich, substantial, and relevant to the problem at hand, usually in narrative form. As a reasonable amount of data starts to accumulate, the grounded theorist undertakes initial coding and interpretation of the data to gain a sense of the core concepts and the meanings of those concepts. A variety of coding strategies can be pursued, but a common strategy is one of comparing incidents (which we describe later). Throughout this comparison process, the theorist engages in a practice called *memoing,* which involves writing ideas and conceptual notes "in the margins." These memos are consulted at a later time, when the theorist begins to move toward integrating categories, specifying relationships, and delimiting a theory. At each point in the process, the theorist considers the possibility of collecting additional data in ways that complement, expand, or better inform the emerging conceptual structure. This process is referred to as *theoretical sampling.* It ensures that the relevant conceptual universe has been thoroughly explored. All of this eventually leads to theory construction. In grounded theory, the tasks of coding, comparing, memoing, integrating concepts, and theoretical sampling are key.

In contrast to grounded theory, emergent theory approaches are not tied to symbolic interactionism. Emergent approaches emphasize description, understanding and explanation, again relying heavily on qualitative, narrative data. According to this perspective, before one can theorize, one must first *describe* the people, events, activities, meanings, contexts, environment, and culture of interest. As one gains a reasonable knowledge base along these lines, one seeks to *understand* what the different objects and events that have been described mean and represent, not only to the actors, but also to the scientist. Armed with such understanding, the theorist then seeks to *explain* why people behave or think as they do.

Imagine, for example, traveling to a remote area of South America and encountering a group of people who have been isolated from the rest of the world. To explain the activities of this group, you might first write copious notes that describe the different people, events, activities, and contexts that you observe over an extended period of time. You might also learn to speak their language and gather as much information as you can about their history, by, for example, asking elders or examining relevant documents or other historical residues. As you build your descriptive accounts, you try to understand what the different events, activities, and contexts mean to the people—that is, how they go about interpreting and orienting themselves to their environment. From this data, you build explanations of their behaviors—why they do what they do. It is within the context of such description, understanding, and explanation that theory emerges.

QUALITATIVE RESEARCH AND WAYS OF KNOWING

Many discussions of quantitative and qualitative research tie the approaches to specific worldviews or philosophies of science. Most often, quantitative methods are said to be dominated by logical positivism, determinism (cause-and-effect analysis), and confirmatory approaches to testing theory. By contrast, qualitative approaches are said to focus on exploratory theory development and to embrace one or more broad-based "ways of knowing" such as constructionism, symbolic interactionism, phenomenology, feminist theory, pragmatism, or deconstructionism (Wertz et al., 2011). These broad-based orientations create a lens through which qualitative data are framed and interpreted. In this sense, their use impacts theory development (see Chapter 12 for elaboration). Too often, however, caricatures of the knowledge systems of quantitative or qualitative research are offered and then unfairly critiqued. In our experience, science in practice rarely fits neatly into simple dichotomies (such as qualitative versus quantitative; logical positivism versus constructivism, confirmatory versus exploratory). Rather, scientists often blend approaches in different ways to differing degrees for different problems and with differing levels of complexity.

Both qualitative and quantitative research seeks to understand our world and build meaningful narratives about it in the form of theory. Both collect data that researchers hope are trustworthy. A scientist interested in analyzing causes and effects can use both quantitative and qualitative research, just as can scientists who adopt purely constructionist perspectives. Quantitatively oriented social scientists can adopt confirmatory or emergent orientations to theory, as can qualitatively oriented scientists. Quantitative scientists summarize data using both prose and numerical indices, as is the case for many qualitative scientists, although the latter tend to emphasize prose over numbers. Be cautious of those who argue that to gain deep understanding, you must adopt a particular form of thought, a particular data collection method, or a particular type of data analysis. As emphasized in Chapter 3, there are many ways of "knowing," and no single approach is necessarily the correct or best way. We return to this point in Chapter 12.

FRAMING THE PROBLEM

A common first step in building a grounded theory is to specify the problem area that one wants to address, the question that one wants to answer, or the phenomena that one wants to understand and explain (Spiggle, 1994). This is typically done in general terms because the framing of the problem and question might change as one gains firsthand knowledge in the field. The goal of many theorists at this step is to avoid imposing preconceived ideas onto the problem. There are, of course, exceptions to this, such as when an existing theory is only partially developed and the scientist might seek to further develop it through additional exploration and probing. In this case, the extant theory can shape the framing of the questions to be addressed. On the other extreme, some emergent theorists avoid framing a problem statement at all, instead intending only to obtain a sense of "what's going on." But more often than not, emergent and grounded theorists begin with a statement of the general problem area or questions they want to address.

Emergent and grounded theorists recognize that it is impossible to approach theory construction with a completely blank slate, a *tabula rasa*. By definition, scientists bring to theory construction a set of concepts and meanings that are learned from birth and that allow them to make sense of the world in which they grew up and are now experiencing. An American social scientist may have a different "lens" through which to view events than a French social scientist or a Japanese social scientist. But the spirit of the emergent and grounded theory approaches is to try to set aside preconceived notions so as to be open to new concepts and relationships, all the while being cognizant of the "filters" that impact the interpretations that are ultimately imposed. Strauss and Corbin (1998) speak of the construct of *theoretical sensitivity,* which refers to the researcher's capacity, based on his or her experience, to focus on constructs that are central to the phenomena of interest.

An important part of framing the problem is specifying the population that you intend to study. For example, one might seek to study alcohol use among inner-city

Latinx youths in the United States; the relationship between economic ideology and economic practices among the Mayan peoples of the western highlands of Guatemala; or the behavioral mechanisms surrounding the spread of HIV and AIDS among young gay men in the United States. In each case, the specification of the group about which one wants to theorize delimits the scope of theory. To be sure, the target population might change as one proceeds further into data collection and analysis, but some delimitation of the population of interest inevitably occurs at the outset.

THE ROLE OF PAST LITERATURE

Like other approaches to theory construction, the timing as to when one should access relevant background literature is subject to some controversy in grounded theory frameworks. Some theorists argue that one should approach a problem after being fully informed by the extant literature, whereas others believe that this only channels and biases one's thinking. For example, Glaser (1978) recommends reading widely, but not pursuing the literature most closely related to the problem being researched so as to avoid channeled thinking. Some grounded theorists note that researchers may not even know at the outset the literature that will later be relevant.

Despite this orientation, the most common view is that past literature is an important resource that needs to be consulted prior to data collection. To most scientists, it only makes sense to have a good working knowledge of the relevant theories and past research as they approach a given problem area. Indeed, the process by which master's thesis proposals, dissertation proposals, and grant proposals are evaluated at most institutions demands careful consideration of the extant literature before embarking on fieldwork or data collection. The key is to ensure that such knowledge does not channel one's thinking narrowly. In some ways, the existing literature is a form of emergent data, just as archival records, interviews, focus groups, and observations are. The aim of the theorist is to compare the existing literature to the theory that emerges from data. Just as other data are subjected to coding and memoing, so should past literature be approached in this way, as one evolves a theory from all the different informational sources.

Of course, no matter what the orientation of theorists is to past literature, when they write their theories, they include a scholarly and comprehensive consideration of past research in their writings. The issue being discussed here is the timing of when to bring the extant literature to bear on the researcher's thinking. We return to this topic later in this chapter.

COLLECTING QUALITATIVE DATA

Given a problem statement, the grounded/emergent theorist collects data to provide perspectives on the phenomena of interest. The data sought are intended to cast a wide net, as one seeks to describe, understand, and explain the phenomena. The term *ethnography* is used in anthropology to refer loosely to a broad class of qualitative methods applied with the purpose of providing a detailed, in-depth description of everyday life and practice. Because the theory construction process itself is so strongly tied to the data one collects, we briefly characterize some of the major methods that comprise ethnographies to provide a sense of the diverse sources of data one might consult for constructing a theory.

Archival Records

Archival records are an important source for understanding the historical roots and contexts of many phenomena. If one wants to study adolescent drug use in the United States, for example, it may be helpful to explore as background the different policies and approaches to drug use that have been used in past decades, how the lives of adolescents over past generations have been affected by drug use, and the ways in which society has viewed and sanctioned adolescent drug use. In the field of anthropology, ethnohistorical methods have evolved that allow scientists to build an understanding of groups and societies through the historical study of maps, music, paintings, photography, folklore, oral tradition, ecology, archeological materials, museum collections, language, and place names. Archival data can be sought from many sources. Municipal and state governments often have a wealth of archival data about business transactions, real estate transactions, zoning, and court cases, all of which can be revealing about a community's past. Newspapers, magazines, web pages, and other forms of media from the past also offer a wealth of information.

Good historical methodology requires that one not only gather historical information from multiple sources but also critically evaluate those sources. For example, no person alive today personally knew Leonardo da Vinci, so how can we know anything about him today? We have access to diaries, letters that he wrote, and portraits of him, and we know what other people have said about him. However, all of these materials must be put together and interpreted. When we examine a document, it is essential that we evaluate the credibility of the source and the context in which the source is making his or her observations. Historians must consider when the source materials were produced, the conditions under which those materials were produced, the intentions that motivated the source, and the reliability of the source. They also must consider the broader historical context in which the documents were produced—the events that preceded and followed the creation of the documents—because the significance of any document depends as much on what comes after it as what came before it.

With the availability of high-speed computers and noninvasive scanners, archival materials are becoming increasingly available and accessible to researchers. Primary materials from the past are a rich source of ideas for theory building about current-day issues, and you will undoubtedly benefit from a study of historical and ethnohistorical methods and principles.

Direct Observation

Another rich source of qualitative data is *direct observation*. This takes many forms, including observing people at a single point in time to the classic method of participant observation. Sometimes people know they are being observed as part of a study and other times they do not. Sometimes the observer is physically present; sometimes the "observations" are recorded by an external device, such as a camera or a recorder, without the observer being present. Sometimes only the behavioral traces or behavioral residues that people leave behind are "observed" (e.g., studies that analyze the contents of people's garbage). Sometimes the scientist becomes a full-fledged member of the group being observed, indistinguishable from other group members. Other times the scientist tries to "blend in" as much as possible, but stands out in a recognizable way, such as the North American anthropologist who lives among the indigenous people of Guatemala to try to better understand their customs and day-to-day activities. Scientists may observe people for only a short time or continuously for extended periods of time. Researchers may select a specific location at a specific time and observe all that happens at that time in that setting, or they may follow people to different locations to observe their behavior. Crucial decisions with respect to observational methods include determining whom to observe, in what contexts to observe them, when to observe them, how to observe them, how often and how long to observe them, and in what format to make a record of those observations.

Observation can take many forms, and there is a degree of creativity in choosing the form of observation to pursue. For example, an academic social psychologist interested in understanding social influence processes took time off from his position at a major university and sought employment as a car salesman, an insurance salesman, a charity fundraiser, an intern in an advertising company, and a retail salesperson—all with the idea of learning about influence strategies used in these professions. As another example, a number of academic researchers in the field of consumer behavior traveled in small mobile homes as a group for almost a year across the United States to many diverse locations, making extensive observations about their own and others' shopping experiences. Each night they would meet as a group and discuss what had transpired during the day, with the idea of formulating a comprehensive theory of consumer behavior. Neither of these observational enterprises is typical of formal observation methods, yet both resulted in insightful accounts of the phenomena the researchers were studying. We discuss observational methods in more detail in Chapter 14.

Structured and Unstructured Interviews and Surveys

Interviews can be *structured* or *unstructured*. They are unstructured to the extent that there is no detailed script for asking questions independent of the answers a research participant provides. Instead, the line of questioning is at the discretion of the interviewer and takes different directions, depending on the answers provided. By contrast, structured interviews have an a priori set of questions that is asked in a given sequence. The questions are formulated by the scientist ahead of time, so as to directly address the issues of interest, and the order of questions is minimally affected by the answers that are provided. Qualitative interviews typically record a person's responses verbatim, but occasionally the respondent is asked to choose between a small number of preestablished response categories.

Some interviews are completely structured, whereas others are completely unstructured, but more often than not, there is a balance between the two in qualitative research. It is not uncommon for the first part of an interview to be unstructured and then to turn to a more structured format in the second part of the interview. A synthesis of structured and unstructured interviews creates the *semistructured* interview. Semistructured interviews have a range of topics and questions to be asked but allow for new questions to be raised spontaneously by the interviewer, depending on what the interviewee says.

One popular type of interview is the *life history*. It is a somewhat unstructured interview that is designed to elicit a sense of the life of the person being interviewed. The idea is that by understanding the life histories of key members of the target population, one will have a better understanding of the contexts in which behaviors are performed. Life histories have different structures. A format that we find particularly useful has several facets. After a set of introductory comments that establishes the focus for telling a life story, the respondents are asked to think about their life in terms of its "main chapters" and to tell us about those chapters, in whatever way they want. This part of the interview is unstructured. Next they are asked to identify a few key events that stand out in their life and to elaborate on each of them (e.g., what happened, how it happened, when it happened, with whom it happened, and what was special about it). After this discussion, respondents are asked to identify and talk about an event that defined the high point of their lives, an event that defined the low point of their lives, an event that was a turning point in their lives, their earliest memory, their most important childhood event, their most important event during adolescence, and their most important event as an adult. Each event is thoroughly explored. Respondents are then asked to describe the single greatest challenge in their lives and then the biggest influences on their lives in terms of other people. Next, respondents are asked to consider their future and to describe it first in terms of hopes and dreams and then in terms of fears. Respondents are then asked to describe their values, political orientations, morals, and the spiritual side of their lives and how these have changed over time. The interview concludes with a final exploration of the respondents' lives in general as well as a solicitation for any other things we should know about to understand their lives. By the conclusion of the interview, we have a rich sense of the individual's life.

A comparable type of interview to the life history focuses on *labor histories,* but in this case, the line of questioning focuses on jobs and economic matters rather than life more generally. In addition to life and labor histories, unstructured and semistructured interviews typically are used to focus more directly on the phenomena of interest to the theorist.

Dick (1990) describes a structured interviewing method called *convergent interviewing* in which two experienced theorists interview two informants, with one theorist interviewing one informant and the other theorist interviewing the other informant, each asking the same questions. The two theorists then compare notes, identifying common themes and points of agreement and disagreement between the two informants. The interview is then revised for the next pair of interviews, so as to include probe questions to seek exceptions to the prior identified points of agreements as well as to seek explanations for the disagreements. The interview structure is dynamic and shifts from pair to pair, as provocative issues are identified by the different theorists.

Many types of specialized interviewing strategies have evolved in different disciplines. For example, *laddering* is a technique that has its roots in psychology and that has become popular in advertising and in the analysis of consumer behavior (Veludo-de-Oliveira, Ikeda, & Campomar, 2006). This technique involves in-depth, one-on-one interviewing that focuses on eliciting fundamental values underlying the choices people make. The respondent is led through a sequence of questions, each time involving probes focused on "Why is this important to you?" and "What does it mean to you?" For example, a graduate student might be asked why he or she prefers one school over another, to which the answer might be because it is more affordable. The next question might be "Why is a school being affordable important to you?" Every answer the respondent gives is pushed further back to a more basic value by continually asking "Why is that important?" following each response that is given.

Focus Groups

Another popular tool for qualitative researchers is the *focus group*. Questions are posed to a small group of individuals, usually 7–12 in number, in a group setting, and the group members provide their reactions and perspectives for all members to hear. For example, a focus group might be conducted with a group of students to explore how they view teachers, and a separate focus group of teachers might be conducted to explore how they view students. Like interviews, focus groups vary in terms of how unstructured or structured they are. Participants usually are selected because they share certain characteristics that relate to the topic at hand. Focus groups are conducted by a moderator, who creates a permissive and nurturing environment that encourages different points of view. Multiple focus groups are often conducted on the same topic, with the composition of the groups sometimes varied strategically. The interactions are usually video- or audiotaped, and written transcriptions are derived from these recordings.

Focus groups can take many forms beyond the traditional focus group format. Some examples include (1) a two-way focus group, where one focus group observes another focus group and discusses the observed interactions and conclusions; (2) a "dueling moderator" focus group, where two moderators take opposite sides on an issue; (3) a participant-moderated focus group, where one of the participants assumes the role of the moderator; (4) a teleconference focus group, where the participants are linked via teleconferencing; and (5) an online focus group, where computers and Internet connections are the main source of communication.

Focus groups can be useful in that the ideas and thoughtful expressions of one member of the group can serve as a catalyst for the ideas and thoughtful expressions of other group members. At the same time, the public forum may inhibit responses and frankness. With online focus groups, members can remain anonymous at the cost of losing some richness in communications. A dominant personality or influential member also can undermine a focus group. Sometimes the conversations in a focus group can become sidetracked and off point, in which case the moderator needs to keep participants "on task." Despite its weaknesses, the focus group can be a rich source of qualitative data.

Virtual Ethnographies

Virtual ethnographies extend the traditional notion of an ethnography to technologically mediated interactions in virtual settings and virtual communities. The physical boundaries of a virtual community can span the entire world. Just as ethnographers immerse themselves in the world of a target community defined in physical terms, the ethnographer studying virtual communities tries to do the same.

Virtual communities can be based on memberships in news groups, mailing lists, e-mail patterns, participation in virtual conferences, multisite users of a web page, or memberships or participation in chat rooms, to name a few. Basic ethnographic questions about a virtual community include how many people belong to it, how long it has existed, how it defines itself, what its focus is, and who belongs to it. Many virtual communities are defined around topics; the nature and scope of these topics need to be documented. Often there is a special vocabulary or jargon that evolves in virtual communities, as well as rules for communication, called "netiquette" (Mason, 1996).

A researcher can collect virtual ethnographic data by participant observation (e.g., by being a member of that virtual community) and by saving e-mails and/or listserv messages sent to, and received from, community members. One also can conduct electronic surveys and in-depth interviews of individuals, usually over the Internet, as well as download and analyze graphics and structures of web pages.

There are virtual communities on an incredibly diverse range of topics. As the influence of the Internet and virtual technologies continues to grow, this will be an additional source of data and information about many phenomena related to the social sciences. Recently, one of our anthropological colleagues was surprised to discover the widespread existence of web pages for many of the villages she has studied for years in remote areas of Central America.

Directive Qualitative Methods

Some qualitative methods assign research participants tasks to perform and then use the data produced in the context of those tasks to construct a theory. An example of this approach is the metaphor elicitation technique (MET) developed by Zaltman for advertising research (Zaltman & Coulter, 1995). This method focuses on a product (broadly construed as a "topic") and asks participants to collect, prior to the main interview, photographs and/or pictures from magazines, books, newspapers, or other sources that indicate what the assigned topic means to them. Upon completing the task, a 10-step process is pursued using the pictures and images the person brings to the interview. Step 1 is called *storytelling* and involves having respondents tell how each picture is related to the topic. Step 2 focuses on *missed issues and images,* in which respondents describe any issue they were unable to find a picture about and to describe a picture that would capture that "missed issue." In Step 3, respondents perform a *sorting task,* where they are asked to sort the pictures into meaningful piles and to provide a label for each pile. There are no restrictions on the number of piles or the number of pictures in each pile. Step 4 is *construct elicitation,* wherein respondents articulate the differences between pairs of piles. In addition, the laddering technique discussed earlier is applied. In Step 5, respondents identify *the most representative image* and elaborate on why it was their choice. In Step 6, respondents characterize *the opposite image*; that is, they describe pictures that might typify the opposite of the task they were given. Step 7, called *sensory imaging,* asks respondents to use other sensory modalities to represent the topic. In Step 8, respondents work with the interviewer to create a *mental map,* based on everything that has been discussed in previous steps. This is a graphical device that positions each key construct identified in the previous steps in a separate rectangle or box and then connects the boxes with lines to show the linkages (or lack of linkages) between them. In Step 9, respondents create a *summary image* in which they make a montage of their images, putting them together so as to express issues important to them. Finally, in Step 10, called *making a vignette,* respondents create a vignette or story that communicates important issues related to the topic.

In sum, there are many methods for collecting qualitative data that can yield rich accounts of the phenomena of interest to a theorist. A detailed discussion of these methods is the topic of a research methods book, not a theory construction book. Our intent is to provide you with a sense of the types of qualitative data grounded or emergent theorists work with when they are formulating their theories. Even this is an inadequate representation, as there are many other forms of qualitative data that we have not mentioned (e.g., video recordings, collections of folklore and oral traditions, case studies). Theory construction from qualitative data can be challenging because it relies heavily on human observations and judgment that can be subject to bias. For examples of some of the biases that must be overcome, see Appendix 10.1.

FIELD NOTES AND MEMO WRITING

As noted earlier, memo writing occurs at various phases of the data collection and theory construction processes. Researchers write down field notes to themselves about ideas and insights they have "on the spot," which they later consult when analyzing their data, or when they formally construct their theory. One type of memo, a *code memo,* is a note relevant to the creation or coding of categories. A *theoretical memo,* by contrast, focuses on theoretical propositions linking categories or variables. *Operational memos* contain directions about the evolving research design and data collection strategies. Memo writing occurs in the field during both data collection and data analysis.

Memo writing does not have to take the form of formal notes. For example, Zaltman (Zaltman & Coulter, 1995) sometimes writes memos in the form of vignettes that he thinks capture the kinds of metaphors that apply to his participants, or he draws images that graphically capture important dynamics that he observes.

Memos have a central role in grounded theory because they are often a crucial link between the data and the writing of the theory. They are a core part of the process of theory construction. For a practical introduction to constructing memos, see Saldaña (2016).

BOX 10.1. Anthropology and the Ethnographic Tradition

Emergent theory has had a central place in the historical development of anthropology as a field. The "father" of anthropology is generally recognized as Franz Boas, a German-born academic who was a professor first at Clark University in 1889 and later at Columbia University in 1899. Boas (1897) conducted research among the Kwakiutl Indians in British Columbia, Canada, and in the process developed new conceptualizations on race and culture. Boas felt that it was important to study all aspects of culture and that theory construction should be deferred until a group had been described as completely as possible. His meticulous and detailed ethnographies of the Kwakiutl reflected this orientation. Based on his emphasis on comprehensiveness, Boas advocated the "four-field approach" to anthropology, which emphasized human evolution, archeology, language, and culture. Each of these areas has since become a major subfield in anthropology. Boas was a highly influential figure on the conduct of ethnographies and the collection of qualitative data as a basis for understanding human behavior.

George Murdock was another influential anthropologist throughout the 1900s who advocated combining qualitative and quantitative methodologies. Murdock focused on comparative analyses of different cultures. He compiled ethnographies from around the world, and in 1949, in conjunction with other researchers at Yale University, he established the Human Relations Area Files. In 1954, Murdock published a list of every known culture, entitled the *Outline of World Cultures*. In 1957, he published the *World Ethnographic Sample*, a dataset of 30 variables for each of 565 cultures. In 1969, he worked with Douglas White to publish a dataset of 186 cultures with approximately 2,000 variables describing each one. The Human Relations Area Files, now maintained by an independent research organization, consists of large data sets and extensive ethnographies of over 365 different cultural groups from around the world. The ethnographies alone consist of over 800,000 pages of indexed information about different societies. An extensive indexing system allows the ethnographies to be readily accessed and searched for purposes of comparative analysis.

As one might imagine, Murdock's work has been controversial among anthropologists, in part because of its combined quantitative and qualitative emphasis. However, one cannot deny his early impact on the field. Other notable anthropologists in the history of the field who embraced ethnographic analysis include Kroeber, Lévi-Strauss, Malinowski, Mead, and Radcliffe-Brown, to name only a few.

THEORETICAL SAMPLING

Grounded and emergent theorists emphasize the importance of theoretical sampling in the context of constructing theory from data. This is purposive sampling that often occurs after initial data have been collected and preliminarily analyzed. The goal of theoretical sampling is to strategically increase the diversity of one's sample with the idea that this diversity will provide new information that will help one better appreciate and define the evolving constructs and propositions. The motivation behind theoretical sampling is not to obtain representativeness, but rather to seek out new information that provides perspectives on the boundaries and nature of concepts and relationships between them (Charmaz, 2006).

Some grounded and emergent theorists emphasize analyzing qualitative data so as to understand the "three mosts"—that is, most of the thinking of most people most of the time (Zaltman & Coulter, 1995). This approach focuses attention on such matters as how many people mention certain constructs or certain themes. Theoretical sampling augments this orientation by encouraging the seeking out of new constructs, even if they are atypical, and exploring the limits of one's conceptions.

Related to the concept of theoretical sampling is *theoretical saturation*. This term refers to the decision to stop data collection because more data will not add anything new to the theory that has been, or is being, created.

The notions of theoretical sampling and theoretical saturation underscore another feature of grounded theory approaches: that data collection and data analysis often are dynamically linked. It is only through the continual interplay between data collection and data analysis that one can make judgments about theoretical saturation and the need for additional sampling.

ANALYZING AND CODING DATA

A key activity in theory construction with qualitative data occurs at the level of data analysis. It is here that the scientist combines the insights gained during the act of data collection, the insights gained from reading past literatures, the field notes, and the information contained in the data to derive a theory. There is no single, correct way to abstract theory from qualitative data. Some theorists work solely at the level of narratives derived from a careful review of the data; other theorists rely on formal data coding; and yet others do both. Some researchers prefer a "top-down" approach, starting with identifying general themes and then focusing on increasingly concrete representations within those themes. Other researchers prefer a "bottom-up" approach, starting with the concrete activities that people perform or thoughts they express and then deriving more general themes from them. Some researchers embark on the process by avoiding, as much as possible, the imposition of an a priori framework on data interpretation; other researchers apply a simple, flexible framework to start analyses, and still other theorists impose a detailed framework, but always with a willingness to amend, adapt, augment, and drop categories and concepts.

An Example from Anthropology

Here, we provide an example of one strategy for deriving theory from the coding of data that will make the above concrete, recognizing that it is only one of many different strategies that could be pursued. In this example, the researcher, Professor Liliana Goldin, is an anthropologist studying the impact of globalization on Mayan families and culture in the highlands of western Guatemala. The particular research we discuss is a study analyzing the impact of maquila factories on Mayan families (Goldin, 2009).

The western highlands of Guatemala are a largely rural area, with townships and a few small cities located throughout. The traditional means of subsistence is through agriculture, in which a family grows crops on a small parcel of land, lives off a portion of the crops, and barters or sells the remaining crops at market. According to Mayan inheritance traditions, land is passed down to all the children in the family, with the land parcel divided equally among them. With a high birthrate, this makes smaller plots of land available to each successive generation. The use of pesticides and certain types of fertilizers has made land productive for the Maya in the short run, but in the long run it has undermined the fertility of the soil. In addition, throughout history, the federal government has seized much of the most productive land of the Maya. Coupled with other political and natural events (e.g., genocide during civil wars, devastating earthquakes), many Maya have had to find means of survival other than agriculture.

With the advent of globalization and the extremely low wages paid to the indigenous Maya people, maquila factories (also called export processing factories) have begun to appear in the highlands. These are foreign-owned factories that specialize in using unskilled labor to prepare exports for sale and use in other countries. For example, parts of clothing are sent from the United States to Guatemala, where the factory workers sew them together. The assembled clothes are then sent back to the United States, tax free, and sold to the American public, all while retaining the marketable label of "made in America."

The factories tend to hire young adolescent girls who work long hours under oppressive conditions, typically for about $6 a day. The workers are thankful for the opportunity to earn a steady wage, although turnover is high: about 50% every 6 months. Many workers are fired (for not being productive enough, for doing poor quality work, for complaining, or for attempting to organize), and others quit because of the hardships of employment or for personal reasons.

The presence of the factories in communities is having a profound impact, not only economically, but also on the Mayan culture. For example, whereas an adolescent female previously spent time helping her parents in the field and around the house, this form of labor has changed. The girl who works in the factory now is a source of steady income and contributes to the household in new ways. Often the money she earns is used to pay for the education of boys, to buy food, and to help with general household expenses. The girl is usually given a small discretionary amount of money to spend on herself. The adolescent girl who does maquila work gains a certain sense of independence. The gender dynamics in the household are changing as a result of the factories, and this, in turn, is affecting other facets of Mayan life.

Professor Goldin has conducted research in the Mayan communities for over 30 years. She lived in the townships with local families for 2 years and has returned to the area every year for extended stays. She is fluent in both Spanish and the Mayan language spoken in the area. Over the years, she has gained considerable knowledge of the people, the culture, and the many changes they have experienced. She also has researched their history through archival analyses, examining records dating to the invasion of the Spaniards in the 16th century.

The data for her study of the impact of the maquila factories include archival analyses; focus groups with maquila workers and nonworkers; interviews (including life and labor histories) of workers, nonworkers, and their families; discussions with owners; physical observations of the factories (though access is restricted by the factory owners and management); maps of the region and the locations of the factories on those maps; photographic accounts; and formal quantitative surveys. As an example, we now consider a strategy she used to analyze interview data. For pedagogical reasons, we present a simplified account of the coding/analysis process.

Goldin started with a typology of the general areas that she wanted to explore. These included, for example, the effects of the maquilas on economic and labor practices, economic ideology, wealth and resources, gender dynamics, health, and family dynamics. She began by reading through all of the interviews so as to gain a general sense of their content and to see if any initial themes, propositions, or "story lines" jumped out. She then read each interview in earnest, placing a color-coded tag next to any segment that mentioned or dealt with economic issues, a different colored tag next to any segment that dealt with gender dynamics, and so on, for each category of her typology. A given segment could be classified into more than one category. We call these level 1 categories.

Goldin defined a "segment" as any important thought or expression that the respondent made about a given topic. Such segments could be several paragraphs, a single paragraph, or a sentence in length, or they could even be a partial sentence. A key decision by a theorist analyzing qualitative data is specifying how a segment will be defined and how to identify the beginning and end of a segment. Some theorists define segments on a word-by-word basis in order to pursue a formal linguistic analysis of the data. Goldin defined a segment as a meaningful thought about a topic.

In the course of classifying segments into level 1 categories, additional areas on which Goldin focused suggested themselves, thereby creating new level 1 categories. For example, in her early studies with the Maya, it was serendipitously discovered that religious conversions from Catholicism to Protestantism were associated with the type of economic strategies that people tended to pursue. Further exploration of this result revealed a complex and fascinating story of the interplay between religious ideology and economic practice. A level 1 category on religion was therefore added to the framework.

Next, Goldin focused on a specific category 1 topic, say gender dynamics, and collected all those tagged segments that focused on that topic. The segments for this topic were reread, and a typology of themes within the gender dynamic topic area was developed. In other words, a set of level 2 categories was created within each level 1 category. The level 2 categories were derived, in part, using what grounded theorists call the *method of segment contrasts* or, more simply, the *method of contrasts* (Strauss & Corbin, 1998, also use the term *constant comparison* to refer to this method). In the method of contrasts, the theorist compares one segment with another segment, noting to him- or herself what is common and what is different about the two segments. This process is repeated many times, comparing different pairs of segments (in principle, all possible pairs of segments) until a conceptual framework for a typology starts to emerge, based on the many observed commonalities and differences. During the process, notes are taken about the similarities and differences between segments and their possible implications. At some point, a formal typology of the level 2 themes within a level 1 category evolves. Goldin carefully reviewed her notes, elaborating and clarifying the typology accordingly. She then assigned descriptive labels to the different categories or themes, a process that grounded theorists refer to as *naming,* and abstracted the major ideas being expressed. With the tentative typology in place, Goldin then repeated the process of reading each segment within the given level 1 category, but instead of comparing one segment to another, she now compared each segment to the taxonomic structure to determine which level 2 category fit it. Called the *method of classification,* this process led to further enhancements and refinements of the typology. Finally, the different segments were color-coded and tagged as to which level 2 categories they represented, thereby completing the level 2 categorization process. This process was repeated for each level 1 category.

The strategy for creating level 2 categories is next repeated to create level 3 categories. A given level 2 category is selected, and all segments that are tagged as members of the category are collected together. After an initial reading of all segments, the method of contrasts and the method of classification are applied, together with memo writing, to produce a typology of level 3 categories within each level 2 category. Figure 10.1 presents a tree diagram of the resulting structure.

The process can be repeated yet again for the level 3 categories to create a fourth level of categories, and so on. At some point, the theorist makes the decision that further layering is beyond the scope of what he or she is trying to accomplish.

Once these steps are complete, theorists typically step back from the more micro-level analyses and think about the interconnections between the level 1, level 2, and

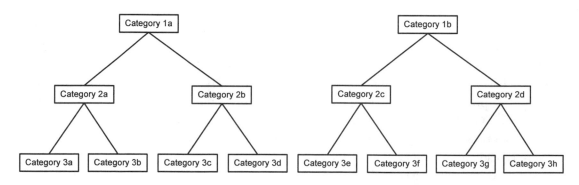

FIGURE 10.1. Tree diagram of category levels.

level 3 categories more generally, in light of all the information processed. The idea is to adopt a "big picture view" and to examine the different phenomena as an interconnected system rather than focusing on its component parts. Indeed, knowing that this type of "big-picture" analysis eventually will take place, researchers typically include notes and thoughts about the larger dynamics during the process of memo writing at the earlier stages. Ultimately, all of this lays a rich foundation for the final theory construction steps, described later in the context of deduction, induction, and abduction.

Computer-Assisted Analysis

We described the process referring to color-coded tags assigned to segments in order to flag the different categories of the segment at each category level. In point of fact, not only did Goldin do this, but she also created computer codes for each category (corresponding to each type of tag) for use in a computer program. Specifically, a given interview was broken down into segments, and each segment was then assigned a level 1, level 2, or level 3 category code. Multiple codes could be assigned if a segment fell into more than one category. This process was repeated for every interview, and then the data for all interviews were merged into a single data file. Next, a computer program was used to sort through the segments to isolate almost instantly all segments associated with a given category at a given level. For example, when Goldin wanted to examine all segments focused on spousal interactions (a level 2 category) reflecting gender dynamics (a level 1 category), the computer sorted through the database and showed only these segments, with a respondent identifier for each one. In pre-software days, this process was pursued rather clumsily by sorting through index cards, with one segment written on each card.

For the method of contrasts, the computer can display all possible pairs of segments at any given category level. or it can display a random sample of the segment pairs or some systematically defined subset of pairs. This is important for several reasons. First, sometimes the sheer amount of information is overwhelming when pursuing the method of contrasts. For example, suppose there are 40 different segments to compare. In this case, there are 780 combinations of two segments to compare, which is a great deal of information to process. If 10 interviews are conducted and each interviewee mentions 10 segments in a given category, then there are 100 segments to compare. In this case, there are 4,950 unique combinations of two segments. It simply is not feasible for the human mind to process this amount of information. By forming all possible pairwise combinations of segments and then selecting a random sample of these using a computer, the task of systematically comparing pairs of segments is manageable.

In sum, computers permit flexible and efficient accessing and pairing of segments. Instead of fumbling with index cards, pages of text, and tags, or instead of relying on memory, segments can be grouped and processed in diverse ways with a few keystrokes. This can facilitate theory development. Some of the more popular qualitative software programs include AnSWR, Atlas.ti, C-I-SAID, Decision Explorer, Ethnograph, N6, Nudist, NVivo, and MAZQDA. For a practical account of coding for these programs, see Saldaña (2016).

Defining and Manipulating Segments

In the preceding example, Goldin defined a "segment" as any important thought or expression that the respondent made about a given topic. Segments can be conceptualized using different criteria. Some researchers conceptualize segments broadly and others conceptualize them narrowly. Some researchers think about segments in terms of semantic meanings, others in terms of their affective content, others in terms of the processes they reflect, others in terms of who the actors are, and still others, at whom the action is being directed. Theorists do not necessarily choose between these different schemes; rather, they use all of them. Thus, multiple codes can be assigned to a segment, with codes variously focusing on the meaning of the segment, on processes occurring in the segment, on the affective content of the segment, and so on. With the help of computers, segments can be accessed almost instantly using any given segment conceptualization that has been coded.

For example, one might have the computer focus on the affective content of all segments across all people interviewed and show first the text of all segments that are expressions of positive affect and then all segments that are expressions of negative affect. This procedure could be pursued across all segments or perhaps focusing only on segments within a given level 1 category (e.g., those segments pertaining to gender dynamics); only for segments within a specified level 2 category (e.g., within gender dynamics, focusing on spousal interactions); or only for specified level 3 categories.

To make matters more complex, the accessing of segments also can vary as a function of individual differences of the people interviewed. For example, the theorist might request that the computer show all segments expressing positive affect in the area of gender dynamics for male participants. This could then be repeated for female participants to make gender comparisons.

Guiding Questions and Coding Families

When thinking about defining and characterizing segments, some grounded theorists encourage analysts to use orienting questions to help them think about possible codes to assign and how to define segments. For example, Glaser (1978) described 18 "coding families" that researchers can use to develop codes and segments. Strauss (Strauss & Corbin, 1998) described a coding family of "Six Cs" that stresses causes, consequences, and boundary conditions. Strauss and Corbin (1998) describe a set of diverse heuristics, much like those described in Chapter 4, as a way of exploring the different interpretations and conceptualizations one might apply to data.

Open Coding, Axial Coding, and Selective Coding

Expositions of grounded theory offer a framework for coding data that is similar to the approach used by Goldin, but somewhat different. Distinctions are made between three types of coding: open coding, axial coding, and selective coding (Strauss & Corbin, 1998). *Open coding* involves developing initial categories for the words, sentences, phrases, or paragraphs under consideration. *Axial coding* involves imposing a coding scheme onto the categories from open coding that identifies connections between the categories. Strauss and Corbin draw the analogy of "putting an axis through the data" to connect the various categories identified in open coding. The connections between categories can come in the form of (1) conceptualizing the categories as causally related, (2) conceptualizing the categories as different aspects of a common dimension, and/or (3) conceptualizing the categories as part of a process, among others. *Selective coding* involves identification of the central themes and integrating the open and axial categories accordingly. The term *selective* is used because the analyst concentrates on a subset of core categories and connections around which to build the theory.

In sum, a great deal of thought is required regarding how to code qualitative data for later review and synthesis. Theorists can exercise considerable creativity in the ways in which they define and manipulate segments. Qualitative analysis is time consuming and difficult, but it offers many rewards in terms of theory construction. The major challenge facing theorists once the data have been analyzed is that of abstracting and formalizing a theory from it, that is, deriving a set of propositions that meet the criteria of a good theory as discussed in Chapter 3 and that makes a theoretical contribution.

CONSTRUCTING THEORY IN QUALITATIVE RESEARCH

We have described methods that qualitative researchers use to collect, process, and categorize data for purposes of theory construction. However, we have not elaborated a key facet of theory construction in qualitative research, namely, how one abstracts theoretical propositions from data once categorization has been accomplished. Qualitative research yields detailed descriptions of the phenomena being studied. Such descriptions are useful for clarifying concepts and providing context, but theory is more than just description; theory seeks to explain what has been described. Tavory and Timmermans (2014) argue that many textbooks on qualitative research focus too much on specifying rules for data collection and data processing at the expense of explicating the fundamental task of how to abstract theoretical assertions from such activities. Collins and Stockton (2018) stress the importance of theory development in qualitative research by describing orientations of researchers toward theory and method in the form of a quadrant:

	Weak emphasis on theory	Strong emphasis on theory
Strong emphasis on optimal methodology	Overemphasis on technique Often lacks insight	Offers data-driven insights into worldviews
Weak emphasis on optimal methodology	Simplistic, lightly descriptive Reads like a monthly report	Conceptual but uninformed by empirics; seeks to be seen as data driven to gain credibility

The cell on the upper right reflects the use of qualitative methodological rigor coupled with the derivation of rich theory from data. It is key to advancing theory. The remaining cells are more limited in what they accomplish. For example, in the cell on the upper left, researchers engage in meticulously designed qualitative research but are weak in linking the data to *innovative* theory development, thereby limiting the added-value contribution of the research (see Chapter 3). Collins and Stockton echo the point of Tavory and Timmermans (2014) that greater emphasis on training qualitative researchers about how to derive theory from data is needed. In this section, we address this matter, first by revisiting our discussion of deduction and induction from Chapter 4, then by introducing an approach based on abduction, and finally by considering process-oriented approaches to theory construction.

Deduction and Induction Revisited

People in general often make inferences about regularities based on their personal experiences, so it might be helpful to first consider how everyday people go about making generalizations. Suppose Tom visits two doctors in a foreign country and is struck by how formal and business-like they are. Tom sees them each for a second visit, and again, they are formal and business-like. Tom thinks that perhaps doctors in this country are formal and business-like, but he tells himself that he can't make such a generalization because the characteristic could be unique to these particular doctors. Months later, Tom sees another doctor who also is formal and business-like. His initial impression is substantiated but now with yet a different doctor. On still another occasion, the same experience occurs for a fourth doctor. Tom's "rule" or "generalization" continues to be reinforced. Later, in a conversation with a colleague who knows the medical community well in the country, the colleague comments on how formal and business-like doctors are. Tom now feels even more confident that doctors in the country are formal and business-like. In future visits with physicians, this also turned out to be the case, except on one occasion where Tom encountered a doctor without these qualities. Tom decided this was a fluke because the doctor was inexperienced and had not yet fully assumed the role requirements of being a doctor. And, of course, there are always some exceptions to the rule.

This scenario illustrates how people abstract principles or make generalizations from their experiences using both inductive and deductive reasoning. *Inductive reasoning,* at essence, fomulates a general assertion from specific cases or exemplars (see Chapter 4 for more detail). Tom's experience with four different doctors all were exemplars consistent with the proposition that doctors in the country are formal and business-like. Tom's conversation with his colleague represented the use of *deductive reasoning,* namely, using premises to derive a conclusion: Premise 1: My colleague believes doctors in this country are formal and business-like; Premise 2: My colleague knows the medical community in this country well; Conclusion: Therefore, doctors are indeed formal and business-like. Tom considered possible contraindications to his conclusion during the belief formation process. Perhaps when interacting with the first physician, the doctor was formal and business-like just because of the mood the doctor was in. However, the doctor exhibited the same style on a second occasion months later. Perhaps it was just this particular doctor who was like this, but then Tom experienced it with other doctors as well. Did Tom's colleague really know the medical community all that well? Yes, Tom decided, he did. What about the exception that occurred? Tom had an explanation to account for it, although in doing so, he had to qualify his "rule" somewhat.

Tom's thought processes, it turns out, are very much like those used by theorists when they abstract theoretical principles from qualitative data. To be sure, the cognitive processes may not be explicit, they may sometimes occur outside the theorist's awareness, and they may occur at lightning-fast speeds in one's mind, but they nevertheless often operate much as they do in everyday life. During data analysis in the maquila factory example described earlier, and after processing the data and creating categories and segments, a theorist might segregate out from the interviews all the statements and narratives about family-related stresses associated with work in the factories by young female employees. After reading the statements, just as Tom formed an impression that doctors are formal and business-like, the theorist might formulate the impression (i.e., the theoretical proposition) that young women bringing steady cash into the household through maquila work creates tension with the male members of the household due to a disruption of traditional gender roles. Just as Tom encountered multiple occurrences of doctors who were formal and business-like, the theorist now searches through the many narratives to determine if there exist multiple exemplars of the theoretical assertion. Suppose there are. The theorist might then examine households where the dynamic was not evident and carefully think about these "exceptions to the rule." The theorist wonders if the exceptions are sufficient to undermine making the theoretical proposition. If there are a few exceptions, the theorist might decide to qualify his or her proposition as being applicable to "most households." However, with further thought, the theorist might formulate ideas about extenuating circumstances, that is, about boundary conditions, just as Tom did. The analyst then rereads the narratives to determine if they support her suspicions about these boundary conditions. A careful analysis (using both deduction and induction) might suggest to the theorist that the assertion is viable but that some qualifications are needed to account for exceptions. In the process of reaching this decision, the theorist might also conclude that he or she needs additional data to gain further insight into the exceptions. The theorist therefore interviews more factory workers and household members to explore the matter in more depth. This latter action underscores the previously noted interplay between theory and data in qualitative research; method often drives theory and theory often drives method.

As the theorist uses his or her creativity and insight to abstract theoretical assertions from qualitative data, field notes, memos, and recollections, there is a constant tension between locating and analyzing affirmations of the assertion through deductive and inductive reasoning versus trying to find fault with the premises underlying inductions or the applicability of exemplars for the deductions. Of course, reasoning processes other than induction and deduction can be used. For example, Chapter 4 discussed the use of reasoning by analogy. In the final analysis, theorists strive to find in the data reasons that support their assertions as well as reasons against them, and then argue for or abandon the assertions based on careful consideration of these reasons. Theorists examine the frequency of occurrence of the phenomena addressed in the assertion as well as the consistency of the assertion across people, time, and contexts within the data. Exceptions are embraced, not ignored. Ultimately, the degree of confidence in the assertion is settled upon. The "accepted" assertions by the theorist are then pieced together into an overall coherent theoretical narrative.

At this point, feedback from colleagues might be sought before theory finalization. The researcher might also share the theory with members of the population being studied, as appropriate, or with other relevant parties for their reactions. He or she might have someone else work through the data independently and see if that person arrives at the same theory, exploring with each other any disparities that occur (see Wertz et al., 2011, for a fascinating example of such a process). When presenting results, the various "accepted" theoretical propositions are described in conjunction with representative exemplars from the data for each assertion.

Abduction Analysis

Tavory and Timmermans (2014) used the classic work on abduction and pragmatism by Charles Peirce (1903/1998) to suggest an alternative (but overlapping) approach to abstracting theoretical propositions from data. Peirce proposed *abduction* in place of induction and deduction. Abduction is used, Peirce said, when one encounters data that are difficult to account for using existing theory and there is a need to make sense of that data:

> A mass of facts is before us. We go through them. We examine them. We find them a confused snarl, an impenetrable jungle. We are unable to hold them in our minds. We endeavor to set them down on paper; but they seem so multiplex intricate that we can neither satisfy ourselves that what we have set down represents the facts, nor can we get any clear idea of what it is that we have set down. But suddenly, while we are pouring over our digest of the facts and are endeavoring to set them into order, it occurs to us that if we were to assume something to be true that we do not know to be true, these facts would arrange themselves luminously. That is abduction. (pp. 531–532)

The essence of abduction is to engage in "creative brainstorming" to generate viable explanations for theoretically difficult data and then focus on the explanation that appears to be the simplest and best for further exploration in the data. Deduction and induction may be involved when initially choosing an explanation, but they are not requisite: One essentially asks "What if _____ were the case? Would this explain the data?" and if the answer is yes, the explanation is further pursued. Abduction combines flashes of insight with later logical analysis.

Contrary to traditional grounded theory approaches, abduction analysis does not require that one approach qualitative research with a conceptual blank slate. Abduction analysis, according to Tavory and Timmermans (2014), instead emphasizes attending to "surprises" when constructing theory by uncovering data contrary to theories of the day. This ensures a theoretical contribution as long as one can make sense of the surprises. Using this approach, one might supplement traditional qualitative data collection with strategies explicitly designed to discover exceptions or surprises. Extant theories serve as a key referent during the first pass through the data so as to identify results that are contrary to them. These results then guide second and third passes through the data as one determines if the chosen explanations through abduction are viable. In essence, one seeks to build new theory, not confirm existing theory, although confirmation can occur in the process. For a detailed discussion of abductive analysis, see Tavory and Timmermans (2014).

Process Analysis

Many grounded and emergent theorists emphasize process-oriented perspectives in their theorizing. Surprisingly little, however, has been written on how to think in terms of processes on a practical level. We discussed such matters briefly in Chapter 4 and consider them again in Chapter 12, but some observations are offered here.

Webster's Dictionary defines a *process* as "a systematic series of actions directed to some end" (e.g., the process of homogenizing milk) and as "a continuous action, operation, or series of changes taking place in a definite manner" (e.g., the process of decay). The essence of these definitions involves the notions of action and change—that is, describing actions that lead entities from Point A to a different Point B. Charmaz (2006) suggests that the following questions be addressed when thinking in terms of process:

1. How does the person act while engaged in this process (i.e., what are the actions and states that describe the process)?

2. How does this process develop?

3. How does the person claim to think and feel in this process?

4. What might the person's observed behavior indicate or signify while engaged in the process?

5. When, why, and how does the process change?

6. What are the consequences of the process?

Note how causal thinking tinges some of these questions.

A useful tool for thinking about processes is the *process map*, a graphical device, much like a flowchart, that summarizes the flow of a process. Constructing process maps helps the theorist see the sequence of events, the branches that can occur in a process, and how all the different events in a process are related to one another. It can be a useful heuristic for theory construction because the sheer act of creating one often leads to insights that might not otherwise be gained. Here are the major steps involved in creating a process map: (1) determine the start and termination points of the process, (2) list the different events in the process, (3) sequence the events, and then (4) think about the logical relations among the events. The process map is then drawn using a conventional symbol notation, as shown in Figure 10.2. In constructing process maps, the theorist must think about how detailed the events in the process map should be. The more specific and detailed the events are, the more intricate the mapping. Variants of process maps used in qualitative research include flowcharts, decision trees, and kinship maps.

We consider additional strategies for thinking about change and processes in Chapter 12. As we have stated here and in earlier chapters, it is rare to find emergent theories that focus exclusively on process. Rather, there usually is a blending of process- and variable-oriented thinking that draws upon many of the tools for explanation that we have discussed thus far.

In sum, one can approach the abstraction of theoretical principles from qualitative data using logic based in deduction, induction, or other forms of reasoning. One also can use abduction and/or seek to describe phenomena in process-like terms. Our presentation of these cognitive strategies has been brief, but it is a starting point from which you can evolve your own heuristics as you approach theory construction.

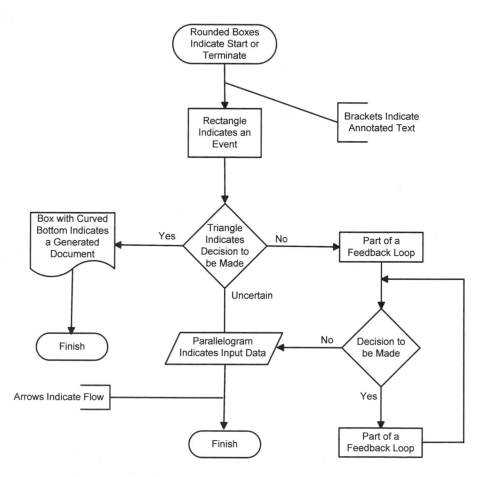

FIGURE 10.2. Conventional symbols for a process map.

MIXED-METHODS RESEARCH

Mixed-methods research, namely, research that uses both qualitative and quantitative methods to build and test theories, has become increasingly popular. Johnson, Onwuegbuzie, and Turner (2007) reviewed 19 definitions of mixed-methods research and found considerable variation in (1) the scope of mixing, (2) what methods were mixed, (3) when the mixing occurred, and (4) the purpose and rationale of mixing. Creswell and Plano Clark (2017) defined mixed methods as the use of both qualitative and quantitative methods either concurrently or sequentially either in a single study or in a program of research in a way that frames the methods through a common theoretical lens.

Plano Clark (2010) analyzed mixed-methods research funded by 25 different agencies in the National Institute of Health and found that the most common type was research that included both an experimental or controlled trial component and a qualitative component tied to the trial. We refer to these as *mixed-methods randomized trials*. A randomized trial that uses only qualitative methods is called a *qualitative randomized trial*. A qualitative randomized trial studies individuals who are randomized to one of two (or more) conditions, usually a treatment versus a control group, or perhaps to one treatment protocol versus another treatment protocol. Individuals in each group typically are interviewed about their experiences and lives before the trial began, during the trial proper, and after the trial is complete; that is, data are collected longitudinally. In addition, direct observations of the study participants might be undertaken in participants' homes or some other setting. Indeed, any of the standard qualitative methods for data collection can be used. In a mixed-methods randomized trial, these qualitative methods are used in conjunction with standard (quantitative) measures typically gathered in randomized trials for purposes of quantitative analysis.

Creswell and Plano Clark (2018) describe three types of designs that can be used when mixing qualitative and quantitative research (1) an *explanatory sequential design* in which the quantitative study is conducted first, with a follow-up qualitative study to supplement, enrich, and qualify the results from the quantitative study; (2) an *exploratory sequential design* in which the qualitative research is conducted first, which then informs the quantitative study; and (3) a *convergent parallel design* in which the qualitative and quantitative data are collected concurrently for purposes of comparing results.

Mixed-methods research has many advantages. A simple example can be illustrated using an exploratory sequential design. All of us have encountered the concept of sampling error in political opinion surveys reported by the media. Polling results often report the percentage of people endorsing a policy or candidate, coupled with an index of the margin of error for that percentage. For example, we might be told that the percentage of people who endorse a given candidate is 40% with a margin of error of plus or minus 5%. This means that because the poll used a sample instead of the entire population, the true population percent could actually be somewhere between 35 and 45%. The larger one's sample size, the smaller the margin of error, everything else being equal. If a poll has a large margin of error, it is of little informational value. Suppose a qualitative researcher interested in understanding problems people experience at home when being treated for cancer conducts in-depth interviews with a sample of 30 patients.

Based on those interviews, the researcher constructs a typology of 15 problem areas that patients report. This typology will undoubtedly be useful to programs providing support services to cancer patients. Suppose the researcher wants to make theoretical statements surrounding the most frequently occurring problems in the typology. The researcher might intuit subjectively from the qualitative data which problems are most common, or he or she might formally compute from the data the percentage of people who report each problem. A limitation of this approach is that the percentages are based on a sample size of only 30 people, so they will have large margins of error. It turns out that for a sample size of 30, the margin of error is about plus or minus 22%, which is too large. A solution to this limitation is to conduct a follow-up quantitative study with a large sample that efficiently assesses if people experience each problem in the typology and then estimate the percentage of people who experience them using the quantitative data. The larger sample size produces a smaller margin of error; for example, a sample size of 350 yields margins of error close to plus or minus 5%. This puts the theorist in a stronger position to make theoretical statements about the relative frequencies of problem occurrence. The two studies, together, form a stronger package.

As another example, a qualitative researcher might study female youth who choose to participate in high school sports programs to determine the positive or negative effects of such participation on young women's lives. Female teens who participate in sports programs are interviewed, and the researcher identifies a host of positive outcomes that the athletes report about sports program participation, including developing increased feelings of positive self-esteem, learning to be disciplined, learning the importance of teamwork, and developing a greater commitment to school because satisfactory grades are necessary for program participation. The link between school performance and participation in sports might be particularly intriguing to school administrators and educators. There is a problem, however, with concluding that participation in sports might be beneficial to school performance based on the beliefs expressed by the female athletes. It turns out that female teens who come from two-parent families are more likely to participate in high school sports programs than female teens from single-parent families. Female teens from two-parent families also tend to achieve higher grades in school. As such, the potential benefit suggested in the qualitative study could reflect family structure effects rather than sports participation effects, despite the claims of study participants. As well, White female teens are more likely to participate in sports programs than non-White female teens, so differences in school performance might reflect ethnic effects rather than sports participation effects. Finally, family income is related to teen female participation in high school sports, with female teens from families with higher levels of income being more likely to participate in sports. Instead of sports participation effects, differences in school performance between female athletes and nonathletes might reflect income effects.

These alternative explanations can be addressed in a follow-up quantitative study and in ways that would be difficult in a purely qualitative study. Specifically, a larger quantitative study that examines the relationship between sports participation and school performance could be pursued that statistically controls for family structure, ethnicity, and income as well as their interactions with one another. If, after simultaneously controlling for these variables and their interactions, there is still a difference in school performance as a function of sports program participation, one has increased confidence that the suggested link from the qualitative study is viable. By supplementing the qualitative study with the quantitative study, we retain the richness of the characterizations from the qualitative research coupled with the descriptions of what sports participation means to female athletes. However, we also extend the work by exploring the intriguing suggestion that female participation in athletics and school performance are linked, using quantitative research to control for complex patterns of confounds that would be extremely difficult to do in a qualitative study.

Many additional examples could be articulated, but the one described here makes our general point: Coordinated mixed-methods studies often offer greater theoretical potential than either quantitative or qualitative studies alone.

PRODUCTS OF QUALITATIVE AND MIXED-METHODS RESEARCH

When a qualitative or mixed-methods study is completed, it can make many types of theoretical contributions. Chapter 3 discussed 16 such contributions for social science research in general, and we list them here again. A qualitative study can (1) clarify, refine, or challenge the conceptualization of a variable/concept, (2) create a new variable or constellation of variables that are of theoretical interest, (3) identify one or more explanatory variables that have not been considered in prior work, (4) identify the mechanisms or intervening processes responsible for an effect of one variable on another, (5) identify the boundary conditions of an effect of one variable on another, (6) identify variables that moderate the effect of one variable on another, (7) extend an existing theory or idea to a new context, (8) identify nuanced functional forms of relationships, (9) identify unenunciated/unanticipated consequences of an event, (10) enrich and deepen the understanding of established quantitative associations, (11) develop typologies/taxonomies, (12) import or apply grand theories and frameworks from other disciplines, (13) synthesize multiple theories into a unified framework, (14) develop theories of measurement, (15) pit and resolve opposing theoretical explanations against one another, and/or (16) propose alternative explanations to established phenomena. More generally, qualitative research can affirm, challenge, or extend extant theory. It can extend extant theory in smaller incremental ways or in ways that are major.

Qualitative research also can be used with cause-and-effect thinking to formulate complex causal theories in the spirit of Chapter 7. As an example, by virtue of the close relationships that Professor Goldin established with families of indigenous people in the highlands of Guatemala over her 30 years of work there, she found that she was able to talk with men and women in those families (as well as their adult children whom she knew growing up) about husband physical abuse, a topic that normally would be extremely difficult to get Mayan people in this region to discuss (Goldin, Copeland, & Padilla-Medina, 2015). Professor Goldin collected extensive qualitative data about why husbands physically abuse their wives, analyzing the data in ways much like her research on the maquila factories and in ways described in this chapter. The analyses and theoretical propositions ultimately were presented and organized around the influence diagram in Figure 10.3. According to the theory, husband physical abuse is impacted by the husband's embrace of machismo, alcohol use, marital infidelity on the part of the male, and perceived norms about the role of males in the household. Low self-esteem and insecurity in males were found to be contributory to their use of alcohol and marital infidelity and, as such, were indirect influences on physical abuse. Patrilocality, another relevant variable that emerged in the analysis, refers to the residency custom that directs a newly married couple to move into the home of the husband's parents until the couple becomes fully capable of supporting themselves independently. This practice, it was found, can lead to low self-esteem and feelings of insecurity on the part of the male as well adherence to traditional norms supportive of aggression against a female spouse. Finally, racism and the embracement of traditional local values about women encouraged marital infidelity which, in turn, made it more likely that males would abuse their wives. Every link in Figure 10.3 was evolved and reported upon in the context of the rich narratives provided by study participants. The result of the qualitative work was an intriguing theory of marital violence for this understudied population, captured in an influence diagram but elaborated with qualitative data.

SUMMARY AND CONCLUDING COMMENTS

A major approach to theory construction is that of grounded or emergent theorizing. Whereas the dominant method of scientific analysis in many areas of the social sciences is based on confirmatory frameworks (i.e., using data to test theory), emergent theory emphasizes a process of letting theory emerge from data. Grounded theory is associated with the classic work of Glaser and Strauss (1967), with early approaches

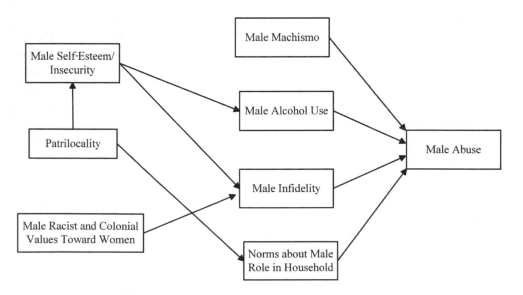

FIGURE 10.3. Theory of determinants of husband abuse.

emphasizing its link to the theory of symbolic interactionism. However, many emergent theory frameworks are not tied to symbolic interactionism, and, indeed, the discipline of anthropology has a longstanding tradition in emergent theorizing that is distinct from grounded theory. The emphasis in anthropology is on description, understanding, and explanation.

Grounded/emergent theory construction typically begins by framing the research problem. Data collection then commences, usually taking the form of qualitative data. The methods used include archival research, direct observation, structured and unstructured interviews, focus groups, and virtual ethnographies, to name a few. The data sought are intended to cast a wide net, as one seeks to describe, understand, and explain the phenomena of interest, broadly construed. The term *ethnography* is used in anthropology to refer loosely to a broad class of qualitative methods applied with the purpose of providing a detailed, in-depth description of everyday life and practice.

As a reasonable amount of data start to accumulate, the grounded theorist undertakes initial coding of the data to gain a sense of the core concepts and the meanings that seem to be operative. The coding and analysis of data often involve defining segments. Typically, a "segment" is any important thought or expression that a research participant makes about a given topic. However, segments can be defined using a variety of criteria. A common strategy for analyzing the meaning of segments is the method of contrasts, which involves comparing segments and creating categories from this comparison process. At some point, a formal typology is developed, and then the researcher compares segments with the evolved taxonomic structure. This is called the method of classification.

Memo writing occurs throughout the research process; researchers record notes to themselves about ideas and insights they have "on the spot." Grounded theorists also emphasize the importance of theoretical sampling, which is a purposive type of sampling that often occurs after initial data have been collected and preliminarily analyzed. The purpose of theoretical sampling is to increase the diversity of one's sample, with the idea that this diversity will provide new information that will help one better appreciate and define the constructs and propositions that will constitute the theory.

After analysis of the data and memos, the scientist creates the formal theory. The thought processes involved in doing so are, in some ways, similar to those used by everyday people when they make generalizations from their personal experiences. Deduction and induction are key. However, abduction and process thinking also can be used. It often is useful to formulate theory from research that uses both qualitative and quantitative approaches possessing a common theoretical lens. Such mixed-methods approaches are becoming increasingly popular.

Grounded and emergent theorizing are useful, productive approaches to building theories. It is hard to argue with the idea that a powerful strategy for building a theory is to immerse yourself in as rich and meaningful a way as possible in the phenomena you are studying and the lives of the people directly involved with those phenomena. Some argue that one loses objectivity with such immersion, but from the perspective of theory construction, it is unclear if this argument justifies abandoning such an obviously rich source of ideas. There are, of course, some areas where grounded theory approaches are limited. For example, researchers who study the neuroscience of attitudes with the goal of mapping electrical activity in the brain associated with drug addiction probably are not going to get very far by pursuing grounded theory approaches that interview people about why they use drugs and the meaning and place of drugs in their lives. Or are they? Perhaps the nature of electrical activity in the brain is tied to the way in which people construe and think about drugs, with different parts of the brain being activated in different ways as a function of these different ways of thinking about things. Keep an open mind as you think about ways to build your theory. Just maybe the approaches that your first reaction is to dismiss will turn out to be the basis for a novel insight.

SUGGESTED READINGS

Barber, R. J., & Berdan, F. (1998). *The emperor's mirror: Understanding cultures through primary sources.* Tucson: University of Arizona Press.

—A discussion of strategies for archival data analysis.

Creswell, J., & Plano Clark, V. (2018). *Designing and conducting mixed methods research* (3rd ed.). Thousand Oaks, CA: SAGE.

—An excellent introduction to mixed-methods research.

Denzin, N., & Lincoln, Y. (2017). *The SAGE handbook of qualitative research* (5th ed.). Thousand Oaks, CA: SAGE.

—A major resource for a variety of qualitative methods. See also the *Handbook of Emergent Methods* and the *Handbook of Mixed Methods in Social and Behavioral Science Research* as well as the *Journal of Mixed Methods Research.*

Duneier, M., Kasinitz, P., & Murphy, A. (2010). *The urban ethnography reader.* New York: Oxford University Press.

—A reader of diverse qualitative research on city life. A nice read to get a sense of qualitative research in action.

Glaser, B. G. (1992). *Basics of grounded theory analysis: Emergence versus forcing.* Mill Valley, CA: Sociology Press.

—A rebuttal of a grounded theory approach advocated by Strauss and Corbin that highlights points of controversy in the grounded theory framework.

Glaser, B. G., & Strauss, A. L. (1967). *The discovery of grounded theory: Strategies for qualitative research.* Chicago: Aldine.

—A comprehensive and classic exposition of the grounded theory approach.

Kahneman, D., Slovic, P., & Tversky, A. (1982). *Judgment under uncertainty: Heuristics and biases.* Cambridge, UK: Cambridge University Press.

—A reader on basic biases identified by cognitive and social psychologists, as discussed in the appendix. See also D. Kahneman (2011), *Thinking fast and slow.* New York: Macmillan.

Kelle, U. (1996). *Computer-aided qualitative data analysis: Theory, methods and practice.* Thousand Oaks, CA: SAGE.

— A book of readings on computerized methods for analyzing qualitative data.

Locke, K. (2001). *Grounded theory in management research.* London: SAGE.

—A clear, short introduction to grounded theory.

Miles, M., Huberman, A. M., & Saldaña, J. (2013). *Qualitative data analysis: An expanded sourcebook* (3rd ed.). Thousand Oaks, CA: SAGE.

—A classic on qualitative data analysis.

Saldaña, J. (2016). *The coding manual for qualitative researchers* (3rd ed.). Thousand Oaks, CA: SAGE.

—A useful, practical guide to coding and memo writing.

Strauss, A. L., & Corbin, J. (1997). *Grounded theory in practice.* Thousand Oaks, CA: SAGE.

—An edited book with 10 chapters illustrating grounded theory construction principles.

Tavory, I., & Timmermans, S. (2014). *Abductive analysis: Theorizing qualitative research.* Chicago: University of Chicago Press.

—A thoughtful application of pragmatism and abduction analysis to emergent theorizing.

Wertz, F. J., Charmaz, K., McMullen, L. M., Josselson, R., Anderson, R., & McSpadden, E. (2011). *Five ways of doing qualitative analysis: Phenomenological psychology, grounded theory, discourse analysis, narrative research, and intuitive inquiry.* New York: Guilford Press.

—An interesting book that analyzes the same dataset from five different perspectives.

KEY TERMS

grounded theory (p. 267)

emergent theory (p. 267)

symbolic interactionism (p. 269)

memoing (p. 269)

theoretical sampling (p. 269)

ethnography (p. 271)

archival records (p. 272)

direct observation (p. 272)

structured/unstructured interviews (p. 273)

life history (p. 274)

labor history (p. 274)

convergent interviewing (p. 274)

laddering (p. 275)

focus groups (p. 275)

virtual ethnographies (p. 276)

code memo (p. 277)

theoretical memo (p. 277)

operational memo (p. 277)

theoretical saturation (p. 279)

method of contrasts (p. 282)

method of classification (p. 282)

open coding (p. 284)

EXERCISES

Exercises to Reinforce Concepts

1. How does an emergent theory approach differ from the confirmatory approach to science?

2. Provide an overview of the grounded theory approach to theory construction.

3. What are the key points that you should take into account when framing a problem in emergent theory construction?

4. Briefly characterize the major methods for qualitative data collection.

5. What is a life history interview?

6. Describe different kinds of focus groups.

7. What is a virtual ethnography?

8. What is memoing? Why is it important?

9. What is theoretical sampling? What is theoretical saturation? How are the two related?

10. Describe the process of creating multiple levels of categories when coding data.

11. What is the difference between the method of contrasts and the method of classification?

12. In what ways can computers assist in the processing of qualitative data?

13. What are the advantages and disadvantages of using family codes and guiding questions?

14. How is theory construction with qualitative data similar to how everyday people make generalizations from their personal experiences?

15. What is deductive and inductive reasoning? How are they used in theory construction with qualitative data?

16. What is abduction, and what are the implications of it for the collection of qualitative data and the construction of theories from qualitative data?

17. What is mixed-methods research? Name some of the advantages of it.

18. What is the difference between an explanatory sequential design, an exploratory sequential design, and a convergent parallel design in mixed-methods research?

19. What form can some of the products of qualitative research take?

Exercises to Apply Concepts

1. Find an example in the research literature of a study that presents a theory based on either grounded or emergent theory approaches. Describe the theory in depth and the methods the theorist used to evolve the theory. Evaluate the processes the theorist used to construct the theory, as best you can.

2. It is not feasible to conduct a full ethnographic accounting of a phenomenon and then develop your own theory about it in the context of a one-semester course on theory construction. However, you can expose yourself to features of the approach on a small scale. For example, you might go to a church, a fraternity party, a cafeteria, a factory, a community center, a classroom, or some other setting and make observations about a phenomenon of interest to you. Use all of the principles discussed in this chapter to make your observations and then try to derive a small-scale theory based on these. Conduct relevant literature reviews.

3. In the first class I ever taught as a new professor, I (Jaccard) assigned a large class of 250 students the task of thinking of a social norm and then going out and breaking it during the ensuing week. The students were to write a report of how people reacted to it and, just as important, what their own reactions were while breaking the norm. Based on this experience, the students were to write an analysis of social norms and, in essence, build a minitheory of social norms. I felt that the exercise combined many interesting features of a field study that would serve class discussion. It was not until the next class, when the students reported some of the activities in which they engaged, that I realized I had made a serious mistake, essentially giving students a valid excuse for acting quite strangely. This once-in-a-Jaccard-lifetime assignment was quite successful in the theoretical insights it yielded as well as the recognition by students of how powerful norms are in American society. We are *not* assigning this exercise to you here.

The Limits of Information Processing

In emergent theory construction, social scientists rely on their ability to observe others and derive theoretical insights from those observations. Psychologists have identified limitations to human information processing that can bias and shape the ways we think about things. In this appendix, we describe a number of these processing limitations, so that you can be aware of how they might color your view of the world as you approach the theory construction process. These limitations may cause you to think more narrowly than you want, make faulty inferences, or focus on concepts or ideas to the exclusion of others that are important. A good grounded/ emergent theorist will be aware of these tendencies as he or she approaches field observations and does his or her best to avoid bias because of them. Indeed, this is true of any theorist who relies on observation or inference to form theoretical propositions.

THE MAGIC NUMBER 7 PLUS OR MINUS 2

One important class of limitations for making inferences is the limitation of human memory and information processing. Psychologists often think of human memory as being like a computer. The computer receives information from the environment (a keyboard), converts that information into a specialized code, the code is stored in immediate memory (random access memory or RAM), and then some is saved to a hard disk. Later, the information is retrieved, either from RAM or from the hard drive. Humans are exposed to information from the environment. They encode this information and then store it in temporary memory. Some of this information is passed to more permanent memory, which can then be retrieved for later use.

Psychologists distinguish four types of memory. *Sensory memory* stores all stimuli that register on the senses (e.g., touch, sight, hearing). Information typically is held in sensory memory for only a fraction of a second to 3 seconds. If the sensation does not draw the attention of the individual, the memory vanishes forever. If attention is drawn to it—that is, if we notice it—it is encoded and then passed into short-term memory and, in turn, possibly working memory. *Short-term memory* is a temporary storage system, where a piece of information is stored and held for perhaps 10 seconds or so, after which it fades away and is lost. Some of the information in short-term memory is acted on by *working memory,* which interprets the information in short-term memory, analyzes it relative to one's goals, and might augment it with information from long-term memory to facilitate interpretation and processing. Some of this information in short-term and working memory is passed to *long-term memory,* which is a more permanent memory that can hold vast amounts of information. Working memory is not just a passive bin of storage for sensory input information. Rather, humans "move" memories from long-term memory and short-term memory into working memory and then manipulate the contents in complex ways. Working memory is a dynamic information-processing center.

What is the capacity of working memory? In a classic paper, George Miller (1956) argued that humans can hold about 7 chunks of information in working memory. He refers to "the magic number 7 plus or minus 2" because across a wide range of studies and tasks, the evidence suggests people can simultaneously hold between 5 and 9 chunks of information in working memory. To be sure, sometimes a chunk of information can be composed of many organized bits of information (e.g., a chess master's vision of a chessboard with all the pieces organized in a well-known configuration), but the human mind has clear limitations as to the number of chunks of information it can process in working memory at one time. Simon (1974) has suggested that the magic number 7 might actually be somewhat less, closer to 4 or 5.

This limitation is important because it suggests that scientists are restricted in the number of variables, concepts, and relationships to which they can attend at any given instant. For theoretical analyses that are complex, scientists must rely on recording information externally and then processing that information sequentially. There also is evidence that people do not necessarily process information in the ways they think they are processing it. For example, when making judgments, people tend to think they use more information than they actually do, and they tend to think they use it in more complex ways than they actually do (Wiggins, 1973). All of this underscores the importance of using thinking aids to assist in processing large amounts of information when constructing a theory (e.g., aids such as an influence diagram discussed in Chapter 7, a process map, or a systemized strategy of note recording). It also underscores the importance of mixed-methods research that can take advantage of multivariate statistical methods that can simultaneously process relationships between hundreds of pieces of information. The human mind, unassisted, is simply incapable of doing this.

The point we wish to stress is the importance of recognizing that we are limited in our abilities to process large amounts of information at a given point in time, and we need to approach our data collection and theorizing strategies knowing these limitations exist. We need to be that much more vigilant about overcoming these limitations.

CONDITIONAL SYMMETRY BIAS

People often process probabilistic information, but they do not always do so in conformity to objective probability theory. An example is the *conditional symmetry bias.* You may have heard the assertion that marijuana is a gateway drug that leads to heroin use. As evidence, some cite the fact that the proportion of heroin users who have smoked marijuana is large. This proportion represents what statisticians call a conditional probability, symbolized as $p(M|H)$, where M is past use of marijuana and H represents using heroin. The symbol $p(M|H)$ is read as "the probability that a person has used marijuana, given that the person is a heroin user"; this conditional probability is usually quite large, near .95. But this in no way means that the reverse conditional probability, $p(H|M)$, is also large: $p(H|M)$ is the probability that someone is a heroin user given that the person has smoked marijuana. As it turns out, this probability is quite small (near .05). The conditional probabilities are not symmetrical (i.e., equal in value) even though many people assume they are. The tendency to assume such equal conditional probabilities is called the *conditional symmetry bias*.

As another example, a survey of 74 CEOs working for Fortune 500 companies led a scientist to conclude recently that there may be a link between childhood pet ownership and future career success. About 95% of all the CEOs as children had possessed a dog, a cat, or both. The CEOs who were interviewed commented on how pet ownership had helped them to develop many of the positive character traits that made them good managers, such as responsibility, empathy, and respect for other beings. Note that the datum being reported is p(owned pet in childhood|CEO) = .95. Because this probability is large, the inference is made that the two variables are linked. But what we want to focus on as well is p(CEO|owned pet as child): that is, given that you owned a pet as a child, what is the probability that you will become a CEO? This is very small. Here again is the erroneous assumption of symmetric conditional probabilities.

We have found several cases of conditional symmetry bias in scientific reports and in scientific theories. When inferring relationships, one must be careful not to commit this logical fallacy. For details, consult any introductory book on probability theory. Although emergent theorists rarely formally calculate conditional probabilities, they do make inferences about relationships based on observations they have made and notes they have taken. The inference of a relationship might be based on a subjective or intuitive representation of a conditional probability. For example, after interviewing a large number of heroin users, the scientist might make the observation that almost all of them started their drug habit using marijuana. The inference of marijuana as a gateway drug may then be formulated, even though we know that such an inference cannot be made from such data.

WHEN RANDOM IS NOT RANDOM

Random events happen all the time, but people sometimes find it difficult to recognize randomness. People impute meaning into random events and build theories around them as if they were systematic, usually because they do not understand randomness. As an example, suppose we flip a coin four times. Which of the following sequences is more likely to occur:

Sequence *A*:   H   H   H   H
Sequence *B*:   H   T   T   H

Most people will say sequence *B*. The correct answer, however, is that they are equally likely to occur. Each has a probability of .0625 of occurring. This is obvious if we list the 16 different outcomes that could occur on the four flips:

H   H   H   H
H   H   H   T
H   H   T   H
H   H   T   T
H   T   H   H
H   T   H   T
H   T   T   H
H   T   T   T
T   H   H   H

```
T   H   H   T
T   H   T   H
T   H   T   T
T   T   H   H
T   T   H   T
T   T   T   H
T   T   T   T
```

Note that the probability of sequence A is 1 out of 16 = .0625; so too is the probability of sequence B.

In a random process such as multiple coin flips, people think that the number of heads will equal the number of tails, and when this expectation is violated grossly, they tend to make attributions of nonrandomness that can be incorrect. In this example, on how many trials in the four coin flips do we get an equal number of heads and tails? From this listing, of the 16 possible outcomes, six have two heads and two tails. Thus, the probability of observing two heads and two tails is 6/16 = .375. This means that it is almost twice as likely that one will *not* observe an equal number of heads and tails in a given random sequence of four flips than it is that one will observe two heads and two tails. This is counterintuitive to most people.

Many features of randomness are nonintuitive, and we need to be careful not to let our intuitions about randomness lead to attributions of systematic relations in what are essentially random events. Training in probability theory helps one to appreciate these nuances.

COMPOUND PROBABILITY BIAS

Another common bias is the *compound probability bias*. Suppose a woman has just started using birth control pills. Let A be the event of a minor side effect occurring, say, innocuous cramps, and suppose that the probability of this event is .80. Let B be the event of her boyfriend approving of the use of the birth control method and suppose that the probability of this event also is .80. What is the probability of both events occurring; that is, what is the probability that both the minor side effect and boyfriend approval will occur? Most people will say it is .80, but is this correct?

It turns out that the correct answer is .64. In probability theory, if events A and B are independent (which is reasonable to assume in this case), then it can be shown that $p(A \text{ and } B) = p(A) p(B)$. That is, the probability of both events occurring equals the product of the two probabilities that each event will occur in isolation. The compound probability fallacy is that people tend to overestimate the joint occurrence of events, given their perceptions of the probabilities of each individual event.

Here is another example. Suppose you are in charge of a complex missile system whose successful functioning depends on each of 500 parts working correctly. Suppose, too, that the probability of a part functioning correctly the first time it is used is .99. What is the overall probability that the system will work the first time it is used? Most people would say it is quite high. Assuming independence, however, the probability is $.99^{500}$, which equals about .01. The chances that the missile system will work the first time are about 1 in 100, or 1%! Just as laypeople are susceptible to the compound probability bias, so may scientists be susceptible to such bias when conducting field observations and making judgments about joint events.

AVAILABILITY OF INFORMATION FROM MEMORY

When we are asked to make a judgment about something, we frequently search our memory and then formulate a judgment based on the information that is retrieved from memory. The information that influences our judgments most is the information that is easily retrieved from memory. The problem is that information that is most available in memory is not always the best information on which to base a judgment. What factors influence availability of information to memory? There are many. One factor is how recently we have been exposed to, or thought about, the information. For example, Higgins, Rholes, and Jones (1977) primed participants in an experiment by having half of them read lists of positive attributes and the other half read lists of negative attributes. Later that day, when they were asked to make attributions of behaviors performed by a person in a different experiment, the research participants were more likely to use categories and words that had been primed in the prior experiment. Identical behaviors were interpreted as "self-confident" or "arrogant," depending on whether positive or negative words had been used in the prior experiment. Such "priming effects" can have obvious implications for judgments a scientist might make in the field because such judgments can be colored by the information to which the scientist has been exposed (i.e., primed with) prior to making the observations.

Unique events also stand out, and hence, they are more likely to capture our attention and be encoded and passed to long-term memory or retrieved from long-term memory. Suppose we read to you the following list of names:

Steve Smith

Joan Gerber

Bill Clinton

Jeanne Weiss

John Glass

Martha Smith

George Bush

Glenn May

Michelle Gayle

Lilly Stanton

After we read the list aloud to you, we might ask you how many males were on the list. This is the task that Kahneman and Tversky (1972) used in their research. They read lists of names to people and then asked them to estimate the number of males or females on the list some time later, without forewarning people they would be asked. The correct answer for the list we gave is five males and five females; that is, half the list has male names. In the Kahneman and Tversky study, most people said the number of males was two or three. The research participants judgments were biased toward the number of famous males in the list (Bill Clinton and George Bush) because these names were more prominent and hence more "available" in memory.

ORDER EFFECTS

Suppose we describe the same person to two different individuals. The description provided to the first person is that the target individual is intelligent, sincere, honest, conceited, rude, and nervous. The description provided to the second person is that the target individual is nervous, rude, conceited, honest, sincere, and intelligent. Note that the exact same information has been provided for each person, and only the order of it has been changed. For the first person, the positive descriptors come first, followed by the negative descriptors (pro–con). For the second person, the order is reversed (con–pro). One would expect that the reactions to, and evaluations of, the described individual would be the same, on average, since exactly the same information has been presented. But this is not the case. When people are presented descriptors in the pro–con order, they tend to form more favorable impressions of the individual than when they are presented the descriptors in the con–pro order. The order in which we are presented or exposed to information can bias the judgments we make. Scientists are just as susceptible to these order effects as laypeople, and care must be taken to counteract this bias when making field observations and collecting and analyzing data.

IGNORING INFORMATION

Sometimes we are exposed to information, but we want to ignore it or not take it into account when making judgments. For example, in some court cases, jurors are told something by a lawyer, the opposing lawyer makes an objection, the objection is sustained, and then the jurors are instructed to ignore the information. But do they? Cialdini (2001) describes a study in which people were randomly selected from jury lists and then exposed to a recording of a trial about a woman who was injured in a car accident by a reckless driver. Jurors were randomly assigned to one of three conditions. In one condition, the juror heard the case and no information was provided about whether the driver had liability insurance. In a second condition, the juror heard the case, and it was revealed that the driver had liability insurance. In the third condition, the juror heard the case, it was revealed that the driver had liability insurance, and then the judge disallowed the information and asked the jurors to ignore it. If people ignore the information, then judgments in the third condition should be the same, on average, as judgments in the second condition. The mean award by jurors for pain and suffering in the first condition was about $33,000, for jurors in the second condition it was about $37,000, and for jurors in the third condition it was about $46,000. Not only did the jurors fail to disregard the information, they apparently gave it more weight by being told to ignore it. Later studies revealed that jurors tended to give such information more weight because they saw it as "privileged" information.

Just because we want to ignore information does not mean that we can indeed ignore it when forming judgments. When judging the type of soil in a plot of land for making planting decisions, farmers are told that they should ignore the moisture content of the soil samples. Yet invariably, the moisture content impacts their judgments about how much of the core components of the soil is present (e.g., the amount of sand particles, the amount of clay particles). And if we are told by an informant that information is special, we tend to give it more weight in our judgments, even if the information is not special (Cialdini, 2001). Such biases can color the judgments scientists make in their field observations, and they need to be dealt with.

ADDITIONAL PROCESSING LIMITATIONS

Psychologists have identified a wide range of additional limitations that people bring to bear as they process information and make judgments, including (1) the base-rate fallacy (the tendency to ignore base-rate information when making frequency judgments), (2) the confirmation bias (the tendency to seek information that will confirm one's expectations or beliefs), (3) the egocentric bias (the tendency to see oneself as the center of attention and to see oneself and one's activities as unique), (4) the false consensus bias (the tendency to overestimate the degree to which other people agree with oneself), (5) halo effects (the tendency to evaluate the specific attributes of an object based on one's overall evaluation of the object), (6) illusory correlation (the tendency to see two unrelated events as being related), (7) the negativity bias (the tendency to weigh negative information more heavily than positive information), (8) the self-serving bias (the tendency to attribute successful outcomes to self and failures to extenuating circumstances), (9) unrealistic optimism (the tendency to distort reality in a direction that enhances self-esteem and maintains personal efficacy and optimism), (10) wishful thinking (the tendency to see desirable outcomes as more probable and undesirable outcomes as less probable), and (11) causal attribution bias (the tendency to attribute one's successes to one's own abilities but the successes of others to luck, chance, or situational influences and the tendency to attribute one's failures to bad luck, chance, or situational influences but the failure of others to the other's lack of ability or own doings). All of these can impact the judgments of the people who report on the world about them as well as the judgments of the scientist directly.

When being trained in disciplines that emphasize qualitative methods, we believe it is important for students to be aware about the limitations of human information processing and how such biases should be dealt with in research contexts (we also believe this is important for quantitative researchers as well). We encourage you to make learning and keeping up on this literature part of your training and professional growth as a scientist.

11

Emergent Theory
Quantitative Approaches

It is a capital mistake to theorize before one has data.
Insensibly one begins to twist facts to suit theories,
instead of theories to suit facts.
                    —SIR ARTHUR CONAN DOYLE

Emergent theory is core to many forms of qualitative research. Rather than approach research as a means of theory testing, emergent theory collects data in systematic ways that allows theory to emerge from data rather than impose one's theory onto data. In qualitative research, one garners ideas for theory through careful exploration of data, culminating in a set of theoretical propositions. Chapter 10 elaborated principles for constructing theory using qualitative methods. Quantitative researchers also have tools to help them evolve theory from data and to stimulate theoretical thinking. The present chapter describes some of these tools. The thesis is that data exploration can be a rich source of ideas for theory and can thus be part of the theory construction process. The tools described are *not* a means of theory testing, at least when used as outlined here. Rather, they are "idea generators" that help you think about conceptual matters in new ways and that assist the theory construction process. Some purists feel that theory should not evolve through data snooping (also called "data fishing" or "data butchery"). However, we distinguish theory construction from theory testing, recognizing that ideas evolve from a variety of sources, one of which is data.

Quantitative data can be collected to formally test a theory, or it can be collected for exploratory purposes. For the latter, researchers usually have a topic of interest in mind, with data collection then being guided by a framework that encompasses many domains within that topic area. Large secondary databases often are of this character. In this sense, exploratory analyses of quantitative data rarely are completely atheoretical. Some conceptual filtering takes place in the choice of variables to measure in the data. In this chapter, we assume you are working with a dataset that has an exploratory focus. Nevertheless, exploratory analyses also can be performed on datasets designed for theory-testing purposes.

When working with exploratory data, one might begin with an initial theory linking variables that is reasonably well thought out. One seeks to refine the theory, bring innovation to it, and think about it more deeply with the aid of exploratory analyses. In other situations, the initial theory is vague, and one may not even be certain about which explanatory variables to focus on. One might know the outcome one wants to understand and broad classes of variables to consider as explanations, but beyond that, we need the help of exploratory analyses to choose the variables to theory construct about.

In this chapter, we move from the use of exploratory analyses for a semi-well-defined theory to increasingly broad exploratory analyses, eventually discussing the case where we seek to isolate constructs from a large set of variables to theorize about. Initially, we link our presentation to concepts from Chapter 7 on causal frameworks, describing exploratory methods for the analysis of direct causal relationships and moderated relationships. We then consider exploratory analyses in other contexts, such as cluster analysis, factor analysis, and machine learning. We conclude by considering chance effects in exploratory analyses. Although there are many other statistical methods that inspire theory construction, we focus on only a sampling. Table 11.1 presents the methods we cover.

This chapter is statistically oriented, but we minimize formulae and statistical theory in favor of providing a general appreciation of how the methods can be used. Some may be unhappy with the absence of statistical technicalities, but our primary goal is to raise awareness of methods that can bring innovation to the theory construction process. The suggested readings at the end of the chapter are good follow-ups. All of the statistical methods described in this chapter can be executed through a simple point-and-click interface that is compatible with SPSS or Excel or ASCII file input. The supple-

TABLE 11.1. List of Exploratory Methods

Analysis	Purpose
Single direct effect	
Smoothers	Identify complex functions between cause and effect
Quantile regression	Explore causal effects in different portions of the outcome distribution
Multiple direct effects	
Dominance analysis	Identify the relative importance of different causal effects
Moderated effects	
Regression mixture modeling	Identify unknown moderators
Interaction smoothers	Identify nonlinear interaction/moderator forms
Cluster analysis	Construction of taxonomies
Factor analysis	Identify underlying dimensions of variables
Data mining/machine learning	Identify key explanatory variables from a set of many

mental materials at *www.theory-construction.com* contain videos that walk you through each analysis as well as detailed primers.

Methodologists often associate exploratory data analysis with creative graphical formulations of data that drive home the adage "a picture is worth a thousand words." Noted statistician John Tukey wrote a classic book in 1977 titled *Exploratory Data Analysis* that contained ingenious graphical (and algebraic) approaches for discerning trends in data. Although the methods we discuss do not follow this tradition, there certainly is some overlap. Our focus is on methods that should stimulate your thinking for theory construction purposes.

Some examples will help set the stage. Conscientiousness is the extent to which people are dependable, persistent, organized, and goal directed. Research typically has found a positive correlation between this quality and job performance in organizational settings. In exploratory analyses, Le and colleagues (2011) analyzed the relationship between worker conscientiousness and job performance in ways that allowed for nonlinearity and found evidence for a curvilinear effect: Job performance was positively related to conscientiousness up to a point. Extremely conscientious workers, it turned out, showed decrements in job performance. Research has now confirmed that when workers are excessively conscientious, they can be rigid, inflexible, and compulsive perfectionists who pay too much attention to small details and who may overlook important job-related goals, all of which can negatively affect job performance. Exploratory statistical tools that reveal nonlinear relationships between variables can thus suggest interesting possibilities to theorists.

As another example, a study of over 21,000 White and Black adults in the United States collected data on their dietary habits for 107 different food items (Judd, Letter, Shikany, Roth, & Newby, 2015). Of interest was whether there were distinct groups or "clusters" of people with similar eating habits. Using exploratory analytic methods, Judd and colleagues (2015) identified five dietary patterns. These patterns were not derived from theory but rather "emerged" from the data based on empirics. The patterns as they summarized were (1) the "convenience" pattern, characterized by a wide mix of dishes, including meat, pasta, Mexican food, Chinese food, pizza, red meat, soup, and potatoes; (2) the "plant-based" pattern, characterized by elevated levels of fruits, vegetables, and fish; (3) the "sweets/fats" pattern, characterized by elevated levels of sweet snacks, desserts, and fats and oils; (4) the "Southern" pattern, characterized by elevated levels of fried foods, organ meat, and sweetened beverages; and (5) the "alcohol/salads" pattern, characterized by elevated levels of beer, wine, liquor, and salads. Interesting theories surrounding the determinants and health consequences of the different patterns have evolved.

EXPLORATORY ANALYSES OF DIRECT EFFECTS

In this section, we assume that you have identified one or more direct causal effects in your theory but that you seek to explore facets of these effects in ways that innovate your theory. The direct effects may be part of a larger causal theory you have formulated, but we set aside that larger theory and focus on just the direct effects. We first review the basic linear model that often is used to think about and analyze direct effects. We then present exploratory analytic tools that move you beyond traditional thinking about them.

In causal modeling, a direct effect is represented by an influence diagram as follows:

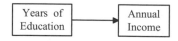

In this depiction, the number of years of education middle-aged adults have achieved is thought to influence their annual income. This relationship might be framed as a linear one, which can be expressed statistically using the linear model

$$\text{Income}_i = \alpha + \beta \text{ Years Education}_i + \varepsilon_i$$

where α is an intercept, β is the (unstandardized) regression or path coefficient, ε is a disturbance or error term that reflects all factors other than education that independently impact income, and i refers to individual i. Suppose our target population consists of middle-aged adults who have years of education ranging from 10 to 16. We can segregate individuals into those who have 10 years of education, those with 11 years of education, and so on. Suppose for each segment, we calculate the mean annual income and obtain the following:

Education	Mean Annual Income
10	$22,000
11	$24,000
12	$26,000
13	$28,000
14	$30,000
15	$32,000
16	$34,000

The mean income increases by $2,000 for each additional year of education. The value for the regression coefficient in the linear model is thus 2,000. This coefficient provides perspectives on mean changes per unit increase in predictor values and in this case reflects the worth of a year of education. It is our experience that many researchers fail to appreciate the fact that linear regression is, at its core, an analysis of means and how means change across predictor profiles. Each of the means in our example is a *conditional mean*, that is, the mean value conditional on the predictor equaling a given value. For example, the mean income conditional on 10 years of education is $22,000, and the mean income conditional on 11 years of education is $24,000.

The relationship between predictor values and conditional means does not have to be linear. Here is a different relationship we might observe:

Education	Mean Annual Income
10	$22,000
11	$22,000
12	$22,000
13	$24,000
14	$26,000
15	$28,000
16	$30,000

Note that there is a floor effect for mean income, with the mean not changing at the lower end of years of education. This is a nonlinear function that traditional regression mischaracterizes.

The same concepts apply to dichotomous outcomes. Consider the case where the outcome is the probability that adolescents will smoke marijuana in the ensuing year and the predictor is the age of adolescents, ranging from 12 to 17 in units of one. We want to characterize the probability of smoking marijuana for youths who are age 12, age 13, age 14, and so on. Here are the empirically derived probabilities:

Age	Proportion Who Smoked Marijuana
12	0.025
13	0.050
14	0.075
15	0.100
16	0.125
17	0.150

The probability of smoking marijuana is 0.025 conditional on age being 12; the probability of smoking marijuana is 0.050 conditional on age being 13; and so on. The regression coefficient is 0.025; for every 1-unit age increase, the probability of smoking marijuana increases by 0.025 units. This model is called a *linear probability model* because the function is linear. Logistic regression, an alternative analytic approach, assumes the function is nonlinear and has the shape of a sigmoid (S) function (see Chapter 8). Which function is more appropriate? This is an empirical question, and so the answer can vary across populations and contexts.

With this as background, we now turn to exploratory analytic methods that can be used to foster your theory construction efforts relative to direct effects.

A Single Direct Effect

Smoothers

When we posit a direct causal relationship between two quantitative variables, we usually have a general sense of whether the relationship is positive or negative, but we may not think through the specific form of the relationship. Traditional regression analyses assume the relationship is linear, but perhaps it is not, as with the conscientious-ness and job performance example. In Chapter 3, we discussed strategies researchers use to make a theoretical contribution, one of which is *identifying nuanced functional forms of relationships*. A statistical tool to help identify such functional forms is called a *smoother* (Wilcox, 2017). There are many types of smoothers. Here we describe first a crude approach to smoothing to give you a sense of smoothers, and then we introduce more sophisticated types.

Suppose we posit that youth who have positive attitudes toward using drugs will develop negative attitudes toward school. For 750 youth, we obtain an index of atti-tudes toward using drugs and then measure their attitudes toward school 6 months later. School attitudes are measured on a 0 to 50 scale, with higher scores indicating more positive attitudes (a score of 25 is a neutral attitude). Drug attitudes are on a 0 to 15 scale, with higher scores indicating more positive attitudes and a score of 8 as the neutral point. School attitude scores are the average of many items and therefore include decimals. Attitudes toward drugs are measured in integers. We want to examine the relationship between the two variables in an emergent theoretical sense.

Figure 11.1 presents a traditional scatterplot from SPSS, with attitudes toward school on the *Y*-axis and attitudes toward drugs on the *X*-axis. The scatterplot is not very helpful for visualizing the dynamics at play. We can instead create a *smoothed scatter-plot* that will be more revealing. Using drug attitudes as the predictor, the (conditional) school attitude mean is calculated at each value of the drug attitude. We then plot these mean values as a function of the drug attitudes. Figure 11.2 presents the scatterplot with a smoothed fit line.

There is a curvilinear trend in the data. When attitudes toward using drugs are neg-ative (near 0), attitudes toward school are positive. The more positive attitudes toward using drugs become, the less positive are attitudes toward school, but this effect dimin-ishes at the higher end of the drug attitude scale. Specifically, there is a flattening of the effect at the higher levels of drug attitudes. We need to ask ourselves as theorists if this

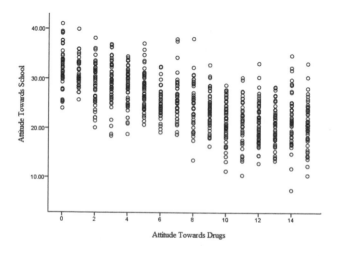

FIGURE 11.1. SPSS scatterplot.

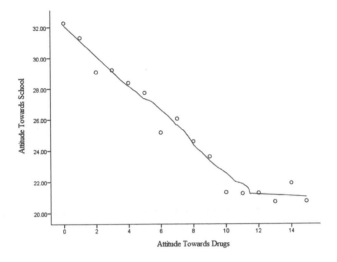

FIGURE 11.2. Scatterplot with smoother.

flattening makes conceptual sense and whether to incorporate it into our theory. In this example, we might argue that negative attitudes toward school have a "floor" beyond which drug attitudes are unlikely to have much effect.[1]

More elegant smoothing techniques exist that can reveal nonlinear trends in the data (see Wilcox, 2017). Figure 11.3 presents one such smoother, called a *binary outcome smoother*, that explores the relationship between levels of young adult depression and the probability of using professional services at a mental health clinic (Munson, Jaccard, Cole, Ben-David, & Ramirez, 2018). The relationship between mental health need (level of depression) and use of professional services generally has been characterized in the literature as linear: those most in need are most likely to be treated. The smoother suggests that this presumption is incorrect. At low levels of depression, depression is unrelated to service use probably because depression is not severe enough to motivate individuals to seek help. The curve is flat. At some point, when depression likely becomes sufficiently problematic for individuals (corresponding to a score of 10 on the depression measure), increases in depression lead to (linear) increases in service use. At another point further up the depression continuum, a ceiling sets in, such that further increases in depression do not increase service use, again reflected by a flat curve. Finally, there is a downturn in service use at the highest levels of depression, likely because of the high levels of apathy and hopelessness associated with extreme depression. If you are apathetic and life is hopeless, why seek treatment? The smoother-identified function makes theoretical sense and contrasts with conventional thinking. Positing this dynamic in a theory would be innovative.

Instead of assuming a linear relationship for direct effects or only specifying general monotonic relationships for them, exploratory smoothers can lead to theoretical innovation by identifying nonlinear functions to consider during theory construction. The

---

[1]As an aside, variability about each mean is not shown in Figure 11.2, but it is in Figure 11.1. Such variability reflects unpredictability at the level of individuals.

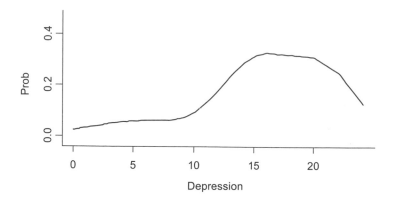

FIGURE 11.3. Binary outcome smoother.

use of smoothers raises the issue of *overfitting*. Overfitting occurs when we assume that the data trends are theoretically meaningful when they might just represent sampling error in the data. Perhaps the true function in our example on drug attitudes and school attitudes is linear and the flattening of the curve at the higher end of drug attitudes is nothing but sampling error. Some analysts stress the need to cross-validate smoother functions in another sample. At a minimum, one needs a coherent rationale or a conceptual logic model for the function. With smoothers, one usually does not take every small "bump" or "change in direction" of the smooth literally; rather, it is the general trends suggested by the smoother that are interpreted.

Quantile Regression

When we analyze data using traditional regression or analysis of variance methods, the focus is on group differences in means. For example, the regression example for the effects of years of education on annual family income analyzed means for those with 10 years of education, those with 11 years of education, and so on. However, instead of theorizing at the level of central tendencies, one might choose to theorize about other portions of an outcome distribution, such as the lower or upper parts of it. It is possible that there are different effects of a direct cause on an outcome at the outcome distribution extremes rather than in the middle of the distribution, which is what a mean reflects. Suppose our focus is on the (direct) effect of gender on math achievement in middle school students. A typical result is that males tend to perform better on tests of mathematical achievement than females. Here is an influence diagram for this theoretical relationship:

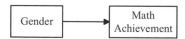

This theory presupposes a simple gender difference in performance on math tests. However, perhaps the function is more complex. For example, perhaps there is a negligible gender difference for students who tend to score poorly in math; a modest gender difference for those in the middle of the math achievement distribution; and a substantial gender difference for those at the upper end of the math achievement distribution. Stated another way, males are no more likely than females to be poor in math, but they are much more likely to be top math students than females. Averaging across everyone shows that there is a medium difference in math achievement for males versus females. However, a theoretical narrative that simply asserts a gender difference in math performance is somewhat misleading because the gender difference is concentrated at the upper end of the math achievement distribution. Theory construction might benefit from thinking not just about what is happening in the middle of an outcome distribution, but also about how variables (like gender) relate to what is happening in different portions of the distribution. Such thinking and innovation can be aided by exploratory analyses using *quantile regression*. We now elaborate its mechanics.

Quantiles are points from the cumulative distribution of a variable. The 0.10 quantile is the value in the distribution that 10% of the individuals have scores less than or equal to it; the 0.25 quantile is the value in the distribution that 25% of the individuals have scores less than or equal to it; and the 0.50 quantile is the value in the distribution that 50% of the individuals have scores less than or equal to it. If we measure annual income of new assistant professors and the 0.25 quantile is $45,000, this means that 25% of the new hires have an annual income of $45,000 or less. If the 0.50 quantile is $55,000, this means that 50% of the new hires have an annual income of $55,000 or less.

A quantile is analogous to a concept most know as *percentiles*. Informally, a percentile is a score or point in a distribution that a specified percentage of individuals score less than or equal to. If we tell you a GRE score of 161 defines the 80th percentile, this means that 80% of individuals score 161 or less on the GRE. Statisticians typically use the term *quantile* instead of percentile, refer to it with the letter q, and state it in probability or proportion terms rather than as percentages. For example, the 0.80 quantile ($q = 0.80$) for the GRE is a score of 161. *Deciles* of a distribution are the 0.10, 0.20, 0.30, 0.40, 0.50, 0.60, 0.70, 0.80, and 0.90 quantiles.

In our example linking number of years of education to annual income, we focused on how mean annual income varies with the number of years of education. We might instead build theories about how education impacts income at the lower or upper end of the income distribution. For example, here are 0.90 quantiles for the different education segments:

Education	0.90 quantile of annual income
10	$42,000
11	$47,000
12	$52,000
13	$57,000
14	$62,000
15	$67,000
16	$72,000

In this case, for every one-year education increases, the 0.90 quantile increases by $5,000, yielding a regression coefficient of $5,000 instead of the $2,000 that we documented earlier. The effect of education on income is different for the top 10% level of earnings than for the mean income. Why might this be the case? Can we build a theory that takes this into account? By only considering means and central tendencies via traditional practice, we limit the richness of theoretical questions we can seek answers to.

Comparing quantiles for different groups can be a good source of theoretical ideas, especially for understanding ethnic and gender disparities. For example, we used the National Longitudinal Study of Adolescent Health and performed a quantile regression to compare Black and non-Latinx White families on the 0.10 quantile for annual income in 1995. For Blacks, the 0.10 quantile was $7,384 and for non-Latinx Whites it was $15,432, a difference of about $8,000. For the 0.90 quantile, the values were $70,421 and $90,653, respectively, a difference of about $20,000. Thus, the income disparity between Blacks and non-Latinx Whites was much larger at the higher end of the income distribution than at the lower end. What theory might you create to explain this finding? Interestingly, some economists argue that income disparities should be examined using income ratios rather than income differences. At the 0.10 quantile, non-Latinx Whites earn about twice as much as Blacks (15,432/7,384 = 2.01). At the 0.90 quantile, non-Latinx Whites earn about 1.3 times as much as Blacks (90,653/70,421 = 1.29). Some economists would argue that income disparity *decreases* rather than increases at the higher end of the income distribution based on the analysis of income ratios. Which do you think is the more compelling narrative, ratios or differences? How would this dynamic affect your theorizing and the way you might construct a theory surrounding income disparities? It turns out that a simple modification of quantile regression can shift the focus to ratios rather than differences.[2]

Figure 11.4 presents an example of distributions for two groups (one plotted with dashed lines and the other with a solid line) that have the same mean on an outcome variable but differ at both extremes. The analysis of deciles would detect these differences, but the analysis of means would not. Exploratory analyses of quantile differences can be a rich source for idea generation.

Multiple Direct Effects

The given examples with smoothers and quantile regression focused on the case of a single direct cause. However, often we work with theories that specify several direct causes for an outcome. One can extend both smoothers and quantile regression to the case of multiple direct effects, but doing so is beyond the scope of this book (see the Suggested Readings for this chapter and the supplemental materials on our website). In this section, we introduce another exploratory method that might spark theoretical ideas, a method known as *dominance analysis*. This method is used when we want to theorize about the relative importance of different causes of an outcome. For example, a theorist

---

[2]This is accomplished by applying quantile regression to the log of income rather than income per se. See our companion website *www.theory-construction.com* and the primer for quantile regression for details.

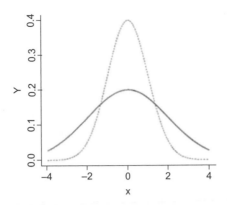

FIGURE 11.4. Plot of two distributions with equal means but different deciles.

might specify six possible determinants of reading skills in children and seek to build a theory about an importance hierarchy of these determinants. Or a theorist might identify five possible determinants of consumer decisions to purchase solar energy products and seek to build a theory surrounding the relative importance of those determinants. For five causes, there are at least 120 different importance orderings of causes that can occur, and for six causes, there are 720 such orderings. Initial exploratory analyses using dominance analysis might suggest a few viable orderings and, in doing so, spark the generation of ideas about importance hierarchies.

One common analytic approach used to compare the importance of presumed influences (hereafter referred to as predictors) is to examine their standardized regression/path coefficients when the outcome is regressed onto the predictors collectively. Predictors with larger absolute standardized coefficients are seen as more important than those with smaller standardized coefficients. This is appropriate, it is argued, because all of the predictors are on a common metric (a mean of zero and a standard deviation of 1.0). The strategy is problematic for many technical reasons that we do not elaborate here (see Blanton & Jaccard, 2006; Bring, 1994; Darlington, 1968; Johnson & LeBreton, 2004). Johnson and LeBreton (2004) review a large number of relative importance indices and ultimately recommend dominance analysis (Azen & Budescu, 2003, 2006). It is not perfect, but it often provides a reasonable sense of viable importance hierarchies for theory construction purposes.

Dominance analysis relies on multiple regression in which an outcome variable is regressed onto each of the direct causes, considered collectively. It documents how much a given predictor contributes to the overall squared multiple correlation in the equation, taking into account both the predictor's correlation with the criterion and its relationship to other predictors. Dominance analysis identifies the extent to which a given predictor "dominates" the other predictors in the regression analysis. As an example, suppose our interest is in three predictors of women's attitudes toward using a new method of birth control: (1) perceived effectiveness of the method in preventing pregnancy, (2) perceived cost of using the method, and (3) perceived convenience of using

BOX 11.1. Robust Statistics

A quiet revolution has been taking place in the field of statistics for decades. It has been quiet in the sense that alternatives to many of our traditional statistical methods have been developed that have more statistical power, make minimal population assumptions, and are relatively outlier resistant, but these (robust) methods are rarely used in many social science disciplines. Professor Rand Wilcox wrote a classic article titled "How Many Discoveries Have Been Lost by Ignoring Modern Statistical Methods?" (1998) to encourage the use of robust methods. However, more than 20 years later, they are still relatively infrequently used. Smoothers evolved out of the robust statistical literature, as did quantile regression, both topics of which are discussed in this chapter. There are robust counterparts of cluster analysis and factor analysis, and, indeed, there are robust analogs to most traditional statistics that dominate current social science research. Why constrain ourselves to models that assume linearity when robust tools are available that are not so constrained? Why miss important theoretical leads because outliers are masking fundamental trends in the data? Why constrain ourselves to methods that lead us astray in the presence of heavy-tailed distributions? As you pursue exploratory analyses for theory construction, we encourage you to add robust analytic methods to your toolbox. Some analysts believe that current statistical approaches are only mildly affected by outliers and assumption violations. Although this is the case in some scenarios, it often is not true, as a reading of the work of Wilcox will quickly reveal (e.g., Wilcox, 1998, 2017).

One striking example of disparate results that can occur from traditional statistical indices is Cohen's d, a commonly used index of effect size when two means are compared (Wilcox & Tian, 2011). Cohen's d translates a raw mean difference into a standardized metric expressed in units of standard deviations (e.g., a Cohen's d of 0.50 means the raw mean difference is half a standard deviation in magnitude). The left panel of Figure B11.1 shows two normal distributions, with Cohen's d equal to 1.0 for the mean difference between the two distributions. The right panel shows two

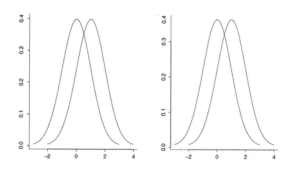

FIGURE B11.1. Cohen's d for two examples.

(continued)

(non-normal) distributions with slightly heavy tails but with the exact same means as the left panel; but now Cohen's d is 0.30. The difference between a Cohen's d of 1.0 and a Cohen's d of 0.30 is typically judged to be dramatic; but the figures suggest the mean differences are comparable. Cohen's d can be deceptive. Wilcox (2017) describes robust analogs to Cohen's d that are not impacted by heavy tails of the distributions. We highly recommend the textbooks and articles, both introductory and advanced, that Professor Wilcox has written on robust statistics and encourage you to incorporate these methods into your statistical toolbox for both exploratory and conventional analyses.

the method. Using the exploratory database that assessed these constructs, dominance analysis calculates the increase in R^2 for predicting attitudes that perceived effectiveness yields over and above perceived convenience; the increase in R^2 that perceived effectiveness yields over and above perceived cost; and the increase in R^2 that perceived effectiveness yields over and above perceived convenience and perceived cost together. The average of these increases in R^2 is the index of dominance of the effectiveness predictor over the cost and convenience predictors. This process is repeated for perceived convenience to determine its dominance over perceived effectiveness and perceived cost, and, again, for perceived cost to determine its dominance over perceived effectiveness and perceived convenience. The dominance indices are then transformed to sum to 100 to reflect the percentage of the squared correlation attributable to each predictor.

As an example, Stolz, Barber, and Olsen (2005) evaluated the effects of six parenting variables on female adolescent antisocial behavior (measured by adolescent ratings of items such as "I steal things from places other than home"; "I lie or cheat"; "I use alcohol or drugs for nonmedical purposes"). The predictor variables (direct causes) included *parental support* (measured by adolescent ratings of items such as "My mother makes me feel better after talking over my worries with her"; "My mother enjoys doing things with me"); *parental monitoring and supervision*; and *parental psychological control* (measured by ratings of items such as "My mother changes the subject whenever I have something to say"; "My mother is always trying to change how I feel or think about things"). All the measures were scored in a direction that higher scores would be associated with higher antisocial behavior. Each dimension was assessed separately for the mother and the father.

The six parenting variables (three for the mother and three for the father) accounted for 32% of the variance in antisocial behavior, which is substantial. The results of the dominance analysis appear in Table 11.2. Behavioral monitoring and supervision tended to be the most dominant parenting dimension predictor, followed by psychological control and then support. Why might this be the case? What conceptual logic model could be introduced for this importance hierarchy? What are the mechanisms underlying the

TABLE 11.2. Dominance Analysis	
Variable	**Dominance**
Father monitoring/supervision	35.5
Mother monitoring/supervision	22.6
Father psychological control	12.9
Mother psychological control	12.9
Father support	12.9
Mother support	6.5

ordering? It is one thing to posit a theory that each of the six parenting dimensions is relevant, but can the theory be taken a step further and address why some parenting dimensions are more dominant causes than others? Note also that the father dimensions tended to be more dominant than the mother dimensions. Can your theory articulate why this might be the case? Does this type of analysis stimulate new or more refined ideas about the multiple direct effects? After conducting an exploratory dominance analysis, interesting theoretical questions might emerge that can be thought about.

In sum, as one constructs theories with several direct effects of an outcome, it may be fruitful to think conceptually in terms of an importance hierarchy for the multiple determinants. There are many ways of conceptualizing importance, but one approach is to frame it as the dominance of a cause in accounting for explained variance in the outcome relative to other causes. Exploratory analyses can be conducted to suggest possible operative importance hierarchies, and these can then be used as a basis for generating theoretical ideas. There are, of course, complexities to defining "importance" in this way as well as some challenging technicalities with respect to dominance analysis per se (see Grömping, 2015, 2016). However, as an idea-generation heuristic, dominance analysis can be of value.

EXPLORATORY ANALYSES OF MODERATED RELATIONSHIPS

Moderated relationships occur when the effects of one variable on another vary as a function of a third variable. For example, the impact of stress on anxiety might differ depending on how much social support individuals receive from significant others when dealing with that stress: Stress will have less of an impact on anxiety for people who have good support networks than on people with poor support networks. Chapter 3 described strategies that can be used to make a theoretical contribution, one of which is to *identify variables that moderate the effect of one variable on another*. In this section, we describe exploratory tools to assist you in thinking about moderated relationships. First, we describe mixture regression and then we revisit smoothers.

Mixture Regression

Suppose we postulate the somewhat mundane theoretical proposition that how much a couple argues about raising their children impacts their marital satisfaction. We wonder if there might be moderators for this effect, such that the effect is stronger for some groups or types of people than for others. What if we could conduct exploratory analyses in a dataset that would test for the presence of such moderation without even knowing the content of the moderator variable? And what if after determining that such an unknown moderator likely exists, we could classify people in the dataset into the groups or categories defined by that unknown moderator? Such information could be quite useful when trying to generate ideas about potential moderators. Mixture regression provides such information. For any given direct effect or set of direct effects in a dataset, regression mixture analysis provides information about (1) whether a moderator variable likely exists for the direct effect, (2) the number of categories the moderator variable likely has, and (3) which people in the dataset likely belong in which category. It is then up to you as a theorist to figure out the content of the moderator variable(s) and the content of the categories based on this information.

Regression mixture analysis belongs to a broader class of statistical methods known as mixture modeling (Kim, Vermunt, Bakk, Jaki, & Van Horn, 2016; Muthén, 2001b; Wedel & Desarbo, 1994). However, regression mixture analysis has special qualities, so we focus exclusively on it. The statistical theory underlying regression mixture analysis is quite complex, but we can provide a sense of it here. Suppose that in the population you are studying there is, in fact, a meaningful moderator variable for the relationship you are targeting. This means there are segments in the population with regression or path coefficients that differ in value for the causal effect. For example, suppose that, unbeknownst to us, there is, in fact, a gender difference in the effect of arguing about childrearing on marital satisfaction such that the effect is stronger for wives than it is for husbands. If we were to analyze the data as a whole ignoring gender, the resulting regression analysis would mix these two heterogeneous segments together and, as a result, obscure the true value of the path/regression coefficient for husbands as well as for wives separately. Such an analysis typically will yield a value that is near the average of the true values of the two coefficients. To be sure, if the two groups have the same coefficient value (i.e., there is no moderation), then no harm is done. However, if the two segments are heterogeneous in the values of their path/regression coefficients, then ignoring this heterogeneity can be misleading.

Statisticians have developed indices of the likelihood that the values in one's data for an outcome variable (in this case, marital satisfaction) would result if a specified causal dynamic (i.e., a model) is operating and people are randomly sampled from a population where the model is true. For example, we can calculate such a likelihood for (1) a model that assumes marital satisfaction is impacted by how much couples argue about childrearing *and* there are no underlying segment differences in the strength of this effect and (2) a model that assumes marital satisfaction is impacted by how much couples argue about childrearing *and* there are exactly two segments in the population who differ in the strength of this effect. We can also calculate the likelihood of the data occurring for (3) a model that assumes there are three segments with differing coefficients, (4) a model that assumes there are four such segments, and so on up to as many segments as we desire. The likelihood indices are called *log likelihoods* in the statistical literature because they involve calculating logarithms of the model likelihoods, but at their core, the indices are likelihoods. In regression mixture analysis, we perform this task for models that assume differing numbers of segments and then examine the (log) likelihoods for each of the models. We choose the model that has the highest likelihood of producing the data and that is most parsimonious. If the model with the highest likelihood is a model that posits no heterogeneity (the one-segment model), then one concludes there is no moderator variable. If the highest likelihood is for the model that posits two heterogeneous segments, then one assumes there are one or more moderator variables that differentiate these two segments. If the highest likelihood is for the model that posits the existence of three heterogeneous segments, then one assumes there is one or more moderator variables that differentiate these three segments; and so on. Once a final model is selected, the statistical theory allows us to classify individuals in the dataset into a given segment. The analyst can then use this classification to explore possible correlates of segment membership. As these correlates are isolated, the nature of plausible moderators emerge.

As an example, suppose we predict heavy smokers' motivation to quit smoking from two variables: (1) their overall personal attitude toward quitting smoking (reflected by individuals' perceived advantages and disadvantages of quitting) and (2) normative pressures from important others to quit smoking. Suppose each variable is measured on a 0 to 10 metric, with higher scores indicating higher motivation to quit, more positive personal attitudes toward quitting, and increased normative pressures to quit, respectively. The regression model (using sample notation) is

$$\text{Motivation} = a + b1 \text{ Attitudes} + b2 \text{ Norms} + e$$

Suppose we perform a regression analysis on the total sample and observe the following regression coefficients:

$$\text{Motivation} = 0.01 + 0.34 \text{ Attitudes} + 0.36 \text{ Norms}$$

These results suggest that both attitudes and norms contribute to the motivation to quit smoking and do so about equally. When we apply mixture regression analysis to the data, we find support for a three-segment model with the following regression coefficients:

$$\text{Segment 1: Motivation} = 0.01 + 0.71 \text{ Attitudes} + 0.01 \text{ Norms}$$
$$\text{Segment 2: Motivation} = 0.01 + 0.01 \text{ Attitudes} + 0.73 \text{ Norms}$$
$$\text{Segment 3: Motivation} = 0.02 + 0.32 \text{ Attitudes} + 0.33 \text{ Norms}$$

with 34% of the sample in the first segment, 31% of the sample in the second segment, and 35% of the sample in the third segment. A different narrative emerges than that for the total sample analysis. There is a sizeable segment of individuals for whom personal attitudes are the primary determinant of their motivation and for whom norms are irrelevant. There is also a sizeable segment of individuals for whom norms are the primary determinant of their motivation and for whom personal attitudes are irrelevant. Finally, about a third of the sample maps onto the narrative for the total sample where both attitudes and norms are coequal determinants of motivation to quit smoking. The total sample analysis mischaracterizes about two-thirds of the people in the sample. Clearly, there are one or more moderator variables that we need to bring into our theory to account for the results and that can differentiate the segments. The task of the theorist is to figure out what these moderator variables might be. Given these results, what would be your guesses?

There are several personality traits that reflect attention to and concern for what other people think about oneself, such as public self-consciousness and self-monitoring. As well, people with high self-esteem are often thought to be less concerned with what other people think about them. Might the three segments be differentiated on one or more of these variables? For example, perhaps people in Segment 1 (primarily attitudinal influence) score relatively low on public self-consciousness and self-monitoring and high on self-esteem; people in Segment 2 score relatively high on public self-consciousness and self-monitoring and low on self-esteem; and people in Segment 3 score moderately on all the measures. If our dataset included these measures, we could formally evaluate if this is the case. Or, suppose we found gender differences in segment membership, with males being more likely to be in Segment 1 than the other two segments. Would this be theoretically meaningful?

Regression mixture modeling is a powerful exploratory tool to help determine if there are potential moderators operating and, if there are, it provides an array of "clues" about what the moderator variables might be based on the patterning of the regression coefficients and correlates of segment membership. Regression mixture analysis is not for the statistically faint of heart, but it is a tool worth learning. An interesting application examining the effects of family resources on child academic outcomes is described in Van Horn and colleagues (2009). Desarbo, Jedidi, and Sinha (2001) use the framework in marketing to identify consumer segments with different personal values linked to product use. Ding (2006) presents an introductory application for educational settings. Regression mixture analysis is useful for theory construction because it can stimulate ideas about population heterogeneity for causal effects and it provides a means to gain insights into the bases of that heterogeneity.

Smoothers

Earlier, we introduced smoothers as a tool for assessing nonlinear effects for direct causes. Smoothers also can be used to explore the functional form of moderated effects, which, in turn, can stimulate theory construction. Suppose that we have already identified a moderated relationship we are interested in but that we want to explore it in more depth to gain a deeper understanding of it. As an example, suppose we are interested in the effect of the time that workers in manufacturing plants are allotted to complete their work on the quality of the products they produce: Less allotted time adversely affects product quality and more allotted time increases product quality. Suppose we have a theoretical hunch that the effect of allotted time on product quality varies as a function of gender. Using an exploratory dataset, we can calculate a smoother for these two variables separately for males and females, and then we can plot the smoothers on the same graph. Figure 11.5 presents a plot with separate smoothers for females (solid line) and males (dashed line). The quality of the work is on the y-axis (ranging from low to high) and the perceived time within which the worker feels he or she has to complete work on the product is on the x-axis. The figure reveals several interesting dynamics that might be the basis for theory construction.

First, the separation between the two lines at a given point on the X-axis reflects the gender difference in the mean quality of products produced at that point; that is, it is a conditional mean difference in the quality of work for males versus females at that particular point on X. The larger the separation, the larger the gender difference in the quality of work. Note that when the felt time pressure to finish a task is 15 minutes or less (which management of these particular manufacturing plants considers to be a fairly quick finish time), there are negligible gender differences in work quality because the lines are close to one another. However, at around 15 minutes, as the felt allotted time increases, the quality of work by females starts to exceed that of males, and increasingly so with more time. The smoothers suggest an interesting theory that implies the existence of a threshold point (15 minutes) below which gender differences in work quality are negligible but above which women produce increasingly higher quality work than men. Why might this be the case? Could such a trend operate more broadly? Can you build an interesting theory around this finding? As it turns out, research suggests that when men in manufacturing jobs have more time to finish their work, the quantity of their output tends to increase but the quality does not. By contrast, women in this same

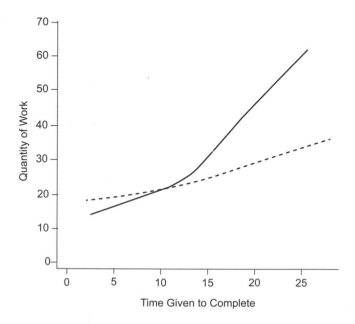

FIGURE 11.5. Time pressures and quality of work. Solid line, females; dashed line, males.

situation tend to improve the quality of their output rather than increase its quantity (Shurchkov, 2012). The analysis of the two smoothers on the same plot suggests interesting possibilities for theory construction.

Let's examine Figure 11.5 from a different perspective: namely, what the shape of the smoother is for females as compared to the shape of the smoother for males. In this case, there is a curvilinear relationship between time given to finish a job and work quality for women, with a relatively flat slope below 15 minutes but with a sharp acceleration in quality with more time after 15 minutes. For males, the same trend holds, with the acceleration in product quality after 15 minutes, but much less so.

These alternative ways of looking at the side-by-side smoothers provide insights into (1) the moderating dynamics of time pressure for the effects of gender on job performance or (2) the moderating effects of gender for the effects of time pressure on job performance. Either way, use of the smoothers can stimulate creative thinking about moderated relationships.

CLUSTER ANALYSIS

Another interesting exploratory tool for theory construction is *cluster analysis* (Everitt, Landau, Leese, & Stahl, 2011; King, 2014). In Chapter 3, we identified *constructing a meaningful typology or taxonomy* as a strategy for making a theoretical contribution. Cluster analysis is an exploratory strategy for doing so. This strategy can be viewed from many different perspectives, but some find it instructive to think of it as identifying "types of people." For this reason, it is sometimes referred to as a *person-centered framework*. In this section, we convey the spirit of cluster analysis initially by using a crude example that does not do justice to formal clustering algorithms but nonetheless provides a sense of what you end up with after performing a cluster analysis.

Suppose a researcher observes teachers and rates them on three dimensions: (1) how strict the teacher is, (2) the warmth of the teacher toward his or her students, and (3) the teacher's overall concern for his or her students. We can classify teachers as "low" or "high" on each of these three dimensions by using, say, a median split on each dimension. We then form all combinations of the dimensions, calculating the percentage of teachers in each group:

High on strictness, high on warmth, high on concern:	4%
High on strictness, high on warmth, low on concern:	4%
High on strictness, low on warmth, high on concern:	22%
High on strictness, low on warmth, low on concern:	21%
Low on strictness, high on warmth, high on concern:	22%
Low on strictness, high on warmth, low on concern:	2%
Low on strictness, low on warmth, high on concern:	3%
Low on strictness, low on warmth, low on concern:	22%

Note that four major teacher configurations occur, with the other configurations being relatively rare. In the language of cluster analysis, each configuration represents a *cluster,* with teachers in a particular cluster being similar to one another on the three dimensions but distinct from teachers in other clusters. As examples, the last configuration (low strictness, low warmth, low concern) includes teachers who might be said to be disengaged. Teachers in the configuration of high strictness, low warmth, and low concern are authoritarian teachers. Based on this cluster analysis, we might focus theorizing on the most prominent "teacher types" and construct a theory about how these particular types are related to student outcomes. We also might theorize about factors associated with teacher membership in a particular cluster, such as teacher gender or teacher ethnicity. The other clusters may be of less interest because they occur so infrequently, but sometimes we might be interested in them and theorize accordingly.

Formal cluster analytic methods do not use median splits or artificial dichotomies as we did above; doing so discards useful information. A variety of algorithms are available to classify people into clusters, but all the methods share a common goal: namely, to cluster together people who are similar on the target variables but distinct from people in other clusters. Some algorithms assign everyone to a cluster, but other algorithms only do so if the data justify it; that is, there can be outliers who do not quite fit into any grouping. Still other algorithms classify all individuals into a group/cluster but also provide a probability estimate of cluster membership for each cluster. Figure 11.6 shows an example of a cluster plot from what is known as a trimmed mean cluster analysis (Garcia-Escudero, Gordaliza, Matran, & Mayo-Iscar, 2010). For this example, we analyzed two variables focused on political ideology: (1) the extent to which individuals value societal-level freedom without government regulation and interference and (2) the extent to which individuals value a government emphasis on equality, that is, equal

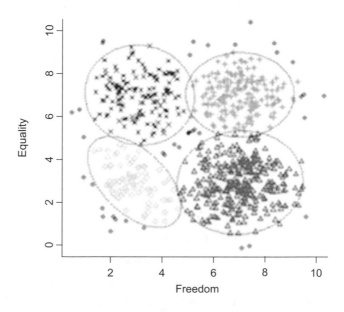

FIGURE 11.6. Cluster plot.

opportunity and equal access to resources. The analysis yielded four clusters. The cluster plot has an ellipse around individuals in the same cluster in the two-dimensional space. Outliers who do not fit into clusters are outside the ellipses.

The cluster structure is well articulated, showing good separation between clusters. Ideally, within-cluster standard deviations on each variable are small. One cluster places high value on equality and low value on freedom, which roughly maps onto communistic orientations. A second cluster places low value on equality and high value on freedom, which roughly fits a capitalist orientation. A third cluster places high value on freedom and high value on equality, which fits with socialism. The fourth cluster places low value on equality and low value on freedom, which fits with fascist orientations. This cluster analysis suggests a typology of political ideology that accounts for major political systems in the world.

Cluster analysis has many possible applications. Researchers have analyzed consumer values to identify consumer segments; studying styles of students; clustering of gene expressions for understanding the biological bases of behavior; policy orientations of countries; stereotypes of different ethnic groups; types of abusive men; clustering of depressive symptoms; clustering of political candidates; and types of homeless people, to name but a few applications. Cluster analysis can be applied to binary variables, categorical variables, quantitative variables, or mixtures of them.

One also can apply cluster analysis to the same variable measured longitudinally to identify patterns of change over time. For example, patients might receive cognitive-behavioral therapy for anxiety and be classified as either "responders" (improved significantly) or "nonresponders" (did not improve much) at an immediate posttest. At 6- and 12-month follow-ups, the patient's level of improvement from baseline is again measured, and the patient is again classified as either a "responder" or "nonresponder" at that particular time point. This yields eight clusters of patients:

- Cluster 1: Responder at posttest, responder at 6 months, responder at 12 months
- Cluster 2: Responder at posttest, responder at 6 months, nonresponder at 12 months
- Cluster 3: Responder at posttest, nonresponder at 6 months, responder at 12 months
- Cluster 4: Responder at posttest, nonresponder at 6 months, nonresponder at 12 months
- Cluster 5: Nonresponder at posttest, responder at 6 months, responder at 12 months
- Cluster 6: Nonresponder at posttest, responder at 6 months, nonresponder at 12 months
- Cluster 7: Nonresponder at posttest, nonresponder at 6 months, responder at 12 months
- Cluster 8: Nonresponder at posttest, nonresponder at 6 months, nonresponder at 12 months

Cluster 1 represents patients who respond to treatment and maintain that positive response for the ensuing year. Cluster 8 represents patients who do not respond to treatment and remain that way over the ensuing year. Cluster 5 represents patients who are "delayed responders"; that is, they did not respond until 6 months after treatment, but ultimately they did so and maintained that response thereafter. Cluster 4 are those patients who respond to treatment but who with time experience loss of treatment effects. And so on. Of interest are the percentage of patients in each cluster, the identification of variables that predict cluster membership, and the identification of nonanxiety outcomes that might be associated with cluster membership. In a randomized controlled trial that includes a treatment and control (treatment-as-usual) condition, one also can test for group differences in the type of change patterns over time. For example, one can test if the treatment group has a greater percentage of patients in Cluster 1 than the control group and a smaller percentage of patients in Cluster 8 than the control group. This example used data based on a small number of binary variables measured over time, but it readily extends to the case of continuous variables measured in a longitudinal context (see Lackner et al., 2018).

Cluster analysis can also be used to build upon extant theories about "types" of people. A popular personality theory distinguishes two personality types, Type A and Type B (Friedman, 1996; Smith & Gallo, 2001). Type A people are individuals who are competitive, highly organized, ambitious, impatient, and anxious. Type B people live for the moment, are relatively relaxed, are less organized, and tend to be worry free. Research has linked these two personality types to a variety of health outcomes, including heart attacks and coronary disease (Smith & Gallo, 2001). People with Type A personality, for example, are more likely to have heart attacks than those with Type B personality. (Which type better describes you?) Suppose we conduct an exploratory study in which we measure competition, organization, ambition, impulsivity, and anxiety and then subject the measures to a cluster analysis. Would the two personality types emerge in the analysis? Or would other personality types (clusters) suggest themselves? If so, perhaps the theory can be augmented accordingly. What percentage of the population would fall into each cluster? How would the additional cluster types relate to health outcomes? How might this affect your theorizing about the link between personality and coronary disease? Suppose we measured an additional dimension that is not normally included in the Type A versus Type B distinction, namely, the tendency to "hold in" or suppress one's feelings. How would this dimension integrate into the personality types as reflected by a cluster analysis? How might this affect your theorizing?

Yet another possibility for theoretical innovation is to choose a well-known measure that has distinct subscales and then cluster analyze the subscales to identify people with different subscale profiles. As examples, social support is often measured with four subscales: (1) emotional support, (2) tangible support, (3) informational support, and (4) companionship support. Measures of risk-taking propensities often use four subscales: (1) social risk taking, (2) physical risk taking, (3) financial risk taking, and (4) ethical risk taking. Depression is often measured in terms of (1) affect, (2) cognitions, (3) somatization, and (4) apathy. What would be the results of cluster analyses on these subscales? The list of constructs with subdimensions is extensive, and theory construction surrounding emergent clusters or profiles for them might be fruitful.

We could describe other innovative uses of cluster analysis, but the gist of our discussion should be clear. When you have multiple variables and it is theoretically reasonable to think in terms of profiles across the variables, a cluster analysis may be a good source of ideas for theory.

Recent approaches to cluster analysis called *latent profile analysis* (which is applied to continuous variables) and *latent class analysis* (which is applied to binary or categorical variables) use statistical theory based on mixture modeling (Lubke & Muthén, 2005; Muthén & Muthén, 2000; Vermunt & Magidson, 2002). These methods are distinct from traditional cluster analytic methods and have the advantage of being part of the broader framework of structural equation modeling (SEM), which facilitates analyses linking the clusters to external variables.

FACTOR ANALYSIS

Factor analysis is a well-known analytic method used for many purposes. Our focus here is on the use of factor analysis to identify higher-order constructs that underlie a set of variables and that can be of theoretical interest in their own right. In Chapter 3, two strategies mentioned for making a theoretical contribution were *to clarify, refine, or challenge the conceptualization of a variable/concept* and *to create a new variable or constellation of variables that are of theoretical interest*. The present section bears on both.

Factor analysis is somewhat misunderstood. It was originally developed by psychologist Charles Spearman (1863–1945) to explain the correlations among student performance on different aptitude tests, such as tests of math ability, verbal ability, general reasoning, and spatial ability. Spearman, observing that scores on the tests were often moderately correlated, hypothesized that these correlations were due to a shared common cause, namely, general intelligence, also known as *g*. To be sure, Spearman recognized that each test has unique variance unrelated to general intelligence and that is specific to the type of ability being assessed. However, the reasons the tests are correlated, Spearman argued, is because they share *g* as a common cause.

Spearman justified the existence of a general intelligence construct based on studies that showed a single unmeasured latent variable or "factor" (presumably *g*) could indeed explain the correlations between the ability tests. Here is the logic that was used. Suppose we administer four different ability tests to a group of students: (1) a math ability test, (2) a verbal ability test, (3) a test of general reasoning, and (4) a spatial ability test. The correlations between the variables are shown in Table 11.3. Suppose that a single unmeasured variable is, in fact, a common cause of each measured variable and that this unmeasured variable is the sole source of the correlation between them. If we could measure this latent variable and then partial it out from each of the measured variables, all the correlations between the measured variables would reduce to zero. In this sense, the unmeasured variable explains their correlations. It turns out that if there is such a single "factor" underlying the observed measures that accounts for their correla-

TABLE 11.3. Correlations between Variables

	Math ability	Verbal ability	Reasoning	Spatial ability
Math ability (MA)	1.00			
Verbal ability (VA)	0.72	1.00		
Reasoning (R)	0.63	0.56	1.00	
Spatial ability (SA)	0.45	0.40	0.30	1.00

tions, then the correlation matrix between the measured variables should show certain regularities. For example, it can be shown mathematically that the ratio of the correlation between math ability and reasoning divided by the correlation between math ability and spatial ability (0.63/0.45) should equal the ratio of the correlation between verbal ability and reasoning divided by the correlation between verbal ability and spatial ability (0.56/0.40). This is the case in Table 11.3—0.63/0.45 = 0.56/0.40 = 1.40. The technical details of why this regularity should exist need not concern us here. However, the way a single-factor model is tested is to determine whether the predicted regularities by a one-factor model are reasonably approximated by the data.

Sometimes a single underlying factor cannot account for the correlations between variables. If this is the case, there may be two common cause "factors," not just one, that impact the measured variables and that exclusively shape the correlations between them. If we could measure the two unmeasured factors and partial them out of the measured variables, all of the correlations between the measured variables would reduce to zero. It turns out that a two-factor model also predicts regularities in the patterning of correlations between the measured variables and that these are distinct from a single-factor model. The two-factor model, like the one-factor model, is tested by determining whether the predicted regularities are reasonably approximated by the data. The same is true of a three-factor model, a four-factor model, and so on. By testing each of these models, we can determine the minimum number of factors needed to adequately account for the correlations between the variables.

Once we have determined the number of factors, we need to figure out what the factors represent. In Spearman's case, where a single-factor model reasonably accounted for the data, he felt the underlying factor was g. However, matters are not always so straightforward. For example, studies of posttraumatic stress (PTS) in soldiers returning from war have documented a wide range of experienced symptoms associated with PTS. Some symptoms co-occur with one another; hence, there are correlations between them. Factor analyses of the symptoms have suggested four factors underlying them that can reasonably account for the correlations. What do these four factors represent?

A useful by-product of the mathematics of factor analysis is that one can estimate the correlation or strength of association between each unmeasured factor and each measured variable. For example, one factor in PTS studies tends to correlate highly with symptoms like having distressing and unwanted memories of the traumatic events, having vivid nightmares about the events, and experiencing flashbacks. A second factor correlates highly with symptoms of avoiding activities, places, and people that might bring back memories of the trauma. A third factor correlates highly with symptoms associated with losing interest in positive activities, feeling distant from others, and experiencing difficulties having positive feelings. The fourth factor correlates highly with symptoms associated with difficulty sleeping, feeling irritable, quickly losing one's temper, having concentration difficulties, and feeling constantly on-guard. After careful consideration of these correlational patterns, theorists have concluded that the four factors represent generalized proclivities for (1) reexperience of the traumatic events, (2) avoidance of the events, (3) emotional numbing, and (4) hyperarousal.

Armed with these general factors, one can then build a theory surrounding them rather than having to focus on all of the individual symptoms per se. One can ask, for example, what social consequences are associated with each of the factors as well as what causes one factor to dominate in some war veterans but not in others. Not only does the factor analysis refine our conceptualization of PTS symptoms, but we also can bring the identified factors into a theoretical network and study those factors in their own right.

Parenthetically, when relating the four factors to a future outcome (e.g., job performance, marital adjustment), it might be interesting to apply dominance analysis to gain perspectives on their importance hierarchy. Or one could use smoothers to determine if the relationships of the four factors to the outcome are nonlinear. Or one could use quantile regression to determine if the effects of the four factors on the outcome vary as a function of where on the outcome distribution one looks. Or one could apply mixture regression to the direct effects to explore the possibility of segment heterogeneity. By combining the exploratory tools discussed in this chapter, rich theories can result that provide novel insights into complex phenomena.

BIG DATA, DATA MINING, AND MACHINE LEARNING

Occasionally you may find yourself in situations where you have one or more outcomes you want to understand, a large number of possible explanatory variables (perhaps from a secondary dataset), and little theory to guide you on the choice of explanatory variables that can be the focus of your theory. You would like to conduct exploratory analyses to identify empirically the most promising constructs. In our view, it is best to avoid this scenario to the extent possible. Instead, you should read the relevant literature about the topic, conduct qualitative research on it (if the topic is amenable to such research), think long and hard about the variables in your dataset, and then try to generate conceptual logic models for purposes of choosing a subset of explanatory variables. However, if you want the additional vantage point of data-driven suggestions for promising explanatory variables, we discuss possible approaches here.

Sometimes you will be in situations where you have data with a large number of variables coupled with a large sample size. In other cases, you will have data with a large number of variables but a small sample size, even to the point where the number of variables may far exceed the number of cases. The scenario of many predictors with small sample sizes is called *high dimensionality* or the *curse of dimensionality*. This scenario will be our primary focus. The social sciences have struggled with the curse of dimensionality for decades. Recently, advances in solving the problem have been made in the field of artificial intelligence and subareas within it known as *big data, data mining,* and *machine learning.* These overlapping domains have broader implications for theory construction per se, so we first comment briefly on them to sensitize you to their possibilities in this regard.

Recent advances in technology have led to unprecedented opportunities to collect extremely large amounts of data for processing and analysis. Sources of such "big data" include genome mapping, search behavior on the Internet, Facebook postings, text messaging, Twitter content, and geospatial data sources, to name but a few. In some cases, the amount of information in the datasets is staggering. Facebook, for example, maintains an average of about 150 megabytes of information about each of its two billion users; the 1,000 Genomes Project has about 200 terabytes of data about genetic variation in humans (Pearl & Mackenzie, 2018). As we seek to answer questions using such "big data," the development of effective strategies for data mining has taken center stage. One such strategy is machine learning.

At a general level, the logic of machine learning is simple. Suppose you seek to "teach" a computer (the machine) to recognize faces of people who walk into stores from images recorded on a store camera at the front door. You want the computer to encode the face of each person and then compare it against a database of faces to determine if the person has been at the store before. You first provide the computer with algorithms to encode and identify if the event on the camera is a person walking into the store and then how to locate that person's face. You also provide algorithms for the computer to encode cues from the face and then compare those cues against a database of faces for purposes of facial recognition. These steps are called the *training phase* of machine learning. After being "trained" (i.e., programmed) with these algorithms, the computer is put into action. While in the field, the machine receives input (an image from the store camera) and generates output (the face is a match or not a match with the database) based on intermediate steps (noting the object the camera is seeing is a person, locating the face, encoding the cues, and checking the database). This is called the *testing phase.* Sometimes the computer will accomplish its task correctly, and sometimes it will make an error. With machine learning, we seek to teach the computer to decipher when an error has occurred and then have the computer change its algorithm so that the error will not occur in the future. In essence, the machine "learns" from its successes and its mistakes. Often, such learning requires human supervision, but it also can occur independent of human input, reflecting what in artificial intelligence is called *deep learning* (Pearl & Mackenzie, 2018). Over time and with enough experience, the machine becomes proficient, potentially exceeding what a human is capable of in terms of speed and accuracy.

Machines can perform many types of tasks in such contexts. These tasks include pattern recognition, classification, pattern association (relating one pattern to another pattern), and prediction. At essence, however, data mining and machine learning approaches formulate prediction models rather than models or theories aimed at explanation. Some striking innovations have resulted from these prediction models, such as self-driving cars, search strategies used by search engines, spam filtering in e-mails, speech recognition, and medical advances associated with genetic mapping, to name but a few. All the same, the focus of theory is explanation, an enterprise that extends well beyond algorithm-driven prediction associated with big data, data mining, and machine learning. To be sure, prediction often leads to explanatory insight. For example, data mining can help refine the questions we ask and reveal patterns that spark new ideas and insights. However, those looking for big data, data mining, and machine learning to *explain* complex phenomena may ultimately be disappointed. Eminent artificial intelligence scientist Judea Pearl has been a strong advocate of what he considers the next generation of artificial intelligence, namely, teaching machines how to engage in causal reasoning and, ultimately, to have free will and agency (Pearl & Mackenzie, 2018). He views current big data, data mining, and machine learning as merely a first step rather than the pièce de résistance for building intelligent machines.

The more general point we emphasize here is that big data, data mining, and machine learning ultimately can be a source of idea generation as new and complex prediction algorithms are derived and as machines modify those algorithms in the machine learning process. Algorithm development requires careful attention to minute details and can lead to insights of phenomena along the way. As machines learn and adapt to successes and mistakes in the context of deep learning, we may actually learn useful information from the machines.

Although explanation is not its focus, modern data mining methods have evolved to help focus attention on variables that are potentially relevant to an outcome variable when one is faced with a large number of candidate predictors in high-dimensionality scenarios. Data mining perspectives on variable selection in such contexts focus on two processes, (1) variable screening and (2) variable selection. (In the data mining literature, variables often are called *features*.) *Variable screening* (also called *filtering*) reduces the number of explanatory/predictor variables to a "workable" number prior to selecting variables that are to be included in a formal prediction model. *Variable selection* chooses the final set of variables for the prediction model, after variable screening has taken place. Sometimes, the two tasks are combined so that both screening and selection occur simultaneously in one step.

There is overlap between the data mining methods that have evolved in artificial intelligence and predictor selection strategies developed by statisticians for the social sciences. However, unique approaches to the curse of dimensionality have been proposed in artificial intelligence that may be profitably used by social scientists. As an example, consider an approach offered by Cai, Tsay, and Chen (2009). Their approach uses linear models, which, of course, are widely used in the social sciences. Suppose one has 50 possible predictors to choose from but a sample size of only 200 in the dataset. Setting aside sample-size considerations for the moment and focusing purely on prediction, we can approach the identification of the best subset of predictors by computing all possible linear regressions (e.g., all possible models with two predictors, all possible models with three predictors, all possible models with four predictors, and so on) and then choosing the most parsimonious model that achieves the highest level of prediction when applied to a validation sample, much like traditional cross-validation studies in the social sciences. However, with 50 predictors, there are $2^{50} - 1$ possible linear models to compare with each other, which yields billions of comparisons. This approach is unworkable. Social scientists in such scenarios sometimes resort to stepwise regression or variants of it, but the curse of dimensionality usually undermines the use of these approaches, as do shortcomings in the methods themselves. Another approach is to screen variables solely on the basis of their zero-order correlations with the outcome, but this ignores variable redundancy in the predictors.

Cai and colleagues' (2009) suggest a solution that divides the predictors into non-overlapping smaller groups, say, seven groups of seven predictors each, except for one group that has eight predictors. Assignment of predictors to groups can be either random or theory based. For a given set of seven predictors, there are 2^7 or 128 different model combinations, which is workable from a "compute-all-possible-regressions" perspective. Many software packages have efficient algorithms for evaluating all possible linear models with ten predictors or less that use algorithms that include well-reasoned penalty functions for model complexity. For each group of predictors, all possible linear regressions are computed, and the "winning" model is identified for each group. The predictors from each of these winning models are pooled into a new predictor pool, a pool that is inevitably smaller than the original pool by virtue of this variable screening process. The new predictor pool is then subjected to the same process; that is, the predictors are grouped into smaller groups, and then each group is evaluated as before to identify the "winning model" for that group. The predictors from each of these new "winning models" are then combined into yet another new predictor pool, with the process being repeated over and over until no new variables are added to the predictor pool. The process is repeated across multiple iterations until the resulting predictor pools consistently overlap with one another. These are the final variables that can then be worked with for purposes of theory construction. Cai and colleagues describe variations of this approach and show that it outperforms a number of more computationally demanding strategies that are widely used in data mining contexts. A concrete example is provided on our companion website at *www.theory-construction.com*.

Other clever strategies for variable screening and variable selection in data mining exist (e.g., the one covariate at a time method; decision trees), but we do not consider them here (see Brick, Koffer, Gerstorf, & Ram, 2018; Cai et al., 2009; Chudik, Kapetanios, & Pesaran, 2018). Again, most of these methods place a premium on prediction over explanation, and none can guarantee selection of the optimal prediction model, only an approximation to it. Parenthetically, some of these methods have been adapted for mediator screening in mediation analyses (see Serang, Jacobucci, Brimhall, & Grimm, 2017). For extensions of SEM to machine learning contexts, see Buckler and Hennig-Thurau (2008).

The big data and data mining fields are changing perspectives on the way some scientists think about theory and data. Consider the comments of Brown and Botstein (1999):

> Exploration means looking around, observing, describing and mapping undiscovered territory, not testing theories or models. The goal is to discover things we neither knew nor

expected, and to see relationships and connections among the elements, whether previously suspected or not. It follows that this process is not driven by hypotheses and should be as model-independent as possible. We should use the unprecedented experimental opportunities that the genome sequences provide to take a fresh, comprehensive and open-minded look at every question in biology. If we succeed, we can expect that many of the new models that emerge will defy conventional wisdom. (p. 36)

Not all scientists share this viewpoint, advocating instead for the importance of theory-driven data collection and analysis (Mazzocchi, 2015; Pearl & Mackenzie, 2018). Having said that, the fields of big data, data mining, and machine learning clearly have elevated the role of exploratory analyses in science.

CHANCE RESULTS

Data analysis as presented in this chapter focuses on idea generation and theory construction, not on formal theory testing. As one approaches exploratory analyses, care must be exercised about treating the data as validating theory. It is perfectly fine to design, conduct, and publish exploratory studies for theory construction purposes. However, formal theory tests generally require collecting data on independent samples. To be sure, the extent to which this is necessary is somewhat controversial, with Bayesians being more open to accepting post hoc explanations based on the data from which those explanations were derived (see Chapter 15). However, most scientists would agree with economist Gregg Easterbrook (1999), who warns: "Torture numbers enough and they'll confess to anything" (p. 42). Theory construction and idea generation are a central part of the scientific process. Although there is nothing wrong with using data to assist that process, ultimately statistics do not generate theory—theorists do.

When conducting exploratory analyses for idea generation, some methodologists argue for invoking controls for chance effects. For example, they suggest using specialized statistical adjustments (e.g., Bonferroni corrections) if one conducts multiple contrasts so as to control for inflated Type I error rates across contrasts, controls that usually demand large sample sizes. Other methodologists argue that such controls should not be used in exploratory contexts; if anything, they state, one might even consider using somewhat looser significance standards because, after all, we are just trying to get ideas and stimulate our thinking, not assert theory validity. How one approaches this matter depends, in part, on the goals of the research and on the conclusions one seeks to make after analyzing the data.

Whichever orientation you adopt, you should be cautious about overfitting data and about making too much of what could be chance effects. If a result surprises you, approach that result with healthy scientific skepticism by thinking about other ways you might analyze your data to further affirm or disconfirm the result. Statisticians encourage what they call *sensitivity analyses*. These analyses can take different forms, but one of them involves analyzing the same question in data using a variety of statistical approaches, each of which might make different assumptions or provide different vantage points on the answer to the question. One then determines if conclusions are "sensitive to" the method of analysis. Try to triangulate wherever possible; that is, approach a conclusion from multiple perspectives and vantage points.

Throughout this chapter, we have liberally associated causality with correlational analytic methods. We fully recognize that this approach is not always justifiable, but again, our focus is on idea generation, not rigorous causal inference. Having said that, you should always be thinking about confounds and alternative explanations to the trends you observe in your exploratory analyses.

SUMMARY AND CONCLUDING COMMENTS

Just as qualitative researchers allow theory to emerge from data, so too can quantitative researchers. A wealth of powerful and flexible statistical tools can be used for purposes of generating ideas and constructing theories in the context of exploratory analyses. Every method described in this chapter is easy to apply (go to our companion website at *www.theory-construction.com*). If your theory is already reasonably developed, you can pursue exploratory analyses to help you be more innovative for portions of that theory. For example, for direct effects, you might consider using smoothers to gain deeper insights into the functional form linking cause and effect. You might use quantile regression to explore direct effects at the lower and upper ends of an outcome distribution rather than restricting your thinking to the middle of that distribution. For multiple direct effects, you might use dominance analysis to help you theorize about importance hierarchies. For moderated relationships, you can use regression mixture modeling to sensitize yourself to possible population heterogeneity surrounding causal effects and the need to incorporate moderator variables into your theory to accommodate that heterogeneity. You also can plot multiple smoothers on the same graph to better delineate and elucidate the functional form of moderation. Cluster analysis is a person-centered approach that encourages you to think theoretically in terms of different types of people (or entities). You can then theorize about why people are the type they are as well as the implications and consequences of being one type of person versus another. Factor analysis can be used to explore dimensionalizing constructs or introducing new constructs (factors) into a theory. Finally, big data, data mining, and machine learning approaches have opened up new possibilities for variable identification and variable combinations in theory construction. When faced with scenarios where you want empirical guidance on possible variables to focus your theory on, approaches for variable screening and variable selection from these literatures might be helpful.

SUGGESTED READINGS

Brown, T. A. (2015). *Confirmatory factor analysis for applied research* (2nd ed.). New York: Guilford Press.

—A solid introduction to confirmatory factor analysis, with a discussion of exploratory factor analysis as well.

Everitt, B. S., Landau, S., Leese, M., & Stahl, D. (2011). *Cluster analysis.* New York: Wiley.

—A classic book on the basics of cluster analysis.

Fabrigar, L., & Wegener, D. (2012). *Exploratory factor analysis.* New York: Oxford University Press.

—A good conceptual introduction to exploratory factor analysis.

Grömping, U. (2015). Variable importance in regression models. *WIREs Computational Statistics, 7,* 137–152.

—A good review of methods for analyzing variable importance in regression; a bit technical.

Han, J., Kamber, M., & Pei, J. (2012). *Data mining: Concepts and techniques.* New York: Elsevier.

—A good introduction to data mining and analysis of big data. For a more social-science-oriented but less comprehensive resource, see Attewell, P. A., & Monaghan, D. (2015). *Data mining for the social sciences: An introduction.* Oakland: University of California Press. Journals devoted to data mining and machine learning include *Data Mining and Knowledge Discovery, IEEE Transactions on Knowledge and Data Engineering,* and *Knowledge and Information Systems.* Judea Pearl's and Dana Mackenzie's book, *The Book of Why,* is a gem.

Hao, L., & Naiman, D. (2001). *Quantile regression.* Newbury Park, CA: SAGE.

—A good, brief introduction to quantile regression.

Johnson, J., & LeBreton, J. (2004). History and use of relative importance indices in organizational research. *Organizational Research Methods, 7,* 238–257.

—A good review of methods for analyzing variable importance in regression.

Koenker, R. (2005). *Quantile regression.* Cambridge, UK: Cambridge University Press.

—A classic and thorough reference for quantile regression.

Wilcox, R. (2012). *Modern statistics for the social and behavioral sciences: A practical introduction.* Boca Raton, FL: CRC Press.

—An introductory treatment of robust methods of analysis.

Wilcox, R. (2017). *Introduction to robust estimation and hypothesis testing* (4th ed.). San Diego, CA: Academic Press.

—A somewhat more technical discussion of smoothers and quantile regression as well as robust statistics more generally.

KEY TERMS

conditional mean (p. 310)

linear probability model (p. 311)

smoother (p. 312)

smoothed scatterplot (p. 312)

binary outcome smoother (p. 313)

overfitting (p. 314)

quantile regression (p. 315)

quantile (p. 315)

EXERCISES

Exercises to Reinforce Concepts

1. What is a conditional mean? In what sense is regression analysis a method for analyzing conditional means?

2. For the analysis of direct effects, what are the advantages of examining relationships using smoothers? In what ways are smoothers useful for idea generation and theory construction?

3. What is overfitting? Why is it bad?

4. What is the difference between a quantile, a percentile, and a decile?

5. What is quantile regression? When would you use it? What are its advantages? In what ways is it useful for idea generation and theory construction?

6. What is dominance analysis? When would you use it? What are its advantages? In what ways is it useful for idea generation and theory construction?

7. What is regression mixture modeling? When would you use it? What are its advantages? In what ways is it useful for idea generation and theory construction?

8. How can you use smoothers for the analysis of moderation? What are the advantages of doing so? In what ways is it useful for idea generation and theory construction?

9. Describe the basic logic of cluster analysis. In what ways is it useful for idea generation and theory construction? How might you apply it in a longitudinal study?

10. Describe the basic logic of factor analysis. What is its primary purpose? In what ways is it useful for idea generation and theory construction?

11. Characterize the general framework and logic of machine learning.

12. What is the difference between variable screening and variable selection? Discuss approaches to each, including their strengths and weaknesses.

13. When conducting exploratory analyses, it is good to invoke statistical controls for chance effects due to multiple contrasts. Do you agree or disagree with this statement? Why?

Exercises to Apply Concepts

1. Pick a topic and identify some variables you would be interested in studying. Design an exploratory study that you might conduct to help you generate novel ideas and construct theory. Describe your population, the variables you would measure, the kinds of questions you would ask of the data, and the data analyses you would pursue.

2. Find a study in the literature that uses structural equation modeling in a way that the model includes a direct effect between two continuous variables. For each such direct effect in the model, imagine if you applied a smoother to it. What kind of functional forms might you expect? Why?

3. Find a study in the literature of interest to you that used multiple regression analysis. Now think about what you might find if you analyzed it using quantile regression. What quantiles would you focus on and why? What different conclusions might you reach, or do you think the conclusions would be the same? Explain your answer.

4. Find a study in the literature that used cluster analysis. Summarize it.

5. Using a database you have access to, try applying some of the techniques described in this chapter to it.

12

Historically Influential Systems of Thought

A hunch is creativity trying to tell you something.
—Frank Capra (1956)

There are many ways of thinking about the world, and we have tapped into only a few of them. In this chapter, we briefly describe historically influential systems of thought that large numbers of social scientists have used to theorize about diverse phenomena. We also consider some lesser known but still influential thinking strategies that might be of use as you approach the theory construction process. We advocate what is sometimes known as *meta-triangulation* in theory construction, or the building of theories from the perspective of multiple paradigms (Lewis & Grimes, 1999). After introducing you to a dozen or so different systems of thought, we encourage you to think about the phenomena in which you are interested from each perspective. That is, think about the phenomena through the lenses of different thought systems and see what new ideas and insights result. To be sure, not all of the systems will "work" for you, but even if only a few do, you will be that much further ahead.

We do not describe the different systems in depth; doing so would require book-length manuscripts on each topic. Instead, we expose you to the spirit of each framework. As you become more familiar with the frameworks in the course of your studies, they may take on greater or lesser import in your scientific efforts. There are ardent critics of each framework, including some who would be appalled that we even mention a given framework. Similarly, some critics will feel that we have left out an important framework. Whatever the case, we believe that each framework has something of value to contribute.

The frameworks are an eclectic group that can be organized in multiple ways. We grouped together one set of frameworks under the general rubric of "grand theories" as discussed in sociology and anthropology. These frameworks include materialism, structuralism, functionalism, symbolic interactionism, and evolutionary perspectives, along with a critical commentary of these grand theories from the perspective of postmodernism. Next, we discuss frameworks that draw heavily on metaphors. These include neural networks and systems theory. We then consider frameworks that emphasize the analysis of change followed by two psychological frameworks. We conclude with the discussion of frameworks inspired by methodological innovations, namely, multilevel modeling and person-centered theorizing.

Some of the frameworks are more popular in some disciplines than others. For example, materialism is more widely used to analyze phenomena in sociology and anthropology than in psychology. This should not, however, deter you from using a framework, no matter what your discipline. Also, some of the frameworks are dated, their dominance in a given discipline having waned with time. This, too, should not deter you from using the framework as a way of possibly generating new perspectives and ideas about the phenomena you are studying.

GRAND THEORIES

In the fields of anthropology and sociology, distinctions often are made between grand theories and middle-range theories (Mills, 1959). Although the characterizations of these two approaches vary, grand theories are seen as comprehensive, inclusive theories of human behavior and society, whereas middle-range theories are more focused accounts of specific phenomena (but for an alternative characterization, see Alford, 1998). Most of the social sciences currently operate at the level of middle-range theories, but there are notable grand theories that theorists often draw upon in formulating their middle-range theories. The present section considers a selection of these grand theories: materialism, structuralism, functionalism, symbolic interactionism, and evolutionary perspectives. We also discuss postmodernism, though it certainly is not a grand theory in the tradition of the other frameworks. Rather, it is a critical commentary on some of the fundamental assumptions underlying the grand theories.

Materialism

Materialist theories emphasize the analysis of human behavior and social institutions from the perspective of the material aspects of society. This approach has its roots in the work of Karl Marx and Friedrich Engels. Although Marxist theory has been used primarily to motivate political ideologies and political analysis, it also has been used as a form of scientific analysis (Plattner, 1989). Marxist frameworks emphasize the concepts of history, ideology, and the analysis of inequalities in social power and wealth. To understand human behavior, one examines the types of ideologies that people have held and how these ideologies are shaped by inequalities in wealth and the means of producing wealth. A materialist pays careful attention to who creates the products that society values and how they go about doing so, how products are converted into wealth, and how the wealth is distributed among different segments of society.

According to Marx, economic inequalities often are structured along social lines that ultimately define socioeconomic classes. In capitalist societies, wage workers comprise one class and capitalists another. In materialistic models, class distinctions also are extended to other groups, such as men versus women and the elderly versus youth, based primarily on their control over the means of production. Materialism involves careful analysis of the historical context in which these relations emerge and change over time, as well as those aspects of ideology, production, and class that have remained stable. Also of importance is identifying the ideological means by which members of the lower class have accepted their positions and by which members of the upper class justify their high status. These systems of beliefs, also called *hegemonies,* are an integral part of materialist analysis.

At the most general level, materialist frameworks highlight the central role of economic issues in impacting behavior and society. One of the authors (Jaccard) remembers early in his career explaining his research on teen pregnancy to a cultural anthropologist with a Marxist bent. He described how he analyzed teens' beliefs and attitudes about sexual activity, the peer pressures that teens experience, the emotions and affect surrounding adolescent sexual relationships, the impact of sexuality issues on the self-concept of adolescents, and, finally, the important role of feelings of efficacy. The anthropologist politely listened for about half an hour, even though at times she looked bewildered by all the jargon being thrown about. She responded with a two-sentence reaction: "Jim, it's class. It's all about social and economic class." Of course, there is more to adolescent pregnancy than class issues, but the comment started Jaccard thinking about the broader contexts of the sexual risk behavior of adolescents. Further reflection led to an analysis of the economic underpinnings of adolescent risk behavior and the class dynamics involved.

Numerous useful analyses have adopted materialist perspectives. For example, Sidney Mintz (1986) conducted a thorough study of sugar production in the Caribbean and highlighted the ways in which the introduction of this commodity changed world economic relations, generated new forms of labor, augmented the slave trade, and completely transformed Caribbean economies. The newly acquired tastes of the English ruling elites for sugar led to global needs for sugar and contributed to a forceful new dynamic in the world economy. In the typical form of a materialist, Mintz focused on history, power relations, and the economy to provide a complex and integrated analysis of social, cultural, and economic processes surrounding sugar production.

In another insightful analysis, June Nash (1989), in her book *From Tank Town to High Tech: The Clash of Community and Industrial Cycles,* studied deindustrialization in the northeastern United States, documenting the impact on a town of the closing of a General Electric plant that built products for the military. She showed how the changes associated with the closure paralleled changes in the country and in the world more broadly and how these macrolevel changes could be used to make sense of the local developments. Her analyses emphasized economic dynamics at the local, national, and world levels and their impact on the lives of individuals.

The materialist framework is not without its critics, but one cannot deny the potential centrality of the kinds of questions it poses when analyzing cultural and societal influences on behavior. Consider carefully how different goods related to the phenomena in which you are interested are produced, allocated, and valued in society. Pay attention to the sources of power, who controls them, and how that power is exercised and transferred. Think about potential conflicts between groups over the allocation of goods and the monopolization of sources of power. Consider how all of these factors permeate political ideologies, economic systems, religion, and educational systems and how these, in turn, impact behavior. As you do, be flexible in conceptualizing what constitutes "goods." For example, suppose you are studying abortion. How is abortion made available, allocated, and valued in society? Who are the sources of power with respect to abortions (e.g., hospitals, clinics, government, religious organizations, Planned Parenthood)? Who controls these organizations (e.g., owners of hospitals, owners of clinics, politicians, religious leaders)? How is control of these organizations exercised and passed on from one year or one generation to the next? What types of conflicts have occurred between which groups over the *Roe v. Wade* decision that made abortions widely available to women? How do political ideologies, economic systems, religion, and educational systems impact access to abortion? The materialist framework encourages you to think about your phenomena on a more societal level in the context of issues of power, class relations, and control of resources.

Structuralism

Structuralism is a system of thought that derives from linguistics and is most strongly associated with the writings of Claude Lévi-Strauss. It is related to the theory of transformational-generative grammar developed by Noam Chomsky (1965, 1972), which we use as an analogy for describing structuralism (though Chomsky based his analysis, in part, on the work of Lévi-Strauss). According to Chomsky, underneath the surface structure of language is a "deep structure" that represents a finite set of organizing principles that serve as a universal linguistic blueprint for all languages. By carefully analyzing the surface structure of different languages, one can isolate this blueprint. Chomsky argues that analyses of languages at the surface structure make them appear more diverse than they really are. At a deeper level, all languages have a small number of organizing principles, and the task of the linguist is to discover these principles.

Lévi-Strauss, an anthropologist, approached the analysis of culture from this same perspective. Although cultures appear diverse on the surface, he argued that there is a core set of underlying organizing principles and structures. Structural analysis of a phenomenon focuses on isolating the basic underlying structural principles associated with it. Lévi-Strauss stressed the importance of both the conscious and the unconscious when considering human behavior.

Lévi-Strauss conceptualized human thought in terms of the principle of binary opposites (good–evil, light–dark, tall–short); that is, he argued that people think in a binary or dialectical manner. Thoughts are expressed differently in cultures through transformations, but such transformations are constrained by the structural operations of the human mind. Structuralism focuses on discovering *how* people think rather than *what* they think. Lévi-Strauss used the metaphor of code, emphasizing the importance of decoding surface structure events into their deeper meanings. In doing so, Lévi-Strauss argued that the scientist should seek analysis of contrasts and opposition.

As an example of a structuralist perspective, Ortner (1974) conducted an analysis of why women have subservient roles and are judged as being inferior relative to men across many cultures. She argued that the disparity derived from oppositional ideologies that associated women with nature and men with culture. She used these opposing associations to articulate structuralist arguments in support of her thesis. Ortner's work has been controversial and her thesis has been refuted, but her work crystallized questions and new perspectives on gender and culture (e.g., MacCormack & Strathern, 1980). As another example, Goldin (1987) conducted a structural analysis of Spanish and Mayan assumptions about markets and exchange in western Guatemala. She identified two contrasting interpretive frameworks used by the Spaniards and the Maya. Whereas the Spaniards preferred enclosed, elevated, artificially illuminated market environments in which to sell goods and the goods organized in accord with Spanish classifications, the Maya preferred open markets, with goods laid out on the ground, natural lighting, and a categorization system consistent with Mayan culture. Goldin's analysis of these views highlighted the oppositional nature of the underlying logic of the two cultures, which is consistent with a structuralist perspective.

Structuralist thinking has its strong and weak points, but for purposes of this book, we highlight the following structuralist principles: (1) think about your phenomena by finding the deeper structure underlying the seemingly diverse surface structure events surrounding it; (2) consider the potential role of both conscious and unconscious factors that might be operating; and (3) think about matters in binary or dialectical terms, focusing on opposites and contrasts (see Rychlak, 1994, for an interesting application of dialectical thought).

Functionalism

Functionalism has been an influential conceptual framework in sociology and anthropology. Notable functional theorists include Émile Durkheim, E. E. Evans-Pritchard, Bronisław Malinowski, Thomas Merton, Talcott Parsons, and Alfred Radcliffe-Brown. There are two major types of functionalist theory, one focused on the societal level (as typified by the work of Durkheim) and the other focused on the individual level (as typified by the work of Malinowski), although the two overlap. Some refer to societal-based frameworks as *structural functionalism* and individual-based frameworks simply as *functionalism*.

Every society has functional requirements for its survival. Functional analysis explores social institutions and segments of society in terms of the functions they serve to this end and conceptualizes society as a system of interdependent parts that tend toward equilibrium. A society is in equilibrium if there is no conflict, if people know what is expected of them, and if societal expectations are met. Parsons (1951, 1971) argued that equilibrium is attained through socialization processes and through social control—that is, sanctions imposed either informally through norms and peer pressure or through formal organizations, such as schools and prisons. Functionalists think of society as a collection of systems within systems. For example, Parsons discusses the personality system within the small-group system, the small-group system within the community system, the community system within society, and societal systems within the world system.

Merton (1968) distinguished between latent and manifest functions. Latent functions are consequences of a cultural or institutional action that are not explicitly intended or recognized by members of a society. Manifest functions are consequences that contribute to equilibrium and that are intended and recognized by societal members. An example of a latent function was described by Edwards (1979), who contrasted the "efficiency movement" with the "human relations movement" in the field of industrial relations. The former movement traditionally was thought to emphasize efficiency in organizational settings through strict control of the workers, whereas the latter movement was thought to downplay control in favor of a more humanistic orientation toward increasing productivity. Edwards's analysis showed that when examined at the latent level, the human relations movement exerted just as much control over workers as the efficiency movement, but in different and subtler ways.

Functionalism has fallen into disrepute in some areas of the social sciences. For example, the idea of a society functioning to achieve equilibrium has been criticized because so many segments in society seem to operate independently of other segments. Functionalism also has been criticized for being ahistorical, focusing on the functions that institutions serve at present rather than on how they evolved over time and the historical forces that shaped them. Despite these limitations, we sometimes find it useful to think about a phenomenon or an entity in terms of the kinds of functions it serves, say, for the individual, family, school, neighborhood, or community. Instead of asking about the causes of something, inquire into what functions it serves. Think of the systems in which the phenomena are embedded and ask what functions those systems serve. As you articulate functions, think in terms of those that contribute to bettering the individual, community, and/or society. What are the manifest functions that are operating, and what are the latent functions? Needs are important components of functional analyses (e.g., social needs, economic needs), because functions often are associated with meeting such needs. What needs define a functional analysis for your topic area? Consistent with criticisms of functionalist approaches, think of whether there is conflict and lack of equilibrium in the organization, institution, or problem you are considering. Is the conflict intrinsic and productive, or is it dysfunctional?

An example of a nontraditional application of functionalism is the work of Katz (1960), who developed a functionalist theory of attitudes. According to Katz, an attitude can serve one or more of four functions for the individual: (1) an ego-defensive function (that protects one's ego), (2) a value-expressive function (that allows one to express one's values), (3) a knowledge function (that allows one to be informed about matters), and (4) a utilitarian function (that allows one to gain positive consequences or have pleasing experiences). Katz theorized that the strategy a change agent (e.g., an advertiser, a health educator) should use to change an attitude depends on the function the attitude is serving. For example, if an attitude largely serves an ego-defensive function, then the advertising or educational strategy used will be different than if that attitude serves a knowledge function. As part of his theory, Katz described the persuasion strategies appropriate for each function.

Symbolic Interactionism

Symbolic interactionism is an influential theory in sociology, anthropology, education, and political science, and it incorporates useful perspectives for theory construction. It often is linked to grounded theory frameworks, but its applications extend far beyond such theories. Our discussion of symbolic interactionism follows closely the classic work of Herbert Blumer (1969).

Symbolic interactionism is based on three premises: (1) that people act toward things based on the meanings of those things to them; (2) that meaning is derived from social interactions (i.e., the meanings of objects emerge socially through our interactions with others); and (3) that meaning is the result of an interpretive process used by people to deal with the stimuli they encounter. The interpretation of stimuli has two phases. First, the actor indicates to him- or herself the things toward which he or she is acting. Second, the actor selects, checks, suspends, regroups, or transforms the meanings in light of the situation. Symbolic interaction occurs when one individual interprets the meaning of another individual's actions or gestures.

According to symbolic interaction theory, interaction involves mutual role taking in which each person tries to see things from the other's point of view. Only through such role playing can you communicate meanings because you must understand the frame of reference of the other individual for communication to occur. The self also is a critical concept in theories of symbolic interactionism. People are the object of their own actions, and as a result, they have a self-concept. The self-concept derives from how you think others view you. By having a self, you can interact with yourself and make indications to yourself. This sets humans apart from animals.

Human action is the result of a person's interpreting the events that transpire in a situation and then forming plans of action given those events. Symbolic interactionism focuses on understanding how individuals construe the environment about them and how they then choose to act upon that environment. The image is not one of individuals being "pushed around" by this or that cause, but rather of an active, interpreting individual, choosing actions to take.

According to symbolic interactionism, our experience of the external environment is subjective, the result of the meanings we impose on it. Objects in the environment are, in this respect, social creations. They are defined and construed in terms of the images we have of them in our mind. But symbolic interactionists also recognize that the empirical world can "talk back" and can challenge or resist our images of it. This, in turn, may lead to a new image.

Blumer (1969) argues that social scientists rarely have firsthand knowledge of the empirical worlds they study. Academics who study drug addiction usually have not lived the life of a drug addict, nor have they directly experienced the world in a way a drug addict does. Blumer emphasizes the inherent outsider role of social scientists and the need for these scientists to experience as closely as possible the world they are studying. Blumer emphasizes the central role of exploratory analysis, participant observation, and intensive case studies in the pretheory construction stages. Such activities help the researcher form the concepts, images, and ideas used in a theory. Blumer believes it is both arrogant and egocentric of social scientists to impose their view of the world on a phenomenon with which they have limited experience. Social scientists must first gain relevant experiences and get as close to the phenomenon as possible before they can adequately theorize about it.

As you construct your theories of human behavior, even though you may not adopt a formal symbolic interactionist perspective, it might be useful to think about your theory in these terms. How do the actors in your theory construe their world and the key elements within it? What meanings are they using, and how do they communicate these meanings to others with whom they interact? How do they view themselves, and how are they forming action plans in light of their interpretations? What are those action plans? How is the setting impacting the meanings that the individuals extract and use? How do the meanings of one actor overlap with, or differ from, the meanings of another actor?

Evolutionary Perspectives

Evolutionary theories of human behavior have a long and somewhat controversial history in the social sciences. Although some might argue that evolutionary perspectives do not constitute a grand theory, they certainly have been used to explain a diverse set of phenomena in many disciplines. The process of evolution can be defined as gradual changes over time in the organic structure of organisms. It was hypothesized to operate by biologists long before Darwin formulated his famous theory of evolution. Darwin's primary contribution was to specify the mechanisms by which evolution occurred. Central to evolutionary approaches are the concepts of *adaptation* and *natural selection*. Adaptation is the product of inherited characteristics of a species that have come into existence through natural selection (Buss, Haselton, Shackelford, Bleske, & Wakefield, 1998). Natural selection has three defining characteristics: (1) variation, (2) inheritance, and (3) selection. *Evolutionary variation* refers to the fact that organisms within a species vary in a large number of ways. Such variation allows evolution to operate. Some of these variations are genetically transferred from parents to offspring across multiple generations. This is the process of *inheritance*. Some of the inherited attributes are better suited to reproduction and survival than other attributes. Organisms with such adaptive attributes produce more offspring, on average, than those lacking these attributes, because they are more likely to survive and reproduce as a result of them. Across many generations, the result is natural *selection* toward the adaptive attributes. As one example, scientists have speculated that pregnancy sickness (food aversion, nausea, vomiting) during the first trimester is the result of selection to protect the embryo against maternal ingestion of teratogens. In essence, natural selection acts like a sieve that filters out problematic and nonadaptive behaviors (Dawkins, 1976). Over many generations, the result is a set of behaviors that interacts with the environment so as to promote reproduction and survival of species.

In addition to adaptive attributes, evolution produces *by-products of adaptation*. By-products are attributes that do not solve adaptive problems but that are confounded with attributes that do. For example, the whiteness of bones is a by-product of the fact that bones contain large amounts of calcium, which is associated with bone strength and which has evolved through natural selection mechanisms. Finally, there are behaviors that are neither adaptive nor by-products of adaptation, and these are viewed as random noise in the evolutionary process. Evolutionary scientists differ in how they classify behavior into these three categories. For example, some view language as a by-product of large brains, whereas others view language as adaptive in its own right.

Evolutionists emphasize that there are constraints on adaptation so that optimal adaptation seldom results. Adaptation is a slow process that may take thousands of years. Lack of genotypic variation can constrain the course that adaptation takes. Some adaptations have both costs and benefits associated with them, resulting in the evolution of costs as well as benefits to the species. Finally, adaptations do not operate in isolation and must be coordinated with other adaptations. This process of coordination can result in compromises that undermine optimal evolution. For all these reasons (time lags, restricted variation, accompanying costs to benefits, and coordination), adaptation does not always function optimally.

Bereczeki (2000) emphasizes three fundamental scientific orientations of evolutionary analysis: (1) adaptation, (2) ultimate causation, and (3) individualism. In terms of adaptation, the evolutionist seeks to identify how a behavior functions historically to increase survival and/or reproduction of the species. The focus is thus on a functional analysis of behavior rather than on the attempt to identify the causes of behavior in a classic cause–effect framework. What functions could the behavior have served in terms of survival and reproduction? In what ways could the behavior enhance survival or increase reproduction? Such functional analysis is a hallmark of evolution theories.

A second important characteristic of evolutionary analysis is a focus on *ultimate causation* (Bereczeki, 2000). Social scientists explore the causes of behavior at many different levels. Most social scientists are interested in specifying the proximal determinants of behavior and give less importance to understanding more distal determinants. By contrast, evolutionists search for the "ultimate causes" of behavior by tracing them to natural selection and the function they serve to promote survival of the fittest.

A third feature of evolutionary analysis is an emphasis on individualism. In traditional theories of evolution, the emphasis was on the idea of group selection; namely, that individuals evolved so as to act for the good of the group. In the 1970s, a group of biologists shifted this focus toward individualism, that is, the view that selection works mainly at the level of the individual so as to enhance an individual's own genetic fitness. These individual interests, in turn, determine the social institutions that emerge from them.

Evolutionary perspectives on human behavior have critics, and some of the critiques are themselves a rich source of ideas. For example, Lickliter and Honeycutt (2003) criticized genetic–evolutionary accounts of human development by noting that the cellular machinery of humans probably has more control over genes than genes do over the cellular machinery of humans. Lickliter and Honeycutt review evidence for the fundamental importance of developmental regulatory systems and posit an epigenetic approach to behavior that promotes systems-based analysis that goes beyond simple views of causality.

Evolutionary perspectives can be applied to any human phenomena and are not restricted to biologically based behaviors. Evolution, as a metaphor, can be used to construct many interesting questions (e.g., How do relationships evolve? How do attitudes evolve? How do personalities evolve?). How might evolutionary perspectives be used to analyze the growth of a business or an organization? Some businesses and organizations "survive" whereas others do not. Could an evolutionary perspective be adapted to analyze such dynamics?

As an example of the use of the evolutionary framework for analysis of nonbiological processes, Mahfouz, Philaretou, and Theocharous (2008) analyzed interpersonal attraction using evolutionary metaphors. According to these theorists, variation is represented by exposing oneself to a pool of available mates; selection takes place through learning courting mechanisms and socialization processes that maximize the mate's level of physical attractiveness; and retention is reflected in the initiation of strategies for ensuring the successful carrying out of the dating process, with the ultimate purpose being that of generating a long-term commitment. Their analysis yielded several insights into dating that are not apparent in traditional theories of dating. Evolutionary perspectives also have been offered on such diverse phenomena as schizophrenia (Pearlson & Folley, 2008), teachers' negative affect toward gifted students (Geake & Gross, 2008), the development of authoritarianism (Hastings & Shaffer, 2008), violent crime (Barber, 2008), and on-site web-page preferences and navigation (Stenstrom, Stenstrom, Saad, & Cheikhrouhou, 2008), to name a few.

What are the ultimate causes of the phenomenon you are studying? Do any of your variables, concepts, or processes have a basis in the survival of the species? What systems might constrain or regulate the impact of the ultimate causes you identify? What are the roles of time lags, limited variation, accompanying costs, and coordination in explaining your phenomenon?

Postmodernism: A Critical Commentary on Grand Theories

Postmodernism is not a formal system of thought but instead a critical commentary on assumptions frequently made in social science theories and research. It is controversial even among postmodernists. The term *postmodernity* means "after modernity" and reflects a rejection of the basic tenets of an orientation called *modernity*. *Modernism* is associated with the Renaissance era and evolved essentially at the same time as the capitalist state. As applied to social science, Gergen (2001) argues that postmodernists question three major tenets of modernism. First, in traditional modernist thought, humans are seen as having the capacity for reasoned and rational deliberations. According to this viewpoint, the thoughts and subjective knowledge of people are key to understanding behavior because a person's thoughts mirror reality, albeit sometimes imperfectly so. Postmodernists question the concept of rationality as traditionally conceived. According to postmodernists, a community judges a person to be rational only if he or she adopts the particular codes of discourse common to that community. For example, scientists are judged as being rational by the scientific community only to the extent that they adopt the discourse rules of the community of science. From this point of view, rationality is relational rather than absolute and can shift from one discourse community to another. Being rational is nothing more than a form of communal participation. Rationality is relative.

Second, in the modernist tradition, distinctions are made between the inner world of the mind and the external world of the material. An objectively knowable and rational world is believed to exist that contains systematic cause-and-effect relationships. In contrast, postmodernism emphasizes a social constructionist viewpoint (see Chapter 2). To speak of the world at all requires language. The words of a language are not mirrors of the world but rather arbitrary parts of a language system. To describe an external reality of causal relations reflects nothing more than participation in a language that draws upon the repository of thoughts and knowledge of a particular cultural tradition. Reality, like rationality, is relative.

Third, modernism holds that language is a means of conveying knowledge to others and hence, it is "the bearer of truth" (Gergen, 2001). The postmodernist view is that language is the result of a cultural process that is generated within the context of human relationships. Language becomes meaningful not from its subjective or objective underpinnings but from its use in action.

Postmodernists are suspicious of authoritative declarations or statements of "truth." They view such declarations as oppressive and silencing, especially for oppressed groups, such as females, members of certain ethnicities, and Third World peoples. For postmodernists, understanding is individualized, and an infinite number of interpretations are possible. To declare one interpretation as correct is to oppress others. Gergen (2001) captures this philosophy as applied to psychology as follows:

> As psychological theories are exported to the culture more generally, what are the reverberations in cultural life? When one holds that the primary ingredients of the mind are cognitive, when one views behavior as genetically prepared, when one distinguishes between pathology and normalcy, which doors are opened within the culture, and which are shut . . . Who is helped and who is hurt when psychologists distinguish between the intelligent and unintelligent, the pathological and normal, the prejudiced and unbiased? What form of culture is created when exploitation, infidelity, and rape are viewed as biologically prepared actions of the male? (p. 808)

Gergen argues that it is important for theorists to think about how they are framing problems and how this might impact other members of society. This, in turn, might impact the choices one makes in framing a problem. Gergen goes on to emphasize the liberating role of postmodernism for psychological theory:

> If scientific descriptions and explanations of the world are not demanded by the nature of the world itself, then one is released from the shackles of the taken for granted. Most importantly, one is invited into a posture of theoretical creativity. Scientists are liberated from the task of being mere mirror holders to the world as it is and challenged to articulate new and

potentially transformative conceptions. The task is not simply that of describing what currently exists but of creating intelligibilities that may foster worlds to come. Metaphorically, the function shifts from that of scribe to poet. (p. 810)

Postmodernists vary in the extremity of their positions within postmodern philosophy. Some reject any attempt at theory construction as futile because everything is relative, whereas others view theory construction as another form of dialogue among an infinite number of possible dialogues. The postmodernist approach emphasizes the importance of understanding the cultural context in which behavior occurs and in which interpretations of behavior are made.

Postmodernists often engage in a process called *deconstruction,* a strategy of analysis associated with philosopher Jacques Derrida (Thomassen, 2006). Derrida objects to attempts to turn deconstruction into a coherent analytic strategy, but there are themes associated with it that many have sought to depict. As applied to textual narratives, deconstruction focuses on identifying what the text represses—what it does not say—and its incongruities. Rosenau (1992) suggests that deconstruction involves (1) finding an exception to a generalization and pushing it to the limit so that the generalization is undermined, (2) interpreting arguments in a text in their most extreme form, (3) avoiding all absolute statements and seeking to make statements that are striking, (4) denying the legitimacy of categories because one can always find exceptions, (5) accepting nothing and rejecting nothing, and (6) using new and unusual terminology to avoid the surplus meaning associated with more established terms.

Although we have difficulty with several tenets of postmodernism, we find it healthy at times to think about concepts, relationships between concepts, and processes from this perspective. As you choose variables, concepts, and processes to study and elaborate theoretical narratives about them, what groups or viewpoints are you affecting by the way you frame the underlying issues? How are your viewpoints filtering your questions and observations? If you rejected the three major tenets of modernism (that people are rational, that there is an objective reality, and that language is a mirror of that reality) and adopted the perspective of the postmodernist, how would this perspective shape the kinds of variables, concepts, and processes you study? How would this impact your explanations of events? What would happen if you tried to deconstruct the narrative account of your theory? Sometimes we write out a theory and then subject it to the deconstruction process, with the result being new insights or perspectives.

In sum, the grand theories of materialism, structuralism, functionalism, symbolic interactionism, and evolution, as well as the critical approach of postmodernism, represent very different lenses through which to view human behavior. There is no question that if you make a sincere effort to think about the phenomena you are interested in from each of these perspectives, you will derive a range of intriguing insights. Our characterizations of these theories are necessarily brief and superficial and we strongly urge you to embark on a program of study for each approach. The more you master them, the more useful they will be. They are good tools to have in your theory construction toolbox.

FRAMEWORKS USING METAPHORS

In this section, we describe two general systems of thought that make use of biological metaphors. The first is the framework of *neural networks*, which combines causal analysis and process analysis in ways that are distinct from the theory construction processes described in previous chapters. The second framework, *systems theory*, has its roots in metaphors from physiology. Physiologists view the human body as a collection of interacting systems, each with its own combination of functions and purposes. These include the nervous system, the musculoskeletal system, the circulatory system, the respiratory system, the gastrointestinal system, the integumentary system, the urinary system, the reproductive system, the immune system, and the endocrine system. These systems coordinate to promote the survival and effective functioning of individuals over time. In systems theory frameworks, one analyzes a phenomenon in terms of the system in which it is embedded and then how that system interacts with other systems to impact outcomes of interest.

Neural Networks

Neural network theories do not have the "track record" of the grand theories described in the previous section, but they are becoming increasingly influential in the social sciences. They use neural mechanisms as metaphors for analyzing a range of behaviors and mental phenomena. We present the core elements of a neural network approach in abstract form, weaving in an example to make it more concrete. Neural networks are popular in the analysis of learning, memory, and information processing. They can be readily applied to decision making, attitude formation, prejudice, and most any phenomenon that involves the processing of information by individuals. The framework also can be adapted to describe relationships between organizations and organizational structures.

The basic unit in a neural network theory, a *neuron,* is connected to other neurons. The neurons are organized into layers, with the first layer representing the *input layer* and the last layer representing the *output layer.* The layers of neurons in between are called *hidden layers.* For example, in a neural network model of impression formation, each neuron at the input level might be a unit reflecting the different pieces of information that a person is given about a stranger. Suppose we describe a teacher to a prospective student using three personality traits and then ask the person how much he or she would like the teacher. Each piece of trait information is viewed as a separate neuron in the first layer, and then these propagate to the neurons in the second layer, and so on, until the final output layer is reached. Essentially, the neurons at the first level are predictors, and the neurons or units in the last layer are outcomes. The input and output layers are usually observable (the input information and the output response), and the layers in between usually are not observable—hence the terminology *hidden layers.*

Any given neuron can be active or inactive. Activation is binary in character; that is, it takes on the value of 1 (active) or 0 (not active). The presentation of the trait information activates some neurons, called *input neurons,* but not others. An activated input neuron reaches a neuron at the next layer through *threshold units*. There is a separate threshold unit for each output neuron. A threshold unit can be active or inactive. When the threshold unit becomes active, it "fires" like a synapse to activate the next neuron it is connected to. The threshold unit has an activation index that reflects its accumulated energy toward activation. The threshold unit also has a threshold value relative to its activation index, such that when the threshold value is exceeded by the activation index, the threshold unit fires, thereby activating the next neuron. Multiple neurons can feed into the threshold unit, each through a weighted connection, to impact its activation index. The connection can be either excitatory (the input neuron can increase the activation index) or inhibitory (the input neuron can decrease the activation index). The larger the weight of the connection, the greater the contribution of the neuron to the threshold unit.

Figure 12.1 presents a simple schematic of the process. Information is presented about traits 1, 2, and 3, and these activate input neurons 1, 2, and 3, respectively. These neurons are linked to a hidden layer neuron (liking for the teacher), and this neuron is linked to an output neuron (taking a class from the teacher). Input neurons 1, 2, and 3 feed into the threshold unit for the layer 1 neuron. Their contribution to the threshold

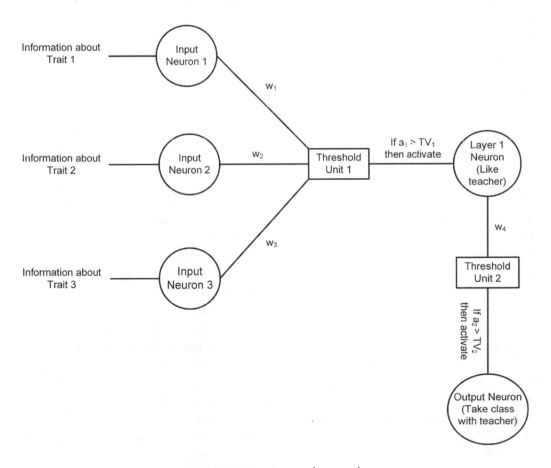

FIGURE 12.1. A neural network.

unit is reflected by the weights of the connections (w_1, w_2, and w_3). The more the weight for a given neuron deviates from 0, the greater the contribution it has for potentially activating the neuron to which it is connected. For example, the neuron for trait information 1 might have a larger weight (w_1) than the neuron for trait information 2 (w_2). The activation index of the threshold unit is signified by a_1, and its value is determined by the weighted combination of the connections from each of the input neurons. If the value of a_1 exceeds the threshold value of the threshold unit (TV_1), then a synaptic-like firing occurs, and the layer 1 neuron is activated. The same process occurs linking the layer 1 neuron to the output neuron.

This is a simplistic representation that is intended to convey the basic processes involved in a neural network. The example we described could be expanded so that other layer 1 neurons impact the output. Also, through the acquisition of experience, the weights of the connections (w_1, w_2, and w_3) can change. Thus, neural networks can "learn" as the strength of connections increases or decreases. For example, if a person is told by several different individuals that a teacher has a particular trait, then this repetition may strengthen the connection between that trait's input neuron and neurons in other layers. Neural network theorists have described a wide variety of learning strategies that neural networks can incorporate. A specialized branch of mathematics and statistics has evolved for the analysis and structuring of neural network approaches. Neural network models take many forms and can be quite complex.

Interesting examples of neural network models abound in the social sciences. For example, Marshall and English (2000) applied neural network analysis to model the association between social workers' overall assessments of the risk status of children in child protective services and information about 37 separate risk factors from the state of Washington's risk assessment matrix. Marshall and English found complex relationships between the risk information available and caseworker judgments of risk that were not evident from more traditional modeling strategies. The neural network analysis indicated that caseworkers actually used only a small number of the 37 risk factors when making their judgments and, as a result, the state of Washington revised its risk assessment matrix. In addition, new training methods were implemented to reemphasize the importance of certain risk factors (e.g., history of domestic violence) known to be related to recidivism but which the neural network analysis showed were not being used by caseworkers in their decision to place a child in foster care. Neural networks map closely onto another type of model, called connectionist models.

You may find it constructive to reconceptualize your theory using a neural network metaphor. What would constitute the neurons for the input layer in your theory? What would be the neurons in the output layers? What are the hidden layers, and how are they organized? What neurons are connected directly to other neurons? How much does it take to activate a neuron (as reflected by the threshold value of the threshold unit connected to it)? Do some of the threshold units in your network have higher threshold values than others, and if so, why? Do some neurons contribute more to a threshold unit than other neurons (as reflected by their different weights, w_i)? What can you conjecture about these differential weights and the sources of the differences? There is an extensive literature on neural network modeling that can assist you in answering these and other questions (see Abdi, Valentin, & Edelman, 1999, for an introductory treatment).

Systems Theory

General systems theory was introduced in the 1940s by Ludwig von Bertalanffy, who presented the theory using biological metaphors. Systems thinking is pervasive in everyday life, as evidenced by such concepts as the health care system, family systems, political systems, ecological systems, and banking systems. General systems theory has been subject to a wide range of interpretations. Sadovski (1974) found over 35 different definitions of what a "system" is in scientific writings. It is impossible to convey a unified view of systems theory in light of this state of affairs. Indeed, one of the main complaints against general systems theory is that it is too vague. We emphasize here systems concepts that reflect different ways of thinking about phenomena relative to the other frameworks discussed in this chapter.

At the simplest level, one can think of a system as an organized entity whose interrelated elements interact with one another so as to achieve some common goal. There are many types of systems: a *static* system remains invariant over time; a *dynamic* system is constantly changing; a *closed* system has limited or no interaction with the environment or other systems; an *open* system interacts with the environment or other systems, exchanging inputs and outputs.

Systems theory adopts a holistic approach rather than a reductionist approach to analysis. It seeks to gain insights into the functioning of the overall system by examining the interrelationships and connections between the component parts of the system. It is not enough, for example, in a family system to separately analyze the mother, the father, the son, and the daughter. Rather, one must examine how these elements interact and study the interconnections between them to more fully understand family functioning. Systems theory emphasizes understanding processes rather than causes. Instead of analyzing *why* families communicate, for example, the focus is on *how* families communicate and how this changes as a function of settings and contexts.

Systems theory also emphasizes the concept of feedback. *Feedback* refers to a circular process in which the system transforms input into output, and the output is brought back to the system as input. Feedback loops allow a system to regulate its behavior and are integral to system analyses.

Many systems have regulatory mechanisms that strive to maintain *equilibrium*. An analogy is a thermostat that heats a home during winter. The equilibrium point is the temperature at which the thermostat is set. The thermostat monitors the room temperature and sends a signal to the heater to turn on if the room's temperature falls below the equilibrium point and for the heater to turn off if the temperature is above the equilibrium point. Systems analysis examines such regulatory mechanisms, emphasizing the underlying processes that are taking place, the feedback loops that are operating within the system, and the continual adjustments that are being made among the many system elements. Another concept emphasized in systems theory is that of *equifinality*, which refers to the idea that there may be several equally effective ways to achieve a goal (Van de Ven & Poole, 1995).

Brinberg and McGrath (1985) discuss three facets of systems that theorists can consider when thinking in terms of systems theory, either for the system as a whole or at various levels of a system. First is *system well-being*, which refers to the identification of conditions and behaviors that threaten the health and safety of the system or that constrain the positive development of the system. Second is *system task performance effectiveness*, which refers to conditions and barriers that hinder the system from carrying out its tasks or achieving its goals. Third is *system cost*, which refers to expenditures of energy and resources in pursuit of task performance.

There are many examples of systems theory approaches in the social sciences. In the field of criminal justice, for example, Van Gigch (1978) used systems theory to analyze major components of criminal justice (police, courts, and corrections) and the agencies and institutions that serve those components. He identified the inputs and outputs of each institution and argued that these were regulated by the needs of the overall criminal justice system. Van Gigch's theory emphasized that the criminal justice system as a whole was greater than the sum of its parts. He also argued that the criminal justice system is itself a subsystem within larger political, economic, educational, and technical systems, all of which impact how the criminal justice system functions. Kraska (2004) argued that the systems approach to criminal justice facilitates macrolevel analyses of criminal justice and offered numerous suggestions for reform based on such analyses. Bernard, Paoline, and Pare (2005) offer a theory of criminal justice based on nine propositions that derive from systems theory perspectives.

As another example, in the 1980s, questions were raised in Canada about the health risks of a herbicide called Alachlor. Three different stakeholders performed what each characterized as objective, scientific assessments of the risks of Alachlor, but each came to a different conclusion. Hatfield and Hipel (2002) used systems theory to isolate the bases of the differing conclusions and advocated for the use of general systems theory in risk assessments more generally.

Systems theory is widely used in analyses of families (Freeman, 1993; Wood, 2002) and organizations (Takahashi, Kijima, & Sato, 2004). Thinking about your theory, what happens if you think about matters in terms of processes performed by systems rather than variables? What insights do you gain by describing how things function rather than by trying to describe why things function as they do? Are there feedback loops? Are there regulatory mechanisms? In what ways is the whole larger than the functioning of the individual parts? As noted earlier, the human body has a nervous, skeletal, circulatory, and respiratory system, and a multitude of other systems. These systems are interrelated and work together toward the common goal of keeping a person alive. Can you use this example as a metaphor for the phenomena you are studying? What are the core systems in your theory? How are they interrelated, and how do they interact with one another? How does one system depend on the other? What are the functions of each system, and what processes take place in the system to allow these functions to be fulfilled?

FRAMEWORKS EMPHASIZING STABILITY AND CHANGE

Although all of the frameworks discussed in this chapter can be applied to the analysis of change, there are perspectives on stability and change worth mentioning that stand apart from these systems of thought. Van de Ven and Poole (1995, 2005) describe four conceptual orientations to process-based analyses of change. First, there is a *life-cycle model* in which the developing entity (an individual, a couple, a social group, an organization) is thought to move through a set of preconfigured or preprogrammed phases from beginning to end. For example, human development is often thought to progress from infancy to childhood to adolescence to young adulthood to adulthood to older adulthood, with noteworthy cognitive, moral, emotional, social, and physical changes associated with each phase of development. A second framework for process analyses of change identified by Van de Ven and Poole is a *teleological model,* which conceptualizes individuals as moving toward a goal or end state in a purposeful way; the person specifies a goal and takes action to reach it. In a third framework, a *dialectical model,* the person or entity is viewed as being influenced by opposing events and forces, some promoting change and others promoting stability. Change is interpreted in the context of the balance of power between these opposing forces. The final framework, an *evolutionary model,* emphasizes cumulative change, as discussed earlier in the context of evolutionary perspectives.

These four approaches to process-based analyses of change are not mutually exclusive. All four mechanisms, or some combination of them, can operate to produce or characterize change. Van de Ven and Poole (1995) described 15 different frameworks that involve various combinations of the four mechanisms.

Related to the life-cycle model of Van de Ven and Poole (1995) are *stage theories* of change. These theories conceptualize people as moving through sequential stages in their progress toward some outcome or end state. Unlike the life-cycle model, however, progression through the stages is not necessarily predetermined. A stage theory specifies what the stages are, the criteria used to classify a person (or other entity) as in one stage as opposed to another stage, and the processes or requirements that must be mastered or achieved to move from one stage to the next. Stage theories are common in disciplines such as developmental science, health, and organizational studies. As an example, in the area of smoking cessation, the transtheoretical model identifies five stages through which a person is presumed to progress (Prochaska, DiClemente, & Norcross, 1992). The first stage is the *precontemplation stage,* where a smoker has no intention of quitting smoking in the next 6 months. In the *contemplation stage,* a smoker is thinking about quitting sometime in the next 6 months but does not plan to quit in the next month. The *preparation stage* marks the smoker's intention to quit within the next month and includes at least one unsuccessful 24-hour quit attempt in the past year. In the *action stage,* the smoker successfully quits smoking for any time between 1 day and 6 months. After 6 months of being smoke free, the ex-smoker is said to have reached the *maintenance stage.* According to the transtheoretical model, the type of intervention that one uses to help a person stop smoking differs depending on his or her "stage of change."

For example, someone in the precontemplative stage will need different information and support than someone in the maintenance stage.

Stage theories differ in at least five ways. First, some stage theories permit the entity (e.g., a person, a family, an organization) to revert back to previous stages, whereas other stage theories dictate a forward progression only. Second, some stage theories require that entities spend a fixed minimum amount of time in a stage, whereas other theories permit movement through stages with no time constraints. Third, some stage theories define stages in terms of categories along a single continuum, whereas other stage theories define the stages multivariately. For example, the first three stages of the transtheoretical model represent a trichotomization of the intention to quit smoking along a time dimension (never, within 6 months, within 1 month). By contrast, Freud's psychoanalytic theory of the stages of psychosexual development (the oral, anal, phallic, latency, and genital stages) involves distinctly different dimensions at each stage. Fourth, some stage theories permit entities to skip an intermediate stage, whereas other theories require that each entity progress through each stage in sequence. Finally, some stage theories characterize movement from one stage to another in terms of large, dramatic shifts in behavior, whereas others view the passing from one stage to the next as a more gradual process.

Dixon and Moore (2000) discuss stage theories from the perspective of the developmental ordering of two or more skills or types of knowledge. Consider two different but interdependent skills, A and B. Dixon and Moore argue that if acquisition of one skill is developmentally dependent on the acquisition of another skill, then this, for all intents and purposes, is a stage theory. If the development of skill B is dependent on the development of skill A, then skill A is the first stage and skill B is the second stage. Dixon and Moore suggest different models of developmental ordering for stage theories. *Developmental synchrony* occurs when both skills begin development at the same time and basically develop at the same rate. One skill is dependent on the other, but the dependence is instantaneous. *Partial developmental priority* occurs when the two skills start at the same time, but one develops at a faster rate than the other. The level of skill B might be dependent on the level of skill A, but there is a lag between the acquisition of a level of skill B and the acquisition of a certain level of skill A. The lag may not be complete in that only a certain level of mastery of skill A is required for skill B to start developing. *Complete developmental priority* occurs when skill A must be fully mastered before skill B can begin to develop.

There are many examples of stage theories in the social sciences, with the transtheoretical model described in this section being one. As another example, Duck (1982) developed a stage-like theory of relationship dissolution that consists of six phases. First, there is a *breakdown phase* where one or both partners become distressed over the way the relationship is being conducted. This eventually leads to an *intrapsychic phase* that is characterized by brooding about the relationship. Nothing is said to the partner at this time, but the focus is on one's feelings that the relationship is damaged. This phase, which is characterized by uncertainty, anxiety, and hostility, is followed by the *dyadic phase,* where partners confront each other and talk through their feelings about the relationship. If a decision is made to break up, they move to a *social phase,* where they tell others of their decision and seek social support. This, in turn, leads to the *grave-dressing phase,* where the relationship is seen as being "dead," with the recognition that it must be "put away." During this phase, the individual builds a narrative about what the relationship was, reinterpreting it and labeling it in light of his or her current feelings. Finally comes the *resurrection process* in which the individual re-creates a sense of his or her social value and defines what he or she wants out of future relationships. This theory was recently updated and enhanced by Rollie and Duck (2006), who emphasize predominant processes throughout the dissolution experience and elaborate on the role of communication at each phase.

In your theory construction efforts, consider if you want to conceptualize any of your variables or phenomena using a life-cycle, teleological, dialectical, or evolutionary model. Consider imposing a "stage" framework. If you think in these terms, elucidate the criteria for defining stages and make decisions about the evolution of stages using the dimensions we discussed on how stage theories differ. Can people revert back to previous stages? Must people spend a fixed minimum amount of time in a stage? Can your stages be defined in terms of a single dimension, or must they be defined multivariately? Can people skip a stage? Are the shifts from one stage to the next gradual or dramatic? What is the developmental ordering of the "skills," "knowledge," or "events" in your theory in the spirit of the Dixon and Moore analysis?

PSYCHOLOGICAL FRAMEWORKS

Several influential frameworks in psychology offer unique perspectives relative to the frameworks we have discussed thus far. We focus on two systems of thought: reinforcement theory and positive psychology. Although other theories are either more contemporary or more influential historically, we focus on these two frameworks because they complement those that have already been discussed.

Reinforcement Theories

Reinforcement theory achieved prominence primarily in psychology, but it also has been applied in education, sociology, political science, and public health. *Reinforcement theories* emphasize the concepts of *stimulus* and *response.* A stimulus is an external or internal event that leads to the performance of a behavior, which is termed the response. Stimuli have three functions: (1) elicitation, (2) discrimination, and (3) reinforcement. An *eliciting stimulus* evokes an instinctual, natural response, such as the sight of food-stimulating salivation. A *discriminative stimulus* does not directly elicit a response but sets the stage for the response. It signals to people that they should respond in a certain way. For example, when a child is eating at the dinner table, he or she may exhibit different table manners when the mother is present than when the mother is absent. The mother, in this case, is a discriminative stimulus. *Reinforcing stimuli* occur as a posi-

BOX 12.1. Collaboration

Theory construction often benefits from collaborating with other individuals. Through the exchange of ideas and perspectives, it is possible for individuals involved in the collaboration to gain insights that they may not have obtained working on their own. When we think of collaboration, we usually think of collaborations between scientists, between professors and students, or between students. But collaborative partnerships can be broader than this and can include collaborations between a social scientist, on the one hand, and journalists, policymakers, representatives from institutions or agencies, and key individuals in professional organizations, on the other hand.

Levine and Moreland (2004) have reviewed the research literature on effective collaborations and state that collaborations tend to be more successful if they include both similar and dissimilar orientations of participants. You don't want a collaborator who merely echoes what you think. Instead you want someone who can add to your knowledge base and who can complement the points of view that you bring to the collaboration. On the other hand, if the collaborator has a very different way of characterizing matters, it may be difficult for you to communicate effectively with him or her, as neither of you can transcend the specialized jargon ingrained in your training.

Usually, effective collaborations happen with individuals who are similar in terms of life stage, status, values, and interaction style (Levine & Moreland, 2004). By contrast, similarity on dimensions such as knowledge and abilities inhibits creativity, as it narrows the pooled knowledge base (Farrell, 2001). Farrell (2001) found that more successful collaborations tend to happen in dyads or triads. With a large number of collaborators, usually a natural pairing off of smaller dyads occurs, and it is in these dyads where much of the creative work happens (Farrell, 2001).

When brainstorming ideas as part of a larger group, several disadvantages have been noted. These include evaluation apprehension, production blocking, and a reluctance to discuss unshared ideas. These obstacles can be overcome by talking about them at the outset of the collaboration, and it usually is easier to do so in dyads, where each participant feels comfortable with the other person. The key is to create the right environment for intellectual exchange.

Within a dyad, some people collaborate by writing text together, side-by-side at a word processor, with one person doing the typing. Debates not only focus on ideas but also on such matters as word choice and sentence structure. Alternatively, one person might write an initial draft and then this and subsequent drafts are exchanged, with each person providing feedback to the other. Whichever approach is used, the key is to develop a communal orientation to theory construction rather than one of just exchanging ideas in a linear, noncommunicative way. In general, it is important that both members have a sense of ownership of the ideas and a sense that a true collaboration has occurred. This outcome fosters sustained collaboration.

(continued)

An important part of collaboration is not just generating ideas but also identifying ideas that are good enough for further consideration in the research. Being open to, as well as being willing to give, constructive criticism is important in this regard. Joseph Bordogna, a deputy director of the National Science Foundation, emphasizes the importance of (1) building trust among partners, (2) making sure everyone has something to gain from the collaboration, and (3) ensuring a diversity of perspectives.

tive or negative consequence of a response. Reinforcement theories focus on identifying the roles of relevant stimuli as being eliciting, discriminatory, and/or reinforcing. For example, if a child acts aggressively, reinforcement theory focuses on identifying what stimuli in the environment are serving to positively reinforce such behavior and what discriminative cues are present that signal the permissibleness of aggressive behavior.

In some (but not all) reinforcement theories, the concept of *drive* is important. Clark Hull (1943) proposed that there is an underlying, unlearned, biological source of core needs related to metabolic processes, such as the need for food, water, and sexual contact. When a person is deprived of the satisfaction of these needs, a drive force is created that activates behavior in the direction of trying to satisfy them. When satisfaction of the need is obtained, reduction in the drive occurs. Dollard and Miller (1950) identified two types of drives: (1) primary or innate drives and (2) secondary drives that are the product of learning (e.g., a drive toward monetary rewards or a drive toward verbal rewards). Another facet of reinforcement theory is to analyze the fundamental drive states, both primary and secondary, that may underlie behavior.

A fundamental tenet of reinforcement theories derives from *Thurstone's law of effect*. This law states that if positive consequences follow an individual's response to a stimulus, then he or she will probably repeat that response in the presence of the stimulus on future occasions. Conversely, if a response to a stimulus is followed by negative consequences, then the individual will avoid repeating that response to the stimuli in the future. One can increase or decrease the probability of a behavior occurring by manipulating reinforcers of the behavior. *Positive reinforcers* are stimuli that strengthen the response, whereas *negative reinforcers* are stimuli that strengthen the response when they are removed. For example, if an aversive stimulus is removed in response to a behavior, then the removal of that stimulus serves as a negative reinforcer. *Punishments* are stimuli that reduce the strength of the response. When analyzing behavior, reinforcement theorists also analyze what stimuli may be operating as reinforcers for the behaviors and what stimuli might be operating to punish the behavior. By identifying these stimuli, one begins to understand the bases of the behavior.

The effectiveness of a reinforcer in shaping behavior depends, in part, on the schedule of its administration. There are two broad types of reinforcement schedules: *continu-*

ous and *intermittent*. Continuous reinforcement occurs when a behavior is reinforced each time it occurs. Research suggests that continuous reinforcement is the fastest way to establish new behaviors or eliminate undesired behaviors. Intermittent schedules occur when only some instances of a desired behavior are reinforced.

Stimulus generalization is an important process in reinforcement theories. It refers to the situation in which a novel stimulus evokes a response that was previously learned in relation to a different, though similar, stimulus. For example, if two situations are very similar to each other and individuals learn to respond in a certain way in one of the situations, they probably will respond the same way in the other situation. *Discrimination* refers to an individual's ability to differentiate stimuli and respond differently to them. Generalization and discrimination go hand in hand: They allow individuals to economize their behavior by generalizing stimuli, on the one hand, yet make important distinctions and respond differentially, on the other hand. Another key point of analysis for reinforcement theories is the analysis of stimulus generalization and how reinforcement histories from one context may generalize to another context.

Extinction is another important process in reinforcement theories. It refers to the progressive decrement in a response under continual nonreinforcement. Thus, if a response is no longer reinforced in the presence of a stimulus, then the response will eventually extinguish. Some people extinguish responses quicker than others. Resistance to extinction is a function of (1) the amount of prior reinforcement, (2) the strength of the drive to obtain the reinforcer during extinction, (3) the amount of work or effort involved in performing the response, and (4) the schedule that was used to reinforce the behavior initially.

Although reinforcement theories have their critics, we often find it useful to "put on the hat of a reinforcement theorist" and think about how such a scientist would analyze the outcome variables in which we are interested. More often than not, explanatory constructs suggest themselves that otherwise would not have. What stimuli are eliciting the behavior? What reinforcers are operating to encourage the behavior? Are there any potential negative reinforcers? What punishments are operating to discourage the behavior? Are there any basic drive states that may be impacting the behavior? What are the operative reinforcement schedules? That is, what is the dynamic process by which reinforcers are being administered? Are there discriminative stimuli operating that point to one type of behavior in the presence of those stimuli but a different behavior in the absence of those stimuli? Is the behavior impacted by a person's history in situations similar to the ones we are studying? To what situations might the effects of variables generalize? If we want to extinguish a behavior, how would we go about removing reinforcers? What would make some people more (or less) resistant to extinction? Trying to answer these questions, even if you are not a reinforcement theorist, can often be a rich source of ideas and perspectives.

Reinforcement theory and the many variants of it are widely used in behavioral interventions to impact inappropriate and destructive behaviors in children, adolescents, and adults (e.g., Durand, 2002; Kazdin, 2008; Patterson, 1975). These interventions identify the behaviors that need changing and then analyze these behaviors in terms of the questions noted above. As relevant reinforcers affecting the behavior are identified, they are either removed or new reinforcers are added. If a desired reinforcer is being administered only intermittently, then a more effective reinforcement schedule is implemented. Or if the child, adolescent, or adult is responding inappropriately only in the presence of a certain discriminative cue, then attempts will be made to eliminate that cue. If the child, adolescent, or adult performs appropriate behaviors in one setting, then methods for generalizing that response to other situations will be introduced.

Reinforcement theory is no longer a cornerstone of mainstream psychology, which, ironically, makes it all that more useful for generating unique perspectives on behavior relative to more dominant theories. Reinforcement theories typically are used to analyze the behavior of individuals, but there is nothing to prevent you from thinking about groups, organizations, or other larger units in these terms. For example, when studying relationships within or between hierarchically structured organizations, how does one department or unit affect another from the perspective of reinforcement theories? Not all of the concepts we outlined apply, but many of them do. Again, try to use the different theoretical perspectives we are presenting in creative ways that go beyond the routine application of them.

Humanism and Positive Psychology

A longstanding approach to the analysis of human behavior is that of *humanism*, which recently has been reinvigorated by a movement in psychology called positive psychology (Bacon, 2005; Kimble, 1984). Positive psychology focuses on understanding strengths and virtues, positive emotions, and positive institutions within society (Seligman & Csikszentmihalyi, 2000). It seeks to understand what factors contribute to these phenomena and how they can be nurtured and developed. It has its roots in psychology in the classic work on client-centered therapy as espoused by Carl Rogers (1961). This theory emphasizes people's innate tendencies to seek self-actualization and health, when conditions permit.

Seligman (2002) presents a positive psychology framework that emphasizes the concept of *strengths,* which he believes are distinct from other psychological constructs, such as traits and abilities. According to Seligman, strengths are valued in their own right and are characteristics or attributes that parents want for their children. Strengths tend to be valued in all cultures. Examples include creativity, wisdom, bravery, leadership, humility, and integrity. Peterson and Seligman (2004) present a taxonomy of 24 strengths that are organized in terms of six higher-order virtues. Bacon (2005) presents an alternative taxonomy that emphasizes focus-oriented strengths and balanced-focused strengths. *Focus-oriented strengths* emphasize individual growth and development, whereas *balance-oriented strengths* emphasize bringing about harmony within the self and between the self and others.

A major contribution of positive psychology is that it has focused theorizing on outcome variables that have a positive character to them. Whereas much of social science is aimed at understanding negative outcomes, such as unhealthy behavior, prejudice, family dissolution, suicide, drug use, HIV-related behaviors, conflict, and survival under adversity, positive psychology shifts the focus to how normal people flourish under normal or benign conditions. Thus, this framework impacts the kinds of outcome variables on which you might choose to focus your theories.

Positive psychology also has implications for the kinds of causes you might focus on and the strategies you use to develop interventions. This point is illustrated in research on adolescent problem behaviors. Most interventions aimed at addressing such behavior are problem-specific. For example, there are school-based interventions aimed at preventing sexual risk taking, smoking, drug use, and alcohol use. These programs focus on the beliefs and attitudes of adolescents toward the problem behavior in question, peer influences on these behaviors, and opportunity structures that make it easier to perform the behaviors. An alternative approach to intervention design is one that emphasizes not the problem behaviors of youths but rather the positive features of adolescent development (Catalano, Berglund, Ryan, Lonczak, & Hawkins, 2002). Known as positive youth development (PYD) programs, these interventions assume that the same individual, family, school, and community factors that influence positive outcomes in youth also impact youth-related problem behaviors. PYD interventions focus not on problem behaviors but instead on promoting bonding, resilience, spirituality, social skills, moral competence, self-efficacy, belief in the future, prosocial norms, and other general orientations toward life that serve the positive development of youths. The idea is that youths who have such positive orientations will be less likely to engage in problem behaviors. In this case, a "positive" focus on human behavior impacts the kinds of explanatory variables one chooses to emphasize relative to the more traditional problem-related beliefs, attitudes, and norms.

We believe that positive psychology perspectives are worth considering when thinking about outcome variables and factors that impact them. If your theory is focused on a negative outcome state, might you also consider adding positive states to your theory? When thinking about ways of reducing a negative state, what positive factors might you try to enhance to do so? Instead of reducing the negatives, might your theory be expanded to increase the positives?

FRAMEWORKS INSPIRED BY METHODOLOGY

Multilevel Modeling

Social scientists in many disciplines have long advocated the importance of incorporating into theories the broader contexts in which individuals behave. Research adopting such perspectives has increased exponentially with the recent advent of a statistical method of analysis called *multilevel modeling*. To be sure, the rudiments of multilevel modeling have been around for decades, but it is only in the last 25 years or so that reasonably user-friendly software has become available to make sophisticated multilevel modeling accessible to social scientists. This, in turn, has shaped the kinds of multilevel questions that scientists ask. In this section, we describe multilevel thinking with the idea that bringing such frameworks to bear on the phenomena you study may provide you with new insights and perspectives.

Consider the case in which we wish to explain student performance on math achievement tests. One set of explanatory variables focuses on individual differences, such as gender. A theorist might offer the proposition that, on average, boys score higher than girls because of a host of socialization factors, which we do not discuss here in the interest of space. This proposition can be diagrammed using a path model (see Chapter 7), as in Figure 12.2a.

Students attend different types of schools, and it is possible that the type of school they attend also impacts their test performance. For example, students who attend private schools might perform better on math achievement tests than students who attend public schools by virtue of the smaller class sizes and more individualized attention they receive. The type of school is a contextual variable in that students are "nested within" different types of schools. This influence can be diagrammed in conjunction with the gender effect as shown in Figure 12.2b.

Finally, the theorist might argue that the type of school moderates the impact of gender on math achievement scores. Specifically, the theorist reasons that in private schools, where students receive more individualized attention, the gender difference between boys and girls is lessened compared with public schools. This yields the revised path diagram shown in Figure 12.2c.

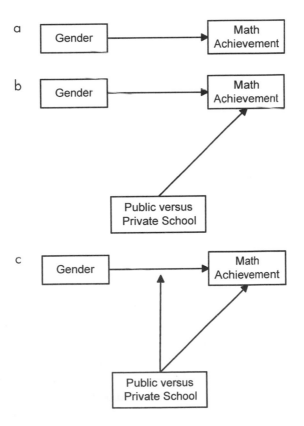

FIGURE 12.2. Examples for multilevel modeling. (a) Level 1 analysis; (b) multilevel model; (c) multilevel model with moderation.

Figure 12.2c (and Figure 12.2b) represents a two-level model. Units in the first level (students) are nested within units of the second level (schools), and the characteristics of the second-level units (i.e., characteristics of the schools) are thought to influence the level 1 outcome variable (math achievement) and/or influence the way in which level 1 characteristics (gender) impact the outcome variable.

Multilevel modeling invokes a frame of mind in which theorists think about explanatory variables at different levels, focusing on cases where level 1 units are nested within level 2 units. There are many such examples. Students are nested within schools, and characteristics of both the students and the schools can influence performance on tests. Employees are nested within organizations and characteristics of both the employees and the organization can influence employee behavior. Patients are nested within hospitals, and characteristics of both the patients and the hospitals can influence patient recovery. Infants are nested within families, and characteristics of both the infants and the families can influence infant development.

These are examples of two-level models. Multilevel theorists also work with three-level models in which level 1 units are nested within level 2 units, which, in turn, are nested within level 3 units. For example, students are nested within schools, which, in turn, are nested within counties. Characteristics of the students, the schools, and the counties all can influence test performance. As another example, in organizational analyses, employees might be nested within departments, which, in turn, are nested within organizations. Characteristics of the employees, the departments in which they serve, and the organizations all can influence job performance.

The relationships between variables at the different levels can be expressed in a variety of ways, such as through the use of propositions in narratives, path diagrams (per Figure 12.2), and/or via mathematical equations. The essence of multilevel modeling, however, is a focus on nested units and the explanatory variables at each level of nesting.

In some theories, level 2 variables are treated as aggregations of level 1 variables. For example, the morale of a family (level 2) might be the average morale across the different family members (level 1), and the cohesiveness of a family (level 2) might be the variance of the morale across family members (e.g., in some families, all members have the same level of morale, whereas in other families, morale differs considerably from one family member to the next). In other cases, the level 2 variables are defined independently of the level 1 variables, such as the case where a school is public or private, or whether the school has a strict or lax policy for expelling students caught with marijuana.

There is a robust literature on multilevel analysis. As you think about the phenomena in which you are interested, consider if they are amenable to multilevel analysis. What are your level 1 units, what are your level 2 units, and what are your level 3 units? What explanatory variables are relevant at each level? Within a given level, what are the causal relations between the variables? What are the causal relations across levels? If you adopt a causal framework, are there moderated effects? Are there mediated effects? Are your level 2 variables simple aggregates of your level 1 variables, or are they defined independent of them? Are your level 3 variables simple aggregates of your level 2 variables, or are they defined independently of them? The multilevel framework encourages you to think about explanatory variables in ways that differ from more traditional forms of analysis and that may therefore enrich your theory.

A unique application of multilevel modeling is the analysis of "growth curves." This application reconceptualizes temporal dynamics by viewing individuals as level 2 units and assessment occasions as level 1 units nested within the level 2 units. For example, consider the data for three individuals in Figure 12.3, where the outcome variable at a given occasion is a behavioral count, namely, the number of alcoholic drinks consumed in the past 2 weeks. This behavior is measured at each of four occasions: the beginning of the first, second, third, and fourth years of high school. All three individuals show a linear change in alcohol consumption over time, and all three have roughly the same average level of drinking across the four time periods. However, the individuals vary in the sharpness of the increase in alcohol consumption across time, as reflected by the differing slopes of the lines plotting their behavioral trajectories. Individual A shows no increase in drinking, Individual B shows a moderate increase in drinking, and Individual C shows a more marked increase in drinking across time. The individuals with the steeper slopes progress toward higher levels of drinking more quickly than the individual with the flatter slope. Instead of explaining individual differences in the average drinking score across time, the focus of this multilevel model might instead be on explaining individual differences in the slope of the line that describes how drinking changes over time. Such "growth curve" analyses are becoming increasingly common in the social sciences. For example, in education research, there often is interest in how reading or math skills change over time and the kinds of trajectories that children show as they move from kindergarten through the elementary school grades. Thus, another option for building theories is to focus on behavioral trajectories over time.

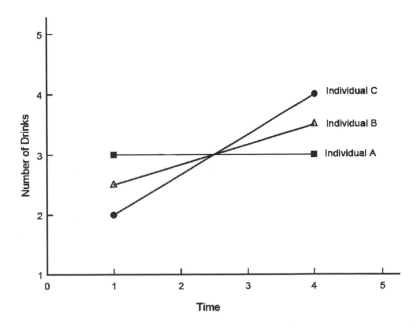

FIGURE 12.3. Example of the analysis of behavioral trajectories.

Person-Centered Theorizing

Whereas variable-centered approaches to theorizing focus on identifying relationships between variables, person-centered approaches emphasize the identification of groups or "clusters" of individuals who share particular attributes in common. The statistical methodological technique most often associated with person-centered theorizing is cluster analysis and its variants, which we discussed in Chapter 11. To review, *cluster analysis* applies statistical algorithms to measures of constructs to identify "clusters" of individuals who exhibit common profiles across those measures. As an example, developmental science has identified numerous key parenting dimensions, including (1) expressions of warmth and affection, (2) exertion of control versus laxness, (3) engagement with one's child in shared activities, (4) use of reasoning and explanation during disciplining, (5) use of monitoring and supervision, and (6) quality of communication (Schaefer & DiGeron, 2000). If one conceptualizes parents as being "low," "medium," or "high" on each dimension, there are 3^6, or 729, possible parenting styles defined by the combination of the six dimensions with three levels each. In practice, not all of these styles occur with equal frequency, and indeed, some combinations may not occur at all. Cluster analysis is a method that quickly and efficiently identifies parents who share common profiles across the six dimensions and thereby permits scientists to identify the most commonly occurring parenting styles in a population. Such strategies can be applied to any area of study where multiple variables are of interest. For example, many person-centered analyses of health behavior have identified health-based lifestyles of the U.S. population as well as healthy and unhealthy lifestyles in other countries (Clatworthy, Buick, Hankins, Weinman, & Horne, 2005). Similarly, person-centered analyses have been used to identify clusters of social groupings in social network analysis (Freeman, 2006).

In marketing, cluster analysis is often used to identify market segments for purposes of developing tailored advertising strategies. Segmentation in marketing typically is pursued using four variable categories (Kotler, Roberto, & Lee, 2002): (1) demographic segmentation, which divides populations into segments based on variables such as age, gender, income, occupation, education, religion, ethnicity, and cohort (e.g., generation Y, echo boomers); (2) geographic segmentation, which divides populations into segments according to geographical areas, such as states, regions, counties, cities, and neighborhoods as well as related elements, such as commuting patterns, places of work, and proximity to landmarks; (3) psychographic segmentation, which divides populations into segments based on social class orientation, personality, values, and lifestyle; and (4) behavioral segmentation, which divides populations into segments based on knowledge, attitudes, and practices relevant to the product being marketed (e.g., user status, usage rate, loyalty status, readiness for change). Segments are defined based on some combination of these variable classes. Cluster analysis is used to help marketers identify large population segments that are likely to be receptive to a product, that can be reached in cost-effective ways, and that can be targeted using a common advertising strategy.

As you theorize, consider if a person-centered perspective advances your efforts. Are there multiple dimensions or groups of variables where it would help to identify segments of individuals (or segments of other entities, such as families or organizations) who share common profiles across those dimensions? If so, what profiles or pattern of clusters across the dimensions do you expect to observe and why? Which clusters or profiles do you think will occur most frequently in your population? Why? As you begin to think about "segmenting" your population as a function of response patterns across variables, you may gain new insights into the phenomena you are addressing. For introductions to cluster analysis, see Everitt, Landau, Leese, and Stahl (2011) and Kaufman and Rousseeuw (2005). For a discussion of recent extensions of cluster analysis to procedures that integrate person-centered and variable-centered theorizing, see Lubke and Muthén (2005), Muthén (2001a), and Muthén and Muthén (2000). Chapter 11 also discusses numerous applications of cluster analysis.

SUMMARY AND CONCLUDING COMMENTS

We have considered over a dozen different perspectives for thinking about human behavior, including materialism, structuralism, functionalism, symbolic interactionism, evolutionary perspectives, postmodernism, neural networks, systems theory, stage theories, reinforcement theories, humanism, multilevel modeling, and person-centered theorizing. These frameworks complement and augment the frameworks of causal thinking, mathematical modeling, simulations, and emergent theory described in Chapters 7–11, as well as the strategies discussed in Chapter 4 for idea generation. We use the frameworks presented in this chapter by role-playing a scientist who embraces the particular system of thought, and then thinking about how that scientist would analyze the phenomenon in which we are interested. Sometimes this leads to new and productive insights, and sometimes it does not. But by forcing ourselves to invoke each of the perspectives, it helps us think through our phenomena in more depth and often yields insights we would not have thought of otherwise. Of course, there will be some phenomena for which a given framework simply does not seem relevant, and there is no reason to force the matter. But usually we find that a couple of the frameworks are both applicable and useful.

SUGGESTED READINGS

Abbott, A., & Alexander, J. C. (2004). *Methods of discovery: Heuristics for the social sciences.* New York: Norton.

—This book includes a chapter that adopts an approach similar to that used in the present chapter in which readers are encouraged to think about phenomena from different schools of thought. However, Abbott focuses on different frameworks and takes a dialectical approach.

Abdi, H., Valentin, D., & Edelman, M. (1999). *Neural networks.* Thousand Oaks, CA: SAGE.

—An introduction to neural network theories.

Blumer, H. (1969). *Symbolic interactionism: Perspective and method.* Berkeley: University of California Press.

—A classic book by a leading expert on symbolic interactionism.

Buss, D., Haselton, M., Shackelford, T., Bleske, A., & Wakefield, J. (1998). Adaptations, exaptations, and spandrels. *American Psychologist, 53,* 533–548.

—A general introduction to evolutionary perspectives in the social sciences.

Everitt, B., Landau, S., Leese, M., & Stahl, D. (2011). *Cluster analysis.* New York: Wiley.

—An introduction to the statistical technique of cluster analysis, which forms the cornerstone of many person-centered theory construction approaches.

Gergen, K. (2001). Psychological science in a postmodern context. *American Psychologist, 56,* 803–813.

—A central article for the application of postmodern perspectives to the social sciences, with a focus on psychology.

Klein, K., Tossi, H., & Cannella, A. (1999). Multilevel theory building: Barriers, benefits and new developments. *Academy of Management Review, 24,* 243–248.

—A special issue on multilevel modeling theories in organizational studies.

Lickliter, R., & Honeycutt, H. (2003). Developmental dynamics: Toward a biologically plausible evolutionary psychology. *Psychological Bulletin, 129,* 819–835.

—An insightful critique of evolutionary perspectives.

McGee, J., & Warms, R. (2003). *Anthropological theory: An introductory history.* Boston: McGraw-Hill.

—An introduction to such systems of thought as materialism and structuralism.

Merton, R. (1968). *Social theory and social structure.* New York: Free Press.

—A classic on structuralist–functionalist thinking.

Parsons, T. (1971). *The system of modern societies.* Englewood Cliffs, NJ: Prentice-Hall.

—Another classic on structuralist thinking.

Raudenbush, S., & Bryk, A. (2001). *Hierarchical linear models: Applications and data analysis methods.* Newbury Park, CA: SAGE.

—An insightful and useful discussion of multilevel analysis from the perspective of mathematical and statistical modeling.

Seligman, M., & Csikszentmihalyi, M. (2000). Positive psychology: An introduction. *American Psychologist, 55,* 5–14.

—The lead article of a special issue on positive psychology. The collection of articles also discusses humanistic perspectives more generally.

Skinner, B. F. (1965). *Science and human behavior.* New York: Free Press.

—A classic on behaviorism, a major reinforcement theory in psychology.

Weinstein, N., Rothman, A., & Sutton, S. (1998). Stage theories of health behavior: Conceptual and methodological issues. *Health Psychology, 17,* 290–299.

—A discussion of the core properties of stage theories.

KEY TERMS

materialism (p. 341)

structuralism (p. 343)

functionalism (p. 344)

symbolic interactionism (p. 346)

evolutionary variation (p. 347)

inheritance (p. 347)

selection (p. 347)

by-products of adaptation (p. 347)

ultimate causation (p. 348)

postmodernism (p. 349)

modernism (p. 349)

deconstruction (p. 351)

neural networks (p. 352)

systems theory (p. 352)

neuron (p. 352)

input layer (p. 352)

output layer (p. 352)

hidden layer (p. 352)

threshold unit (p. 353)

threshold value (p. 353)

activation index (p. 353)

static system (p. 355)

dynamic system (p. 355)

closed system (p. 355)

open system (p. 355)

feedback (p. 355)

equilibrium (p. 355)

equifinality (p. 355)

life-cycle model of change (p. 357)

teleological model of change (p. 357)

dialectical model of change (p. 357)

evolutionary model of change (p. 357)

stage theory (p. 357)

developmental synchrony (p. 358)

partial developmental priority (p. 358)

complete developmental priority (p. 358)

reinforcement theories (p. 359)

stimulus (p. 359)

response (p. 359)

eliciting stimulus (p. 359)

discriminative stimulus (p. 359)

reinforcing stimulus (p. 359)

drive (p. 361)

Thurstone's law of effect (p. 361)

positive reinforcers (p 361)

negative reinforcers (p. 361)

punishment (p. 361)

continuous reinforcement schedule (p. 361)

intermittent reinforcement schedule (p. 362)

stimulus generalization (p. 362)

discrimination (p. 362)

extinction (p. 362)

humanism (p. 363)

focus-oriented strengths (p. 363)

balance-oriented strengths (p. 363)

multilevel model (p. 364)

cluster analysis (p. 368)

EXERCISES

Exercises to Reinforce Concepts

1. Describe the basic tenets and principles of materialism.

2. Describe the basic tenets and principles of structuralism.

3. Describe the basic tenets and principles of functionalism.

4. Describe the basic tenets and principles of symbolic interactionism.

5. Describe the basic tenets and principles of evolutionary perspectives.

6. Describe the basic tenets and principles of postmodernism.

7. Describe the basic tenets and principles of neural networks.

8. Describe the basic tenets and principles of systems theories.

9. Describe the basic tenets and principles of stage theories.

10. Describe the basic tenets and principles of reinforcement theories.

11. Describe the basic tenets and principles of humanism.

12. Describe the basic tenets and principles of multilevel modeling.

13. Describe the basic tenets and principles of person-centered theorizing.

Exercises to Apply Concepts

1. Pick an existing theory in an area of interest to you and try to recast it using at least one of the frameworks described in this chapter.

2. Pick an outcome variable and analyze it from the perspective of any two of the frameworks described in this chapter. Compare and contrast the approaches and the conclusions you make.

Part IV

THEORY AT THE LEVEL OF MEASUREMENT

13

Theory and Measurement

General Frameworks

*I feel passionately about measurement—about how difficult it is,
about how much theory and conceptualization is involved in
measurement and indeed, how much politics is involved.*
    —SIR ANGUS DEATON, Nobel Laureate in Economics

Measurement and observation are at the heart of science. Despite the centrality of measurement, philosophers of science and scientists themselves disagree about how to define measurement, what is measurable, and the necessary conditions that make measurement feasible. When we measure a construct (e.g., depression), we specify a *theory* that links the observed measure to the underlying construct that the measure is thought to reflect (true depression). When we confront the problem of measurement error in a study, we formulate a *theory* about factors that impact measurement error and then we seek to address those factors to make our measures better. As such, theory construction is relevant to measurement. Although many social scientists see measurement as the province of methodology and/or a simple task of choosing a good measure, the fact is that researchers must rely on *theories* of measurement to effectively measure constructs in empirical research. In this chapter, we elucidate a theory construction mindset for you to use when thinking about measurement and when choosing measures to use in your research. After reading this chapter (and Chapter 14), we hope you will better appreciate the theoretical underpinnings of measurement and why you need to think about it from a theory construction perspective.

Before elaborating such perspectives, we must first present some background material, namely, how measurement is traditionally defined, the classic distinctions about levels of measurement, and revisiting (from Chapter 5) the importance of concept mapping. After doing so, we present the basics of classic test theory, a fundamental theory of measurement that emphasizes the concepts of reliability and validity. This theory allows us to then articulate approaches to constructing theories of measurement within that context. Chapter 14 complements the current chapter, but it approaches measurement theory construction at a more microlevel, focusing on self-reports, observer reports, and "objective" measures. The current chapter is the view of the measurement theory forest; Chapter 14 is a view of the trees inside that forest.

Measurement theory is traditionally associated with quantitative research, and our initial discussion will adopt this frame. However, the concepts are essential for qualitative research as well. We make this explicit after developing key points using quantitative research perspectives. Readers with a more qualitative emphasis—be patient. If you conduct mixed-methods research, then the material in this chapter is directly relevant to your focus.

DEFINING MEASUREMENT

Measurement traditionally has been defined as the assignment of people or "objects" to numerical categories according to a set of rules (Stevens, 1951). The *metric* of a measure refers to the numbers or units that are used to reflect the variable (e.g., a 1 to 5 scale; a 0 to 10 scale; a 0 to 100 scale). The metric for grade point average in the United States in many schools is 0 to 4 (4 = A, 3 = B, 2 = C, 1 = D, 0 = E/F). The metric for whether someone reports having ever used drugs might be 0 or 1 (0 = no, 1 = yes). Metrics for variables are human inventions that people agree represent a reasonable benchmark for the variable. For example, the ancient Egyptians measured height in units of "hands," and this standard was adopted by various communities in order to provide a common benchmark for describing height. Height was determined by laying hands side by side next to the object to be measured (one hand is about 4 inches or 0.10 meters wide). Current-day metric benchmarks for many physical phenomena are as arbitrary as "hands," but they are quite precise and strictly regulated by world governments and treaties. The General Conference on Weights and Measures (CGPM), established in 1875, oversees the international kilogram system. In 1983, the meter was redefined as the distance traveled by light in free space in 1/299,792,458 of a second. In 1960, by agreement of the governments of the United States, the United Kingdom, Australia, and South Africa, the yard was redefined as being 0.9144 meters. The kilogram was redefined in 2018 by a consensus of 60 countries to tie its definition to Planck's constant, the smallest possible unit of energy in quantum physics. Metrics used in the social sciences often lack such oversight, consensus, and precision; however, and as a result, measurement can be more of a metric "free for all."

A major approach to measurement during the early 1900s emphasized mapping relationships between objects onto relationships between numbers. Measurement theorists focused on theories for measuring magnitudes of an underlying dimension, such as height (how tall something is), velocity (how fast something moves), weight (how heavy something is), or length (how long something is). They sought to map numerical relations derived from algebra onto known relations between objects relative to those magnitudes and relied on mathematical proofs to accomplish the mappings. Scholars working in this tradition often argued that relations among the measured objects did not always correspond to relations governed by the rules of algebra, so that measurement was possible for only those objects that did so. Many concepts were thus deemed unmeasurable. Considerable disagreement occurred about what conditions had to exist for meaningful measurement to occur and what could be measured.

This somewhat narrow view of measurement was liberalized by S. S. Stevens (1946, 1951) when he introduced his now classic distinction between levels of measurement (nominal, ordinal, interval, and ratio). He proposed that measurement was indeed applicable to a broad range of objects as long as one did not demand that measures conform to all of the formal rules of algebra. In Stevens's system, *nominal measurement* uses numbers merely as labels. For example, an investigator might classify a group of people according to their religion—Catholic, Protestant, Jewish, and all others—and use the numbers 1, 2, 3, and 4 for these categories. The numbers have no special quality; they are merely labels. *Ordinal measurement* assigns numbers to objects in ways that allow the objects to be ordered on an underlying continuum. For example, if on the SAT test that measures verbal ability you are told you scored in the 50th percentile and someone else scored in the 48th percentile, you know you have more verbal ability than that person, but you have no idea by how much. When cast in a metric of percentiles, the SAT represents an ordinal measure. *Interval-level measurement* assigns numbers in ways that have ordinal properties, but with an additional mathematical property: the difference between two consecutive numbers will reflect the same amount of the underlying dimension as any other two consecutive numbers. For example, on a Fahrenheit scale of temperature, the difference between 32 and 33 degrees reflects the same amount of heat as the difference between 45 and 46 degrees. *Ratio-level measurement* has all the properties of interval-level measurement, but in addition, ratio statements are meaningful. For example, for the metric of distance in miles, 4 miles is twice as far as 2 miles and 20 miles is twice as far as 10 miles. This property does not necessarily hold for interval-level measures. Stevens's system is important because the answers to certain questions using statistical analyses can require different levels of measurement (see Davison & Sharma, 1988, 1990; Townsend & Ashby, 1984; Vellman & Wilkinson, 1993).

The history of measurement is a fascinating topic. For our purposes here, we rely on the working definition of measurement as "the assignment of people or 'objects' to numerical categories according to a set of rules," while also making use of Stevens's classification scheme.

CONCEPTUAL DEFINITIONS AND MEASUREMENT

The measure one uses to represent a construct should be guided in large part by the conceptual definition of the construct. In many cases, this mapping is straightforward. A person's registered political party affiliation and weight are two such examples. By contrast, other variables represent content domains that are not as straightforward, potentially large, and challenging to measure. For example, the concept of intelligence is complex and multifaceted because there are many types of intelligence. Even if an investigator limits interest to one type of intelligence, say mathematical intelligence, one could generate a measure of it in many ways. When measuring a variable, it is important that researchers adequately specify its universe of relevant content and then decide what to sample from that universe for measurement purposes (see Chapter 5). For example, if a conceptualization of social support specifies four types of support (tangible, emotional, informational, companionship), then these four domains need to be represented in a measure unless an investigator is interested in only a specific type of support. The extent to which a measure adequately represents the totality of a construct is called *content validity* (Nunnally, 1978). As Cronbach, Gleser, Nanda, and Rajaratnam (1972, p. 380) state, "if one claims that observations represent a universe, one ought to define the universe clearly. Readers should agree that the conditions appearing in the study fit within the universe and that they are reasonably distributed over its whole range, not confined to some narrow sub-universe."

Inevitably, a healthy "give and take" exists between conceptual definitions and measurement, with conceptual definitions guiding the choice of measures and the choice of measures nuancing more abstract conceptual definitions embraced by a study. Consider the case of poverty, which might be defined conceptually as the state of being very poor. How might this state be measured? A researcher might measure poverty using income, with income values below a cutoff standard (sometimes called the "poverty line") used to reflect poverty. Another researcher might agree with this approach but further reason that people may have limited income and yet own considerable assets that enable them to live quite comfortably. As such, this researcher might factor assets into a measure of poverty as well. How should he or she weight the different assets, such as home ownership, car ownership, and access to health care? In agricultural communities in developing countries, those who own horses, cows, or a truck often are deemed to possess key assets. Are these assets taken into account when assessing poverty in studies of people living in an agricultural community? What about urban areas? As we examine more closely what assets the researcher measures and how they are quantified and combined to form an index of poverty, we gain a more nuanced sense of the concept of poverty that is invoked in the study.

In the United States, the poverty line is set by the Census Bureau and is defined as the minimum amount of income needed to cover basic needs (in 2018, it was about $25,000 for a family of four). However, countries define poverty using different criteria. For example, many countries currently define poverty lines based on the concept of how much it costs people to have enough to eat. Having enough to eat is often quantified as 2,000 calories per day, but this value might be adjusted upward or downward depending on circumstance. Policymakers then calculate the smallest amount of money necessary to buy a food bundle with 2,000 calories. Other countries base the index on the cost of purchasing essential living necessities that include factors other than just having enough to eat. What are these necessities? These also vary from country to country. In most European countries, the poverty line is set at 60% of the median income of the country. Using yet another approach, in research in small rural towns, one might measure poverty by asking residents to identify the poorest individuals in the township. These subjective nominations constitute yet another measure of poverty. In all of these cases, the conceptual meaning of poverty is "the state of being very poor," but the meaning of "very poor" is somewhat different and nuanced. In one case (nominations by others) it is subjective, while in other cases it is based on different criteria with different cutoffs. Measurement and conceptual definitions go back and forth, with measurement often giving greater clarity to the meaning of a concept in a study but with the essential meaning of the concept driving the choice of measures.

CLASSIC TEST THEORY: THE BASICS

Having presented this background, we now describe classic test theory—a theory of measurement that emphasizes the concepts of reliability and validity (Lord & Novick, 1968). The theory focuses not so much on how to construct a measure of a variable/concept and the challenges of doing so, but rather on whether the constructed measure has certain desirable psychometric properties. The theory is mathematical in form, but we present it conceptually. We begin by formally defining the concepts of reliability and validity, introducing the notions of random error and systematic error in so doing. We then represent classic test theory as an influence diagram and proceed to "theory construct" using the diagram as a frame.

Reliability

Ideally, a person's score on a measure of a construct is impacted by that person's true standing on the underlying dimension being measured and on nothing else. Unfortunately, this is often not the case. Sometimes the observed score is influenced by both the true score of the individual and other factors that represent *measurement error.* There are different types of measurement error, one of which is called *random measurement error.* These errors are random events that arbitrarily push an individual's observed score up or down when the measurement is taken. The events likely will not repeat themselves in the same way for the same individual on a different assessment occasion because the events are, after all, random. For example, a person might happen to misread an item on a survey and answer it differently than would otherwise be the case. Think of the last time you missed a question you knew the answer to on an exam, but you got it wrong because you misread it. Or you might happen to be in a particularly bad mood on the day of the exam, and this mood might influence your response to a question. The wording of a question might be ambiguous, so you can interpret the question differently at different points in time depending on your frame of mind. These random influences are unpredictable, they can artificially raise *or* lower scores, and they are unsystematic. The *reliability* of a measure is the extent to which it is free of random error. Psychometricians quantify reliability using an index called the *reliability ratio,* which ranges from 0 to 1.00. It reflects the degree to which a measure is *not* affected by random error. If the reliability ratio (or more simply, the reliability) of a measure is 0.70, then 70% of the variation in the measure is systematic and 30% is random error. If the reliability ratio is 0.90, then 90% of the variation is systematic and 10% is random error.

Measurement unreliability can distort the inferences we make from a measure and, obviously, is undesirable. If we want to determine the degree of association between the quality of mother–adolescent relationships and adolescent drug use and if both measures have a reliability of 0.50 (half of the variability in each measure is random noise), then we are probably going to significantly underestimate the true association between the constructs. When we conduct a statistical analysis that seeks to control for a confound by including a measure of that confounding variable in a regression analysis, if the measure is contaminated by random error, then perhaps we really have not adequately controlled for the confound. For example, to the extent measures of socioeconomic status (SES) are subject to random error, then analyses that seek to control SES statistically may not adequately do so.

How unreliable can a measure be to still be considered scientifically useful? If a measure is contaminated by 30% random noise, is that acceptable? How about 20%? Or how about 10%? The answer is not straightforward because differing amounts of random error have different consequences, depending on the questions one seeks to answer. Nunnally (1967/1978; Nunnally & Bernstein, 1994) has argued that correlations of the magnitude typically observed in the social sciences are not much affected as long as the reliability of measures is 0.80 or higher. Cortina (1993) notes that reliability estimates of 0.70 or greater in scientific reports usually are presented without comment or qualifications about unreliability. Rogosa (1999) describes a case where if a national aptitude test, like the SAT or GRE, has a reliability of 0.85, a student whose true score is in the 50th percentile will have only a probability of about 0.25 of scoring between the 45th and 55th percentile. That is, the percentile rank of the test taker can be nontrivially compromised. Tests such as the SAT and GRE often are determining factors in college admissions, so random error in them is disconcerting. For research purposes, some analytic methods (e.g., structural equation modeling [SEM]) often allow us to take measure unreliability into account when estimating means, standard deviations, correlations, and regression coefficients. Even so, it is good practice to maximize the reliability of measures to the extent possible.

It turns out that it is difficult to know the true reliability of many measures, but psychometricians have derived (imperfect) methods for estimating it. These estimation strategies include test–retest methods, split-half methods, alternate form methods, methods based on SEM, and coefficient alpha for multi-item scales. Consideration of these methods is beyond the scope of this book; interested readers are referred to Price (2016) and Furr (2017). Note that some scientists confuse reliability estimation methods with the concept of reliability per se. For example, some researchers describe reliability as the extent to which a measure at one point in time is highly correlated with or reproduces scores for that same measure at another point in time, assuming the construct remains stable. This is not reliability. It is the test–retest method for *estimating* reliability. Different estimation methods can be sensitive to different types of random error and make different assumptions, but ultimately, our goal is to estimate the extent to which a measure is free of random error.

Validity and Systematic Error

In addition to random error, there is another type of measurement error, called *systematic error*. Systematic error is not random and, unless countered, can repeat itself on multiple occasions for the same individuals. As one example, *constant error* occurs if measured scores are biased upward (or downward) by a constant value for everyone, such as when a scale to measure weight is consistently 5 pounds too heavy. Another type of systematic error, socially desirable response tendencies, refers to an individual difference variable that reflects a propensity to want to create good impressions on others. Individuals who are high on this trait are more likely to systematically underreport such things as drug use, unprotected sex, and depressive symptoms and to overreport income, life satisfaction, and accomplishments. Systematic error can bias estimates of means, correlations, and other statistics when we conduct theory tests. For example, social desirability response tendencies might impact self-reports of both drug and alcohol use, thereby inflating the estimated correlation between the two variables due to the common cause of social desirability on both measures. Or the presence of variation due to social desirable response tendencies in an outcome might weaken the ability of other variables to predict the contaminated scores of that outcome. A common strategy for dealing with systematic error variance is to obtain a measure of its source and then include that measure as a covariate in one's statistical model. For example, measures of social desirability response tendencies (Stoeber, 2001) can be gathered in a study and then used as a covariate in a regression analysis by including the measure in the prediction equation. Ideally, however, measures are constructed in ways that minimize systematic measurement error to begin with.

A measure is said to be valid or have *validity* to the extent that it is free of both random error and systematic error; that is, the only thing causing variation in it is the true variance of the construct the measure is thought to reflect.

Figure 13.1a presents a diagram of this measurement theory. The observed (measured) scores are a function of three constructs: (1) people's true scores on the underlying dimension being measured, (2) people's random error scores, and (3) people's systematic error scores.[1] Technically, this theory is not directly testable because we rarely know the true scores of individuals, nor can we directly assess either of the error scores. Nonetheless, the framework can be used to evaluate measures and to form useful "theories of measurement," so it has heuristic value. Figure 13.1b presents an expanded representation of the theory that will be used in the remainder of this chapter and that underscores the role of theory construction in measurement. As will be seen, a host of factors can impact the amount of random error in a measure. When pursuing measurement, we need to theorize about what these factors are and, if research bears out their relevance, try to eliminate them when we conduct research. There also are a host of factors that impact the amount of systematic error in a measure, and we also need to theorize about them. Sometimes it is not possible to eliminate the sources of systematic error, so we need to theorize about variables or strategies that will allow us to mitigate their impact. That is, we need to identify addressable moderators of their impact on observed scores and then use our knowledge of those moderators to reduce the effects of error.

Our goal in the remainder of this chapter is to help you think about measurement theoretically from the perspective of Figure 13.1b and ultimately to adopt a theory-construction mindset for random and systematic error for every project you pursue. Some social scientists publish research on their "theories of measurement" about factors that impact random and systematic error so that others can take advantage of the theory they have developed. We discuss much of this research in this chapter.

---

[1] Technically, classic test theory is based in variance decomposition, but we take some liberties here in the interest of pedagogy.

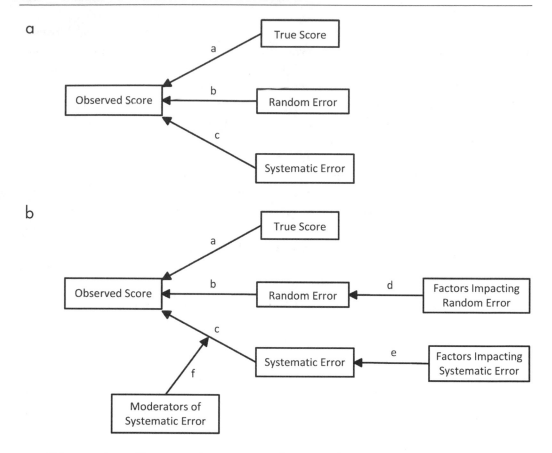

FIGURE 13.1. Classic test theory. (a) Brief version; (b) theory construction version.

Parenthetically, measurement theory extends well beyond a focus on paths *d*, *e*, and *f* in Figure 13.1b. For example, a branch of psychometrics focuses on path *a*, namely, the function that relates true scores to measured scores. Often, we assume that this function is linear (which is the case for interval or ratio measures), but perhaps it is nonlinear monotonic (which is the case for ordinal measures). Quite elegant theories have been developed surrounding path *a*, but consideration of these theories is beyond the scope of this book (go to our companion website *www.theory-construction.com* for a discussion of them). Our focus here is primarily on the boxes associated with paths *d* and *e*, coupled with a discussion of ways to either eliminate a given source of measurement error or, if it cannot be eliminated, invoke strategies to minimize their influence.

THE FACETS OF MEASUREMENT AND THEORY CONSTRUCTION

Often scientists speak of the reliability and validity of a scale. Technically, however, this is not a correct frame of reference. When we administer a scale, we do so in a specific setting, for a specified population of individuals, and at a given point in time. The reliability and validity of a set of observations are functions of each facet of measurement, inclusive of scale. A scale can be reliable and/or valid for one population but not for another. It can be reliable and/or valid when given in one type of setting but not in another. It can have good psychometric properties at one point in time but not at another. In this sense, we should generally reference the reliability and validity *of a set of observations* rather than a scale per se. An important extension of classic test theory is a theory known as *generalizability theory* (Brennan, 2001; Cronbach, Nageswari, & Gleser, 1963; Shavelson & Webb, 1991), which is grounded in the idea that measurement error potentially varies as a function of these facets of measurement.

We can give many examples of the impact of measurement facets on the reliability and validity of measures. For example, there is controversy about whether intelligence tests are valid indicators of general intelligence for different ethnic groups (Onwuegbuzie & Daley, 2001). Studies also have explored whether web-based administration of a scale alters the reliability and validity of the observations produced by that scale relative to traditional face-to-face administrations (Meade, Michels, & Lautenschlager, 2007). Research has found that the reliability and validity of a scale can change with the age of a child as children mature and acquire different levels of cognitive and emotional ability (Borgers, de Leeuw, & Hox, 2000). Research also has documented differences in the validity of self-reports of physical activity by adults as a function of their educational levels (Annemarie et al., 2015). These examples underscore the importance of keeping in mind each facet of measurement when you theory construct about sources of random and systematic error in measures. Think about what characteristics of the testing situation might impact random or systematic error. Think about what characteristics of the broader context might be a source of random or systematic error. Think about how the timing of the assessment might impact random or systematic error. Think about features of the scale itself that might encourage random or systematic error. All of these considerations are key to good theory construction. To conduct quality research, not only must we think about theory at the conceptual level, so too must we think about theory at the level of measurement.

MEASUREMENT THEORY CONSTRUCTION

We now illustrate approaches to measurement theory construction. We focus first on theory construction surrounding random error and then on systematic error.

Constructing a Theory of Random Error

Our first target of theorizing is to think about factors that increase the random error (unreliability) in a measure you plan to use in a given assessment setting for a given set of individuals at a given point in time. Once these factors are identified, you will want to adopt practices to negate them so as to increase the reliability of the measure. In this section, we illustrate the theory construction process focusing on examples with self-reports. However, the spirit of the approach applies to observer and "objective" measures as well, as elaborated later and in Chapter 14.

Suppose we plan to ask adolescents questions about their beliefs about smoking marijuana using a 5-point disagree–agree rating scale for each of 10 belief statements, as well as questions about their use of alcohol and of marijuana (separately) during the past month. One way random error can occur is if an individual becomes distracted when reading an item, such as by a noise or some other interruption, causing a misreading of the question. This possibility can be addressed by ensuring a quiet, distraction-free assessment setting. If you plan to administer an unsupervised web survey to respondents in their home, it is more difficult to ensure such an environment. Your task then is to problem-solve a way to do so. For example, using instructions given at the outset of the study, you might tell respondents how important a distraction-free environment is and encourage them to find such a setting to complete the survey, perhaps suggesting possibilities.

Another source of random error might be question ambiguity; if the meaning of a word or phrase in a question is ambiguous, people might interpret it differently, depending on whatever happens to be salient in their minds at that particular point in time. For example, the question "how many times have you used marijuana in the past month" contains several sources of ambiguity. The phrase "the past month" could be interpreted as meaning the past 30 days, or it could mean since the first day of the month (e.g., February 1). The phrase the "number of times" could be interpreted as the number of days irrespective of whether the respondent smoked marijuana multiple times on the same day. Should marijuana use on two separate occasions on the same day be counted as "2" times or "1" time? Some people may interpret the question using one interpretation, while other people might interpret it the other way. Does "use" refer to smoking marijuana, eating marijuana in a food product, vaporizing it, or some other form of ingestion? Clearly, this question can be rephrased to eliminate these ambiguities. For example, we might decide that using marijuana on multiple occasions on the same day is not crucial to our theory, and then we might ask the question "During the past 30 days, on how many days did you use marijuana (in any form, such as smoking, eating in a food product, etc.?)."

Ambiguity also can result from omissions. For example, if not made explicit in a question, respondents will often impute their own time frames and other contextual information into questions, leading to unreliable responses. The item "Joining a gang would be good" can elicit a different response than the item "For me, joining a gang in my neighborhood at this time would be good." The first statement not only fails to indicate a time period, it also fails to clarify whether the respondent is being asked about his or her own gang-related decision or the decisions of people in general. Vague or abstract questions invite random noise to enter into responses.

Yet another source of random error might be warm-up effects for scale usage. People in a study may not be familiar with, say, a 5-point rating scale, and it may take them a few items to get comfortable using it. The initial items rated may thus contain random error due to scale unfamiliarity. This random error can be minimized by providing a few practice items that allow people to adjust to the scale. Another source of random error might be people misreading items because they are in a hurry to finish the task. This can be countered by ensuring that people have plenty of time to complete the survey and that they know this is the case. Another source of random error might be boredom, as respondents grow weary of answering so many questions. This error can be minimized by keeping the survey to a manageable length or by "breaking up" sets of questions to reduce monotony (perhaps by splitting the survey into different packets and allowing for short breaks between packets). Yet another source of random error might be coding errors—staff members who code the completed survey into the computer may make recording errors. This problem can be addressed by using two independent coders for the same data and comparing their entries. Alternatively, one might store responses into a database directly from a computer-administered survey, thereby avoiding the step of data coding (although computer errors are possible as well).

Figure 13.2 presents the measurement theory that results by incorporating the ideas from the above theory construction process. In the research that we conduct, we make it routine practice to engage in this type of theory construction for every measure we intend to use, drawing, in part, on the research literature of published theories of factors that affect measure unreliability. We then think about ways to counteract the identified factors that promote random error variance in each measure. The examples of sources of random error described above are illustrative, not exhaustive. Again, you need to theory construct about the most likely and important sources of random error for your particular research study. To reduce clutter, we have not integrated the strategies for dealing with each source of random error into Figure 13.2. But the spirit of our approach should be evident: Build a theory about the sources of random measurement error and then do your best to nullify them.

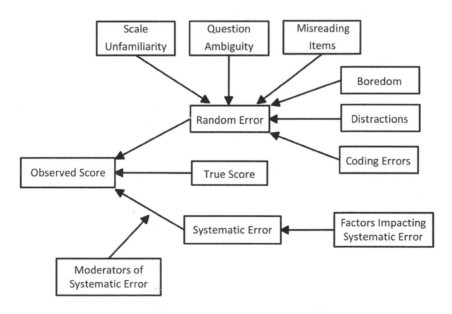

FIGURE 13.2. Augmented diagram for random error.

Constructing a Theory of Systematic Error

For systematic error, we repeat the same process, but now we theory construct about systematic error for each measure. If we are asking sensitive questions, then one obvious source of systematic error is social desirability bias, described earlier. Social desirability is often viewed as a relatively stable, trait-like characteristic of individuals that is difficult to change. If we suspect it is relevant in a given measurement context, then we typically use the following procedures to lessen its impact by situational means (that serve as moderators): (1) use a self-administered as opposed to a face-to-face reporting format so that respondents do not have to report sensitive behaviors directly to an interviewer; (2) use anonymous/confidential conditions and provide respondents assurances that identifying information will not be associated in any way with their data; (3) stress that results in research reports will only be reported for groups of people, not for individuals; (4) provide motivational instructions at the outset that encourage honest reporting (e.g., how the quality and ability of the research to "make a difference" depends on people giving honest answers); (5) instruct respondents not to answer a question if they are not going to be truthful (and then use specialized analytic methods to handle the missing data); and (6) obtain a measure of social desirability tendencies to use as a statistical covariate.

Another potential source of systematic error is the *response style* or *response set* that some people use. In a study with a large international sample, Baumgartner and Steenkamp (2001) identified five response styles: (1) acquiescence (the tendency to endorse items/questions, independent of their content), (2) disacquiescence (the tendency to disagree with items/questions independent of their content), (3) extreme (the tendency to use the extremes of a rating scale independent of item/question content), (4) midpoint (the tendency to use the midpoint of a rating scale independent of item/question content), and (5) noncontingent (the tendency to respond to items carelessly, randomly, or nonpurposefully). These researchers found that the response styles accounted for an average of about 25% of the variation in 14 different consumer behavior constructs. To be sure, debate has arisen over the extent to which response styles are problematic for social science research (e.g., Lance, Dawson, Birkelbach, & Hoffman, 2010; Podsakoff, MacKenzie, & Podsakoff, 2012; Spector & Brannick, 2009; Van Vaerenbergh & Thomas, 2013). However, we believe it is good practice to consider the possibility that response styles operate and then introduce correctives, should evidence for response set bias be present (see below). A common strategy for dealing with response styles is to obtain a measure of the tendency and then statistically control for it when analyzing the data (see Baumgartner & Steenkamp, 2001; Podsakoff et al., 2012; Van Vaerenbergh & Thomas, 2013; Weijters, Geuens, & Schillewaert, 2008).

Yet another source of systematic error is the use of leading questions that encourage research participants to respond in certain ways. A classic example comes from Loftus and Palmer (1974). In their study, students watched a film of a traffic accident and afterward described what happened as if they were eyewitnesses. They were then asked specific questions, one of which was "About how fast were the cars going when they contacted each other?" In another condition, everything was the same except individuals responded to the question "About how fast were the cars going when they smashed into each other?" The average speed estimate for the first question was 32 miles per hour, but for the second it was 42 miles per hour. The latter question encourages respondents to communicate a faster speed by using the word "smashed." We always review questions with an eye toward determining if they have this quality.

Race or gender matching of the interviewer and respondent is another potential consideration for systematic error variance. Lamb and Garretson (2003) studied forensic interviews of alleged child abuse victims and found that girls between the ages of 4 and 14 tended to provide more information to female than to male interviewers; boys did not respond differently to male and female interviewers. Barnes and colleagues (2008) found that White interviewers asking Blacks questions about discrimination tended to yield lower estimates of discrimination than was found with Black interviewers. Sometimes, however, race matching interviewers and respondents can also produce biased responses. For example, research in political science has found that Blacks tend to overreport their voting behavior in elections and that this tendency is more prevalent when Blacks are interviewed by Black interviewers than by White interviewers (Jenkins, White, Hanmer, & Banks, 2018). A possible interpretation of this finding is that positive norms toward "Black" political participation are activated by the presence of Black interviewers, thereby creating the overreporting (Jenkins et al., 2018). Schaeffer, Dykema, and Maynard (2010) reviewed the literature on interviewer effects more generally and concluded that sensitive, ambiguous, complex, and open-ended questions are more likely to be biased by interviewer effects than questions that are simple, straightforward, and closed-ended (see also West & Blom, 2017). These reviews underscore the importance of interviewer training to remove interviewer effects. If matches or mismatches are thought to be problematic for your research but you are unable to address them procedurally, then they often can be handled through statistical covariates using race of the respondent and the interviewer in statistical modeling.

Another type of systematic error is the order in which questions are asked. A classic example was described by Iyengar and Kinder (1987), who found that when people were first asked "What is the most important problem facing the nation?," the answer they gave became the basis for their answer to the next question asking about approval or disapproval of a presidential candidate. This phenomenon is called a *priming effect*. The ordering of questions also may be impactful if respondents try to appear consistent, purposely making their answers to later questions consistent with prior answers. Some methodologists suggest dealing with order effects by randomizing the order of questions, but this can be a nightmare for data coders: it can create awkward sequences of questions (if questions form natural groupings), and it might even create increased random error as respondents try to deal with the constant shifting of their frames of mind to answer questions. An alternative strategy is to place similar questions together in a block and to counterbalance the order of presentation of blocks (using a Latin square design per Maxwell, Delaney, & Kelley, 2003) and then statistically control for ordering during data analysis.

Another form of systematic measurement error is *source effects*. The idea is that depending on the source of the measure, variance unique to that source can bias the observed measures relative to the true scores. For example, reports of levels of anxiety of an adolescent might be obtained from a parent, a friend of the adolescent, a teacher, and a clinician. Generally, the correlations among such reports are relatively low, suggesting the presence of source effects (Silverman, Kurtines, Jaccard, & Pina, 2009). Some interpret this lack of convergence as indicative of systematic error, but it also is possible that the "source" effects are substantively meaningful. For example, in anxiety research, different sources are exposed to different behaviors of adolescents in different contexts, and anxiety might manifest itself differently in these contexts. Rather than being artifactual, "source effects" might be of substantive interest. When planning a study, it is good practice to theorize about potential artifactual source effects and, if they are likely, to develop procedures to counteract them. Well-crafted instructional sets can help sources rise above their biases (see De Los Reyes, Augenstein, Wang, Thomas, & Drabick, 2015); statistical correctives during data analysis can also be used (via SEM).

Source effects are a broader type of systematic error called *method variance* or *method effects*. Method effects occur when a person's inferred standing on a dimension based on an observed measure varies by the method of assessment. In essence, method variance reflects variance attributable to the measurement method rather than to the construct the measure supposedly represents. The mechanisms responsible for hypothesized method effects need to be specified in order to be dealt with. For example, when a supervisor completes evaluative ratings of a worker's productivity, the supervisor's ratings might be impacted by *halo effects*—bias in which one's overall impression of a person ("he or she is very likeable") impacts evaluations of that person's performance independent of actual performance. A more objective measure of worker productivity, such as quantity of products made or sold by the worker, might not be subject to such method effects. As is the case with response styles, there is debate about how problematic method variance is in social science research (e.g., Lance et al., 2010; Podsakoff et al., 2012; Spector & Brannick, 2009), but as before, we believe it is good practice to a priori theorize about method effects and then address them procedurally or statistically.

Figure 13.3 is an expanded depiction of Figure 13.2 and includes the above concepts based on our theory construction process surrounding systematic error (to avoid clutter, we omit the moderators we discussed). Again, as you develop and evaluate measures for use in your research, you will want to build a theory of both random and systematic error variance for each measure, using the facets of measurement as a potential organizing frame. Note that the variables in Figure 13.3 represent characteristics of the questions (e.g., leading questions), of the population (e.g., social desirability and response sets), or of the broader testing context (e.g., interviewer effects, question order). The theory you generate may include some of the factors elaborated here as well as other factors; be sure to take into account the idiosyncratic features of your research. As with random error, we don't just select a measure that has been found to be relatively free of systematic error in a prior study and then assume all is fine. Rather, we engage in thoughtful theory construction surrounding the sources of systematic error in our planned study and all the facets of measurement associated with it.

Gaining Perspectives on True Score Variance

Invariably, you will need to make a case (both to yourself and to others) that the measure of a construct you are using is dominated by true score variance. Without access to true scores, how can we know this? One strategy for asserting measure validity is to

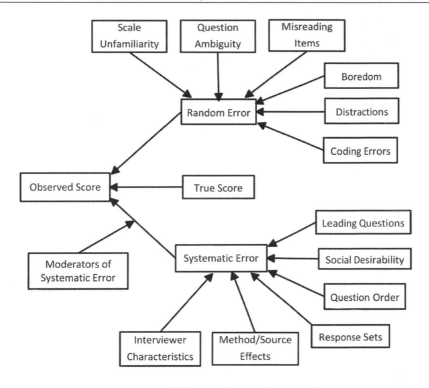

FIGURE 13.3. Augmented diagram for random and systematic error.

correlate the measure with valid measures of other constructs that are known, without ambiguity, to be associated with the target construct. If the measure is correlated with things it is supposed to be correlated with, we will have more confidence in its validity. Psychometricians have identified several such strategies, with the main ones being *convergent validity* ("Does the measure correlate with other measures of the same construct?"), *concurrent validity* ("Does the measure correlate with other constructs it is supposed to be related to when both are measured concurrently?"), and *predictive validity* ("Does the measure prospectively predict other constructs it should predict?"). If we develop a new, brief measure of intelligence, for example, we expect it, based on hundreds of prior studies, to be related to performance in school to a moderate degree. If, however, we correlate the new measure with a valid index of grade point average and observe a trivial correlation, we will question the validity of the measure.

Another approach to establish validity is to correlate the measure with valid measures of other constructs that are unambiguously known to be *unrelated* to the target construct. If a correlation between the measure and these other constructs is observed, questions about the validity of the measure arise. For example, it is well established that there are no gender differences in general intelligence among youth (Nisbett et al., 2012). If our new measure of intelligence finds a notable gender difference, then this result will raise questions about its validity. This type of validity is sometimes called *discriminant validity*. When examining discriminant validity by showing a lack of association, it obviously is not sufficient to select an irrelevant construct (e.g., eye color) and empirically demonstrate the absence of an association. Rather, the validating construct must be grounded in a larger, meaningful, multivariate theoretical network and be shown to behave in that network in ways that are expected based on past research, in terms of both expected correlations and expected lack of correlations. This type of analysis is referred to as *construct validity* or *nomological validity*.[2]

As you theorize about a measure from the perspective of classic test theory, it often is useful to identify variables that can help establish construct validity or that strengthen confidence in validity through convergent, concurrent, or predictive validity. We routinely seek to include such variables in our research to build a stronger psychometric case for our measures, although practical constraints sometimes restrict our ability to do so.

In sum, a theory-construction mindset to address random error, systematic error, and measure validity is key for high-quality research.

EMERGENT THEORY BUILDING IN MEASUREMENT: COGNITIVE TESTING, EXPERT INTERVIEWS, AND PILOT RESEARCH

As you build a theory to address random and systematic error, it may be helpful to conduct a small, preliminary study to help you build that theory and to develop correctives. One approach to doing so is *cognitive response testing* (Beatty & Willis, 2007; DeMaio & Rothgeb, 1996; Lapka, Jupka, Wray, & Jacobsen, 2008; Willis, 2004). Cognitive response testing is a form of qualitative research that allows one to identify assessment problems by asking people to paraphrase items and discuss thoughts that come to mind when answering questions and by offering suggestions for improvement. Even if this feedback is obtained from only a few individuals, the benefits can be considerable.

One such technique, called the *think-aloud method,* asks people to verbalize their thoughts while answering questions. The session is recorded, and data are analyzed on a question-by-question basis. Here is an example script (Willis, 2000):

> INTERVIEWER: (*reading survey question to be tested*) How many times have you talked to a doctor in the last 12 months?
>
> RESPONDENT INSTRUCTED TO DO THINK-ALOUDS: I guess that depends on what you mean when you say "talked." I talk to my neighbor, who is a doctor, but you probably don't mean that. I go to my doctor about once a year, for a general check-up, so I would count that one. I've also probably been to some type of specialist a couple of more times in the past year—once to get a bad knee diagnosed, and I also saw an ENT about a chronic coughing thing, which I'm pretty sure was in the past year, although I wouldn't swear to it. I've also talked to doctors several times when I brought my kids in to the pediatrician—I might assume that you don't want that included, although I really can't be sure. Also, I saw a chiropractor, but I don't know if you'd consider that to be a doctor in the sense you mean. So, what I'm saying, overall, is that I guess I'm not sure what number to give you, mostly because I don't know what you want.

---

[2] You may encounter different definitions of the various validity terms; there is inconsistent use of them. But the core ideas described here are commonly agreed upon strategies for documenting validity.

BOX 13.1. Measuring Sex and Gender

When framing questions to respondents about a construct, the level of precision and detail needed depends on the broader goals of the study. In most national surveys, for example, people are asked to self-report their biological sex and are provided a few response categories to choose from (usually "male" and "female"), which are considered sufficient for study purposes. However, assessing biological sex is quite another matter in professional women's sports. Richard Raskind was a tennis star as a youth who also played on the United States Tennis Association professional circuit for men over age 35. In 1975, he underwent a sex-change operation, changed his name to Renee Clarke, and in 1976 played in a women's regional tournament, where he completely dominated the defending tournament champion in the finals. Clarke later changed her name to Renee Richards and applied to play in the 1976 Women's United States Open, causing a national controversy. The United States Tennis Association, in response to her application, implemented a rule requiring all women competitors to take a sex chromosome test. Richards sued and the U.S. Supreme Court upheld her arguments that the requirement was unfair and discriminatory. She ultimately played in the U.S. Open, but lost decisively in the first round to Virginia Wade.

Sex testing has a long and troubled history in the Olympics and in track events sponsored by the world track governing body, the International Association of Athletics Federations. Biologically, the view that there are two and only two distinct sexes is scientifically questionable. Fetuses begin as sex undifferentiated and begin developing "male" or "female" characteristics depending on a complex process of protein synthesis, with a gene known as the *SRY* gene playing a critical role. The generation of proteins by the *SRY* gene is impacted by a variety of hormones such that people can develop hormonally or phenotypically as a male or as a female, but to varying degrees. Initial Olympic tests tested for *SRY* dynamics, but ultimately these tests were found to be scientifically suspect and were abandoned. Testosterone testing was introduced as a replacement, with the intent of identifying cases where testosterone levels were elevated above an arbitrary chosen level that was felt to advantage some women athletes. (Testing for advantaging testosterone levels is not performed in men, to the chagrin of many.) A test result above the criterion level is termed *hyperandrogenism*. The focus thus shifted from sex determination to the identification of hyperandrogenism, which itself has been controversial (per the recent case of world-class South African middle-distance runner Caster Semenya).

Many social scientists describe sex as the relatively unchanging biology of being male or female (although such dichotomous thinking itself can be problematic), while gender refers either to social roles based on the sex of the person, to one's sex-role identity, or both. Most survey researchers ask people to self-identify their sex by indicating whether they are male or female and leave it at that. However, critics have argued for more elaborated questions and response options.[a] Gender categories

(continued)

_____

[a]In some person-to-person surveys, sex is determined by the interviewer based on observation.

include, among others, heterosexual male, heterosexual female, lesbian, gay, bisexual, and transgender, with possible distinctions within some categories. Critics argue that failing to distinguish sex from gender does not allow us to explore, for example, whether certain health risks are more closely related to biological differences traditionally associated with men and women or to the experiences of living or identifying as a woman, a man, or some other sex role (Westbrook & Saperstein, 2015). The challenge for researchers is to settle upon questions to ask about sex and gender based on the broader theoretical questions one seeks to address. What may seem to some like a very straightforward question turns out to require careful analysis, depending on the substantive questions being addressed.

Note that the respondent tries to "count up" each prior visit individually, the implications of which we discuss in Chapter 14. The respondent has difficulty determining if a visit is within the specified time frame, perhaps because the time period is too long. Another problem is that the respondent is unclear about whether the question refers only to contacts about health and whether the type of physician/provider matters. Respondents who participate in think-aloud cognitive response testing need to be trained in how to "think aloud" to maximize information gain. Some people find the task difficult and have a hard time staying on task, but with training, it is viable.

Another approach to cognitive response testing is *verbal probing,* which relies on verbal probes about the interpretation of questions, judgment strategies used, and rating scale usage. With this method, after a person answers a question, the researcher asks a series of pointed questions focused on seven categories (Willis, 2000), (1) comprehension and interpretation (e.g., "What does the term 'doctor' mean to you?"), (2) paraphrasing ("Can you repeat the question I just asked in your own words?"), (3) confidence ("How sure are you of your answer? Why?"), (4) recall probe ("How did you remember that you went to the doctor five times in the past 12 months?"), (5) specific probes ("I noticed that you hesitated at one point—tell me what you were thinking when you hesitated"), (6) general probes ("How did you arrive at that answer? Was the question easy or hard to answer?"), and (7) improvement probes ("Can you think of ways we can improve the question?"). In some variants of the strategy, called *retrospective probing,* verbal probes are asked only after the entire interview is finished rather than after each individual question (the latter of which is called *concurrent probing*). A set of scripted probes is usually asked of everyone and planned a priori, in addition to spontaneous probes tailored to a particular reaction by a particular respondent.

Cognitive response testing helps identify sources of random error and systematic error, as shown in Figure 13.1. It is a good source for measurement-oriented theory construction. Although critics of the approach note that it is not the ultimate solution to identifying problems in question design (Foddy, 1998), we find that the strategy provides useful perspectives. For a detailed description of an application using cognitive response testing, see Pepper, Hodgen, Lamesoo, Kõiv, and Tolboom (2018); for a review of cognitive testing methods, see Beatty and Willis (2007); and for a computer-assisted analysis of cognitive response testing data, see Bolton and Bronkhorst (1996).

In addition to cognitive response testing, another helpful device for constructing a relevant measurement theory is to ask experts to provide feedback and ideas on your intended questions/measures, with the explicit task of identifying sources of random and systematic error. One set of experts would be those who have substantive expertise in the content area you are studying; a second set are specialists in psychometrics.

Multiple other strategies have been suggested in the literature to determine whether a question is problematic, such as (1) the use of response latencies to computer-administered questions (if the response latency is slow, this might indicate that people are having difficulties with question comprehension; however, longer response times also may be associated with more careful reading and processing of questions; see Andersen & Mayer, 2017, and Presser et al., 2004); (2) the use of eye-tracking technologies to determine what elements of a question and response options are attended to; and (3) behavioral coding of respondents during the interview process to document such factors as requests for clarification, hesitancies, and refusals to answer (see Ongenal & Dijkstra, 2006). Most of these methods are best suited to identifying questions in need of repair rather than helping you build a theory of measurement per se.

Once we have a final assessment tool, we often conduct an additional small-scale pilot study in which we administer the survey to a representative sample of our target population. We include measures of social desirability response tendencies and relevant response sets with the idea that if they have trivial relationships in the pilot study with our core measures, we can exclude the measures from the main study to streamline it. We also include measures that allow us to address construct validity with the idea that, by demonstrating construct validity in the pilot study, we do not need to do so in the main study, again in the interest of streamlining the main study. We include open-ended questions at the end of our pilot study about general reactions to the survey to obtain a final sense of respondent reactions.

In our broader research program, as we reuse measures with the same or similar populations and assessment contexts, both cognitive response testing and pilot studies become less necessary because we can rely on the cumulative knowledge gained from the prior studies.

Parenthetically, although this discussion centers on self-reports, the core ideas also apply to observer reports, but now the target is the observer rather than the person being observed. Thus, cognitive response testing on observers who make behavioral observations with formal coding schemes can be conducted.

USING EXTANT MEASURES

Often researchers use extant measures in their research with the idea that the validity of the measures has already been established and therefore need not be addressed. For example, there are well-developed measures of depression, financial literacy, brand loyalty, political ideology, alcohol use, and health-related expectancies, all of which have documented favorable reliability and validity data. When deciding whether you can reasonably use an extant measure, you need to think about whether the facets of measurement used in the prior reliability and validity studies map onto the measurement facets of your study and whether any disparities in that mapping matter. If reliability and validity were established using college students, but your study uses economically disadvantaged, inner-city youth of color in middle school, does the prior documented reliability and validity of the measure apply to your research? If not, you will need to build a case for the reliability and validity of the measure as applied in your study.

In this regard, it is important to keep in mind a subtle implication of classic test theory, namely, that measure reliability and validity can be impacted by the amount of true score variability in your population. We illustrate this concept using an extreme example. Suppose the true number of hours people exercise per week is 10 hours and this is the case for everyone in the population. This means there is no true score variance because all true scores are identical. If we ask people to self-report the amount of hours they exercise each week and find that the variability of the self-reports is 3.0 hours, then all of the variability in the measure is error variance. The reliability of the self-report measure is zero. Suppose instead that the true number of hours exercised per week had a variance of 7.0 hours but that the amount of error variance was the same as before, namely, 3.0. Now the observed score variance will be 7.0 + 3.0 = 10.0, and only 30% of it is random noise (i.e., the reliability of the measure is 0.70). This example illustrates that measurement error is more or less consequential, depending on how much true score variance is present; the larger the true score variance, the less the impact of error.

Now suppose a psychometric study designed to provide reliability data on a measure of attitudes toward abortion used the general population of adults in the United States to estimate reliability and found it to be 0.80. There is undoubtedly considerable true score variance in such attitudes, given the controversial nature of abortion in the United States. If your study measures attitudes toward abortion but focuses just on Democratic females in New York City, the true attitudes are likely to be much less variable as compared to attitudes in the general population. Even if the sources and amount of error variance are comparable in your own and the general population, the reliability (and hence, validity) of the attitude measure will differ because of the restricted range of true score variability in your target population relative to the U.S. population in the original psychometric study. When evaluating the applicability of previously documented reliability and validity data for a scale you are considering, it also is useful to consider possible differences in true score variance for your population as compared to those of prior psychometric studies.

When we evaluate extant measures for possible use in our own research, we routinely subject them to a careful analysis as illustrated in Figures 13.1 and 13.3 and also perform cognitive response testing on them. If we find nontrivial problems with the measure or with the response metric, we alter the measure to improve its psychometric properties. This practice is somewhat controversial. For example, doing so limits our ability to invoke previously reported data on reliability and validity for the measure because the prior data technically used a different instrument than our altered version.

Also, making changes can interfere with using scale norms (if they exist) as well, performing comparative analyses with prior studies. Still, we do not think it wise to move forward with a measure that we know has flaws and can be improved.

OTHER CRITERIA FOR MEASURE EVALUATION

Reliability and validity are not the only criteria to use when evaluating the utility of measures. Other substantive and practical criteria can be used as well. When discussing the characteristics of a good measure of economic well-being at a country level, Sumner (2004), an economist, states that the measure should "be policy-relevant (i.e., meaningful to policymakers), a direct and unambiguous measure of progress, specific to the phenomena, valid, reliable, consistent, measurable, user friendly, not easily manipulated, cost effective and up-to-date." Sumner's list not only includes reliability and validity, but also multiple practical criteria.

Another criterion outside of classic test theory is the level of measurement of a measure: namely, whether the measure has ordinal-, interval-, or ratio-level properties. One should prefer measures that are higher up on the measurement hierarchy, everything else being equal. Also, be careful not to equate ratio-level properties of a measure on one dimension with it having ratio properties on your target dimension. For example, in computer-assisted surveys of attitudes, some researchers use the amount of time it takes to respond to an attitudinal question (in milliseconds) as an index of attitude accessibility in working memory; shorter response latencies reflect more accessible attitudes (Fazio, 1995; Mulligan, Grant, Mocabee, & Monson, 2003). Although 5 seconds is twice as long as 2.5 seconds when measuring time, it is not necessarily the case that an attitude for a person who responds in 2.5 seconds is twice as accessible as that for a person who responds in 5 seconds. Indeed, it is not even clear if interval-level properties exist for the time metric as an indicator of attitude accessibility.

Blanton and Jaccard (2006) argue that, in addition to reliability and validity, good measures have *nonarbitrary metrics*; that is, the values of the measure should have intuitive meaning that is tied to meaningful benchmarks. Metric arbitrariness can exist independently of reliability and validity. This point can be illustrated by analogy. Consider height of individuals as expressed in meters. Most residents of the United States, if told that a person is 1.83 meters tall, will have no sense of how tall such an individual is. Yet, expressing height in meters uses a scale that is completely valid and reliable. If told that another individual is 1.52 meters tall, one knows the latter individual is shorter than the former individual, but by how much? Most U.S. citizens would have no idea. This is because, for them, the metric of meters is arbitrary. Many self-report measures have this arbitrary quality. Given a choice between a measure with a nonarbitrary metric (e.g., On how many days in the past 30 days have you smoked cigarettes?) or an arbitrary metric (e.g., On a rating scale, indicate "how often you have smoked cigarettes in the past 30 days," with response options, "not at all," "a few times," "a moderate amount of the time," "quite a bit," and "everyday"), our preference is for the former. For a discussion of how to make arbitrary metrics nonarbitrary, see Jaccard and Bo (2019).

CLASSICAL TEST THEORY AND QUALITATIVE RESEARCH

Our emphasis thus far has been on measurement theory in the context of quantitative research, but the tenets of classical test theory apply equally to qualitative research. When people are interviewed as part of a qualitative study, investigators want to ensure that their answers to queries are not biased by random error, such as by misunderstanding a question due to distractions in the environment, ambiguous wording of questions, simple boredom, warm-up effects, or coding errors. Systematic measurement error also can bias responses to open-ended questions in qualitative contexts, including socially desirable response tendencies, general response sets (e.g., a tendency to disagree with whatever they are asked about), the inadvertent use of leading questions, interviewer characteristics that might bias the kinds of answers one gets, possible source or method effects, and order effects. In short, we want people's answers and characterizations to be free of both random and systematic error. We want responses by informants to be valid and capture the true thoughts and feelings of the interviewee. When we make observations of others or events in qualitative contexts, we do not want our observations to be impacted by random error, transient factors, or systematic error (e.g., halo effects or by our own values and biases).

If a qualitative researcher formulates a set of open-ended questions for use in an interview, such as life history questions followed by more topic-directive questions, or for use in a focus group, good scientific practice is to formulate a theory of potential random error and systematic error influences relative to those questions. One then problem-solves ways of negating the influence of the identified factors. The questions can be subjected to cognitive response testing to help build a relevant measurement theory about them and ultimately to improve the questions.

WRITING REPORTS TO JUSTIFY MEASUREMENT CHOICES

When writing research reports, dissertation proposals, or dissertations, it is important to make a strong case for the measures you used or are going to use in your research. A common reason for rejection of submissions to journals and grant agencies is poor measurement or inadequate measure justification. For dissertation proposal defenses, we routinely ask our students to promise that they will not use "faulty measurement" as an excuse during their final defense if a hypothesis is not supported. Our intent is to send the message that their measurement house should be in order *before* conducting a major research project.

In journal reports of studies that rely on multi-item scales, researchers frequently justify measure viability by citing a statistic called coefficient alpha for the chosen scale, either from past research or as calculated in the reported study. Coefficient alpha is an (imperfect) reliability estimate of a measure. By reporting it alone for measure justification, one essentially ignores matters of systematic measurement error and validity. This is unsatisfactory. You need to make a strong case for measure reliability *and* validity. Reliability is only a part of the larger measurement narrative to be addressed. Too many articles report an alpha coefficient for a scale and leave it at that.

When writing reports, we like to discuss all major threats to measurement validity in our study and describe how we counteracted each of them (if we can't counteract a threat, it becomes part of our limitations section in the Discussion). We seek to assure readers that we have been scientifically rigorous in the execution of the research and that using solid measurement practices is part of doing so. Unfortunately, journal page limits often mitigate against detailing measurement rigor. In addition, some readers do not want to wade through such details (imagine that!). We therefore make liberal use of journal options to place supplemental materials online to explicate such details. For dissertations by our students, we have them write up such information in either the main text or the appendices.

EMPIRICAL TESTS OF MEASUREMENT THEORY

The theories you construct relative to measurement can, of course, be subjected to empirical tests and published in the scientific literature so that other researchers can benefit from the measurement-related knowledge you have gained. Sometimes your theory will be narrow in scope and will apply only to your research domain or your specific project. Other times, it will be broad in scope and apply to many measurement scenarios. Journal editors generally will be more open to publishing measurement theory tests that are broad in scope.

When we generate theory about measurement relative to a particular research project we are conducting, we usually do not empirically test every (untested) theoretical expression to give it scientific standing. Doing so would sidetrack us from our main purpose, which is to test or build upon substantive theory in our primary study. Instead, we usually invoke common sense or past measurement research as a means of presuming the viability of the measurement theory we generate. Having said that, we almost always conduct a preliminary measurement-oriented research project to address measurement issues and to test some of the measurement-oriented theoretical expressions we generated. On occasion, we have published that research for others to benefit from, but more often than not, it is only used to refine measurement in our primary study. There are scientists who make careers formulating measurement theories and publishing empirical tests of those theories. Such work is extremely important for advancing research in the social and health sciences.

SUMMARY AND CONCLUDING COMMENTS

Theory construction is an essential activity for measurement purposes. Classical test theory is a general framework that can help you think theoretically about core measurement issues. It focuses your theory construction efforts on identifying factors that impact random and systematic measurement error, while also taking into account the generalizability of those properties across measurement facets. It encourages you to think about your specific study context and to identify likely sources of measurement error that you then problem-solve to remove, either procedurally or statistically. There is no unified set of measurement error factors that applies in all contexts. You need to theorize about them relative to your particular study. Our discussion focused primarily on random and systematic error analysis for individual-based self-reports, but the concepts of reliability and validity apply with equal vigor to observer reports, "objective" indicators of a construct (e.g., formal arrest records of adolescents as an index of delinquency), and more macrolevel variables often studied by sociologists and economists, such as country indicators of poverty, city indicators of quality of life, or community indicators of employment. The classic test theory framework is a useful heuristic for guiding more specific measurement-oriented theory construction to improve measurement practices in research.

The definition of reliability is the extent to which a measure is free of random error. The reliability ratio for a measure is the proportion of variation in a measure that is *not* due to random error or the extent to which a measure is free of random error. Too much random error in a measure can bias the inferences we make when we test hypotheses of relationships between variables based on measures. We can never know the true reliability of a measure, but we can *estimate it* using a variety of strategies developed by psychometricians. Importantly, the reliability of a measure can shift depending on the facets of measurement, including the study population, question formats or characteristics, testing context, and timing of assessment. For individually focused self-reports, factors that might impact random error include distractions in the test environment, question ambiguity, scale unfamiliarity, misreading of items, boredom with the task, and coding errors. As you build a theory of sources of random error, you should develop strategies for dealing with them so as to maximize measure reliability.

Validity is defined as the extent to which a measure is free of both random error and systematic error; that is, the measure assesses what it is supposed to measure and nothing else. Validity, like reliability, can vary as a function of the facets of measurement. For individual focused self-reports, factors that impact systematic error might include social desirability response tendencies, response sets, the use of leading questions, characteristics of the interviewer (including interview matching), method/source effects, and the ordering of questions. Like random error, as you build a theory of sources of systematic error, you need to develop strategies for dealing with those sources so as to maximize measure validity.

Measurement theory construction can be facilitated by conducting qualitative research in the form of cognitive response testing and by consulting experts to assist you in the theory construction process. Pilot psychometric studies also can help you streamline your primary study as the pilot studies help you eliminate the possibility of different sources of measure contamination (so you do not have to measure and statistically control for them in the primary study). They also allow you to build a case for your measures by demonstrating construct validity. Some of your measures may be created just for your study, and others may represent extant measures that have a psychometric track record. For the latter, you want to make a case that the facets of measurement for prior psychometric studies map reasonably onto the facets of your study, at least for those facets that matter. You will want to choose measures that have high reliability and validity, but you also might seek to maximize other criteria, such as interval/ratio properties, nonarbitrary metrics, practicality, and applied significance.

The basic tenets of reliability and validity are as relevant to qualitative research as they are to quantitative research. One does not want verbal reports of informants to be impacted by either random error or systematic error; we want them to reflect the true thoughts and feelings of informants. To achieve this objective, qualitative researchers must construct measurement theories of factors that create random and systematic error in their research contexts and then develop strategies to minimize them. The factors may overlap with or be distinct from those that we have discussed in this chapter, but ultimately, measurement-oriented theory construction is important to the quality of the research effort.

Classic test theory offers useful perspectives for improving measurement practice in research, but it is not without its critics. Many of these criticisms are directed at the vagueness associated with the concept of a true score and exactly what it represents (Borsboom, 2005). When grounded in the philosophy of science, formal classic test theory does indeed have conceptual ambiguities. All the same, the theory has been highly influential and, at the general level discussed here, yields a useful framework for thinking about how to improve measurement practices by theory construction.

SUGGESTED READINGS

Bandalos, D. L. (2018). *Measurement theory and applications for the social sciences.* New York: Guilford Press.

—A very good introduction to measurement theory that emphasizes classic test theory but discusses many topics beyond it.

Borsboom, D. (2005). *Measuring the mind: Conceptual issues in contemporary psychometrics.* Cambridge, UK: Cambridge University Press.

—A nice treatment of the philosophical foundations of measurement emphasizing three measurement theories: classic test theory, latent variable models, and representational measurement.

Gescheider, G. (2015). *Psychophysics: The fundamentals.* New York: Psychology Press.

—A good introduction to psychophysics.

Lord, F. M., & Novick, M. R. (1968). *Statistical theories of mental test scores.* Reading, MA: Addison-Wesley.

—This is a classic book on classical test theory and one of the original sources. Although it is dated and somewhat mathematical, it is a great resource for key tenets of classic test theory.

Shavelson, R. J., & Webb, N. M. (1991). *Generalizability theory: A primer.* Thousand Oaks, CA: SAGE.

—Generalizability theory is a technical, complex mathematical theory of the facets of measurement. This book provides a good introduction to it.

Willis, G. (2004). *Cognitive interviewing: A tool for improving questionnaire design.* Thousand Oaks, CA: SAGE.

—A nice introduction to cognitive response testing.

KEY TERMS

metric (p. 376)

nominal measurement (p. 377)

ordinal measurement (p. 377)

interval-level measurement (p. 377)

ratio-level measurement (p. 377)

content validity (p. 378)

measurement error (p. 379)

random measurement error (p. 379)

reliability (p. 379)

reliability ratio (p. 379)

systematic error (p. 380)

constant error (p. 380)

validity (p. 381)

generalizability theory (p. 383)

response sets (p. 386)

priming effect (p. 387)

source effects (p. 387)

method variance (p. 388)

method effects (p. 388)

halo effects (p. 388)

convergent validity (p. 389)

concurrent validity (p. 389)

predictive validity (p. 389)

construct validity (p. 390)

discriminant validity (p. 389)

nomological validity (p. 390)

cognitive response testing (p. 390)

think-aloud method (p. 390)

verbal probing (p. 392)

retrospective probing (p. 392)

concurrent probing (p. 392)

nonarbitrary metrics (p. 395)

EXERCISES

Exercises to Reinforce Concepts

1. Define measurement.

2. What are Stevens's four levels of measurement? Define them.

3. What is concept mapping? Why is it important? How is it related to content validity?

4. What is reliability, and how does one interpret the reliability ratio?

5. Is test–retest reliability the same as reliability? Explain.

6. What are some factors that are a source of random error? Name at least three. How might each of them be addressed to reduce their impact?

7. Give some examples of factors that represent systematic measurement error. Name at least three. How might each of them be addressed to reduce their impact?

8. What is validity of a measure?

9. Name three different response sets and characterize them. How might we remove their effects?

10. What is interviewer–interviewee matching? Does it lead to bias or reduce bias?

11. What are source effects? What are method effects? What is the difference between them?

12. What is the difference between convergent validity, concurrent validity, predictive validity, and construct validity?

13. Characterize cognitive response testing and the different forms it can take.

14. What is generalizability theory, and why is it important?

15. What are major factors you should consider when deciding to use an existing measure of a construct in your study?

16. What is a nonarbitrary metric?

17. Why is it important to apply classic test theory to qualitative research?

Exercises to Apply Concepts

1. Find a study of interest to you in the literature and read the section on the primary measures used in that study. For each measure, describe the reliability and validity of it or note if the investigator failed to provide information about the reliability and validity of the measure.

2. In the study you chose above, pick out one of the measures to focus on. Are there practices the investigator did not mention that he or she could have used to improve the reliability or validity of the measure? What are they? That is, how could you have improved the measurement practices of the study?

3. In the study you chose above, pick out one of the measures to focus on. Does the measure have nominal, ordinal, interval, or ratio properties? How do you know? Did the investigator discuss level of measurement at all? (If there is no mention of it, read Chapter 14 for how to gain perspectives on the matter.)

4. In the study chosen above, did the investigator report any pilot research on the primary measures, such as cognitive response testing, or a pilot study of psychometric properties? If not, is the decision not to do such work justifiable? Why or why not?

5. Pick out an extant measure of a construct you are interested in. Find someone you know and do a cognitive response test on the measure using verbal probes. Then do a second cognitive response test on another person but use the think-aloud method (develop any training materials you might need to use it). Compare and contrast what you learned in each approach. Which was better?

14

Theory and Measurement
Types of Measurement Strategies

I have been struck again and again by how important
measurement is to improving the human condition.
                    —WILLIAM GATES (2013)

The concepts of reliability, validity, and measure generalizability are core to measurement theories. Chapter 13 described theory construction perspectives that can help you identify factors that impact the reliability and validity of measures and also help you select extant measures for your research. However, it did not consider measure and scale construction per se, that is, theory that drives the formal construction of measures. The present chapter does so. As with Chapter 13, our intent is not to provide a checklist of good measurement practices, although you will learn about such practices as you progress through the chapter. Rather, we stress that to measure a construct well, you need to adopt a theory construction mindset that specifies determinants of key measurement properties and that takes into account, at minimum, the population you are studying, the structure and content of the measures you use or construct, and the assessment context that you will ultimately use.

Our focus is on self-reports, observer reports, and "objective" measures that collectively form the backbone of research in the social sciences. Although our discussion is dominated by quantitative research orientations, much of what we cover is relevant to qualitative research; it certainly bears on mixed-methods research that combines qualitative and quantitative methodologies. As in Chapter 13, we emphasize idea generation rather than formal tests of those ideas. Although you could pursue such tests and potentially publish their results, our goal is to encourage and elaborate a theory construction mindset. We omit the complex topic of multi-item scale construction using approaches such as item response theory, Thurstone scaling, and Guttman scaling. These topics are beyond the scope of this chapter (they are discussed on our companion website at *www.theory-construction.com*). In addition, we do not attempt to provide comprehensive theories of self-reports, observer reports, and "objective" measures, given the inevitable complexity of such theories. Again, our goal instead is to create a mindset about the use of theory construction for measurement and to provide guidelines and examples to help you think along such lines.

CONSTRUCTING A THEORY OF SELF-REPORTS

Self-reports are widely used in the social and health sciences. Three processes underlie self-reports for organizing one's theory construction efforts. First, people must understand the question posed to them as intended by the researcher; that is, there must be *comprehension*. Second, people must form or retrieve from memory judgments and opinions in response to the posed question to form an answer in their minds. This *judgment* process typically involves cognitive and affective mechanisms playing themselves out in working memory. Third, once the judgment/opinion is formed, people must communicate it to the researcher. Sometimes people provide their responses in an open-ended format and other times on a rating scale. The act of communicating one's answer to the investigator is called *response translation*. Measurement theorizing about comprehension, judgment, and response translation can shape how you ask questions and how you structure response options. We have found that organizing our thinking around these processes is a useful theory construction frame. In the next sections, we specify factors that impact each process separately.

Constructing Theories of Comprehension

Your first step is to construct a theory of comprehension relative to your measures. Comprehension of a question obviously is impacted by a person's vocabulary. If a question is posed in a language you do not know, you will have little sense of what the question means. At the same time, the human mind has a remarkable capacity to bring past experience to bear to make sense of what is technically gibberish as the brain fills in gaps and reorganizes "nonsense to sense" in text processing. As evidence, read the following text:

> Aoccdrnig to rscheearch at Cmabrigde Uinervtisy, it deosn't mttaer in waht oredr the ltteers in a wrod are, the olny iprmoetnt tihng is taht the frist and lsat ltteer be at the rghit pclae. The rset can be a total mses and you can sitll raed it wouthit porbelm. Tihs is bcuseae the huamn mnid deos not raed ervey lteter by istlef, but the wrod as a wlohe. Amzanig huh?

Such "fill-in" processing is a two-edged sword, sometimes working in favor of good measurement and other times not.

To effectively construct questions that are understandable, we ultimately need a theory of comprehension and text processing. What factors impact comprehension of a question, text, or a preamble? How can you address these factors to maximize comprehension? Components of your theory might generalize across different substantive domains, but you also undoubtedly will need to introduce nuances specific to your research area. Our discussion emphasizes general factors that impact comprehension to help stimulate idea generation on your part. To organize our framework, we draw on the core measurement facets from Chapter 13, namely, characteristics of the population, characteristics of the questions, and characteristics of the assessment context that can affect comprehension.

Population Characteristics

Characteristics of your population will impact your respondents' ability to comprehend the questions you pose. As such, you need to theorize about these characteristics. What guidance can extant social science and measurement theories provide as you think about this matter? Let's consider some relevant factors.

Literacy. One variable that has been found to affect comprehension is *literacy*. Literacy is defined as the ability to read and write, but the concept is sometimes nuanced further via the concepts of *functional literacy* and *functional illiteracy*. Functional illiteracy refers to having trouble in everyday life because of reduced reading and writing skills. Distinctions often are made between specific types of literacy, such as health literacy, financial literacy, e-digital literacy, and numeracy. In terms of general literacy, research in the United States suggests that a person's reading level is usually three to five grade levels below the highest grade the person has completed (Agency for Healthcare Research and Quality, 2015). If your target population is juniors and seniors in high school, for example, you probably can assume about a seventh-grade reading level and write your questions accordingly. This heuristic does not always apply, so it should be used only as a rough guideline. For example, in Detroit, a workforce studying illiteracy found that about half of those who were functionally illiterate had high school degrees (Detroit Regional Workforce Fund, 2011). Several brief assessment tools for literacy can be used in pilot testing to gain a better understanding of the literacy of your population, if need be (e.g., Davis et al., 1993). Even if questions are to be read to respondents, literacy may be relevant. For example, it has been shown that learning to read reinforces other key abilities, such as verbal and visual memory, phonological awareness, and visuospatial and visuomotor skills (Ardila et al., 2010), all of which impact information processing.

Computerized readability formulas, such as the Flesch–Kincaid readability index available in Microsoft Word, can be applied to a question or text to gain a sense of its reading level. These indices are limited because they focus on the length of words and sentences rather than comprehension per se; shorter words and shorter sentences are assumed to be more readable. As a general guideline, it has been suggested that material written at the fourth- to sixth-grade level based on these indices is easy to read; seventh- to ninth-grade materials are of average difficulty; and material at or above a tenth-grade level is deemed difficult (Agency for Healthcare Research and Quality, 2015).

As noted, there are many subtypes of literacy that can impact the way you approach question design. The number of content-oriented literacy types is considerable (e.g., food literacy, health literacy, financial literacy, social literacy). In some ways, these different forms of literacy reflect how knowledgeable people are in different topic areas. Thinking about such matters relative to your research topic may help you determine terms you can safely use in questions.

One type of literacy that generalizes across many content domains is that of *numeracy* (Reyna, Nelson, Han, & Dieckmann, 2009). Numeracy is the ability to understand and use numbers, including the ability to perform simple arithmetic operations, compare numerical magnitudes, and to understand fractions, proportions, percentages, and probabilities. Numeracy is relevant, for example, if your questions include percentages (e.g., agreement or disagreement with the statement "This new treatment controls cancer in about 40% of cases like yours") or if your response metric uses percentages ("If women use birth control pills for 6 months, what percentage of them do you think will accidentally become pregnant?"). In a study of patients considering a new treatment with a 40% cure rate, Weinfurt and colleagues (2005) found that 72% correctly interpreted the percentage; 16% of patients interpreted the statement to mean either the doctor was 40% confident the treatment would work or that the treatment would reduce disease severity by 40%; and 12% indicated they did not understand the statement at all. If your population has low numeracy, it may be best to avoid questions with these formats (Reyna et al., 2009).

Working Memory Capacity and Cognitive Skills. Another potentially relevant consideration is working memory capacity. Psychologists distinguish three types of memory: short-term memory, working memory, and long-term memory. *Short-term memory* refers to the short-term storage of information without actively processing that information. *Working memory* refers to processes to interpret, elaborate, and act on a subset of the information that is in short-term memory. The cognitive processes used by working memory include attention, encoding, integration, processing, and retrieval of information from long-term memory, all of which are used to interpret the information (which is part of the comprehension process), and, ultimately, to form judgments. *Long-term memory* is our permanent storehouse of memories in the brain, which also can be accessed by working memory.

The processes used in working memory are central to comprehension and reasoning when answering a question that has entered short-term memory. Short-term memory can store information for about 10 seconds unless working memory processes or "manipulates" it (Miller, 2003). Unless acted upon by working memory, information in short-term memory decays rapidly. It is difficult to specify the capacity of short-term/working memory, but Miller's (1956) classic work suggests that for adults it is 7 bits of information, ± 2. More recent work indicates that the limit may be lower, whereas others have argued that it is impossible to know because of phenomena like information chunking (e.g., where the numbers 1, 2, 3 are chunked into 123; Miller, 2003). Still, it is safe to say that the amount of information people can keep in their conscious mind is time sensitive and rather limited and that Miller's 7 ± 2 is a rough guideline for appreciating the limits of conscious information processing. Consideration of working memory limitations in question design is particularly relevant for research with children and the elderly, because comprehension is hindered by limited working memory capacities.

With such populations, questions must be that much shorter, simpler, and more concrete.

In addition to working memory, other cognitive skills relevant to comprehension include processing speed (how quickly one digests new information); attention (the ability to sustain focus); verbal reasoning (the ability to understand linguistic information); abstract thinking (the ability to think abstractly); verbal memory (how efficiently one encodes and recalls linguistic information); and visual memory (how efficiently one encodes and recalls visual-spatial information). Are any of these skills relevant to the measurement strategies in your research? How? How would respondent limitations on one or more of these skill(s) shape the questions you design?

Language Diversity. Migration has increased in many countries, and with it has come linguistic diversification. Individuals who do not have a good speaking knowledge of the native language in which questions are written or phrased may have difficulties comprehending questions. Kleiner, Lipps, and Ferrez (2015) found that resident foreigners were more likely to have comprehension problems due to reduced language mastery *and* reduced motivation to conscientiously complete an interview, presumably because of task difficulty. In some cases, you may need to offer versions of your survey in different languages. Methods for effectively translating surveys use *forward–back translation* methodology. This involves expert translation to the new language, followed by independent retranslation of the translated survey back to the original language. The original version and the back-translated versions are then compared to each other, and the disparities found signal potential translation issues. See the World Health Organization (2018) website for elaboration of the steps in the forward–backward translation approach. Peytcheva (2008) argues that the language used in a survey can itself create a cultural lens for interpreting and responding to questions (see also Johnson, Holbrook, & Cho, 2006).

Attention and Motivation. People will be more likely to miscomprehend questions if they do not attend to them, partially attend to them, or read/listen to them superficially. As such, respondent motivation to take the assessment task seriously is another factor that can affect comprehension. Providing research participants with motivating instructions (e.g., stressing how important it is to attend to everything carefully and how their participation will contribute to science and/or society) can help. Remuneration is often used as a task motivator, although research suggests that the effect of payments on task motivation is complex (Bonner, Hastie, Sprinkle, & Young, 2000). Wenemark, Persson, Brage, Svensson, & Kristenson (2011) apply formal motivation theory to the analysis of survey responses. What factors might impact the motivation to work conscientiously on the self-report tasks in your research?

In sum, it is important for you to construct a theory of question comprehension as you plan your research. What characteristics of your study population might impact question comprehension and how you approach measurement? What is the literacy level of your population? What specific types of literacy are relevant to your questions? What cognitive skills does your population need to answer your questions, and how do you adjust for low skills in question design? Is the working memory capacity of your population limited? Does your population include people whose native language is different from the language you intend to use? Do you need different language versions of your questions? What can you do to increase motivation to work conscientiously on your task?

Characteristics of Questions

The survey research literature offers many ad hoc but common-sense principles for improving question comprehension. For example, Alwin and Beattie (2016) discuss research supporting the KISS principle—"Keep it simple, stupid"— to encourage question designers to be brief and to the point in constructing questions. Other tips include the following: (1) avoid technical terms, jargon, and slang (e.g., many respondents might refer to marijuana as "weed," but it is unwise to assume this term is universally understood); (2) avoid abbreviations (e.g., the item "I know the whereabouts of my child 24/7" might fit the way many parents talk, but it might be confusing to some parents); (3) avoid words with ambiguous meanings; (4) strive for wording that is specific and concrete as opposed to general and abstract; and (5) avoid questions with single or double negations (e.g., "I am not disapproving of legislation restricting access to abortion")

Lexical and Semantic Processing. One can think about question comprehension linguistically at two levels: the lexical and the semantic. At the *lexical level,* concern is with how people understand the individual words in the question. At the *semantic level,* concern is with the meaning of the overall question/sentence or portions of it based on those words. Sentence meaning is not a simple function of the individual words that make up the sentence. Rather, there is an interplay between lexical and semantic processes in shaping individual word interpretation and the implied meanings of a sentence. In the question "How many tobacco cigarettes did you smoke yesterday?," the focus is on the action of smoking a tobacco cigarette. People may be able to provide meaningful and accurate definitions of the words *cigarette* and *smoking* but differ in how they comprehend and interpret the act of "smoking a tobacco cigarette." Suessbrick, Schober, and Conrad (2000) found that 23% of respondents said the question referred to only cigarettes one had finished, 23% felt it included cigarettes one finished or partly smoked, and 54% defined it as taking even one puff from a cigarette. The counts that people report in response to this question can differ depending on their understanding of the implied action. In web-based or computer-assisted surveys, some researchers allow people to click on terms or collections of terms embedded in questions if they are unsure of their meaning, at which point a pop-up bubble is shown on the screen that defines the clicked terms. In our opinion, researchers ideally should frame their questions so that such clarifications are not necessary, but such prompts might nevertheless serve as useful comprehension aids.

Language Structure. Variables related to linguistic structure also can affect comprehension. Sentence complexity impacts reading fluency, which, in turn, can affect comprehension, perhaps by undermining task motivation because people find the task difficult or too time consuming. Thompson and Shapiro (2007) emphasize the importance of the order in which major elements appear in a sentence. For example, it is easier to process the sentence "John (S) kicked (V) the ball (O)" than "The ball (O) was kicked (V) by John (S)" or "It was the ball (O) that John (S) kicked (V)." Lenzner, Kaczmirek, and Lenzner (2010) identified text features that detract from comprehension, including (1) the use of low-frequency words (people understand words that occur more frequently in their language); (2) the use of vague relative terms, like *many, often, rarely,* and *substantially*; (3) the use of vague or ambiguous noun phrases (e.g., "John showed the boy a picture of his mother," which is ambiguous with respect to whether the picture was of John's mother or the boy's mother); (4) complex syntax (in which a sentence contains both a dependent clause with words like *if, when, while, after, before, because,* coupled with an independent clause, yielding something like "I voted for Donald Trump because it would help the economy"—which is confusing for someone who voted for Donald Trump but not because he or she thought it would help the economy); (5) complex logical structures (sentences that include numerous logical operators, like *or,* which can require respondents to keep a large amount of information in mind); (6) low syntactic redundancy (using uncommon grammatical structures); and (7) bridging inferences (needing to make inferences from one part of the sentence to another). Graesser, Cai, Louwerse, and Daniel (2006) developed software that automatically evaluates questions for the presence of most of these features. We recommend its use.

Assessment Context Characteristics

Features of the assessment context are another source of question miscomprehension. Any facet of the context that detracts from people paying attention to questions (noise, interruptions, poor lighting, the presence of others, smells) can affect question comprehension. Similarly, facets of the assessment context that reduce respondent motivation to approach the task conscientiously are relevant because they lessen attention to the task at hand. Sometimes these facets can be subtle, such as when question ordering impacts task motivation. For example, the conventional wisdom is that (1) initial questions in a survey should be simple and build rapport; (2) questions at the beginning should address the topics described during informed consent; (3) questions on the same topic should be grouped together; and (4) questions on sensitive topics should occur at the end of the survey (Krosnick & Presser, 2010). For online surveys, respondents often become more conscientious when prompted by a pop-up message reminding them to read items carefully if the computer detects they are making too many item nonresponses, not differentiating their responses to questions (answering them all in the same way), or answering questions too quickly so as to suggest only casual reading (Zhang & Conrad, 2016).

In face-to-face interviewing, methodologists distinguish between *standardized interviewing* and *conversational interviewing* (Schober & Conrad, 2002). In standardized interviewing, interviewers are required to read a question exactly as worded and provide only neutral answers to respondent probes. This approach has the advantage of reducing inappropriate interviewer influence and ensuring that everyone responds to the same "stimuli." In conversational interviewing, interviewers read questions as worded, but they then use whatever clarifications are necessary to convey the meaning of the question. This often improves responses by ensuring that all respondents interpret the question in the same way. Conversational interviewing thus tends to increase comprehension but at the risk of interviewers inappropriately putting words into the respondents' mouths. Conversational interviews generally take longer than standardized interviews and require more interviewer training (Schober & Conrad, 2002). Replication of results has become an issue in some social science disciplines (Earp & Trafimow, 2015), which also raises concerns about the use of conversational interviewing. Which approach is best for your research?

In sum, good measurement practice requires you to theory construct about factors that impact question comprehension for your research and then use that theory to guide your approach to measurement. Relevant variables in your theory will include characteristics of your target population, characteristics of the questions per se, and characteristics of the assessment context you intend to use, among others. We have elaborated general variables in each of these domains to help stimulate your thinking. These variables are summarized in Figure 14.1, which is a simplified representation

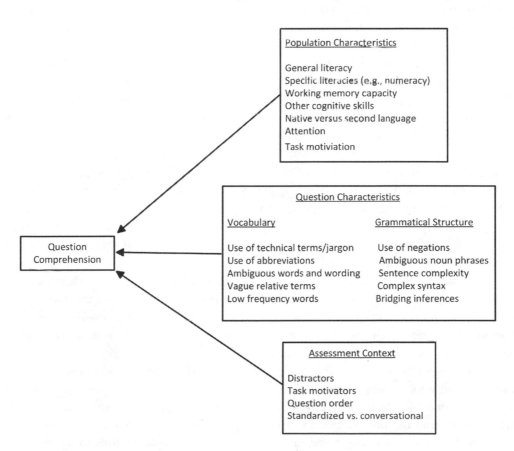

FIGURE 14.1. Factors impacting comprehension.

because it omits likely interactive/moderated relationships between factors and dependencies between the various causes.

Constructing a Theory of Judgment

Once a question has been understood, people form an answer in their minds. Although it may seem counterintuitive, understanding how people formulate judgments and answers also can impact question design. This fact reveals, again, the need for theory construction for measurement purposes, but now around the judgment process. Social scientists have studied so many types of judgments that we cannot begin to consider this topic comprehensively. Instead, we illustrate the process using a common question type in social science research, namely, that of asking people the number of times they have performed a behavior or experienced an event in the past (e.g., the number of times they have seen a doctor in the past year; the number of days they used marijuana in the past month).

When individuals are asked to recall the number of times they have performed a behavior or experienced an event over a specified time period, they might use several cognitive strategies. One strategy is to think of the relevant time period and then try to recall each occurrence of the event, counting them up as each event is recalled. Individuals could either begin with the most recent event and count backward in time, called a *think backward strategy*, or they could start at the beginning of the time period and count recalled instances that occur sequentially since the inception date, called a *think forward strategy* (Loftus & Fathi, 1985). Some studies favor the use of think backward strategies to maximize recall accuracy because the cues for recent events are more readily available in memory and can serve as cues for accurate recall of the earlier events (Loftus, Smith, Klinger, & Fiedler, 1992). Other studies favor a think forward strategy because it involves recalling events as they unfolded over time, providing a more natural structure (Loftus & Fathi, 1985). Overall, research tends to favor think backward strategies for maximizing recall accuracy, but there are exceptions (Bradburn, Rips, & Shevell, 1987). For both strategies, the memory of one event may interfere with the memory of another event. In addition, there may be order effects, with events that occur more recently having a greater impact on the final judgment. Whatever the case, the fundamental nature of this judgment process is episodic in that individuals try to recall specific episodes of the event and then count them up.

A second mental strategy is to use a rule-based judgment process. In this case, the individual invokes a stored rule or algorithm from memory that is used to generate the requested frequency without recourse to recalling specific episodes of the event. For example, asked how many days you have smoked marijuana in the past month, you may reason you do so every day and therefore report a frequency of 30.

Other cognitive strategies involve a combination of episodic and rule-based processes. When adolescents make a judgment of the frequency of marijuana use during the past 12 months, they may think episodically of the number of times they smoked marijuana during the past month and then adopt a generating rule that multiplies this result by 12. They also might cognitively invoke "correction" factors to account for months when unusual events occurred, such as being away on a family vacation.

These processes have implications for the choice of a time period over which to measure the count. Questions focused on short time intervals, such as 1 month, probably encourage episodic recall strategies, which can be reasonably accurate for individuals who engage in the behavior infrequently (Blair & Burton, 1987). However, a focus on counting individual episodes may be counterproductive for individuals who engage in the behavior frequently because of episode interference and the difficulty of keeping the episodes distinct in memory. A longer time frame (e.g., 3 months or 6 months) might yield more accurate recall because individuals who engage in the behavior infrequently will still rely on episodic cognitive strategies, whereas those who engage in the behavior more frequently will adopt a rule-based process that is less subject to episodic distortion, presuming individuals use reasonably accurate rule-generating criteria. If the focal time period becomes too long, such as recall over a period of 1 or more years, then those who engage in the behavior infrequently may have trouble recalling episodes that occurred in the distant past, and those who use rule-generating criteria may apply a rule that is appropriate for recent events (e.g., the past 3 or 4 months) but not for such a broad time base. These considerations led Jaccard, McDonald, Wan, Dittus, and Quinlan (2002) to predict that recall accuracy would be best for *moderate* time periods (3 or 6 months) as compared to short (1 month) or long (12 months) periods when young adults were asked to recall their frequency of sexual intercourse. (Of course, when the time period is extremely short, such as 1 day, recall should be accurate because individual episodes are distinct and readily recalled by all). Note that the Jaccard et al. prediction is counter to the common-sense notion that shorter recall periods, by fiat, lead to greater accuracy. Their predictions were borne out in their data.

Often, when we measure past behavior, we do so with the idea of measuring the behavioral proclivities of individuals, such as the tendency to smoke marijuana a great deal, a moderate amount, or very little/not at all. If the time frame used in the question is very short, then occurrence of the behavior may reflect idiosyncratic, situation-specific influences rather than a general behavioral proclivity on the part of the individual. For example, if the time interval is a week, a person might smoke marijuana during that week while away visiting a distant friend who has marijuana readily available and who pressures the person to smoke; however, this is a situational exception rather than a general behavioral proclivity. A longer time period gives a better "sampling" of behaviors for identifying a behavioral proclivity. If the time period is too long, however, then the underlying proclivity might change between the start of the period (when the proclivity was, say, high) and where the individual is now (when the proclivity is low). This logic also favors the use of moderate time frames, unless one is specifically interested in situational influences.

Finally, with longer time frames, individuals may have greater difficulty keeping clear in their minds the precise time period on which they should focus. This is typically addressed by using psychological "landmarks" (such as a birthday or an important or notable event) that define the beginning of the period and serve as a reference point for the individual (Shum, 1998). Even in the presence of such landmarks, however, an individual's thoughts might drift to periods outside the landmarks. Such cognitive drifting is more likely to occur when the time period is long in duration.

An interesting phenomenon that sometimes occurs for count judgments is *cognitive rounding* or *cognitive heaping* (Smitherman, Martin, Penzien, & Lipton, 2013). When making judgments about the number of days on which an event occurred over the past 3 months, for example, individuals tend to round estimates to the nearest 5 days once the frequency exceeds 10 days; above 20 to 30 days, rounding tends to occur to the nearest 10 days. This "cognitive heaping" can yield an ill-shaped distribution of scores; it can bias means and standard deviations; and it raises questions about whether a reported score of, say, 27 (someone who did not round) is truly distinct from a score of 25 (someone who likely rounded). Research has observed individual differences in cognitive rounding. For example, in a study of reports of headache frequency, Smitherman and colleagues (2013) found that women were more likely to cognitively heap than men; younger patients were more likely to cognitively heap than older patients; and depressed patients were more likely to cognitively heap than nondepressed patients. Cognitive rounding can be addressed by using shorter time frames (heaping is less likely to occur at lower frequencies, and a shorter time frame will produce lower frequencies); using daily diaries in place of longer recall periods (thereby reducing the recall time to one day but then aggregating entries across many days to better represent behavior proclivities); or making statistical adjustments during data analysis.

As a whole, this discussion clarifies some of the theoretical issues one must consider when framing questions about recall of event frequencies. What time interval should you use in your question to maximize recall accuracy? If you want to study behavioral proclivities, what time interval will allow for an adequate "sampling" of behavior but not be too protracted? Will recall accuracy be maximized by people using episodic strategies (behavior occurs infrequently) or rule-based strategies (behavior occurs frequently)? How can you, or should you, try to encourage one or the other through question phrasing or instructional sets? If respondents are likely to use episodic strategies, should you encourage a think backward or think forward strategy through instructional sets or question wording, or should you say nothing at all and leave it to the respondent to do whatever comes naturally? For longer time periods, should you use "landmarks" and, if so, what landmarks should you use? How will you handle cognitive rounding?

On a more general level, when a question is posed to a person, the verbatim question enters short-term memory and working memory then extracts the gist of the question (Reyna et al., 2009). Relevant information from long-term memory is accessed by the individual based on this gist, coupled with the processing of information in the surrounding context as respondents formulate an answer to the question. Cognitive scientists distinguish two appraisal systems that operate in any given situation (Gross, 2007; Smith & Kirby, 2000). The first system is a cognitive appraisal system, where we interpret the situation we are in, make note of who is present, think about the intentions and orientations of the people who are present, and formulate other cognitions about the context. The second system is an affective appraisal system that alerts us to the emotions, feelings, and affective reactions we are experiencing and that, in turn, may predispose us to act or interpret matters in certain ways. These cognitive and emotional appraisals happen at lightning-fast speeds, often automatically, and sometimes without awareness. These appraisals and the question posed to us form the basis of the informa-

BOX 14.1. Quantifying Love

Early in my career, I (Jaccard) interacted with traditional anthropologists who were skeptical (to put it mildly) of quantitative methods. One of them would repeatedly and defiantly say "let's see you quantify love!" It turns out that numerous theories of love have been offered by social scientists (e.g., Hatfield & Walster, 1978; Lee, 1973; Rubin, 1970; Sternberg, 1997). Sternberg (1997) posited a theory of love with three major components: passion, intimacy, and commitment. Passion is associated with physical arousal and emotional stimulation, whereas intimacy is associated with feelings of closeness and attachment; commitment is associated with a conscious decision to be together over the long run. According to Sternberg, different types and stages of love are represented by different combinations of these components. One couple might be high in passion and high in intimacy, but low in commitment; another couple might be low in passion and low in intimacy, but high in commitment. As part of his research program, Sternberg developed three scales, one for each component, consisting of 15 items per scale. Each item was rated on a 9-point disagree–agree scale. Total scores on each subscale were based on a sum of the items. Sample items for passion are "Just seeing _____ excites me"; "My relationship with _____ is very romantic"; "I find _____ to be very personally attractive"; "I especially like physical contact with _____"; Sample items for intimacy are "I have a warm relationship with _____"; "I communicate well with _____"; "I feel close to _____"; "I feel that I really understand _____." Sample items for commitment are "I know that I care about _____"; "I am committed to maintaining my relationship with _____"; "I have confidence in the stability of my relationship with _____"; "I could not let anything get in the way of my commitment to _____."

Suppose you want to describe love for couple members in the United States with a specific focus on these three dimensions. You might decide you need a random sample of 1,000 couples to have a reasonable representation of the population. A qualitative study of that magnitude would be a massive undertaking, especially if you wanted to compare subgroups on the dimensions based on gender, ethnicity, age, and social class. Granted, a summary score for each of the three components is limited. But if primary interest is with these three dimensions per se, the quantitative approach is not unreasonable for a study of that magnitude. Sternberg went to great lengths to establish the reliability and validity of these measures.

Interestingly, Sternberg later altered his measurement approach (Sternberg, Hojjat, & Barnes, 2001). He noted that people typically are exposed to large numbers of diverse stories about love, either love stories by and of themselves or love stories embedded in larger stories. The stories come from observing people in relationships, experiencing one's own relationships, watching television and movies, reading novels, and so on. Based on these stories, Sternberg reasoned, people create their own stories or narratives about what love is or should be. Potential partners may "fit" a person's personal stories to a greater or lesser degree. Sternberg felt that relationships

(continued)

might be more stable and satisfying if there was a match in the personal love stories of the couple members. Based on extensive qualitative interviews and content analyses of media, Sternberg identified 25 kinds of stories that people might have about love. These stories encompassed the three dimensions of passion, intimacy, and commitment, but they were far more nuanced and qualitatively rich. Sternberg developed an assessment tool that asked individuals to rate how much they embraced themes in each of the 25 stories. He acknowledged that story content and relevance would be culturally dependent, and he encouraged research to explore this position, leading to cultural specific assessments. In your opinion, does this approach to measuring love have merit? Can we measure love or are my anthropologist friends correct?

tion we access from long-term memory for purposes of constructing an answer. Note our use of the word *constructing*: Answer formulation is a constructive process; it is not a simple process of finding the relevant information in long-term memory and passively reporting it. People actively construct answers based on their appraisals and on the information they have in working memory. When we theorize about measurement, we find it helpful to think about the cognitive and affective appraisals respondents are likely to make and the type of information likely to be accessed from long-term memory when formulating an answer to a question.

Elements of the above were evident in our prior analysis of count recall. By thinking through each question in this kind of depth, you will be better able to construct a measurement theory of judgment to guide effective question design. Research has elaborated many factors that can potentially impact accurate recall. Relevant variables include, among others, (1) cognitive abilities; (2) age; (3) mood; (4) stress and anxiety; (5) attention; (6) the salience, vividness, and distinctiveness of the information or events to be recalled; (7) the frequency and recency of exposure to the information or events to be recalled; and (8) factors that promote confusion with other information/events. The importance and relevance of these factors for accurate recall can vary as a function of the facets of measurement in your study (e.g., the population you are studying, the assessment context, the substantive topic). Of course, often you will be interested not in maximizing the accuracy of recall but rather in the judgments people make about prior, current, or future events per se independent of accuracy. Generally, as you structure questions, a thoughtful analysis of the type of judgments and judgment processes you are activating will ultimately help you frame questions and potentially interpret answers to those questions.

Constructing a Theory of Response Translation

Once an individual formulates an answer to a question, he or she needs to convey that answer to the researcher or interviewer. In quantitative research, this task is often accomplished using rating scales. Rating scale formats are useful if we intend to process data for large numbers of people in multivariately complex ways for purposes of theory testing or describing populations. Rating scales are foreign to many people. People must learn how to use them and forge a strategy for translating their judgments onto them. Two people may make identical cognitive judgments but give different answers on the rating scale if they interpret and use the rating scale differently. This is a potential source of measurement error and needs to be addressed. How we accomplish accurate response translation requires a theory of the response translation process. Again, theory construction and measurement go hand in hand. In this section, we focus primarily on rating scales. We consider issues of metric precision, anchoring, use of adverb qualifiers, the problem of response satisficing, practice effects, and the identification of "mischievous" responders. All focus on the fundamental process of response translation.

Metric Precision

An important distinction in measurement theory and statistics is that between a *discrete variable* and a *continuous variable*. Often, the number of values that a variable can assume is relatively small and finite, such as the number of people in one's family. Such variables have a finite number of values that can occur between any two points. For example, consider the number of people who donate blood at a blood drive during the first hour of the drive. Only one value can occur between the values of 1 person and 3 persons, namely, 2 persons. We do not think of there being 1.5 or 2.7 persons. Variables for which only a finite number of values can occur between any two points are called discrete variables. In contrast, a continuous variable can theoretically have an infinite number of values between any two points. Reaction time to a stimulus is an example of a continuous variable. Even between the values of 1 and 2 seconds, an infinite number of values can occur (1.870 seconds, 1.8703 seconds, 1.87035 seconds, and so on). Many measures we use in the social sciences are discrete in character, but they are thought to reflect an underlying continuous construct. Satisfaction with a product might be measured on a 7-point scale ranging from very dissatisfied to very satisfied, but the construct it is thought to reflect (satisfaction) is continuous in character.

When measuring agreement with a statement on an opinion survey, the underlying construct of agreement is continuous, but researchers might use a different number of discriminations to assess agreement. Some researchers might use a 2-point metric (0 = disagree, 1 = agree); others might use a 3-point metric (0 = disagree, 1 = neither, 2 = agree); and still others might uses a 5-point metric (1 = strongly disagree, 2 = moderately disagree, 3 = neither, 4 = moderately agree, 5 = strongly agree). The number of categories/discriminations of a measure refers to the *precision* of that measure, with more categories being more precise. More precise measures have the advantage of better identifying individuals who truly differ in their opinions or judgments, while less precise measures can artificially lump together people who are meaningfully different into the same measurement category. A 2-point agree–disagree scale lumps into the same category and treats as the same people who strongly disagree with a statement, people who moderately disagree with the statement, and people who only slightly disagree with it. Such "lumping" can lead to misleading inferences. For example, consider the concept of behavioral intent. People who only slightly agree with the statement "I intend to vote in the upcoming presidential election" often behave differently in their voting behavior than those who strongly agree with this statement. As a result, many social scientists conceptualize behavioral intentions as a continuous construct and measure such intent using more precise metrics than 2-point scales (see Fishbein & Ajzen, 2010).[1]

Simulation studies that have addressed issues of scale coarseness suggest that five to seven categories often are enough for many empirical applications. For example, in a classic study focused on Pearson correlations, Bollen and Barb (1981) created on a computer a very large "population" of individuals where the true population correlation between two continuous variables was either 0.2, 0.6, 0.8, or 0.9. Bollen and Barb then created coarse measures from the continuous measures for each population by breaking the continuous measures into anywhere from 2 to 10 categories. For example, a normally distributed continuous variable that ranges from –3 to +3 can be turned into a 2-point scale by assigning anyone with a score of 0 or less a "0" and anyone with a score greater than 0 a "1." Bollen and Barb computed the correlations using these "coarse" measures and examined how close they were to the case where the correlation was computed using fully continuous metrics. They found that the true correlations were relatively well reproduced by the coarse measures as long as the coarse measures had five or more categories. For example, the reproduced correlations for five-category measures were within about 0.06 correlation units of the continuous-based correlations when the true correlations were 0.60. Bollen and Barb concluded that five categories were probably sufficient for many applications. This recommendation has been replicated in many other studies using different analytic contexts (although some research suggests seven or more categories may be best in some scenarios; see Green, Akey, Fleming, Hershberger, & Marquis, 1997; Lozano, García-Cueto, & Muñiz, 2008; Lubke & Muthén, 2004; Taylor, West, & Aiken, 2006). Thus, coarse measurement of continuous constructs is not necessarily problematic unless it is very coarse. Having said that, the requisite precision needed for a measure is dependent on the research question and context.

In the literature on question design, you will encounter conflicting statements about the relationship between precision and reliability, with some methodologists suggesting that more precise measures lead to lower reliability and other methodologists suggesting the opposite. Our recommendation is to think through the needed precision for the substantive questions you are addressing (which usually will be five or more discriminations) and then to use assessment practices that maximize reliability relative to that level of precision (see Chapter 13 for a discussion of such practices). Sometimes, the construct you study will require only a few discriminations, such as whether a person voted or whether a person purchased a product. However, if your construct is continuous, then you want a reasonably precise measure. If you work with populations where rating scales are not viable (because of literacy issues), with some ingenuity, you can still ask questions orally in ways that yield precise answers. For example, one might

---

[1] Sometimes, greater precision leads to lower reliability as individuals grapple with having to choose from among many discriminations. Later in this chapter we discuss strategies for circumventing this dilemma.

avoid the use of rating scales altogether and orally ask a question in two steps. At Step 1, you ask if the person "agrees" or "disagrees" with a statement or concept. If the person states "agree," you follow up by asking, "Do you strongly, moderately, or only slightly agree with it?" If the person states "disagree" at Step 1, you follow up by asking, "Do you strongly, moderately, or only slightly disagree with it?" When the two steps are combined, the result is a 6-point agree–disagree metric.

Anchoring

Cognitive judgments often are impacted by *cognitive anchors,* namely, a reference point against which judgments are made. At auctions, the opening bid is an anchor or standard against which later bids are evaluated. In negotiations, the first position stated becomes an anchor for counterpositions. Rating scales typically have endpoint descriptors that serve as anchors for how one uses the scale. One commonly used rating format is a *visual analog scale* (VAS). A VAS is a horizontal line, usually 100 millimeters in length, anchored by verbal descriptors. There are many variants, but here is a common example used in pain research to rate experienced pain associated with an event (e.g., a medical condition):

Respondents are instructed to mark a point on the line that best describes the pain they experience. A score between 0 and 100 is assigned based on the number of millimeters from the left that the mark is made. (*Note:* This example is not drawn to scale.) Pain researchers almost always use "no pain" as the left anchor, but they vary the descriptor for the right anchor. Usually, the maximal anchor is extreme to avoid ceiling effects (i.e., everyone marking the upper end of the scale), but not too extreme to the point people can't comprehend it. Research finds that as the maximal anchor becomes more extreme, pain ratings decrease (Seymour, Simpson, Charlton, & Phillips, 1985), which makes sense because with an extreme right anchor, individuals essentially are pushed away from the right extreme of the scale when making their ratings.

Qualitative studies have examined the painful events that people mentalize as maximum pain anchors. These tend to vary across individuals (de Williams, Davies, & Chadury, 2000). For example, adult females tend to use events associated with childbirth, whereas men use events associated with injuries (Robinson et al., 2004). Some people imagine events they think would be painful, while others recall a painful event that they experienced. These individual differences are important because two individuals can make the same cognitive judgments of pain but will translate it differently onto the rating scale if the mental representation of the maximum anchor is not the same, with more extreme representations lowering pain ratings. Indeed, the same individual may use different anchors at different time points in a longitudinal study, artificially producing change in pain ratings when no true pain change has occurred. Good psychometrics provides individuals with common anchors by defining anchors and providing referents. This is true for most rating scales, not just VASs.

Use of Adverb Qualifiers

Sometimes a VAS will include numerical demarcations on the line as reference points, as follows:

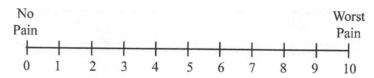

Although this format reduces precision, it can enhance reliability and equal interval properties of the metric as people have clear demarcations to indicate their marks on, and hopefully, they apply numerical properties to the scale points (such as equal intervals between numbers). Other researchers eliminate the line altogether, as in the following:

| No | | | | | | | | | | | | Worst |
| Pain | 0 | 1 | 2 | 3 | 4 | 5 | 6 | 7 | 8 | 9 | 10 | Pain |

People circle the number that best captures their judgment. The use of numbers assumes some degree of numeric literacy. To reduce such reliance, some researchers add *adverb qualifiers* to the scale at different points:

| 0 | 1 | 2 | 3 | 4 | 5 | 6 | 7 | 8 | 9 | 10 |
| Not at All Painful | | | Slightly Painful | | | Quite Painful | | | Extremely Painful | |

The idea is that individuals will first orient themselves to the adverb qualifier that best captures their judgment and then circle a number above that qualifier, but with the flexibility to rate somewhat lower or somewhat higher by circling a nearby number instead. Indeed, instructional sets are often given to use the scale in exactly this fashion. Numerous studies and meta-analyses have supported the addition of verbal descriptors to numerically labeled scales to increase reliability and validity (Bendig, 1953; Rodgers, Andrews, & Herzog, 1992; Saris & Gallhofer, 2007). Finally, some researchers eliminate the numbers to rid numeracy from the mix but at the cost of losing precision, as in the following:

_____ Not at all painful

_____ Slightly painful

_____ Quite painful

_____ Extremely painful

A classic scale format that also does not use numbers is called the *semantic differential* (Snider & Osgood, 1969), which appears as follows for rating a political candidate:

Candidate A

bad	____:____:____:____:____:____:____	good
weak	. . . . . .	strong
passive	____:____:____:____:____:____:____	active

The labels *extremely, quite,* and *slightly* are used for the three leftmost categories and *slightly, quite,* and *extremely* for the three rightmost categories as well to create symmetry. The middle category is labeled *neither or both*. Instructional sets usually are given that link these adverbs to the categories (see Snider & Osgood, 1969), but sometimes the adverbs are written below each category. Sometimes both labels and numbers (e.g., –3 to + 3) are associated with each category. Many different combinations are used in practice.

When choosing adverbs to use in rating scales, one should use adverbs that connote roughly equal intervals across the underlying dimension. For example, when rating the importance of each of several factors that entered into a decision, a commonly used format for each rating is:

____ Very important

____ Somewhat important

____ Not very important

____ Not at all important

Note that there seems to be unequal "psychological spacing" between these qualifiers. The difference between "not very important" and "somewhat important" seems slight compared to the difference between "somewhat important" and "very important." The choice of these particular adverbs creates an ordinal metric. There are large literatures in psychometrics that can guide the choice of adverbs to produce roughly equal intervals across the underlying dimension (Beckstead, 2014; Rohrmann, 2015). For example, using psychophysical scaling methods, Cliff (1959) found that describing something as "slightly good" is generally perceived to be about 0.50 times as "good" than the simple, unmodified "good." Adverbs can be selected based on such qualifying values to approximate equal intervals (taking into account, as well, linguistic distinctiveness and comprehension of the adverb). Rohrmann (2015) presents adverb analyses in English, German, and Chinese for dimensions of frequency (e.g., never, seldom, sometimes, often, always); intensity (not at all, a little, moderately, quite a bit, very much); probability (certainly not, unlikely, about 50:50, likely, for sure); quality (bad, inadequate, fair, good, excellent); and agreement (fully disagree, mainly disagree, neutral, mainly agree, fully agree). Beckstead (2014) summarizes research on qualifying values for frequency judgments and magnitudes. We do not recommend interpreting qualifying values in these reports as strictly applicable to your research because studies have shown that qualifying values can vary as a function of the different measurement facets (McClelland, 1975). However, published studies such as these can serve as rough guidelines. Coupled with common sense that is sensitive to creating equal psychological differences between categories as well as proper cognitive response testing, reasonable adverb choices can be made to produce approximately equal interval metrics.

As an aside, rating scales can be unipolar (from not having a property to having much of it) or bipolar (rating an object on polar adjective opposites, such as sad–happy, dominant–submissive). Here is an example of a bipolar format:

−5	−4	−3	−2	−1	0	1	2	3	4	5
Very Sad		Moderately Sad		Slightly Sad		Slightly Happy		Moderately Happy		Very Happy

For bipolar scales, it is important that the adjectives are, in fact, polar opposites. Research suggests that formal antonyms are not always perceived as psychological antonyms (Yorke, 2001). For example, some perceive the antonym pair calm–angry as not constituting polar opposites. Early research on prototypical personalities treated masculinity and femininity as polar opposites, but this conceptualization was later rejected with the introduction of the concept of androgynous personality styles (namely, having both male and female qualities; see Lubinski, Tellegen, & Butcher, 1983). In addition, use of negative numbers in bipolar scales implies numeracy, which may be problematic. One can address this by eliminating numbers and using just the label "neither or both" for the midpoint, yielding a 7-point metric.

Satisficing

Herbert Simon was awarded the Nobel Prize in economics in 1978 for his extensive work in decision making. Earlier, in 1957, he coined the term *satisficing* (a combination of the words "satisfy" and "suffice") to refer to decision contexts where instead of carefully thinking about all available decision options, people only do what is sufficient to obtain a satisfactory result. For example, in choosing a bank, a person may open an account at the first bank that seems satisfactory rather than explore the merits of bank after bank. In the context of questionnaires, satisficing refers to the tendency to choose the first acceptable response option for a question because doing so requires the least effort.

Satisficing can take different forms. If a consumer psychologist asks people to rate different ice creams on 0 to 10 scales, a person might just rate them all 8 because he or she likes ice cream in general. Galesic and Yan (2011) used eye-tracking technology to follow people's eye movements as they read items on questionnaires. They found that about 10% of survey takers never looked at the last two response options in a 12-category list of preferred products and that they spent far more time looking at options in the first half of the list. Strategies for dealing with satisficing include (1) use of instructional sets to encourage conscientious responding, (2) keeping questions or response options short and simple, (3) splitting complex questions that have many response options into multiple questions, and (4) including checks to diagnose satisficing. For the latter, for example, Adams and colleagues (2006) included the following item among 42 items rated on 5-point disagree–agree scales: "We use this question to discard the survey of people who are not reading the statements. Please select option 4 to this item." Individuals are more likely to satisfice if they feel time pressure to complete the task, if they find the task difficult, or if they are bored.

Practice Effects and Scale Comprehension

As noted, your population may have little experience with rating scales, in which case it may take time for them to become comfortable with the scales. To remove these warm-up effects, we find it helpful, where feasible, to include a few practice items. After the warm-up items, we also include a few items that serve as comprehension checks for rating scale use. These are items where we know what response the individual should make if he or she understands the rating scale properly (e.g., a rating on a good–bad scale of something that is obviously good). If the correct response is not given, we know we must review the rating scale instructions with the respondent. Finally, we have found that people sometimes object to frequent shifts in scale formats. Such changes may be necessary, but wherever possible, we try to use one format (e.g., a 5-point agree–disagree scale with adverb qualifiers) for most items. Doing so also limits the number of anchoring examples and practice tasks.

Mischievous Responders

Research has documented the existence of what are known as mischievous responders (Robinson-Cimpian, 2014). These are individuals who comprehend a question, make a valid judgment in their minds, but then deliberately report a false judgment, often in outlandish ways, in order to be "mischievous." Fish and Russell (2018) documented an example in the National Longitudinal Study of Adolescent Health (Add Health). They noted that an unusually high number of middle and high school youth in the study had reported they were not heterosexual. In addition, the number of students who reported being nonheterosexual but changed their answer to being heterosexual in a one-year follow-up interview was unusually high. Fish and Russell developed a mischievous index based on methods suggested by Robinson-Cimpian (2014) that used response patterns to 10 low base-rate items unrelated to sexual identity within Add Health. If people responded affirmatively to a large number of these items, it raised the possibility that they were being "mischievous." Using this index and response triangulation from multiple questions about sexual identity, Fish and Russell identified those individuals who were engaging in mischievous responding. They then used this information as a covariate in analyses of health disparities between heterosexual and nonheterosexual youth. They found evidence for only a small proportion of "mischievous" youth, but, importantly, one of the five health disparities they had documented in prior analyses became statistically nonsignificant when the mischievousness index was included as a covariate. Mischievousness can probably best be counteracted through the use of instructional sets that discourage it and that encourage honest responding and also through including items that will detect it in the survey.

Concluding Comments on Response Translation

Many types of rating scales are used in social science research that allow people to translate their judgments and opinions into brief, quantitative formats that can be analyzed effectively. You need to theory construct about ways to facilitate that translation process for your particular research domain. We have provided general guidelines to stimulate your thinking, and these are summarized in Figure 14.2. This figure, like Figure 14.1, is a simplification because it ignores potential moderated and interactive relationships between constructs. Inevitably, some considerations will be unique to your substantive domain and your chosen scale formats.

Concluding Comments on Theory Construction for Self-Reports

In sum, when using self-reports in a research project, it is helpful to adopt a theory construction mindset as you think about the measures using three processes as a theory generation frame: comprehension, judgment, and response translation. We make it a practice to theory construct around these processes, explicitly taking into account the particular measurement facets of our study (who the population is, what the assessment context is, etc.). We engage in such theory construction not only for measures we develop but also for extant scales that purportedly have solid psychometric histories. Sometimes those "histories" do not hold up when they are subjected to rigorous analysis. More often than not, we find ourselves engaging in preliminary psychometric studies designed to provide insights into the best way to structure the measures we will use in our main study.

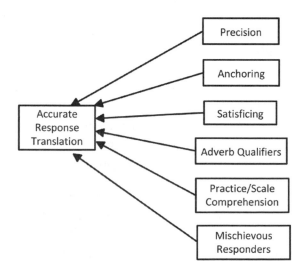

FIGURE 14.2. Factors impacting response translation.

CONSTRUCTING A THEORY OF OBSERVER REPORTS

Many studies do not rely on self-reports but instead use trained observers to record information (e.g., make behavioral counts) and/or to make judgments about people's behavior (e.g., rate a child's behavior in a playground on a rating scale reflecting how aggressive the behavior is). There are many types of observational research contexts in the social and health sciences. Sometimes observations are made in natural settings and other times in laboratory settings. Sometimes observers are hidden from view, and sometimes research participants are aware of their presence and can visually see the observer. Sometimes observers code behaviors using dichotomous formats (e.g., the behavior performed expressed positive affect or it did not), and sometimes the behaviors are rated on scales or are subject to some other form of quantification. Sometimes observers make judgments about a person's behavior, and sometimes they make inferences about psychological states (e.g., anxiety). Sometimes observations are made about people, and sometimes they are made about settings, such as the quality of a child's home environment. In our view, self-reports are a form of observer reports; it is just a matter of who the "observer" is—the person being studied (self-report) or someone else (observer report).

External observers fundamentally use the same processes that we have described for self-reports. First, observers must have a clear understanding of the behaviors/constructs they are to observe (comprehension). They then must make judgments about the person's behavior relative to those constructs (judgment). Finally, they must communicate those judgments to the researcher by translating them onto a rating scale or some other response format (response translation). As such, the theory construction frame we described for self-reports applies with equal vigor to observer reports. For example, most factors we have identified as determinants of question comprehension for self-reports also impact the comprehension of instructions to observers about what they are to observe and how they are to make their observations. If observers use ratings scales, the factors we have described for response translation for self-reports also apply to observers, namely, the need to have precise metrics; to use well-defined anchors; to use adverb qualifiers strategically selected to approximate equal interval metrics; to implement practices in order to increase observer task motivation and eliminate satisficing; and to deal with potential practice and warm-up effects.

Developing effective measurement strategies using trained observers means you need to theorize about observer comprehension, judgment, and response translation. Theorizing about these processes will inevitably invoke consideration of characteristics of (1) the observers, (2) the research participants, (3) the research context, (4) the behavioral context, and (5) the judgments to be made. These five categories form a starting point for your measurement theory construction for observer reports.

One important difference between self-reports and observer reports lies in the kinds of factors that impact the cognitive judgments made by observers. The literature in organizational psychology suggests potential biases on the part of supervisors when judging the behaviors of employees and, although made in slightly different contexts, these biases are also of potential relevance for observer reports more generally. The biases include (1) a *halo effect,* a bias whereby the overall impression of a person ("he or she is very good") impacts evaluations of the person's performance independent of actual performance; (2) a *horn effect,* a bias that is the same as the halo effect but is focused on an overall negative impression, leading one to evaluate behaviors more negatively; (3) a *central tendency bias,* the tendency to judge everyone as average; (4) a *leniency bias,* the tendency to "go easy" on people by judging most everyone positively; (5) a *strictness bias,* the tendency to "be hard" on people by judging most everyone negatively; (6) a *contrast effect,* the tendency to see someone who stands apart from others as more different than they actually are, such as judging a person to be a very good performer if that person is surrounded by people who are poor performers; (7) an *assimilation effect,* the tendency to see someone who is slightly different from others as being more like those others than is actually the case, such as judging a person to be a poor performer if that person is surrounded by people who are poor performers; (8) a *recency bias,* the tendency to judge performance based on the most recently observed performances rather than the total performance; (9) a *primacy bias,* the tendency to judge performance based on the initially observed performances rather than the total performance; (10) *stereotyping,* the tendency to allow stereotypes of the groups a person is a member of, such as gender and ethnicity, to impact judgments of that person; and (11) an *expectancy effect,* the tendency to base judgments on what the observer expects to happen. Which of these biases might be relevant to your research that uses observers? What other biases may be relevant for your research project that are not listed here? What is your theory of judgment bias? When you are training observers, how might you address such biases and eliminate their impact to improve measurement validity? The operation of these biases may differ depending on characteristics of the observer, the target person, the research context, the behavioral context, and the judgment dimensions. As you plan your measurement strategy, think through these theoretical facets.

A concept of some importance in studies using trained observers is *observer drift* (Smith, 1986). Most definitions of drift state that it occurs when observer understandings of the behavioral codes or coding criteria they are to use change over time. Other researchers use the term *drift* to refer to such changes between the time observers finish training and the time they begin observing. In either case, it is important to ensure that observers maintain consistency across time, that is, to theorize about factors that might impact drift in one's research.

Sometimes observers are used who have not undergone formal training in the target observational tasks. For example, teachers might be asked to rate or make judgments about individual students for research purposes, and parents might be asked to rate or make judgments about their children. In such cases, one must be particularly sensitive to observer bias. Perhaps one can ask questions of these observers or use instructional sets in ways that minimize bias. As stated earlier, lack of convergence of reports by these different "observers" may not reflect observer bias, but instead may indicate that the observers have access to different behavior samples of the target person. Parents who are asked to rate the anxiety levels of their children see their children in different contexts than teachers do. Disparities in ratings between multiple observers often are regarded as problematic, but in some cases, they are meaningful.

Just as cognitive response testing can be used to good effect for self-reports (see Chapter 13), it also can be used for observer reports. After observers have been trained and execute a few observations in a training session, verbal probes about the interpretation of behavioral codes, judgment strategies used, and response translation can be helpful in building your measurement theory and provide insights into factors that need to be addressed.

CONSTRUCTING A THEORY OF "OBJECTIVE" MEASURES

In addition to self-reports and observer reports, another measurement approach uses "objective" measures that directly indicate one's standing on a construct. For example, there are biomarkers to indicate if a woman is pregnant, if a person has cancer, viral loads for HIV, if a person has consumed alcohol in the past 30 days, and the amount of physical exertion during an activity, to name but a few. Formal records of people's text messaging or search patterns on the Internet also do not require self-reporting or direct observer reports. Examination of the accuracy of "objective" measures like these often reveals the possibility of bias; there can be false positives or false negatives in them, that is, measurement error. For example, urine tests for opioid use can yield a false positive if the person taking the test consumes a large amount of poppy seeds prior to the test. False positive urine tests for some illicit drugs also can occur if people taking the test consume cold medications containing pseudoephedrine. False negatives for urine tests of illicit drug use can occur through tampering (e.g., adding water to dilute the sample or adding soap to the sample), taking diuretics, or drinking large amounts of water before the test. A urine test for cannabis use will test positive for 1 to 3 days after a single use of marijuana, but not longer, indicating the time-restricted nature of these tests. Given that "objective" measures are subject to measurement error, it follows that a theory construction mindset surrounding that error is required. Accurate use of biomarkers for research purposes often requires considerable expertise.

"Objective" measures are not always sensitive to the behavioral dimension of theoretical interest to a social scientist. For example, there is no biomarker of the number of days in the past 30 days that someone has smoked marijuana, so if one is interested in understanding the frequency or patterns of marijuana use, biomarkers are of little help. A theory of "objective" measurement also should articulate such boundary conditions.

Researchers often use official records as "objective" measures of constructs, such as school records to document grade point averages of students, arrest records for drunk driving or some form of criminal activity, and death certificates to index mortality. In some cases, these indices will contain relatively little measurement error, but in other cases, this will not be so. For example, many people drive drunk but never get arrested for it. Official arrest records for drunk driving are thus poor measures of it. As another example, in 2015, official death certificates in the United States were found to overlook more than half of the people killed by police (Feldman, Gruskin, Coull, & Krieger, 2017), indicating a source of bias in using such certificates as an index of mortality rates.

Scientists are skeptics, and it is best to approach any "objective" measure with a mindset of potential fallibility. A theory construction mindset of potential sources of error and how to rectify them is as applicable to "objective" measures as it is to self-reports and observer reports.

THE IMPORTANCE OF A THEORY CONSTRUCTION MINDSET TO MEASUREMENT

In sum, as you approach measurement matters in your research, we strongly urge you to adopt a theory construction mindset, namely, strive to construct theories of measurement for every question you ask or every measure you use by making use of the thinking strategies and heuristics elaborated in the current and previous chapters. As you evaluate measures for possible use, bring that measurement theory to bear. To the extent that important psychometric issues are theoretically unresolved, you may need to conduct preliminary research to gain perspectives on them before you move forward with your main study. If you encounter poor psychometric practice for a standard scale (e.g., the scale fails to provide adequate anchors, it does not use appropriate adverb qualifiers, or it pays inadequate attention to precision), consider altering the measure if you believe the changes will improve its psychometric properties.

As per our discussion of measurement theory in Chapter 13, the theories you construct about self-reports, observer reports, and objective reports can be subjected to empirical tests and published in scientific journals for other researchers to benefit from. However, as noted in Chapter 13, we usually do not go about the task of empirically testing every core (untested) theoretical expression in our measurement theory because doing so would sidetrack us from our main purpose of building substantive theory in our main study. We instead rely heavily on common sense and past measurement research for measure evaluation, but we also invariably end up conducting a preliminary measurement-oriented research project to address measurement issues (and to test some of the theoretical expressions we generated) to improve the primary study.

MEASUREMENT AND QUALITATIVE RESEARCH

Our discussion thus far has emphasized quantitative measurement, but the issues of comprehension, judgment, and response translation apply just as strongly to qualitative research, either when asking people questions, when making your own observations, or when training others to make observations for you. In qualitative research, as in quantitative research, it is important that the questions we pose to people are comprehended. In addition, if we have some sense of the cognitive and affective processes people use when processing and answering our questions, or if we can discover what those processes are, we might be able to better structure questions and probes to yield answers that provide a deeper understanding of the phenomena we are studying. Finally, it is important for qualitative researchers to appreciate the difference between people's understanding of their environment, as represented by the concepts they have in mind, and their description of that environment per se, as represented by the symbols or words they use to describe their thoughts, that is, response translation.

Qualitative researchers, like quantitative researchers, probably can benefit from the use of cognitive response testing of their interview-based questions to ensure that their questions will be understood properly when posed to informants. As well, many of the factors discussed above that impact comprehension, judgment, and response translation directly apply to qualitative research contexts. For example, how might issues of statisficing and task motivation be addressed when questions are posed in unstructured interviews in qualitative research? Are questions phrased in ways that encourage bipolar or unipolar responses, and if bipolar, are the opposites truly opposites from the respondent's perspective? Is it necessary to provide examples of "anchors" for people to establish reference points for certain open-ended questions? What should those anchors be? A theory construction mindset for measurement is as relevant to qualitative researchers as it is to quantitative researchers.

Qualitative researchers often engage in a strategy known as *informal interviewing* (Bernard, 2017). For example, Connolly (1990) studied children who live, eat, and sleep on the streets in Guatemala City by just hanging out with them and talking with them informally during his everyday interactions to learn about their lives. At the end of each day, Connolly wrote extensive field notes based on his observations and his conversations with the children. Our discussion of theory construction surrounding observer reports directly applies to this scenario.

Unstructured interviewing also is common in qualitative research. Such interviews have a different quality than informal interviewing because the researcher typically sits with the informant and asks specific questions. To be sure, unstructured interviews are "structured" in the researcher's mind in that he or she invariably has certain goals that are constantly salient during the course of the interview. However, the general spirit of unstructured interviews is to get people talking about a topic and then stay out of the way as they express their thoughts, feelings, recollections, and hopes.

Key to unstructured interviewing is the act of *probing*, that is, knowing when, how, and how often to ask for clarification and elaboration, or knowing how to re-focus interviewees to get them back on topic. Is there a "theory of probing" you can use to help you approach this important facet of unstructured interviewing? If you were to construct a "theory of probing" for your particular research project, what would it be? Are there different types of probes one can use? What is the typology describing probe differences? Are there nonverbal probes in this typology (e.g., the nod of one's head, a look of surprise)? Are some types of probes better in some contexts and for certain types of people and certain topics? How do you effectively probe without interjecting your own views into the interviewee's thinking? How do you know people are quiet because they are reflecting on the topic at hand as opposed to being quiet because they have finished expressing their thoughts? Are the three processes of comprehension, judgment, and response translation relevant to probes?

Although formal measurement theory has been dominated by psychologists, anthropologists have offered important insights into such theories as well. Instead of thinking of a measure as a static "object" or "thing," anthropological perspectives often think of the act of completing a measure as a behavior in its own right that is subject to the same types of ethnographic-based descriptions and explanations as any other behavior (Hubley & Zumbo, 2017; Maddox, Zumbo, Tay-Lim, & Qu, 2015). Theorizing is not restricted to measurement principles brought to bear per traditional psychometric theory; it also expands such analysis to include broader situational, cultural, and ecological facets pertinent to assessment. Would doing so help in your theory construction efforts?

SUMMARY AND CONCLUDING COMMENTS

Testing creative and novel theories often requires that you develop your own measures of constructs. These measures can take the form of self-reports, observer reports, or "objective" measures. When constructing (or evaluating) measures, you need to invoke a measurement theory. As such, theory construction at the level of measurement is important.

Three fundamental processes are involved when people provide self-reports: (1) they must comprehend the questions you are asking, (2) they must form answers and judgments relevant to those questions, and (3) they must report those answers and judgments to you. There is considerable room for theory construction surrounding these processes of comprehension, judgment, and response translation. Question comprehension is potentially impacted by characteristics of the population you are studying, the structure and nature of the questions you are asking, and the broader assessment context in which the questions are asked. Factors within each of these domains that may come into play are summarized in Figure 14.1. These factors may be nuanced and augmented depending on your substantive application and research questions and, as such, you need to theory construct relative to them. Judgment and answer formulation ultimately involves cognitive and affective processes that operate in working memory of individuals. The content of working memory is determined by a person's cognitive and affective appraisals of the assessment context and questions being posed as well as information retrieved from long-term memory, which is then used to construct one's answers. Careful analysis of these judgment processes can often help researchers frame questions in ways that will maximize their information yield, reliability, and validity. Response translation takes many forms, but a ubiquitous format is that of the rating scale. Rating scales take many different forms (e.g., requiring unipolar versus bipolar judgments), and how people interpret and use rating scales is critical. Two people may make identical judgments cognitively but may differ in the responses they make on a rating scale, depending on scale interpretation. Similarly, individuals may make different cognitive judgments but give the same response on the rating scale depending on scale interpretation. Factors that impact rating scale interpretation and utility include metric precision, anchoring, the choice of adverb qualifiers, the use of satisficing response strategies, and scale familiarity. As you approach measurement in your research, you will need to theory construct about judgment processes and response translation, just as you theory construct about question comprehension, and then, based on these theories, formulate optimal measurement strategies to achieve your broader research goals. Measurement is complicated, and so it demands high-quality theory construction to do it right.

Observer reports typically use trained observers to record behavioral observations of a target person or to make judgments about the person's observed behaviors. External observers fundamentally use the same processes described for self-reports. First, observers must have a clear understanding of the behaviors/constructs they are to observe (comprehension). They then must make judgments about the person's behavior relative to those constructs (judgment). Finally, they must communicate those judgments to the researcher by translating them onto a rating scale or some other response format (response translation). As such, the theoretical issues addressed for self-reports often apply with equal vigor to observer reports. However, the observers' biases can impact the accuracy of their recorded observations, including halo effects, horn effects, central tendency bias, leniency bias, strictness bias, contrast effects, assimilation effects, recency bias, primacy bias, stereotyping, and expectancy effects. Observer drift, through which observer interpretation of behavioral codes changes over time, also is of concern. "Objective" measures do not require observation in the sense that self-report and observer reports do, and they include such approaches as biomarkers, formal search indices on the Internet, and a wide range of unobtrusive measures or behavioral traces left behind by people. Close examination of these measures often reveals sources of measurement error in them, requiring that scientists maintain a skeptical attitude when considering them as measures to include in their research. For both observer-based and "objective" measures, you will need to theory construct about potential sources of error and then adopt practices to counter them.

SUGGESTED READINGS

Abrams, W. (2000). *Observational research handbook: Understanding how consumers live with your product.* New York: McGraw-Hill; and Yoder, P., & Symons, F. (2018). *Observational measurement of behavior.* Baltimore: Brookes.

—Two useful books on a wide range of issues to consider when conducting observational research.

Aiken, L. (1996). *Rating scales and checklists: Evaluating behavior, personality, and attitudes.* New York: Wiley.

—An informal and engaging writing on rating scales in the social sciences.

Bernard, H. R. (2017). *Research methods in anthropology: Qualitative and quantitative approaches.* Lanham, MD: Rowman & Littlefield.

—Includes chapters that provide practical and thoughtful accounts of measurement principles from an anthropological perspective.

Edwards, A. L. (1957). *Techniques of attitude scale construction.* New York: Appleton-Century-Crofts.

—A dated but incredibly clear exposition of the classic scaling methods of Guttman, Likert, and Thurstone.

Marsden, P., & Wright, J. (Eds.). (2010). *Handbook of survey research*. Bingley, UK: Emerald Group.

—A thorough reference on survey research and questionnaire design.

Oakhill, J., Cain, K., & Elbro, C. (2015). *Understanding and teaching reading comprehension: A handbook*. New York: Routledge.

—Although this book is focused on teaching reading skills to children, it is filled with useful concepts and principles that can benefit comprehension issues in question design.

Schober, M. F., & Conrad, F. G. (1997). Does conversational interviewing reduce survey measurement error? *Public Opinion Quarterly, 61*, 576–602.

—An overview of the advantages of conversational interviewing. See also Lavrakas, P. (2008). Conversational interviewing. In *Encyclopedia of survey research methods*. Thousand Oaks, CA: Sage.

Weldon, R. B., Corbin, J. C., Garavito, D. M. N., & Reyna, V. F. (2017). The gist is sophisticated yet simple: Fuzzy-trace theory's developmental approach to individual differences in judgment and decision making. In M. Toplak & J. Weller (Eds.), *Individual differences in judgment and decision making from a developmental context* (pp. 67–84). New York: Routledge.

—A nice introduction to how people extract gists from information and the role of gists in memory and judgment.

Wingfield, A., & Byrnes, D. L. (1981). *The psychology of human memory*. New York: Academic Press.

—A good introduction to the basics of short-term memory, working memory, and long-term memory.

KEY TERMS

comprehension (p. 403)

judgment (p. 403)

response translation (p. 403)

literacy (p. 404)

functional literacy (p. 404)

functional illiteracy (p. 404)

numeracy (p. 405)

short-term memory (p. 405)

working memory (p. 405)

long-term memory (p. 405)

forward–back translation (p. 406)

lexical level (p. 407)

semantic level (p. 407)

standardized interviewing (p. 408)

conversational interviewing (p. 408)

think backward strategy (p. 410)

think forward strategy (p. 410)

cognitive rounding/heaping (p. 412)

discrete variable (p. 415)

continuous variable (p. 415)

metric precision (p. 415)

cognitive anchors (p. 417)

visual analog scale (p. 417)

adverb qualifiers (p. 418)

semantic differential (p. 419)

satisficing (p. 420)

halo effects (p. 424)

horn effects (p. 424)

central tendency bias (p. 424)

leniency bias (p. 424)

strictness bias (p. 424)

contrast effect (p. 424)

assimilation effect (p. 424)

recency bias (p. 424)

primacy bias (p. 424)

stereotyping (p. 424)

expectancy effects (p. 424)

observer drift (p. 424)

informal interviewing (p. 427)

unstructured interviewing (p. 427)

probing (p. 427)

EXERCISES

Exercises to Reinforce Concepts

1. What are the three cognitive processes that underlie self-reports? Characterize each of them.

2. What are literacy and functional literacy? Why is it important to consider them in question construction?

3. What is numeracy? How is it important for question design?

4. What is the role of working memory in the question construction process? How does it work with short-term and long-term memory to affect question comprehension and the formulation of answers to questions?

5. What is the method of forward–back translation?

6. What is the difference between standardized interviewing and conversational interviewing? What are the strengths and weaknesses of each?

7. You are going to ask people to recall the number of times they ate dinner out at a restaurant during the past 3 months. What factors would you take into consideration in framing this question to them?

8. What is the difference between a think forward and think backward strategy? Which one tends to work best?

9. Give some examples of factors that represent systematic measurement error. Name at least three. How might each of them be addressed to reduce their impact?

10. What is the validity of a measure?

11. What is cognitive heaping? How might you deal with it?

12. What is metric precision? In general, what is the minimum number of scale categories you need for a measure of a continuous variable?

13. What is a visual analog scale? Describe some of the different variants of it.

14. What is anchoring? Why is it important psychometrically?

15. How might you choose adverbs for rating scales to help approximate interval-level properties? What principles would you take into account in choosing adverbs?

16. What is satisficing? Why is it important in question design? How can you prevent it?

17. Why is it important to remove practice effects when you are using rating scales?

18. Name five biases that can bias observer reports, and define each of them.

19. What is observer drift? How can you prevent it?

20. Why are the processes of comprehension, judgment, and response translation important in qualitative research?

Exercises to Apply Concepts

1. Find a study of interest to you in the literature and read the section on the primary measures used in that study. Critique the measurement section as if you were reviewing the article for a journal. Write out constructive suggestions to the author for how to improve his or her measurement. If you want to draw on principles from Chapter 13 as well, do so.

2. Locate a copy of a dissertation that collected original data, from either your school library or on the Internet. Role-play that you are on the student's dissertation committee and that the student gave you the section on measurement in the dissertation during his or her *proposal* defense. What recommendations would you make to the student to improve his or her measurement?

3. Pick out an extant measure of a construct you are interested in that uses a rating scale. Find someone you know and do a cognitive response test on the measure using verbal probes. Use the material you learned in this chapter to shape the probes you ask.

4. Find a study that used trained observers to do behavioral observations. Critique the observer report strategies used in the study. How might you improve what the study did?

5. Construct a theory of probing for a research topic and population of interest to you.

Part V

CONCLUDING ISSUES

Theory Revision

Before I got married I had six theories about raising children;
now, I have six children and no theories.
                    —JOHN WILMOT, Earl of Rochester

In the early 1800s, Alexis Bouvard, an astronomer, charted the orbit of the planet Uranus, the most distant planet in our solar system known at the time. Using principles from Newtonian mechanics, he predicted future positions of Uranus during its orbit, but these predictions did not bear out. An undergraduate student of mathematics, John Adams, learned of the disparities and entertained the possibilities that they might be due to (1) measurement error, (2) the sun's gravity, or (3) an undiscovered outer planet that was causing a "pull" on Uranus. Adams became intrigued by the latter possibility and used mathematics and Newton's law of gravitation to deduce the mass, position, and orbit of the perturbing body that would be the source of the deviations (calculations also were performed, independently, by Urbain Le Verrier, a French mathematician). Johann Galle, an astronomer at the Berlin Observatory, used these results to discover that a new planet did in fact exist and that it was located exactly where Adams had predicted. Such was the discovery of Neptune, a new planet in the solar system. Noted philosopher of science, Karl Popper, interpreted these events as an example of a critical test of Newton's theories of gravitation, referring to the event as "the most startling and convincing success of any human intellectual achievement" (Thornton, 2018, p. 14). Popper (1968, 1970, 1983) advocated for the central role of such critical tests in science via his principle of falsification, namely, that a theoretical proposition should have the capacity to be falsified. As straightforward as this principle may seem, it has been a source of controversy about how scientists orient themselves to disconfirming evidence.

When we collect data designed to test a theory, results can emerge that call the theory into question. We then need to revise the theory or abandon it altogether. Faced with disconfirming or partially supportive data, there are thinking strategies one can use that impact decisions about whether and how to revise a theory. These strategies are the primary topic of this chapter. We begin by discussing Popper's framework on theory disconfirmation. Within that context, we consider ambiguities in the principle of falsification, the identification of boundary conditions for a theory, and replication research. We then discuss the importance of these principles for qualitative research. Next, we describe Bayesian perspectives on theory revision, providing a general appreciation for Bayesian epistemology. We then turn to the topic of automated theory revision. This work is in its infancy, but the idea is to rely on computer algorithms to make decisions about how to revise a theory in the face of disconfirming data, lessening the role of humans in the process. Finally, if a theory is to be revised, there are desiderata that the revised theory should seek to satisfy. We discuss these desiderata, drawing on our discussion in Chapter 3 about what constitutes a "good" theory. We also briefly describe theory revision at the level of broad paradigm shifts via the work of Thomas Kuhn.

DISCONFIRMATION AND THEORY REVISION

Faced with theory-disconfirming evidence in a study, researchers typically respond to it by (1) reducing confidence in the theory itself and/or (2) reducing confidence in the procedures used to test the theory. Popper (1968, 1970, 1983) has written extensively about these two alternatives in the philosophical literature but in ways that are somewhat abstract relative to current, everyday research activities in the social sciences. In this section, we take some liberties with Popper's ideas, but much of what is presented is grounded in his principles.

Popper describes the choice between these two options as the *disconfirmation dilemma*. He describes the tendency by researchers to resolve the dilemma by discounting the methods used to test the theory as the *dogmatic approach*, whereas the tendency to discount the theory itself is called the *critical approach*. Both tendencies have virtues and vices, with Popper emphasizing the importance of the critical approach for scientific advancement.

Popper argues that theories cannot be verified but instead they can only be falsified (unless they are untestable). For example, we might have a theory that alcohol use is a cause of depression in middle school youth in the United Sates. From this theory, we derive the hypothesis that if we measure alcohol use and depression in a sample of middle school youth living in the United States, we should observe a positive correlation between the measures. If we conduct a study and observe a positive correlation between them, then the data are consistent with the theory. However, this does not prove that alcohol use is, in fact, a cause of depression. There are many rival explanations that could produce the correlation. For example, perhaps depression causes youth to "self-medicate" by drinking alcohol, so causality is in the opposite direction to what the theory states. The hypothesized correlation would be produced by this rival explanation. According to many philosophers, there will always be rival explanations of some kind, even if they seem remote. Strictly speaking, they argue, absolute verification is impossible. This is even true for clinical trials or laboratory studies that use randomization because factors like attrition, missing data, testing effects, regression to the mean, and manipulation confounds can create interpretational ambiguities.

If our study of alcohol and depression failed to yield a correlation between the two constructs, then we might meaningfully say the theory is disconfirmed. Popper provides convincing examples of where this logic applies and argues for the centrality of falsification in theory tests. Leary (1979) and others, however, have noted that disconfirmation also can be difficult to demonstrate because studies can falsely produce results counter to theoretical predictions. For example, perhaps the theoretical proposition that alcohol use is a cause of depression is true but the measures of depression and alcohol use in the study were flawed and produced a near-zero correlation. Philosopher Imre Lakatos (1970, 1978) argues that critical tests do not exist in the sense that Popper envisioned. Using the discovery of Neptune as an example, Lakatos invoked a counterfactual and asked what would have happened if Galle had not found Neptune. Lakatos doubts that Newtonian physics would have been abandoned or that scientists of the time would have believed that Newton's theory had been falsified. Failure to find the planet could be attributed, he conjectured, to the interference of the Earth's atmosphere with the telescope, to the presence of an asteroid belt, and so on. Lakatos argued that high-level scientific theories are relatively resistant to falsification and fall into disrepute only in the context of broader research programs that cumulate disconfirming evidence. Given that disconfirmation, like confirmation, within any one study will likely be ambiguous, we ultimately are almost always faced with directly addressing Popper's disconfirmation dilemma, one way or the other.

Popper (1968, 1983) specified what he called *methodological rules* that, if followed, prevent theories from being immunized against disconfirmation. These rules, stated by Popper in abstract terms, have been criticized and reinterpreted extensively in the philosophy of science literature. A more modern translation of the concept for the social sciences is the long list of threats to internal validity, external validity, construct validity, and statistical conclusion validity that can lead to false confirmation or false disconfirmation of a theory; see Shadish, Cook, and Campbell (2002) for an excellent discussion of these "methodological rules" as well as on our companion website (*www. theory-construction.com*). Our own orientation to the disconfirmation dilemma in the research we conduct is to anticipate as many methodological objections as possible when designing a study, make a list of these objections, prioritize their importance as threats to theory tests, and then deal with as many of the threats as possible (in order of priority) either procedurally or statistically. We include those objections that we are unable to address in the limitations section of our report, or we conduct a second study to rule them out and then publish both studies together as a single article. The intent of these "methodological rules" for the planned study is to make a dogmatic orientation impossible; if data do not conform to the theory, one *must* reject the theory with a high level of confidence. A heuristic we sometimes invoke is to envision a hostile group of highly expert reviewers (e.g., a hostile dissertation committee) who will question everything we do and every conclusion we make. Our task is to design the study so that we can counterargue any methodological argument the reviewers make.

Rather than question the methodology of the disconfirming study, another option is for a theorist to amend the theory to accommodate the disconfirming data. Thus, the data are reinterpreted as only partially disconfirming and theoretical adjustments are made, thereby preserving the original theory, albeit in modified form. Einstein used the strategy of adding a "cosmological constant" to his initial mathematical formulations of general relativity to accommodate data he could not explain unless he accepted the idea of an expanding universe, something he was loath to do at the time. (Einstein later referred to this reluctance as the biggest blunder of his career; ironically, the constant has recently been brought back into his theory to help explain the existence of dark energy.)

BOUNDARY CONDITIONS AND THEORY REVISION

Some theories are conceptualized as universals, whereas other theories are thought to only apply to certain individuals in certain contexts and at certain points in time. When a theory makes such qualifications, the qualifications are said to represent the *boundary conditions* of the theory. The boundary conditions of a theory can be specified as a formal part of the theory, or they can be invoked in ad hoc ways, such as after a study has been completed and one needs to invoke boundary conditions in order to preserve the original theory; the theory holds, but just not as broadly as previously presumed. Resorting to the specification of boundary conditions is thus a strategy theorists sometimes use when faced with convincing disconfirming data. This is not necessarily inappropriate—many theories likely have boundary conditions—but it does limit the generalizability of the theory.

An interesting illustration of the complex dynamics surrounding boundary conditions and theory revision is captured in the work of Henrich, Heine, and Norenzayan (2010). These authors criticized mainstream psychology for building a psychological science based primarily on societies they characterized as WEIRD (Western, Educated, Industrialized, Rich, and Democratic). Henrich and colleagues note that about 70% of respondents in published psychology research come from the United States and that 96% of them hail from Western, industrialized societies. The countries in this research, they note, represent about 12% of the world's population. In the *Journal of Personality and Social Psychology,* a premier research journal of the American Psychological Association, about 70% of the respondents in studies conducted in the United States are undergraduate college students enrolled in introductory psychology courses, leading some to suggest that over the years we have built a strong psychological science of undergraduate psychology students (Arnett, 2008). Henrich and colleagues reviewed cross-cultural studies in areas of psychology on visual perception, fairness, cooperation, spatial reasoning, categorization/inferential induction, moral reasoning, reasoning styles, self-concepts, and the heritability of IQ. They concluded that there was little generalizability in results across cultures, even when basic processes were the target of study.

A classic example they highlighted is the *Müller–Lyer illusion,* a core part of several visual perception theories. In one version of the illusion, individuals are shown two horizontal lines in a drawing, like this:

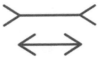

The two lines in the inner shaft are of equal length, but the illusion makes the first line appear longer than the second line. Participants in studies of the illusion are asked if the lines representing the shafts in the drawings are equal in length. If the individual answers no, he or she is asked to adjust the shaft of the lower diagram to make them of equal length. In an early study, Segall, Campbell, and Herskovits (1966) determined the point of subjective equality (PSE) in 18 different societies/groups. The PSE is the percentage that the lower shaft line needs to be extended for the two shaft lines to be said by the person to be equal in length. Figure 15.1 presents the results (the right-most data points are for a U.S. sample of undergraduates from Northwestern University and a community sample in Evanston, Illinois). There are large societal differences, with the PSE being largest in the U.S. samples and the European South African sample from Johannesburg. By contrast, for the foragers of the Kalahari, it was not even an illusion: their PSE was functionally zero.

Some theories explaining the Müller–Lyer illusion were called into question based on these results, but importantly, a potential boundary condition for the remaining viable theories needed to be introduced in conjunction with a viable conceptual

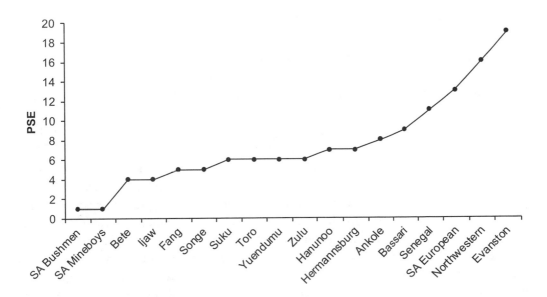

FIGURE 15.1. Societal differences in visual perception.

logic model. Segall and colleagues (1966) undertook the challenge of specifying the dynamics underlying the boundary condition. They noted the angular nature of the lines creating the illusion and speculated that the illusion would occur primarily in "carpentered environments" that contain many right angles, such as urban environments. Segall and colleagues argued that perceptual systems emerge developmentally as children mature and that these systems should be affected by increased exposure to angled stimuli. Although there was some ensuing empirical support for the explanation of Segall and colleagues, rival explanations soon emerged that attributed the effect instead to retinal pigmentation and the density of pigmentation in the eye (Jahoda, 1971; Pollack, 1970). Interestingly, the Müller–Lyer effect was recently demonstrated in pigeons and parrots (Nakamura, Fujita, Ushitani, & Miyata, 2006; Pepperberg, Vicinay, & Cavanagh, 2008), creating a "reverse boundary condition" in which the effect has wider applicability than previously thought (i.e., it applies to animals as well as humans). Segall and colleagues' thesis became less tenable because it could not account for such data.

The literature on the Müller–Lyer illusion as a whole reveals the diverse ways in which boundary condition identification can affect theory revision, the seeking of meaningful explanations of those boundary conditions, the potential occurrence of reverse boundary conditions, and even broader reflections on research practices and theory development in an entire discipline (psychology's study of WEIRD people). Our own takeaway from this literature is not to think of the dogmatic and critical orientations identified by Popper as an either–or dichotomy. Rather, scientists should adopt both orientations, bringing healthy skepticism to both the extant theory being questioned and the disconfirming data that are questioning it.

REPLICATION AND THEORY REVISION

Another potential source of theory disconfirmation is the failure to replicate a prior affirmative result, suggesting that the original study may have been nothing more than a false positive. According to some, replication failures often occur because of the practice of *p hacking* in the original study (Head, Holman, Lanfear, Kahn, & Jennions, 2016). This refers to when researchers apply multiple statistical analyses to a dataset to evaluate a theoretical proposition and then selectively report only those that produce favorable, significant results but without alerting readers to the tests that failed to yield statistical significance. Simmons, Nelson, and Simonsohn (2011) describe *researcher degrees of freedom* as the many decisions that scientists make when they implement a study design, such as whether to collect more observations, which outcome measures to analyze, and what covariates to include in a given analysis as statistical controls. These decisions often are made prior to conducting a study, but sometimes they are made as the study unfolds or at the time of data analysis. In this context, some researchers experiment with different study tactics until the desired result occurs, ultimately yielding *p* values that might reflect false positives that will not replicate.

The issue of replication failure has been particularly salient in psychology, where recent failures to replicate experiments for prominent theories have created controversy in the discipline as a whole. For example, an effort was recently made to replicate 21 psychology-oriented studies published between 2010 and 2015 in the journals *Nature* and *Science* (Camerer et al., 2018). Only 13 of the 21 studies (62%) were replicated. The Open Science Collaboration (2015) sought to replicate 100 studies that had been published in three top-tier journals in psychology. Less than 50% of these studies were replicated. As the number of failed replications has accumulated, criticisms of the replication studies themselves have mounted, focusing on the competence of the researchers conducting the replications, whether the studies reflect "close-enough" replications, and a host of statistical issues. Critics, for example, have argued that some replications used smaller sample sizes than the original study and that it was the subsequent reduced power that led to failure to replicate rather than problems with the theory.

Sensitive to these arguments, Camerer and colleagues (2018), in an attempt to replicate published social science studies in *Nature* and *Science,* used sample sizes in each replication that were considerably larger than the original studies. They also sought approval of the replication methodologies from the original investigators. They not only failed to replicate over a third of the studies, but their average effect sizes were about half the size as the original studies. The back-and-forth on this issue between the original authors and those who conducted the failed replications represents the Popper disconfirmation dilemma playing itself out in sometimes contentious ways and on a disciplinary level (see, e.g., Anderson et al., 2016; Gilbert, King, Pettigrew, & Wilson, 2016a, 2016b).

Replication studies have an important place in science. This has proven true in innumerable cases, such as the infamous case in the 1980s of the discovery of a method to produce cold fusion that would have yielded an unlimited supply of energy for the world. Having said that, replication studies in the social sciences can be difficult to publish no matter what the study finds due to editors seeing the work as unoriginal. No replication study can repeat the conditions of the original study precisely in every detail. Just as studies of boundary conditions evaluate the generalizability of a theory across targeted dimensions, such is also the case for replication studies. The difference is that boundary condition research actively seeks to create differences on theoretically relevant dimensions to evaluate generalizability, whereas replication studies seek to minimize those differences to test a restricted form of generalizability, namely, replicability. In either case, the results of replication studies have implications for theory and theory revision. Again, we advocate for healthy skepticism of both the target theory and the methodology of the replications when one is evaluating the implications of replication studies.

DISCONFIRMATION AND QUALITATIVE RESEARCH

Our emphasis to this point has been on theory revision in the face of disconfirming data for quantitative research. The core ideas also apply to qualitative research that leads to

BOX 15.1. Strong Inference

In 1964, the noted physicist John Platt published a classic article in *Science* titled "Strong Inference." Platt advocated for experiments that pit two or more theories against one another. The idea was that testing a single proposition from a single theory was not as strong as experiments with different outcomes that would definitively favor one theory or the other. The approach yields disconfirming data for one of the theories and support for the other.

Consider an example from marketing in which a new product is described to people in terms of its qualities or attributes. Suppose we index how positive or negative each attribute is on a −3 to +3 metric, where 0 is neutral, negative numbers indicate negative attributes, and positive numbers indicate positive attributes. Many cognitive scientists contend that, when forming attitudes (in this case toward the product), people mentally "tally up" the evaluative qualities of the attributes associated with it using a form of "cognitive algebra." Scientists, of course, do not think people actually do formal algebra in their heads; but the mental processes involved, they argue, can be modeled via algebra and then used to make interesting predictions.

Some theorists argue that the cognitive algebra people use takes the form of an averaging process, where the individual evaluations are psychologically averaged. Other theorists contend that the process is summative. Thus, there are competing theories. We can devise an empirical test pitting the two theories against one another via strong inference. Suppose we describe a product to individuals using three attributes, all of which are very positive: +3, +3, and +3. Later, we describe a second competing product using the exact same attributes, but we add a slightly positive attribute to the description, +3, +3, +3, and +1. If an averaging integration rule holds, we would predict individuals to have a more positive attitude toward the first product because the average attribute evaluation for it is $(3 + 3 + 3)/3 = 3.0$, but for the second product it is $(3 + 3 + 3 + 1)/4 = 2.5$. If a summation integration rule holds, we predict the opposite; the sum for the first product is $3 + 3 + 3 = 9$, and for the second product it is $3 + 3 + 3 + 1 = 10$. Note that an averaging model leads to a counterintuitive prediction that adding a piece of positive information about a product can actually make attitudes toward the product more negative if the new information is not positive enough; an ad to increase product attitudes can unwittingly backfire.

Competitive tests of the two theories used experimental paradigms that mapped onto this scenario. For example, in one condition, a new product was described with three very positive attributes (+3, +3, +3). In another condition, the product was described with four positive attributes—the same three as the first condition plus one that was slightly positive (+3, +3, +3, +1). The averaging and summation theories make opposite predictions about which conditions should yield the more positive attitude. Research using this or similar paradigms initially found support for averaging, but summation theorists objected, claiming that the additional piece of information may have led people to give less weight to the other attributes in ways that summa-

(continued)

tion could account for the results. In addition, they argued that people may infer that the product has other attributes based on the information presented, and depending on the evaluations of the inferred attributes, the summation model could account for the results. Proponents of the averaging model complained about lack of parsimony due to these required auxiliary assumptions. However, when later research under different test conditions found support for summation over averaging, the averaging proponents introduced their own set of auxiliary assumptions to account for the data. As research accumulated, it became evident that people sometimes "average" and sometimes "sum," depending on the situational context. The spirit of strong inference was undermined as theoretical adjustments were made to account for disconfirming data by each opposing camp of theorists or methodological issues were raised. What often sounds good in theory (strong inference) sometimes can be difficult in practice.

conclusions that contradict an existing theory. Faced with disconfirming qualitative data, scientists can adopt the dogmatic or critical orientations, or some combination of the two. From a dogmatic perspective, critics might fault the interpretation of the previous theory; the sampling of populations or contexts of the disconfirming study (arguing they are not appropriate relative to theory specification); the measures or recording of data in the disconfirming study; a too-small sample size in the disconfirming study (failing to reach theoretical saturation); or an inappropriate content analysis strategy. As with quantitative studies, when designing qualitative research, an approach to confronting a disconfirmation dilemma is to anticipate as many objections as possible when designing the study, make a list of the objections, prioritize their importance as threats to adequately documenting and evaluating theoretical propositions that might emerge, and then deal with as many of the threats as possible (in order of priority).

Just as the issue of replication is relevant to quantitative research, such is also the case for qualitative research. If a researcher repeats a qualitative research project with as much fidelity as possible to the original study and fails to replicate the theoretical conclusions, what would this say about the original theory? What might it say about the methodology of the replication?

BAYESIAN PERSPECTIVES IN THEORY REVISION

Distinct from Popperian perspectives of theory revision is an approach based on Bayesian epistemology. The approach is rooted in Bayes' theorem, a probability theorem developed by the Reverend Thomas Bayes, a statistician, philosopher, and minister born in 1701. Actually, Bayes never published his theorem. He published only two works in his lifetime, one on religion and the other a defense of the mathematical work of Isaac Newton. The probability theorem Bayes became famous for was disseminated after his death by Pierre-Simon Laplace, a French mathematician, physicist, and astronomer, from notes Bayes had left. Bayes would never know the major impact his work would have on statistics, science, and epistemology.

Bayes' theorem works with probabilities, odds, and conditional probabilities, so we first develop these concepts as background. (We assume readers have had exposure to the concept of probability.) We then delve into the implications of Bayes' theorem for theory revision in light of disconfirming data, taking some liberties with notation in the interest of pedagogy.

Probabilities, Odds, and Conditional Probabilities

Probabilities range from 0.00 (impossible) to 1.00 (certain). If the probability of rain tomorrow is zero, this means there is no chance it will rain. If the probability of rain tomorrow is 0.50, this means it is as likely it will rain as it is it won't rain. If the probability of rain tomorrow is 1.0, then we are certain it is going to rain. Probabilities, in some respects, reflect our confidence that something will happen or that something is true.

Another way of expressing a probability is as an *odds*. We convert a probability to an odds by dividing it by 1 minus the probability. For example, if the probability of a 50-year-old man in the United States seeing a doctor in the ensuing 12 months is 0.667, then the probability of him not doing so is 1 − .667 = 0.333. The ratio of these two probabilities is the odds—0.667/0.333 = 2.0—or, in the more common vernacular, the odds are "2 to 1" (i.e., it is twice as likely that 50-year-old men living in the United States will see a doctor in the next 12 months than they will not).

An odds value can be less than 1. For example, if the probability of teenagers smoking marijuana is 0.20, the odds of teenagers smoking marijuana is 0.20/0.80 = 0.25. The odds value of 0.25 means the probability of smoking marijuana is one-fourth the probability of not smoking marijuana. If the probability of Black men being convicted of a crime is 0.25, the odds of Black men being convicted of a crime are 0.25/0.75 = 0.33. An odds of 0.33 means the probability of being convicted is one-third that of not being convicted. Characterizing events as probabilities or odds is a matter of preference; they are different ways of expressing the same thing.

A *conditional probability* indicates the likelihood of an event given some other event occurs or has occurred. The general symbolic form for a conditional probability is $P(A \mid B)$, where P stands for probability, A is event A, B is event B, and | is read as "given that." For example, if we want to express the conditional probability that people are happy with their marriage given that they are happy with their job, we would focus just on people who are happy with their jobs. For these people, we would calculate the proportion of them that are happy with their marriages, yielding the conditional probability $P(\text{happy with marriage} \mid \text{happy with job})$. The probability that people vote for a candidate given the candidate is a Democrat would be written as $P(\text{vote for candidate} \mid \text{candidate is a Democrat})$.

Bayes' Theorem

Bayes' theorem has been highly influential in the social sciences and has been used for many purposes. One application has been as an alternative framework for data analysis to traditional null hypothesis testing. Another application has been the formulation of a general "theory of knowledge" known as *Bayesian epistemology*. It is this latter use that is of interest here, with a particular focus on theory revision in light of disconfirming data. The challenges that face Bayesian data analysis are not the same as those that face Bayesian epistemology (although there is some overlap). Our treatment targets only epistemology. We begin with an exposition of Bayes' theorem per se. We then discuss how the approach differs from Popper's approach in terms of thinking about theory-disconfirming (and confirming) data.

Bayesian epistemology views knowledge as probabilistic rather than certain and self-evident. Bayesians frame knowledge in terms of the likelihood or probability a proposition is true, essentially reflecting one's confidence that the proposition does, in fact, hold. Before a study is conducted to test a theoretical proposition, a Bayesian seeks to specify the degree of confidence he or she has in that proposition based on all relevant prior research and the cumulative knowledge base to date. This likelihood can be expressed as either a probability or an odds, with the latter being called the *prior odds* of the proposition. As an example, suppose a theory posits that cancer patients' adherence to postsurgery recovery protocols is reduced if patients are depressed. Based on established theory, past research, and a convincing conceptual logic model, the prior odds of this proposition being true might be judged to be 2 to 1. This means that it is twice as likely the proposition holds than it does not hold. If the prior odds were 1 to 1, this means that it is just as likely the proposition holds as it is that the proposition does not hold. If the prior odds were 0.50, this means it is half as likely the proposition holds than that it does not hold.[1]

Suppose an empirical study is conducted and, based on the study results, we revise the prior odds because the results are supportive of the theory, yielding what are called *posterior odds*. Posterior odds are the odds that the proposition holds after taking into account the results of the study. For example, it might be that the prior odds of a theoretical proposition were 2 to 1, but after the study is conducted, the results are convincing enough that the odds the proposition holds are revised to 3 to 1. Or, perhaps the results of the study are disconfirming so that the prior odds shift from 2 to 1 to 1 to 1. As a rule, if the posterior odds are greater than the prior odds, study results are confirming, more or less. If the posterior odds are less than the prior odds, study results are disconfirming, more or less. If the posterior odds equal the prior odds, then the study was *uninformative*.

Bayes' theorem uses the concepts of both prior odds and posterior odds but does so in conjunction with yet another concept known as the *Bayes factor*.[2] The value of the

---

[1] How these prior odds are determined in practice is beyond the scope of this chapter and not relevant to our key points. Interested readers can consult Howard, Maxwell, and Fleming (2000).

[2] The Bayes factor is often called the *likelihood ratio*, but we prefer the "Bayes factor" terminology because the term *likelihood ratio* is also used for entirely different contexts in statistics.

Bayes factor determines how much we revise the prior odds of our theory (either upward or downward) given the results that occurred in our study. It is best explained by showing it in the context of the full Bayesian theorem, which is as follows:

$$Posterior\ Odds = (Bayes\ Factor)\ (Prior\ Odds)$$

In this equation, the Bayes factor is a multiplicative factor that "adjusts" the prior odds in light of the study results to yield the posterior odds. When the Bayes factor is equal to 1.0, the posterior odds will equal the prior odds, and the study is seen as providing no new information regarding the theoretical proposition. The results are uninformative. If the Bayes factor is larger than 1.0, then the study results increase our confidence in the proposition. For example, if the prior odds were 2.0 and the Bayes factor is 1.5, then the posterior odds are (2.0)(1.5) = 3.0. If the Bayes factor is less than 1.0, the study results decrease our confidence in the proposition. For example, if the prior odds were 1.5 and the Bayes factor is 0.5, then the posterior odds reduce the prior odds to (1.5)(0.5) = 0.75.

The Bayes factor is formally defined as the ratio of two conditional probabilities. One conditional probability is the likelihood that we would have obtained the results we did in the study if the theoretical proposition is, in fact, true. We signify this conditional probability as P(results | theory is true). The other conditional probability is the likelihood that the study results would have occurred if the theoretical proposition is false. We signify this probability as P(results | theory is false). The Bayes factor is thus

$$BF = \frac{P(Results\mid Theory\ is\ true)}{P(Results\mid Theory\ is\ false)}$$

Let's examine the properties of the Bayes factor more closely using our prior example on depression and alcohol use in middle school students. Suppose our theory is that alcohol use causes depression. We conduct a study and examine the correlation between alcohol use and depression, which turns out to be moderately positive: higher levels of alcohol use are associated with higher levels of depression. The numerator of the Bayes factor is the probability of obtaining this result given that alcohol use does, in fact, cause depression. Suppose that we and other scientists judge this conditional probability to be large, say 0.90 for the sake of exposition. Based on this, the data seem to support the theory.

However, key to declaring theory support is not just the numerator of the Bayes factor but also the denominator, namely the probability of obtaining the study result given that alcohol use does not cause depression, or P(results | theory is false). Suppose a critic argues that the (self-report) measure of alcohol use in the study is flawed because it is impacted by social desirability response tendencies (see Chapter 13) and that this also is true of the measure of depression. Alcohol use and depression will be positively correlated, the critic contends, even if the theory is false because the two measures share a common cause, social desirability response tendencies. This argument implies that the probability of the study result (a moderately positive correlation between alcohol use and depression) might be large, say 0.90, even if the theory that alcohol use causes depression is false because of the flawed measurement of the constructs. The Bayes factor, the critic argues, is 0.90/0.90 = 1.00 and the study results are uninformative. The study does not provide support for the theory.

Suppose we suspect this criticism as a possibility when designing our study, so we decide to obtain a measure of social desirability response tendencies in the study and then statistically control for it when calculating the correlation between alcohol use and depression. Suppose the correlation is still moderately positive when we do so. We now argue that the numerator of the Bayes factor is large, say 0.90, but the denominator is small because any effect of social desirability on the measures has been removed; if our theory that alcohol use causes depression is false, the probability of observing a moderately positive correlation between measures of them is low. The net result is a large Bayes factor and the study therefore increases our confidence in the theory.

But suppose yet another critic argues that instead of alcohol use causing depression, a reverse causal dynamic might operate, namely that depression causes alcohol use because alcohol use serves as a way of coping with depression. This argument implies that the probability of the study result (a moderately positive correlation between alcohol use and depression) will be large, say 0.90, even if the original theory that alcohol use causes depression is false, again producing a Bayes factor of 1.00 or near 1.00. The challenge for us is to design the study in a way that this alternative theory can be ruled out so that the Bayes factor can be diagnostic rather than uninformative. (It is indeed possible to design such a study, but we do not get sidetracked on this matter here.)

The essence of the Bayes factor is important. To raise the prior odds of a theory, the study result must be diagnostic, that is, the result should occur if the theory holds *and* it should not occur if the theory does not hold. Bayes factors of 1.00 mean the study results are uninformative. The more the Bayes factor deviates from 1.0 in either direction, the more the study results are diagnostic. It is against this standard that the results of a study are judged when using Bayesian logic. The numerator of the Bayes factor focuses on whether the result is consistent with the theory. The denominator focuses on whether there are credible alternative explanations of the results. The dynamic interplay between these considerations takes the form of a ratio of the respective conditional probabilities, which is the Bayes factor.

Again, do not get too concerned with discerning the actual numerical values of the Bayes factor or prior odds. Focus instead on the general logic of the Bayesian approach and the conceptual meaning of the Bayes factor, prior odds, and the need to consider both when evaluating the implications of study results for a theory. Researchers in practice rarely posit specific values of these elements. However, they often make a case that their study results are meaningfully diagnostic (in one direction or the other) and they often explicitly take into account the weight of prior evidence for the theory when making conclusions.

Implications of Bayesian Epistemology for Theory Revision

With that discussion as background, we now turn to the implications of Bayesian epistemology for theory revision in light of disconfirming data. In doing so, we do not delve further into the underlying mathematics of Bayes' theorem, nor do we consider the strategies and challenges of deriving specific values for the prior odds and the Bayes factor. Rather, we emphasize the broader conceptual implications of the framework.

Implication 1

One implication of the Bayesian approach is that knowledge is seen as probabilistic rather than as all or none. For a Bayesian, theories are not "accepted" or "rejected" based on study results; science is not a dichotomous enterprise. Rather, results from a study change one's confidence in a theoretical proposition, with that confidence sometimes changing a little, sometimes moderately, or sometimes a good deal, in either direction. By contrast, many researchers approach theories by making "accept" or "reject" judgments as a function of study results. Bayesians are more nuanced than this. Disconfirmation is a continuum. The same is true of confirmation.

Implication 2

By introducing the concept of prior odds into the theory revision framework, Bayesians tend to be conservative about discounting theoretical propositions that have considerable prior empirical support in the face of a study that produces disconfirming results. If a theory has strong prior support (i.e., a large prior odds), the posterior odds will remain relatively high even if the Bayes factor is somewhat or moderately below 1.0 (i.e., the results are somewhat disconfirmatory). By the same token, a theoretical proposition that has little prior support and that initially lacks credibility will have difficulty producing large posterior odds unless the Bayes factor is considerably larger than 1.0. Bayesian formulations remind researchers to keep the degree of prior evidence for a proposition front and center when interpreting the results of a study.

Implication 3

The disconfirmation dilemma described by Popper applies in Bayesian frameworks, but it involves a somewhat different mindset than that advocated by Popper. When study results are contrary to a theory (i.e., a Bayes factor less than 1.0 occurs), those who adopt the dogmatic approach often react with arguments designed to convince other scientists that the Bayes factor actually equals 1.0 so as to render the study uninformative. For example, suppose in our study of alcohol use and depression, the study yielded a zero correlation between alcohol use and depression. The numerator of the Bayes factor for this case should be near zero, that is, the probability of the study result given that alcohol use causes depression should be quite low. A theorist bent on saving the theory might argue that the study used flawed measures or was poorly implemented and this is why the result occurred. Stated differently, this theorist would argue that the probability of the study result (a zero correlation) is actually large if the theory is true because the study was poorly designed.

Those who adopt the critical approach, by contrast, will tend to stand by the Bayes factor being less than 1.0, and they will reduce their confidence in the theoretical proposition proportional to the prior odds of the proposition. Note that it is not a question of completely rejecting the theory in the face of disconfirming results for those who adopt the critical approach. Rather, one's confidence is shaken. The arguments between those with a dogmatic orientation and those with a critical orientation essentially focus on trying to convince other scientists as to the likely values of (1) the Bayes factor and/or (2) the prior odds of the theoretical expression.

Implication 4

To a Bayesian, confirmatory data require theory revision just as disconfirmatory data do. When we observe study results consistent with a theory, we revise our confidence in that theory upward. When you read a study that is confirmative, think about how much your confidence in the theory improves as a result of the study. For Bayesians, the amount that confidence increases is impacted by (1) the confidence you had in the theory prior to the study and (2) the quality of the study design, the quality of study execution, and the study results vis-à-vis their impact on the Bayes factor. When you design research for purposes of testing a theory that is already reasonably well accepted, perhaps the study can still make a theoretical contribution by increasing that much more the scientific community's confidence in the theory.

Implication 5

According to a Bayesian framework, even studies that have confounds can be informative and confirming as long as the Bayes factor is larger than 1.0. To be sure, confounds reduce the information yield of a study, but they do not necessarily eliminate information yield completely. If a confound is present but is presumed to be unlikely to have much impact, the Bayes factor can remain meaningfully above 1.0 (see Brinberg, Lynch, & Sawyer, 1992, for an elaboration of this point).

Implication 6

Traditional falsificationists value a priori predictions more than post hoc explanations of a study result. The argument is that post hoc "hypotheses" or explanations can never be inconsistent with the observed data because they literally are derived from the data. As such, they violate the principle of falsification, at least for the study at hand. Creative researchers, the argument goes, can generate post hoc explanations of nearly any result, making those explanations less scientific.

Bayesians, by contrast, argue that the timing of an explanation is irrelevant. Rather, one's confidence in an explanation should be based on the broader theoretical context surrounding the observed effect in the study as well as the prior evidence that supports the (post hoc) explanation, that is, the Bayes factor and the prior odds of the explanation (Dienes, 2011). If a researcher develops a post hoc explanation tailored to the data but that explanation is seen as unlikely given past research or if it makes implausible assumptions, then the prior odds of the explanation should be low, yielding low posterior odds. If the trend in the data that is used to generate the post hoc explanation is as likely to be observed if the explanation is true as when the explanation is false, the Bayes factor will be 1.0 and the study results will not be confirmatory. Indeed, for a Bayesian, we might even find ourselves in situations where we actually prefer an a priori explanation that does not fit the data all that well to a post hoc explanation that does if the prior odds of the a priori explanation are higher than the post hoc explanation and the Bayes factor for the post hoc explanation is near 1.0. The Bayesian philosophy is that, for any given explanation, one thinks about its prior odds and the Bayes factor relative to the study, not the timing of when that explanation is offered (see Schlesinger, 1991, for arguments in support of this philosophy, as well as Dienes, 2011).

In sum, keep the following (Bayesian) points in mind as you consider theory revision in light of disconfirming data: (1) Rather than thinking about theoretical propositions or explanations in all-or-none terms, it probably is better to think about them in terms of degrees of confidence or certainty. (2) Confirming and disconfirming data are not all or none in terms of their effects on one's confidence in a theoretical proposition— disconfirming data shakes our confidence in a proposition, but how much it does so depends on our confidence in the proposition to begin with as well as the quality, design, and execution of the study (as reflected by the Bayes factor). (3) In some sense, confirmatory data require theory revision just as disconfirmatory data does. When we observe study results consistent with a theory, we revise our confidence in that theory upward. When you read a study that is confirmative, think about how much your confidence in the theory has improved as a result. (4) Just because a study contains a confound does not mean the study cannot increase our confidence in a theoretical proposition; the presence of confounds does not, by fiat, render a situation hopeless for gaining information about the viability of a theory (it all depends on the value of the Bayes factor). (5) Faced with disconfirming data, you should think long and hard about your prior confidence in the theoretical proposition and the basis of that confidence; you should also think about the quality of study design and its implementation in terms of the Bayes factor. Finally, (6) just because an explanation is offered post hoc does not necessarily mean it is of reduced value. According to Bayesians, you should not, by fiat, apologize for formulating a compelling post hoc explanation.

Your task as a scientist is to convince others to take your study results seriously and to "buy into" your arguments either for or against a theoretical proposition. Your arguments, if based on Bayesian epistemology, should be framed around the prior odds of the proposition and the Bayes factor associated with the study. As such, Bayesian epistemology is one mindset you can use to think about issues of theory revision in light of confirmatory or disconfirmatory data. It is not without its critics, but it does offer many interesting perspectives to take into account in the theory revision process.

A LOOK TO THE FUTURE:
COMPUTER AUTOMATION AND THEORY REVISION

In this section, we look forward to the not-too-distant future and describe a fascinating direction in which theory revision is headed. The approach is grounded in causal analysis using structural equation modeling (SEM), but it eventually will extend its reach as traditional statistical analysis and SEM become more integrated (which, in our opinion, is inevitable). To describe the logic of the innovations, we use a simplified causal theory that is unrealistic relative to typical applications. After establishing the logic, we consider more complex theories.

Suppose an education researcher is studying the experiences of sexual minority youth (those whose sexual identity, orientation, or practices differ from those of the majority of society, such as lesbian, gay, or bisexual youth) and formulates a theory that sexual minority students (SMSs) who feel connected to their school will be more likely to develop positive relationships with their teachers. School connectedness is defined as the extent to which students feel engaged with school, involve themselves in school activities, feel a sense of loyalty toward their school, and have an overall positive attitude toward it. Positive student–teacher relationships are defined as the extent to which students feel personally accepted, respected, and supported by their teachers, as a whole. The researcher further theorizes that more positive student–teacher relationships will lead to better student performance in school as reflected by the grades students achieve. The theory is summarized using the influence diagram in Figure 15.2. The straight arrows in the figure indicate presumed causal relationships. Path *a* signifies a presumed causal effect of school connectedness on student–teacher relationships; path *b* signifies the presumed causal effect of teacher–student relationships on school performance. The figure explicitly recognizes that many other factors influence teacher–student relationships other than school connectedness; these factors are formally parameterized in the theory in d1. Similarly, d2 reflects factors other than teacher–student relationships that impact school performance (such as student abilities and parental supervision of homework). These two sets of disturbances are assumed to be uncorrelated—an assumption that may or may not be reasonable.

The model in Figure 15.2 traditionally would be evaluated using SEM. To use SEM in this case, one first identifies the two outcome variables in the theory: (1) teacher–

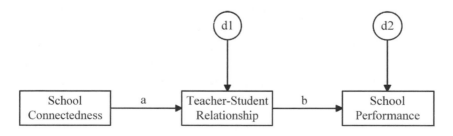

FIGURE 15.2. Model of school performance.

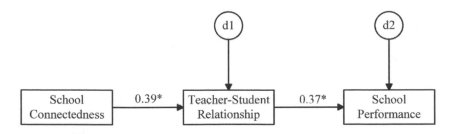

FIGURE 15.3. Model of school performance with coefficients.

student relationships, which is an outcome for school connectedness, and (2) school performance, which is an outcome for teacher–student relationships. One regresses each outcome onto its predictors or presumed determinants, that is, any variable that has an arrow going directly to the outcome. In this case, we regress school performance onto teacher–student relationships and teacher–student relationships onto school effectiveness. The regression coefficients are called path coefficients (see *a* and *b* in Figure 15.2). Figure 15.3 repeats Figure 15.2 but with the standardized coefficient values shown.

The theory in Figure 15.3 predicts that both regression/path coefficients should be statistically significant, and this is indeed the case (* indicates $p < .05$). In this respect, the data are consistent with the theory, although the results do not *prove* the theory. The advantage of using SEM instead of traditional regression strategies is that SEM allows for an additional perspective on theory viability beyond these simple predictions. Using the mathematics of SEM, we can show that, for this particular theory, the correlation between school connectedness and school performance should equal the product of the two path coefficients. That is, if the theory is correct as expressed in Figure 15.2, the correlation between school connectedness and school performance should equal (0.39) $(0.37) = 0.14$. This is called the *predicted correlation* between school connectedness and school performance based on the theory. How does it compare to the actual correlation between these variables as observed in the data? Suppose the *observed correlation* was 0.56. The disparity between the predicted and observed correlations is $0.56 - 0.14 = 0.42$. This is a sizeable disparity and suggests that the theory, considered as a whole, is probably wrong; if the theory was correct, we would not see this type of disparity. This is a nice feature of SEM. It often provides tests of a theory that go beyond simple examination of the statistical significance of regression/path coefficients.[3]

Given this disconfirming data, the theory needs revision. But how? Remarkably, SEM software makes explicit suggestions to researchers for ways to revise the theory so as to produce a better fit with the data, that is, a revision that lowers the discrepancy between the predicted and observed correlations. The computer makes these suggestions knowing nothing about past literatures or about extant knowledge, nor does it

---

[3]Some analysts think that the primary advantage of SEM over traditional regression is that SEM can adjust for measurement error. Although this is true in some cases, SEM also is advantageous because it provides critical theory tests that traditional regression analysis does not, as illustrated here.

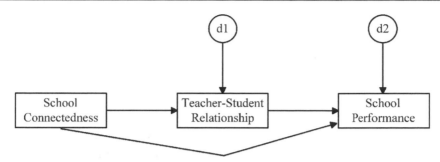

FIGURE 15.4. Modified models.

know the topic that is being studied or the substantive content of the variables. Each suggestion the computer makes takes the form of a numerical index called a *modification index,* with larger values indicating a stronger urging by the computer to consider the suggested change associated with that index.

For the current example, the computer made multiple suggestions as to how the theory might be revised, each with equal strength. One of the suggestions is shown in Figure 15.4. Figure 15.4 represents the suggestion to add a direct causal path from school connectedness to school performance. How should a theorist react to this suggestion? This is a controversial issue.

Some analysts recommend that the suggestions should be ignored. After all, it is substantively uninformed and made by a computer ignorant of theory construction principles and substantive nuances. Other analysts treat the suggestions as theory diagnostics that can be used as a starting point for thinking about theory revision. The theorist examines what the computer is suggesting, then thinks about the viability of the suggested revisions relative to prior research, logic, and extant knowledge. If all line up, perhaps the theorist will make the revision. Granted, the revision will be post hoc, but in the spirit of Bayesian epistemology, perhaps such timing may matter less than theoretical coherence. With this in mind, let's examine the suggestion more closely.

In Figure 15.4, the suggested change makes salient the idea that the original theory presumed that any effect of school connectedness on school performance must be through its effect on teacher–student relationships. In the language of Chapter 7, teacher–student relationships completely mediate the effects of school connectedness on school performance. It may be possible, however, that school connectedness influences school performance through other mechanisms. For example, a student feeling connected to his or her school may engage in more after-school activities at school, thereby spending less adult-unsupervised time outside of school where drinking, drug use, and other such activities that interfere with school performance could occur. School connectedness also might encourage the formation of friendships with other like-minded students, and these "positive peer groups" might then promote effort in school and, in turn, school performance. Based on such logic, the researcher might decide that the intellectually vacuous suggestion made by the computer via Figure 15.4 may actually work well after all because of the omitted mediators that are captured, in part, by introducing partial mediation.

Some technical complications confront the effective use of modification indices for theory revision. First, as noted, some of the suggestions are nonsensical; these can just be ignored by the theorist. Second, even after such screening, there can be redundancies in some of the suggestions such that the ill fit in the model can be reduced in several ways; one suggestion will reduce the same source of the ill fit as another suggestion. The question then arises as to which theoretical revision to adopt in order to reduce the ill fit. One might choose one suggestion over the others based on the theoretical desiderata described below. Or one might adopt several of the suggestions, not just one.

The current example was simplistic. Causal theories in the social sciences are generally much more complex, and sorting through the vast number of modification indices within them can be challenging. Modification indices not only address omitted paths but also omitted correlated disturbances in a theory, such as a correlation between d1 and d2 in Figure 15.3 (see Chapter 7 for a discussion of such correlations). Consider the latent variable theory presented in Chapter 7 and reproduced in Figure 15.5, which

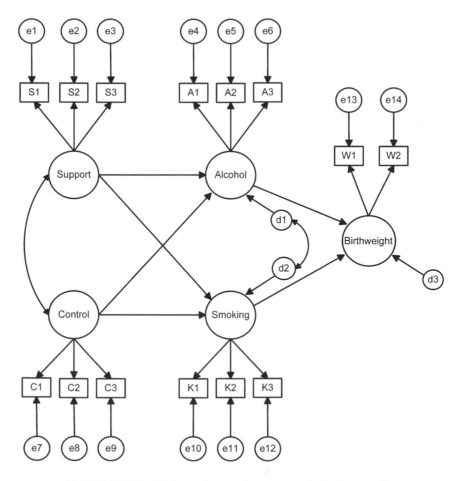

FIGURE 15.5. Birthweight, smoking, and alcohol example.

focused on pregnant women trying to quit smoking and drinking during their pregnancy so as to lessen the likelihood of having a low birthweight baby. Their success in reducing drinking and smoking is thought to be impacted by (1) the social support they have from others to help them quit smoking and drinking and (2) the locus of control of the woman, that is, her generalized belief that she can control what happens to her rather than be the pawn of luck or fate. Four of the variables have multiple indicators (three indicators each), so the broader theoretical specification also includes a measurement theory. (Details are provided in Chapter 7.) If this model were analyzed in SEM, it would yield 336 modification indices for omitted parameters (paths or correlated errors) that could be considered for inclusion in the theory. This is a bit overwhelming, and so it makes sense to try to help the theorist sort through the mass of indices in a systematic, intelligent way.

We believe that the techniques currently being developed in artificial intelligence, data mining, and machine learning (see Chapter 11) hold promise for automating theory revisions in SEM, perhaps to the point that much less human input will be necessary. Such automation is an intriguing "out-of-the-box" idea, the foundations for which are just now being laid. The earliest (unsuccessful) automated theory revision strategies in SEM have been described and explored by MacCallum (1986). More recently, Marcoulides and Ing (2012) have suggested a number of interesting automated strategies using multiple analogies. For example, one approach is known as *ant colony optimization* (Dorigo & Stützle, 2004). Ants are quite facile at finding the shortest distance between a food source and their nest. They begin by randomly trying different paths from the nest to the source while leaving traces of a chemical called pheromone on the ground for each path tried. The pheromone accumulates faster on the most direct path as more and more ants reach the food source more quickly and return to the nest with food. Each ant is sensitive to the accumulation of pheromone, leading them to prefer the path with the larger accumulation of pheromone on it, which is the most direct path. Marcoulides and Drezner (2003) explored theory revisions in SEM by building a large number of slightly altered model configurations from the original theory/model and then assessed the ability of each new model to accurately reproduce the observed correlations. For each path in each new model, a pheromone analogy was used that increased a weight for paths (initially set to zero) that contributed most to accounting for good model reproduction of the observed correlations. As these weights accumulated across the many different model configurations, the most important paths for good model fit across all the models emerged. These identified paths were then compared to the original model, and theory revisions were derived by focusing on the "best" paths that had accumulated the largest weights.

Marcoulides and Ing (2012) describe other analogies for use in automated theory revision, including one based on genetic algorithms that promote survival of the fittest, a second one based on Tabu searches from machine learning, and a third based on melting metals. All the approaches are somewhat crude, but the stage has been set. With the new technologies before us via machine learning and with some human ingenuity, we believe it is just a matter of time until theory revision becomes highly (but not completely) automated.

THEORETICAL DESIDERATA FOR REVISED THEORIES

In Chapter 3, we discussed the properties of a good theory. When we contemplate revising a theory in light of disconfirming data, we need to hold the revised theory to the same standards we seek for theories in general. These standards include the following: The new theoretical expression (1) should be logically consistent, (2) should be in agreement with other known facts and amenable to scientific consensus, (3) should be testable in future studies, (4) should strive to be appropriately parsimonious, (5) should ideally have a potentially wide scope in terms of its implications and applications, and (6) should ideally have potential for generating interesting future research. When evaluating plausible theoretical alternatives or revisions that can account for disconfirming data, we prefer alternatives or revisions that have these properties.

PARADIGM SHIFTS

Thomas Kuhn (1962, 1970, 2000) has written a series of books on scientific paradigms and the structure of scientific revolutions. He defined a paradigm as a set of commonly agreed-upon assumptions, meanings, and methods for characterizing and summarizing phenomena. According to Kuhn, the evolution of a paradigm is influenced by many factors, true science being just one of them. Historical, social, and political factors also come into play. Kuhn described scientific revolutions as passing through four stages. In the first stage, *normal science,* ordinary scientific research and scientific progress occur. The dominant paradigm sets the agenda for the type of theorizing and research that is pursued, and it shapes scientific thinking accordingly. The second stage is the *appearance of anomaly.* Some problems are harder to solve than others by the prevailing paradigm, and this can induce a period of crisis. Or flaws in the dominant paradigm start to build up that lead to some scientists beginning to question it. The third stage is *crisis.* If a problem or finding provokes a crisis, the grip of the paradigm on science weakens. A few especially creative scientists break out of the confines of the dominant paradigm, rejecting one or more of its defining tenets and proposing new ones. The final stage is *revolution,* during which the advocates of the emerging paradigm gain control of the power structure in science, namely, journal editorships, granting agencies, and textbooks. The old paradigm is replaced by the new one, beginning the cycle again with that of normal science.

Critics of Kuhn's analysis contend that change in science is more complicated than what he portrays. They argue, for example, that Kuhn does not give sufficient attention to competing models within a paradigm and that paradigms are rarely ever fully discarded and replaced. Nevertheless, elements of his analysis ring true. It is not our purpose to discuss broad issues surrounding paradigm shifts in the social sciences. This belies our goal of providing you with practical heuristics for thinking about and generating theory in your everyday practice. However, being aware of the dominant paradigms in your research areas and the way your thinking can be channeled by those paradigms is useful for breaking through to make creative contributions.

SUMMARY AND CONCLUDING COMMENTS

Theory revisions in the face of disconfirming data are often met with two orientations: one that maintains theory viability by criticizing the methodology of the study that produced the disconfirming data and one that questions the theory in light of the evidence. Perspectives from the philosophy of science suggest that it is difficult, on strict technical grounds, to fully confirm or fully disconfirm a theory. When you are designing research to test a theory, it is useful to think of all the arguments critics might amass to dismiss study findings and then try to address them as best as you can for your study, either procedurally or statistically.

When faced with disconfirming data from a theory test, theories are often rescued by introducing the concept of boundary conditions. Post hoc specified boundary condition identification must be accompanied by compelling logic models for those conditions. Disconfirming data also can take the form of replication failures. Failed replications can occur either because the prior theoretical affirmations were the result of false positives or because the replications were poorly conducted. It is important to carefully think about each of these possibilities when evaluating replication studies.

Bayesian epistemology provides additional perspectives on theory revision. Bayesians view knowledge as probabilistic, preferring to think about theoretical propositions in terms of degrees of confidence rather than in "all-or-none" terms. Revisions in confidence in a theoretical proposition are impacted by the degree of confidence we have in the proposition to begin with and the information value of the study that evaluates it. Bayesians are not as concerned with the timing of when a theory revision is offered (a priori or post hoc) as much as the overall coherence of the explanation.

In the field of structural equation modeling, use of automated theory revision is often used. Theory revision is based, in part, on suggestions made by a computer, even though the computer has no knowledge about principles of theory construction, the topic you are studying, or the particular variables you are working with. Current practice is to listen to the computer suggestions but to exercise human logic and knowledge of past research to decide whether to adopt or adapt a suggestion. The stage has been set for sophisticated automatic theory revision to aid theorists in the revision choices they make.

When we consider making revisions to theories, we should take into account theory desiderata more generally. These include logical consistency, agreement with known facts, testability, parsimony, scope, and generation of future research and applications. Theory revisions as they accumulate ultimately can lead to fundamental paradigm shifts in science.

Most of these theory revision considerations are applicable to both quantitative and qualitative research, unless that research is purely descriptive.

SUGGESTED READINGS

Center for Open Science at *https://cos.io.*
—A website worth looking at for a wide set of resources on replications.

Henrich, J., Heine, S. J., & Norenzayan, A. (2010). The weirdest people in the world? *Behavioral and Brain Sciences, 33,* 61–83.
—A fascinating article on generalizability and boundary conditions, followed by many replies and reactions to the lead article.

Howard, G. S., Maxwell, S., & Fleming, K. (2000). The proof of the pudding: An illustration of the relative strengths of null hypothesis testing, meta-analysis, and Bayesian analysis. *Psychological Methods, 5,* 315–332.
—An excellent gentle introduction to Bayesian thinking. For a step up and a discussion of Bayesian statistical analysis, see Kruschke, J. (2015). *Doing Bayesian data analysis: A Tutorial with R, JAGS, and Stan.* New York: Academic Press.

Kline, R. B. (2016). *Principles and practice of structural equation modeling* (4th ed.). New York: Guilford Press.
—A solid introduction to structural equation modeling.

Kuhn, T. S. (1962). *The structure of scientific revolutions.* Chicago: University of Chicago Press.
—Kuhn's classic piece on paradigm shifts in science. For a reflection on reactions to his book, see Kuhn, T. S. (2000). *The road since structure: Philosophical essays, 1970–1993, with an autobiographical interview.* Chicago: University of Chicago Press.

MacCallum, R. C. (1986). Specification searches in covariance structure modeling. *Psychological Bulletin, 100,* 107–120.
—A dated but useful precursor to automated theory revision in structural equation modeling. For a more current treatment, see Marcoulides, G. A., & Ing, M. (2012). Automated structural equation modeling strategies. In R. H. Hoyle (Ed.), *Handbook of structural equation modeling* (pp. 690–704). New York: Guilford Press.

Popper, K. (2014). *The logic of scientific discovery.* Mansfield Center, CT: Martino Publishing.
—A book that does not make for light reading but is a classic, with many gems.

KEY TERMS

disconfirmation dilemma (p. 436)

dogmatic approach (p. 436)

critical approach (p. 436)

methodological rules (p. 437)

boundary conditions (p. 438)

Müller–Lyer illusion (p. 439)

p hacking (p. 440)

researcher degrees of freedom (p. 440)

odds (p. 440)

conditional probability (p. 444)

Bayes' theorem (p. 445)

Bayesian epistemology (p. 445)

prior odds (p. 445)

posterior odds (p. 445)

EXERCISES

Exercises to Reinforce Concepts

1. What is the disconfirmation dilemma and the two major orientations researchers can take to disconfirming data?

2. Is it ever possible to truly confirm a theory? Is it ever possible to truly disconfirm a theory? Explain your answers.

3. What are Popper's "methodological rules"? How can you make use of the concept when designing a study?

4. What is a boundary condition? Discuss the role of post hoc versus a priori identification of boundary conditions in theory revision.

5. Describe the research on the Müller–Lyer illusion and discuss its implications for the analysis of boundary conditions and strong inference.

6. Why does the study of non-WEIRD people matter?

7. How are replication and boundary condition paradigms similar? How are they different?

8. Discuss why theory revision in the face of disconfirming data is important for qualitative research.

9. Characterize Bayesian epistemology in general terms. What are the most important elements and implications of Bayesian epistemology?

10. Can studies with confounds be informative? Why or why not?

11. What type of theory test does structural equation modeling offer that goes beyond simple evaluation of statistical significance of path/regression coefficients? Describe the logic.

12. Describe the logic of automated theory revision.

13. What is a modification index? How is it used in automated theory revisions?

14. Describe the ant colony optimization principle in automated theory revision.

15. What are the theoretical desiderata one should invoke when evaluating a theory revision?

16. What are the different stages of a paradigm shift in science, according to Kuhn?

Exercises to Apply Concepts

1. There are many instances in the research literature of an article being published and then being followed by a critique and a reply to the critique by the original author. Find such an exchange and analyze it from the perspective of Popper's framework as discussed in this chapter. Evaluate the quality of the exchange. Whose side do you take and why?

2. Locate a research article of interest to you and read it from the perspective of a researcher who fully embraces Bayesian epistemology. Did you gain any different insights?

3. Pick out an article of interest to you in which the data were not fully supportive of the theory or hypotheses being tested. Read the discussion section carefully. Analyze how the author(s) dealt with the disconfirming data and how they approached theory revision from the perspective of the Popperian framework discussed in this chapter. Also think about it from a Bayesian perspective.

4. Find a study that uses structural equation modeling and modification indices. Do a critical analysis of the theory revisions the authors made based on the modification indices. Did the authors build a strong case for adopting the automated suggested revisions?

5. Find a study that was a failed replication of another study (these are, unfortunately, fairly easy to find with Internet searching). Critically analyze the faithfulness and methodological quality of the replication study. What are your conclusions based on it? How would you revise the original theory in light of it, if at all?

16

Reading and Writing about Theories

The ability to express an idea is well nigh as important as the idea itself.
—Bernard Baruch (1942)

Throughout your career as a scientist, you will read research reports that describe theories. Many of you will write articles that summarize or describe your own theories or the theories of others. In this chapter, we discuss practical issues to consider when you read and write about theories. We focus first on reading theories and then on writing about theories.

The way in which theories are written in professional reports differs by discipline. In disciplines that emphasize experimentation and empirical efforts to test theories, the theories appear as central elements of the empirical tests, but they are accompanied by information about the tests of the theory per se. In disciplines that emphasize emergent/ grounded theories, the theories usually are written in narrative form in a context that does not have the "tone" of a theory test. To be sure, the emergent theory is consistent with the collected data because, after all, the theory was derived from that data. In our discussion of reading about theories, we separate the two approaches, first describing how you will typically see theories presented in outlets emphasizing formal theory tests and then considering how theories are written about in outlets emphasizing grounded and emergent theorizing. We encourage readers to work through both sections no matter what your orientations are toward theory construction.

READING ABOUT THEORIES

Reading about Theories in Outlets Emphasizing Theory Tests

Journal articles are probably the most common source of information about theories. These articles typically contain four major sections: introduction, methods, results, and discussion. In this chapter, we consider each section and how to read and extract from all of them information about a theory. We do *not* consider methodological matters, such as research design and evaluating the quality of empirical tests of theories. That is a matter for methodological texts. We focus instead on how to identify and clarify the theory being tested. It may seem unusual to consider methods for extracting theories from research reports because one would think that articles would be clear about the theories being considered. Unfortunately, this is not always the case. We adopt a variable-centered and causal thinking approach in this section because these are dominant.

The Introduction Section

The *Introduction section* describes the general problem, reviews the relevant literature on the problem, develops the theory to be tested, and presents the hypotheses to be tested. Statements also are made about how the research will advance knowledge not only about the problem area but also about the theory. The essence of theories in most reports of this type is their variables and the posited relationships between them. A useful strategy for mapping out the theory being tested is to first make a list of all the major variables the author mentions in the measurement section of the Methods section. These are almost always the core variables that are addressed in the theory test. To be sure, the Introduction may discuss other variables to provide context and, if they seem relevant, add them to your list. After doing so, write out the formal conceptual definition of each variable/concept. Sometimes the author will provide an explicit conceptual definition, but other times, the conceptual definition is assumed to be known because the concept is used so often in the scientific literature that there is widespread consensus about its definition. In such cases, you might still write out the conceptual definition so you can be explicit about the theory, but that is a matter of choice. If the author does not provide a conceptual definition and you are not aware of a consensual definition, then generate your own "working definition" based on your reading of the article and your past knowledge of the problem area.

Once the concepts/variables and definitions are in place, on a separate sheet of paper draw an influence diagram of the causal relationships between the variables based on the information in the introduction. Use the methods for diagramming described in Chapter 7 that make use of influence diagrams. The influence diagram might include direct causal relationships, indirect causal relationships (with either partial or complete mediation), moderated causal relationships, reciprocal causation, spurious relationships, and/or unanalyzed relationships. As you draw the diagram, you may be surprised to find that the theorist does not specify causal links that you think should be addressed. Or you may find that the theorist is vague about certain relationships. As we discuss later, you may still be able to "complete the theory" based on material in other sections of the report. The idea is to draw the influence diagram as best you can based on the presented material.

Usually, a conceptual logic model will accompany each link in a theory. You also should write out the conceptual logic model and evaluate it using the approaches discussed in Chapter 4. Our companion website (*www.theory-construction.com*) provides multiple examples of extracting influence diagrams from articles and evaluating their conceptual logic models.

The Method Section

In the *Method section*, the researcher describes methodological features of the empirical study that was conducted to test the theory. This typically includes subsections that describe the research participants, the measures used in the study, how the data were collected, and any other procedural facet that is scientifically relevant. The subsection on the characteristics of the study participants is important theoretically because it suggests the population to which the theory is applicable. To be sure, the author may envision the theory as applying to populations broader than the one reflected by the particular sample studied, but at the very least, the sampled population provides some sense of whom the theory applies to.

As noted, the section on measures also is of interest. It is here that the researcher provides concrete instantiations of the constructs being studied. If the researcher was vague about a conceptual definition in the introduction section, here you can examine the measure for the concept and formulate a conceptual definition based on that measure because the measures usually are specific and concrete. For example, a researcher might theorize about the construct of intelligence in the introduction section, but never define it. In the method section, you discover that the researcher measured intelligence using the Peabody Picture Vocabulary Test (PPVT). As it turns out, the PPVT emphasizes the verbal aspects of intelligence and focuses on the breadth of vocabulary and facility with words. Use of this measure implies a certain conceptual commitment to the meaning of intelligence, and, in this case, the conceptual definition might be construed as one that reflects verbal intelligence.

Sometimes you will be surprised at the way a construct is discussed in the introduction section compared to the instantiation of it that appears in the method section. The measure may reflect a narrower conceptualization than you think is appropriate, or it may reflect a broader conceptualization than what you expected. For example, when discussing the concept of intelligence in the introduction, the researcher might use it in a context that reflects more than verbal intelligence, but when examining the measure, you discover that the PPVT was used.

Next to each variable you listed in the introduction section, modify any conceptual definitions you initially wrote after examining the measure for it. Then write a brief description of the measure that was used for each construct (or the strategy that was used to manipulate it) next to the conceptual definition. Revisit the concept as it was presented in the introduction, the conceptual definition written next to it, and the measure that was used to assess it. Based on these, you should be able to derive a reasonably clear sense of the variables involved, their conceptual meanings, and how reasonably the measures reflect or represent those meanings.

The Results Section

The *Results section* typically reports how the collected data were analyzed and the ensuing results. In most cases for these types of articles, results sections describe the application of statistical techniques. If a researcher was vague or fuzzy about relationships between variables in the introduction section, it is here that he or she must be more explicit. Almost all major statistical methods focus on characterizing relationships between variables. Just as measures are more specific instantiations of variables, statistical tests are more specific instantiations of presumed relationships between variables. Appendix 16.1 describes how different statistical tests map onto different causal models and how they can be used to infer the causal models addressed.

The Discussion Section

The *Discussion section* addresses, among other things, whether the empirical tests were consistent with the theory. If the theory was not supported, then revisions to the theory might be suggested. If the theory was supported, then the researcher often highlights the implications of the results and what future research is needed. Typically, the researcher will encourage the future study of new direct causes, mediators, moderators, extensions to new outcomes, or application of the theory to other contexts and populations to establish generalizability. The researcher often builds a case for the importance and implications of the research. Evaluate the quality of his or her arguments.

Reading about Theories in Outlets Emphasizing Grounded/Emergent Approaches

Articles that publish reports of grounded or emergent theories have a somewhat different format than articles based on confirmatory approaches that report theory tests. Although some grounded/emergent theory articles represent a blending of qualitative and quantitative approaches, our discussion here elaborates traditional grounded/emergent theory styles of presentation that emphasize qualitative data.

Articles using grounded/emergent theory typically begin with a statement of the problem, brief background material to provide a context, and a characterization of the relevant past literature. Prior to describing the method and results, many writers provide an overview of the major conclusions that were reached in the study, so the reader can keep the "big picture" in mind as the particulars are developed. It represents a glimpse of the theory that evolved. This is followed by a method section that describes how the data were collected, who the data were collected on, the strategy used for writing field notes, and how the data were analyzed. It is here that authors build a case that they involved themselves adequately for purposes of conducting an informed grounded/emergent analysis. The results are then presented in which the different theoretical assertions are provided, coupled with exemplars that justify the conceptual logic model underlying them. The examples are representative and often vivid and image provoking.

The article typically ends with a section that places the emergent theory in context relative to other theories and that draws out its theoretical/practical implications.

As with any scientific report, one expects the emergent theory to be clearly developed and articulated. In cases where the emergent theory is variable-centered, one can use the same principles described earlier to clarify the constructs and their interrelationships. For process-oriented theories, one can consider creating a process map, as discussed in Chapter 10. As with the variable-centered approach, it often is useful to write out the key concepts and propositions in the theory. The method section of articles often provides details that might clarify definitions that are vague. We find it useful to make a list of each major theoretical proposition and the key arguments in favor of and against it.

Evaluating the Quality of the Theory You Are Reading

When you read about theory, you want to critically evaluate its quality and assess the extent to which the theory being addressed makes a contribution. The material we covered in Chapter 3 is key to this process. Chapter 3 articulated 16 ways in which researchers can seek to make a theoretical contribution. As you read an article, determine which of those approaches the article is pursuing. To reiterate from Chapter 3, the strategies include (1) clarifying, refining, or challenging the conceptualization of a variable/concept; (2) creating a new variable or constellation of variables that are of theoretical interest; (3) identifying one or more explanatory variables that have not been considered in prior work; (4) identifying the mechanisms or intervening processes responsible for an effect of one variable on another; (5) identifying the boundary conditions of an effect of one variable on another; (6) identifying variables that moderate the effect of one variable on another; (7) extending an existing theory or idea to a new context; (8) identifying nuanced functional forms of relationships; (9) identifying unenunciated/unanticipated consequences of an event; (10) enriching and deepening the understanding of established quantitative associations; (11) developing typologies/taxonomies; (12) importing or applying grand theories and frameworks from other disciplines; (13) synthesizing multiple theories into a unified framework; (14) developing theories of measurement; (15) pitting opposing theoretical explanations against one another; and/or (16) proposing alternative explanations to established phenomena, among others (see Chapter 3 for an elaboration of each strategy). Does the theory in the target article successfully accomplish any of these?

Chapter 3 also described the qualities of a good theory, including the extent to which it is logically consistent, in agreement with prior data, testable, appropriately parsimonious, broad in scope, novel/original, useful, and likely to stimulate research by others. Does the theory you are reading meet these criteria? Chapter 3 also described three criteria that editors and reviewers often use to judge the theoretical contribution of an article: (1) novelty or originality, (2) practical utility, and (3) scope. How does the theory you read about fare on these particular dimensions?

BOX 16.1. PowerPoint Presentations of Theories

PowerPoint presentations are commonplace, and you often will present a theory using this form of media. Here is a list of 40 things to consider as you prepare a PowerPoint presentation:

1. Make your first or second slides an outline of your presentation.
2. Follow the order of your outline for the rest of the presentation.
3. Use one or two slides per minute of your presentation.
4. Write in point form, not complete sentences.
5. Include no more than four or five points per slide.
6. Avoid wordiness: Use key words and phrases only.
7. If possible, show one point at a time by adding points dynamically to the same slide:
   • This helps the audience concentrate on what you are saying.
   • This prevents the audience from reading ahead.
8. Do not use distracting animation.
9. Use at least an 18-point font.
10. Use different-sized fonts for main points and secondary points.
11. Use a standard font such as Times New Roman or Arial.
12. Place words in all capitals only when necessary—it is difficult to read.
13. Use a color of font that contrasts sharply with the background.
14. Use color to reinforce the logic of your structure (e.g., light blue title and dark blue text).
15. Use color to emphasize a point, but only occasionally.
16. Using color for decoration is distracting.
17. Use backgrounds that are attractive but simple.
18. Use backgrounds that are light.
19. Use the same background consistently throughout your presentation.
20. Data in graphs are easier to comprehend and retain than are raw data.
21. Always title your graphs.
22. Minor gridlines on graphs usually are unnecessary.
23. Proof your slides for spelling mistakes, the use of repeated words, and grammatical errors.
24. If your presentation is not in your first language, have a native speaker check it.
25. Use a strong closing and summarize the main points of your presentation.
26. Consider ending your presentation with a "question slide" that invites your audience to ask questions or that provides a visual aid during the question period.

(continued)

27. Show up early for your talk. Check whether your equipment works properly.
28. Check whether the projector's resolution is the same as your laptop's. If it isn't, then your slides may be cropped, may jump, or may lose scan lines.
29. Don't leave Standby Power Management on your laptop on; make sure that your laptop does not turn off if you're inactive for a while during your talk.
30. Don't leave your screen saver on.
31. Don't use the mouse as a pointer. Moving a mouse on a slide show may cause a pointer to appear that is suboptimal in terms of performance.
32. Don't use the edges of the slide. Some projectors crop slides.
33. Do not assume your presentation will work on another person's laptop. Disk failures, software version mismatches, lack of disk space, low memory, and many other factors can prevent this. Check these out before your presentation.
34. Practice moving forward and backward within your presentation. Audiences often ask to see the previous screen again.
35. If possible, preview your slides on the screen you'll be using for your presentation. Make sure that they are readable from the back-row seats.
36. Have a Plan B in the event of technical difficulties (e.g., transparencies and handouts).
37. Practice with someone who has never seen your presentation. Ask him or her for honest feedback about colors, content, and any effects or graphics you've included.
38. Do not read from your slides.
39. Do not speak to your slides. Face the audience, not the slides.
40. When possible, run your presentation from a hard disk rather than a floppy disk or a flash drive. Using a floppy disk or flash drive may slow your presentation.

Note. Compiled from the following websites: *www.iasted.org/conferences/formatting/Presentations-Tips.ppt; www.anandnatrajan.com/FAQs/powerpoint.html;* and *kinesiology.boisestate.edu/kines442/tips_for_making_effective_powerp.htm*

When evaluating a theory, one should ask if each of the core constructs in the theory is clearly defined. Are the constructs "fuzzy" or ambiguous? As discussed in Chapters 4 and 10, theoretical propositions should have strong conceptual logic models based in either deductive reasoning, inductive reasoning, analogic reasoning, abduction, or some other viable logic system. Is this the case for the theory you are reading? Chapter 6 on thought experiments stressed the importance of theories being clear about the nature of the relationships between concepts or variables. Is this the case for the theory you are reading?

WRITING ABOUT THEORIES

In this section, we identify points to consider when presenting your theory, focusing on general points relevant to all reports. Later, we discuss issues specific to certain outlets.

How You Say It Can Be as Important as What You Say

Over the course of our careers, we have seen articles by colleagues with very good ideas be rejected for publication, and we have seen articles with what we thought were weak ideas published in highly competitive journals. Although there are many reasons for this variability, one particularly important reason is how the theory is "packaged" in the written product—that is, how the theory is presented. A description of a theory is not unlike the telling of a story, with some people being better storytellers than others. We wish the world was such that it was purely the quality of the idea that mattered. But it is not. If you can't communicate your ideas well, and if you can't get people excited about your ideas, then you are going to have a difficult time publishing your work. You need to be both clear and engaging when presenting ideas.

In graduate school, one of the authors (Jaccard) was taken aside by a senior graduate student who, somewhat tongue in cheek, decided to tell the struggling first-year student the secret to writing scientifically. "Try to think of the most boring and dryest way you can say something in the fewest words possible, and you will be a successful scientific writer." In essence, the message was to get to the point and to be concise in getting there. I (Jaccard) was taught as a graduate student by my mentors to avoid "cute titles" for articles and instead to include the main variables in the title so that the title would be informative. I also was taught to avoid journalistic tricks, such as starting an article with a gripping, real-life event of an individual who had experienced the phenomenon I was studying (or something related to it), and then using this as a lead-in to the presentation of the science. The strategy of giving phenomena memorable labels (e.g., "fundamental attribution error") also was viewed pejoratively as "marketing." Despite the more conservative training I received, there are those who believe otherwise. Sternberg (2003) and Peter and Olson (1983), for example, suggest a mindset for scientific writing that is similar to that of an advertiser: "Keep in mind that you have something to sell, namely your ideas, and sell it" (Sternberg, 2003, p. 22). Scientists are only human, the logic goes, and if they have to listen to someone tell a story, they would rather hear it from a good storyteller than a bad one. There are reasonable arguments on both sides of this issue.

Briefer Is Better, But Don't Be Too Brief

Readers appreciate papers that are concise and to the point. A lengthy theoretical description is often greeted with dread and sometimes hostility. Yet, you need to make your case and provide background to your theory. Don't be afraid to use the space you need; just make sure you need it. For a variety of reasons, most journals have strict limits on the number of manuscript pages that can be published. You typically will find your hands tied because of this restriction. Sometimes you may elect to publish in an outlet not only because the outlet reaches your intended audience, but also because it does not have strict limits on the number of pages. The journal may be less prestigious, but at least you can say what needs to be said and build your case effectively. The bottom line is that you need to be scholarly and thorough while at the same time being as brief and concise as possible.

Prepare an Outline

Many people benefit by preparing an outline of the section of the manuscript where the theory is presented (and for that matter, the entire article) prior to actually writing about it. An outline helps you keep the logical sequence of your presentation in mind as you write. It also makes it easier to recognize if you have omitted something crucial. Writing from an outline can help prevent the inclusion of irrelevant thoughts. Some people like to write brief outlines consisting of only key terms or phrases; others prefer to write complete-sentence outlines.

Provide a Roadmap

It often is useful to provide readers at the outset with a "roadmap" of where you are headed in the narrative. This usually consists of a short paragraph, strategically placed after some introductory orientation, such as: "In this article, we first discuss the prevalence of adolescent drug use. Next, we consider . . .". In other words, provide an overview of the structure of the theoretical presentation. It also helps readers if you make liberal use of headings and make the headings reasonably descriptive.

Provide a Succinct Review of Current Knowledge

It goes without saying that you need to review past research and summarize current knowledge about the topic area you are addressing. The omission of a key article or result from prior work in your characterization of the literature will be problematic. For journal articles, you usually will not have the luxury of writing about all relevant past research in depth. You might do so in a dissertation but not in a journal article. If a large body of literature already exists on your topic, try to cite and incorporate published literature reviews. The primary objective of your literature review is to provide a good sense of what is already known about the topic you are addressing so as to set the stage for describing how your theory will make a contribution relative to this body of work.

Discuss the Implications and Importance of Your Theory

The importance and implications of your theory may be clear to you, but this does not mean that your readers will automatically recognize them. It helps to be explicit about what new insights and perspectives your theory has to offer. Directly answer the question "What is new here?" and envision a reader who is constantly saying "So, who cares, anyway?" Consider adding a section in the introduction at a strategic location (e.g., at the end of the introduction), titled "Summary, Innovations, and Implications."

Earlier, we presented a listing from Chapter 3 of the strategies researchers use to make theoretical contributions. Consider telling the reader the strategy or strategies you are using (in the introduction) or used (in the discussion) and make a case for why the strategies you chose are important. Chapter 3 also emphasized the importance of the originality, scope, and utility of a theory to reviewers and readers. Humbly build a case for these criteria in your presentation of the theory in the introduction section and reiterate it in the discussion section. Good theories generate future research, so it is important to include a description of the future research implications of the work in the discussion section.

Keep Your Audience in Mind

Before writing a paper, it helps to have made a decision, at least tentatively, about the journal to which you plan to submit the paper for possible publication. This defines your "audience." Various criteria can be used as the basis for selecting a journal. A common strategy used by those who are at an early point in their careers is the quantitative impact factor of the journal. This index reflects how often articles published in the journal typically are cited by other researchers and are frequently thought to be indicative of the "prestige" of the journal. There are many limitations to such indices, and we tend not to rely on them when we are making placement decisions. To be sure, we seek to publish in journals that are rigorous and reputable in our discipline, but we form such judgments based on our own readings of the journals and in consultation with senior colleagues whose opinions we respect. When selecting a journal to submit an article to, we think more in terms of the audience we want to reach, that is, who the typical readers are of a particular journal and how large that audience will be. We also think about the likely backgrounds and orientations of the readers because these can affect how we ultimately structure and frame our theory to them. The type of scientist who reads a journal can best be determined by examining who publishes in the journal, the type of articles published in it, and who cites work published in that journal. A sense of the type of scientist who reads a journal and the types of articles published in it can be determined by examining recent issues of the journal. A sense of who cites the work can be garnered by choosing an article from the journals and then using Google Scholar to reveal other articles that have cited it.

Before a target audience will ever see a paper, however, it must first be accepted for publication. This means that you must also write with another audience in mind, namely, the likely reviewers of the article. If your theory is well articulated, clearly laid out, and makes a contribution, then these strengths will count a great deal toward your paper being accepted by a reviewer. With a complex theory and a complex study (or set of studies) surrounding a theory, it sometimes is difficult to anticipate all the reactions and issues that two or three diverse reviewers will have. Having a draft of a paper reviewed by your colleagues for purposes of feedback can help in this regard. A heuristic we often use is to assume we will be assigned an expert but hostile reviewer who seeks to find every fault he or she possibly can with our work and who is determined to reject our manuscript. Our task is to write the article in a way that addresses every concern the reviewer might have and to convert the reviewer to an advocate rather than a critic.

Using Figures

Because journal space is limited, editors typically discourage the use of many diagrams or figures. Articles generally contain only two or three figures, if any. For variable-centered frameworks that rely on causality, an influence diagram can speak a thousand words, theoretically. Some theorists provide the influence diagram early in the introduction section and then use it to organize an ensuing narrative that considers each path or a cluster of paths in the diagram. The relevant literature is reviewed for each path to provide a sense of current knowledge about it, and then the contributions of the study to be reported are developed relative to this literature. Other theorists present a narrative organized in this way, but reserve the presentation of the formal diagram until the end of the narrative, as a multivariate summary of the prior discussion.

Some theorists list theoretical propositions and label them with phrases like "Proposition 1." Such propositions formalize a theory and highlight its most important points. One can translate an influence diagram into propositions and present the logic verbally rather than using a figure. For example, in the case of mediated relationships, consider the assertion that the impact that watching violence on television has on aggression is mediated by the perceived legitimacy of acting aggressively. The mediational chain can be stated verbally as:

Proposition 1: The more televised violence that people view, the more legitimate they perceive it is to act aggressively.

Proposition 2: The more legitimate viewers perceive aggression to be, the more aggressively they behave.

Proposition 3: The more televised violence that people watch, the more they will behave aggressively.

Some scientists prefer presenting theoretical propositions in this format, whereas others prefer influence diagrams with supplementary narratives.

Cite Sources for Your Ideas, Text, and Related Items

Section 3.1.3 of the Council of Science Editors' (2012) White Paper on Promoting Integrity in Scientific Journal Publications defines plagiarism as "the use of text or other items (figures, images, tables) without permission or acknowledgment of the source of these materials" (p. 39). All of us are familiar with plagiarism. Many are not as familiar with "piracy," however, which the White Paper defines as "the appropriation of ideas, data, or methods from others without adequate permission or acknowledgment. The intent is the untruthful portrayal of the ideas or methods as one's own" (p. 39). In other words, not only is it unethical to use the exact words of another author without permission, it also is unethical to use ideas originated by others without adequate permission or acknowledgment.

Both authors, as well as a number of our colleagues, have been subject to blatant idea theft and, in some instances, plagiarism as well, and it is frustrating. Although many scientific societies and professional organizations have codes of ethics prohibiting plagiarism, a lesser number have corrective mechanisms for handling the problem. All too often, there is not much one can do about plagiarism or piracy.

That said, sometimes it is hard to remember the sources of your ideas. Moreover, there are instances (as with introductory texts, including this one) where providing citation after citation would burden readers. Furthermore, some journals place limits on the number of citations one can use, so that authors submitting work to such journals sometimes are left in a quandary as to which prior works to cite and which to ignore. So, piracy is not always a cut-and-dry matter. However, you should always approach your writings in the spirit of giving credit where credit is due.

Do Not Engage in HARKing

Norbert Kerr (1998) coined the term *HARKing* (*H*ypothesizing *A*fter the *R*esults are *K*nown) to refer to scientists who write up a study as if the significant results were anticipated and hypothesized prior to data analysis when, in fact, the "hypotheses" were derived only after analyzing the data. HARKing can have the unfortunate effect of causing readers to presume higher levels of initial confidence in a proposition prior to conduct of the study, which, if one adopts Bayesian perspectives, can be detrimental to theory evaluation (see Chapter 15 as well as the broader discussion of HARKing by Rubin [2017]). It also is intellectually dishonest. We do not encourage the practice.

Spelling, Grammar, Typos, and Punctuation

If your manuscript has spelling errors, poor grammar, and/or "typos," then some readers will conclude that you are "sloppy" and don't care enough about your science. Scientists are noted for being careful and methodical thinkers, and these attributes should generalize to other areas of the scientific process, even to the level of spelling, grammar, typos, and punctuation. It is best to be compulsive in this regard.

In sum, when presenting your theory, good communication is the key. How you say something can be just as important as what you say. Being brief and to the point is preferred, but not at the expense of being scholarly. Many theorists benefit by creating outlines prior to writing. If you are developing many ideas, be sure to provide an overview of what you will be covering and make liberal use of headings. State the general problem and then do a succinct review of current knowledge. In addition to presenting the theory, be sure to discuss its implications and importance. As you do so, keep your target audience and reviewers in mind, give credit where credit is due, and correct those typos! In the final analysis, the best way to get a sense of writing styles is to read first-hand articles in the outlets where you will be publishing your work. It is through such readings that you will get a sense of the organizational structures and writing styles that typify successful writing in the areas of study you pursue.

The Role of the Abstract

The abstract of an article allows for only a few sentences about your theory. However, it is critical in that it usually is the first exposure readers and reviewers will have to your theory, and it can shape their impressions accordingly. An abstract that leads to the reader's reaction that your work is mundane is not a good starting point. This means you need to think carefully about how to summarize the essence or "big picture" view of your theory in a few sentences. Don't trivialize the role of the abstract. Decisions about whether an article is worth reading often are at stake.

GRANT PROPOSALS, TECHNICAL REPORTS, AND PRESENTATIONS

Social scientists write for different outlets, although by far the most common one is the scientific journal. All the principles discussed in this chapter will usually serve you well independent of the outlet for which you are writing. Technical reports usually include an "executive summary" that is intended to capture the essence and main conclusions of the larger project in one to three pages. The idea is that a top-level executive usually is too busy to read about the details: He or she just wants to get to the bottom line quickly and efficiently—but have the entire report available should he or she desire to read in greater detail.

It is common for researchers to seek funding for their research efforts. Grants can be pursued either from federal or state governments or from private, not-for-profit organizations. Typically, the social scientist writes a formal grant proposal and submits it for review by the agency that ultimately decides to fund (or not fund) the research. The level of detail and the description of the underlying theories guiding the research vary considerably, depending on the funding source and the goals. Many agencies focus on applied problems and are most interested in addressing those problems rather than advancing science or helping to accumulate knowledge about a problem area. In short, their focus is on solutions. Other agencies understand the importance of building a strong knowledge base through both theory and research and demand that strong theories guide the efforts of the research they fund. If you pursue funding for your research, look carefully at the proposal guidelines developed by the funding agency, determine the focus and goals of the agency, and try to find examples of successful proposals in your field to see how theory was presented in those proposals.

In terms of oral presentations, you typically will give presentations that are either 15 minutes long (e.g., at a scientific convention) or 45–50 minutes long (e.g., at a job talk or a colloquium). Usually, only a small portion of this time is used to describe your theory—perhaps one-fourth or one-third of the allocated time. In oral presentations, you might spend a few minutes on a literature review that summarizes current knowledge, a few minutes laying out the theory itself, a few minutes describing what is new and innovative about the theory you propose, and a few minutes on its implications. The book by Alley (2003) in the Suggested Readings section provides numerous useful strategies for structuring presentations. Our companion website (*www.theory-construction. com*) has links to videos about preparing presentations and posters at conferences.

SUMMARY AND CONCLUDING COMMENTS

When reading theories in scientific reports, we want to capture the essence of the theory being addressed. For variable-centered theories, a useful strategy is to make a list of the variables in the theory, write out their conceptual definitions, and then draw a path diagram to reflect the presumed causal relationships that operate between the variables. A well-specified theory will clearly articulate the concepts on which it focuses, the nature of those concepts, and the relationships between variables. If the theorist is vague or unclear about these matters, you often will find clarity as the researcher instantiates his or her theory in the methods and results sections. For process-oriented theories, you should list the relevant processes and try to characterize each, perhaps using the process map described in Chapter 10.

When writing about your theory, you need to follow several key imperatives, notably: (1) attend not only to what you say but also to how you say it, (2) be brief and to the point, but not at the expense of good scholarship, (3) work from outlines, (4) provide readers with an overview of the organization of the paper, (5) make liberal use of headings, (6) provide a succinct review of the literature and characterize the current state of knowledge about the phenomena you are studying, (7) discuss the implications and importance of your theory, (8) always keep in mind the target audience and reviewers, (9) give credit for ideas where credit is due, and (10) do not HARK. The best way to get a sense of good scientific writing is to read articles in journals where you intend to publish and take note of the styles used.

SUGGESTED READINGS

Alley, M. (2003). *The craft of scientific presentations*. New York: Springer.

—A host of strategies for making effective scientific presentations, based on the techniques of scientists who are effective presenters.

Becker, H., & Richards, P. (2007). *Writing for social scientists: How to start and finish your thesis, book, or article*. Chicago: University of Chicago Press.

—A well-written book about practical writing strategies for social scientists. One of the better resources on the topic.

Council of Science Editors. (2012). White paper on promoting integrity in scientific journal publications. Retrieved from *www.councilscienceeditors.org/wp-content/uploads/entire_whitepaper.pdf.*

—An excellent source of information on the roles and responsibilities of authors, editors, reviewers, sponsoring societies, and media in regard to publishing scientific papers.

Friedland, A., & Felt, C. (2000). *Writing successful science proposals*. New Haven, CT: Yale University Press.

—Strategies for writing grant proposals.

Locke, L., Silverman, S., & Spirduso, W. (2010). *Reading and understanding research, 3rd ed.* Thousand Oaks, CA: SAGE.

—A very clear exposition of strategies and principles for reading research articles.

Peter, J. P., & Olson, J. (1983). Is science marketing? *Journal of Marketing, 47,* 111–125.

—A discussion of the importance of selling readers on your ideas.

Silva, P. (2015). *Write it up: Practical strategies for writing and publishing journal articles.* Washington, DC: American Psychological Association.

—A "how to" for writing articles and working through the publication process.

Sternberg, R. (2003). *The psychologists' companion: A guide to scientific writing for students and researchers* (4th ed.). New York: Cambridge University Press.

—A book filled with ideas for more effective writing by social scientists.

KEY TERMS

Introduction section (p. 462)

Methods section (p. 463)

Results section (p. 464)

Discussion section (p. 464)

E X E R C I S E S

Exercises to Reinforce Concepts

1. Describe the strategy you would use to discern a theory from the introduction section of a journal article.

2. In what ways can you use the method section to help give clarity to a theory?

3. Describe what you think are the most important points to keep in mind when writing about a theory.

Exercises to Apply Concepts

1. Choose an article that empirically tests a theory and write a short summary of that theory. Identify points in the theory that need clarification or elaboration.

2. Write a report that presents either a theory of your own or an existing theory from the literature using all the principles discussed in this chapter.

3. Prepare a PowerPoint presentation of a theory and present it to someone.

Appendix 16.1

Inferring Theoretical Relationships from the Choice of Statistical Tests

This appendix describes how to discern presumed theoretical relationships between variables based on the statistical methods that were chosen by the theorist to analyze data. In doing so, we adopt a causal framework as our point of analysis. We assume you are familiar with each statistical test we discuss. If not, skip the section describing that test.

T-TEST

A *t*-test examines a quantitative outcome variable and whether the mean scores on that outcome differ between two groups. For example, one might want to determine if there are gender differences in attitudes toward restricting the legalization of abortion. The two groups, males and females, represent an independent variable or a presumed "cause," and the variable whose means are computed and compared (attitudes toward restricting the legalization of abortions) is the presumed "effect." The underlying causal model that typically motivates the analysis is a direct causal relationship, as shown in Figure 16.1a. This is true for both the independent group's *t*-test and the correlated group's *t*-test. The direction of the mean difference isolates the nature of the relationship, and the magnitude of the effect (in raw score units) is the magnitude of the absolute mean difference. Cohen's *d* is typically used to index the strength of the relationship in a standardized metric. Thus, if a researcher applies an independent group's *t*-test to data or a correlated group's *t*-test, the model in Figure 16.1a is probably the theory that motivates the analysis.

ONE-WAY ANALYSIS OF VARIANCE

The one-way analysis of variance is an extension of the *t*-test, and it, too, has an underlying causal model that usually reflects a direct causal relationship. The different groups comprising the factor represent the independent variable or the presumed "cause," and the variable whose means are compared is the presumed "effect." The underlying causal model that motivates the analysis is shown in Figure 16.1b.

For example, a one-way analysis of variance might be performed to compare three religious groups—Catholics, Protestants, and Jews—on their attitudes toward having large families. The

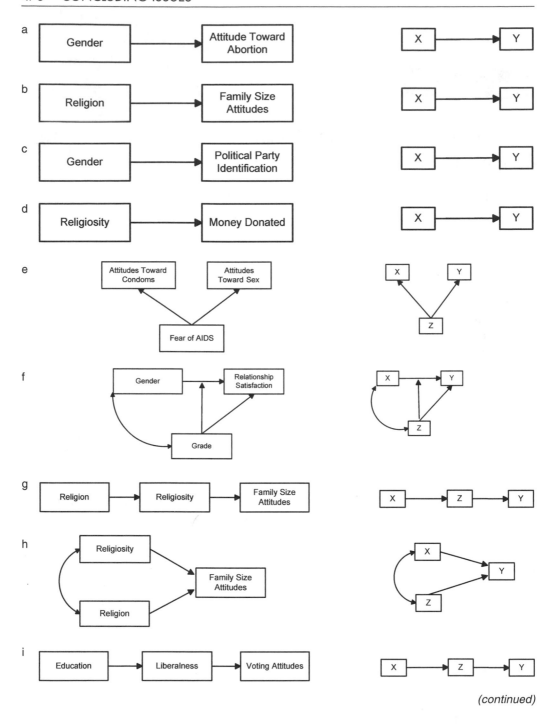

(continued)

FIGURE 16.1. Causal models underlying statistical tests (text example on left, generic form on right). (a) Two-group/condition *t*-test; (b) one-way analysis of variance; (c) chi-square test of independence and test of proportions; (d) Pearson correlation/linear regression: direct cause model; (e) Pearson correlation: common cause or spurious effect model; (f) two-factor analysis of variance; (g) one-way analysis of covariance: mediation; (h) one-way analysis of covariance: independent influence and error reduction; (i) partial correlation: mediation.

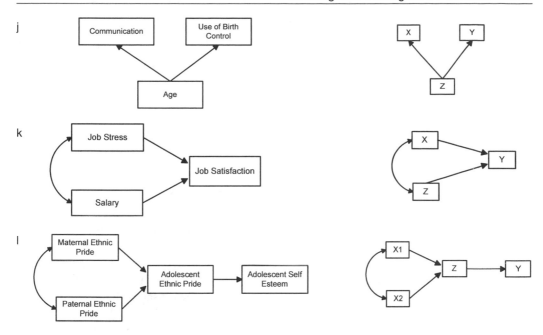

FIGURE 16.1. *(continued)* (j) partial correlation: common cause or spurious effect model; (k) multiple regression; and (l) hierarchical multiple regression: mediation.

overall *F*-test reveals whether there is a relationship between religion (the independent variable) and family size attitudes (the outcome variable). If the overall or omnibus *F*-test is statistically significant, then we conclude there is such a relationship (at least, in terms of means). If the test is not statistically significant, then we cannot conclude that such a relationship exists. Pairwise comparisons of group means isolate the nature of the relationship, and indices such as omega squared or eta squared measure the strength of the relationship in standardized metrics. This underlying causal model holds for both between-groups and repeated measures analysis of variance. Thus, if a researcher applies a one-way analysis of variance to data, the model in Figure 16.1b is probably the theory that motivates the analysis.

CHI-SQUARE TEST OF INDEPENDENCE AND TESTS OF PROPORTIONS

The chi-square test of independence examines the association between two categorical variables. For example, a theorist might believe that there are gender differences in political party identification and test this hypothesis using the chi-square test of independence. Gender is the independent variable or the presumed "cause," and political party identification is the presumed "effect." A statistically significant omnibus chi-square test is consistent with the proposition that a relationship exists. Figure 16.1c presents the causal model that motivates this analysis. Follow-up comparisons focused on specific cells of the contingency table isolate the nature of the relationship, and indices such as Cramer's *V* or the phi coefficient measure the strength of the relationship on a standardized metric.

A variant of the chi-square test of independence is a test of the difference between two proportions. For example, a researcher might compare the proportion of male seventh graders who have engaged in sexual intercourse with the proportion of female seventh graders who have engaged in sexual intercourse. The significance test roughly maps onto the chi-square test of independence in a 2×2 contingency table, with gender as rows and whether the individual has had sex as columns. Thus, the model in Figure 16.1c also captures the causal model that typically motivates a test of the difference between two proportions.

In sum, if a researcher applies a chi-square test of independence or a test of the difference between two proportions to data, the model in Figure 16.1c is probably the theory that motivates the analysis.

PEARSON CORRELATION AND/OR LINEAR REGRESSION

A Pearson correlation examines the degree to which the relationship between two variables approximates a linear relationship. The predictor variable, X, is the presumed "cause," and the criterion variable, Y, is the presumed "effect." For example, a researcher might compute the correlation between individuals' degree of religiosity and how much money they donate to religious organizations over the course of a year. Figure 16.1d presents the causal model that often motivates a correlation analysis, which is a direct causal relationship.

Another model that might motivate the calculation of a correlation coefficient is a spurious effect or "common cause" model. If two variables are thought to be related because they share a common cause, then there should be a correlation between them. For example, if fear of AIDS impacts both attitudes toward using condoms and attitudes toward having sex, then one would expect attitudes toward condoms and attitudes toward having sex to be correlated. A statistically significant correlation between two variables is consistent with the proposition that they share a common cause. The "common cause" or spurious correlation model motivating a correlation coefficient appears in Figure 16.1e.

There are other models that might motivate a bivariate correlation analysis (e.g., to identify a variable as a potential confound or to document an unanalyzed relationship), but these two models are by far the most common ones motivating the calculation of a correlation. Usually, you can discern which of the two theoretical orientations the researcher has adopted based on material from the introduction and/or discussion section.

FACTORIAL ANALYSIS OF VARIANCE

We describe the case of factorial analysis of variance (FANOVA) using a two-factor design. Extensions to three-factor or four-factor designs are straightforward. In a two-factor analysis of variance, the quantitative dependent variable whose means are being computed and compared is the outcome variable or the presumed "effect." We refer to one of the factors as X and the other factor as Z; these are the presumed "causes." In FANOVA one typically examines three "effects": the main effect of X, the main effect of Z, and the interaction between X and Z. There are separate omnibus F-tests for each effect. As an example, let X be gender, Z be grade in school, and the outcome variable be adolescents' degree of satisfaction with their relationship with their mother. The FANOVA tests if there is a significant mean difference in satisfaction as a function of gender (collapsing across grade in school), a significant mean difference in satisfaction as a function of grade in school (collapsing across gender), and if the gender difference in satisfaction varies significantly as a function of grade in school. Figure 16.1f presents the causal model that typically motivates a FANOVA. The main effects reflect direct causes, and the interaction effect reflects a moderated relationship. A researcher who conducts a factorial analysis of variance usually is testing if the data are consistent with the causal paths noted in Figure 16.1f. This underlying causal model holds for both between-groups and repeated measures of factorial analysis of variance.

ONE-WAY ANALYSIS OF COVARIANCE

A one-way analysis of covariance (ANCOVA) is comparable to a one-way analysis of variance (ANOVA), except that a covariate is included in the analysis. For example, a researcher might analyze the same variables as the one-way ANOVA (described starting on page 477) by comparing three religious groups (Catholics, Protestants, and Jews) on attitudes toward having large families. However, a covariate is introduced into the analysis, namely, each individual's degree of religiosity. The comparisons are conducted on group differences in attitudes toward large families, holding constant (or covarying out) religiosity.

The underlying causal model for this analytic method usually takes one of two forms. The first is a mediation model and is illustrated in Figure 16.1g. The covariate is thought to be a (complete) mediator of the effect of the "factor" on the dependent variable. For example, the effect of religion on family size attitudes is thought to be mediated by the fact that religious groups differ, on average, on how religious their members are. If, after holding the covariate constant, the effect of the factor on the outcome variable is no longer statistically significant, then this is consistent with the proposition that the covariate is a complete mediator of the effect. If the effect of the factor on the outcome variable remains statistically significant, then this is consistent with the proposition that the factor has independent effects on the outcome variable over and above the covariate.[1] Thus, some form of mediational model often motivates an analysis of covariance.

The second causal model commonly underlying analysis of covariance is shown in Figure 16.1h. In this model, the researcher views the factor and the covariate as each having independent influences on the outcome variable. Including the covariate in the analysis reduces bias in the parameter estimates (by avoiding left-out variable error) and also reduces the error term, which can increase the power of the statistical test. Mediation is not an issue in this model. The focus instead is on assessing the effect of the factor while simultaneously taking into account the effect of the covariate.

Although other causal models can motivate a one-way analysis of covariance (e.g., a spurious effect model), these two (or a combination of them) are the most common motivators of this test. If a researcher conducts an analysis of covariance, it usually is with one of these two models in mind. More often than not, you can discern which of the two models the researcher is using from the text in the introduction and discussion sections.

---

[1] Formal statistical tests to evaluate partial or complete mediation are more complex than simple covariate-based procedures such as the ones described in this section. This does not alter the fact that mediational models often are the motivating sources of covariate-based analyses, such as analysis of covariance, partial correlation, and hierarchical regression.

FACTORIAL ANALYSIS OF COVARIANCE

A factorial analysis of covariance is comparable to a factorial analysis of variance, except that a covariate is included in the analysis. The causal model underlying the factorial analysis of covariance is the same as that for the factorial analysis of variance (see Figure 16.1f), except for the additional role of the covariate. Like the one-way ANCOVA, the covariate is typically seen as taking on the role of a mediator or as an independent influence on the outcome, whose inclusion in the model reduces error and increases the statistical power of the test.

PARTIAL CORRELATION

A partial correlation analysis is similar to a Pearson correlation analysis but includes a covariate. One of two causal models typically motivates a partial correlation analysis. The first model is a mediational model and is illustrated in Figure 16.1i. A researcher might want to test if a variable Z is a partial or complete mediator of the effect of X on Y. For example, to test if liberalness mediates the relationship between education and attitudes toward voting for a Democratic presidential candidate, a partial correlation between years of education and attitudes toward the candidate might be computed, partialing out liberalness. A statistically significant partial correlation is consistent with the proposition that education has an independent effect on attitudes toward voting for the Democratic presidential candidate over and above liberalness. If a statistically significant correlation between education and voting attitudes becomes nonsignificant when liberalness is partialed out, then this is consistent with the proposition that liberalness mediates the relationship between education and voting attitudes (but see footnote 1).

The second causal model that often motivates a partial correlation analysis is a common cause or spurious effect model. For example, a researcher might argue that the relationship between parent–adolescent communication about birth control and adolescent intentions to use birth control is spurious due to the common cause of age of the adolescent: As adolescents get older, parents are more likely to talk with them about issues surrounding the use of birth control. As adolescents get older, they also are more likely to use birth control, often for reasons that have nothing to do with parental communication. So the argument might be that any association between parent–adolescent communication and use of birth control is spurious. If one calculates a partial correlation between parent–adolescent communication and adolescent use of birth control using age of the adolescent as a covariate, a statistically significant correlation is consistent with the proposition that the correlation is not spurious, per Figure 16.1j.

As before, other types of causal models may motivate the use of partial correlation analysis, but these two models are the most common bases for partial correlation.

MULTIPLE REGRESSION

Multiple regression analysis involves regressing an outcome variable, Y, onto two or more predictor variables. Figure 16.1k presents the causal model that typically motivates this analytic method. As an example, a researcher might regress job satisfaction onto two variables: (1) how stressful the job is and (2) how much an individual gets paid, as reflected by his or her annual salary. A statistically significant regression coefficient for a given predictor is consistent with the proposition that there is a causal path between the presumed "cause" (the predictor variable) and the presumed "effect" of job satisfaction.

It is possible to use multiple regression to pursue moderated relationships using product terms and a wide variety of other types of causal relationships. However, traditional applications of multiple regression with several predictors evaluate models of the form in Figure 16.1k.

HIERARCHICAL REGRESSION

Hierarchical regression analysis is typically used to address either mediation or covariate control. For the case of mediation, the researcher typically enters the mediators on the first step of the analysis and then the more distal causes on the second step. In the case of complete mediation, the prediction is that the increment in the multiple correlation at the second step will not be statistically significant. A statistically significant increment in the squared multiple correlation implies that one or more of the distal causes has an independent effect on the outcome variable over and above the mediators.

For example, a researcher might study self-esteem as an outcome variable in adolescent Latinos. The researcher theorizes that self-esteem is influenced by ethnic pride (i.e., how much pride the adolescent takes in being Latino). The adolescent's ethnic pride, in turn, is thought to be a function of the ethnic pride of his or her mother and father. The impact of maternal and paternal ethnic pride on adolescent self-esteem is thought to be mediated by adolescent ethnic pride. Figure 16.1l presents the underlying causal model. The analyst performs a hierarchical regression by first regressing adolescent self-esteem onto adolescent ethnic pride. A statistically significant regression coefficient should be observed. If more than one mediator is thought to be operating, then all the mediators are entered into the regression equation at this first step. At the second step, the researcher adds the two distal variables to the equation, hypothesizing that the regression coefficients for the two distal variables will not be statistically significant, but for the mediators, the regression coefficients will remain so.[2]

For the case of covariate control, the covariates that are to be controlled are entered on the first step of the analysis, and then the key "causes" of interest are entered on the second step. If the key causes impact the outcome over and above the covariates, then the increment in the multiple correlation should be statistically significant. If a significant increase in the multiple correlation is observed, then this is consistent with the proposition that there is an effect of the "causes" on the outcome variable over and above the covariates. The fundamental causal model for this analysis is the same as for multiple regression (see Figure 16.1k), with the covariates representing one set of predictors and the key "causes" representing the other set of predictors, all in the same equation.

As is true of all the methods discussed, one can usually discern the underlying model motivating a hierarchical regression analysis from the introduction and discussion sections. Although other models can motivate hierarchical regression, the ones described above are those you will most typically encounter.

---

[2]There are better ways of testing the mediation model than hierarchical regression: these make use of structural equation modeling. Nevertheless, you occasionally will encounter use of hierarchical regression to test mediation.

LOGISTIC REGRESSION AND THE GENERALIZED LINEAR MODEL

Logistic regression is analogous to multiple regression but focuses on the case where the outcome variable is dichotomous. The generalized linear model extends regression-like analyses to count variables (e.g., Poisson regression; negative binomial regression), categorical outcomes with more than two categories (e.g., multinomial logistic regression), or ordinal outcomes (e.g., ordinal regression). The fundamental causal model that motivates all these techniques is the same as that depicted in Figure 16.1k for multiple regression. When hierarchical tests are conducted in the context of these models, causal models similar to those discussed for hierarchical regression typically motivate the analysis.

STRUCTURAL EQUATION MODELING

Structural equation modeling (SEM), an analytic method designed to evaluate the viability of causal models, can be drawn in the form of path diagrams. The theoretical structure the researcher is using when SEM methods are pursued is usually evident from the accompanying path diagrams.

You will encounter other statistical tests, but the ones described in this appendix represent a good sampling of the major statistical tests used by social scientists. Once an investigator applies one or more of these tests, he or she usually is invoking a causal model of the form that we described for each test. If a researcher has not made clear the presumed theoretical relationships between variables or the underlying causal model that is the focus, then you can often discern this by examining the statistical tests that the researcher reports in the results section.

17

Epilogue

The most important fundamental laws and facts of physical science have all been discovered, and these are now so firmly established that the possibility of their ever being supplemented in consequence by new discoveries is exceedingly remote.
—ALBERT MICHELSON, noted German scientist (1903);
stated before Einstein's groundbreaking work in physics

We have covered a large number of topics throughout this journey. Admittedly, book-length treatments of almost every topic could be written, and our colleagues undoubtedly will not agree with all of our characterizations and conceptualizations. Our goal was not to provide an in-depth treatment of topics related to theory construction, which is why we provided a section on suggested readings in each chapter. Rather, we sought to expose you to a wide range of concepts that not only give you a sense of the nature of theory construction in all its complexity, but that also provides you with practical, concrete suggestions for how to construct theory as you pursue your career as a research scientist or practitioner. As you relate the ideas to your substantive domain of interest, hopefully you will gain new insights and evolve your own frame for how to think conceptually about the problems and questions that are important to you.

In closing, we want to offer some thoughts about career considerations relative to the pursuit of creative theory construction. Creative research that pursues big ideas can be greeted with resistance and skepticism by scientists entrenched in the dominant scientific paradigms. The work may initially be difficult to publish, and it may take years to build an empirical base in support of the new theory. This is not true of research that accepts standard presuppositions and then builds on scientific knowledge in more modest and traditional ways. If asked, most scientists would not admit to a bias against "crowd-defying" ideas; but the reality is that scientists are trained to think in terms of a common paradigm, and this paradigm dominates their evaluation of other ideas. As such, there inevitably is some bias against crowd-defying ideas. This bias has implications for career development.

Consider the traditional path of a student pursuing doctoral training in the social sciences with the idea of securing an academic career in a research-oriented college or university. Typically, a PhD is obtained after 4 years of advanced study. At this time, doctoral students seek to transition to the role of assistant professor via a position at a college or university. Knowing that universities and colleges must make decisions about which applicants to interview, applicants must set themselves apart from other applicants in terms of the quality and quantity of their scientific publications. A typical position at the assistant professor level will have 75 or more applicants, although this figure varies depending on the discipline. In some universities and subfields, there may be as many as 300 applicants. Initial decisions are generally made by a search committee, which reviews the vitae that applicants submit. Usually the top three or four candidates are invited for in-person interviews. These interviews generally occur within the first few months of the fourth or final year of one's graduate training. This means that research you conduct during your fourth year is less likely to be considered when it comes time to apply for jobs because this research has not been accepted for publication at the time your vitae is considered by the search committee. The time frame for a graduate student to produce publications is, in reality, 3 years, not 4 years (unless one extends graduate training beyond the customary 4-year period).

For a research project to be published, the scientist must develop an idea, collect and analyze data to test or explore the idea, and then write a research report and submit it to a journal for publication. This process takes a minimum of 6 months and usually longer. Once the paper is submitted for publication, it must be peer reviewed (which, depending on the journal, takes 3 months or more), the result of which usually is an editorial decision to "revise and resubmit" before final acceptance (which takes an additional 3 months). Thus, the minimum time lag between when a research idea is formed and when a research report is accepted for publication typically is about 1 year. This time lag means that only research that is started *before* the early part of the third year of graduate study has a chance of being accepted for publication in time to have an impact on your job prospects. The bottom line is that it is the first 2 years of graduate study that are crucial for deciding one's career prospects, and these years need to be research focused. Most students spend their first year of study taking required courses and gaining scientific knowledge and background to better prepare themselves for conducting research. In the typical 4-year program, this leaves the precious second year of graduate study as the one that ultimately has a major impact on one's career.

One way that graduate students adapt to these demands is to become involved in the research programs of their major professor. By working in an already established research program, students can produce joint authored publications with their major professors at a competitive and reasonably rapid pace.

It is against this backdrop that one must face the realities of developing and conducting research related to a crowd-defying idea. Given the possible resistance to such an idea and the time it takes to lay the groundwork and empirical base for such a theory, it is unlikely that a graduate student who pursues this type of research will be competitive on the job market when his or her graduate studies are completed because it is unlikely that this work will be completed in time to be published. Our suggestion is to strike a balance between the idealistic and practical sides of science. By all means, pursue your big ideas. Take the risk and see where it leads you. Science needs this type of creative pursuit. But while you are doing so, also develop a second research program that will lead you to the publications, training, and contacts you need to be competitive in the job market. This will require extra work on your part, but hopefully it will be worth it. We are not suggesting that your "second" research program be something in which you are not interested or something to which you are not committed. Indeed, it often can supplement or be a smaller part of your crowd-defying idea. But in making the choice to pursue a big idea, we suggest that you give practical considerations their due weight; otherwise you may find yourself with no viable prospect for a job in academia. Idealists may not like this advice. It may indeed be possible for you to carve out your own, highly innovative program of research without regard to a second research program of the nature we are describing. However, this will be rare, and it requires an exceptional student, an exceptional major professor (who is willing to support the student), an exceptional graduate program, and an exceptional set of environmental supports.

These same time demands are equally oppressive for new faculty hired as assistant professors. In our opinion, the pressure is even greater because such faculty can no longer rely as much on their major professors, at least in the way they did during graduate school. New professors typically work for 7 years and then are evaluated for tenure. If they are granted tenure, they are given a lifetime contract. If they are not granted tenure, they are fired. If denied tenure, it is difficult to obtain another academic position. So tenure decisions are critically important for new professors. Because institutions want to provide you with a year to find a new job should you be denied tenure, the formal tenure review process typically starts at the beginning of your sixth year of employment, not your seventh year. At this time, you are expected to have established an independent research program, and, depending on your particular discipline and the type and prestige of your host institution, you are expected to have published anywhere from 5 to 35 high-quality publications in your field. Given the time lags associated with publishing described earlier, any research you conduct near the end of your fifth year probably will be too delayed to count toward your tenure decision. This means that you have 4–4½ years to produce. Your first year as an assistant professor usually is consumed by the logistics of moving to a new location, preparing lectures for the courses you will teach, and getting a research program set up (e.g., recruiting graduate and undergraduate students to help, buying equipment). This reduces the time you have to conduct research to gain tenure to years 2–4. To make matters worse, the faculty who ultimately evaluate you for tenure start to form impressions of how productive you are from the beginning of your employment, so if you produce nothing in your first year or two, this often leads to a negative impression. It is against this backdrop that you must decide to pursue a crowd-defying idea, with its attendant time delays and risks.

Our advice to young scientists in these circumstances is the same as what we gave the graduate student. Pursue your big ideas, but also develop a second research program that respects the practical constraints in which you are operating. If you do not, you may end up being fired with no prospect of pursuing the big ideas you treasure.

These scenarios vary from one discipline to the next, but the bottom line is the same. You need to be both an idealist and a realist. If you pursue only the idealistic side of science (the side that we love and that emphasizes advancing knowledge in creative and fulfilling ways), your career may come to a screeching, unexpected halt, and you may find yourself unable to do what you love. If you pursue the practical side only, you may find yourself poorly equipped to pursue an independent research program that makes sufficient contributions to science. Indeed, you may not receive tenure because your research is considered pedestrian. Find a balance between idealism and realism, but never let go of your idealism. Pursue it with a vengeance when opportunities present themselves.

A PROGRAM OF SELF-STUDY

Throughout this book we have made reference to a "theoretical toolbox" and identified areas wherein it would be useful for you to pursue further reading over and above your substantive domains of interest. The areas are diverse, and it is rare to find a graduate program that emphasizes all of them. A summary list of these areas follows. It is not that areas omitted from this list are unimportant. Rather, we believe that the list serves as a starting point. In these days of electronic search and access to articles and books, it is much easier to set aside regular time to update oneself in these areas, even if one must do so fleetingly.

We suggest five strategies to stay current on these topics. First, once or twice a year, conduct an electronic search through reference databases in libraries and examine all abstracts of articles and books in a given topic area. Flag a subset to obtain and read. By reading the abstracts and titles, you will gain a sense of "what is out there," even though you may not choose to read every article. Read review articles and/or articles/books that you judge will most impact your substantive work. Our electronic searches include not only major electronic library-based databases (such as Medline, PsychInfo, Sociological Abstracts, and Social Work Abstracts), but also major sellers of books (e.g., *amazon.com*). For the latter, when you select a book to examine, many sellers display related books and books that others who purchased that book also purchased. This can facilitate the process of identifying potentially relevant books.

Second, identify a small group of scientists whose work you have come to admire and whom you judge to be particularly creative and insightful. Every year, conduct an electronic search to examine the abstracts of all articles they published that year. Obtain and read a subset of these articles, focusing on those that seem interesting or useful. A variant of this strategy is the identification of web pages of certain individuals or professional organizations (e.g., the American Academy of Pediatrics) to regularly consult for information and leads about further study and relevant literatures.

Third, identify certain journals that consistently publish important articles in a given target area. Make a point of scanning the abstracts of every article published in those journals in a given year, again with the idea of then identifying a subset of articles to obtain and read.

Fourth, use several search engines (e.g., Google, Yahoo!) to conduct electronic searches of the areas of study. This strategy taps into web pages that people have created to address different topics and can lead to a wealth of information about a topic area that is not in the formal scientific literature. To be sure, there is a great deal of misinformation on the web, and one must be careful in this regard. But there also is a tremendous amount of useful information to be found.

Fifth, talk to colleagues about their work and attend colloquia sponsored in your department and other departments as much as possible, especially when the topics are included in the list that follows. Many researchers also find it useful to attend professional conferences and their workshops.

In no particular order of importance, here we list a suggested program of self-study (that we personally use) of areas of which you might keep updated on over and above your substantive domains of interest:

1. *Creativity.* Read current literatures on creativity that may give you new thinking strategies.

2. *Psychometrics.* Read literatures in psychometrics that help you define and think about constructs in general as well as in your substantive areas of study.

3. *Philosophy of science.* Read the classics in philosophy of science as well as more current-day perspectives on science from the point of view of philosophers.

4. *Causality and causal modeling.* Read literature on statistical, methodological, conceptual, and philosophical issues on causality in general as well as moderation, mediation, spuriousness, reciprocal causality, longitudinal modeling, and latent variables in particular.

5. *Simulation methods.* Read about simulation methodology, especially as it applies to emerging technologies.

6. *Mathematical modeling.* In addition to mathematical modeling in general, read literatures on chaos theory and catastrophe theory.

7. *Grounded/emergent theory construction.* Read literature on strategies for constructing grounded theories and qualitative data analysis.

8. *Rhetoric and communication theory.* Read literature on methods of argumentation, logic, and theories and methods of debate.

9. *Cognitive biases and limitations of information processing.* This literature tends to appear mostly in cognitive psychology, social psychology, consumer behavior, and decision making. It will help keep you attuned to biases that can enter into your thinking.

10. *Historical methodology.* For research involving analysis of primary sources and archival materials, staying abreast of good historical methodological practices is important.

11. *General systems of thought.* Touch base with the literatures on all of the topics discussed in Chapter 12. These include neural networks, stage theories, reinforcement theories, humanism and positive psychology, symbolic interactionism, systems theory, materialism, structuralism, functionalism, postmodernism, and evolutionary perspectives.

12. *Statistics.* Stay on top of recent developments in probability theory, exploratory statistical methods, structural equation modeling, nonlinear modeling, multi-level modeling, and longitudinal methods.

13. *Measurement theory.* As discussed in Chapter 13, there is a connection between concepts on the one hand and the measurement of those constructs on the other hand that can facilitate theory construction and rigorous scientific thinking more generally. We find it useful to keep updated on measurement theory and to bring innovations in it to bear as we think about substantive phenomena.

14. *Scientific and nonscientific writing techniques and presentation strategies.* Strive to find more effective ways of presenting your theories.

In addition to staying abreast of these literatures, we also make it a point to stay current on our substantive areas of interest and, as time permits, to read biographies and auto-biographies and other works of fiction and nonfiction that may expand our thinking.

CONCLUDING COMMENTS

As you pursue your career and strive to develop theories, we want to underscore the importance of being resilient. You will face criticism and negative feedback. All of us do. The key is not to let this feedback grind your efforts to a halt or get you too discouraged. Listen to it, work with it, decide what is worthwhile, and keep a forward focus. The classic characterization of reaction to reviewer and editorial feedback by the famous psychologist Benton Underwoood (1957, p. 222) is as much applicable today as it was over 60 years ago:

> The rejection of my own manuscripts has a sordid aftermath: (a) One day of depression; (b) one day of utter contempt for the editor and his accomplices; (c) one day of decrying the conspiracy against letting truth be published; (d) one day of fretful ideas about changing my profession; (e) one day of re-evaluating the manuscript in view of the editor's comments followed by the conclusion that I was lucky it wasn't accepted.

Despite the ups and downs you ultimately will experience, if you stay with it and be resilient, and if you approach your science with curiosity, an open mind, and a diverse theoretical toolbox from which to work, positive contributions probably are in your future.

References

Aassve, A., Goisis, A., & Sironi, M. (2012). Happiness and childbearing across Europe. *Social Indicator Research, 108,* 65–86.

Abbott, A., & Alexander, J. C. (2004). *Methods of discovery: Heuristics for the social sciences.* New York: Norton.

Abdi, H., Valentin, D., & Edelman, B. (1999). *Neural networks.* Thousand Oaks, CA: SAGE.

Abraham, C., & Michie, S. (2008). A taxonomy of behavior change techniques used in interventions. *Health Psychology, 27,* 379–387.

Acevedo, B. (2007). Creating the cannabis user: A post-structuralist analysis of the reclassification of cannabis in the United Kingdom (2004–2005). *International Journal of Drug Policy, 18,* 177–186.

Achinstein, P. (1983). *The nature of explanation.* New York: Oxford University Press.

Ackoff, R. L. (1991). *Ackoff's fables.* New York: Wiley.

Adams, W. K., Perkins, K. K., Podolefsky, N. S., Dubson, M., Finkelstein, N. D., & Wieman, C. E. (2006). New instrument for measuring student beliefs about physics and learning physics: The Colorado Learning Attitudes about Science Survey. *Physical Review Special Topics—Physics Education Research, 2*(1).

Agency for Healthcare Research and Quality. (2015). Be cautious about using readability formulas. Retrieved from *www.ahrq.gov/professionals/quality-patient-safety/talkingquality/resources/writing/tip6.html.*

Ajzen, I., & Fishbein, M. (1980). *Understanding attitudes and predicting social behavior.* Englewood Cliffs, NJ: Prentice-Hall.

Alford, R. (1998). *The craft of inquiry: Theories, methods, evidence.* New York: Oxford University Press.

Alley, M. (2003). *The craft of scientific presentations.* New York: Springer.

Alwin, D. F., & Beattie, B. A. (2016). The KISS principle in survey design: Question length and data quality. *Sociological Methodology, 46,* 121–152.

Amabile, T. M. (1983). *The social psychology of creativity.* New York: Springer-Verlag.

Andersen, H., & Mayer, J. (2017). Desirability and undesirability effects on survey response latencies. *Bulletin of Sociological Methodology, 135,* 68–89.

Anderson, C., Bahník, S., Barnett-Cowan, M., Bosco, F. A., Chandler, J., Chartier, C. R., et al. (2016). Response to comment on "Estimating the reproducibility of psychological science." *Science, 351,* 1037.

Anderson, N. H. (1965). Primacy effects in personality impression formation using a generalized order effect paradigm. *Journal of Personality and Social Psychology, 2,* 1–9.

Anderson, N. H. (1991). *Contributions to information integration.* Hillsdale, NJ: Erlbaum.

Anderson, N. H., & Hubert, S. (1963). Effects of concomitant verbal recall on order effects in personality impression formation. *Journal of Verbal Learning and Verbal Behavior, 2,* 379–391.

Annemarie, N. E., Winckers, J., Mackenbach, J. D., Compernolle, S., Nicolaou, M., van der Ploeg, H. P., et al. (2015). Educational differences in the validity of self-reported physical activity. *BMC Public Health, 15,* 1299–1307.

Ardila, A., Bertolucci, P., Braga, L. W., Castro-Caldas, A., Judd, T., Kosmidis, M. H., et al. (2010). Illiteracy: The neuropsychology of cognition without reading. *Archives of Clinical Neuropsychology, 25,* 689–712.

Arnett, J. (2008). The neglected 95%: Why American psychology needs to become less American. *American Psychologist 63,* 602–614.

Arnheim, R. (2004). *Visual thinking.* Berkeley: University of California Press.

Azen, R., & Budescu, D. (2003). The dominance analysis approach for comparing predictors in multiple regression. *Psychological Methods, 8,* 129–148.

Azen, R., & Budescu, D. (2006). Comparing predictors in multivariate regression models: An extension of dominance analysis. *Journal of Educational and Behavioral Statistics, 31,* 157–180.

Babbie, E. R. (1973). *Survey research methods.* Belmont, CA: Wadsworth.

Bacon, S. (2005). Positive psychology's two cultures. *Review of General Psychology, 9,* 181–192.

Baker, D. W., Parker, R. M., Williams, M. V., Clark, W. S., & Nurss, J. (1997). The relationship of patient reading ability to self-reported health and use of health services. *American Journal of Public Health, 87,* 1027–1030.

Barber, N. (2008). Evolutionary social science: A new approach to violent crime. *Aggression and Violent Behavior, 13,* 237–250.

Barnes, L., Mendes de Leon, C. F., Lewis, T., Bienias, J. L., Wilson, R. S., & Evans, D. (2008). Perceived discrimination and mortality in a population-based study of older adults. *American Journal of Public Health, 98,* 1241–1247.

Barron, F., & Harrington, D. (1981). Creativity, intelligence, and personality. *Annual Review of Psychology, 32,* 439–476.

Barry, A. (1997). *Visual intelligence: Perception, image, and manipulation in visual communication.* Albany: State University of New York Press.

Bassili, J. N., & Brown, R. (2005). Implicit and explicit attitudes: Research, challenges, and theory. In D. Albarracin, B. Johnson, & M. Zanna (Eds.), *The handbook of attitudes* (pp. 543–574). Mahwah, NJ: Erlbaum.

Baumgartner, H., & Steenkamp, J. B. E. M. (2001). Response styles in marketing research: A cross-national investigation. *Journal of Marketing Research, 38,* 143–156.

Beatty, P., & Willis, G. (2007). Research synthesis: The practice of cognitive interviewing. *Public Opinion Quarterly, 71,* 287–311.

Becker, H. (2003). *Tricks of the trade: How to think about your research while you're doing it.* Chicago: University of Chicago Press.

Beckstead, J. (2014). On measurements and their quality: Paper 4. Verbal anchors and the number of response options in rating scales. *International Journal of Nursing Studies, 51,* 807–814.

Bednar, J., & Miikkulainen, R. (2003). Learning innate face preferences. *Neural Computation, 15,* 1525–1557.

Bem, D. J. (1970). *Beliefs, attitudes, and human affairs.* Belmont, CA: Brooks/Cole.

Bendig, A. W. (1953). The reliability of self-ratings as a function of the amount of verbal anchoring and the number of categories on the scale. *Journal of Applied Psychology, 37,* 38–41.

Bereczki, T. (2000). Evolutionary psychology: A new perspective in the behavioral sciences. *European Psychologist, 5,* 175–190.

Bergh, D. (2003). From the editors: Thinking strategically about contribution. *Academy of Management Journal, 46,* 135–136.

Bernard, H. R. (2017). *Research methods in anthropology: Qualitative and quantitative approaches.* Lanham, MD: Rowman & Littlefield.

Bernard, T., Paoline, E., & Pare, P. (2005). General systems theory and criminal justice. *Journal of Criminal Justice, 33,* 203–211.

Blair, E., & Burton, S. (1987). Cognitive processes used by survey respondents to answer behavioral frequency questions. *Journal of Consumer Research, 14,* 280–288.

Blalock, H. M. (1964). *Causal inferences in non-experimental research.* Chapel Hill: University of North Carolina Press.

Blanton, H., & Jaccard, J. (2006). Arbitrary metrics in psychology. *American Psychologist, 61,* 27–41.

Blanton, H., & Jaccard, J. (2008). Unconscious prejudice: A concept in pursuit of a measure. *Annual Review of Sociology, 34,* 277–297.

Blumer, H. (1969). *Symbolic interactionism: Perspective and method.* Berkeley: University of California Press.

Boas, F. (1897). *The social organizations and secret societies of the Kwakiutl indians* [Report to the U.S. National Museum].

Bodenhausen, G., & Lambert, A. (Eds.). (2003). *Foundations of social cognition: A Festschrift in honor of Robert S. Wyer, Jr.* Hillsdale, NJ: Erlbaum.

Bohrnstedt, G. W. (1970). Reliability and validity assessment in attitude measurement. In G. F. Summers (Ed.), *Attitude measurement* (pp. 80–99). Chicago: Rand McNally.

Bollen, K. A., & Barb, K. (1981). Pearson's r and coarsely categorized measures. *American Sociological Review, 46,* 232–239.

Bolton, R., & Bronkhorst, T. (1996). Questionnaire pretesting: Computer-assisted coding of concurrent protocols. In N. Schwarz & S. Sudman (Eds.), *Answering questions: Methodology for determining cognitive and communicative processes in survey research* (pp. 37–64). San Francisco: Jossey-Bass.

Bonner, S. E., Hastie, R., Sprinkle, G. B., & Young, M. (2000). A review of the effects of financial incentives on performance in laboratory tasks: Implications for management accounting. *Journal of Management Accounting Research, 12,* 19–64.

Borenstein, M., Hedges, L., Higgins, J., & Rothstein, H. (2009). *Introduction to meta-analysis.* New York: Wiley.

Borgers, N., de Leeuw, E., & Hox, J. (2000). Children as respondents in survey research: Cognitive development and response quality. *Bulletin of Sociological Methodology, 66,* 60–75.

Borsboom, D. (2005). *Measuring the mind: Conceptual issues in contemporary psychometrics.* Cambridge, UK: Cambridge University Press.

Bradburn, N. M., Rips, L., & Shevell, S. K. (1987). Answering autobiographical questions: The impact of memory and inference on surveys. *Science, 236,* 157–161.

Brennan, R. L. (2001). *Generalizability theory.* New York: Springer-Verlag.

Brick, T. R., Koffer, R., Gerstorf, D., & Ram, N. (2018). Feature selection methods for optimal design of studies for developmental inquiry. *Journals of Gerontology, Series B: Psychological Sciences and Social Sciences, 73,* 113–123.

Brinberg, D., & Hirschman, E. (1986). Multiple orientations for the conduct of marketing research: An analysis of the academic/practitioner distinction. *Journal of Marketing, 50,* 161–173.

Brinberg, D., Lynch, J., & Sawyer, A. (1992). Hypothesized and confounded explanations in theory tests: A Bayesian analysis. *Journal of Consumer Research, 19,* 139–154.

Brinberg, D., & McGrath, J. (1985). *Validity and the research process.* Newbury Park, CA: SAGE.

Bring, J. (1994). How to standardize regression coefficients. *The American Statistician, 48,* 209–213.

Brodbeck, M. (1968). *Readings in the philosophy of the social sciences.* New York: Macmillan.

Brown, P. O., & Botstein, D. (1999). Exploring the new world of the genome with DNA microarrays. *Nature Genetics, 21,* 33–37.

Buckler, F., & Hennig-Thurau, T. (2008). Identifying hidden structures in marketing's structural models through universal structure modeling: An explorative neural network complement to LISREL and PLS. *Marketing Journal of Research and Management, 2,* 49–68.

Bunge, M. (1961). Causality, chance, and law. *American Scientist, 69,* 432–488.

Buss, D., Haselton, M., Shackelford, T., Bleske, A., & Wakefield, J. (1998). Adaptations, exaptations, and spandrels. *American Psychologist, 53,* 533–548.

Busse, C., Kach, A., & Wagner, S. (2017). Boundary conditions: What they are, how to explore them, why we need them, and when to consider them. *Organizational Research Methods, 20,* 574–609.

Cacioppo, J. T. (2004). Common sense, intuition, and theory in personality and social psychology. *Personality and Social Psychology Review, 8,* 114–122.

Cai, A., Tsay, R., & Chen, R. (2009) Variable selection in linear regression with many predictors. *Journal of Computational and Graphical Statistics, 18,* 573–591.

Camerer, C. F., Dreber, A., Holzmeister, F., Ho, T., Huber, J., Johanneson, M., et al. (2018). Evaluating the replicability of social science experiments in *Nature* and *Science* between 2010 and 2015. *Nature: Human Behavior, 2,* 637–644.

Carlin, J. (1962). *Lawyers on their own.* New Brunswick, NJ: Rutgers University Press.

Carnap, R. (1936). Testability and meaning. *Philosophy of Science, 3,* 419–471.

Carnap, R. (1937). Testability and meaning. *Philosophy of Science, 4,* 1–40.

Carnap, R. (1971). A basic system of inductive logic: Part 1. In R. Carnap & R. C. Jeffrey (Eds.), *Studies in inductive logic and probability* (Vol. 1, pp. 18–39). Berkeley: University of California Press.

Cartwright, N. (2007). *Hunting causes and using them.* New York: Cambridge University Press.

Catalano, R., Berglund, L., Ryan, J., Lonczak, H. S., & Hawkins, J. D. (2002). Positive youth development in the United States: Research findings on evaluations of positive youth development programs. *Prevention and Treatment, 5*(1), Article 15.

Cederman, L. (2005). Computational models of social forms: Advancing generative process theory. *American Journal of Sociology, 110,* 864–893.

Centers for Disease Control and Prevention. (2018). HIV by group. Retrieved March 2018, from *www.cdc.gov/hiv/group/index.html.*

Chaplin, J. P., & Krawiec, T. S. (1960). *Systems and theories of psychology.* New York: Holt, Rinehart & Winston.

Charmaz, K. (2006). *Constructing grounded theory: A practical guide through qualitative analysis.* Newbury Park, CA: SAGE.

Chestnut, R. W., & Jacoby, J. (1980). Product comprehension: The case of permanent versus term life insurance. *Advances in Consumer Research, 7,* 424–428.

Chetty, S., Steppner, M., Abraham, S., Lin, S., Scuderi, B., Turner, N., et al. (2016). The association between income and life expectancy in the United States, 2001–2014. *Journal of the American Medical Association, 315,* 1750–1766.

Chia, R., & Tsoukas, H. (2002). On organizational becoming: Rethinking organizational change. *Organization Science, 13,* 567–582.

Chomsky, N. (1965). *Aspects of the theory of syntax.* Cambridge, MA: MIT Press.

Chomsky, N. (1972). *Language and mind.* New York: Harcourt Brace Jovanovich.

Chudik, A., Kapetanios, G., & Pesaran, H. (2018). A one covariate at a time, multiple testing approach to variable selection in high-dimensional linear regression models. *Econometrica, 84,* 1479–1512.

Cialdini, R. (2001). *Influence: Science and practice.* Boston: Allyn & Bacon.

Cialdini, R. (2003). Crafting normative messages to protect the environment. *Current Directions in Psychological Science, 12,* 105–109.

Clatworthy, J., Buick, D., Hankins, M., Weinman, J., & Horne, R. (2005). The use and reporting of cluster analysis in health psychology: A review. *British Journal of Health Psychology, 10,* 329–358.

Clement, J. (1988). Observed methods for generating analogies in scientific problem solving. *Cognitive Science, 12,* 563–586.

Clement, J. (2006). Thought experiments and imagery in expert protocols. In L. Magnani (Ed.), *Model-based reasoning in science and engineering* (pp. 1–16). London: King's College.

Clement, J. (2008). *Creative model construction*

in scientists and students: The role of imagery, analogy, and mental simulation. Mahwah, NJ: Erlbaum.

Cliff, N. (1959). Adverbs as multipliers. *Psychological Review, 66,* 27–44.

Cohen, B. (1956). *Franklin and Newton: An inquiry into speculative Newtonian experimental science and Franklin's work in electricity as an example thereof.* Philadelphia: American Philosophical Society.

Cole, J. W., & Wolf, E. (1974). *The hidden frontier: Ecology and ethnicity in an Alpine valley.* Berkeley: University of California Press.

Coleman, J. (1994). *Foundations of social theory.* Boston: Harvard University Press.

Collins, C., & Stockton, C. (2018). The central role of theory in qualitative research. *International Journal of Qualitative Methods, 17,* 1–10.

Conlon, E. (2002). Editor's comments. *Academy of Management Review, 27*(4), 489–492.

Connolly, M. (1990). Adrift in the city: A comparative study of street children in Bogotá, Colombia and Guatemala City. In N. A. Boxill (Ed.), *Homeless children: The watchers and the waiters* (pp. 129–149). New York: Haworth Press.

Cook, S. D. N., & Brown, J. S. (1999). Bridging epistemologies: The generative dance between organizational knowledge and organizational knowing. *Organization Science, 10,* 381–400.

Coombs, C., Dawes, R., & Tversky, A. (1970). *Mathematical psychology: An elementary introduction.* Englewood Cliffs, NJ: Prentice-Hall.

Cooper, R., & Law, J. (1995). Organization: Distal and proximal views. *Research in the Sociology of Organizations, 13,* 237–274.

Copi, I. M., & Cohen, C. (2005). *Introduction to logic.* New York: Prentice-Hall.

Corley, K. G., & Gioia, D. (2011). Building theory about theory building: What constitutes a theoretical contribution? *Academy of Management Review, 36,* 12–32.

Cornelissen, J. (2004). What are we playing at?: Theatre, organization, and the use of metaphor. *Organization Studies, 25,* 705–726.

Cortina, J. M. (1993). What is coefficient alpha?: An examination of theory and applications. *Journal of Applied Psychology, 78,* 98–104.

Cosentino, M. (2007). *Case in point: Complete case interview preparation.* Needham, MA: Burgee Press.

Council of Science Editors. (2012). *White paper on promoting integrity in scientific journal publications.* Retrieved from *http://www.council-*

scienceeditors.org/wp-content/uploads/entire_whitepaper.pdf.

Creswell, J., & Plano Clark, V. (2017). *Designing and conducting mixed methods research*. Thousand Oaks, CA: SAGE.

Cronbach, L. J., Gleser, G. C., Nanda, H., & Rajaratnam, N. (1972). *The dependability of behavioral measurements*. New York: Wiley.

Cronbach, L. J., & Meehl, P. E. (1955). Construct validity in psychological tests. *Psychological Bulletin, 52*, 281–302.

Cronbach, L. J., Nageswari, R., & Gleser, G. C. (1963). Theory of generalizability: A liberation of reliability theory. *British Journal of Statistical Psychology, 16*, 137–163.

Cunningham, J., & Macan, T. (2007). Effects of applicant pregnancy on hiring decisions and interview ratings. *Sex Roles, 57*, 497–508.

Cylwik, H. (2001). Notes from the field: Emotions of place in the production and interpretation of text. *International Journal of Social Research Methodology, 4*, 243–250.

Darlington, R. (1968). Multiple regression in psychological research and practice. *Psychological Bulletin, 69*, 161–182.

Darr, W., & Johns, G. (2008). Work strain, health, and absenteeism: A meta-analysis. *Journal of Occupational Health Psychology, 13*, 293–318.

Davis, J., Bingham, C., & Eisenhardt, K. (2007). Developing theory through simulation methods. *Academy of Management Review, 32*, 480–499.

Davis, J., Eisenhardt, K., & Bingham, C. (2005). *Complexity theory, market dynamism, and the strategy of simple rules*. Unpublished manuscript, Stanford Technology Ventures Program, Palo Alto, CA.

Davis, M. S. (1971). That's interesting! *Philosophy of Social Science, 1*, 308–344.

Davis, T. C., Long, S. W., Jackson, R. H., Mayeaux, E. J., George, R. B., Murphy, P. W., et al. (1993). Rapid estimate of adult literacy in medicine: A shortened screening instrument. *Family Medicine, 25*, 391–395.

Davison, M., & Sharma, A. (1988). Parametric statistics and levels of measurement. *Psychological Bulletin, 104*, 137–144.

Davison, M., & Sharma, A. (1990). Parametric statistics and levels of measurement: Factorial designs and multiple regression. *Psychological Bulletin, 107*, 394–400.

Dawkins, R. (1976). *The selfish gene*. Oxford, UK: Oxford University Press.

Dawson, R. E. (1963). Simulation in the social sciences. In H. Guetzkow (Ed.), *Simulation in social sciences* (pp. 221–252). Englewood Cliffs, NJ: Prentice-Hall.

De Cock, C., & Sharp, R. (2007). Process theory and research: Exploring the dialectic tension. *Scandinavian Journal of Management, 23*, 233–250.

De Los Reyes, A., Augenstein, T., Wang, M., Thomas, S., & Drabick, D. (2015). The validity of the multi-informant approach to assessing child and adolescent mental health *Psychological Bulletin, 141*, 858–900.

de Williams, A. C., Davies, H. T., & Chadury, Y. (2000). Simple pain rating scales hide complex idiosyncratic meanings. *Pain, 85*, 457–463.

DeMaio, T. J., & Rothgeb, J. M. (1996). Cognitive interviewing techniques: In the lab and in the field. In N. Schwarz & S. Sudman (Eds.), *Answering questions: Methodology for determining cognitive and communicative processes in survey research* (pp. 155–176). San Francisco: Jossey-Bass.

Desarbo, W. S., Jedidi, K., & Sinha, I. (2001). Customer value analysis in a heterogeneous market. *Strategic Management Journal, 22*, 845–857.

Detroit Regional Workforce Fund. (2011). *Addressing Detroit's basic skills crisis*. Retrieved from *https://skilledwork.org/wp-content/uploads/2014/01/BasicSkillsReport.pdf*.

Deutsch, M., & Krauss, R. (1960). The effect of threat upon interpersonal bargaining. *Journal of Abnormal and Social Psychology, 61*, 181–189.

Dick, R. (1990). *Convergent interviewing*. Brisbane, Australia: Interchange.

Dienes, Z. (2011). Bayesian versus orthodox statistics: Which side are you on? *Perspectives on Psychological Science, 6*, 274–290.

Ding, C. (2006). Using regression mixture analysis in educational research, *Practical Assessment Research and Evaluation, 11*, 1–11.

Dittus, P., & Jaccard, J. (2000). The relationship of adolescent perceptions of maternal disapproval of sex and of the mother–adolescent relationship to sexual outcomes. *Journal of Adolescent Health, 26*, 268–278.

Dixon, J., & Moore, C. (2000). The logic of interpreting evidence of developmental ordering: Strong inference and categorical measures. *Developmental Psychology, 36*, 826–834.

Dollard, J., & Miller, N. E. (1950). *Personality and psychotherapy*. New York: McGraw-Hill.

Dorigo, M., & Stützle, T. (2004). *Ant colony optimization*. Cambridge, MA: MIT Press.

Driessen, E., & Hollon, S. D. (2010). Cognitive behavioral therapy for mood disorders: Efficacy, moderators and mediators. *Psychiatric Clinics of North America, 33,* 537–555.

Dubin, R. (1976). Theory building in applied areas. In M. D. Dunnette (Ed.), *Handbook of industrial and organizational psychology* (pp. 17–39). Chicago: Rand McNally.

Duck, S. W. (1982). A topography of relationship disengagement and dissolution. In S. Duck (Ed.), *Personal relationships 4: Dissolving personal relationships* (pp. 112–139). London: Academic Press.

Durand, M. (2002). *Severe behavior problems: A functional communication training approach.* New York: Guilford Press.

Earp, B., & Trafimow, D. (2015). Replication, falsification, and the crisis of confidence in social psychology. *Frontiers in Psychology, 6,* 621. Retrieved from *www.frontiersin.org/articles/10.3389/fpsyg.2015.00621/full.*

Easterbrook, G. (1999). Our warming world. *New Republic, 221,* 42.

Edin, K., & Kefalas, M. (2005). *Promises I can keep: Why poor women put motherhood before marriage.* Berkeley: University of California Press.

Edwards, R. (1979). *Contested terrain.* New York: Basic Books.

Einstein, A. (1934). *Essays in science.* New York: Philosophical Library.

Einstein, A. (1956). Autobiographische skizze. In C. Seelig (Ed.), *Helle zeit—dunkle zeit* (pp. 9–17). Zurich, Switzerland: Europa Verlag.

Eisenhardt, K. E. (1989). Building theories from case study research. *Academy of Management Review, 14,* 532–550.

Ellet, W. (2007). *The case study handbook: How to read, discuss, and write persuasively about cases.* Boston: Harvard Business School Press.

El-Shamy, S. (2005). *Role play made easy: 25 structured rehearsals for managing problem situations and dealing with difficult people.* New York: Pfeiffer.

Enzensberger, H. M. (1974). A critique of political ecology. *New Left Review, 84,* 3–32.

Epstein, C. F. (1983). *Women in law.* Garden City, NY: Doubleday.

Everitt, B., Landau, S., Leese, M., & Stahl, D. (2011). *Cluster analysis.* New York: Wiley.

Farmer, J., & Geanakoplos, J. (2002). *Beyond equilibrium and efficiency.* New York: Oxford University Press.

Farrell, M. P. (2001). Collaborative circles: Friendship dynamics and creative work laboratories to collaboratories: A new organizational form for scientific collaboration. *European Journal of Social Psychology, 31,* 707–729.

Fazio, R. H. (1995). Attitudes as object-evaluation associations: Determinants, consequences, and correlates of attitude accessibility. In R. Petty & J. Krosnick (Eds.), *Attitude strength: Antecedents and consequences.* Mahwah, NJ: Erlbaum.

Feldman, J., Gruskin, S., Coull, B., & Krieger, N. (2017). Quantifying underreporting of law-enforcement-related deaths in United States vital statistics and news-media-based data sources: A capture–recapture analysis. *PLOS Medicine, 14,* e1002449.

Fish, J., & Russell, S. (2018). Have mischievous responders misidentified sexual minority youth disparities in the National Longitudinal Study of Adolescent to Adult Health? *Archives of Sexual Behavior, 47,* 1053–1067.

Fishbein, M., & Ajzen, I. (1975). *Beliefs, attitudes, intentions and behavior.* Reading, MA: Addison-Wesley.

Fishbein, M., & Ajzen, I. (2010). *Predicting and changing behavior: The reasoned action approach.* New York: Psychology Press.

Fishbein, M., Triandis, H., Kanfer, F., Becker, M., Middlestadt, S., & Eichler, A. (2001). Factors influencing behavior change. In A. Baum, T. Revenson, & J. Singer (Eds.), *Handbook of health psychology.* Mahwah, NJ: Erlbaum.

Fisher, G., & Aguines, H. (2017). Using theory elaboration to make theoretical advancements. *Organizational Research Methods, 20,* 438–464.

Foddy, W. (1998). An empirical evaluation of in-depth probes used to pretest survey questions. *Sociological Methods and Research, 27,* 103–133.

Fogel, R. (1964). *Railroads and American economic growth.* Baltimore: Johns Hopkins University Press.

Folger, R., & Turillo, C. J. (1999). Theorizing as the thickness of thin abstraction. *Academy of Management Review, 24,* 742–758.

Frank, P. (1961). *Modern science and its philosophy.* New York: Collier Books.

Freeman, B. (1993). *Substance abuse treatment: A family systems perspective.* Thousand Oaks, CA: SAGE.

Freeman, L. (2006). *The development of social network analysis.* Vancouver, BC, Canada: Empirical Press.

Friedman, M. (1996). *Type A behavior: Its diagnosis and treatment.* New York: Plenum Press.

Friedman, M., & Rosenman, R. H. (1974). *Type A behavior and your heart.* New York: Plenum Press.

Fromkin, H. L., & Streufert, S. (1976). Laboratory experimentation. In M. Dunnette (Ed.), *Handbook of industrial and organizational psychology* (pp. 415–466). Chicago: Rand McNally.

Furr, M. (2017). *Psychometrics: An introduction.* Thousand Oaks, CA: SAGE.

Fussell, P. (1983). *Class: A guide through the American status system.* New York: Touchstone.

Gaiha, G. D., Rossin, E. J., Urbach, J., Landeros, C., Collins, D. R., Nwonu, C., et al. (2019). Structural topology defines protective CD8(+) T cell epitopes in the HIV proteome. *Science, 364,* 480–484.

Galesic, M., & Yan, T. (2011). Use of eye tracking for studying survey response processes. In M. Das, P. Ester, & L. Kaczmirek (Eds.), *Social and behavioral research and the internet: Advances in applied methods and research strategies.* London: Routledge Taylor & Francis.

Garcia-Escudero, L. A., Gordaliza, A., Matran, C., & Mayo-Iscar, A. (2010). A review of robust clustering methods. *Advances in Data Analysis and Classification, 4,* 89–109.

Geake, J., & Gross, M. (2008). Teachers' negative affect toward academically gifted students: An evolutionary psychological study. *Gifted Child Quarterly, 52,* 217–231.

Gergen, K. J. (1985). The social constructionist movement in modern psychology. *American Psychologist, 40,* 266–275.

Gergen, K. J. (2001). Psychological science in a postmodern context. *American Psychologist, 56,* 803–813.

Gergen, M., & Gergen, K. (2003). *Social construction: A reader.* London: SAGE.

Gilbert, D., King, G., Pettigrew, S., & Wilson, T. (2016a). Comment on "Estimating the reproducibility of psychological science." *Science, 351,* 1037–1038.

Gilbert, D., King, G., Pettigrew, S., & Wilson, T. (2016b). A response to the reply to our technical comment on "Estimating the reproducibility of psychological science." Retrieved from *https://gking.harvard.edu/files/gking/files/gkpw_response_to_osc_rebutal.pdf.*

Gilbert, N., & Abbott, A. (2005). Introduction. *American Journal of Sociology, 110,* 859–863.

Glaser, B. (1978). *Theoretical sensitivity: Advances in the methodology of grounded theory.* New York: Sociology Press.

Glaser, B. (1992). *Basics of grounded theory analysis.* Mill Valley, CA: Sociology Press.

Glaser, B., & Strauss, A. (1965). *Awareness of dying.* Chicago: Aldine.

Glaser, B. G., & Strauss, A. L. (1967). *The discovery of grounded theory: Strategies for qualitative research.* Chicago: Aldine.

Goffman, E. (1959). *The presentation of self in everyday life.* New York: Anchor Books.

Goffman, E. (1967). *Interaction ritual: Essays on face-to-face behavior.* New York: Doubleday.

Goldin, L. R. (1987). The "peace of the market" in the midst of violence: A symbolic analysis of markets and exchange in Western Guatemala. *Ethnos, 3,* 368–383.

Goldin, L. R. (2009). *Global Maya: Work and ideology in rural Guatemala.* Tucson: University of Arizona Press.

Goldin, L., Copeland, R., & Padilla-Medina, D. (2015). *Behind Maya doors: Gender violence, acceptance, and resistance in Highland Guatemala.* East Lansing: Gender, Development and Globalization Program, Center for Gender in Global Context, Michigan State University.

Goldin, L., & Jaccard, J. (2019). Transitory and dispositional facets of ethnic identity in Latino adolescents: A mixed method analysis. *Journal of the Society for Social Work Research.* Manuscript submitted for publication.

Golding, P., & Murdock, G. (1978). Theories of communication and theories of society. *Communication Research, 5,* 339–356.

Goleman, D. (1995). *Emotional intelligence.* New York: Bantam Books.

Gooding, D. (1992). The procedural turn: Or, why do thought experiments work? In R. Giere (Ed.), *Cognitive models of science* (pp. 45–76). Minneapolis: University of Minnesota Press.

Gottman, J. M. (1994). *What predicts divorce?* Hillsdale, NJ: Erlbaum.

Graesser, A. C., Cai, Z., Louwerse, M. M., & Daniel, F. (2006). Question understanding aid (QUAID): A web facility that tests question comprehensibility. *Public Opinion Quarterly, 70,* 3–22.

Green, E. (2018). What are the most-cited publications in the social sciences (according to Google Scholar)? Retrieved from *https://blogs.lse.ac.uk/impactofsocialsciences/2016/05/12/what-are-the-most-cited-publications-in-the-social-sciences-according-to-google-scholar.*

Green, P., & Tull, D. S. (1975). *Research for*

marketing decisions. Englewood Cliffs, NJ: Prentice-Hall.

Green, S. B., Akey, T., Fleming, K., Hershberger, S. L., & Marquis, J. (1997). Effect of the number of scale points on chi square fit indices in confirmatory factor analysis. *Structural Equation Modeling, 4*, 108–120.

Greenberg, J. (1987). A taxonomy of organizational justice theories. *Academy of Management Review, 12*, 9–22.

Gregory, R. (1997). *Eye and brain*. Princeton, NJ: Princeton University Press.

Grömping, U. (2015). Variable importance in regression models. *WIREs Computational Statistics, 7*, 137–152.

Grömping, U. (2016). Variable importance in regression models, Corrigenda. *WIREs Computational Statistics, 8*, 154–157.

Gross, J. (2007). *The handbook of emotion regulation*. New York: Guilford Press.

Guetzkow, H., Akger, C. F., Brody, R. A., Noel, C., & Snyder, R. C. (1963). *Simulation in international relations*. Englewood Cliffs, NJ: Prentice-Hall.

Hambrick, D. C. (2005). Upper echelons theory: Origins, twists and turns, and lessons learned. In K. G. Smith & M. A. Hitt (Eds.), *Great minds in management: The process of theory development* (pp. 109–127). New York: Oxford University Press.

Hannerz, U. (1993). *Cultural complexity: Studies in the social organization of meaning*. New York: Columbia University Press.

Hastings, B., & Shaffer, B. (2008). Authoritarianism: The role of threat, evolutionary psychology, and the will to power. *Theory and Psychology, 18*, 423–440.

Hatfield, A., & Hipel, K. (2002). Risk and systems theory. *Risk Analysis, 22*, 1043–1057.

Hatfield, E., & Walster, G. W. (1978). *A new look at love*. Latham, MA: University Press of America.

Head, M. L., Holman, L., Lanfear, R., Kahn, A., & Jennions, M. D. (2016). The extent and consequences of p-hacking in science. *PLOS Biology, 13*, e1002106.

Headland, T. N., Pike, K. L., & Harris, M. (Eds.). (1990). *Emics and etics: The insider/outsider debate*. Newbury Park, CA: SAGE.

Henrich, J., Heine, S. J., & Norenzayan, A. (2010). The weirdest people in the world? *Behavioral and Brain Sciences, 33*, 61–83.

Higgins, E. T., Rholes, W., & Jones, C. (1977). Category accessibility and impression formation. *Journal of Experimental Social Psychology, 13*, 141–154.

Hill, D. (2006). Theory in applied social psychology: Past mistakes and future hopes. *Theory and Psychology, 16*, 613–640.

Ho, Y., & Hartley, J. (2016). Classic articles in psychology in the Science Citation Index Expanded: A bibliometric analysis. *British Journal of Psychology, 107*, 768–780.

Hoffman, D. (2000). *Visual intelligence: How we create what we see*. New York: Norton.

Hollander, E. P. (1967). *Principles and methods of social psychology*. Oxford, UK: Oxford University Press.

Hossenfelder, S. (2018). *Lost in math: How beauty leads physics astray*. New York: Basic Books.

Howard, G. S., Maxwell, S., & Fleming, K. (2000). The proof of the pudding: An illustration of the relative strengths of null hypothesis, meta-analysis, and Bayesian analysis. *Psychological Methods, 5*, 315–332.

Hoyer, W. D., & Jacoby, J. (1983). Three-dimensional information acquisition: An application to contraceptive decision making. In R. P. Bagozzi & A. Tybout (Eds.), *Advances in Consumer Research, 10*, 618–623.

Hubley, A., & Zumbo, B. D. (2017). Response processes in the context of validity: Setting the stage. In B. D. Zumbo & A. Hubley (Eds.), *Understanding and investigating response processes in validation research*. New York: Springer.

Huff, A. S. (1999). *Writing for scholarly publication*. Thousand Oaks, CA: SAGE.

Hull, C. (1943). *Principles of behavior*. New York: Appleton-Century.

Hume, D. (1975). *An enquiry concerning human understanding* (3rd ed.) (P. N. Nidditch, Ed.). Oxford, UK: Clarendon Press. (Original work published 1777)

Hume, L., & Mulcock, J. (2004). *Anthropologists in the field: Cases in participant observation*. New York: Columbia University Press.

Hutchins, E. (1996). *Cognition in the wild*. Cambridge, MA: MIT Press.

Idler, E., & Benyamini, Y. (1997). Self-rated health and mortality: A review of twenty-seven community studies. *Journal of Health and Social Behavior, 38*, 21–37.

Iyengar, S., & Kinder, D. (1987). *News that matters*. Chicago: University of Chicago Press.

Jaccard, J. (1974). Predicting social behavior from personality traits. *Journal of Research in Personality, 7*, 358–367.

Jaccard, J. (2009). *Unlocking the contraceptive conundrum: Reducing unintended pregnancies in emergent adulthood*. Washington, DC: National Campaign to Prevent Teen and Unplanned Pregnancy.

Jaccard, J., & Bo, A. (2018). Prevention science and child/youth development: Randomized explanatory trials for integrating theory, method, and analysis in program evaluation. *Journal of the Society for Social Work and Research, 9*, 651–687.

Jaccard, J., & Bo, A. (2019). *Making outcome measures more useful in clinical trials: Addressing the problem of arbitrary metrics*. New York: Silver School of Social Work, New York University.

Jaccard, J., Dodge, T., & Guilamo-Ramos, V. (2005). Meta-cognition, risk behavior, and risk outcomes: The role of perceived intelligence and perceived knowledge. *Health Psychology, 24*, 161–170.

Jaccard, J., Levitz, N., Kantor, L., Levine, D., Morfesis, J., & Kohn, J. (2018). *Pregnancy ambivalence and contraceptive use: Implications for contraceptive counseling of young women*. New York: Silver School of Social Work, New York University.

Jaccard, J., McDonald, R., Wan, C., Dittus, P., & Quinlan, S. (2002). The accuracy of self reports of condom use and sexual behavior. *Journal of Applied Social Psychology, 32*, 1863–1905.

Jackson, J., Rand, D., Lewis, K., Norton, M., & Gray, K. (2017). Agent-based modeling: A guide for social psychologists. *Social Psychological and Personality Science, 8*, 387–395.

Jacoby, J. (1975). Perspectives on a consumer information processing research program. *Communication Research, 2*, 203–215.

Jacoby, J. (1977). Information load and decision quality: Some contested issues. *Journal of Marketing Research, 14*, 569–573.

Jacoby, J. (1984). Perspectives on information overload. *Journal of Consumer Research, 10*, 432–435.

Jacoby, J. (2002). Stimulus–organism–response reconsidered: An evolutionary step in modeling (consumer) behavior. *Journal of Consumer Psychology, 12*, 51–57.

Jacoby, J., & Chestnut, R. (1977). *Amount, type and order of information acquisition in purchasing decisions*. Final report for the National Science Foundation, GI-43687.

Jacoby, J., & Chestnut, R. (1978). *Brand loyalty: Measurement and management*. New York: Wiley.

Jacoby, J., Jaccard, J., Currim, I., Kuss, A., Ansari, A., & Troutman, T. (1994). Tracing the impact of item-by-item information accessing on uncertainty reduction. *Journal of Consumer Research, 21*, 291–303.

Jacoby, J., Jaccard, J., Kuss, A., Troutman, T.,

& Mazursky, D. (1987). New directions in behavioral process research: Implications for social psychology. *Journal of Experimental Social Psychology, 23*, 146–174.

Jacoby, J., Morrin, M., Jaccard, J., Gurhan, Z., & Maheswaran, D. (2002). Attitude formation as a function of incremental information input: A procedure for studying on-line processing models of attitude formation. *Journal of Consumer Psychology, 12*, 21–34.

Jacoby, J., Speller, D. E., & Berning, C. (1974). Brand choice behavior as a function of information load: Replication and extension. *Journal of Consumer Research, 1*, 33–42.

Jacoby, J., Speller, D. E., & Kohn, C. (1974). Brand choice behavior as a function of information load. *Journal of Marketing Research, 11*, 63–69.

Jahoda, G. (1971). Retinal pigmentation, illusion susceptibility and space perception. *International Journal of Psychology, 6*, 199–207.

James, W. (1890). *The principles of psychology*. New York: Holt.

Jarvis, P. (1998). *The practitioner-researcher: Developing theory from practice*. San Francisco: Jossey-Bass.

Jenkins, C. M., White, I. K., Hanmer, M. J., & Banks, A. (2018). *Vote over-reporting while black: Identifying the mechanism behind black vote overreporting*. Working paper, Department of Political Science, George Washington University, Washington, DC.

Jessor, R. (1994). Problem–behavior theory and the life course in adolescence: Epistemology in action. *Medicine and Mind, 8*, 57–68.

Jessor, R., & Jessor, S. L. (1977). *Problem behavior and psychosocial development: A longitudinal study of youth*. New York: Academic Press.

Johar, G. V., Jedidi, K., & Jacoby, J. (1997). A varying parameter averaging model of on-line brand evaluations. *Journal of Consumer Research, 24*, 232–247.

Johnson, J., & LeBreton, J. (2004). History and use of relative importance indices in organizational research. *Organizational Research Methods, 7*, 238–257.

Johnson, R., Onwuegbuzie, A., & Turner, L. (2007). Towards a definition of mixed methods research. *Journal of Mixed Methods Research, 1*, 112–133.

Johnson, T. P., Holbrook, A., & Cho, Y. (2006). The effects of acculturation on survey question comprehension among Latino respondents in the U.S. *ASA Section on Survey Research Methods*, pp. 3186–3192.

Judd, S. E., Letter, A. J., Shikany J., Roth, D., & Newby, P. (2015). Dietary patterns derived using exploratory and confirmatory factor analysis are stable and generalizable across race, region, and gender subgroups in the REGARDS study. *Frontiers in Nutrition, 1.* Retrieved from *www.frontiersin.org/article/10.3389/fnut.2014.00029.*

Kahneman, D., & Tversky, A. (1972). Subjective probability: A judgment of representativeness. *Cognitive Psychology, 3,* 430–454.

Kahneman, D., & Tversky, A. (1973). On the psychology of prediction. *Psychological Review, 80,* 237–251.

Kalick, S. M., & Hamilton, T. (1986). The matching hypothesis reexamined. *Journal of Personality and Social Psychology, 51,* 673–682.

Kaplan, A. (1964). *The conduct of inquiry.* San Francisco: Chandler.

Katz, D. (1960). The functional approach to the study of attitudes, *Public Opinion Quarterly, 24,* 163–204.

Kaufman, L., & Rousseeuw, P. (2005). *Finding groups in data: An introduction to cluster analysis.* New York: Wiley.

Kazdin, A. (2008). *The Kazdin method for parenting the defiant child.* New York: Houghton Mifflin.

Kelinman, S., & Copp, M. (1993). *Emotions and fieldwork.* Newbury Park, CA: SAGE.

Kenny, D. A., Kashy, D. A., & Cook, W. L. (2006). *Dyadic data analysis.* New York: Guilford Press.

Kerr, N. L. (1998). HARKing: Hypothesizing after the results are known. *Personality and Social Psychology Review, 2*(3), 196–217.

Kiesling E., Gunther, M., Stummer, C., & Wakolbinger, L. (2012). Agent-based simulation of innovation diffusion: A review. *Central European Journal of Operations Research, 20,* 183–230.

Kim, M., Vermunt, J., Bakk, Z., Jaki, T., & Van Horn, M. L. (2016). Modeling predictors of latent classes in regression mixture models. *Structural Equation Modeling, 23,* 601–614.

Kimble, G. A. (1984). Psychology's two cultures. *American Psychologist, 39,* 833–839.

King, R. S. (2014). *Cluster analysis and data mining: An introduction.* Herndon, VA: Mercury Learning and Information.

Kleiner, B., Lipps, O., & Ferrez, E. (2015). Language ability and motivation among foreigners in survey responding. *Journal of Survey Statistics and Methodology, 3,* 339–360.

Kotler, P., Roberto, N., & Lee, N. (2002). *Social marketing: Improving the quality of life.* Thousand Oaks, CA: SAGE.

Kowalski, B. (2006). *Computational logic as a dual process model of thought.* London: Imperial College.

Kraska, P. (2004). *Theorizing criminal justice.* Long Grove, IL: Waveland.

Krosnick, J. A., & Presser, S. (2010). Question and questionnaire design. In P. Marsden & J. Wright (Eds.), *Handbook of survey research* (pp. 263–314). Bingley, UK: Emerald Group.

Kruglanski, A. W. (2004). The quest for the gist: On challenges of going abstract in social and personality psychology. *Personality and Social Psychology Review, 8,* 156–163.

Kuhn, T. S. (1962). *The structure of scientific revolutions.* Chicago: University of Chicago Press.

Kuhn, T. S. (1970). Logic of discovery or psychology of research? In I. Lakatos & A. Musgrave (Eds.), *Criticism and the growth of knowledge* (pp. 1–22). Cambridge, UK: Cambridge University Press.

Kuhn, T. S. (2000). *The road since structure: Philosophical essays, 1970–1993, with an autobiographical interview.* Chicago: University of Chicago Press.

Lackner, J., Jaccard, J., Keefer, L., Brenner, D. M., Firth, R. S., Gudleski, G. D., et al. (2018). Improvement in gastrointestinal symptoms after cognitive behavior therapy for refractory irritable bowel syndrome. *Gatsroenterology, 155,* 47–57.

Lakatos, I. (1970). Falsification and the methodology of scientific research programmes. In I. Lakatos & A. Musgrave (Eds.), *Criticism and the growth of knowledge.* Cambridge, UK: Cambridge University Press.

Lakatos, I. (1978). *The methodology of scientific research programmes.* Cambridge, UK: Cambridge University Press.

Lamb, M. E., & Garretson, M. E. (2003). The effects of interviewer gender and child gender on the informativeness of alleged child sexual abuse victims in forensic interviews. *Law and Human Behavior, 27,* 157–171.

Lance, C. E., Dawson, B., Birkelbach, D., & Hoffman, B. J. (2010). Method effects, measurement error, and substantive conclusions. *Organizational Research Methods, 13,* 407–420.

Langley, A. (1999). Strategies for theorizing from process data. *Academy of Management Review, 24*(4), 691–710.

Lapka, C., Jupka, K., Wray, R., & Jacobsen, H. (2008). Applying cognitive response testing in message development and pre-testing. *Health Education Research, 23*(3), 467–476.

Lave, C. A., & March, J. G. (1975). *An introduction to models in the social sciences.* New York: Harper & Row.

Lavie, S., Narayan, K., & Rosaldo, R. (1993). *Creativity/anthropology.* Ithaca, NY: Cornell University Press.

Le, H., Oh, I., Robbins, S., Ilies, R., Holland, E., & Westrick, P. (2011). Too much of a good thing: Curvilinear relationships between personality traits and job performance. *Journal of Applied Psychology, 96,* 113–133.

Leary, M. R. (1979). Levels of disconfirmability and social psychological theory: A response to Greenwald. *Personality and Social Psychology Bulletin, 5,* 149–153.

Lee, J. A. (1973). *Colors of love.* Toronto, ON, Canada: New Press.

Lenzner, T., Kaczmirek, L., & Lenzner, A. (2010). Cognitive burden of survey questions and response times: A psycholinguistic experiment. *Applied Cognitive Psychology, 24,* 1003–1020.

Levine, J. M., & Moreland, R. L. (2004). Collaboration: The social context of theory development. *Personality and Social Psychology Review, 8,* 164–172.

Lewis, C. I. (1929). *Mind and the world order: Outline of a theory of knowledge.* New York: Dover.

Lewis, D. (2000). Causation as influence. *Journal of Philosophy, 97,* 182–197.

Lewis, M., & Grimes, A. (1999). Metatriangulation: Building theory from multiple paradigms. *Academy of Management Review, 24,* 672–691.

Lickliter, R., & Honeycutt, H. (2003). Developmental dynamics: Toward a biologically plausible evolutionary psychology. *Psychological Bulletin, 129,* 819–835.

Loftus, E., & Fathi, D. C. (1985). Retrieving multiple autobiographical memories. *Social Cognition, 3,* 280–295.

Loftus, E. F., & Palmer, J. C. (1974). Reconstruction of auto-mobile destruction: An example of the interaction between language and memory. *Journal of Verbal Learning and Verbal Behavior, 13,* 585–589.

Loftus, E. F., Smith, K., Klinger, M., & Fiedler, J. (1992). Memory and mismemory for health events. In J. Tanur (Ed.), *Questions about questions: Inquiries into the cognitive bases of surveys* (pp. 102–137). New York: Russell Sage.

Lomi, A., & Larsen, E. (2001). *Dynamics of organizations: Computational modeling and organization theories.* Cambridge, MA: MIT Press.

Lord, F. M., & Novick, M. R. (1968). *Statistical theories of mental test scores.* Reading, MA: Addison-Wesley.

Lozano, L. M., García-Cueto, E., & Muñiz, J. (2008). Effect of the number of response categories on the reliability and validity of rating scales. *Methodology: European Journal of Research Methods for the Behavioral and Social Sciences, 4,* 73–79.

Lubinski, D., Tellegen, A., & Butcher, J. N. (1983). Masculinity, femininity, and androgyny viewed and assessed as distinct concepts. *Journal of Personality and Social Psychology, 44,* 428–439.

Lubke, G., & Muthén, B. (2004). Applying multigroup confirmatory factor models for continuous outcomes to Likert scale data complicates meaningful group comparisons. *Structural Equation Modeling, 11,* 514–534.

Lubke, G. H., & Muthén, B. (2005). Investigating population heterogeneity with factor mixture models. *Psychological Methods, 10,* 21–39.

Luce, R. D., & Raiffa, H. (1957). *Games and decisions.* New York: Wiley.

Luke, S., Cioffi-Revilla, C., Panait, L., & Sullivan, K. (2004). *MASON: A new multi-agent simulation toolkit.* In *Proceedings of the 2004 Swarmfest Workshop* (pp. 181–187). Ann Arbor: University of Michigan.

MacCallum, R. C. (1986). Specification searches in covariance structure modeling. *Psychological Bulletin, 100,* 107–120.

MacCormack, C., & Strathern, C. (1980). *Nature, culture, and gender.* New York: Cambridge University Press.

MacCorquodale, K., & Meehl, P. (1948). On a distinction between hypothetical constructs and intervening variables. *Psychological Review, 55,* 95–107.

Maddox, B., Zumbo, B., Tay-Lim, B., & Qu, D. (2015). An anthropologist among the psychometricians: Assessment events, ethnography, and differential item functioning in the Mongolian Gobi. *International Journal of Testing, 15,* 291–309.

Mahfouz, A., Philaretou, A., & Theocharous, A. (2008). Virtual social interactions: Evolutionary, social psychological and technological perspectives. *Computers in Human Behavior, 24,* 3014–3026.

Manicas, P. T. (2006). *A realist philosophy of science: Explanation and understanding.* Cambridge, UK: Cambridge University Press.

Marcoulides, G. A., & Drezner, Z. (2003). Model specification searchers using ant colony optimization algorithms. *Structural Equation Modeling, 10,* 154–164.

Marcoulides, G. A., & Ing, M. (2012). Automated structural equation modeling strategies. In R. H. Hoyle (Ed.), *Handbook of structural equation modeling* (pp. 690–704). New York: Guilford Press.

Marshall, B., & Galea, S. (2015). Formalizing the role of agent-based modeling in causal inference and epidemiology. *American Journal of Epidemiolology, 181,* 92–99.

Marshall, D., & English, D. (2000). Neural network modeling of risk assessment in child protective services. *Psychological Methods, 5,* 102–124.

Marx, K. (1887). *Das kapital* (Vol. 1). Moscow: Progress Publishers.

Marx, M. (1951). *Psychological theory: Contemporary readings.* New York: Macmillan.

Mason, B. (1996). Moving toward virtual ethnography. *American Folklore Society News, 25,* 4–6.

Masten, A. S. (2014). *Ordinary magic: Resilience in development.* New York: Guilford Press.

Matysiak, A., Mencarini, L., & Vignoli, D. (2016). Work–family conflict moderates the relationship between childbearing and subjective well-being. *European Journal of Population, 32,* 355–379.

Maxwell, J. (2004). Using qualitative methods for causal explanation. *Field Methods, 16,* 243–264.

Maxwell, S. E., Delaney, H. D., & Kelley, K. (2003). *Designing experiments and analyzing data: A model comparison perspective.* New York: Routledge.

Mayo, C., & LaFrance, M. (1980). Toward an applicable social psychology. In R. F. Kidd & M. J. Saks (Eds.), *Advances in applied social psychology* (pp. 282–298). Hillsdale, NJ: Erlbaum.

Mazzocchi, F. (2015). Could big data be the end of theory in science?: A few remarks on the epistemology of data-driven science. *EMBO Reports, 16,* 1250–1255.

McClelland, G. H. (1975). Psychological processing of evaluative meaning of adverb-adjective combinations. *Dissertation Abstracts International, 35*(11-B), 5697.

McGrath, J. E., & Altman, I. (1966). *Small group research: A synthesis and critique of the field.* New York: Holt, Rinehart & Winston.

McGuire, W. J. (1968). Personality and susceptibility to social influence. In E. F. Borgatta & W. W. Mabert (Eds.), *Handbook of personality theory and research* (pp. 1130–1187). Chicago: Rand McNally.

McGuire, W. J. (1976). Some internal psychological factors influencing consumer choice. *Journal of Consumer Research, 2,* 302–319.

McGuire, W. J. (1997). Creative hypothesis generating in psychology: Some useful heuristics. *Annual Review of Psychology, 48,* 1–30.

McGuire, W. J. (2004). A perspectivist approach to theory construction. *Personality and Social Psychology Review, 8,* 173–182.

McIntyre, A. (2007). *Participatory action research.* Thousand Oaks, CA: SAGE.

Mead, G. (1932). *Mind, self and society from the standpoint of a social behaviorist.* Chicago: University of Chicago Press.

Mead, M. (2001). *Coming of age in Samoa: A psychological study of primitive youth for Western civilization.* New York: Harper.

Meade, A., Michels, L., & Lautenschlager, G. (2007). Are internet and paper-and-pencil personality tests truly comparable?: An experimental design measurement invariance study. *Organizational Research Methods, 10,* 322–335.

Menzies, P. (2017). Counterfactual theories of causation. In *Stanford encyclopedia of philosophy.* Retrieved from *https://plato.stanford.edu/archives/win2017/entries/causation-counterfactual.*

Merton, R. (1968). *Social theory and social structure.* New York: Free Press.

Michie, S. M., Richardson, M., Johnston, C., Abraham, C., Francis, J., Hardeman, W., et al. (2013). The behavior change technique taxonomy (v1) of 93 hierarchically clustered techniques: Building an international consensus for the reporting of behavior change interventions *Annals of Behavioral Medicine, 46,* 81–95.

Miller, G. A. (1956). The magical number seven, plus or minus two: Some limits on our capacity for processing information. *Psychological Review, 63,* 81–97.

Miller, G. A. (2003). The cognitive revolution: A historical perspective. *Trends in Cognitive Sciences, 7,* 141–144.

Millman, A., & Smith, C. (1997). Darwin's use of analogical reasoning in theory construction. *Metaphor and Symbol, 12,* 159–187.

Mills, C. W. (1959). *The sociological imagination.* New York: Oxford University Press.

Miner, H. (1956). Body ritual among the Nacirema. *American Anthropologist, 58,* 503–507.

Mintz, S. (1986). *Sweetness and power: The place of sugar in modern history.* New York: Penguin.

Mintzberg, H. (2005). Developing theory about the development of theory. In K. G. Smith & M. A. Hitt (Eds.), *Great minds in management: The process of theory development* (pp. 355–372). Oxford, UK: Oxford University Press.

Mohr, L. (1982). *Explaining organizational behavior.* San Francisco: Jossey-Bass.

Morgan, S., & Winship, C. (2007). *Counterfactuals and causal inference.* New York: Cambridge University Press.

Morrin, M., Jacoby, J., Johar, G., He, X., Kuss, A., & Mazursky, D. (2002). Taking stock of stock brokers: Exploring investor information accessing strategies via process tracing. *Journal of Consumer Research, 29,* 188–198.

Mueller, W. (2006). Exploring precalculus. Retrieved from *www.wmueller.com/precalculus/index.html.*

Mulligan, K., Grant, J., Mocabee, S., & Monson, J. (2003). Response latency methodology for survey research: Measurement and modeling strategies. *Political Analysis, 11,* 289–301.

Munson, M., Jaccard, J., Cole, A., Ben-David, S., & Ramirez, L. (2018). *The role of cognitions and emotions in the relationship between objective need and mental health service use.* New York: Silver School of Social Work, New York University.

Murdock, G. P. (1954). *Outline of world cultures.* New York: Taplinger.

Murdock, G. P. (1957). World ethnographic sample. *American Anthropologist, 59,* 4–28.

Murdock, G. P., & White, D. R. (1969). Standard cross-cultural sample. *Ethnology, 8,* 329–369.

Muthén, B. O. (2001a). Latent variable mixture modeling. In G. A. Marcoulides & R. E. Schumacker (Eds.), *New developments and techniques in structural equation modeling* (pp. 1–33). Mahwah, NJ: Erlbaum.

Muthén, B. (2001b). Second-generation structural equation modeling with a combination of categorical and continuous latent variables: New opportunities for latent class–latent growth modeling. In L. M. Collins & A. G. Sayer (Eds.), *New methods for the analysis of change* (pp. 291–322). Washington, DC: American Psychological Association.

Muthén, B. (2011). Applications of causally defined direct and indirect effects in mediation analysis using SEM in Mplus. Retrieved March 2011 from *www.statmodel.com/download/causalmediation.pdf.*

Muthén, B. O., & Muthén, L. K. (2000). Integrating person-centered and variable-centered analysis: Growth mixture modeling with latent trajectory classes. *Alcoholism: Clinical and Experimental Research, 24,* 882–891.

Nakamura, J., & Csikszentmihalyi, M. (2001). Catalytic creativity: The case of Linus Pauling. *American Psychologist, 56,* 337–341.

Nakamura, N., Fujita, K., Ushitani, T., & Miyata H. (2006). Perception of the standard and the reversed Müller-Lyer figures in pigeons (*Columba livia*) and humans (*Homo sapiens*). *Journal of Comparative Psychology, 120,* 252–261.

Nash, J. (1989). *From tank town to high tech: The clash of community and industrial cycles.* Albany: State University of New York Press.

Nersessian, N. (2002). Maxwell and "the method of physical analogy": Model-based reasoning, generic abstraction, and conceptual change. In D. Malament (Ed.), *Essays in the history and philosophy of science and mathematics* (pp. 129–166). La Salle, IL: Open Court.

Nersessian, N. (2008). *Creating scientific concepts.* Cambridge, MA: MIT Press.

Newell, A., & Simon, H. A. (1972). *Human problem solving.* Englewood Cliffs, NJ: Prentice-Hall.

Nisbett, R. E., Aronson, J., Blair, C., Dickens, W., Flynn, J., Halpern, D., et al. (2012). Intelligence: New findings and theoretical developments. *American Psychologist, 67,* 130–159.

Nisbett, R. E., & Wilson, T. (1977). Telling more than we can know: Verbal reports on mental processes. *Psychological Review, 84,* 231–259.

North, M. J., & Macal, C. (2005). Escaping the accidents of history: An overview of artificial life modeling with Repast. In A. Adamatzky & M. Komosinski (Eds.), *Artificial life models in software* (pp. 115–141). Heidelberg, Germany: Springer.

Nunnally, J. C. (1978). *Psychometric theory.* New York: McGraw-Hill. (Original work published 1967)

Nunnally, J. C., & Bernstein, I. H. (1994). *Psychometric theory.* New York: McGraw-Hill.

Ongenal, Y., & Dijkstra, W. (2006). Methods of

behavior coding of survey interviews. *Journal of Official Statistics, 22,* 419–451.

Onwuegbuzie, A., & Daley, C. (2001). Racial differences in IQ revisited: A synthesis of nearly a century of research. *Journal of Black Psychology, 27,* 209–220.

Open Science Collaboration. (2015). Estimating the reproducibility of psychological science. *Science, 349,* 1129.

Ortner, S. (1974). Is female to male as nature is to culture? In M. Rosado & L. Lamphere (Eds.), *Woman, culture and society* (pp. 68–87). Palo Alto, CA: Stanford University Press.

Osborn, A. (1963). *Applied imagination* (3rd ed.). New York: Scribner's.

Oswald, F. L., Mitchell, G., Blanton, H., Jaccard, J., & Tetlock, P. (2015). Using the IAT to predict ethnic and racial discrimination: Small effect sizes of unknown importance. *Journal of Personality and Social Psychology, 108,* 562–571.

Pabón, M. (2010). Ethnic identity development in Latino youth: A meta analysis of the research. Retrieved from *https://conservancy. umn.edu/bitstream/hanndle/11299/172788/ Pabon_umn_0130E_11185.pdf;sequence=1.*

Pap, A. (1962). *An introduction to the philosophy of science.* Glencoe, IL: Free Press of Glencoe (Macmillan).

Parsons, T. (1951). *The social system.* New York: Free Press.

Parsons, T. (1971). *The system of modern societies.* Englewood Cliffs, NJ: Prentice-Hall.

Patterson, G. (1975). *Families: Applications of social learning to family life.* Champaign, IL: Research Press.

Paulhus, D. L., & Williams, K. (2002). The dark triad of personality: Narcissism, Machiavellianism, and psychopathy. *Journal of Research in Personality, 36,* 556–563.

Pawson, R., & Tilley, N. (1997). *Realistic evaluation.* London: SAGE.

Pearl, J. (2009). *Causality: Models, reasoning, and inference.* New York: Cambridge University Press.

Pearl, J., & Mackenzie, D. (2018). *The book of why.* New York: Basic Books.

Pearlson, G., & Folley, B. (2008). Schizophrenia, psychiatric genetics, and Darwinian psychiatry: An evolutionary framework. *Schizophrenia Bulletin, 34,* 722–733.

Peirce, C. S. (1998). Pragmatism as the logic of deduction. In The Peirce Edition Project (Eds.), *The essential Peirce* (Vol. 2). Bloomington: Indiana University Press. (Original work published 1903)

Pepper, D., Hodgen, J., Lamesoo, K., Kõiv, P., & Tolboom, J. (2018). Think aloud: Using cognitive interviewing to validate the PISA assessment of student self-efficacy in mathematics. *International Journal of Research and Method in Education, 41*(1), 3–16.

Pepperberg, I., Vicinay, J., & Cavanagh, P. (2008). The Müller-Lyer illusion is processed by a grey parrot (*Psittacus erithacus*). *Perception, 37,* 765–781.

Peter, J. P., & Olson, J. C. (1983). Is science marketing? *Journal of Marketing, 47,* 111–125.

Peterson, C., & Seligman, M. E. P. (2004). *Character strengths and virtues: A classification and handbook.* New York: Oxford University Press/Washington, DC: American Psychological Association.

Petty, R. E., & Cacioppo, J. T. (1986). *Communication and persuasion: The central and peripheral routes to attitude change.* New York: Springer-Verlag.

Peytcheva, E. (2008). Language of administration as a source of measurement error. *ASA Section on Survey Research Methods,* 4314–4124.

Plano Clark, V. (2010). The adoption and practice of mixed methods: U.S. trends in federally funded health related research. *Qualitative Inquiry, 16,* 428–440.

Platt, J. (1964). Strong inference. *Science, 146,* 347–353.

Plattner, S. (1989). *Economic anthropology.* Palo Alto, CA: Stanford University Press.

Podsakoff, P. M., MacKenzie, S. B., & Podsakoff, N. (2012). Sources of method bias in social science research and recommendations on how to control it. *Annual Review of Psychology, 63,* 539–569.

Poincaré, H. (1952). *Science and hypothesis.* New York: Dover.

Pollack, R. H. (1970). Müller-Lyer illusion: Effect of age, lightness contrast, and hue. *Science, 170,* 93–95.

Poole, M., & Van de Ven, A. (1989). Using a paradox to build management and organization theories. *Academy of Management Review, 14,* 562–579.

Popper, K. R. (1963). *Conjectures and refutations: The growth of scientific knowledge.* London: Routledge & Kegan Paul.

Popper, K. R. (1968). *The logic of scientific discovery.* London: Hutchinson.

Popper, K. R. (1970). Normal science and its dangers. In I. Lakatos & A. Musgrave (Eds.), *Criticism and the growth of knowledge* (pp. 51–58). Cambridge, UK: Cambridge University Press.

Popper, K. R. (1983). *Realism and the aim of science*. London: Routledge.

Pound, P., & Campbell, R. (2015). Exploring the feasibility of theory synthesis: A worked example in the field of health related risk-taking. *Social Science and Medicine, 124*, 57–65.

Presser, S., Couper, M., Lessler, J., Martin, E., Martin, J., Rothgeb, J. M., et al. (2004). Methods for testing and evaluating survey questions. *Public Opinion Quarterly, 68*, 109–130.

Price, L. R. (2016). *Psychometric methods: Theory into practice*. New York: Guilford Press.

Prochaska, J. O., DiClemente, C. C., & Norcross, J. C. (1992). In search of how people change: Applications to addictive behaviors. *American Psychologist, 47*, 1102–1114.

Radecki, C. M., & Jaccard, J. (1995). Perceptions of knowledge, actual knowledge, and information search behavior. *Journal of Experimental Social Psychology, 31*, 107–138.

Randall, W. (2007). From computer to compost: Rethinking our metaphors for memory. *Theory and Psychology, 17*, 611–633.

Reason, P., & Bradbury, H. (2001). *Handbook of action research: Participative inquiry and practice*. Thousand Oaks, CA: SAGE.

Reason, P., & Bradbury, H. (2007). *The SAGE handbook of action research: Participative inquiry and practice*. Thousand Oaks, CA: SAGE.

Repenning, N. (2002). A simulation-based approach to understanding the dynamics of innovation implementation. *Organization Science, 13*, 109–127.

Reyna, V., Nelson, W., Han, P., & Dieckmann, N. (2009). How numeracy influences risk comprehension and medical decision making. *Psychological Bulletin, 135*, 943–973.

Robins, G., Pattison, P., & Woodstock, J. (2005). Small and other worlds: Global network structures from local processes. *American Journal of Sociology, 110*, 894–936.

Robinson, M. E., George, S. Z., Dannecker, E. A., Jump, R. L., Hirsh, A. T., Gagnon, C. M., et al. (2004). Sex differences in pain anchors revisited: Further investigation of "most intense" and common pain events. *European Journal of Pain, 8*, 299–305.

Robinson-Cimpian, J. P. (2014). Inaccurate estimation of disparities due to mischievous responders: Several suggestions to assess conclusions. *Educational Researcher, 43*, 171–185.

Rodgers, W. L., Andrews, F. M., & Herzog, A. R. (1992). Quality of survey measures: A structural modeling approach. *Journal of Official Statistics, 8*, 251–275.

Rogers, C. (1961). *On becoming a person*. New York: Houghton Mifflin.

Rogosa, D. R. (1999). *Accuracy of individual scores expressed in percentile ranks: Classical test theory calculations* (CRESST Technical Report 509). Los Angeles: National Center for Research on Evaluation, Standards, and Student Testing (CRESST), Center for the Study of Evaluation (CSE), Graduate School of Education and Information Studies, University of California, Los Angeles.

Rohrmann, B. (2015). Designing verbalized rating scales: Sociolinguistic concepts and psychometric findings from three cross-cultural projects. Retrieved from *www.rohrmannresearch.net/pubsq.html*.

Rollie, S., & Duck, S. (2006). Divorce and dissolution of romantic relationships: Stage models and their limitations. In M. Fine & J. Harvey (Eds.), *Handbook of divorce and relationship dissolution* (pp. 531–563). Mahwah, NJ: Erlbaum.

Root-Bernstein, R. S., & Root-Bernstein, M. (1999). *Sparks of genius: The thirteen thinking tools of the world's most creative people*. New York: Mariner.

Rosaldo, R. (1993). *Culture and truth: The remaking of social analysis*. New York: Beacon.

Rosenau, P. (1992). *Post-modernism and the social sciences*. Princeton, NJ: Princeton University Press.

Rosnow, R. L., & Rosenthal, R. (1989). Definition and interpretation of interaction effects. *Psychological Bulletin, 105*, 143–146.

Rubin, D. (1974). Estimating causal effects of treatments in randomized and nonrandomized studies. *Journal of Educational Psychology, 66*, 688–701.

Rubin, D. (1978). Bayesian inference for causal effects: The role of randomization. *Annals of Statistics, 6*, 34–58.

Rubin, D. (2005). Causal inferences using potential outcomes: Design, modeling decisions. *Journal of the American Statistical Association, 100*, 322–331.

Rubin, M. (2017). When does HARKing hurt?: Identifying when different types of undisclosed post hoc hypothesizing harm scientific progress. *Review of General Psychology, 21*, 308–320.

Rubin, Z. (1970). Measurement of romantic love. *Journal of Personality and Social Psychology, 16*, 265–273.

Runkel, P. J., & McGrath, J. E. (1972). *Research on human behavior: A systematic guide to method*. New York: Holt, Rinehart & Winston.

Russell, B. (1931). *The scientific outlook*. London: Allen & Unwin.

Rychlak, J. (1994). *Logical learning theory: A human teleology and its empirical support*. Lincoln: University of Nebraska Press.

Rynes, S. (2002). From the editors: Some reflections on contribution. *Academy of Management Journal, 45*, 311–313.

Sadovski, V. (1974). *Foundations of general systems theory*. Moscow: Nauka.

Saldaña, J. (2016). *The coding manual for qualitative researchers*. Thousand Oaks, CA: SAGE.

Salmon, W. C. (1984). *Scientific explanation and the causal structure of the world*. Princeton, NJ: Princeton University Press.

Salmon, W. C. (1989). Four decades of scientific explanation. In P. Kitcher & W. C. Salmon (Eds.), *Scientific explanation* (pp. 3–196). Minneapolis: University of Minnesota Press.

Salmon, W. C. (1998). *Causality and explanation*. New York: Oxford University Press.

Salovey, P., & Grewal, D. (2005). The science of emotional intelligence. *Current Directions in Psychological Science, 14*, 6–12.

Salovey, P., & Mayer, J. D. (1990). Emotional intelligence. *Imagination, Cognition, and Personality, 9*, 185–211.

Saris, W. E., & Gallhofer, I. (2007). Estimation of the effects of measurement characteristics on the quality of survey questions. *Survey Research Methods, 1*, 29–43.

Sastry, M. A. (1997). Problems and paradoxes in a model of punctuated organizational change. *Administrative Science Quarterly, 42*, 237–275.

Sayer, A. (1992). *Method in social science: A realist approach*. New York: Routledge.

Scarr, S. (1985). Constructing psychology: Making facts and fables for our times. *American Psychologist, 40*, 499–512.

Schaefer, C., & DiGeron, T. (2000). *Ages and stages: A parent's guide to normal childhood development*. New York: Wiley.

Schaeffer, N. C., Dykema, J., & Maynard, D. W. (2010). Interviewers and interviewing, In J. Wright, P. Marsden, & V. Bingley (Eds.), *Handbook of survey research* (2nd ed., pp. 437–470). Bingley, UK: Emerald Group.

Scheerer, M., Rothmann, E., & Goldstein, K. (1945). A case of "idiot–savant": An experimental study of personality organization. *Psychology Monographs, 58*, 1–63.

Schelling, T. C. (1971). Dynamic models of segregation. *Journal of Mathematical Sociology, 1*, 143–186.

Schlesinger, G. N. (1991). The credibility of extraordinary events. *Analysis, 51*, 125.

Schober, M., & Conrad, F. (2002). A collaborative view of standardized survey interviews. In D. Maynard, H. Houtkoop-Steenstra, N. C. Schaeffer, & J. van der Zouwen (Eds.), *Standardization and tacit knowledge: Interaction and practice in the survey interview* (pp. 67–94). New York: Wiley.

Schubert, G. (1960). *The public interest*. Glencoe, IL: Free Press.

Segall, M. H., Campbell, D. T., & Herskovits, M. J. (1966). *The influence of culture on visual perception*. New York; Bobbs-Merrill.

Seligman, M. E. P. (2002). *Authentic happiness: Using the new positive psychology to realize your potential for lasting fulfillment*. New York: Free Press.

Seligman, M. E. P., & Csikszentmihalyi, M. (Eds.). (2000). Positive psychology [Special issue]. *American Psychologist, 55*, 234–244.

Serang, S., Jacobucci, R., Brimhall, K., & Grimm, K. (2017). Exploratory mediation analysis via regularization. *Structural Equation Modeling, 24*, 733–744.

Seymour, R. A., Simpson, J. M., Charlton, J. E., & Phillips, M. (1985). An evaluation of length and end-phrase of visual analogue scales in dental pain. *Pain, 21*, 177–185.

Shadish, W. R., Cook, T., & Campbell, D. (2002). *Experimental and quasi-experimental designs for generalized causal inference*. Boston: Houghton Mifflin.

Shavelson, R. J., & Webb, N. M. (1991). *Generalizability theory: A primer*. Thousand Oaks, CA: SAGE.

Shaw, M., & Costanzo, P. (1982). *Theories of social psychology*. New York: McGraw-Hill.

Sheluga, D. A., & Jacoby, J. (1978). Do comparative claims encourage comparison shopping?: The impact of comparative claims on consumers' acquisition of product information. In J. Leigh & C. Martin (Eds.), *Current issues and research in advertising* (pp. 166–181). Ann Arbor: University of Michigan Press.

Sheth, J. N. (1967). A review of buyer behavior. *Management Science, 13*, B718–B756.

Shurchkov, O. (2012). Under pressure: Gender differences in output quality and quantity under competition and time constraints. *Journal of the European Economic Association, 10*, 1189–1213.

Shum, M. (1998). The role of temporal landmarks in autobiographical memory processes. *Psychological Bulletin, 124,* 423–442.

Sierra, J., & Hyman, M. (2006). A dual-process model of cheating intentions. *Journal of Marketing Education, 28,* 193–204.

Silverman, E., & Bryden, J. (2007). From artificial societies to new social science theory. *Advances in Artificial Life, 22,* 565–574.

Silverman, W. K., Kurtines, W. M., Jaccard, J., & Pina, A. A. (2009). Directionality of change in youth anxiety treatment involving parents: An initial examination. *Journal of Consulting and Clinical Psychology, 77,* 474–485.

Simmons, J. P., Nelson, L. D., & Simonsohn, U. (2011). False-positive psychology: Undisclosed flexibility in data collection and analysis allows presenting anything as significant. *Psychological Science, 22*(11), 1359–1366.

Simon, H. A. (1974). How big is a chunk? *Science, 183,* 482–488.

Simon, H. A., & Newell, A. (1956). Models: Their uses and limitations. In L. D. White (Ed.), *The state of the social sciences* (pp. 61–83). Chicago: University of Chicago Press.

Simonton, D. K. (1988). *Scientific genius.* New York: Cambridge University Press.

Simonton, D. K. (2004). *Creativity in science: Chance, logic, genius, and zeitgeist.* New York: Cambridge University Press.

Skinner, B. F. (1957). *Verbal behavior.* Englewood Cliffs, NJ: Prentice-Hall.

Skurka, C., Byrne, S., Davydova, J., Kemp, D., Safi, A. G., Avery, R. J., et al. (2018). Testing competing explanations for graphic warning label effects among adult smokers and nonsmoking youth. *Social Science and Medicine, 211,* 294–303.

Slater, M. D., & Gleason, L. S. (2012). Contributing to theory and knowledge in quantitative communication science. *Communication Methods and Measures, 6,* 215–236.

Slife, B., & Williams, R. (1995). *What's behind the research?: Discovering hidden assumptions in the behavioral sciences.* Thousand Oaks, CA: SAGE.

Smith, C. A., & Kirby, L. D. (2000). Appraisal as a pervasive determinant of anger. *Emotion, 4,* 133–138.

Smith, E. R., & Conrey, F. (2007). Agent-based modeling: A new approach for theory building in social psychology. *Personality and Social Psychology Review, 11,* 87–104.

Smith, E. R., & DeCoster, J. (2000). Dual process models in social and cognitive psychology: Conceptual integration and links to underlying memory systems. *Personality and Social Psychology Review, 4,* 103–131.

Smith, E. R., Zarate, M., & Branscombe, N. (1987). *Affect, ideology, and action: A dual-process model of attitude responses.* Technical report, Purdue University, West Lafayette, IN.

Smith, G. A. (1986). Observer drift: A drifting definition. *Behavior Analysis, 9,* 127–128.

Smith, T. W., & Gallo, L. C. (2001). Personality traits as risk factors for physical illness. In A. Baum, T. Revenson, & J. Singer (Eds.), *Handbook of health psychology* (pp. 139–172). Hillsdale, NJ: Erlbaum.

Smitherman, T. A., Martin, V., Penzien, D. B., & Lipton, R. B. (2013). Rounding behavior in the reporting of headache frequency complicates headache chronification research. *Headache, 53,* 908–919.

Smolin, L. (2006). *The trouble with physics: The rise of string theory, the fall of a science, and what comes next.* New York: Houghton, Mifflin & Harcourt.

Snider, J. G., & Osgood, C. E. (1969). *Semantic differential technique: A sourcebook.* Chicago: de Gruyter.

Sorensen, I. (1998). *Thought experiments.* New York: Oxford University Press.

Sowa, J. (2000). Processes and causality. Retrieved from *www.jfsowa.com/ontology/causal.htm.*

Spatig, L., Parrott, L., Kusimo, P., Carter, C., & Keyes, M. (2001). We roll deep: Community and resistance in the lives of Appalachian girls. *Journal of Appalachian Studies, 7,* 64–92.

Spector, P. E., & Brannick, M. T. (2009). Common method variance or measurement bias?: The problem and possible solutions. In D. Buchanan & A. Bryman (Eds.), *The SAGE handbook of organizational research methods* (pp. 346–362). Los Angeles: SAGE.

Spiggle, S. (1994). Analysis and interpretation of qualitative data in consumer research. *Journal of Consumer Research, 21,* 419–503.

Starr, W. (2019). Counterfactuals. In *Stanford encyclopedia of philosophy.* Retrieved from *https://plato.stanford.edu/archives/spr2019/entries/counterfactuals.*

Stein, M. (1974). *Stimulating creativity: I.* Oxford, UK: Academic Press.

Stein, M. (1975). *Stimulating creativity: II. Group procedures.* Oxford, UK: Academic Press.

Steinberg, L. (2008). A social neuroscience perspective on adolescent risk-taking. *Developmental Review, 28,* 78–106.

Stenstrom, E., Stenstrom, P., Saad, G., &

Cheikhrouhou, S. (2008). Online hunting and gathering: An evolutionary perspective on sex differences in website preferences and navigation. *IEEE Transactions on Professional Communication, 51,* 155–168.

Sterman, J. (2000). *Business dynamics: Systems thinking and modeling for a complex world.* New York: McGraw-Hill.

Sternberg, R. J. (1985). Implicit theories of intelligence, creativity, and wisdom. *Journal of Personality and Social Psychology, 49,* 607–627.

Sternberg, R. J. (1997). Construct validation of a triangular love scale. *European Journal of Social Psychology, 27,* 313–335.

Sternberg, R. J. (2002). Creativity as a decision. *American Psychologist, 57,* 376.

Sternberg, R. J. (2003). *The psychologist's companion: A guide to scientific writing for students and researchers.* New York: Cambridge University Press.

Sternberg, R., Grigorenko, E., & Singer, J. (2004). *Creativity: From potential to realization.* Washington, DC: American Psychological Association.

Sternberg, R. J., Hojjat, M., & Barnes, M. (2001). Empirical tests of aspects of a theory of love as a story. *European Journal of Personality, 15,* 199–218.

Sternberg, R. J., & Lubart, T. (1996). Investing in creativity. *American Psychologist, 51,* 677–688.

Stevens, S. S. (1946, June 7). On the theory of scales of measurement. *Science, 103,* 677–680.

Stevens, S. S. (1951). Mathematics, measurement, psychophysics. In S. S. Stevens (Ed.), *Handbook of experimental psychology* (pp. 1–49). New York: Wiley.

Stoeber, J. (2001). The Social Desirability Scale–17 (SDS-17): Convergent validity, discriminant validity, and relationship with age. *European Journal of Psychological Assessment, 17,* 222–232.

Stolz, H., Barber, B., & Olsen, J. (2005). Toward disentangling fathering and mothering: An assessment of relative importance. *Journal of Marriage and Family, 67,* 1076–1092.

Strauss, A., & Corbin, J. (1998). *Basics of qualitative research.* Newbury Park, CA: SAGE.

Sturdy, A., & Grey, C. (2003). Beneath and beyond organizational change management: Exploring alternatives. *Organization, 10,* 651–662.

Suessbrick, A., Schober, M. F., & Conrad, F. G. (2000). Different respondents interpret ordinary questions quite differently. In *Proceedings of the American Statistical Association,* *Section on Survey Research Methods.* Alexandria, VA.

Suleiman, R., Troitzsch, K., & Gilbert, N. (2000). *Tools and techniques for social science simulation.* Heidelberg, Germany: Physica-Verlag.

Sumner, A. (2004). *Economic well-being and non-economic well-being: A review of the meaning and measurement of poverty.* Helsinki, Finland: World Institute for Development Economics Research. Retrieved from *www.wider. unu.edu/sites/default/files/rp2004-030.pdf.*

Sun, R. (2006). *Cognition and multi-agent interaction: From cognitive modeling to social simulation.* New York: Cambridge University Press.

Takahashi, S., Kijima, K., & Sato, R. (2004). *Applied general systems research on organizations.* New York: Springer.

Tavory, I., & Timmermans, S. (2014). *Abductive analysis: Theorizing qualitative research.* Chicago: University of Chicago Press.

Taylor, A., West, S., & Aiken, L. (2006). Loss of power in logistic, ordinal logistic, and probit regression when an outcome variable is coarsely categorized. *Educational and Psychological Measurement, 66,* 228–239.

Tetlock, P., & Belkin, A. (1996). *Counterfactual thought experiments in world politics.* Princeton, NJ: Princeton University Press.

Thom, R. (1975). *Structural stability and morphogenesis: An outline of a general theory of models.* Reading, MA: Benjamin.

Thomassen, L. (2006). *The Derrida–Habermas reader.* Chicago: University of Chicago Press.

Thompson, C., & Shapiro, L. (2007). Complexity in treatment of syntactic deficits. *American Journal of Speech–Language Pathology, 18,* 30–42.

Thornton, S. (2018). Karl Popper. In *Stanford encyclopedia of philosophy.* Retrieved from *https://plato.stanford.edu/archives/win2017/entries/popper.*

Thurstone, L. L. (1947). *Multiple factor anaylsis.* Chicago: University of Chicago Press.

Timmermans, S., & Almeling, R. (2009). Objectification, standardization, and commodification in health care: A conceptual readjustment. *Social Science and Medicine, 69,* 21–27.

Torgerson, W. S. (1958). *Theory and methods of scaling.* New York: Wiley.

Toulmin, S. (2003). *The uses of argument.* Cambridge, UK: Cambridge University Press.

Townsend, J. T., & Ashby, F. G. (1984). Measurement scales and statistics: The misconception misconceived. *Psychological Bulletin, 96,* 394–401.

Tracy, M., Cerdá, M., & Keyes, K. (2018). Agent-based modeling in public health: Current applications and future directions. *Annual Review of Public Health, 39,* 77–94.

Tukey, J. (1977). *Exploratory data analysis.* New York: Pearson.

Turner, V. (1967). Carnival, ritual, and play in Rio de Janeiro. In A. Falassi (Ed.), *Time out of time: Essays on the festival* (pp. 74–92). Albuquerque: University of New Mexico Press.

Turner, V. (1970). *The forest of symbols: Aspects of Ndembu ritual.* Ithaca, NY: Cornell University Press.

Tversky, A., & Kahneman, D. (1973). Availability: A heuristic for judging frequency and probability. *Cognitive Psychology, 5,* 207–232.

Tversky, A., & Kahneman, D. (1974). Judgment under uncertainty: Heuristics and biases. *Science, 185,* 1124–1131.

Underwood, B. (1957). *Psychological research.* New York: Appleton, Century, Crofts.

Valeri, L., & VanderWeele, T. J. (2013). Mediation analysis allowing for exposure–mediator interactions and causal interpretation: Theoretical assumptions and implementation with SAS and SPSS macros. *Psychological Methods, 18,* 137–150.

Van de Ven, A., & Poole, M. (1995). Explaining development and change in organizations *Academy of Management Review, 20,* 510–541.

Van de Ven, A., & Poole, M. (2005). Alternative approaches for studying organizational change. *Organization Studies, 26,* 1377–1399.

van der Heide, I., Wang, J., Droomers, M., Spreeuwenberg, P., Rademakers, J., & Uiters, E. (2013). The relationship between health, education, and health literacy: Results from the Dutch Adult Literacy and Life Skills Survey. *Journal of Health Communication, 18,* 172–184.

van Doorn, J., Verhoef, P., & Bijmolt, T. (2007). The importance of non-linear relationships between attitude and behaviour in policy research. *Journal of Consumer Policy, 30,* 75–90.

van Fraassen, B. C. (1980). *The scientific image.* Oxford, UK: Clarendon Press.

van Fraassen, B. C. (1989). *Laws and symmetry.* Oxford, UK: Clarendon Press.

Van Gigch, J. (1978). *Applied general systems theory.* New York: Harper & Row.

Van Horn, M. L., Jaki, T., Masyn, K., Ramey, S. L., Smith, J. A., & Antaramian, S. (2009). Assessing differential effects: Applying regression mixture models to identify variations in the influence of family resources on academic achievement. *Developmental Psychology, 45,* 1298–1313.

Van Vaerenbergh, Y., & Thomas, T. (2013). Response styles in survey research: A literature review of antecedents, consequences, and remedies. *International Journal of Public Opinion Research, 25,* 195–217.

VanderWeele, T. J. (2015). *Explanation in causal inference: Methods for mediation and interaction.* New York: Oxford University Press.

Vellman, P. F., & Wilkinson, L. (1993). Nominal, ordinal, interval and ratio typologies are misleading. *American Statistician, 47,* 65–72.

Veludo-de-Oliveira, T., Ikeda, A., & Campomar, M. (2006). Discussing laddering application by the means–end chain theory. *Qualitative Report, 11,* 626–642.

Vermunt, J., & Magidson, J. (2002). Latent class cluster analysis. In J. Hagennars & A. McCutcheon (Eds.), *Applied latent class analysis.* New York: Cambridge University Press.

Vilorio, D. (2016, March). Education matters. *Career Outlook.* Retrieved from *www.bls.gov/careeroutlook/2016/data-on-display/education-matters.htm.*

Wadsworth, Y. (1998). What is participatory action research? *Action Research International,* Paper 2.

Wallace, J. M., & Bachman, J. G. (1991). Explaining racial/ethnic differences in adolescent drug use: The impact of background and life style. *Social Problems, 38,* 333–357.

Watzlawick, P. (1976). *How real is real?* New York: Random House.

Weber, M. (1904). *The Protestant ethic and the spirit of capitalism* (T. Parsons, Trans.). New York: Scribner's.

Wedel, M., & Desarbo, W. S. (1994). A review of recent developments in latent class regression models. In R. Bagozzi (Ed.), *Advanced methods of marketing research* (pp. 352–388). Cambridge, UK: Blackwell.

Weick, K. E. (1979). *The social psychology of organizing.* Reading, MA: Addison-Wesley.

Weijters, B., Geuens, M., & Schillewaert, N. (2008). Assessing response styles across modes of data collection. *Journal of the Academy of Marketing Science, 36,* 409–422.

Weinfurt, K., DePuy, V., Castel, L., Sulmasy, D. P., Schulman, K. A., & Meropol, N. J. (2005). Understanding of an aggregate probability statement by patients who are offered participation in phase I clinical trials. *Cancer, 103,* 140–147.

Weisskopf, V. (1977). The frontiers and limits of science. *American Scientist, 65,* 405–411.

Wenemark, M., Persson, A., Brage, H., Svensson, T., & Kristenson, M. (2011). Applying motivation theory to achieve increased response rates, respondent satisfaction, and data quality. *Journal of Official Statistics, 27,* 393–414.

Werner, E. (2005). Reslience and recovery: Findings from the Kauai Longitudinal Study. *Research, Policy, and Practice in Children's Mental Health, 19,* 11–14.

Wertz, F. J., Charmaz, K., McMullen, L. M., Josselson, R., Anderson, R., & McSpadden, E. (2011). *Five ways of doing qualitative analysis: Phenomenological psychology, grounded theory, discourse analysis, narrative research, and intuitive inquiry.* New York: Guilford Press.

West, B., & Blom, A. (2017). Explaining interviewer effects: A research synthesis. *Journal of Survey Statistics and Methodology, 5,* 175–211.

West, C., & Zimmerman, D. (1987). Doing gender. *Gender and Society, 1,* 125–151.

Westbrook, L., & Saperstein, A. (2015). New categories are not enough: Rethinking the measurement of sex and gender in social surveys. *Gender and Society, 29,* 534–560.

Westerhoff, F. (2008). The use of agent-based financial market models to test the effectiveness of regulatory policies. *Journal of Economics and Statistics, 228,* 195–227.

Whetten, D. A. (1989). What constitutes a theoretical contribution? *Academy of Management Review, 14,* 490–495.

Whitehouse, H., Kahn, K., Hochberg, M., & Bryson, J. (2012). The role for simulations in theory construction for the social sciences: Case studies concerning divergent modes of religiosity. *Religion, Brain and Behavior, 2,* 182–201.

Wiggins, J. S. (1973). *Personality and prediction.* New York: Longman.

Wilcox, R. R. (1998). How many discoveries have been lost by ignoring modern statistical methods. *American Psychologist, 53,* 300–314.

Wilcox, R. R. (2017). *Introduction to robust estimation and hypothesis testing.* San Diego, CA: Academic Press.

Wilcox, R. R., & Tian, T. (2011). Measuring effect size: A robust heteroscedastic approach for two or more groups. *Journal of Applied Statistics, 38,* 1359–1368.

Willis, G. (2000). Cognitive interviewing: A how to guide. Retrieved from *www.chime.ucla.edu/ publications/docs/cognitive%20interviewing%20 guide.pdf.*

Willis, G. (2004). *Cognitive interviewing: A tool for improving questionnaire design.* Los Angeles: SAGE.

Wood, B. (2002). *Attachment and family systems: Family process.* New York: Wiley.

World Health Organization. (2018). Process of translation and adaptation of instruments. Retrieved from *www.who.int/substance_abuse/ research_tools/translation/en.*

Wyer, R. S. (2004). A personalized theory of theory construction. *Personality and Social Psychology Review, 8,* 201–209.

Yorke, M. (2001). Bipolarit . . . or not?: Some conceptual problems relating to bipolar rating scales. *British Educational Research Journal, 27,* 171–186.

Zaheer, S., Albert, S., & Zaheer, A. (1999). Time scales and organizational theory. *Academy of Management Review, 24,* 725–742.

Zaltman, G., & Coulter, R. (1995). Seeing the voice of the customer: Metaphor-based advertising research. *Journal of Advertising Research, 83,* 35–51.

Zeeman, E. (1976). Catastrophe theory. *Scientific American, 221,* 65–83.

Zhang, C., & Conrad, F. (2016). Intervening to reduce satisficing behaviors in web surveys: Evidence from two experiments on how it works. *Social Science Computer Review, 36,* 57–81.

Zhang, H., & Vorobeychik, Y. (2017). Empirically grounded agent-based models of innovation diffusion: A critical review. *Artificial Intelligence Review, 10,* 1–35.

Author Index

Subject Index

About the Authors

James Jaccard, PhD, is Professor of Social Work at the Silver School of Social Work at New York University. Previously, he was Distinguished Professor of Psychology for 20 years at the University at Albany, State University of New York, and Professor of Psychology at Florida International University for 8 years. Dr. Jaccard has authored or edited numerous books and has published over 200 articles in peer-reviewed journals. He has served on numerous boards and panels for the Health and Medicine Division of the National Academies of Sciences, Engineering, and Medicine and for the National Institutes of Health. Dr. Jaccard's research focuses broadly on attitudes, cognitions, and emotions as they affect decision making, especially in applied settings. This includes research on adolescent decision making, health-related decisions, and a critical analysis of the effects of unconscious influences on adult decision making.

Jacob Jacoby, PhD, until his death in 2018, was Merchants Council Professor of Consumer Behavior at New York University's Stern School of Business. He authored or edited several books and published over 160 articles in peer-reviewed social science and law journals. Dr. Jacoby was a Fellow of the American Psychological Association and a Fellow and past president of the Association for Consumer Research. His research on the factors that affect consumer decision making and behavior was honored by awards from the American Psychological Association, the American Marketing Association, the American Academy of Advertising, the Association for Consumer Research, and the Society for Consumer Psychology. Dr. Jacoby conducted research or consulted for dozens of Fortune 500 companies and other organizations in the United States and internationally. He also worked for federal agencies (including the U.S. Senate, Federal Trade Commission, and Food and Drug Administration) and testified in more than 100 cases heard in U.S. District Courts.